DATE DUE

BRODART   Cat. No. 23-221

SHAKESPEARE'S BLACKFRIARS
PLAYHOUSE

Shakespeare's
BLACKFRIARS
PLAYHOUSE

Its History and Its Design

IRWIN SMITH

Foreword by James G. McManaway

NEW YORK UNIVERSITY

PRESS

ACKNOWLEDGMENTS

I am indebted to many persons for their help in the preparation of this book, and above all to my friend Dr. John Cranford Adams, author of *The Globe Playhouse* and until recently the president of Hofstra University. It was he who first suggested my making a study of the Blackfriars Playhouse. He placed his library of Elizabethan literature at my service, and subsequently gave my manuscript the benefit of his wise and friendly criticism.

Father William A. Hinnebusch, O.P., of the Dominican House of Studies in Washington, has aided me with facts and advice bearing upon the history of the London friary before the Suppression. Miss Marjorie B. Honeybourne, editor of *The London Topographical Record* and an outstanding authority on the topography of medieval London, has given me help available nowhere else with respect to the boundaries and surroundings of the Ludgate precinct in the days of the friars. Mr. R. Gilyard Beer, Inspector of Ancient Monuments in the Ministry of Works, has shared with me his expert knowledge of some of England's historic buildings. Professor John McCabe of New York University has permitted me to study his doctoral thesis on the Blackfriars Playhouse during its tenancy by the King's Men, and Professor J. B. Bessinger has aided me in my translation of the Blackfriars passage in *Piers the Plowman's Creed*. Professor Bernard Beckerman, author of *Shakespeare at the Globe*, has read sections of my manuscript and made many helpful suggestions.

I am grateful to the Folger Shakespeare Library in Washington, and to the Houghton Library at Harvard University, for granting me access to their invaluable collections; and I am not less grateful to the Garden City Public Library, and in particular to its research librarian, Mrs. Muriel Major, through whose interest and diligence I have been able to call upon the resources of all the libraries in the Nassau Library System, the New York State Library in Albany, the Library of Congress in Washington, and other libraries as far away as the Middle West.

Plates I and II are from photographs by F. Frith & Co., Ltd.,

Reigate, Surrey. Plates III through VIII are from photographs by Edwin Smith, Esq., Saffron Walden, Essex.

Finally, I have been greatly aided, both in research and in the preparation of my manuscript, by the generosity of the American Philosophical Society in giving me two grants from its Penrose Fund.

I. S.

Garden City, New York

PREFACE

The Blackfriars story is the history of a community of Dominican friars, of a great hall within their friary where the parliament sometimes sat, and of two playhouses in succession inside the precinct walls.

The religious community was founded by the Black Friars in 1275 on the north bank of the Thames, between Ludgate Hill and the river; it became the scene of important events connected with the Reformation in England. Parliaments assembled in the friary's great hall, and there Henry VIII held the trial preceding his divorce from Katharine of Aragon, a trial that Shakespeare's company of actors was later to reenact in the very room in which it had historically taken place. Of the two theatres, the first was England's first commercial indoor theatre, and as such the forerunner of all the theatres of today. The second and greater Blackfriars Playhouse was England's leading theatre during a great theatrical age, and one of the two playhouses of which Shakespeare was a part owner. He wrote his final plays for its stage, and it left its mark upon them.

The two Blackfriars Playhouses spanned the years that saw the English drama in its greatest glory and the English stage in its greatest transition. Together, with a sixteen-year intermission, they lasted from 1576 until 1642. During those years the art of staging passed from the fixed polyscenic settings of the medieval stage, through the successive settings, effected with properties and without scenery, of the Elizabethan public playhouses, to the changeable painted flats that fathered the scenery of today. In these years the actor and the theatre changed from the amateur to the professional. The status of the actor changed from one of vagabondage to one of respectability, the boy player gave way to the man, and the woman made her debut upon the stage.

This book is the first to tell the Blackfriars history as a continuing story, from the settlement of the Dominican Friars at Ludgate in 1275 until the suppression of the second playhouse under Oliver Cromwell in 1642. It is the first to reconstruct the design and equipment of the two playhouses and their stages, and in so doing is the first also to reconstruct the stage of any "private" playhouse of Elizabethan and Jacobean times. In consequence, it is the first to undertake a thorough inquiry into one of the few areas of Shakespearean research that remain virtually untouched.

Many sixteenth- and seventeenth-century manuscripts survive to give fragmentary information about the topography of the Blackfriars precinct, the relationship of the friary to the Crown, and the history of the two playhouses. Such of the documents as have been printed are distributed among many volumes, only one or two of which were published within the last half century. Those that are most important to the present study are here, for the first time, collected in a single book. Quite apart from the convenience of having them assembled in one volume, they need reprinting, for almost all the books in which they were originally published are out of print, many are hard to come by, and some are ready to crumble at the touch.

As originally printed, the documents make formidable reading. Page follows unbroken page without a paragraph to relieve the congestion of close-packed sentences or to indicate a turn of thought, and often without punctuation. Some editors have printed the documents in type facsimile, retaining the old symbols of abbreviation. Others have gone part way toward modernization by completing the abbreviations and supplying some commas and periods. But halfway methods have slender justification; they are neither one thing nor the other. Study of the documents has convinced me that little is to be gained by stopping short of fully modernized spelling. The documents contain none of those ambiguities or subtleties that send Shakespearean scholars to facsimile reprints of the plays in hopes of finding out exactly what the poet intended; most of them were drawn up by men trained in the law, men who knew precisely what they wanted to say and who usually said it in hackneyed phrases. I have therefore chosen to use modernized spelling and punctuation in reprinting all the documents in the Appendix.[1]

Like legal documents of the present day, those of the sixteenth century were often long-winded and repetitious; in some of them, therefore, I have resorted to frequent and even extensive ellipses. For the most part I have omitted only the later repetitions of such legalistic phrases as these: "his executors admynystrators or assigns or eny of them or eny other person or persons to whom this present lease graunt interest or terme of years or eny parte or parcell thereof shall or may fortune to come at eny time hereafter," or "all & singuler the said messuages and premisses with thappurtenances before in & by theis presents bargained and sould or mencioned to be bargained & sould and euery parte & parcell thereof." When learned counsel wrote these phrases originally, he doubt-less thought them necessary safeguards against all contingencies, but in the intervening centuries they have lost their utility, and they now serve only to make one lose one's way in a maze of technicalities, wearisomely repeated. They now contribute nothing of substantive value.

Dimensions, which are especially important in any attempt to re-construct the Blackfriars precinct and its buildings, are given in the original documents in such varied forms as these: "lxxiiij^n fote" and "ffyftye & two yerds and a half & a half quarter of a yerde and every yerde thereof conteyninge thre fote of Assice." All such dimensions have been transposed into terms of feet and inches in arabic numerals, as 74 feet or 157 feet 10½ inches. Similarly, sums of money, which in the original manuscripts are sometimes stated in such terms as "viij^{c}lxxix^{li}-iij^{s}iiij^d" or "Cvj^{s}viij^d," are here restated as £879 3s. 4d., or £5 6s. 8d.

The texts have been broken into numbered paragraphs to facilitate reference. In every instance, the modernized document is prefaced by a paragraph that tells not only its ultimate source, but also where it can be found in unmodernized printed form.

The documents, as here reprinted as an Appendix to this book, are arranged in their chronological order within four different categories: (1) land surveys and records of real estate transactions; (2) petitions, official regulations, and other documents of control; (3) depositions in legal controversies; and (4) miscellaneous documents. References to the docu-ments are indicated in the body text in parentheses, the first numeral being that of the document itself, and the second, after a colon, being that of a particular paragraph within the document. References to all other sources are given in footnotes.[2]

Four chapters in this book are devoted to reconstructing the design of the auditorium and stage of the Second Blackfriars Playhouse; and that design, having been arrived at through an analysis of Blackfriars plays and other contemporary documents, is stated both in text and in measured drawings. As is the nature of such drawings, they inevitably go beyond the text in explicitness: they assign specific sizes and shapes and positions to individual pieces of timber, glass, and stone. In doing so they are often making an excursion from the area of reasonable assurance into that of mere conjecture, while at the same time, because of that explicitness, they seem to show an authority which, of course, they do not possess. Both the excursions into conjecture and the seeming authority are the consequences of my employing a medium that demands positive statements and prohibits uncertainties, ambiguities, and alternative theories.

In quotations from plays, dialogue is printed in roman, without italicizing proper names, and stage directions are printed in italics, without throwing proper names into roman. All quotations of Shakespearean dialogue are from Kittredge,[3] but stage directors are from the original sources. I follow Chambers in his chronology of Shakespeare's plays.[4]

Completely at a loss for the 1964 equivalent, in purchasing power, of the £600 that James Burbage paid in 1596 for the real property in which the Second Blackfriars was installed, and of the 8 shillings that Edward Kirkham contracted to pay to Henry Evans, I turned for advice to Dr. Giles E. Dawson of the Folger Shakespeare Library. He graciously replied as follows:

No equivalent can be established, and those people who try it all get different answers. The trouble is that relative values in 1600 were totally different from relative values today. A pair of silk stockings cost as much as 40s.; a chicken cost tuppence ha'penny or threppence. In an account book that we have, a man paid (on one page of the book, about 1638) 10d. for a lemon and 2d. for a dog. The First Folio cost £1, but a schoolmaster or a parson was well paid if he got £12 a year (plus, of course, perquisites and fringe benefits that we can't possibly calculate). Black pepper cost some people I know, about 1600, £3 per pound; allspice cost £6 per pound. In short, what was imported, such as lemons and pepper, and what took a long time to make by hand, such as silk stockings (imported silk) and books (imported paper)—these things were expensive. The product of the local farm was cheap, and ordinary unskilled labor was *very* cheap. But then there is another complication: a great nobleman expected to pay a great deal more for a given article than a plain gentlemen would pay for the same article. The farm laborer of course did without that kind of article, and he could live (after a fashion) on very little. There's another consideration, too. Thorold Rogers, in his *History of Agriculture and Prices,* tells us the price of turnips, sugar, shoes, and paper for any year. With turnips the prices would differ little with quality variations, but shoes and paper varied so greatly in quality, size, and the like that unless we know these factors (and we never do, at least not fully), we don't know anything about the price.

Still, money would on the average buy a great deal more then than the same money will buy now, and for convenience we can hardly resist the desire to have a rule of thumb for comparison. If we say that £1 in 1600 was approximately equivalent in purchasing power to $50 today it works out fairly reasonably. It makes the price of the First Folio high, and it makes that dog in 1638 still cheap. It makes the chicken 62.5 cents, a shilling seat in a playhouse $2.50, Henry Evans's 8s. $24, and the Blackfriars property $30,000. But one must always remember that one cannot in fact work out any really meaningful equation.

$30,000 would no doubt be cheap for the same property now; it would probably cost more than ten times that. But it does not seem to me an unreasonably low price for 1600. And you could certainly have fed boys on $1.20 a head. Beef, chickens, eggs, bread, milk, and small beer, which is about what they would have eaten, were the very articles of diet that were cheapest.

For publication details of the various papers, pamphlets, books, and articles mentioned in abbreviated fashion in the footnotes, the reader is referred to the bibliography.

1. I have reached this decision the more confidently since the Folger Shakespeare Library is publishing its *Folger Documents of Tudor and Stuart Civilization* with modernized spelling and punctuation.

2. As used in footnotes, the letters *BR* stand for *Blackfriars Records*, an invaluable little volume published by the Malone Society as Volume II, Part 1, of its *Collections*. The letters are followed by two numbers separated by a colon, as *BR* 17:21. The first numeral refers to a page in the book, and the second to a line upon that page.

3. *The Complete Works of Shakespeare*, ed. George Lyman Kittredge, Boston, 1936.

4. *William Shakespeare*, by E. K. Chambers, Oxford, 1930, Vol. I, pp. 270–71.

FOREWORD

In the career of William Shakespeare as actor-playwright-theatrical manager, there were several climactic events. One occurred when the Lord Chamberlain's Men built and occupied the Globe. There was another when their primacy was recognized by the gift of royal livery and they became the King's Men. The last, and in some ways the most important, was their occupancy of the Blackfriars, for this was the first time that adult professional players in England performed regularly in a private playhouse. Scholars have recognized that the physical conditions of the indoor stage and the taste of the elite audience would have required or permitted important, perhaps radical, changes in methods of production and staging of plays and in the style of acting. At the same time, there were modifications in the theatrical bill of fare: more music, and more sophisticated music, was required; the farcical jig would have less appeal than formerly. Playwrights would produce a different kind of drama. It is important, therefore, to learn as much as possible about the Blackfriars Theatre of the King's Men and its repertory.

It is almost equally important to discover all that can be learned about the earlier theatrical ventures in the Blackfriars and about the children's companies concerned in them. These are controversial matters, about which documentary information is fragmentary.

By a careful study of the remains of other structures built and used by the Friars Preachers, or Black Friars, in England, Mr. Smith has been able to interpret the historical records and archaeological remains of the London buildings with results that challenge respectful attention. The precise location of the rooms that were remodeled to serve as the Second Blackfriars needs to be determined, for the shape and size of the area affect directly both the seating arrangements for the audience and the equipping and operating of the stage.

Previous discussions of the use of the Blackfriars by the King's Men usually deal with the years after 1603 or 1604, when Burbage had to consider the possibility that the Children of the Queen's Revels might be compelled to vacate, and then concentrate on the period after 1609, when the King's Men began to act there. Mr. Smith makes the point that when Burbage acquired the premises in 1597, he had intended to use them for the Lord Chamberlain's Men and had remodelled them accordingly. It would appear that Shakespeare and his fellows would have had the potentialities of the Blackfriars constantly in mind during the decade that was to elapse before they could establish themselves there.

In his examination of the plays known to have been performed at the Blackfriars by the children and adult companies, Mr. Smith has been constantly aware of the need to make his ideas about staging consistent with the physical attributes of the playhouse—and, of course, his sketches of stage and auditorium have necessarily been drawn in conformity with the known requirements of the plays.

It was at the Blackfriars between about 1609 and 1642 that professional actors had the opportunity to adapt some of the techniques of the court masques to the commercial stage, and the post-Restoration development of the English stage can hardly be understood without full knowledge of what had been attempted at the Blackfriars.

James G. McManaway

GLOSSARY

A *monk* is a member of a religious community or brotherhood living apart from the world under vows of poverty, chastity, and obedience, and devoted primarily to contemplation and the performance of liturgical observances. A *friar* takes similar vows, but does not live in equal seclusion from the outside world. In strict usage, *friar* means a member of one of the mendicant orders, of which the chief were the Dominicans or Friars Preachers or Black Friars, the Franciscans or Gray Friars, the Augustinians or Austin Friars, and the Carmelites or White Friars.

A community of monks is a *monastery;* of friars a *friary;* and of nuns, a *nunnery*. A monastery or nunnery is an *abbey* if it is ruled by an abbot or abbess, or a *priory* if ruled by a prior or prioress. A house of friars is always ruled by a prior, and therefore is never an abbey; it is always a friary or priory.

The noun of broadest application with respect to personnel is *religious;* it includes monks, friars, and nuns. Similarly, *religious house* includes the establishments of all three. *Convent* was equally comprehensive originally, but it has tended, without historical justification, to acquire a limitation in popular usage to the houses of nuns. The adjective *conventual*, however, retains a broader application than does its noun; it seems to have resisted the drift toward an association with nunneries exclusively, and to apply to monasteries and friaries as well; and the adjective *monastic*, although its primary association is with monks and monasteries, is acceptable also with reference to friars and friaries. The friars lack any adjective of their own except *friary*, which has only a limited acceptance.

CONTENTS

Contents

ILLUSTRATIONS

Figures in the Text

Plates

xix

SHAKESPEARE'S BLACKFRIARS PLAYHOUSE

The Black Friars of London

FOUR GREAT ORDERS of mendicant friars originated on the mainland of Europe and spread thence to England during the early years of the thirteenth century. First came the Friars Preachers or Black Friars, and after them the Franciscans or Gray Friars, the Augustinians or Austin Friars, and the Carmelites or White Friars.

The monks had come some centuries before the friars, in the darkest days our western civilization has known. In those troublous times they had contributed vigor, stability, and authority to the life of the kingdom. They had stood for sanity and peace in an age of violence. They had given the nation its first hospitals and almonries, its first universities and schools. They had kept classical culture alive by their copying of Greek and Latin manuscripts; they had pioneered in agriculture and in the use of running water for power, irrigation, and sanitation; they had taken the lead in artistic and architectural enterprise. But they had lost their dominant position in many of those fields as the general level of civilization slowly rose. Their eventual eclipse was due partly to the passing of feudalism and the approach of the Renaissance, partly to their falling away from the rigorous rules formulated for their own discipline in the fervor of primitive idealism, and partly to the arrival of the friars and the new religious concepts that they brought with them. Whereas the number of monasteries had increased fourfold during the twelfth century, virtually no new monastic houses were founded after the middle of the fourteenth.

The monastic and the mendicant orders of the Middle Ages had much in common. Monks and friars alike took vows of poverty, chastity, and obedience; all dedicated themselves to a communal life devoted to the service of the church. Their precincts were basically similar. The es-

3

sential components of all were the churches where the brethren worshipped, the chapter houses where they transacted their temporal and spiritual affairs, the dormitories where they slept, the refectories where they ate their meals, the infirmaries where they cared for their sick and aged, the guest houses where they lodged visitors, and the cloisters that bound all these elements together. Furthermore, all orders, whether of monks or friars, commonly arranged these architectural constituents in accordance with the same general plan. The plan had been evolved by the older orders in the formative days of monachism and had proved serviceable, and by the time that the friars came it was hallowed by centuries of observance, and was recommended to them by tradition, prescription, and utility.[1]

But for all these similarities the monks differed from the friars in many respects, and notably in their attitudes toward church and cloister and toward the lay community outside the precinct walls.

Monks were bound by vow to remain within the confines of their own monasteries: the mere fact of lifelong residence within a single cloister was in itself a monastic virtue not less esteemed than poverty, chastity, and obedience. Their days were dedicated to contemplation and liturgical observances; the service of the church was the be-all and end-all of their lives. Their abbeys were hymns of praise to Almighty God in terms of stone and glass, with a splendor of mass and a delicacy of detail that mark them today as the noblest expression of medieval man's aspiration and love of beauty and engineering skill. But their churches existed for the monks, not for the laity. They were not places of congregational worship; the rituals of praise and intercession were functions of the religious alone.

Mendicant friars, on the other hand, dedicated their lives to the service of man as well as to the glory of God. They did not, as did the monks, take vows of stability that confined them to their own precincts; their cloisters were bases of operation, points of departure, not the limits of their lives. Itinerancy was for them not a deviation from the rule, but an integral part of it. They wandered two by two, a preacher and his *socius*, through the countryside and towns, begging their daily bread, hearing confessions, and preaching in marketplaces or town squares or wherever else people might gather to listen; for preaching, while preeminently the province of the Friars Preachers, was a function of all the other mendicants also. The friars preached conduct and doctrine in a racy and virile vernacular. Their sermons were larded with anecdotes or *exempla* calculated to point a moral or adorn a precept, and were a principal source of diversion in an age that offered little by way of entertainment. The friars' special mission as preachers demanded that their own churches should be places where large congregations could hear sermons, not where they could merely witness ritual processions; and this need, as will be seen, greatly influenced their church design.

Other differences between the monks and the friars in the construction of their convents arose from their different interpretations of the doctrine of apostolic poverty. The friars were beggars: in theory they were dependent entirely upon the voluntary gifts of well-wishers and were forbidden to accept rents or revenues. As individuals they could possess nothing, and as communities they could possess only their priories and the land on which the priories stood.[2] Both economy and the rules of the mendicant orders thus demanded moderation in building, and the rules of the Friars Preachers in particular not merely demanded it in general terms, but fixed specific limits. Their early constitutions restricted the height of one-story buildings to 12 feet, of two-story buildings to 20 feet, and of church walls to 30 feet, and limited the use of stone vaulting to the sacristy and choir.[3] Rules such as these were subsequently relaxed, and, even as modified, were often ignored, for the temptation toward grandeur in building seems to have been irresistible. But the rules remained in effect and evasions were sometimes punished by penance. As a result the establishments of the friars tended on the whole to be smaller in size, lighter in construction, less ornate, and less costly, than those of the monks.

The monks built their religious houses, and the friars built theirs, in their days of pristine dedication and austerity. Their churches and cloisters therefore tell what the religious orders adumbrated and stood for, not what they later became. A time was to come when the monastic virtues would here and there be replaced by slackness of discipline, negligence in the performance of divine offices, irresponsibility in temporal administration, and even in some places by scandalous abuses. But the tragic fall from grace was still a long way off when the mendicant friars first set foot on English soil.

The English friars of the Dominican Order were familiarly called Black Friars because they wore long black cloaks over their white habits. They were called Friars Preachers because they were dedicated to the mission of fighting heresy and saving men's souls through preaching. These two names—Black Friars or Friars Preachers, or both—are those by which they are usually designated in the secular English documents of post-Dissolution days. The name Dominican is a modern appellation.[4]

The Order of Preachers was founded by St. Dominic, a Spaniard of Old Castile, and received papal sanction in 1216. The founder believed profoundly in the importance of scholarly training for those who would preach. He looked upon learning as a tool to be used in expounding Catholic doctrine and exposing error, and upon universities as places where his followers could teach and be taught; and in accordance with this principle the Order established its first houses in such centers of learning as Paris, Bologna, and Montpellier. In 1221 the same consideration determined the Order's choice of a site for its first settlement in England, when the second General Chapter, at its meeting in Bologna, voted to dispatch a little band of brethren to set up an English province. The thirteen emissaries, after landing at Dover, halted only briefly at Canterbury and London, the ecclesiastical and political capitals of the kingdom; their destination was Oxford, a university town. For the next three centuries the relations between the Oxford Dominicans and Oxford University remained always close, even if sometimes acrimonious. The friary sent both students and professors to the University.

Figure 1. The escutcheon of the Order of Preachers.

The second English settlement of the Order was in the suburbs of London, outside the west wall of the City in the parish of St. Andrew, Holborn. The land for the friary was donated in 1224 by Hubert de Burgh, Earl of Kent. He was Grand Justiciary of England and the most powerful noble at the royal court during the minority of Henry III. His gift, coming only three years after the arrival of the Friars Preachers on English soil, seems to foretoken the close relationship between the Order and the Court that was to continue almost without interruption until the Dissolution.

The land given by the Earl was a six-acre tract extending from Holborn in the north to Harp Alley in the south, and from Shoe Lane to the Fleet. It was covered with buildings and thickly populated. The friars' first task was to clear it of encumbrances and tenants, and to convert it to the uses of a friary; old buildings must be torn down or adapted, and new ones must be built. The church took six years to build; the domestic buildings took twenty or more; and the conduit, built at the King's expense to bring water from Clerkenwell, needed five. The record of the next few years is a record of the acquisition of new land by gift or purchase, and of constant building and rebuilding to meet the friary's expanding needs; and through all the years of growth, Henry and his nobles continued their benefactions in the form of money or land, of oak for fuel and timber, of lead for roofs and conduits, and of stone and lime. By 1243 the friary at Holborn numbered eighty brethren, as evidenced by the King's Christmas gift of eighty habits and eighty pairs of shoes. Two of the yearly General Chapters of the whole Order were held there. The first was in 1250, with more than four hundred friars present from all parts of Christendom, including Jerusalem. The second was in 1263; and on this occasion the King ordered seven hundred complete habits to be provided from his royal wardrobe for the friars that should attend.[5]

The Holborn priory was still young, as priories go, when the friars decided to abandon it and move to a new location. The reasons for their decision are not obvious. As far as the friars themselves were concerned, the old site was probably just as serviceable as the new, quite apart from its now having a full complement of monastic buildings and the new site's having none. Both sites were north of the Thames and less than a quarter of a mile apart. Both suffered from the stench of the tanneries and slaughterhouses that bordered the Fleet Ditch,[6] the Holborn precinct being just west of the Fleet and the new site just east of it, between Ludgate Hill and the river. Both, presumably, were adequate in area: over the course of fifty years the Holborn site had undoubtedly grown to a size at least equal to that of the Ludgate site as initially acquired; and even if the new site was larger, it is not clear that the priory needed more room, for the Holborn friary, as we have seen, could accommodate eighty brethren, and the Ludgate friary, as far as we know, never needed room for more than ninety.[7] The new precinct could not even offer the important inducement of lying wholly within the City wall. That was not achieved until later, when the wall itself was moved toward the west

7

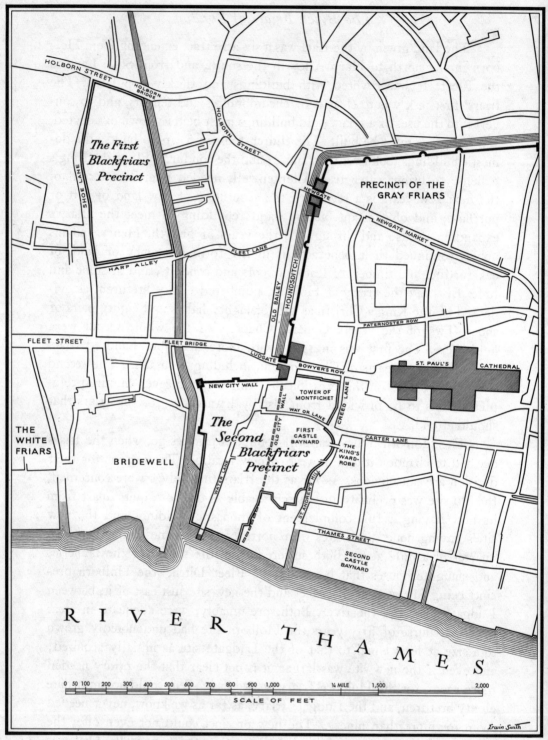

Figure 2. *The sites of the Holborn and Ludgate precincts.*

so as to enclose all the land lying south of today's Pilgrim Street and east of the Fleet.

But the Ludgate site did lie nearer to the heart of the City and to the royal Court; and this, it would seem, was the consideration that led the King—now Edward I—to favor the move. His interest in having the Friars Preachers move to Ludgate is a matter of record: as an incentive and reward for changing their location he granted them the deodands that accrued to the Crown over a period of three years, and a continual flow of remittances from other sources.[8] Throughout his reign his devotion to the Ludgate foundation proved to be so fervid and so sustained as to earn for him and his Queen the right to be accounted its founders.

The move to the "bosome of the Cittie," as the lay inhabitants of the precinct were to term the new situation three centuries later,[9] permitted and encouraged the intermeshing of the affairs of friary and Crown that was to mark the whole subsequent history of the community.

The first purchase of land for the new precinct was made in 1275 by Robert Kilwardby, Archbishop of Canterbury. He was himself a Friar Preacher, and had been the Order's English Provincial until his appointment to the archiepiscopal see. Acting for the Friars, he bought from Robert Fitz-Walter the land on which stood the ruins of Castle Baynard and of Montfichet Tower, with their appurtenances, dikes, and walls.[10] Shortly afterwards he secured from the Lord Mayor and Barons of the City of London their permission to close two lanes adjoining the Castle, and authorization to destroy Montfichet Tower for the stone that it contained.

Plans to construct the friary buildings immediately encountered the opposition of the Dean and Canons of St. Paul's. They disliked having the church of a powerful religious order erected within two hundred yards of their own cathedral, and for three years they succeeded in frustrating every attempt on the part of the friars to start construction. But in 1278 the King's earnest importunities prevailed, and building began; and in that same year Archbishop Kilwardby was authorized by the King to tear down the part of the City wall that ran from Ludgate directly south to the river, and to rebuild it on a new line running from Ludgate west to the Fleet and from there southward to the Thames. John Stow, in his *Survey of London*, tells the story in these words:

Now here is to be noted, that the Wall of *London,* at that time, went straight South from *Ludgate,* downe to the River of *Thames:* But for building of the

Blacke Friers Church, the said Wall in that place was by commandement taken downe, and a new Wall made, straight West from Ludgate to *Fleet-bridge,* and then by the water of *Fleete,* to the River of *Thames.*[11]

The exact run of the original wall is not known, nor the exact extent of the Castle Baynard site. One cannot be sure, therefore, just how much of Kilwardby's initial purchase lay within the City wall and how much lay outside it to the west. One can be sure, however, that when the old wall was torn down and the friars were permitted to take in all the land to the west as far as the Fleet, the size of their precinct was more than doubled. By royal command the new wall was to be built at the expense of the citizens of London, but the people resented the murage tax levied against them and took their time about finishing the job. The wall was still unfinished thirty-seven years later.[12]

The friars lived on at Holborn while their new precinct was being made ready to receive them, in the meantime accumulating other small parcels of land in extension of their Ludgate site. Into the new buildings went a thousand marks from the royal purse,[13] stones from Castle Baynard and Montfichet Tower and the old City wall, oaks out of Windsor Forest and the royal forest of Essex, and lead roofing and piping from Holborn. Late in 1286 the friars diverted their aqueduct so that it carried the water from the spring in Clerkenwell to their house at Ludgate instead of to Holborn, and at about the same time they left their old precinct and moved to their new. The property in Holborn was sold to the Earl of Lincoln for 550 marks.

THE FRIARS PREACHERS AND THE COURT

THE CROWN and the royal family were directly concerned in the founding of nine thirteenth-century Dominican houses—those at Bamburgh, Canterbury, Chichester, Dunstable, Guildford, Ipswich, Salisbury, York, and, as has already been stated, Ludgate in London.[14] Relations between the Friars Preachers and the house of Plantagenet were especially close: Father Jarrett says that the Dominicans were the confessors of successive English monarchs for 144 consecutive years, beginning with the fourth Plantagenet king and ending only with the deposition of Richard II, who was buried in the Church of the Friars Preachers at King's Langley.[15]

Henry IV, fearing that the Dominicans might be too attached to the house that he had overthrown, at first transferred his spiritual allegiance to the Carmelite friars. Eventually he came back to the Friars Preachers, however, and his grandson, Henry VI, also chose them as his confessors. The house of York seems not to have patronized any particular religious order, although two of Edward's children, including one of the two Princes in the Tower, were born in the Dominican friary at Shrewsbury. The Black Friars were spared "the adventurous and intricate task of soothing the scruples" of Henry VIII,[16] but the priory was not for that reason exempted from sharing in some of the crucial events connected with the King's divorce and the English Reformation; and a Dominican friar, Geoffrey Athequa, was confessor to Henry's first unhappy queen.[17]

The royal confessor was expected to be in constant attendance upon his sovereign. He and his *socius* lived at court when the king was at home, and in peace or war they accompanied him upon his travels. The confessor's life as a courtier was one not easily reconcilable with some of his vows as a friar. While residing at court he could not without unseemliness obey those rules that required him to subsist upon alms, to remain silent at the dining table, and to walk afoot when the rest of the king's attendants rode. Some mitigations of the rules were early found to be necessary and were granted by papal dispensation. Thus Pope Innocent IV gave permission in 1250 for the friars in attendance upon Henry III to ride on horseback whenever the King might desire it, and in 1321 King Edward II asked the Pope to grant permission for his confessor to converse at table.[18]

Out of this relationship as penitent and confessor sprang other relationships between kings and friars. Often the friars were called upon to act as ambassadors, negotiators, legates, or messengers. Official records of their embassies show that Friars Preachers often traveled on state business to Ireland, Scotland, and Wales, to France, Flanders, Hungary, Sweden, and elsewhere on the Continent, and over and over again to Rome.[19] Their frequent employment on such errands probably resulted in part from their knowledge of their masters' minds and the trust that the kings reposed in them, in part from their freedom from family ties and political ambition, and in part from their literacy, their contacts with other Friars Preachers in foreign courts, and their skill in the use of the international language, Latin.

Relations between the London Blackfriars and the Court were especially close, for reasons of propinquity if for no other. At London the relationship was not merely one of personal service in a spiritual or a diplomatic capacity; it was one that also involved the regular or occasional use of friary buildings by English kings for national purposes. No friary records survive to tell of this extraordinary relationship. Such records as do survive are those in the rolls of the Exchequer or in other governmental archives, or in the pages of Stow and Hall.

These accounts are undoubtedly incomplete, but they tell, for instance, that in 1311 the Parliament of the realm held its meetings in the friary, and during its sessions King Edward II had his lodging in the priory's hospitium. On August 24 he paid the friars £33 6s. 8d. in aid of maintenance and in recompense for damage done to buildings and grounds. That same year he chose the friary as the place in which to receive the homage of the Earl of Lancaster, and as the place where the Bishop of Worcester should give up the Great Seal of England before going to the General Council of Vienne, and should receive it back on his return.[20]

As early as 1322–1323 the friary served as a depository for state records. In 1322 the king sent his clerks to the house of the Friars Preachers for the purpose of examining and arranging the royal charters of Pontefract, Tutbury, Tunbridge, and the Tower of London.[21]

The Lord Chancellor held his Court of Chancery in the hospitium in 1343, 1370, 1376, and 1378.[22]

In 1358–1359, King David of Scotland, being a prisoner of war, here engaged to pay his heavy ransom.[23]

Beginning, probably, with the reign of Henry IV, a hall in the precinct was set aside for the affairs of the Duchy of Lancaster. The Duchy had its origin in Bolingbroke's desire to keep his ducal patrimony separate from the royal estates when he became king. By the sixteenth century the Duchy had come to possess formidable political power, with rights and estates scattered all over England and Wales. The administration of its affairs required a large staff of receivers, auditors, surveyors, and clerks, operating under the direction of the Chancellor of the Duchy. Much of its business was conducted in a building called the Duchy Chamber, located within the Blackfriars precinct but somewhat apart from the cloistral buildings.[24]

In 1411 a French embassy was accommodated in the hostelry of the Blackfriars; King Henry IV paid £36 for its board and lodging. The next year he made similar payments to the London Dominicans for their entertainment of the ambassadors of the Duke of Brittany, and the representatives of the Dukes of Berry, Orleans, and Bourbon.[25]

The Privy Council met in the friary often, especially during the early years of Henry VI, and on one occasion (July 27, 1426), the record specifically says that the meeting was held *"in refectorio Fratrum Praedicatorum."*[26]

The Parliament of 1450 met at the Blackfriars in London and was adjourned thence to Leicester.[27]

King Henry VIII used the friary buildings more often, and for more important events, than did any of his predecessors. The first notable occasion came in 1522, when he was host to Charles V of Spain, head of the Holy Roman Empire. Charles, the most powerful ruler on the European continent, was the nephew of Henry's Queen, Katharine of Aragon; and the place that Henry chose as lodging for the Emperor was the hostelry of the Blackfriars. Charles and his immediate entourage were accommodated in the friary's guest house, and his retinue of Spanish and German nobles in the new Palace of Bridewell, on the far side of the Fleet. To facilitate communications between Charles and his train, Henry constructed a long tapestry-lined gallery from one building to the other, over the Fleet and through a breach in the City wall.[28] Edward Hall, in his *Chronicle*, relates that the King and the Emperor, after making a triumphal entrance into London and being received by the Archbishop of Canterbury at St. Paul's,

> returned to horseback and came to the Blackfriars, where the Emperor was lodged in great royalty. All his nobles were lodged in his new Palace of Bridewell, out of the which was made a gallery to the Emperor's lodging, which gallery was very long, and that gallery and all other galleries there were hanged with arras. The King's palace was so richly adorned of all things that my wit is too dull to describe them, or the riches of the hangings, or the sumptuous building and gilding of chambers.[29]

Henry's choice of the Blackfriars guest house for the Emperor's personal use is more convincing testimony to its magnificence than anything Hall can say. He can have chosen it for only one reason: he thought of it as being more suitable for the accommodation of his imperial guest than any royal palace at his command.

In 1523 the Parliament convened in the great hall of the Blackfriars. Hall's *Chronicle* designates the place of meeting as the Parliament Chamber:

The xv day of April began a Parliament at the Blackfriars in London, and that day the mass of the Holy Ghost was sung, all the lords being present in their parliament robes. And when mass was finished the King came into the Parliament Chamber, and there sat down in the seat royal or throne, and at his feet on the right side sat the Cardinal of York [Wolsey] and the Archbishop of Canterbury, and at the rail behind stood Doctor Tunstall, Bishop of London, which made to the whole Parliament an eloquent oration declaring to the people the office of a king.[30]

The Commons having chosen Sir Thomas More to be their speaker, Cardinal Wolsey presented the King's demand for an enormous subsidy for prosecution of the war against France—a subsidy of four shillings out of the pound, or one fifth of every man's goods. The Parliament debated for two months and finally appropriated half the amount, and with that the King and Cardinal had to appear to be content.

This Parliament was adjourned to Westminster, amongst the Blacke Monkes, and ended in the Kings Palace there the 14. of August, at 9. of the clocke in the night, and was therefore called the *Blacke Parliament*.[31]

The Parliament met at Blackfriars again in 1525.[32] Its last recorded meeting there was on November 3, 1529, with Sir Thomas More sitting as Chancellor.[33] Not until after that, presumably, did Henry begin to use the Parliament Chamber as the office of the King's Revels and as storehouse for the Revels paraphernalia (13:4).

The Ludgate friary was the scene of some of the decisive events connected with the Reformation in England. Those about to be related continue the story of the London Blackfriars as a religious institution, and bring that story to a close. They show, as earlier events have already shown, that the Crown's relationship with the Blackfriars house at Ludgate was one that permitted it to enjoy privileges and to exact services that went beyond the purely spiritual. In doing so they suggest at the same time that some buildings within the precinct walls were of a sumptuousness more characteristic of royal ostentation than of mendicancy and evangelical poverty. Father Palmer has commented as follows upon the relationship of friary and Crown:

In this Priory, the foundation of a religious house was, in truth, subservient to the erection of offices of state under the guardianship of religious men. The cloistral portion enhanced the grandeur of the national institution, and the

Hospitium for unceasing hospitality to strangers was fit to be the lodging of kings and the residence of nobles. Here was a great Parliament Hall, where the supreme Council of the kingdom sometimes met. Here the Court of Chancery was held, and here were long stored up a part of those grand archives, which now enrich the Public Record Office. Here was the Duchy Chamber, where the business of the Duchy of Lancaster was transacted, and the palatine records were preserved.[34]

This relationship between friary and State will be called upon later in my discussion to support the conjecture that the Parliament Chamber, although within the precinct walls, was no part of the friary proper, but was in fact a possession of the Crown.

THE LONDON BLACKFRIARS AND THE REFORMATION

THE SPARK kindled by Martin Luther in 1517 became a forest fire: within a generation the Church suffered worse ravages than in the previous thousand years. Large areas of central and northern Germany repudiated the authority of the Holy See; so too did some of the Scandinavian countries, and the revolt was still spreading. Almost everywhere it was sanctioned by royalty, and almost everywhere it was accompanied by a breakup of monastic life and the confiscation of monastic property. It was not primarily directed toward the reform of ecclesiastical weaknesses and abuses. Those weaknesses and abuses existed, in England as elsewhere, and they cried out for reform. Men within the Church, men completely orthodox in creed and high in authority, acknowledged the evils and denounced them even more vehemently than did the laity. Churchmen charged their fellow churchmen with greed, sloth, licentiousness, and apostasy; they demanded an end to the laxity that permitted prelates to hold many benefices and draw stipends from them all, to absent themselves from the livings that they held, to confer church preferments upon immature and ignorant boys, to sell indulgences, and to charge exorbitant fees for the administration of sacraments.

But our present concern is not with the larger aspects of the Reformation in England, but only with the part played in it by the Ludgate priory. The priory was first drawn into the path of the approaching conflagration as early as 1382, when it was the scene of the ecclesiastical court that condemned John Wycliffe. Wycliffe had long been a thorn in the flesh of the clergy. He had demanded that the religious orders should return to the full observance of their rules, had denounced them for accumulating wealth while preaching poverty, and in effect had urged that the Church be shorn of all material possessions and power and divorced from the papacy. In the last half of the fourteenth century he had already anticipated every major element of the English Reformation that was to come a century and a half later. In 1382 the Church hit back at this budding protestantism: it summoned Wycliffe to appear before a provincial synod at the Blackfriars in London. The august assembly that confronted him included one archbishop, nine or ten bishops, thirty doctors of theology, and sundry doctors or bachelors of canon or civil law. Bishop Courtenay read twenty-four articles drawn from Wycliffe's writings; the solemn council condemned them and him,[35] and Wycliffe was permitted to die a natural death two years later only because of the protection of John of Gaunt, leader of the anticlerical party and uncle of the King. A generation later another heresy trial was held at Blackfriars. A priest named William Taylor had been condemned as heretical by a clerical court at St. Paul's. Blackfriars concurred, and Taylor was sent to the stake.[36]

The Wycliffe and Taylor trials were matters of internal discipline affecting only the Church; government had no part in them, was asked to have none, and wanted none. From its very beginning the Church in England had insisted upon its right and its competence to regulate its own affairs without lay discussion or civil intervention, and Parliament had respected the Church's insistence upon autonomy and inviolability. But when the Parliament met in 1512 it found public resentment running high against the abuses that had grafted themselves onto the ancient prerogative of benefit of clergy. In its simple original form, benefit of clergy had exempted all ecclesiastical persons from civil punishment for secular crimes, including murder. But clerical privilege had been extended to include all persons who could write, whether or not in holy orders, and even those who sought immunity by getting into orders after committing a crime; and it provided that all clerical criminals, after conviction in a civil court, might be confined only in a bishop's jail, from which escape was not unheard of. By 1512 the Commons and the people felt that the situation had gotten out of control, and the Parliament of that year took some halfhearted steps toward reform. It ruled that criminals could claim benefit of clergy only if they were in the superior orders of bishop, priest, or deacon, and it limited the privileges and exemptions conferred by clerical status in other respects as well. But Parliament qualified even these modest steps by making them effective only until it should meet again.[37]

Its next meeting was in 1515, at Westminster; and on the Sunday before the session was to open, the Abbot of Winchcombe preached a sermon at Paul's Cross in which he charged that the Act of 1512 was against the law of God and the liberty of Holy Church, and that all persons who had supported it were subject to excommunication. In spite of the Abbot's clear warning, the Commons promptly passed a bill to renew the Act of 1512; but the Upper House, where the lords spiritual were in a slight majority over the lords temporal, threw it out. The Commons passed the bill a second time; again the Lords threw it out; and then, at the request of the enraged Commons, the King called a conference to discuss the matter in his presence at Blackfriars.[38] At that meeting a mendicant friar, Dr. Henry Standish, Warden of the Franciscans, spoke in favor of the Act, arguing that clerical privilege should not be allowed to stand in opposition to the weal of the whole realm. In the ensuing debate he was vigorously attacked by the prelates, but he acquitted himself so well that the Commons rallied to his support and demanded that the bishops compel the Abbot of Winchcombe to retract his sermon. They refused, and instead summoned Standish to appear before them in Convocation on suspicion of heresy. Well knowing the nature of the punishment that could follow conviction on that charge, Standish appealed to the King for protection against the consequences of supporting the civil cause in defiance of the ecclesiastical, and his Majesty ordered a commission composed of judges, the Privy Council, certain spiritual and temporal lords, and a few members of the Parliament, to assemble at Blackfriars to try the question.[39]

They met in Michaelmas Term of 1515, at a moment when the whole problem of benefit of clergy had been given a new immediacy and urgency by the death of one Richard Hunne, a London merchant, under gravely suspicious circumstances. The coroner's inquest found that Hunne had been murdered, and named Dr. Horsey, Chancellor of the Bishop of London, as being implicated in the crime. The truth of the matter is not known, but the mere fact of Dr. Horsey's being committed for trial was enough to complicate the situation immeasurably for the prelates assembled at Blackfriars. It not only placed them on the defensive in their relations with King, Parliament, and public, but it forced them to oppose renewal of the Act of 1512 both on principle and in order to protect their colleague from having to stand trial for willful murder before the King's judges. As a first step they challenged Dr. Standish's orthodoxy in a series of six specifications. Some of them he denied, others he explained. He now had the support of Dr. Vesey, Dean of the Chapel Royal, and, with events to help them, the two managed Standish's defense so adroitly that the bishops found themselves to be not the accusers, but the accused. Instead of condemning Standish, the judges ruled that all who had taken part in the proceedings against him had incurred the penalties of Praemunire[40] as being under suspicion of disloyalty to the Crown. This ruling placed the churchmen wholly in the King's power, and Cardinal Wolsey, as spokesman for them all, took the only way out. He knelt before the King and begged for mercy, assuring his Majesty that no member of the clergy had intended to do anything in derogation of the royal prerogative.

The session ended with a series of compromises. The Act of 1512 was not renewed. The King ordered an investigation of the charges against Dr. Horsey and found no real case against him. Convocation dropped its allegations of heresy against Dr. Standish, and the King elevated him to a bishopric over Wolsey's protest.[41] Parliament adjourned after six weeks with little done, but it had at last dared to meddle in a question that affected the privileges of the Church.

The forces that were to give the English Reformation its special character had still not appeared. The first of them began to emerge in 1526 or early 1527, when those who were closest to Henry VIII became aware that he was contemplating a divorce.

The question of the royal succession had long been uppermost in the King's mind. He, and the country with him, dreaded the possibility of a female heir or a disputed inheritance with its threat of another civil war. An illegitimate son would not do: Henry must have a son born in wedlock to him and his lawful queen. By this time, however, it had become obvious that he could have no male heir while Katharine remained his wife. She was now in her forties. She had had eight pregnancies in nine years, two of which had ended in miscarriages, three in stillbirths, and two in the birth of children who had lived only a few weeks; and for all her pains the Queen had nothing to show but the sickly Princess Mary. Henry feared increasingly that his marriage to Katharine had been cursed by God as being incestuous, on the grounds that Katharine had been briefly married, many years before, to Henry's older brother, Prince Arthur. She was sixteen years old at the time, and he was fifteen. He had died a few months later, and Henry, with papal dispensation, had married his brother's widow. But now he had come to fear that a pope's dispensation was impotent in the face of the Biblical prohibition of such marriages and its threat of childlessness as a penalty.[42] His scruples soon combined with a growing infatuation with Anne Boleyn to suggest a divorce and remarriage.

The first overt move toward a divorce was made in 1527, in an appeal to Pope Clement VII to grant an annulment. The appeal confronted the Pontiff with a dilemma that could have no happy solution. To grant the King's request would be to compromise the doctrine of papal infallibility by dishonoring the bull of dispensation that his predecessor had signed. It would dissolve a union that the Pope and the Roman Curia regarded as a true marriage. It would enable Henry to marry a woman with whom he had precisely the same degree of affinity as that upon which he based his claim that his marriage with Katharine was incestuous,[43] and it would infuriate Katharine's nephew, the Emperor Charles V. On the other hand, to refuse the annulment would be to deny Henry and his subjects their legitimate desire for a male heir, to arouse the resentment of a king whose zeal and skill in support of the Church and the Papacy had earned him the title of Defender of the Faith, and to risk —indeed, as events were to prove, to lead to—the alienation of England from Rome. And as if the difficulties inherent in the situation were not enough already, in late 1527 the Emperor's soldiers sacked Rome and took the Pope prisoner.

Pope Clement, always vacillating and weak, found the problem insoluble. He evaded all final decisions in the hope that something might happen—perhaps a cooling of Henry's passion for Anne, or Katharine's retirement to a nunnery—that would remove the need for any decision at all. But Henry redoubled his petitions, and finally he and his chancellor, Cardinal Wolsey, wrung from the Pope his slow leave to have the case submitted to trial in England. The Pope commissioned Cardinal Wolsey and Cardinal Campeggio of Rome to preside at a court of inquiry as papal legates. He empowered them to hear evidence and to decide the issue irrevocably, and he promised Henry that he would confirm their verdict; but at the same time he gave secret instructions to Campeggio to delay proceedings as much as possible and under no circumstances to render a decision without his consent. These were the crippling conditions under which the legatine trial opened in the Parliament Chamber at Blackfriars.

According to the Shakespeare-Fletcher play of *Henry VIII*, it was the King himself who chose the friary as the place of trial:

> The most convenient place that I can think of
> For such receipt of learning is Blackfriars.
> There ye shall meet about this weighty business.
> My Wolsey, see it furnish'd.[44]

Official records show that the Pope's commission was presented to Cardinals Wolsey and Campeggio on May 31, 1529, "in the Parliament Chamber near the convent of the Friars Preachers,"[45] and that the writ of summons to the trial directed Henry VIII and Katharine of Aragon to appear before the two Cardinals "in the Parliament Chamber near the Friars Preachers."[46] In that chamber, beginning on June 18, the King and Queen and Cardinals staged the drama that was to be reenacted by Shakespeare's fellows eighty-four years later in the very hall in which it had historically taken place.

Holinshed describes the scene as follows:

> The place where the cardinals should sit to hear the cause of matrimony betwixt the King and the Queen, was ordained to be at the Blackfriars in London; where in the great hall was preparation made of seats, tables, and other furniture, according to such a solemn session and royal appearance. The court was platted in tables and benches in manner of a consistory, one seat raised higher for the judges to sit in. Then as it were in the midst of the said judges, aloft, above them three degrees high, was a cloth of estate hanged, with a chair royal under the same, wherein sat the King; and besides him, some distance from him, sat the Queen, and under the judges' feet sat the scribes and other officers. . . . Then before the King and the judges, within the court, sat the Archbishop of Canterbury, Warham, and all the other bishops. Then stood at both ends within, the counsellors learned in the spiritual laws, as well the King's as the Queen's. The doctors of law for the King . . . had their convenient rooms. Thus was the court furnished.[47]

While the trial was in progress Henry and Katharine lived across the Fleet, in the same Bridewell Palace that had accommodated the Emperor's retinue seven years before. Proceedings dragged on at a snail's pace. His Majesty tried to hurry them because he had become impatient to marry Anne Boleyn; Wolsey tried to hurry them through fear that the Pope, under pressure from Charles, might revoke the case to Rome before a decision could be reached; Campeggio, for his well-instructed part, did everything in his power to slow matters down. The testimony consisted largely of hearsay gossip as to the connubial relationship of a teen-age boy and girl twenty-eight years before: had or had not Katharine's marriage to Henry's brother been consummated? The whole trial was a legalistic mummery dressed up in spectacular formality and pious pretense; its only moments of honesty were Katharine's appeal to the conscience of the King, and Bishop Fisher's denunciation of the King's cause, an act of courage that was to cost him his head.

> Thus went this strange case forward from court-day to court-day, until it came to the judgment, so that every man expected the judgment to be given upon the next court-day [July 23]. At which day the king came thither, and sat within a gallery against the door of the same that looked unto the judges where they sat, whom he might both see and hear speak, to hear what judgment they would give in his suit.[48]

Cardinal Campeggio rose to his feet; but instead of pronouncing a verdict, he announced a three-month adjournment for a summer recess. Henry and Wolsey were caught napping. Shortly afterwards the Pope recalled the case to Rome.

Henry was furious. Never before had he been crossed in anything. Having identified his own will with the will of God, he was incapable of accepting defeat. Since he had not secured an annulment through the Holy See, he would secure it through some other more pliable agency. Since the Pope had failed him, the Pope must be stripped of all authority within Henry's realm. And since Wolsey had urged the tedious and fruitless resort to Rome instead of shorter and more summary processes at home, Wolsey must go.

His Majesty now charged his able and loyal minister with treason under the Statute of Praemunire, an old statute that made it treasonable to sue in a "foreign" (i.e., papal) court on any matter that might be construed as lying within the jurisdiction of the Crown. Wolsey had done so when he acted as legate for the Pope; he had acquiesced in having a question involving the English succession submitted to a Roman court. He had done so in the King's interest and at the King's command, but those things made no difference to a King who was determined upon Wolsey's ruin. Within three months of the July fiasco at Blackfriars, Wolsey was called to stand trial before a parliament held in the same place that had seen his previous failure.[49] The parliament condemned him

21

in Praemunire. The King confiscated the Cardinal's enormous wealth and gave his chancellorship to Sir Thomas More. For the present he permitted Wolsey to leave London in safety.

Parliament met a week later "at the Black Friars, London, 3 Nov., 21 Hen. VIII [1529], the King being present the first day. Sir Thos. More as chancellor declared the cause of its being summoned . . . in a long and elegant speech . . . and in the end he ordered the Commons in the King's name to assemble next day in their accustomed house and choose a Speaker, whom they should present to the King."[50] Hall tells the same story with an important addition: he identifies the Commons' "accustomed house" with a certain "nether house." He reports the Chancellor as directing the Commons to "'resort to the nether house, and there amongst yourself, according to the old and ancient custom, to choose an able person to be your common mouth and speaker, and after your election so made to advertise his Grace thereof.' . . . After this done, the Commons resorted to the nether house, and they chose for their speaker Thomas Audeley, esquire and attorney for the Duchy of Lancaster; and the same day was the Parliament adjourned to Westminster."[51]

Professor J. E. Neale, author of *The Elizabethan House of Commons,* says (p. 364) that, "oddly enough, there seems to be no clue to the Commons' meeting place in Henry VIII's reign." But the two passages just quoted, taken together, seem to provide the clue that he has lacked, for they make it appear that the "accustomed house" of the Commons was the "nether house" beneath the great Parliament Chamber. We know from other sources that two rooms, called respectively the Hall and the Parlor in the Survey of 1548 (4:6), occupied two thirds of the story immediately below that chamber. They may originally have been a single room;[52] they presumably had an inside width of 46 feet and a combined length of about 70;[53] and one or both of the rooms may have been the accustomed meeting place of the Commons when they met apart from the Lords.

As we have already seen, Parliament had two places of meeting in the reign of Henry VIII, the one at Blackfriars and the other at Westminster. We still lack clues as to why there should have been two and under what circumstances one should have been preferred to the other.

Wolsey, ever since his downfall, had been living far from the Court and almost in penury; but rumors reached Henry from time to time that the Cardinal had been in correspondence with Rome, that he had expressed opinions unfavorable to the King, and that he still possessed large sums of money that he had managed to conceal when the rest of his property was seized. In 1530, therefore, the King sent the Earl of North-ampton to Cawood in Yorkshire to place Wolsey under arrest for high treason, and ordered Sir William Kingston, Constable of the Tower of London, to escort him to London for a trial that, as Wolsey well knew, could end only in conviction and the block. Broken in spirit and in body, Wolsey waxed so sick on the journey that he was divers times likely to have fallen from his mule, and by the time the train reached Leicester Abbey he was spent and could go no farther. Kingston sought to encourage him, but the dying Cardinal refused to be deceived. "Well, well, Master Kingston," quoth he, "I see the matter against me how it is framed; but if I had served God as diligently as I have done the king, he would not have given me over in my grey hairs."[54] These words were later to be adapted by Shakespeare, with Thomas Cromwell substituted for Kingston as the person to whom they were addressed:

> O Cromwell, Cromwell!
> Had I but serv'd my God with half the zeal
> I serv'd my king, he would not in mine age
> Have left me naked to mine enemies.[55]

Quite apart from its association with the play, the incident is of present interest because a few years later, in the partition of the Ludgate friary, Sir William Kingston and his lady were to become the holders of certain houses and parcels of land in what had formerly been the Blackfriars precinct. Sir William will be mentioned more than once in the pages that follow, and Lady Mary has her own short paragraph in the history books; for it was to her, as wife of the Tower Warden, that Queen Anne Boleyn knelt on the eve of her execution and asked a last favor: that she should kneel before Princess Mary and beseech her, in Anne's name, to forgive the wrongs that had come to her through the pride and thought-lessness of a miserable woman.[56]

Cardinal Wolsey's trial at Blackfriars in 1529 was probably the last occasion on which the friary was directly involved in the events of the Reformation until it was itself wiped out at the very end. The story of the great religious struggle during the nine intervening years will be passed over quickly.

The Parliament that began in 1529 lasted until 1536, and by the time that it ended it had broken the ties of the English Church to Rome, placed the Church wholly under royal supremacy, and redistributed a fifth of the national wealth at the Church's expense. Early in the session the bishops dared to lock horns with the King by denying that he or Parliament had the right to intervene in Church affairs. Henry retaliated by threatening to prosecute, as traitors under the Statute of Praemunire, all clergymen who had recognized Wolsey's authority as a papal legate. He would stay prosecution under two conditions: first, confession of guilt and payment of an enormous fine; and second, acknowledgment of the King as the "Protector and Supreme Head of the English Church and Clergy." The clergy offered compromises, but Henry accepted none. Finally, after inserting the qualifying clause "so far as the law of Christ allows," they yielded.

Henry demanded and secured still other anticlerical legislation when Parliament and Convocation reconvened in 1532, and a year later a chastened clergy gave its approval to his divorce from Katharine. He had already secretly married Anne, and the Act of Succession of 1534 made it a capital offense for anyone to question the validity of the new marriage or the legitimacy of its issue. That same year Parliament enacted the Statute of Supremacy that affirmed Henry's sovereignty over Church and State and gave him all the powers that the Church had previously exercised in matters of creed, morals, and ecclesiastical organization; and the bishops took a new oath by which they submitted to Henry unconditionally, without regard to the law of Christ. Except in some remote areas where communication with London was tenuous, the clergy made surprisingly little determined resistance when Henry moved to substitute his own authority for that of the Pope. The rights and wrongs of those anxious years are still disputed by historians and theologians: it may be fair to say that many English priests had long resented the growing power of Rome, and, while they did not relish putting the supreme ecclesiastical authority in the hands of the King, they seized the opportunity to rid themselves of the Pope.

The legislation that Henry had forced through Parliament and Convocation constituted a reformation in a legal and political and administrative sense, but not in doctrine or morals. Henry was still an orthodox Catholic in every respect except recognition of papal authority. He had not the slightest intention of deviating, or of permitting his subjects to deviate, from the essential dogmas of Catholicism: he persecuted those who denied the teachings of the Roman Church no less enthusiastically than he did those who accepted the jurisdiction of the Roman See.

The next step was inevitable, not because the Church was worldly and lax, but because it was wealthy and weak. Its wealth was prodigious. Estimates place its holdings in land at one fifth of all the kingdom,[57] in addition to buildings and sacristy treasures of incalculable worth.[58] And the King needed money sorely. His personal and Court expenses were extravagant, far in excess of his revenue; new taxes were stubbornly resisted by the Commons, and taxation was already high to the point of diminishing returns. The answer to Henry's fiscal problems was obvious; it lay in closing the religious houses and confiscating their property for the Crown.

Cardinal Wolsey had already shown the way. In 1524, with the consent of the Pope, he had closed a score or more of ailing monasteries and nunneries to raise funds for the endowment of colleges in Oxford and in his native Ipswich. His agent in those early suppressions had been the clever but unscrupulous Thomas Cromwell. Henry now took Cromwell into his own service, dignified him with the title of Vicar-General in Spirituals, and gave him power to "treat and examine all causes ecclesiastical." Under this broad authority Cromwell appointed commissions in 1535 to conduct visitations of all religious houses for the purpose of reporting on behavior and good fame, on fidelity to vows and rule, on property and revenue, and on acceptance of royal authority. His investigators were handpicked men whose mission was not to inquire, but to condemn. They pursued that objective with scandalous efficiency. They coerced monks into confessing abuses or implicating their brethren; they omitted to distinguish between fact and gossip, between current irregularities and those long past; they interpreted an absence of incriminating evidence as collusion to conceal the truth; they suppressed reports that were favorable, and they accepted bribes freely. They found, of course, more than enough proof of immorality, lax discipline, and neglect of duty, but the true picture was by no means as black as the picture they painted.

A year before the general visitations were ordered, John Hilsey, Prior of the Black Friars of Bristol, had already come to London and offered his services to the King. As a reward he had been appointed Provincial of the Order of Friars Preachers in England, and on April 13, 1534, he and the Provincial of the Austin Friars were commissioned to make visitations of the mendicant orders and reduce them to acknowledgment of royal supremacy; and this they did with so much persuasiveness that within a week all the London friaries had formally accepted Henry's headship of the English Church. The Ludgate Friars Preachers accepted it on April 17. Their submission was signed by Robert Stroddle, *humillimus prior fratrum praedicatorum*, acting freely and of his own will and with the consent of all his brethren.[59]

Three weeks later the London Dominicans received a bloody reminder of the price of opposition to the King's will, when the headless bodies of two Benedictine monks were brought to their friary for burial. They had been hanged and beheaded at Tyburn, along with Elizabeth Barton, the Holy Maid of Kent, for siding with her in her denunciation of the King's divorce.[60]

Under the leadership of a provincial who was of the King's party, the Dominican priories throughout England surrendered one after another as the visitors approached. A few misguided spirits had the courage and integrity to hold to their convictions, but they were quickly disposed of; one of them was the Prior of the Black Friars of York, who was hanged, beheaded, and quartered at Tyburn.[61] Some of those who could face neither martyrdom nor apostasy took refuge in Scotland or on the Continent, and a few fled to Ireland. Others accepted the inevitable on the conscience-salving theory that the jurisdiction of Rome had after all been a matter of human ordinance rather than of divine precept, and that defection from papal rule involved no repudiation of the doctrines of Catholic faith. The rest joined the headlong rush into schism to save their own skins.

Hilsey was suitably rewarded for helping the friaries to see their way clear to the acceptance of royal headship. To the title of English Provincial, which he already held, the King added those of Master-General of the Order in England, and Prior of London. Stroddle was chagrined at being displaced as prior, and tried to recover the office through the mediation of friends at Court, and especially of Sir William Kingston. But Hilsey had merited more gratitude than Stroddle at the King's hands, and the priorate remained his. The next year he was consecrated Bishop of Rochester, with a pension of £60 a year and a lodging in the London precinct, while still retaining the offices of Master-General, Provincial, and Prior.[62]

Cromwell's visitations had been merely preludes to the final act of suppression and seizure. They had served two useful purposes. To the King and his Vicar-General they had brought reassurance as to the golden harvest to be reaped by confiscation of Church property; and to the abbots and priors they had brought warning of the grim exaction levied by the King for tardiness in yielding to the royal will. The next step followed fast when Parliament met at Westminster on February 4, 1536. Cromwell, armed with the reports of his visitors, asked Parliament to order the suppression of all monasteries and nunneries with an annual income of £200 or less, on the grounds that "manifest sins and vicious and carnal living is daily used in such small abbeys and priories of monks, canons, and nuns, . . . and that in spite of many visitations, no reformation is had hitherto."[63] Parliament consented, and 370 or more lesser houses were closed and their property swept into the royal treasury, and a special Court of Augmentations was created to deal with property that fell to the Crown.

Spoliation of the smaller monasteries met with active resistance in the northern shires. The insurgents, of course, were soon dispersed and their leaders killed, but the rebellions had the effect of sealing the fate of all the remaining religious houses. No new act of Parliament was passed to legalize the new suppressions, but an Act of 1539 ratified all the seizures that the King had made in the past or should make thereafter. The last of the monasteries had been seized by 1540.

Cromwell's choice as chief inquisitor to the Dominicans had been a certain Richard Ingworth, Prior of the Noviciate House at King's Langley. He later was consecrated Bishop of Dover in recognition of his services.[64]

The Ludgate priory of the Black Friars was surrendered on November 12, 1538. It was valued at £104 15s. 5d.[65] The Deed of Surrender of the "House of Friars-Preachers of the Order of St. Dominic, commonly called the Blake Freers in London," was signed by Hilsey as "J. bp. of Rochester, prior commendatory," and sixteen others[66] who presumably were all that remained of a convent that had once numbered eighty or ninety brethren. The keys of the priory were turned over to Sir John Portinary, a gentleman pensioner[67] and resident of the precinct, who got a fee for keeping them. In his own words, "when the said house of Blackfriars was dissolved and came to the King's hands, by order from the King the keys of the said house were delivered to this examinate to keep, who had a fee for the keeping of the said house of friars."[68] The church plate was confiscated and carried to the King's jewel house. The treasures of the library have never been traced.

1. The Carthusian and Cistercian Orders were exceptions to the rule of general conformity. Carthusian settlements were gatherings of individual anchorites rather than communities of brethren, and therefore provided separate cells rather than communal domestic buildings. The Cistercians had two set of domestic buildings, one for the monks and another for the lay brethren or *conversi*. The establishments of both orders must be understood to constitute exceptions to many of the general statements in the pages that follow.

2. Hinnebusch, pp. 232–33.

3. Hinnebusch, pp. 28, 126; Jarrett, p. 25.

4. The official title of the Order was and is *Ordo Praedicatorum*, Order of Preachers.

5. All my information about the Holborn friary is derived from Fr. Palmer's two articles on that subject, and from Fr. Hinnebusch, pp. 20–33.

6. Palmer, "London," p. 37; Jarrett, p. 32.

7. Hinnebusch, p. 55.

8. Palmer, "London," pp. 34–35.

9. The 1619 petition of precinct inhabitants to the Lord Mayor (28:1).

10. Castle Baynard had been razed by King John in 1213 in reprisal for the hostility of its lord, the first Robert Fitz-Walter, marshal of the baronial forces; it was now nothing more than a heap of rubble. A second Castle Baynard was built in 1428, somewhat to the east of its predecessor. This later castle was the one upon whose leads the Duke of Gloucester appeared between two bishops in *Richard III*, III vii.

11. Ed. 1618, p. 688; ed. 1633, p. 405.

12. Hinnebusch, p. 37.

13. Palmer, "London," p. 36.

14. Hinnebusch, pp. 75–85.

15. Holinshed, Vol. III, p. 517; Everyman's ed., p. 50.

16. All my statements about the spiritual relationship of the Order to the Crown are based upon Jarrett, p. 106.

17. At least until 1515, and probably long after, Henry paid an annuity of £20 out of the King's alms to the Friars Preachers of London, of 50 marks to the Friars Preachers of Oxford, and of 25 marks to the Friars Preachers of Cambridge. See the *Letters and Papers of Henry VIII*, Vol. II, p. 299, no. 1128, and p. 301, no. 1141.

18. Hinnebusch, p. 462; Jarrett, p. 108.

19. The relations between the Order and the Court are discussed more fully by Hinnebusch, pp. 458–65 and 470–89, and by Jarrett, pp. 107–28.

20. Palmer, "London," p. 275. Fr. Palmer seldom gives his references, and I have not been able to trace his sources for this item; but the later writers who quote him invariably do so with complete confidence, and I do not question his accuracy as to these events.

21. *Ibid.*

22. *Ibid.*

23. *Ibid.*

24. 4:5, 4:10, 6:21, 6:23; see also Hugh Losse's schedule of Crown rents, as printed in Palmer, "London," p. 286. Neale, in *The Elizabethan House of Commons*, pp. 221–32, discusses the political importance of the Duchy in the time of Elizabeth I.

25. Jarrett, p. 36.

26. *Proceedings and Ordinances of the Privy Council*, Vol. III, p. 209.

27. Hall, ed. 1809, p. 217. Cf. Stow, ed. 1618, p. 653; ed. 1633, p. 373.

28. Stow, p. 1618, pp. 747–48; ed. 1633, p. 436. This was the "decayed gallery" of the 1548 and 1550 Surveys (4:2 and

6:18), and the "ruined gallery" of the Cawarden grant (7:6).

29. Ed. 1548, p. 640.

30. Ed. 1548, p. 652; ed. 1809, p. 106. Cf. *Letters and Papers of Henry VIII*, Vol. III, Part 2, p. 1244, no. 2956.

31. Stow, ed. 1618, p. 653; ed. 1633, p. 374. Cf. Hall, ed. 1548, p. 657. Stow gives the date as 1524 instead of 1523.

32. Stow, ed. 1618, p. 748; ed. 1633, p. 436.

33. See p. 22 below.

34. Palmer, "London," pp. 274–75.

35. Palmer, "London," p. 276; Wheatley, Vol. I, p. 194; Durant, p. 36.

36. Palmer, *loc. cit.*

37. Carter, pp. 32–34; Ferguson, pp. 126, 128.

38. *Letters and Papers of Henry VIII*, Vol. II, p. 351, no. 1313.

39. *Ibid.*, Vol. II, p. 352.

40. See p. 21 below.

41. Hughes, p. 154.

42. Leviticus xx 21: "He that marrieth his brother's wife, doth an unlawful thing; he hath uncovered his brother's nakedness: they shall be without children."

43. Henry had the same impediment to marriage with Anne as he alleged himself to have with respect to Katharine: i.e., affinity arising from a sexual relationship, in the one case through a sister, in the other case through a brother; for Mary, sister of Anne, had been and still was the King's mistress. Thus at the moment when Henry was denying that the previous Pope had the power to remove an impediment arising from affinity, he was asking the present Pope to remove the impediment to his marriage with a woman toward whom precisely the same affinity existed. See Hughes, Vol. I, pp. 159–60, etc.

44. *Henry VIII*, II ii 138–41.

45. *Letters and Papers of Henry VIII*, Vol. IV, p. 2483, no. 5613.

46. *Ibid.*, Vol. IV, pp. 2483–84. The use of the word "near" in these two documents is discussed on p. 99 below.

47. Vol. III, p. 907; Everyman's ed., p. 192. Cf. Hall, ed. 1809, p. 756.

48. Cavendish, Vol. I, p. 164.

49. Stow, ed. 1618, p. 653; ed. 1633, p. 374.

50. *Letters and Papers of Henry VIII*, Vol. IV, p. 2689, no. 6043.

51. Pp. 764–65. I am aware that in the *Chronicle*, p. 784, "nether house" means the Lower House, the House of Commons as a body, not as a place. But in the present instance the phrase "resort to" seems to preclude that interpretation.

52. The Parliament Chamber itself was originally "one great and entire room," but by 1596 it had become "those seven great upper rooms as they are now divided" (19:2).

53. See p. 97 below.

54. Cavendish, Vol. I, p. 320.

55. *Henry VIII*, III ii 454–57.

56. John Lingard, *History of England* (1855), Vol. V, p. 37, as quoted by Durant, p. 560.

57. Ferguson, p. 126, places the figure at one fifth of all the land in England. James, p. 14, says that 650 monasteries owned a quarter of the land. Belloc, p. 117, says that by 1500 the Church owned, on a conservative estimate, about a fifth of all the property in England.

58. This wealth was not shared by the mendicant orders. The friaries had little property and no treasure. They had never had a fixed income, and by the fifteen-thirties voluntary gifts had fallen away to nothing. At the time of the Dissolution many of the friaries were poor to the point of destitution, and their seizure

brought little revenue to the royal purse. Cf. Knowles, Vol. III, pp. 360, 366, 411.

59. Palmer, "London," p. 281; Jarrett, p. 157.

60. Palmer, "London," p. 281; Jarrett, p. 157.

61. Jarrett, p. 159.

62. Palmer, "London," p. 281; Jarrett, p. 165.

63. *Letters and Papers of Henry VIII*, Preamble to the Act of Suppression.

64. Jarrett, p. 156.

65. Stow, ed. 1618, p. 653; ed. 1633, p. 374.

66. *Letters and Papers of Henry VIII*, Vol. XIII, Part 2, no. 809.

67. *Ibid.*, Vol. IV, Part 1, p. 871.

68. *BR* 52:17ff.

Materials for Reconstruction
of the Precinct

THIRTY-EIGHT YEARS after its confiscation, the secularized precinct near Ludgate was the site of the First Blackfriars Playhouse; twenty-four years after that, it was the site of the Second. Both playhouses are milestones in the history of the English stage, and yet neither can be precisely located on the authority of contemporary documents. The First Blackfriars was installed in an upstairs apartment six or seven times as long as it was wide, which occupied parts of the upper stories of two adjoining buildings. This much we know, but the records fail to say whether the playhouse was located in the building called the Old Buttery or in that called the Upper Frater. The Second and greater Blackfriars was on one or the other of two stories in the Upper Frater building, but no record says on which story. The latter point is important, because upon it depends the prior history, size, and architectural character of the hall that James Burbage converted to theatrical purposes. I shall undertake to prove that the playhouse occupied the topmost floor, the "seven great upper rooms" of the Burbage deed of purchase. In holding this opinion I am taking a position at variance with those of the two scholars who have preceded me in a study of the subject. Their theories will be examined on a later page.

The Old Buttery and the Upper Frater have wholly disappeared; their last vestiges perished in the Great Fire of 1666. No pictures of buildings or playhouses are known to exist, and the verbal descriptions of both leave much to the creative imagination. Both buildings can nevertheless be reconstructed with a considerable degree of confidence if all the resources at our command are brought to bear upon the question. Some bare facts are quickly established, as for instance the locations of the two buildings and their dimensions; but other facts of equal importance—as that the Old Buttery was not merely a culinary office, but the guest house of the friary, and that the top floor of the Upper Frater was not designed to be the dining hall of a confraternity of friars, but to be the meeting place of great deliberative assemblies—emerge only upon a study of the two buildings in their relationship to the friary as a whole. The friary too has totally vanished; it too must therefore be reconstructed in its essentials. For this purpose four categories of evidence are available:

First, architectural remains of abbeys and priories as revealing the usual practice of monks and friars in general, and of the Black Friars in particular, in planning their convents;

Second, traces of the actual Ludgate buildings as they have been uncovered by excavation or as they are perpetuated in modern building lines;

Third, surveys and other real estate records relating to the London precinct; and

Fourth, the description of the friary in *Piers the Plowman's Creed*.

Of these the first is the most important, even though the least direct. The excavated relics are intelligible only as they confirm facts otherwise known or surmised; the real estate surveys and deeds give only some post-Dissolution metes and bounds; the *Piers* passage gives vivid details, but no general plan. All these groups of data become comprehensible only when interpreted by the system of cloistral arrangement originally devised by the monastic orders and subsequently adopted, with minor modifications, by the mendicant.

I: *THE CLASSIC TRADITION IN PRECINCT DESIGN*

THE TRADITIONAL system of cloistral arrangement was evolved on the continent of Europe by the monks, was by them brought thence to England, and in the course of centuries acquired a few characteristics peculiar to English practice while still conforming generally to the classic plan. That plan, as it was developed in England by the monastic orders and adapted by the mendicant, is best evidenced by the cloistral remains that survive in England today. Unfortunately, not one precinct survives intact and entire out of the 650 religious houses that are believed to have existed in England when monasticism was at its height. In the years following the Dissolution all suffered grievously, those in the country from neglect, many of those in the cities from deliberate spoliation. Some have disappeared completely, of which the Ludgate priory is one.

Others exist only in magnificent ruin; and of those in condition still to be used for religious purposes, for the most part only the churches remain. But here or there a chapter house or cloister survives as well, or a dormitory or refectory; and although not all the components of a medieval monastery or friary can be found in any one place, each component can be found somewhere in a condition that suggests its original appearance and use.

I have previously spoken of certain philosophical differences between monks and friars, notably in their attitudes toward the world outside their cloisters. The differences in philosophy led to differences in the arrangement and design of their conventual buildings. Because they concerned themselves little with the laity, monks could build their settlements in secluded valleys, far from the converse of men; and because they came early, they had little difficulty in finding sites suitable in size, shape, and contour for the construction of precincts in conformity with the traditional plan.

Friars, on the other hand, were compelled to build in towns. Both their ministry to the masses and their subsistence upon alms demanded that their priories be built where people lived, in centers of population; and their mission of preaching made the further demand that their churches be built not merely in towns, but near the main thoroughfares of the towns. The friars, however, were latecomers, and land of that sort was not easy to get. It was already occupied, and acreage enough for a priory was hard to come by. As a result the friars often had to put up with cramped quarters and ill-shaped sites when they started to build, and to pick up additional parcels piecemeal from time to time as opportunity arose. For the friars, therefore, adherence to the classical pattern of precinct arrangement was more difficult, and departures from it were more frequent.

The architectural remains of the friars' houses are less considerable than those of the monks. Although the mendicant houses numbered about two hundred at the Dissolution, little of them is left, and that little is relatively unimportant and unimpressive, and usually needs searching for. This condition is largely the result of the friaries' location in cities, where land was in demand and where the walls of secularized churches provided useful quarries of dressed stone.

The remains of the Dominican establishments are particularly meager. The Order had between fifty and sixty houses in England and Wales at the Dissolution;[1] of these all but sixteen have disappeared without leaving a trace, and ten of the sixteen have left only fragmentary

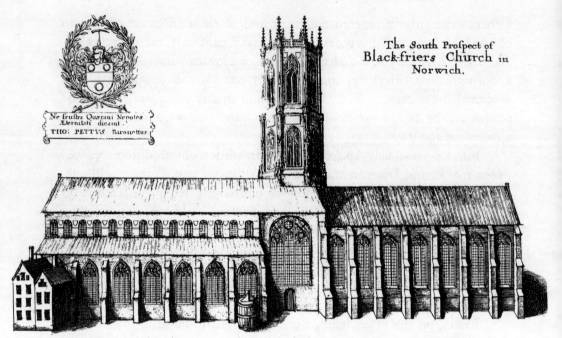

Figure 3. The Blackfriars Church in Norwich. The original church was built in the thirteenth century; when the present nave was built two centuries later, the old church became its chancel or choir. The illustration above is from the 1716 edition of Dugdale's Monasticon Anglicanum, *and shows the church as it was about 1670, before the tower fell. The building, still lacking a tower, is now known as St. Andrew's Hall.*

remains. The only important Dominican monument that survives is the Church of St. John the Baptist at Norwich, now known as St. Andrew's Hall;[2] it is not merely the best of the Blackfriars remains, but is the best example of a friars' church left in England by any of the mendicant orders. At Brecon the choir still stands, serving now as the chapel of Christ College; the nave is gone. At Gloucester and Canterbury the refectories remain, both much altered; Canterbury also has a building that was probably the guest house originally, and Gloucester has an important dorter. A part of the south range stands at Bristol and now serves as a school. The preaching cross survives at Hereford, the only such cross left in England. Foundation walls have been uncovered at Bangor and Cardiff, and traces of vanished buildings have been found at Bamburgh, Beverly, Boston, Cambridge, King's Langley, Newcastle-on-Tyne, Thetford, and Ludgate in London.

Fortunately, architectural remains are not our only source of information with respect to Dominican practice in precinct design. Surveys of some sites were made after the Dissolution on behalf of the Crown or of private landowners, and specifications sometimes survive in wills, deeds, leases, chronicles, and so forth. Drawings or prints are extant of the priory buildings at Bamburgh, Canterbury, Gloucester, Ipswich, Newcastle-on-Tyne, and Rhuddlan. Even so, however, there are vast gaps in our range of knowledge, gaps so deep and wide as to make it dangerous to generalize on the subject of Dominican tendencies. I shall not venture to do so. I shall merely summarize whatever scanty evidence we possess, without intending to suggest that it indicates a settled practice.

The Church

As originated by the monastic orders on the mainland of Europe and transplanted to England, the traditional system of cloistral arrangement provided, to begin with, that the church should lie at the north end of the precinct and on the highest ground, and that it should be cruciform in plan, with nave to the west, chancel to the east, and transepts to the north and south. The northern position was desirable because a church so sited could shelter a cloister to the south of it on a cold winter's day; the high walls of its nave and south transept could ward off the north and east winds and give the cloister the added warmth of the reflected sun—advantages doubly important in an English winter. The church's position on the highest ground was dictated less by the dignity of the sacred edifice than by prosaic problems of drainage. Water supply was a matter of first importance in every precinct; running water must always flow along the outskirts of the group of domestic buildings to sweep away the refuse of kitchen and rere-dorter; and since water seeks the lower ground, the domestic buildings too must seek the lower, and the church, which needed no drainage, must take the higher.

The monks, with their wider choice of desirable sites, were able to place their churches at the north ends of their precincts with a good deal of consistency; the friars did so whenever they could. But sometimes the friars found that their low ground lay at the north, and so were led to forgo the advantages of a warm cloister out of deference to sewage disposal; and sometimes even the requirements of drainage were overridden by the obligation resting upon the friars to make their churches available for public worship. If, therefore, the main highway of the town lay to the south of the precinct, the convenience of lay worshippers commonly outweighed all other considerations, and the church was placed at the south. And when, for any of these reasons, the church was at the

south and the cloister at the north, then all the north-south relationships were reversed, but the east-west relationships remained unchanged:
the church's choir still lay toward the east and its nave toward the west,
with very rare exceptions.[3]

The friars' ministry as preachers led to other deviations from the
monastic norm in church design. In their churches they needed floor
space enough to accommodate large congregations, and visibility for the
preacher from all parts of the nave. To gain the first objective they
moved their choir stalls from the structural nave to the structural choir,
and to gain the second they rejected the massive columns of the monastic
abbey in favor of the slender pillars characteristic of the mendicant
church.

Their churches had two marked peculiarities found in them and nowhere else; both seem to have evolved spontaneously in England and
Wales and to have owed nothing to continental influences. The first was
the general lack of transepts in the churches of the English friars. Occasionally a single transept ran out from the body of the church on the
side away from the cloister, but both arms of the cross were exceedingly
rare.[4]

The second distinctive feature was the walking place or ambulatory,
with the belfry above it, an architectural device "peculiar to English
mendicant churches, and found nowhere else in England or abroad."[5] The
walking place was an internal passageway that traversed the church from
north to south between the choir and the nave, leading toward the public
highway at one end and to the east cloister alley at the other. Within the
body of the church it was enclosed by two parallel walls, each pierced
by a great arch that gave access to nave or to chancel; and high overhead
two secondary walls bridged the space between them so as to form a
four-sided base on which the spire and belfry could rest. The walking
place provided a ready means of communication in mendicant precincts
between the cloister and the outside world; in monastic precincts its nearest equivalent was the slype at the southwest corner of the nave, as will
be discussed later.

The Cloister

The cloister was an open space, usually square or approximately so,
around whose four sides the conventual buildings were organized; the
church enclosed it on one side, and the domestic buildings on the other

36

three.[6] Passage from one building to another was provided by a walk or alley that bordered each side of the quadrangle along its outer edge; the alleys were paved with tile, and roofed against the weather.[7] In monastic construction the roofs over the cloister walks were of the lean-to type, attached to and sloping down from the walls of the adjacent buildings, and sometimes straddled by flying buttresses. The English mendicants, however, and the Dominicans in particular, often deviated from that plan by incorporating their alleys within the lower stories of the domestic ranges, so that the upper stories projected over and covered them. They thus gained more space on their upper floors and at the same time avoided the cost of roofing their cloister alleys.[8]

The alleys framed a grassy garth or lawn, and between garth and alleys ran a series of arcades to support the inner edge either of the pent-house roof or of the overhanging story. In the earliest construction the arcades were left open, but later they were mullioned and glazed. The north alley, sheltered by the church, was the place where warmth was to be found in winter if anywhere in the precinct, and was therefore the monks' living room, their favorite place for reading and study; there they often built stone benches against the church walls, and closets for their books. The friars, since their mission took them outside the cloister, did this less often. Their cloister walks were usually narrower, and among the Dominicans served only as passageways.

Doors opened upon the alleys from all the adjacent buildings. The two that led from the church's nave to the east and west cloister walks were used in some orders for the weekly ceremonial processions. The ritual involved visiting all the altars in the church, passing from church to cloister by way of the east door, making a solemn round of the cloistral buildings to bless each in turn, and then reentering the church by way of the doorway at the head of the west alley. Since the church was normally on the precinct's highest ground, a short flight of steps usually intervened between the cloister walk and the floor of the nave.

The Eastern Range

A continuous range of buildings flanked the east side of the cloister, from the church on the north to the cloister's south alley. In monasteries the northernmost element of the eastern range was the church's south transept, which combined with the nave to form an angle framing the cloister's northeast corner, and which thence extended part way down the

37

cloister's east side. In friaries, on the other hand, with transepts normally lacking, the domestic buildings ran all the way north to make contact with the chancel. They were two stories high.

The ground floor of the eastern range was cut up into several chambers or offices or passageways, each with its opening upon the cloister walk. At the northern end, next to the church, a slype or passageway often cut through the range from the cloister to the cemetery; it commonly served also as a parlor where necessary conversation was permitted, silence being the rule everywhere else. Next to it might come the sacristy where holy vessels and utensils were kept ready for service in the church, and a cubicle for the books needed for study in the cloister. At the midpoint of the range, the vestibule of the chapter house ran through the range from east to west, from the cloister on one side to the vaulted hall on the other. Just south of the vestibule a flight of day stairs led up from the alley to the dormitory on the upper floor. The buildings of the east range usually extended southward beyond the cloister, and the undercroft at their southern end normally held a warming house or calefactory where a fire was kept burning day and night from All Saints until Easter. It provided the only artificial heat that the monks had, except for those who were sick in the infirmary.

The Dorter

The dorter, or dormitory, occupied the entire upper floor of the eastern range, sailing over all the compartments and passages on the level below. It was a long narrow hall usually 20 or 30 feet wide by three or four times that long. Its north end met the church, either at transept or at chancel; and at that point a flight of night stairs led down from the dorter to the church so that the brethren, when roused from their first sleep at midnight for the office of matins and lauds, might troop from their beds to the choir without a long journey through icy corridors.[9] From the night stairs the dorter ran southward without interruption to the southern end of the eastern range.

In early times the dorter was an open hall, with two rows of beds stretching from end to end and a passageway down the center; dwarf partitions were introduced later to give some modicum of privacy. The Black Friars, and perhaps other mendicant orders also, went further. They reduced the rows of beds to one, and opposite each bed they built an alcove large enough to hold a table, chair, and locker, cut off from its neighbors by partitions jutting out from the wall. The carrels in the old Dominican priory at Gloucester are still perfectly preserved.[10]

The Chapter House

The chapter house was second in sanctity and beauty only to the church itself. In position it varied less than any other of the conventual buildings: it stood always on the east side of the cloister, facing west, and usually at about its middle.[11] It was normally deeper, front to back, than any other building in the eastern range; and the magnificent chapter houses built in the thirteenth century were, as a matter of fact, so deep that their primary elements, the halls proper, projected eastward from and stood free of the cloistral range, so that their vaulted roofs could rise clear of the range's upper story. Since the hall thus stood at the rear of the eastern range, entrance to it was by way of a vestibule that passed through the range at ground level beneath the dorter; and the entrance facing the cloister alley was distinguished from its humbler neighbors by its pre-Palladian central door with a window or open arch on either side. The hall itself was sometimes square or oblong in plan; more often it was polygonal or circular. Its walls were lightened with arcading or mural painting, and opened up with windows. Internally it had stone benches running along its sides for the brethren to sit on, and a raised stall at its east end for the abbot or prior. Here the religious community met each day for a service that began with a reading from the Martyrology followed by collects and a chapter[12] of the Rule, discussion of affairs connected with the administration of the convent, and the imposition of penalties for faults against the monastic code of life.

Taken as a group, the chapter houses built in England during the great period give vivid proof of the versatility and structural skill of English builders. Their extraordinary beauty and delicacy, and their relatively small size, have led to their being preserved in some precincts where all the rest of the cloistral buildings have perished.[13]

The Frater

The frater was the refectory or eating hall. Its traditional position was at the south side of the cloister, opposite the church. Usually it paralleled the church's nave and thus constituted the cloister's southern range, but in Cistercian precincts it projected southward at a right angle

39

to the cloister's south edge, with only its narrow north end abutting upon the cloister walk. Always, however, whatever its orientation, the frater adjoined the cloister and had its entrance upon it. Its floor was commonly elevated above ground level, with a vaulted undercroft beneath. It was a hall of considerable size. Of fifty or more monastic and mendicant fraters whose ground plans I have measured, the average inside length of non-Dominican fraters was about 90 feet and their width about 29, to give a square footage of about 2,610. The Dominican refectories were somewhat smaller. Those of which we have knowledge had an average inside length of about 75 feet and a width of 24, to give a floor area of approximately 1,800 square feet.[14]

Assuming that the frater lay in an east-west direction, it was entered from the south walk of the cloister by a door near its western end. A lavatory fronted upon the cloister walk near the frater doorway, and there the brethren congregated upon the sounding of the bell for meals, washed their hands, recited a psalm, and formed in line to mount the stairs to the refectory. The lavatory might take any one of several different forms, but characteristically it was a long lead-lined trough or series of troughs recessed in the refectory wall and separated by arcades from the cloister walk, with a total length of 30 to 50 feet. Often it consisted of two troughs, one on either side of the frater door.[15]

Internally, the western end of the frater was screened to mask the entrances from the cloister and from the kitchen. The eastern end, as with church and chapter house, was the place of special veneration: it held a dais for the table of the abbot and other dignitaries, and the east wall carried a representation in paint or sculpture of the Crucifixion or of Christ in Majesty. (Leonardo's "Last Supper" is frescoed on the east wall of the Dominican frater at Milan.) A reader's pulpit, reached by a flight of steps in the thickness of the wall, projected from the south wall near the dais end; from it a lector read aloud to the brethren during meals.[16] The frater windows were set high, so that their lower edges would clear the penthouse roof covering the adjacent cloister alley.

When we pass from the monastic cloister to the mendicant, we find less uniformity in the siting of the frater; the topography of the individual precinct often demanded that the refectory be placed elsewhere than in the southern range. As for Dominican precincts in particular, the frater is known to have been in the traditional southern range only at Newcastle-on-Tyne. It was in the western range at Canterbury, Gloucester, Ludgate, and probably at Bristol. At Cardiff it was in the northern range, and at Ipswich it was not on the main cloister at all. As to other Dominican refectories information is lacking.[17]

The Porter's Lodge

The church and the domestic buildings encompassed a smaller and stricter close within the wider enclave of the precinct walls. The inner enclosure was entered by a covered passageway leading through the western range at ground level. Its gate was guarded by a porter whose cell adjoined the southwest corner of the church, and from his cell a window was cut through the common wall into the church so that the porter could witness mass and other church functions and ceremonies without leaving his post of duty.[18] The porter's lodge was the ground floor of what was usually a two-story building; the upper floor served a variety of purposes. Since the lodge abutted upon the south side of the church at its western end, it constituted the northernmost element in the western range.

The Guest House

Just south of the porter's lodge was the building whose upper floor commonly served as a guest house. Hospitality to travelers was an obligation enjoined by Rule upon all medieval religious establishments. In its simple original form it involved nothing more than providing a benighted wayfarer with bed and board for a night or two, but in practice the demands upon monastic hospitality were often crippling. Kings and nobles sometimes arrived with their retinues and stayed for weeks at a time, as when Humphrey, Duke of Gloucester, brought his family and a train of three-hundred retainers to St. Albans Abbey for a fortnight in 1423, or when King Henry VI was entertained at Bury St. Edmund's from Christmas of 1453 until the following Easter, in a palace that the abbot had felt constrained to build in expectation of his royal guest's intended visit, and that he staffed with a hundred officers to wait upon the king.[19]

The western position was chosen for the hospitium partly because the west was the place for layfolk, partly because it was near the porter's gate, and partly because, being far from the dorter, a guest house so placed would ensure "that the brethren be not disturbed by the guests who arrive at uncertain hours and who are never wanting in a monastery."[20]

Accommodations for guests were of course on the upper floor of the building, with homely service rooms occupying the undercroft below.[21] But a single hostelry was not enough in any religious house except the smallest, for guests ranged from kings to beggars and could not all be lodged under one roof. Nobles and prelates were often accommodated in the abbot's or prior's house, so that the head of the convent might himself tender the hospitality that the rank of his guests required. Ordinary wayfarers were accommodated in the hospitium, and vagabonds got straw pallets in the almonry.

The Cellarium and the Outer Court

The *cellarium,* the great storehouse of the monastery, occupied nearly the whole lower story of the western range. It was the domain of the cellarer, the general provisioner for the entire establishment. There he dickered with the tradesmen who came to the western court to market their wares, and there, in the cool undercroft beneath the guest house, he stored foodstuffs and other commodities until they were needed in frater, guest house, or firmary. The *cellarium* was usually vaulted from a central row of pillars and divided into several rooms for storage or other domestic purposes.

The ground floor of the western range usually contained a public parlor also, where conversation was permitted between the brethren and their kinfolk; it often was no more than a passageway through the range. Sometimes another and more private passageway cut through the range from the southwest corner of the cloister to the outer court. In the western court was the almonry where food and alms were distributed to the poor and sick of the neighborhood.

The units yet to be discussed were usually off the main cloister. Their placements were dictated by the exigencies of the site more often than by rule.

The Rere-dorter

The rere-dorter, or latrine block, was near the eastern range but never within it; it was always close to the dorter and on the same upper level, and connected with the dorter by a bridge. A stream ran beneath it from end to end through a stone-walled trough. The monastic *necessarium* was no small affair. That at Fountains Abbey was about 110 feet long, at Canterbury 145, and at Lewes 158; and twenty-two rere-dorters, as measured on precinct ground plans, show an average length of about 64 feet and a width of about 22. They had rows of seats against the walls, divided by partitions.

The Firmary

The firmary,[22] or infirmary, cared for the sick, for those too old or infirm to sustain the heavy daily routine of monastic life, and for those who submitted to the periodical bloodletting believed at that time to be necessary to keep a man in health. It was usually east of the great cloister, away from the noise of the western court where the tradesmen came. Its bed-ward was like a church, with the beds in the aisles, heads to walls, and with a chapel at the eastern end. It had its own frater, known as a misericord or place of indulgence, where meat was served, and its own kitchen. It had its own rere-dorter, and fireplaces or a central fire, and commonly a little cloister or garden close for patients to walk in. Of Dominican firmaries, that at Cardiff constituted a separate block to the north of the main cloistral buildings, but connected with them; that at Ludgate was well to the south. Those at Brecon and Bristol may have been to the south, but one cannot be sure.[23]

The Abbot's or Prior's Lodging

Early monastic precept bade the head of a religious house to live with the members of his flock, to dine with them in the frater, and to have his bed with them in the dorter. The precept was little honored in England and Wales after the twelfth century. Sometimes an abbot paid lip service to the rule by having a bed assigned to him in the dorter, but he seldom slept there;[24] sometimes he gave the rule a technical obeisance by dwelling in a building that communicated with the dormitory, even though that communication was only by way of the rere-dorter.[25] But these slender and artificial observances of an outmoded rule were soon discarded, as they deserved to be; for as the monasteries had grown in lands and wealth, their abbots had grown in importance and responsibility; they had come to be feudal lords of consequence in their communities, with complex administrative duties outside their own convents and with the obligation to provide worthy hospitality for distinguished guests. Abbots' lodgings therefore developed into commodious self-contained guest houses, with halls, solars, chapels, living apartments, kitchens—and budgets and retainers—of their own. The houses of priors and provincials

43

in the mendicant precincts followed the same mutation, as evidenced by the use of the word "hospice" in the Bryan grant, to describe the prior's lodging at Ludgate (5:17).

The mansions of abbots, priors, and provincials had no fixed position. Often they were near the guest houses. Sometimes they were associated with firmaries or fraters, and sometimes, by ancient tradition, with dorters and rere-dorters, outside the eastern range.[26]

The Schoolhouse

The usual monastic schoolhouse was designed for the instruction of laymen, and therefore stood west of the cloister in the laymen's outer court. But the mendicant priories, with their special emphasis upon learning, had also other schoolhouses devoted to the training of their own friars and novices. The Constitution of the Dominican Order required every friary to have an instructor of the rank of professor, and required every Friar Preacher, unless he was himself an advanced scholar and specifically exempted by the Master General, to attend lectures. The curriculum included grammar, arts, philosophy, and theology.[27]

A library supplemented the schoolhouse. It usually occupied an upper story, since an upper room was likely to be less damp and therefore less apt to subject the books to mildew. It had no need to be a large room, for books were few; all had been painstakingly transcribed by hand, and many were enriched with exquisite illuminations.

The Ankers House

The Ankers House (the house of an anchorite or anchoress) was a cell occupied by a solitary recluse, and usually was located within the confines of the cemetery. Such hermitages were attached to the Dominican friaries at Dartford, Ludgate, Newcastle, and Salisbury.[28]

The Kitchen

The kitchen was necessarily near the frater, and ideally near the guest house also; but because of its smoky chimneys and its odors of cooking, it was usually outside the frater range, on the side away from the cloister.[29] The fourteenth-century kitchen at Durham survives in its entirety. It is a massive structure of about 50 feet by 57 feet, with fire-places set diagonally in its corners and with intricate vaulting overhead. The existing kitchen at Glastonbury is of similar design.[30]

The more important culinary offices—buttery, pantry, larder, and scullery—were located near the kitchen, often in the undercroft beneath frater or guest house. Bakehouse and brewhouse could be farther removed. And at the periphery of the precinct were scattered such other service buildings as barns, mills, stables, pigsties, hen houses, dovecotes, fish hatcheries, etc., and shops for masons, carpenters, and blacksmiths.

Monastic and mendicant life and ideals underwent a continuing change during the later Middle Ages, with a resultant change in the cloistral buildings. The causes were primarily two. One was a persistent decline in religious fervor and an increase in worldliness. The other was a falling off in the numbers of monks and friars. The first caused, and the second permitted, the growth of a tendency toward material comfort and individual privacy, in direct contravention of the pristine ideals of austerity and the common life. It found expression in many ways, of which the following are representative:

A] As has already been related, the provision of handsome free-standing residences for the heads of houses, apart from the general quarters of the brethren;

B] The division of dorters into separate bedchambers by means of wainscot partitions;

c] The building of more and more fireplaces, with the result that the old warming house no longer served as the only place where cold bones could be thawed out, and became instead a common room for informal meetings;[31] and

D] The increased consumption of meat, with a decreased use of the frater as a result. Under the original monastic rule, the eating of flesh had been permitted only to the sick and to workmen; but the rule was gradually relaxed, until by the end of the fifteenth century it had become the general custom for monks to eat meat three days in the week, except in seasons of fasting. Even as moderated, however, the rule still did not permit meat to be cooked in the common kitchen nor eaten in the frater, and the monks therefore tended to reject the frater in favor of a dining chamber to which the prohibition did not extend.[32]

THREE TIMES in the present century, workmen digging at the site of the Ludgate precinct have brought to light the fragmentary remains of what were once friary buildings.[33] The first find came in 1900,[34] at a place a few feet west and north of the junction of Ireland Yard and Friar Street, in the area where Nos. 5 and 7 Ireland Yard now stand.[35] The remains consisted of a vaulted crypt or undercroft of thirteenth-century workmanship. The crypt ran east and west, and indications of three bays existed. Its north wall was virtually intact for a distance of about 40 feet; it had originally been longer. South of it, and 27 feet away, were traces of a south wall; and midway between the two walls stood the last survivor of a row of handsome shafts of Purbeck marble, four in number, that had supported the stone vaulting overhead; the surviving shaft still carried the south end of a cross rib that stretched across to the north wall and there rested upon a delicate corbel. West of the corbel, the north wall showed the remains of a wall arch enclosing a window designed to admit light from above, and traces of a similar window farther east. The base of the marble shaft was 9 feet below the present ground level; the height from floor to ceiling was about 17½ feet. Nothing remains to suggest the nature or purpose of the building that once surmounted the crypt.

The Purbeck marble shaft is preserved in the Dominican Church at Haverstock Hill, Hampstead. The arch has been reerected at Selsdon Park, near Croydon. A fragment of the south wall remains in situ; the rest has been destroyed.

The second discovery was made in 1915 by workmen digging for new construction on the east side of Water Lane. Dr. Philip Norman reports it as follows:

On the site being excavated the workmen came upon the remains of the west wall of the church of the Dominican Priory. An inner respond marked the line of arcading between the south aisle and the nave. Some tile pavement could be seen undisturbed. The wall, 5 ft. thick, was composed of chalk and rubble. It ran due north, from about the centre of the north wall of the building of which the present banqueting hall forms the greater portion [i.e., Apothecaries' Hall], and which is on the site of the Guest House and the Guest Hall of the Priory. . . . Measurements of the remains discovered were made by [Mr. Alfred W. Clapham] and Mr. [Walter H.] Godfrey. Another wall was

46

found running east and west immediately west of what was the north wall of the Guest House, with a return wall running south. It stood above medieval ground level, and was of rubble, with ashlar quoins at the angle probably of Reigate stone. The stone jambs and mullion of a pointed arched window were in the wall, but it could not be determined if they were in their original position.[36]

The measurements made by Clapham and Godfrey ought to be authoritative as a record of the relationships and dimensions of structures at or near the west end of the Church. But do we have their findings? Certainly they were not published by those two gentlemen themselves. They cannot have been embodied in Clapham's conjectural

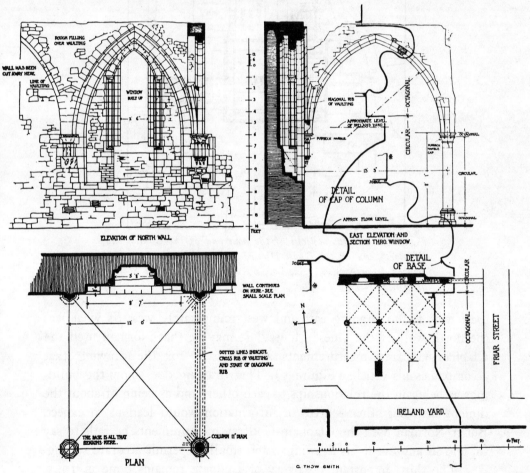

Figure 4. Remains of the Blackfriars subvault unearthed in 1900, as measured and drawn by G. Thow Smith, Esq. Reprinted from Archaeologia, *Vol. 63, by courtesy of the Society of Antiquaries of London.*

reconstruction of the Blackfriars precinct as printed in *Archaeologia 63*, Plate xi, for his drawing antedated the 1915 excavations by three years.[37] Nor are they to be found in his later versions of the same ground plan, for the later follow the earlier with merely trifling differences, and all show their independence of the 1915 excavations by ignoring the wall

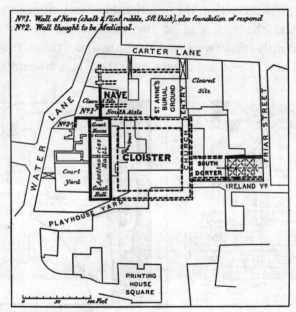

Figure 5. The foundations of the west end of the Church and the north end of the Guest House, as uncovered in 1915. Reprinted from Archaeologia, Vol. 67, *by courtesy of the Society of Antiquaries of London.*

that "was found running east and west immediately west of what was the north wall of the Guest House." It may be that Norman used the Clapham-Godfrey measurements as the basis for the drawing that accompanies his article (Figure 5). That drawing does show the buildings as being in the relationships to each other, and as being of about the dimensions, that other sources of information would lead us to expect. But if Norman used the Clapham-Godfrey measurements he fails to say so, and in any event his drawing is too small to permit accurate scaling.

The third important discovery of Ludgate remains came in 1925, and was reported in 1926 by Mr. William Martin, who saw, measured, and photographed the finds that he describes:

As regards the discoveries of 1925, the area was excavated in September of that year, the area having been covered by Nos. 73 and 74 Carter Lane, E. C. It lay between Carter Lane on the north, . . . the backs of the houses in Friar Street on the east, Church Entry on the west, and a burial ground . . . of the united parishes of St. Ann and St. Andrew-by-the-Wardrobe on the south. The greater part of the excavated area was occupied by a portion of the choir. The east end of the choir, however, being situated below houses in Friar Street, was not included in the area under excavation. In 1925, some operations in connection with sewerage in Friar Street revealed a massive wall of medieval masonry just below the surface along the line of the Street. The wall appeared to be at least 5 ft. in thickness. . . . The total length of the choir, excluding the passage through the church, measured ninety-five feet.

Somewhat at right angles to Church Entry, a short run east and west of apparently a part of the choir was seen to be the only portion of the church *in situ*. It measured some 7 ft. in length, over 3 ft. in height and 3 ft. 3 ins. in thickness. . . . Immediately to the west of the extremity of this walling . . . were found in an upright position, the base and capital of a clustered column. . . . They had been hacked away so as to make them flush with the walling and thus to render them more serviceable.[38]

Mr. Martin's article is accompanied by a ground plan and architectural analysis by Mr. Sidney Toy (Figure 6). The plan[39] shows the 7-foot stretch of wall as lying in an east-west direction 16½ feet north of the line that the wall of the south aisle would follow if it were extended eastward, and directly in line with the presumed position of the row of arcades that separated the south aisle from the nave, as that position was indicated by the respond discovered at the west end of the church in 1915. This correspondence, together with other considerations, suggests to Mr. Toy that "the length of walling recently unearthed at the eastern part of the church . . . is doubtless a portion of the south wall of the chancel." In addition to the 7-foot wall and the clustered column, Toy's ground plan shows two fragments of walling not mentioned by Martin, and indicates that they were parts of the foundation wall of a chapel adjoining the chancel at its south side. He describes them (p. 376) as being 10 feet south of the line of which the 7-foot stretch of wall formed a part, but his drawing shows them as being 11 or 12 feet to the south.

Modern building lines, as they are recorded in the meticulously accurate Ordnance Surveys of the Ludgate district, probably preserve the dimensions and positions of at least a few vanished friary buildings.

Some cellar excavations would have survived the Great Fire, and even some foundation walls, and builders would have been inclined to use old groundworks when they could, rather than dig and build anew. Building lines do tell us the precise position and direction of the south wall of the church, of the north wall of the porter's lodge, and of the

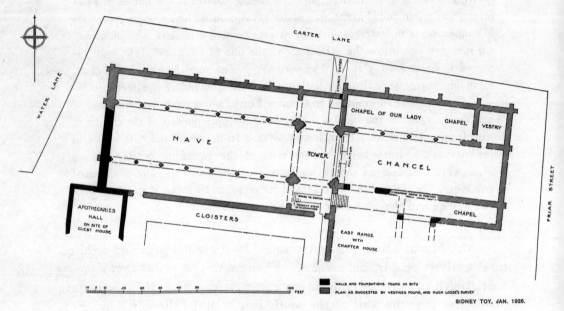

Figure 6. Vestiges of the foundations of the chancel and chapel, as revealed in 1925 and plotted by Sidney Toy, Esq.
Reprinted from The Transactions of the London and Middlesex Archaeological Society, New Series, Vol. V, Part iv, by courtesy of the Society of Antiquaries of London and Mr. Toy.

north and west edges of the cloister, and approximately of the east; and they show that the northwest corner of the cloister was an angle of about 91½ degrees, not 90 degrees. They would probably tell much more if we knew how to interpret their messages; but when a building line approximates, but does not coincide with, a specification derived from other sources—as when, for instance, the Blagrave Survey gives the east-west length of Jane Freemount's tenement as 52 feet (8:3c) and the building line suggests a length of 54 or 55 feet—one hesitates to re-ject a specification of known applicability in favor of one that may or may not apply. I originally intended to take modern building lines into account in drafting my reconstruction of the conventual buildings, but I soon discovered that the Ludgate area, as delineated in the Ordnance Survey, has no pairs of parallel lines and no right angles, and so gave up the attempt.

III: *BLACKFRIARS REAL ESTATE RECORDS*

THE PUBLIC RECORD OFFICE and the Muniment Room at Loseley have preserved the records of hundreds of surveys, grants, sales and rentals of real property in the area of the Ludgate precinct. The documents give a remarkably comprehensive account of the positions, relationships, and dimensions of the principal friary buildings. Gaps exist, of course, that one would wish to have filled, but enough information survives to permit the friary to be reconstructed with a considerable degree of confidence. Fortunately, the surviving information includes the positions and principal dimensions of the buildings with which we are primarily concerned—the range of buildings flanking the western sides of the two cloisters.

Dimensions in the old documents must always be taken with a grain of salt. At best they were made with inexact tools. But the great cause of confusion lies less in inaccuracies than in the failure of the documents to say what any given measurement comprehends. Not once are we told whether the figure is an outside dimension that includes walls, or an inside dimension that excludes them; and when one is dealing with walls 3 to 5 feet thick, the difference is substantial. Another major difficulty is caused by the total absence of vertical measurements of any kind whatsoever.

On the question of outside dimensions versus inside, it seems reasonable to assume that the old surveys, since they deal with land as well as buildings, were made outdoors and that they give outside measurements; and conversely, that the leases of interior apartments give inside dimensions. In my conjectural ground plan of the conventual buildings (Figure 16) I have acted on that assumption with what consistency has been possible.

I have assumed, too, that the exterior walls of domestic buildings were 3 feet thick. This was the thickness of the walls of the Upper Frater, since the breadth of the building was 52 feet (4:5, 6:21, 7:8) and the breadth of the great hall that it contained was 46 (40:3).[40] The walls of the church would naturally have been somewhat thicker. As was related a few pages back, modern excavations have shown that the west wall of the nave was 5 feet thick and the south wall of the choir 3 feet 3 inches; and building lines, as delineated on the Ordnance Survey, indicate that the outer wall of the south aisle had a thickness of between 3 and 4 feet.[41] In Figure 16, however, I have drawn all exterior walls, except the massive west wall of the church, as being just 3 feet thick, and I have treated all interior walls (i.e., walls within some one given building, but not common walls shared by two buildings) as having a thickness of 2 feet.

When the old documents fail to tell anything about the dimensions of some building in the Ludgate precinct, I have whenever possible been guided by the average of the dimensions of corresponding buildings in other Dominican precincts, as shown in the measured drawings in the book by Fr. Hinnebusch.

IV: *THE DESCRIPTION OF THE FRIARY IN*

PIERS THE PLOWMAN'S CREED

LINES 153 to 215 of *Piers the Plowman's Creed* give a vivid contemporary description of a Dominican friary in its prime, "the most graphic purely architectural description in the whole range of English mediaeval literature."[42] Its applicability to an establishment of the Blackfriars is proved by the words "the Preachers" in the second line of the passage:

> Then thought I to question the first of these four orders,   *153*
> And pressed to the Preachers to make proof of their will.
> I hied to their house to hear more about them,
> And when I came to that court I gazed all about.[43]

Nothing in the poem, to be sure, says specifically that the narrative relates to the Preachers' London house in particular, but its relevancy to the Ludgate priory is all but conclusive. In the opinion of a distinguished authority on historical monuments in England, the passage "refers almost certainly to the London house of the Blackfriars, since, whenever the details can be tested, they are found to be accurate."[44] Then, too, the description is so circumstantial that it could have been written only by one who told of things that he had seen, and of all the Blackfriars houses, that in London would presumably have been the one most readily available to the author of the *Creed*, since he is believed to have been a Londoner. For these and other reasons, the identity of the *Creed's* house with the London priory of the Friars Preachers has been accepted as probable or certain by all those who have expressed themselves on the subject, whether as chroniclers of the Dominican Order,[45] architectural historians,[46] writers on the Elizabethan drama,[47] or commentators upon the *Creed*.[48]

The passage in the *Creed* is a lampoon that seeks to discredit the Friars Preachers by contrasting the magnificence of their friary with their vows of poverty and their profession of mendicancy; the poet's method is to pretend a specious admiration for the opulence of the friary buildings, hoping thereby to produce a contrary reaction in the minds of his readers. To be sure, we have no direct testimony but his as to the architectural extravagance of the Ludgate precinct specifically, though we do have as to Dominican extravagance elsewhere in England. Matthew Paris, the Benedictine chronicler who was the severest contemporary critic of the Friars Preachers, railed against the gorgeous palaces that housed the English Blackfriars, and at least twice the Order itself was up in arms against its own excesses. Its first remonstrance came within twenty-nine years after the Friars Preachers set foot on English soil, and was directed against no less a personage than the English Provincial himself. At the General Chapter of the Order held at Holborn in 1250, he was rebuked and penanced for his architectural overambition: "We ordain to the Prior Provincial of England 5 days on bread and water, 5 psalters, 5 masses, 5 disciplines, and let him meddle less in building"; and at the same assembly the prior of the Dominicans at Newcastle-on-Tyne was summarily ejected from office for involving his priory in a building program of such magnificent proportions as to threaten to plunge it into ruinous debt.[49]

But even though no direct evidence testifies to the splendor of the Ludgate friary in particular, the indirect evidence is strong enough to prove the case. A priory in the heart of England's greatest city, probably moved thither at royal request and built partly at royal expense, is not likely to have been built parsimoniously; and Henry's choices of its hospitium for the entertainment of his imperial guest in 1522, and of its

Parliament Chamber for enterprises of great pith and moment throughout his reign, are abundant proofs that the poet's jibes were warranted.
Piers's descriptions bear evidence of direct observation, and bear none of
having been embellished imaginatively for satirical purposes.

1. Bond, Vol. I, p. 167, gives the number as fifty-eight; G. H. Cook, p. 214, gives it as fifty-four; Hinnebusch, p. 56, as fifty-seven, and Jarrett, pp. 22 and 171, as fifty-three.

2. See Fig. 1, which shows the church as of 1670. Recent photographs, showing the church without a tower and with a south porch, are printed in Hinnebusch, opposite p. 129, and Jarrett, opposite p. 66.

3. In eight Dominican priories the church is known or believed to have been placed on the north side of the great cloister: the eight are Brecon, Bristol, Gloucester, London (Ludgate), Newcastle-on-Tyne, Oxford, Rhuddlan, and Stamford. In six priories it was at the south: Bangor, Canterbury, Cardiff, Norwich (second site), and probably at Hereford and Lynn. In all the above priories the axis of the church lay in an east-west direction, and it did so also at Cambridge, Guildford, Ilchester, Salisbury, Scarborough, and Shrewsbury; but with respect to the last six, information is lacking as to whether the church lay to the north or the south of the cloister. At Carlisle it probably formed the eastern wing. At Ipswich it ran north-south and was not on the main cloister at all; in this as in other respects Ipswich was an exception to nearly all the rules. For the above information I am indebted to Hinnebusch, p. 133n.

4. Of Dominican churches specifically, we have evidence of regular symmetrical transepts only at Gloucester. Ipswich had a single shallow transept on the west side of the nave at its northern end. The Dominican churches at Bangor, Brecon, Bristol, Canterbury, Cardiff, London (Ludgate), Newcastle-on-Tyne, and Oxford had none. (Cf. Hinnebusch, p. 144, and ground plans on pp. 13, 39, 41, 122, 125, 138, 143, 160, 162, 168, 177, 194.)

5. Hinnebusch, p. 140. Cf. Clapham, "Friars as Builders," p. 244, and "Architectural Remains," p. 89; and Gilyard-Beer, p. 22.

6. As far as is known, the buildings in Dominican friaries were arranged around the four sides of a great cloister everywhere except at Ipswich, where church and chapter house adjoined a secondary quadrangle north of the main cloister. Cf. Hinnebusch, Fig. 9, p. 138.

7. Photographs of cloister walks are printed in Cook and Smith, Plates LXI and CV; G. H. Cook, Plates V, VI, VII, XXII; and in Crossley, Figs. 48, 57, 60, 61.

8. The English Dominicans incorporated one or more of the cloister alleys within the domestic ranges in their friaries at Bristol, Canterbury, Hereford, and Norwich. A photograph of such a cloister alley, at Bristol, is printed by Jarrett, opposite p. 138. The Dominicans conformed to the older lean-to type of roof at Gloucester, London, and Newcastle-on-Tyne. Cf. Hinnebusch, p. 202.

9. Night stairs are pictured in Plate III in the present book, and in Cook and Smith, Plate XXXIX; G. H. Cook, Plates VIII, IX; and Crossley, Fig. 71.

10. Jarrett, p. 37; Hinnebusch, pp. 171ff.

11. This rule was observed even in some precincts of the Carthusians, who in all other respects followed rules of their own. Dominican chapter houses were in the east range of the great cloister everywhere but at Ipswich, and at its midpoint everywhere but at Cardiff. At Ipswich it was in the center of a secondary east range facing the cemetery. At Cardiff it was in the southern corner of the east range, next the sacristy. Cf. Hinnebusch, p. 186.

12. Whence the name "chapter house." The word "chapter," as meaning a section of the Rule, was transferred to the meeting at which it was read, and thence

to those who met. Cf. *O.E.D.*, *s.v.* "Chapter."

13. Photographs of chapter houses are printed in Cook and Smith, Plate XXIX; G. H. Cook, Plates X-XIV; and Crossley, Figs. 62, 63, 65, 66.

14. We know the sizes of only six Dominican fraters, as follows: Bristol, 69 by 27 feet, 1,863 sq. ft.; Canterbury, 71 by 23 feet, 1,633 sq. ft.; Cardiff, 46 by 20 feet, 920 sq. ft.; Gloucester, 82 by 25 feet, 2,050 sq. ft.; Newcastle-on-Tyne, 83 by 23 feet, 1,909 sq. ft.; and Norwich, 98 by 25 feet, 2,450 sq. ft. All these dimensions are necessarily approximate, since they were arrived at by scaling small ground plans. The first five of the plans are in Hinnebusch, and the sixth in Gilyard-Beer.

15. Photographs of monastic lavatories are printed in this book, Plate V; G. H. Cook, Plate VII; and Crossley, Figs. 69 and 80.

16. Two perfect examples of reader's pulpits survive, at Chester and at Beaulieu. At Shrewsbury the pulpit is the only thing that does remain, all else having perished. Traces of pulpits are to be found in several other ruined abbeys. Cf. photographs in G. H. Cook, Plates XV-XVII, and in Crossley, p. 48 and Fig. 70.

17. Hinnebusch, p. 158.

18. Cf. Hinnebusch, p. 49; Jarrett, pp. 24-25.

19. G. H. Cook, p. 19.

20. From the Rule of St. Benedict, translated by the Rev. Boniface Verheyen, O.S.B., seventh ed. (1933), p. 80.

21. Of the few Dominican guest houses whose whereabouts we know, all were in the west. Those at Cardiff, Gloucester, London, Newcastle, and Norwich were on the west side of the Great Cloister. That at Canterbury was off-cloister, but still to the west. Cf. Hinnebusch, p. 193.

22. Also spelled "farmery," "fermery,"

"fermory," etc. *O.E.D.* recognizes "fermery."

23. Hinnebusch, pp. 191-92.

24. G. H. Cook, p. 74.

25. Gilyard-Beer, p. 33.

26. Photographs of abbots' or priors' houses are printed in the present book as Plate VII; in Cook and Smith, Plate CXXXII; in G. H. Cook, Plate XVIII; and in Crossley, Figs. 84-87.

27. Hinnebusch, p. 198; cf. Jarrett, pp. 49-53.

28. Jarrett, pp. 26-27.

29. The Cistercians differed from the other orders in their siting of frater and kitchen. As has been said, they permitted only the narrow north end of the frater to abut upon the cloister, and by doing so they found space enough to allow the kitchen also to face the cloister at the frater's west side.

30. The kitchen at Glastonbury is pictured in this book, Plate VI. See also Cook and Smith, Plate XLVI, and Crossley, Fig. 77.

31. Gilyard-Beer, pp. 45-57.

32. G. H. Cook, p. 71; Crossley, pp. 48, 60, 61; Graham, p. 86.

33. A plinth and the foundation of a buttress were unearthed in 1855, and a section of walling and a piece of another buttress in 1871, but they have been too vaguely described and located to be of any importance in our present inquiry. Cf. Palmer, "London," pp. 365-66.

34. Cf. Norman, "Mediaeval Remains"; Clapham, "On the Topography," p. 71, with measured drawing on p. 69; Martin and Toy, p. 362; and Hinnebusch, pp. 48-49.

35. The measured drawings of the foundations disagree slightly with respect to site. The ground plan by Dr. Norman (Fig. 5) shows the south edge of the undercroft as almost touching the north edge of Ireland Yard. So do all of Clapham's

plans of the precinct. But the drawing by G. Thow Smith (Fig. 4) shows the south edge as lying about 10 feet north of Ireland Yard; and since it gives evidence of being based upon careful measurements, its placement of the foundations is followed in Fig. 16.

36. "Recent Discoveries," pp. 13–14.

37. Clapham later became Sir Alfred, C.B.E., F.B.A., F.S.A. He was President of the Society of Antiquaries of London from 1939 to 1944, and Secretary of the Royal Commission on Historical Monuments in England from 1933 to 1948. His conjectural ground plan of the Ludgate precinct, drawn to illustrate his article on that subject in *Archaeologia 63* (1912), pp. 57–80, has been widely reprinted in slightly different versions (Harben, Plate III; Clapham and Godfrey, *Some Famous Buildings*, p. 254; *The Site of the Office of the Times*, p. 2, etc.). Sir Alfred drew the plan before some of the pertinent Loseley documents had been published. His drawing is therefore necessarily incorrect in many details; but his ability to come so near the mark, lacking so much information now available, demonstrates his remarkable intuition as an interpreter of cloistral design.

38. Martin and Toy, pp. 365–68.

39. Although Martin says (p. 365) that "the total length of the choir, excluding the passage through the church, measured ninety-five feet," Toy's drawing shows it as measuring 90 feet.

40. Measurements of the ground plans of thirty-one monastic cloisters yield an average thickness of 4 feet for the outer walls of cloistral buildings other than churches. But walls built by friars would have been thinner than those built by monks.

41. This is the distance by which the north wall of Apothecaries' Hall overshoots the neighboring east-west building line. It undoubtedly represents the thickness of the nave's south wall.

42. Clapham, "Friars as Builders," p. 256. See footnote 37 above.

43. Document 44 gives the Blackfriars passage in its original spelling as edited by the Rev. Walter W. Skeat, and also in a translation of which these four lines are a part.

44. Clapham, *op cit.*, p. 256.

45. Fr. Walter Gumbley, O.P., as editor of the revised and abridged edition of Jarrett, p. 43; and Hinnebusch, pp. 40, 121.

46. Clapham, "On the Topography," p. 60; and Martin and Toy, p. 363.

47. Joseph Quincy Adams, "Conventual Buildings," p. 75, and *Shakespearean Playhouses*, p. 196; and Chambers, *Elizabethan Stage*, Vol. II, p. 484, n. 2.

48. A. I. Doyle, "An Unrecognized Piece of *Piers the Plowman's Creed* and Other Works by Its Scribe," *Speculum*, Vol. XXXIV, No. 3 (July 1959), p. 434.

49. Hinnebusch, p. 128; Jarrett, pp. 23, 25.

❧ 3 ❧

The Church and the
Domestic Buildings

T HE PRECINCT of the Blackfriars in London, when his Majesty acquired it by the stroke of Bishop Hilsey's complaisant pen, was an
area of about nine acres. It lay within, but was not coextensive with, the
tract now enclosed by Ludgate Hill and the River Thames at north and
south respectively, St. Andrew's Hill on the east, and New Bridge Street
on the west. Its principal point of entry by land was at about the place
where today's Pilgrim Street, after cutting sharply southward from Ludgate Hill, strikes out toward the west; and from that point the precinct's
northern boundary ran westerly with the City wall of the Middle Ages
and the Pilgrim Street of today. Both the City wall and the precinct
boundary turned southward at the east bank of the Fleet River or Ditch,
which now flows ignominiously through an underground drain beneath
New Bridge Street; and after following the Fleet for about 700 feet, the
wall terminated at Thames-side in a bastion which is shown in both the
Hoefnagel and the Agas maps (Figures 7 and 8). From the mouth of
the Fleet the precinct's southern boundary ran eastward along the river
bank, which at that time was farther north than it is now; but after only
250 feet it took off in a northeasterly direction along the wildly erratic
line that marks the eastern boundaries of both St. Anne's Parish and Farringdon Ward Within. At the west side of St. Andrew's Hill it turned
northward and took a soberer course past the King's Wardrobe, and continued north on Creed Lane almost to Bowyer's Row, now known as
Ludgate Hill; but before reaching Bowyer's Row it turned westward and
ran parallel to that thoroughfare, back to the point of starting.[1] The
precinct's highest land was at the north. From there it dropped 27 feet,
according to the modern Ordnance Surveys, to its lowest point at the edge
of the Thames.[2]

The precinct was walled on all sides, and had four gates. That in the north wall was called the Cemetery Gate because it opened upon the friars' burial ground. That in the south wall was called the Water Gate; it gave entrance to the precinct for those who approached by boat on the Thames. A third gate pierced the east wall directly opposite the King's Wardrobe, at or near the point where Ireland Yard now meets St. Andrew's Hill. Shakespeare was to buy the upper floor of this gatehouse in 1613, either as an investment or with the thought—which however was never realized —of occupying it himself as his London residence.[3] The fourth gate was "the late Blackfriars gate called the New Gate, next unto the lane called Carter Lane,"[4] and therefore about 150 feet farther north.

Two roads in succession crossed the precinct internally from the gate in the north wall to the edge of the Thames. The earlier road (cf. Figures 7, 8, and 13) ran southward in a straight line and divided the precinct into two sections of which the western was twice as large as the eastern. It presumably followed the course of the original City wall. This is suggested by its position and direction and by the words "NB: remnants of old Walls hereabouts" written at its north end in Figure 14. The later surveys (Figures 11, 12, and 14) show only the road's southern half, and show it as extending northward from the river for only a hundred yards or so and as coming to an end in the midst of nowhere.

At the same time, the surveys now show the irregular new road that was called Water Lane in the sixteenth century and is called Blackfriars Lane today. It lay farther west than its predecessor had done, and it bisected the precinct into two parts of which the western was now far smaller than the eastern. The western part held only a few houses and gardens, whereas the eastern held the minster, cloister, and all the friary's domestic buildings.[5]

The Hoefnagel and Agas maps show a covered bridge as traversing St. Andrew's Hill from the Blackfriars precinct to the King's Wardrobe; this presumably was built after the Office of the King's Revels was established in the Parliament Chamber, when easy communications between the Wardrobe and the Revels became needful. The same two maps show another covered bridge as crossing the Fleet near the precinct's northwest corner. I take this to be an erroneous placement, as being too far north, of the remains of the gallery that King Henry VIII built in 1522 to link the friary's guest house with Bridewell Palace. The bridge's correct position is shown in the Leake survey (Figure 11).

Figure 7. This is a section of
the map of London published
in Cologne in 1572 by Braun
and Hogenberg in their Civi-
tates Orbis Terrarum; it is
commonly called the Hoef-
nagel map on the assumption
that its style shows it to be the
work of Georg Hoefnagel. It
was probably copied from an
English original, now lost.
Reproduced by courtesy of the
London Topographical Society
and the Guildhall Library.

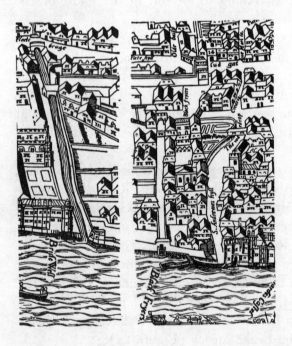

Figure 8. This map, the so-
called Agas map of London,
was probably engraved between
1572 and 1590, but was not
published until 1633. The
Ludgate area occupies neighboring parts of two separate en-
graver's plates whose edges fail
to correspond perfectly; hence
the gutter down the middle of
the map as printed here. Agas
seems to have been influenced
by Hoefnagel in some details,
as for instance in showing a
covered bridge over the Fleet,
and another over St. Andrew's
Hill from the precinct to the
King's Wardrobe.
Reproduced by courtesy of the
London Topographical Society
and the Guildhall Library.

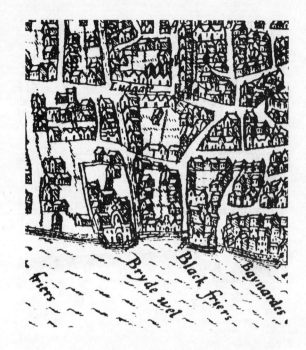

Figure 9. John Norden's first map of London was printed in his Speculum Britanniae *of 1593. It fails to show the City wall as enclosing the Black-friars precinct on its north and west sides, and in other respects also it shows a defective knowledge of the Ludgate district. Reproduced by permission of the Trustees of the British Museum.*

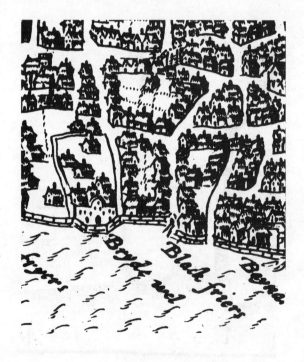

Figure 10. Norden issued a revised map in 1600, engraving it as an inset in his Civitas Londini *panorama. The later map is even less accurate than its predecessor. Among other departures from fact, it shows the Fleet River as being a street. Reproduced by courtesy of the London Topographical Society.*

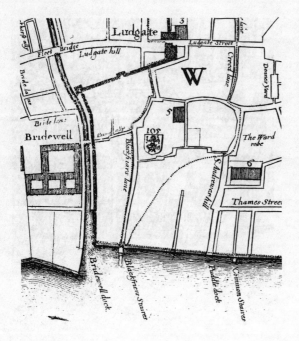

Figure 11. On orders of the Common Council, John Leake and five associates made an "Exact Surveigh" of the area devastated by the Great Fire of 1666, and their map was engraved by Wenceslaus Hollar. This map, for the first time, shows the two sides of the precinct in their correct relative proportions as checked by modern Ordnance Surveys, and shows Blackfriars Lane substantially as it is today.
Reproduced by permission of the Trustees of the British Museum.

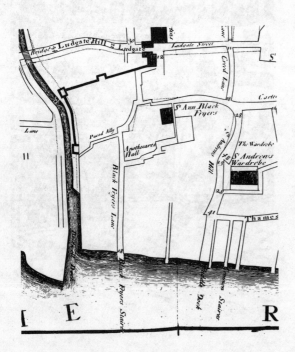

Figure 12. Vertue's engraving of the John Leake map omits some of Leake's details and adds new ones of its own. It gives the widths of some streets, in arabic numerals, as they were before the Great Fire. In showing the course of Blackfriars Lane as running parallel with that of the Fleet, it is less accurate than the map upon which it is based.
Reproduced by courtesy of the London Topographical Society and the Guildhall Library.

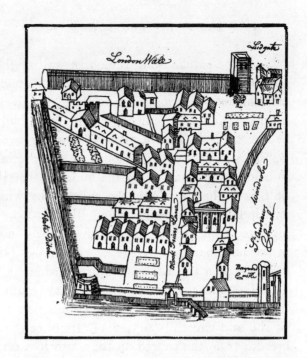

Figure 13. This anonymous sketch, drawn with a quill pen and with ink now faded, is here reproduced for the first time. It is catalogued as No. 106 in Book IV of "'Drawings and Prints Illustrating Some Account of London,' by Thos. Pennant, 4th Edition, 1805," in Sir John Soane's Museum. It is manifestly an amateur's copy of the Agas engraving.
Reproduced by permission of the Trustees of Sir John Soane's Museum.

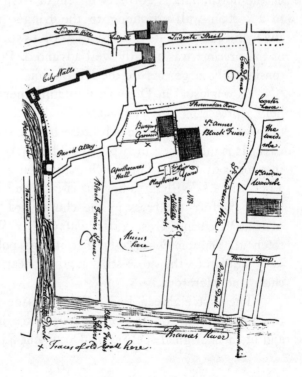

Figure 14. Like No. 106, with which it shares a page in the Pennant volume, this map, catalogued as No. 107, has not hitherto been reproduced. It is based upon the Vertue engraving, but with some added placenames and other notations. Personal observation leads me to believe that the "traces of old wall" at the place marked "X" are the remains of Roman walls embedded in the foundations of Apothecaries' Hall.
Reproduced by permission of the Trustees of Sir John Soane's Museum.

The Gatehouse and Churchyard

Of the gatehouse in the north wall of the Ludgate precinct no description exists except that in *Piers the Plowman's Creed*. Piers does not say that he is describing a gatehouse; he gives no hint of the building's purpose; and this indeed is the only building, of those to which he devotes more than a glancing word or two, that he fails to identify. But it is clearly the gatehouse in the precinct's north wall. Its being so is indicated by its being the building that Piers first encounters when he hies to the Preachers, the building by which he enters the precinct; it is indicated too by his being still outdoors after he has "entrid in" (line 163), in a walled area with posterns and orchards and arbors, and in the neighborhood of the "curious cros" (line 167) that is known to have stood in the Ludgate churchyard.[6]

The churchyard or cemetery lay south of the gatehouse and of the precinct's northern boundary, and "on the north side of the body of the said church" (6:3, 7:3). Its dimensions are given as 90 feet in breadth from the church on the south to a certain brick wall and houses on the north, and as 200 feet in length from certain houses on the west to a certain wall adjoining to the King's highway on the east (6:3, 7:3). But those are its dimensions as of 1550, by which time the partition of the precinct was already well advanced. Probably the churchyard was considerably larger before the Dissolution.

As was usual in Dominican establishments, the cemetery at London held a preaching cross, an outdoor pulpit that permitted the churchyard to serve as a summertime substitute for, or supplement to, the preaching nave. It is mentioned in two wills. The 1410 will of Roger Jaket directs that his body be laid "in the churchyard near the pulpit there," and the 1431 will of William Thorley, citizen and bowyer, directs that he be buried "before the cross in the churchyard."[7] The *Creed's* description of it as "a curious cros, craftly entayled, / With tabernacles y-tight, to toten all abouten," suggests that it was polygonal in form, probably very similar to the cross still standing near the site of the Blackfriars church at Hereford.[8]

The first eighteen lines of the passage from the *Creed*, including the four already quoted on page 52, are given below in translation, and in their original spelling in Document 44.

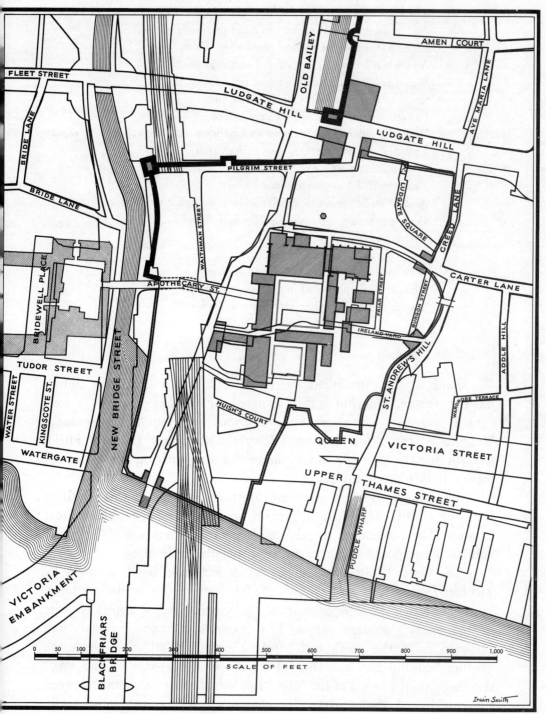

Figure 15. The Ludgate precinct with relation to the streets of modern London.

Then thought I to question the first of these four orders,   153
And pressed to the Preachers to make proof of their will.
I hied to their house to hear more about them,   155
And when I came to that court I gazed all about.
Such a boldly built building raised upon the earth
Saw I never, in certainty, since a long time.
I gazed on that house and eagerly looked
How the pillars were painted and polished full bright,   160
And quaintly were carven with curious knots,
With windows well wrought, lofty and wide.
Then entered I in and forward I went,
And all walled was that dwelling place, though it were wide,
With posterns in private to pass when they list,   165
Orchards and arbors neatly arranged,
And a curious cross, craftily built,
With tabernacles encircled, facing all sides.
The price of a plowland in pennies so round
To embellish that pillar were little indeed.   170

The Church

South of the churchyard was the church, and south of the church was the cloister. The church thus occupied the classical position for conventual minsters, north of the cloister and on the highest ground. Nearness to the main highway (Bowyer's Row, now Ludgate Hill), warmth for the cloister, and drainage for the outlying buildings, all combined to place it there.

The church lay in an east-west direction, with the southern wall of the body of the church abutting upon the northern edge of the Great Cloister. The position of the cloister is precisely known, and by reference to it the position of the church is determinable also.

The Great Cloister was square,[9] 110 feet from north to south by 110 feet from east to west (6:4, 7:4). Its western edge is marked today by the eastern side of Apothecaries' Hall, which now occupies the site of the priory's western range. The cloister's northern boundary ran eastward from the north end of Apothecaries' Hall, first along the existing building line and then along the southern edge of the small detached burial ground of St. Anne; this was the line of contact between the church and the cloister. The cloister's east side ran substantially along the now-irregular east margin of the passageway named Church

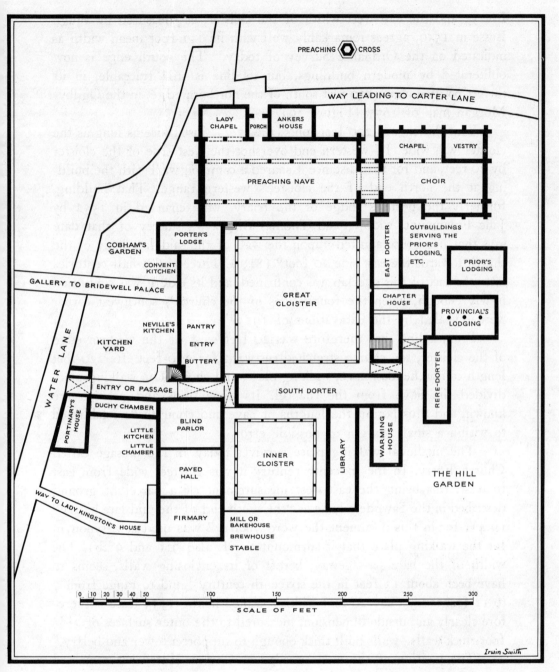

Figure 16. *A conjectural plan of the buildings in the Blackfriars precinct.*

Entry; and the east-west width of the cloister, as measured by Hugh Losse in 1550, agrees remarkably well with its 111-foot mean width as indicated on the Ordnance Survey of today.[10] The south edge is now obliterated by modern buildings, but its line is still traceable, in its correct position about 110 feet south of the northern edge, in the Ogilby-Morgan map of 1677 (Figure 19).

The church was 220 feet long (6:2, 7:2), just twice as long as the cloister was wide. Its western end overshot the west side of the cloister by 20 feet, and for that distance it shared a common wall with the building at the north end of the cloister's western range. That building, formerly the porter's lodge of the friary, was tenanted in 1552 by Jane Freemount, widow; and Thomas Blagrave's survey of that date says that her house abutted "upon the wall of the said late body of the church towards the east side 20 foot" (8:3c). Three and a half centuries later the fact of this overlap was confirmed, and its extent was confirmed nearly enough, when the foundations of the church's southwest corner were revealed by the excavations of 1915.[11]

From a line that therefore was 20 feet west of the western edge of the cloister, the church stretched eastward for 220-feet. Its 220-foot length comprehended nave, walking place, and choir. The walking place divided the nave from the chancel. Its dimensions and position are known, and thus permit the lengths of nave and choir to be established to within a small margin of possible error.

The medieval walking place survives today in the passage called Church Entry. In the sixteenth century it was 20 feet wide from east to west, this being the east-west measurement of a parcel of ground described in the Sawnders lease as "the south end of the said late belfry" (9:4); for in this document the word "belfry" was used as a synonym for the walking place that it surmounted (cf. also 9:1 and 9:2b). The width of the bare passageway, bereft of its enclosing walls, seems to have been about 13 feet in the sixteenth century[12] and to range from 7 to 11 feet today. The 20-foot width specified in the 1553 lease is therefore clearly an outside dimension, measured to the outer surfaces of 3½-foot-thick walls—walls built thick enough to support a tower and belfry.[13]

The position of the western edge of Church Entry has remained unchanged through the centuries. It was and is about 103½ feet east of what was the western side of the Great Cloister, and, since the nave stretched west of the cloister to a distance of 20 feet, it was 123½ feet east of the western end of the nave. Deducting this last measurement from 220 feet as the total length of the church, we find that the western edge of Church Entry was 96½ feet west of the eastern end of the choir. A wall, 3½ feet thick, lay between the nave and Church Entry; and having deducted this from 123½ feet, we are left with 120 feet as the length of the nave. To the east of the western edge of Church Entry lay the passageway itself, 13 feet wide, and another 3½-foot wall; and thus (96½ minus 16½) the chancel is found to have been just 80 feet long.[14] By this process of calculation we arrive at 120 feet as the length of the nave, 20 feet as the width of the walking place with its enclosing walls, and 80 feet as the length of the choir, for the prescribed total of 220.

The church was 66 feet in breadth from north to south, and had two aisles (6:2, 7:2); nave and aisles were roofed with lead (6:12). No contemporary document gives the respective widths of aisles and nave, but their dimensions can be approximated by reference to the discoveries made in 1915 and 1925. The excavations of 1915 exposed the stump of an inner respond jutting out from the west end of the nave on its eastern side, and thus established the position and thickness of the row of arcades that separated the nave from the south aisle.[15] Later excavations uncovered a 7-foot run of wall about 180 feet to the east of the nave's west end, and directly in line with the arcades as their position had been established a decade before; it presumably was a section of the south wall of the chancel.[16] The reports of the two finds give none of the relative measurements verbally; dimensions can be arrived at only by scaling the ground plans drawn by Dr. Norman in 1915 or 1916 and by Mr. Toy ten years later. At no point do their proportions agree precisely, but they do suggest that each outer wall of the church was about 3 feet thick and each aisle about 13½ feet wide, each row of arcades 3 feet thick, and the nave 27 feet wide in the clear. The total is the prescribed 66 feet. The subtotal for each aisle and its outer wall is 16½, and for the nave with its neighboring arcades is 33; and since the chancel walls were in alignment with the rows of arcades, 33 feet was the width of the chancel also. All these north-south dimensions thus are 16½ feet or its multiples, and their accuracy is the more probable since 16½ feet or 5½ yards was a recognized measure of length called a rod, perch, or pole.[17]

The church had no transepts. As we have seen (page 36 above), transepts were rare in mendicant churches and particularly so in Dominican; only one Blackfriars church—Gloucester—is known to have had them. Their absence at Ludgate is indicated not merely by the failure of the surveys and deeds to mention them, but also by the intimation that "the south end of the said belfry and the north end and side of the late cloister adjoining to the said dorter" were separated not by a transept, but only by a "way" or slype (9:2b).

A little chamber and a chapel are described in the Bryan grant as being "adjacent to the church . . . on the south side" (5:8, 5:9), necessarily in the area of the choir. Either the little chamber or the chapel probably adjoined the chancel at its eastern end, and added its depth to the chancel's 33-foot width to give "the end of the said chancel 43 foot" in overall width (9:2a). The other of the two buildings has perhaps left its trace in the two scraps of foundation wall discovered lying some 10 or 12 feet south of the presumed position of the south wall of the chancel in 1925. Whichever of the two buildings was the chapel, it was relatively shallow; and this shallowness, together with its inclusion in the grant to Sir Francis Bryan, who got the Prior's lodging (5:2), suggests that it may have been the personal chapel of the Prior.

A vestry adjoined the chancel "on the north side on the east end of the said church" (6:12), with the eastern faces of vestry and chancel forming a continuous straight line, and with "the east end of the said vestry, taking 22 foot, and the end of the said chancel, 43 foot, [totaling] in the whole at that end from north to south 65 foot" (9:2a). The vestry was roofed with lead (6:12).

A mutilated passage in the Sawnders lease speaks of the vestry as "belonging" to a chapel, and of the chapel as being "annexed" to the vestry (9:1). Since the vestry was on the north side of the chancel, this chapel was there too; either it, or the Lady Chapel soon to be mentioned, was probably the one listed by Hugh Losse as "one chapel on the north side of the said church" (6:7). Its north-south width seems to have been about 22 or 23 feet, as indicated by the lease's giving 56 feet as the width of the church at or near the line of the East Dorter, at which line the measurement presumably included the chancel and the north chapel; and since we have estimated the width of the chancel at 33 feet, 23 are left for the width of the chapel, just 1 foot more than that of the vestry to which the chapel was annexed.[18] The line on which the measurement was taken indicates that the north chapel extended well toward the west (9:2c).

A chapel of Our Lady adjoined the north side of the church at its western end. Its position is fixed, first, by a reference to the "chapel of Our Lady in the cemetery of the Blackfriars," which places it on the north side of the church, and second, by a testamentary request by Robert Castell to be buried in "the church of the Friars Preachers over

70

against (*desuper*) the chapel erected and founded in the same church in honor of the most blessed and glorious Virgin Mary . . . and the west wall of the same church."[19] It seems to have been 24 feet deep from north to south, that being the number which, added to 66, gives a total of 90; for after the church had been destroyed, the length of what had been its west end is given by implication as 90 feet, consisting of the 62 feet by which Scryven's property abutted "east upon a vacant place which was the body of the church" (8:1) and the 28 feet by which Jane Freemount's property abutted "east upon the late body of the church" (8:3a). The east-west width of the chapel is not known.

A "messuage or tenement called the Square Tower, sometime called the Church Porch, and the little gateroom thereunto adjoining" (*BR* 108:22) abutted upon the wall of the church, necessarily on the side away from the cloister. Its dimensions and its exact position are not stated, but it was certainly square, and its position was presumably near, but not at, the church's western end, as is usual for church porches.[20]

The Ankers House was nearby: Hugh Losse, in his 1540 list of Crown rents, describes it as "at the Church door."[21] It was 30 feet wide from east to west (*BR* 113:2) by 24 feet deep from north to south (*BR* 113:32-37).

Fr. Palmer has assembled the names of members of the nobility and gentry, and of the church hierarchy, who are known to have been buried in the Blackfriars church. They include Hubert de Burgh, Earl of Kent, and his wife Margaret, founders of the first house of the Friars Preachers in Holborn, whose bodies were carried from Holborn to Ludgate when the friars moved, and were reinterred in the choir; Sir Thomas Parr and Dame Maude his wife, parents of Henry's sixth queen; Sir John Tiptoft, Earl of Worcester, who was beheaded in 1470, and Margaret his wife, daughter of a King of Scotland; Dame Isabel, sister of Alexander, King of Scotland, and wife of Roger Bigott, Earl Marshal of England; Roger Beauchamp, Lord Chamberlain of the Royal Household, and his lady; William Courtney, Earl of Devonshire; the hearts of Elinor of Castile, Queen of Edward I, and of her son; Elizabeth, wife of William Bohun, Earl of Northampton, mother of the Earl of March and Harford, and of Ellis or Alice, Countess of Arundel; Dame Maude, daughter of Guy, Earl of Warwick, and wife to Sir Geoffrey Say, Admiral of the King's Fleet; the fathers confessor to Edward I and Edward II; two archbishops of Dublin, and bishops of Bangor, St. David's, and Rochester; and so on for over a hundred more.[22]

Sir Alfred Clapham prints the names of a few persons of humbler station, the particulars of whose burials provide information about monuments in the church. Their wills mention a Pardon Chapel, and Chapels of St. Anne and of St. John the Baptist; altars of Our Lady of Grace and of St. Michael the Archangel in the nave, and altars of St. Peter and St. Dominic in places not specified; and images of Our Lady of Grace and of St. Michael the Archangel in the nave, of St. Peter Martyr and St. Erasmus in the north aisle, and of Our Lady of Pity, St. Thomas Aquinas, St. Osyth, and St. Patrick.[23]

Piers Plowman gives twenty lines to his description of the church of the Friars Preachers. His comments are printed in their original spelling in Document 44, and in translation below:

> Then hurried I forth to study the minster,   *171*
> And found it an edifice wondrously built,
> With arches on every side, cleverly carven,
> With crockets on corners, with knots of gold,
> Wide windows[24] wrought with numberless writings,   *175*
> With shapely shields shining to show all about,
> With emblems of merchants mixed in between them,
> More than twenty-and-two, twice numbered o'er.
> There is no herald that hath half such a roll,
> Such as a ragman hath reckoned anew.
> Tombs upon tabernacles raised up aloft,
> Placed in corners, set closely about,
> In armor of alabaster presently clad,
> Made out of marble in different ways
> Were knights in their cognizances clad for the nonce,   *185*
> All, it seemed, saints enshrined upon earth;
> And lovely carved ladies to lie by their sides,
> In many gay garments that were beaten gold.
> Though the tax for ten years were honestly gathered,
> 'Twould not make half that house, as I truly believe.   *190*

The Great Cloister

The Ludgate friary had two cloisters. One was the Great Cloister, situated immediately to the south of the church; the other was the Inner Cloister, smaller than the Great Cloister and farther south, with the South Dorter falling between them.[25]

The Great Cloister at Ludgate was the largest Blackfriars cloister of which we have knowledge. As contrasted with its 110 feet on a side, the cloister at Newcastle-on-Tyne had 90 feet, at Canterbury 82 feet, at Gloucester 80 feet, at Brecon 71 feet, and at Bangor 62 feet.[26] It was unusual too in its failure to incorporate its cloister alleys within the lower stories of buildings fronting on the garth. As we have seen,[27] this recessing of the alleys within the domestic ranges was characteristic of the English mendicant cloisters in general and of the Blackfriars cloisters especially, its purpose being to avoid the cost of roofing the alleys. But the Ludgate precinct did not conform. Its failure to do so is implied in Losse's specification of "the lead of the whole south cloister" (6:12) and in Piers Plowman's reference to a roofing of lead (line 193), both of which indicate that the alleys had roofs of their own and were not built over.

The alleyways[28] were paved (6:7) and arcaded, and had glazed windows (6:9); and somewhere within the boundaries of the Great Cloister was the lavatory where the friars washed their hands before meals. It is mentioned in the will of Sir Robert Southwell, knight, who in 1514 directed that he be buried

> in the Cloister of the Friars Preachers in the City of London, under or near the Lavatory there, nigh to the picture of the holy Crucifix there set;

and Sir Robert further directed that

> that friar of the same place, appointed daily for the work to say there the mass of the Trinity, by the space of xx years next after my decease, say every day a special collect in his mass for my soul, also de profundis with a pater and ave and crede for my said soul . . . at the said lavatory immediately when the convent of the same place, or the most part of them, shall go to dinner. Item, I will that that friar, being a priest, that first happens to come any day during the said xx years in the morning first to the said lavatory to wash his hands and then and there to say de profundis for the souls before said, have for his so doing 1*d*.[29]

William Stalworth, citizen and merchant tailor, also directed in his will, dated 1519, that he be buried in the cloister, and made this strange bequest:

> I will that there shall be distributed to the Friars Preachers every Lent for ten years a barrel of white herrings, and to the young friars of the same house for the same time a frail of figs.[30]

73

As for Piers Plowman, he seems to have gone to the cloister immediately on leaving the church, probably by way of the walking place leading to the east alley. His description of the cloister mentions both the lavatory and the lead roofing of the cloister alleys:

> Then came I to that cloister and gazed all about,   *191*
> How it was pillared and painted and cunningly carved,
> With roofing of lead low to the stones,
> With painted tiles paved, one after another;
> With conduits of clean tin, closed all about,   *195*
> With lavers of latten lovingly wrought.
> The yield of the ground in a great shire, I trow,
> Would not even begin to furnish that place.

The East Dorter

The 1550 Survey mentions an East Dorter and a South Dorter, both of them roofed with slates and tiles (6:8). The East Dorter occupied the upper floor of the eastern range. Night stairs led down to the church from the dorter's north end, and provided the means by which the brethren descended to the choir for their midnight office. The stairs are mentioned incidentally by Hugh Losse, who lists their lead roof in his inventory of building materials—"the lead of a little roof covering the stairs coming out of the church to the dorter" (6:12)—and in doing so indicates that the staircase stood under its own roof and was not an integral part of either the dorter or the church. Blagrave mentions the staircase as "a stair going up . . . into the late east dorter of the said late Black Friars" (9:2b). For him the staircase served as a part of the southern boundary of a certain parcel of ground, and thus is shown to have lain in an east-west direction.

The east range was as long as the cloister, and perhaps longer; its warming house may have extended southward beyond the cloister's southern end, as warming houses often did. We have no direct information as to the width of the building, but (basing our conjecture upon the known dimensions of the Chapter House, as will be explained below) we may suppose it to have been 25 feet wide in outside measurement.

The Chapter House

The Chapter House adjoined the Great Cloister on its eastern side (5:1),[31] probably at or near the midpoint of its east alley. It was 44 feet in length by 22 in breadth (6:5). It therefore was long enough for its hall to project back from the cloistral range into the clear, so that the hall's vaulted ceiling could rise free of the range's upper story. Since the building was 22 feet in width, it presumably extended east of the range by an equal distance, for the halls of chapter houses were usually square or circular in ground plan, or otherwise as deep as they were wide. A 22-foot projection, deducted from an overall length of 44, would leave 22 feet as the length of the vestibule within the range, as measured from the cloister walk to the near side of the range's east wall, or 25 feet to the outer side. This, therefore, may have been the width of the east dorter and the other buildings in the eastern range.[32] Piers Plowman's description of the chapter house runs as follows:

> Then was the chapter house wrought like a great church,
> Carven and covered and quaintly contrived,   200
> With a beauteous ceiling set up aloft,
> Like a Parliament House all painted about.

In the distribution of Crown lands following the Dissolution, the Chapter House was divided between two recipients. Sir Francis Bryan got the vestibule leading from the cloister alley to the hall, his portion being described as "a parcel of the Chapter House there, and adjoining the cloister there on the east side" (5:1); it went eventually to the Bishop of Ely (11:2). Sir Thomas Cawarden got the hall itself (6:5, 7:5).

The Schoolhouse

The Schoolhouse was a "chamber . . . standing at the east end of the great cloister" (2:4); and the fact of its going to Gresham and Boldero, and through them to Lady Anne Gray (11:6), suggests that it was in the neighborhood of the other houses and gardens that followed the same route, and therefore at or near the cloister's southeast corner. It may have been a ground-floor chamber under the East Dorter at its southern end, or under the South Dorter at its eastern end; and of the alternatives the latter is perhaps preferable, since the Schoolhouse windows overlooked a small garden (2:4). The chamber was presumably as wide as the dorter that contained it, but its length is unknown.

Two passageways cut through the east range at ground level, with the upper story of the range covering them. One was at the north, immediately south of the chapel that adjoined the church on its south side (5:9); it was the slype described by Blagrave as "a way . . . leading between the south end of the said belfry and the north end and side of the late cloister adjoining to the said dorter" (9:2b). Such passageways often served dual purposes, as entries and as "parlors" where necessary conversation was permitted, and Blagrave's "way" may therefore have been "our cenacle called a Parlor . . . adjacent to the said chapel on the south side" (5:10). The other was at the south, as proved by its nearness to the gallery of Lady Anne Gray; it is bewilderingly described as "all that entrance . . . containing by estimation 16 feet in length to the door leading to the cloister, and in width by estimation 8 feet, leading to the door in the east side of the dorter," with further specifications that defy reconstruction (2:1). Somewhere between the two passageways, and probably nearer to the south end than to the north, was the day stair leading up from the east cloister walk to the east dormitory.

The Prior's Lodging and Its Outbuildings

In addition to the east range elements already discussed, some two dozen other houses, chambers, galleries, and halls were in or under the East Dorter, or in the grounds that lay between it and "those our two gardens there . . . over the great royal wardrobe there commonly called the King's Great Wardrobe" (5:17). The various houses and halls extended north as far as the church, and far enough south to include the vestibule of the Chapter House.

The Prior's Lodging was the easternmost building in the group, since nothing but the two gardens lay to the east of it; they are described as being "adjacent to the said hospice called the Prior's Lodging on the east side" (5:17). Other units, including the great dining chamber, the cellar called a buttery, the storehouse, the house with a hearth, and the kitchen and larder house (5:11, 5:3–7) had probably served the Prior's Lodging originally in its capacity as hospice. These and other buildings and parts of buildings—a bedchamber, three galleries big or little, eight assorted chambers, a chapel, a hall, a parlor—are described in the Bryan patent as lying north, east, south, or west of each other, or over or under. No dimensions are given. In the absence of any clues as to size, it would be profitless to attempt to depict the units in a ground plan.

The Provincial's Lodging

The Provincial's Lodging or Chamber[33] seems to have been to the south of the Prior's Lodging. It was accessible from the cloister by way of "the door in the east side of the dorter; and from the same dormitory

20 feet in length from the south wall to the first beam towards the north," whatever that may mean (2:1). It was accessible also by way of "one pair of stairs . . . leading by the stone wall south of the said dormitory to the said chamber called the Provyncyall Chamber" (2:2). Both avenues of approach are described with unusual particularity in the Gresham-Boldero grant, but the particulars are stated with reference to unknowables, and therefore are wholly baffling.

It seems probable that the Provincial's Chamber was the building whose foundations were unearthed in 1900,[34] for only two buildings—the Provincial's Lodging and the Rere-dorter—may be supposed to have been located in that general area, and of the two the second is eliminated by the nature of the substructure revealed at the time of excavation. The chamber proper, since it is described as "a certain small chamber" (2:1), presumably occupied only a part of the Lodging.

The Rere-dorter

The Rere-dorter, popularly known as the "common jakes" or the "common privy," was "next to" the Provincial's chamber (2:2). It was undoubtedly near the dorter and connected with it by an upper-level bridge; and since the Ludgate friary had a south dorter as well as an east, the rere-dorter may have been connected with both. It presumably lay in a direction approximately north and south, for the drainage stream beneath it necessarily flowed in that direction, toward the lower ground and the river. No dimensions are available for it nor for any other Dominican rere-dorter; those shown in Figure 14 (64 feet by 22 feet) are the average for twenty-two rere-dorters, as mentioned on page 43 above.

The South Range

So much for the eastern side of the Great Cloister. As for the southern side, its story is quickly told. The Great Cloister was flanked at the south by a range which at the same time flanked the Inner Cloister at the north; it divided the two cloisters one from another. It was 25 feet 1½ inches in breadth (12:5) and two stories in height; its length is not stated. Hugh Losse called it the South Dorter in his 1550 Survey (6:8), and its character as a dorter is further attested by the terms of the lease which gave Sir William Kingston the tenancy of "all the houses and edifices under the dormitory . . . and all that part of the dormitory not assigned nor demised to the Lady Anne Gray, widow, on the north part of the said [Inner] cloister" (1:2), and by a second document which describes Dame Gray's property as "a mansion at the end of the Great Dormitory."[35] It is remarkable that the friary should have had two dorters, and doubly remarkable that one of them should have occupied the range opposite the church, usually the place for the frater.[36]

The buildings at the west side of the Great Cloister will be considered in the next chapter. But they cannot be considered alone; both historically and topographically, they demand to be studied in association with the Upper Frater building to the south of them, which united with them to compose a continuous block of masonry well over 200 feet long. That block stretched far enough south to border the South or Inner Cloister as well as its neighbor to the north, and it will therefore be well to dispose of the Inner Cloister before going on to the three buildings that made up the western ranges.

The Inner Cloister

The Inner Cloister[37] was known also as the Old,[38] the South,[39] and the Little Cloister.[40] Its dimensions are unknown. It adjoined the infirmary, and probably was designed originally for the refreshment of the sick. It was let to the Kingstons in 1540, and thereafter was known as their garden. Its boundaries are given in the Kingston lease as "all the hall, storehouse, and cellar on the north part of the said cloister, and all the house and edifice called the Library on the east part of the said cloister, . . . and also all the house and edifice called the Firmary at the west end of the said cloister, . . . and all the mill and brewhouse adjacent to the said firmary, and one stable situated next to the said brewhouse" (1:2), presumably at the south. Just as the cloister came to be known as the Kingstons' garden, so "the firmary at the west end of the said cloister" came to be known as Lady Kingston's house. It was only a part—the southernmost third—of the range that bounded the Inner Cloister on the west; the rest of the range was composed of "a house called the Upper Frater, . . . abutting south and east to my Lady Kingston's house and garden" (4:5, 6:21, 7:8). The mill and brewhouse undoubtedly adjoined the Firmary at its eastern side, since they would not otherwise have been mentioned in association with the Inner Cloister; the brewhouse cannot, therefore, be identified with that other and perhaps later brewhouse that stood hard by the little house occupied by Bywater, west of the Upper Frater building and near its northern end.[41] As for the stable, it cared for the horses of guests, since the friars presumably had none of their own; they traveled afoot except by special dispensation. But the guests who came to the Blackfriars in London were apt to be substantial citizens rather than casual wayfarers, and the stable needed therefore to be large enough to shelter the mounts of lordly retinues, as, for instance, did the Benedictine abbey at St. Albans, which provided stabling for three hundred horses.[42]

The Library

The Library was on the east side of the Inner Cloister. It was in two sections: the Great or Upper Library (11:5) and the Under or Nether Library (11:5, 6), which seems to have been composed of two chambers and a cellar (1:1). It adjoined the Hill Garden (1:1), and this implies the absence of any buildings immediately to the east of it. Its dimensions are not known, but some of its contents are. A partial list of the books "*In Bibliotheca Praedicatorum Londini*" was compiled in 1536 or thereabouts, and in addition to Scripture and Biblical commentaries it included the works of Master Wycliffe and replies to them, several tragedies of Seneca, a volume or two of Cassiodorus, some of the Chronicles of Giraldus Cambrensis, an illustrated manual on the motion of the heart, and a complete treatise on the life and behavior of comets.[43]

1. In this description of the precinct boundaries I have had the great advantage of consultation, through correspondence, with Miss Marjorie B. Honeybourne of the London Topographical Society. My inquiry as to the reason for the irregular south-east boundary brought this response: "The answer really lies in the position of the Prior of Okebourne's Inn. This lay between the Blackfriars precinct and the Thames, in Castle Baynard Ward. It never became part of the Blackfriars property, for Henry VI gave it to King's College, Cambridge, which he founded. The Blackfriars precinct, in the Ward of Farringdon Within, became the Parish of St. Anne, Blackfriars, and the precinct, ward, and parish boundaries here coincided."

2. Statements about the topography of the area at the present day are based upon Ordnance Surveys TQ-3180-NE and TQ-3181-SE, which combine to cover the Blackfriars precinct and its surroundings.

3. See pp. 250–52 below.

4. *Hist. MSS. Comm.*, 7th Report, p. 665a.

5. Figs. 14, 19, and 20 show an east-west way or lane called Shoemaker Row. This became the western end of Carter Lane in 1866.

6. If any reader should have misgivings lest the first building described by Piers can only have been one of greater dignity and importance than a gatehouse, and if for that reason he should challenge my identification of the two, I invite him to compare the description with the photographs of extant conventual gatehouses listed here: Cook and Smith, Plates XLIV, LXXXI, XCIX, CVI, CVII, CXXIX, CXXX; G. H. Cook, Plates I–IV; Crossley, Figs. 93–97; Gilyard-Beer, Plates X, XI; and James, opposite p. 89.

7. Clapham, "On the Topography," p. 62.

8. Plate II in this book, Plate XXIII in Hinnebusch, and p. 120 in Jarrett.

9. But its traces, as preserved in modern building lines, suggest that no two sides were exactly parallel, and that no corner was a true right angle.

10. The measurement is to the east side of Church Entry. This is now an irregular line, but a straight line running from its northern extremity to its southern is just 111 feet east of the east wall of Apothecaries' Hall.

11. See pp. 46–48 above. Dr. Philip Norman, in his report of the excavations, has omitted to say verbally by how many feet one building overlapped the other, but his little ground plan (Fig. 5) seems to put the distance at about 18 feet. Mr. Sidney Toy's later plan (Fig. 6) puts it at about 17 feet. But since we lack assurance that either dimension is authoritative, I prefer the figure given by Blagrave, and I base all my reckonings and measured drawings upon it.

12. This, as nearly as I can scale it on Plate VI of Harben, is the width of the passageway after its walls had been destroyed. But the small scale of the map makes accurate scaling difficult.

13. Clapham says that as a rule the parallel walls enclosing the walking place "were placed close together, generally some ten feet apart" ("Friars as Builders," p. 244).

14. Dr. William Martin, who had an opportunity to see and measure the remains revealed by the 1925 excavations, says that "the total length of the choir, excluding the passage through the church, measured ninety-five feet" (cf. p. 49 above). One wonders how he arrived at this figure. He was not able to measure the length of the choir, since he says that "the east end of the choir . . . was not included in the area under excavation";

nor is it obvious how he knew the position of the passage, since no discovery reported by him or Toy, nor shown in Toy's measured drawing, indicates its position. A 95-foot measurement *excluding* the passage puts the passage about 9 feet farther west than we know it to have been; the same measurement, *including* the passage, comes close to being right.

15. See pp. 46–48 above, and Fig. 5.

16. See pp. 48–49 above, and Fig. 6.

17. A distance of 66 feet is marked on the floor of the Guildhall in London as an ancient Standard of Length.

18. Or more probably 22 feet, the same as the width of the vestry. The scribe has made an error in addition, in giving fourscore as the sum of 3 plus 56 plus 20 (9:2c); and if we assume that he intended 55 instead of 56, his total becomes a correct 79 and his north chapel becomes the same width as the vestry.

19. *V. C. H. London*, Vol. I, p. 500, and Wills, P.C.C., 40 Holgrave, as quoted by Clapham, "On the Topography," p 64.

20. Joseph Quincy Adams, "Conventual Buildings," p. 67, says that "the Church Porch, later known as the Square Tower, seems to have occupied the usual position on the north side of the Nave at the west end, and to have been in the nature of a small chapel dedicated to Our Lady." But we have no reason to suppose that the church porch was at the nave's northwest corner, and therefore none to suppose that it and the Lady Chapel were the same. Dr. Adams's siting of the porch at the west end of the church is presumably based upon an erroneous identification of the house that John Barnard (or Barnett) owned, with the house that he lived in. He *owned* the Square Tower in the fifteen-sixties, but a certain William Tanner occupied it (*BR* 107:36–42). Barnard

lived *in* a tenement that is described as "on the west end of the same church" (6:2) and "on the west part" of the Great Cloister (6:4), which means that it abutted upon the cloister's western edge. It was probably the same tenement as that later occupied by the Widow Freemount (cf. *BR* 114:28–30).

21. Palmer, "London," p. 286.

22. Palmer, "London," pp. 197–205, 266–69.

23. "On the Topography," pp. 65–67.

24. *Encyclopaedia Britannica, s.v.* "London," speaks of "the arrogant magnificence of the Blackfriars Church, its 'gay glittering glas glowing as the sun.'" The ascription to the Blackfriars is incorrect. The line occurs in a passage of the *Creed* that specifically deals with the Minorites or Friars Minor or Franciscans (line 103).

25. Hugh Losse, the King's surveyor, twice refers to the Great Cloister as the "south cloister" (6:7, 6:12), but it was south only in respect of being on the south side of the church. He cannot have meant the Inner Cloister, for many of the specifications in his survey are appropriate to the Great Cloister but not to the Inner, and the whole purpose of the survey rules out the possibility of its applying to the southernmost cloister. It is concerned with defining the property about to be granted to Sir Thomas Cawarden, who, indisputably, got the Great Cloister and buildings fronting upon it. The Inner Cloister had already, ten years before, been let to Sir William and Lady Mary Kingston (1:2), and it remained in their tenure for many years to come.

26. Hinnebusch, pp. 200–201.

27. P. 37 above.

28. G. H. Cook, p. 59, says that "the average width of the cloister walks was 11 or 12 feet"; but he is talking of the walks in monasteries, not in friaries; the friars,

with their missions outside their precincts, had less need of roomy galleries. Fr. Hinnebusch, pp. 201–02, says that the cloister walks of the Dominican establishments at Cardiff and **Bangor** were 8 feet wide internally, and 8 feet seems to have been about the average for mendicant cloisters. I have accordingly used that dimension in Figure 16, and have represented the cloister bays as being about as wide as they are deep, which again seems to have been customary.

29. Wills, P. C. C., 5 Holder, as quoted by Clapham, "On the Topography," p. 68, and "Friars as Builders," p. 259.

30. *Ibid.*, 22 Ayloffe, as also quoted by Clapham, *loc. cit.*

31. Hugh Losse erroneously described the Chapter House as being "on the west end of the said cloister" in his 1550 Survey (6:5), and his error was translated into Latin by the scribe who wrote the Cawarden patent of 1550. The position of the house is correctly stated in the Bryan grant (5:1) and in Cawarden's *Inquisition Post Mortem.*

32. The average outside width of five Dominican dorters, as arrived at by scaling their ground plans in the book by Fr. Hinnebusch, was about 27 feet. Individual dimensions are: Brecon, 28 feet; Canterbury, 27; Gloucester, 29; Cardiff, 22; and Newcastle, 28. The South Dorter at Ludgate was 25 feet 1½ inches wide (12:5).

33. It is called Lodging in 11:6 and Chamber in 2:1–2.

34. See pp. 46–48 above.

35. The first item in the list of Crown rents, as printed in Palmer, "London," p. 285.

36. This usualness presumably accounts for Sir Alfred Clapham's attaching the label "Frater" to the south range building in all his ground plans of the Ludgate precinct; he had no other reason for doing so, and is clearly in error. Joseph Quincy Adams, "Conventual Buildings," pp. 69–70, is equally in error in postulating two south ranges, one at the south edge of the Great Cloister and the other at the south edge of the Inner. He supposes both to have been dormitories originally and to have been tenanted by the Kingstons later. But his two dorters were undoubtedly one; no evidence exists for any range at the south side of the Inner Cloister.

37. 1:2, 1:3, *BR* 124:34.

38. "*Quoddam Claustrum vocatum vetus Claustrum,*" *BR* 120:3.

39. 11:5.

40. Palmer, "London," p. 285, quoting Losse's list of Crown rents.

41. *BR* 43:4, 43:35, 44:7.

42. Crossley, p. 25.

43. Palmer, "London," pp. 279–80, as abridged and translated by Jarrett, p. 39.

4

The Western Ranges

FROM THE STANDPOINT of theatrical topography, the important part of the Blackfriars precinct was the range of three buildings that flanked the western sides of the Great and Inner Cloisters. The 1548 Survey and its derivatives call them Lord Cobham's House, an Old Buttery, and the Upper Frater (4:4, 4:5). Lord Cobham's House was the most northerly and the smallest of the three; it abutted upon the Church at the northwest corner of the Great Cloister. The Old Buttery was just south of it; the two buildings together composed a continuous range long enough to enclose the Great Cloister along the whole of its western side. The Upper Frater was south of the Old Buttery, with only an entry or passage between (4:4, 6:20). From there it stretched southward to form the western range of the Inner Cloister.

All three names are unsatisfactory and misleading. They must be retained for the present, however, until the true characters of the three buildings can be developed.

In the days of the friars, the lower floor of Lord Cobham's House was the porter's lodge. The upper floor, in all probability, was the friary's first guest house.

The upper floor of the Old Buttery was the original refectory or frater. The lower floor was broken up into several service rooms—the buttery, which later gave its name to the building as a whole, a pantry, and probably bins for the storage of foodstuffs.

The upper floor of the Frater block, flanking the Inner Cloister, was the great chamber where the parliament of the realm sometimes sat. The lower floor held the "nether house" where the Commons assembled when they met apart from the Lords.[1]

But in the course of time some changes were found to be necessary.

The upper floor of the porter's lodge proved to be inadequate as the guest house of the friary, and it did so the earlier because the Ludgate friary was called upon not only to provide such hospitality as was expected of all religious houses, but also to accommodate foreign embassies and other guests of the state with their throngs of retainers. Under such circumstances the hospitium inevitably spilled over into the refectory on the adjoining upper floor of the Old Buttery, and eventually took it over altogether. The top floor of the Old Buttery had clearly become the friars' guest house by the time of the visit of Charles V in 1522.[2]

When the upper floor of the Old Buttery became a hostelry instead of a refectory, the friars were forced to find a new place to eat. They found it in a room on the ground floor of the Upper Frater block. It was smaller than their old refectory had been, but that imposed little hardship, for the number of friars had already begun to dwindle; and they made the move the more willingly because in their new misericord they would be permitted to eat meat three days in the week, whereas they were forbidden to eat it at all in their old refectory.[3] The friars were eating in a room on the lower story of the Upper Frater at least as early as 1532.[4] Another room, or perhaps the same room, was being used by the Commons as their "accustomed house" in 1529; we have no knowledge that it was being so used after that date.

Some of the statements made in the last two pages are certainties; others are conjectures. It now becomes my task to adduce proof of the certainties, and reasons for regarding the conjectures as probabilities. I shall discuss the three buildings in the order in which they lay from north to south.

The Porter's Lodge

I have assumed that the upper floor of the porter's lodge was the first guest house of the friary. This assumption is based upon the following considerations: First, it was suitably located and adapted for that purpose. It was in the west, always the place for layfolk and the preferred place for the guest house as being far removed from the friars' sleeping quarters, and it was directly over the gate of the porter whose duty it was to admit guests. Second, it was far larger than was required to meet the porter's modest needs. He needed a small cell at most, and that on the lower floor; he had no need of a great upper story that could be described as "the large room of the said capital mansion sometime called the Porters Lodge of the said Priory."[5] Third, the Old Kitchen was adjacent to it, and could therefore do the cooking for it as well as for the refectory; and fourth, an upstairs window was cut through the wall into the church under conditions that suggest its having been provided for the convenience of guests. A hall so large and so favorably situated must be presumed to have had some important function from the beginning; and as far as our information goes, everything points toward, and nothing conflicts with, the theory that the top floor of the porter's lodge was the first hospitium of the friars.

The building at Ludgate was located as was usual for porters' lodges, at the southwest corner of the church and at the north end of the western range. It is important to our present inquiry because, under the name of Lord Cobham's house, it is given as the northern boundary of Cawarden's property in the Survey of 1548 and several other documents deriving from it,[6] and because, in marking the north limit of Cawarden's holdings, it also marked the limit of the parcels later to be available to Farrant and to Burbage for conversion to theatrical purposes. It becomes desirable therefore to know just what Lord Cobham's house comprised.

The Cobham deed of 1554 gives its dimensions as 21 feet from north to south by 47 feet from east to west (10:3). Two years earlier, when Jane Freemount tenanted its lower floor, Blagrave gave the dimensions as 21 feet at the side where the tenement abutted east upon the cloister (8:3a) by 52 feet in length (8:3d);[7] and Blagrave gave the further information that the north side of the Widow Freemount's lodging abutted north upon the south wall of the church for a distance of 20 feet (8:3c). Both the 52-foot overall length and the fact of abutment were confirmed when the foundations of the west wall of the church were unearthed in 1915. As reported and sketched by Dr. Norman (Figure 5), the excavations revealed the remains of a foundation wall that stretched east and west for a distance of about 52 feet along precisely the line that the lodge's northern wall must have followed, and that overlapped the south wall of the church for a distance of about 18 feet.[8]

The property seems to have been in the tenure of Lady Jane Guildford from a time well before the Dissolution; she had rented it from the friars at some unknown date, perhaps even as early as 1522, at which time she is known to have been a resident of the precinct.[9] On April 10, 1536, she subleased her tenement or mansion to George Brooke Lord Cobham (3:2); but apparently she had tenure of, and consequently was able to sublet to Cobham, only the building's upper floor. The terms of the lease, as they were sketchily reported afterwards in the deed of 1545 or 1546, do not say so; on the contrary, they give the offhand impression that Lord Cobham acquired the lower story as well as the upper (3:2). But he cannot have done so, for sixteen years later Jane Freemount still held the tenement whereof all the rooms except the entry were "under the lodgings of the Lord Cobham" (8:3a), and not until two years after that did Cobham purchase from Cawarden "all that his nether room, ground, soil, and hereditament . . . under the chambers of the said Lord Cobham, containing in length from the east part to the west part thereof 47 foot, and in breadth from the north part to the south part 21 foot" (10:3). This is the more surprising since Cawarden is not otherwise known to have owned any part of the porter's lodge at any time, in spite of its being sandwiched between two other edifices—the church and the Old Buttery—that went to him in the royal grant of 1550. But Edward VI could not grant the lodge to Cawarden in 1550, because the Crown no longer held it; four years earlier Henry VIII had terminated Lady Jane Guildford's pre-Dissolution lease and had sold the lodge outright to Lord Cobham. The deed of sale, as translated from the original Latin, describes the property as "one tenement or mansion there, with a certain window called the Closet Window looking into the church there, together with all the rooms, kitchens, storerooms, larders, cellars, solars, and all other the houses and buildings . . . which formerly were in the tenure of Lady Jane Guildford" (3:2).

The reference to "the Closet Window looking into the church" is of special interest. As we know, it was usual in monasteries and friaries to have a window cut through the common wall between the porter's cell and the church, so that the porter could theoretically be present at mass and other liturgical offices without leaving his post of duty.[10] But this particular window had not been designed for the convenience of the porter; it was on the wrong story for that. The porter's field of operations, and therefore his window, would necessarily have been on the lower floor; but this window was on the upper, as evidenced by its being listed as a part of the property sold to Cobham in 1545 or 1546, which included only the upper story. The window had therefore presumably been provided for the convenience of guests, possibly of Charles V on the occasion of his state visit.

Incidentally, since the porter's function was to pass upon the admissibility of persons who sought entrance to the cloister, one must suppose that a passageway into the Great Cloister either ran from end to end of the lodge internally, or adjoined it at the south.

By his purchase of a part of the porter's lodge from Henry VIII in 1545–1546 and of the rest from Cawarden in 1554, George Brooke Lord Cobham acquired the entire building and still held it at his death. Together with neighboring parts of the Old Buttery building, it remained in the family for about fifty years. George was succeeded by his son William, the seventh Lord Cobham, who became Lord Warden of the Cinque Ports in succession to Cheyne, was appointed Privy Councillor in 1586, and served as Lord Chamberlain for a few months in 1596–1597. The eighth Lord Cobham, Henry Brooke, was attainted of treason in 1603 for his part in the Raleigh conspiracy, and his properties returned to the Crown. Thereafter the Cobham mansion passed through many hands.[11] Its last change of ownership came in 1632, when Anne Lady Howard of Effingham sold it, together with the building to the south, to the Society of Apothecaries. Both buildings were destroyed in the Great Fire of 1666. The present hall of the Society was built on the same site, and the land and its buildings remain the property of the Society of Apothecaries to this day.[12]

The Old Buttery

The name Upper Frater suggests that the top floor of the Frater block served as the refectory of the friars, but it never did; it was unsuitable for that function in location, in size, and in its lack of facilities for the preparation of food. Not the top floor of the Upper Frater, but the top floor of the Old Buttery, served in that capacity. It was entirely suitable in every respect.

The Upper Frater block was unsuitable in location because it had no frontage upon the Great Cloister. In all orders except the Carthusian, custom, ceremony, and convenience dictated that the frater of a monastery or friary should abut upon the main cloister and have its entrance upon it;[13] the brethren congregated in the cloister before meals, washed their hands at the lavatory near the refectory door, recited a psalm, and formed in line for the march upstairs to the dining hall. As we have seen, the friary at Ludgate did in fact have such a lavatory in the Great Cloister,[14] and by prescription the door to the refectory should have been near it. But the entrance to the Upper Frater was not near it; it did not front upon the Great Cloister at all, but upon the lay yard to the west of the cloistral buildings. It follows therefore that some door other than that, some door near the lavatory, was the door leading to the refectory, and that some building other than the Upper Frater was the friars' dining hall.

87

Secondly, it was unsuitable in size; judged by the average size of fraters in monasteries and friaries alike, the Parliament Chamber was too large to be a refectory. As related on page 40 above, the average floor area of non-Dominican refectories, including those of some of the great monasteries with their hundreds of monks and *conversi*, was about 2,610 square feet; the average for Dominican fraters was about 1,800. But the Parliament Chamber, with its inside length of 101 feet and its width of 46, had a floor area of 4,646 square feet. It was thus more than two and a half times as large as the average for Dominican refectories, and half again as large as the general average. The Ludgate priory cannot have needed so large a hall for the feeding of its ninety brethren.

The top floor of the Old Buttery building, on the other hand, had the suitability that the Parliament Chamber lacked, in respect both of location and of size. Its location was entirely appropriate. Not only did it abut upon the Great Cloister for its entire length, but it abutted upon the side of the cloister that was usual for Blackfriars fraters.[15] As we have seen, the traditional place for a refectory was the south range, opposite the church; but if for some reason a refectory could not be accommodated at the south side of the cloister, the western range was the customary place. It was so at Ludgate. There the south range was preempted by the South Dorter, and under those circumstances the western range was the natural place for the refectory to be.

In size also the Old Buttery block conformed to the norm for refectories. Its top floor was probably about 92 feet long by 26 feet wide internally, for an area of 2,392 square feet. It was thus a trifle smaller than the average for monastic and mendicant establishments generally, and decidedly larger than the average for Dominican. As the dining hall for one of the greatest of the Blackfriars houses, its size was altogether suitable.

Finally, the facilities for the preparation of meals were grouped around the Old Buttery building rather than around the Upper Frater block. The buttery itself, located at the south end of the ground floor of the building to which it gave its name, was only one of them. Another was the Old Kitchen, which abutted against the building on the west side (4:3–4, 6:19–20); and it is noteworthy that both the buttery and the kitchen are characterized as Old, and that the kitchen is also called the Convent Kitchen (14:2), adjectives suggesting that these two offices were parts of the friary's original establishment. Near the buttery was a pantry (12:5), and close by the Convent Kitchen were two houses called Larders

(14:2). The Upper Frater building had no comparable facilities. It did have a kitchen abutting toward the Blind Parlor (4:7), but this kitchen is described as Little; so, too, is the Little Buttery that was located "at the north end of the said seven great upper rooms and on the west side thereof" (19:11). Both may have come later, in consequence of the friars' move from their first frater to their misericord on the lower floor of the Upper Frater building.

That move, as has already been briefly related, came in consequence of the need to expand the guest house, and of the decision to devote the top floor of the Old Buttery to that purpose in addition to the top floor of the porter's lodge. We know that the Old Buttery building was being used as the guest house at the time of the imperial visit of 1522; we know it because we can trace the path followed by the tapestried gallery that connected the Emperor's apartments with the lodgings of his entourage on the far side of the Fleet, and because that path, when extended eastward, leads to about the midpoint of the Old Buttery block. Sir Alfred W. Clapham describes the evidences of the path's course as being contained in

a survey of certain tenements lying on the south side of the lane leading from Blackfriars to Bridewell Bridge, now widened and known as Union Street.[16] They start with a wooden gallery spanning the Fleet ditch immediately to the south of the bridge, 42 ft. long by 14 ft. wide. Then follow a number of tenements of various lengths fronting the street, but all 14 ft. deep, certainly an extraordinary dimension for a house. The solution is that we have here the remains of Henry VIII's wooden gallery from Bridewell to Blackfriars, cut up into tenements. It followed the southern side of Union Street up to Water Lane, immediately opposite the building we have been describing, thus proving that it was the building occupied by Charles V in 1522, for whose convenience the gallery was built.[17]

So much for the history of the Old Buttery prior to the Dissolution. As for its dimensions, it was several feet narrower on the top floor than it was on the floor below. Its ground-level width is given as 36 feet in the two surveys (4:4, 6:20),[18] whereas its upper-level width is given as 25 feet in the Cobham and Farrant leases (15:2, 16:2), as 26 feet 7½ inches in the Neville lease (12:2), and as 27 feet in the Cobham deed (10:2). The minor discrepancies cannot readily be explained. The greater discrepancy, i.e., the difference between these widths and that of the building at ground level, is explained by the existence of a gallery that ran along the west side of the building at the height of the upper story. The Neville lease describes it as "a certain high gallery of stone that is situate and over the foresaid buildings, houses, edifices or walls" (12:13). At the date of the Neville lease (1560) the gallery was already ruinous and likely to fall, and it, or more probably a part of it, was pulled down by Thomas Totnall in 1563 or 1564;[19] but a section described as "one gallery containing in length 40 feet and in breadth 10 feet, lying on the east part of the said kitchen" (14:2) and therefore between the kitchen and the west side of the Old Buttery (4:4, 6:20), was still standing in 1566.[20]

The various figures given as the widths of the upper floor, averaging about 26 feet, are in all probability inside dimensions, since an upstairs apartment would most conveniently be measured within walls. Figure 17 therefore shows the upper floor of the Old Buttery as being 26 feet wide internally and 32 feet wide externally. Under such conditions, the 10-foot-wide gallery would overhang the lower wall by a distance of 6 feet.

The longitudinal dimensions of the Old Buttery will be considered shortly, in connection with those of the Upper Frater block.

Various utility rooms occupied the lower floor of the Old Buttery building. The buttery proper, the unit that gave its name to the building as a whole, was at the south end. North of the buttery came a "pantry, with a little entry leading between them" (12:5); then probably more rooms, and at the north end, next to the porter's lodge, a stepped passageway leading easterly through the range from the Convent Kitchen to the Great Cloister (14:2), and a staircase leading up to Lord Cobham's House on the upper floor of the porter's lodge (10:2). The roof of the Old Buttery was covered with tiles. This is evidenced by three orders given by the Society of Apothecaries for the amending of old tiling and the providing of new, soon after the Society took possession of the building in 1632.[21]

The Burbage deed of 1596, and other real estate records dating from the years after the Old Buttery had ended its role in English theatrical history, speak often of a Pipe Office. It was established by Sir William More in 1591 upon his appointment as one of the Chamberlains of the Exchequer, so that he might have a place where he could store the rolled Exchequer documents, pipelike in appearance, that passed through his hands in his official capacity. It occupied two rooms (20:5, 20:7) on the upper floor of the Old Buttery at its southern end. Among the documents that Sir William stored there were some of those that provide material for this present study.

The Upper Frater

Upper Frater is one of several names applied to the southernmost of the three west-range buildings or to parts of it; others are Frater, Parliament Chamber, and the Seven Great Upper Rooms. So far as we know, the titles Upper Frater and Frater,[22] as names for the building's top floor or for the building as a whole, originated with the anonymous author of the 1548 Survey. He used Upper Frater once, not as designating the building's upper floor, but as designating the building in its entirety— "a house called the Upper Frater" (4:5). He used Frater three times without the Upper, twice as meaning the top story (4:4, 4:6) and once as meaning the whole house (4:10). Two years later Hugh Losse followed the lead of his predecessor in one use of Upper Frater (6:21) and two of Frater alone (6:20, 6:23), and he added two new Fraters on his own initiative, both times as indicating the building as a whole (6:12). The same appellations were subsequently used in other documents that were in the direct line of descent from the 1548 Survey, but not with the same meanings in any documents deriving from other sources.

The Survey of 1548 was written ten years after the Dissolution, and by a man who gives little evidence of having known the functions and names of the friary buildings in the days of the friars: Frater and Cloister are the only purely conventual words that he uses. Frater, as he uses it, is ambiguous; it means both of two different things. Upper, as he uses it, is incomprehensible.

In contrast with the dubious ancestry and sense of Upper Frater as a title, Parliament Chamber as a title is of known parentage and precise meaning. King Henry VIII, who "possessed [the chamber] during his life" (13:6), caused or permitted it to be called by the name of Parliament Chamber in his letters and papers of state.[23] The historian Edward Hall, author of the invaluable *Hall's Chronicle*, called it the Parliament Chamber in his account of the Parliament of 1523;[24] and Sir William More, who in 1562 knew the building both as its owner and as a member of parliament for fifteen years past, called it the Parliament Chamber in his memorandum on the subject of Kempe's claim (13:2). The name unmistakably and consistently means the top floor of the Upper Frater building.

The title Seven Great Upper Rooms is equally precise, and refers to the same top floor. It is used to designate the Parliament Chamber in the Burbage Indenture of 1596, and is used nowhere else. Nearly half a

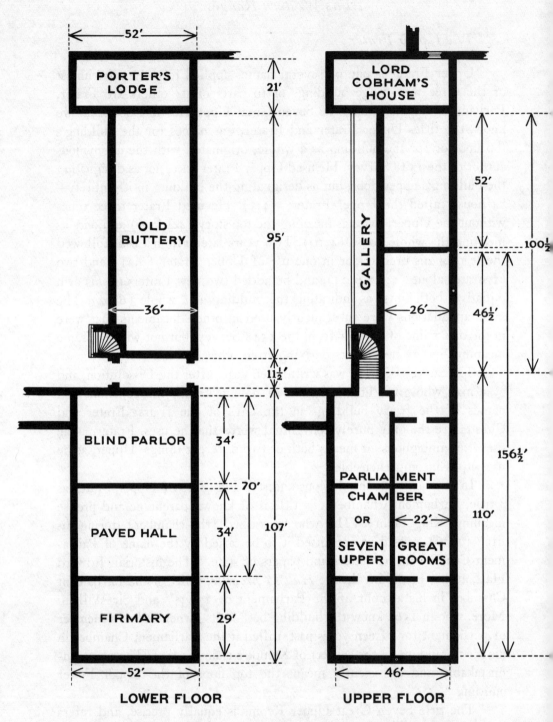

Figure 17. Dimensions of the buildings in the western ranges. Dimensions are in terms of feet. External walls are drawn as being 3 feet thick, and internal walls as being 2.

century earlier, as has already been related, Sir Thomas Cawarden, in seeking to make the great top story "mansionable" for residential purposes, had split it into east and west halves by means of a wall running lengthwise from north to south. By 1571 the east half had been divided into four rooms (15:2) and the west half into three, to make up the total of seven into which the Parliament Chamber was partitioned at the time of the Burbage purchase.

The north-south dimensions of the Upper Frater and the Old Buttery are interrelated, and require to be considered together. Two sets of documents supply the figures. The 1548 Survey and its derivatives give the measurements of the two buildings at ground level; a series of leases gives their measurements on the floor above. After the figures have been assembled and correlated, these facts emerge as the result:

At ground level, the Upper Frater and the Old Buttery were separated by a gap 11½ feet wide, that being the width of an entry or passage that passed between them and then ran westward to Water Lane. On the upper level the two buildings were connected, however; their upper stories bridged the gap and combined to form a continuous floor 213½ feet long by outside measure. These conclusions are based upon the data and computations given in the reduced-type paragraphs that follow:

The 1548 Survey and its derivatives give the size of the Upper Frater as being 107 feet long by 52 feet wide (4:5, 6:21, etc.), and that of the Old Buttery as being 95 feet long[25] by 36 feet wide (4:4, 6:20). These measurements were made in the course of an outdoor survey that dealt with grounds as well as with buildings, and they therefore were unquestionably made at ground level and to the outside surfaces of walls. The presumption that they are outside dimensions is proved correct with respect to the Upper Frater specifically by Hawkins's testimony to the effect that the great hall on the upper floor was 46 feet wide (40:3). The 52-foot measurement thus includes two exterior walls, each 3 feet thick.

The second source of data is the sequence of leases dealing with the lodging that Sir Thomas Cawarden created in 1553 or thereabouts by combining parts of the upper stories of the two buildings into a continuous corridorlike tenement six or seven times as long as it was wide. It occupied the entire length of the Frater's top floor at its eastern side, and the whole width of the Old Buttery's top floor at its southern end. The extant leases give the length of the lodging as 156½ feet. The length of the part that lay within the Upper Frater building is given as 110 feet, and the length of the part that lay within the Old Buttery is given as 46½ feet (15:2).[26] But only the southern portion of the Old Buttery's upper floor was incorporated in the long tenement; the residue—a 52-foot-long hall at the north end of the floor—was excluded, and was later sold by Cawarden independently of the rest (10:2). We thus have 98½ feet as the total of the lengths of two separate sections of the top floor of the Old Buttery, to which total must be added the thickness of an intervening wall. We know that such a wall existed, since Lord Cobham's lease of 1571 authorized him to cut doors through it (15:7). On the assumption that the wall was 2 feet thick, we have a total of 100½ feet as the length of the Buttery's upper floor.

These dimensions were undoubtedly measured within walls; they could not have been measured otherwise, since they deal with interior apartments on an upper floor. In consequence, we find that we have 95 feet as the outside length of the Old Buttery at ground level, as contrasted with 100½ feet as its inside length on the floor above; and we have 107 feet as the outside length of the Frater on its lower floor, as against an inside length of 110 feet on the floor above; to which last dimension must be added 3 feet as the thickness of an outer wall at the south end of the Upper Frater, in order to get the overall length of the building at its upper level.[27] It thus appears that the two buildings, taken together, were 11½ feet longer on their upper floors than on the floors below.

This leads to the conclusion that, while the buildings met at upper-floor level so as to form a continuous long apartment, they were separated at ground level by a gap 11½ feet wide; and this in turn leads to the further conclusion that the gap represents the width of the "entry or passage with a great stair therein . . . with a hall place at the upper end of the stair and an entry there to the frater over the same buttery" (4:4, 6:20). The entry's width as thus determined agrees to within 3 inches with that of the "way leading from the said Water Lane to the tenement now in the tenure or occupation of Richard Frith" on the west side of the Frater's upper floor, which said way is described as containing "in length xxvij yerds & iij quarters of a yerde & in bredeth iij yerds iij quarters" (12:7).[28]

The eastern half of the Frater's upper floor joined the upper floor of the Old Buttery under conditions which suggest that they were in alignment with each other, and thus that the eastern sides of the two buildings formed a continuous straight line. The western side of the Upper Frater therefore extended 16 feet farther west than the west wall of the Old Buttery at ground level.

The Upper Frater stood on ground that sloped down to the Thames, on a decline so steep that the building's top floor had only one story beneath it at the north, but three at the south. The three stories at the south held the triple-decked infirmary, which, as we have seen, eventually went to the Kingstons. The middle story of the three seems to have been thought of as the infirmary proper, since "the firmary had a room above the same which was a lodging for those that were sick, and also one other room beneath the firmary" (13:1).[29] Sir William More said that the firmary was one-third as large as the Parliament Chamber; he probably said it, however, with no thought of being mathematically precise. The figure crops up incidentally in the course of a document that is principally concerned with defining the relationship existing between the Parliament Chamber and the rest of the Upper Frater building, the rest of the friary, and the Crown. It was occasioned by the claim filed by a certain Mr. Kempe, who had acquired title to the infirmary and who used his ownership of it as the basis for a claim to ownership of the Parliament Chamber also, on the plea that the two parcels were parts of the same property. Sir William replied that the two were wholly separate and had always been so, and argued that it was absurd to claim the Parliament Chamber as a consequence of owning the infirmary, in view of the fact that "the parliament chamber . . . ys iij tymes as byg as the said fermerye."[30]

For the remaining two-thirds of its length, the story beneath the Parliament Chamber was divided into two rooms called a hall and a parlor. The parlor was at the north end of the building, near the Old Buttery; it is spoken of as being "blind," which presumably means that it was dark or windowless (4:4). The hall was south of the parlor, between it and the infirmary, and is known to have been paved. I shall therefore call the two rooms the Blind Parlor and the Paved Hall, to distinguish them from parlors and halls in general.

The Burbage deed of 1596 repeatedly uses the phrase "Middle Rooms or Middle Stories" as a designation for certain space beneath the Seven Great Upper Rooms (19:8,9,10). The phrase seemingly applies to the Paved Hall alone. As subdivided into two or more compartments, the Paved Hall could be called the Middle Rooms because it lay between the Blind Parlor—Peter Johnson's two rooms (19:15)—at the north, and the Firmary—now Sir George Carey's house (19:8)—at the south. It could be called the Middle Stories because it was "directly under part of . . . the said seven great upper rooms" (19:8) and over "two vaults or cellars . . . lying under part of the said Middle Rooms or Middle Stories" (19:10).[31]

James Burbage purchased Peter Johnson's two rooms (the Blind Parlor) and the Middle Rooms or Middle Stories (the Paved Hall), but not the Firmary. The wall that divided the Paved Hall from the Firmary was thus the southern limit of his holdings on the lower floor, and its position will be found to have an important bearing upon the position and dimensions of the Second Blackfriars Playhouse that Burbage was to create on the floor above. As indicated in Figure 17, the Blind Parlor and the Paved Hall were of the same size, each of them presumably 34 feet long from north to south by 52 feet wide, with a 2-foot-thick wall between them. The east-west wall that separated Burbage's property from Carey's was therefore 70 feet distant from the building's northern end. The data and computations that lead to these conclusions are given in the ensuing paragraphs printed in reduced type.

The 1548 Survey describes the Paved Hall and the Blind Parlor as "a hall and a parlor under the said frater of the same length and breadth" (4:6). The last phrase is ambiguous. It might be taken to mean that the hall and parlor were of the same length and breadth as the frater, were it not for the fact that the frater is known to have occupied the top floor in its entirety, whereas the hall and parlor together occupied only two-thirds of the floor below. Another interpretation, and the only one that bears close scrutiny, is that the hall and parlor were of the same length and breadth as each other.[32] Two other documents support its validity.

The first is the Burbage deed of 1596. That document describes the Middle Rooms or Middle Stories as "containing in length 52 foot of assize more or less, and in breadth 37 foot of assize more or less" (19:8). The 52-foot figure, of course, is the width of the Upper Frater building, and as such is known to be an outside dimension; we are therefore probably justified in assuming that the 37-foot figure is an outside dimension also, and in taking it to be the north-south breadth of each of the two rooms, with the thickness of a neighboring wall included. The breadth of each of them in the clear would then be 34 feet of assize more or less.

This 34-foot dimension, and therefore the assumptions leading up to it, are strongly buttressed by a notation written by Sir Henry Jerningham in 1562 on the subject of the lodging then occupied by Richard Frith. Frith held one of the two apartments into which the Parliament Chamber, as we have already seen, had been divided; and if we may assume that the two longitudinal sections of the 52-foot-wide chamber were of equal width, then each was 26 feet wide before allowances were made for the thickness of walls. Frith's tenement was the one on the west side of the dividing wall. Beneath him were a half of the Blind Parlor at the north, a half of the Paved Hall in the middle, and a half of the Firmary at the south. The north end of Frith's lodging was consequently over the west end of the Blind Parlor, and that room, as has already been intimated, had been used by the friars as their frater in the later years of the convent's history. It was therefore the Blind Parlor to which

Jerningham applied the name Frater, and the Blind Parlor whose length he gave, when he wrote "As much of Frith's house as standeth over the frater, containing 34 foot in length and 26 in breadth."[33]

By this method of reckoning we arrive at 34 feet as being the north-south measure of each of the two rooms. With a 2-foot wall between them, the Blind Parlor and Paved Hall together occupied the northernmost 70 feet of the Upper Frater building on its lower floor. After deducting another 2 feet as the thickness of the wall between the Paved Hall and the Firmary, 29 feet are left as the depth of the Infirmary between walls. This falls short of being a third of the Parliament Chamber's interior length of 101 feet, but it is perhaps near enough to avoid doing violence to Sir William More's statement that the Parliament Chamber was "iij tymes as byg."

As we have seen, the surveys gave the width of the Upper Frater building as 52 feet (4:5, 6:21), and this accords perfectly with the inside dimension of 46 feet given sixty years later as the width of the great hall that then contained the playhouse (40:3). Earlier, in the days when the chamber was split by an internal wall running lengthwise from end to end, the width of the eastern half was given as 22 feet (15:2, 16:2). This figure suggests that the measurement was taken internally, and that the chamber was divided into two strips of equal width, with a 2-foot-thick wall between them.

I have said that a room on the lower floor of the Upper Frater block served as the friars' dining hall after the original refectory had been taken over for use as a guest house. A part of the proof of this statement is to be found in the testimony of two men called as witnesses in the Poole-More controversy of 1572. At that date the Blind Parlor and the Paved Hall were, or until recently had been, rented to a certain William Joyner for use as a fencing school. In the course of the arbitration proceedings growing out of the controversy, the witnesses were asked whether or not the rooms occupied by Joyner had at any time before the Dissolution been occupied by any person or persons other than the friars themselves; in answer to which question one Edward Muschampe of Newington, aged 59 years or thereabouts, testifying under oath before the Lord Mayor, deposed that

the said house wherein the said William Joyner or his assign doth now keep the said school of fence, was always used since this examinate's remembrance by the friars themselves to their own proper use for a parlor where commonly the friars did use to break their fast, for it stood near the buttery of the said house, and never let out or inhabited by any other person or persons until the said house of friars was dissolved or surrendered, that ever this examinate could perceive.[34]

And Richard Lichfield, sergeant-at-mace attending on the Lord Mayor, aged threescore and four years or thereabouts, testified that the friars used the Parlor not merely to break their fast, but also as a place to dine and sup in. He swore that

the said house and place wherein the said William Joyner now or lately kept the said school of fence, was always since this examinate's remembrance used and occupied by the friars themselves to their own proper use as a parlor to dine and sup in; . . . and . . . the buttery which they commonly used stood fast by the said room, and the said parlor stood so handsome to the buttery and the kitchen and brewhouse that it could not without great inconvenience be spared from the use of the said friars.[35]

The use of the Blind Parlor as a frater receives confirmation from yet another source, a source previously cited on page 96 in a different connection. As we know, Richard Frith in 1562 occupied one of the two long tenements into which the Parliament Chamber had been divided. His was the western half, and beneath it were the western halves of the Blind Parlor and the Paved Hall, which, for reasons given above, are estimated to have been 34 feet long from north to south. It was therefore to one of those rooms that Sir Henry Jerningham applied the word "frater," when he wrote "As much of Frith's house as standeth over the frater, containing 34 foot in length and 26 in breadth."[36]

It appears then that the friars did have a refectory in the Upper Frater building, but not on its upper floor, before the Dissolution and yet within the memory of men living in 1572; and it was this later refectory that the 1548 surveyor presumably had in mind when he used the title Upper Frater as a designation for the building. Nothing suggests that any other refectory occupied any other part of the building at any time.

If, then, the Parliament Chamber was never a refectory of the friars in the days before the Dissolution, what was its purpose originally? We find the answer not in the ecclesiastical records of the cloister, but in the secular records of the Court and of lay individuals. So far as the evidence goes, the Parliament Chamber had no connection with any activity of the friars; it was in the friary but not of it; it existed solely to accommodate the special needs of the Crown. The following considerations point in this direction:

First, the Parliament Chamber had no counterpart in any other English monastery or friary. It was unexampled among conventual halls in its off-cloister site and in its notable size. It was, as a matter of fact, one of the largest halls built in England in medieval times, with an unaisled interior span that few buildings of the era could match. In *The Guildhall of the City of London,* Sir John James Baddeley, Lord Mayor of London in 1921–1922, lists only four medieval English halls as having widths equaling or exceeding the Parliament Chamber's width of 46 feet between walls: the Guildhall itself, with a span of 49½ feet; Hatfield Hall in Durham, with a span of 50; Old Christ's Hospital at Newgate, with a span of 51; and, of course, Westminster Hall in London, with a span of 67 feet 6 inches.

Second, the stairway giving access to the Chamber led up to it "out of the great yard . . . next unto the Pipe Office" (19:5); in other words, out of the layfolks' yard, not out of the cloister. Both the stairway and the Chamber it served were therefore for the use of outsiders, not for the use of the friars.

Third, the Chamber was walled off from contact with even the nearest of the apartments used by the friars. Although it and the infirmary were under the same roof, "the parliament chamber, whereof part is over the room above the firmary, did never pertain to the firmary, . . . also there never was any way or passage to go out of the firmary to the said chamber" (13:2–3).

Fourth, King Henry's special interest in the Parliament Chamber is shown by his keeping it for his own use even when he granted the south end of the same building to the Kingstons: "the said chamber was not rented at the time of the grant nor long after to any person, but kept in the King's hands to the use of the Revels" (13:4).

Fifth, Henry VIII and his Court seemingly thought of the Chamber as being an entity apart from the friary proper, as evidenced by the official use of the word "near," rather than "in," in designating the Chamber as "the Parliament Chamber near the Friars Preachers," and "the Parliament Chamber near the convent of the Friars Preachers" at the time of the divorce trial.[37]

Finally, Sir William More said that "King Henry VIII possessed it during his life; also King Edward did the like until the second year of his reign, at which time he let it by lease to Sir Thomas Cawarden" (13:6, 7). Whether Sir William literally meant Henry's life, or merely Henry's reign, in either event he reported the King as having "possessed" the Parliament Chamber from a time well before the Dissolution. If he meant the former, then Henry possessed the Chamber for forty-seven years before he seized the monasteries; if the latter, for twenty-nine years.

The hall occupied by the Second Blackfriars Playhouse was therefore not a dining hall converted to theatrical purposes, but a room created in the first instance to house great assemblies. It was built by kings, not priors, and built without regard to the limitations imposed by the doctrine of apostolic poverty. Medieval artisans had undoubtedly fashioned it with all the grace and skill of which they were capable in the handling of oak and glass and stone.

Entrance to the Parliament Chamber was by way of a staircase whose descriptions come from sources separated in time by nearly half a century. The Survey of 1548, followed by that of 1550, speaks of

> an entry or passage with a great stair therein, . . . with a hall place at the upper end of the stair and an entry there to the frater over the same buttery (4:4, 6:20).

The Burbage Indenture of 1596 describes it as

> all that great pair of winding stairs, with the staircase thereunto belonging, which leadeth up unto the same seven great upper rooms out of the great yard there which doth lie next unto the Pipe Office (19:5);

and the Neville lease, in describing the pathway leading eastward from Water Lane to the west-range buildings, says that

> the east end thereof spreadeth to greater breadth to serve towards two entries (12:7).

The following points are noteworthy:

A] The Surveys and the Indenture speak of the stair as great, and the Indenture speaks of it as winding.

B] The Surveys say that the stair led up to the Frater, and the Indenture says that it led up to the Seven Great Upper Rooms. No document says that it gave access to the upper floor of the Old Buttery as well.

c] The stair was in an entry or passage.

d] It led up out of the great yard next the Pipe Office; i.e., the yard that lay to the west of the Old Buttery.

e] The hall place at the upper end of the stair, and also the entry to the Frater, were over the Buttery;[38] and

f] One of the two "entries" served by the pathway at its eastern end can only have been the door to the "entry or passage" mentioned in the Surveys, and the other, necessarily farther north and thus facing the great yard next the Pipe Office, was undoubtedly a door leading to the stairs.

Other circumstances combine to suggest that the stairs were assigned to Richard Frith for his exclusive use for an indefinite period during the fifteen-sixties and seventies, and this in turn suggests that the stairs were located at the north end of Frith's lodging in the western half of the Parliament Chamber, and thus at the northwest corner of the Upper Frater block.

The first of these circumstances is the failure of the three extant leases of the long apartment to allude to the stairs in any way whatsoever. If the stairs had been the means of access to that apartment, one would expect the leases to say so, just as the 1548 Survey speaks of the stair as providing entry to the frater, and as the 1596 Indenture speaks of it as leading up unto the seven great upper rooms. But the stairs are not mentioned in the 1560 lease to Sir Henry Neville, nor in the 1571 lease to Sir William Brooke Lord Cobham, nor in the 1576 lease to Richard Farrant. The implication is that the stairs were not a part of the apartment, did not provide access to it, and did not encroach upon it. It follows that the stairs were not on the east side of the Parliament Chamber's dividing wall.

The second circumstance is the high rental that Frith paid for his lodging in the west side of the Chamber, as compared with what Neville paid for his in the east side, with half of the upper floor of the Old Buttery to boot: Frith paid £8 per year, and Neville paid only £6 for a lodging half again as large.[39] On the face of it, this implies that Frith's lodging had conveniences that Neville's had not.

The third circumstance is Neville's causing "great stairs" to be built up to his lodging at his own expense (16:5). It must be remembered that Neville was lessee, not owner; he would therefore have been unlikely to incur so substantial a capital outlay if stairs had been otherwise available.

Stairs located as in Figures 17 and 22 are believed to meet all the known conditions. "The hall place at the upper end of the stair" may have been the room described as "all that one chamber or loft with a chimney therein, being next under the roof where the high gallery of William More, esquire, . . . did stand, which said loft or story is the uppermost and highest story of the tenement or messuage now in the tenure and occupation of Thomas Hall, musician, the which said chamber or story, amongst other, the said Richard Frith hath."[40]

I return for a moment to the subject of those other stairs built by Sir Henry Neville at his own expense. Sir Henry was the second occupant of the long apartment, not the first. Sir John Cheke had preceded him, and he had been able to get to and from his apartment in spite of his not having the use of the stairs that Sir Henry was later to build. It seems probable, therefore, that the great winding stairs originally served the eastern side of the Parliament Chamber as well as the western; and in that event the passage from one side to the other may have been by way of the great round portal in one of the four chambers on the east side of the dividing wall, the chamber described as being "ceiled with wainscot on the east part, south part, and a part of the west, with a great round portal contained within the same chamber" (15:2, 16:3). Perhaps the stairs were turned over to Frith for his exclusive use in December, 1559, when he renewed his lease for an additional thirty-year term.[41] Neville's rental of the apartment on the east side of the dividing wall came just six months later.

We have no direct information as to the height of the Parliament Chamber; but since its history proves it to have been one of the noblest of England's medieval halls and its dimensions prove it to have been one of the largest, we may suppose that it was one of the loftiest also. Of the unaisled halls built in or near London in medieval times, only Westminster Hall and the Guildhall exceeded it in floor area; the Middle Temple and the Great Hall at Hampton Court, which came later, were slightly smaller. These four stately halls have two things in common: all have (or originally had) hammerbeam roofs,[42] and all have side walls between 40 and 46 feet high; and since the Parliament Chamber presumably was a hall of the same sort, we may suppose that it too had a hammerbeam roof and that its vertical walls were about 40 feet in height. Figures 18 and 21 depict it as having a roof with a design and pitch based upon those of Westminster Hall; but to err on the side of conservatism, I have drawn the supporting walls as being only 38 feet tall, instead of 40

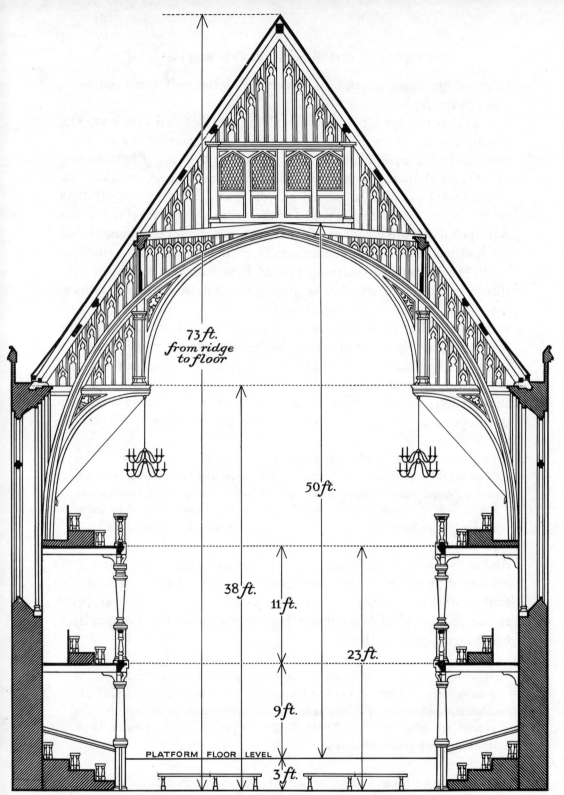

73 ft.
from ridge
to floor

50 ft.

38 ft.

11 ft.

23 ft.

9 ft.

PLATFORM FLOOR LEVEL

3 ft.

Figure 18. A sectional view of the auditorium of the Blackfriars Playhouse, as conjecturally reconstructed. In this drawing, the design of the roof follows that of Westminster Hall.

or more. On these assumptions, the ridge of the roof turns out to be about 73 feet high.

The roof of the Upper Frater building was sheathed with lead. The Loseley documents are specific on this point. The Losse Survey speaks of "the lead that covereth the frater parcel of the said Black Friars" (6:12); Sir William More, in his answer to Kempe's claim, says that "the [Parliament] chamber is covered all with lead, being more worth than all the money he [Kempe] paid for the purchase" (13:8); and James Burbage's indenture gives him the possession, among other things, of "all the lead that doth cover the same seven great upper rooms" (19:2).

This fact of lead sheathing has led Professor Wallace to the conclusion that the roof was flat, an assumption that he explains in a footnote by saying that "steep roofs were covered with tile, and flat roofs with lead."[43] But he is demonstrably mistaken. He is correct up to the point of saying that flat roofs called for lead, but wrong in believing that lead called for flatness; for although lead permitted a flatter pitch than did tiles or slate or thatch, it by no means compelled it. This point is authoritatively covered in letters written to me by Mr. Gilyard-Beer of the Inspectorate of Ancient Monuments in the Ministry of Works:

> Steep-pitched leaden roofs were common in the middle ages. Dissolution inventories show that lead was a common roofing material for monastic churches, and surviving remains show that many of these retained their steep-pitched gables until the 16th century, implying steep-pitched roofs. . . . The steepest possible pitches were achieved in the lead coverings of wooden spires.

And to this last observation about nearly-vertical spires I may add one of my own about the eight great timbers at the corners of the lantern of Ely Cathedral: they are truly vertical, and they are sheathed with lead. With respect to the roof of Westminster Hall in particular, Mr. Gilyard-Beer has written to me as follows:

> When the hall was remodelled at the end of the 14th century and given its present roof, the pitch of which is more than 50°, it was covered with lead; substantial expenditures in the purchase of large quantities of lead for this purpose are recorded in the Patent Rolls for 1391-96. At the present day it is covered with graduated slates.

In view of these and other facts, I dare to say categorically that the roof of the Parliament Chamber was not flat. It had the extraordinary span of 46 feet between the supporting walls. Its frame was oak, not steel. It was covered with a lead sheathing that weighed 16½ fothers (6:12) or almost 33,000 pounds. A flat roof built to such specifications could stand up only if supported by a forest of posts, and a forest of posts would have made the hall wholly unsuitable for use either as a parliament chamber or as a theatre.

The roof was reachable by way of a flight of stone stairs that led up out of the seven great upper rooms unto the leads or roof overhead (19:3). One may confidently assume that they were spiral stairs built within the thickness of the wall, and that they gave access to a battle-mented walkway running along the edge of the roof. The stairs were used not only by persons who had a legitimate interest in inspecting and amend-ing the leads, but also on at least one occasion by boys whom a certain tenant, "either by negligence or otherwise, [suffered] . . . to cut up the lead with knifes or to bore it through with bodkins, whereby . . . the rain cometh through, and the house thereby much annoyed."[44]

In its days as a Parliament Chamber the great hall held at least one gallery; this we know from Cavendish's report of the divorce trial of 1529, on the last day of which "the king came thither, and sat within a gallery against the door of the same that looked unto the judges where they sat, whom he might both see and hear speak, to hear what judgment they would give in his suit."[45] Later, when the Parliament Chamber became the Seven Great Upper Rooms, the gallery was undoubtedly torn down. Sir William More later had a high gallery "next under the roof."[46] But wholly new galleries were probably needed (40:3) when the great hall became the Second Blackfriars Playhouse.

For reasons given at the beginning of this chapter, I have assumed that the upper floor of the Old Buttery was designed originally to serve as the friars' refectory. On this assumption, it was entered from the Great Cloister by a door near its northern end, for normally the entrance to any frater was at the right of the friar as he stood in the cloister with the building before him. Inside the hall, screens masked the entrances from the cloister and from the kitchen that adjoined the building near its northwest corner. A reader's pulpit projected into the hall on the side away from the cloister, from which a lector read aloud to the silent friars during meals. At the south end of the room was a dais for the use of the prior and other church dignitaries, and behind the dais a solid wall of stone stretched across the hall from side to side, decorated in paint or sculpture with a scene from the life or death of Christ; the wall was subsequently torn down when the upper floors of the two neighboring buildings were united. By reason of date, this undoubtedly was the frater that Piers the Plowman described in the following lines:

> Then I fared to the frater, and found there again   203
> A hall for an high king his household to harbor,
> With broad tables about, and benches to boot,   205
> With windows of glass wrought like a church.

After leaving the frater, Piers Plowman "walked further, and went all about." He saw "halls full high," chambers and chapels, kitchens, a dorter, a firmary, and a second frater that may have been that attached to the firmary. All these buildings he might have found to the south and west of the Great Cloister. His description of the friary ends with these lines:

> Then walked I further, and went all about,
> And saw halls full high and houses full noble,
> Chambers with chimneys, and chapels gay,
> And kitchens for an high king in castles to have,   210
> And the dorter provided with doors full strong.
> Firmary and frater, with many more houses,
> All walled with strong stone standing on high,
> With gay garrets and great, and each opening glazed,
> And other houses enough to shelter the queen.   215

The Western Yards

TWO ENTRIES, passages, or ways led easterly from Water Lane to the buildings in the western ranges. One was the passageway that ended in the 11½-foot gap between the Old Buttery and the Upper Frater. The surveys give its length as 84 feet (4:3, 6:19), and the Neville lease as 83 feet 3 inches (12:7). The modern entrance to Playhouse Yard undoubtedly follows the course of the old entry or passage, and thus indicates that it slanted slightly toward the south as it ran eastwards.

The second way or lane was farther south. It was the "way leading to my Lady Kingston's house" (4:7), later to be described as leading both to the house of Sir George Carey Lord Hunsdon and to Burbage's Middle Rooms or Middle Stories (19:9). Its course is unquestionably indicated by the Printing House Lane of today, which shows a strongly marked slant from northwest to southeast.

Three yards lay to the west of the western ranges. The most northerly and the smallest of the three was Lord Cobham's garden. It was bounded on the east by the porter's lodge and the north end of the Old Buttery, on the west by Water Lane, and on the south by a brick wall which abutted upon the west side of the Old Buttery at a point 74 feet north of that building's southern end (4:3, 6:19).[47]

The middle yard was called the Kitchen Yard in the surveys (4:3, 6:19) and the Great Yard next the Pipe Office in the Burbage Indenture (19:5, 19:17, etc.). It abutted north on Cobham's brick wall for a distance estimated at 66 feet, west upon Water Lane for 68,[48] south upon Portinary's house and the more northerly of the two passageways for 84 feet, and east upon the Old Buttery for 74 feet (4:3, 6:19). Originally it probably included all the land that later became Lord Cobham's garden, for it took its name from the Old Kitchen or Convent Kitchen that was "in the south end of the Lord Cobham's lodging" (6:8) in the days when his lodging extended no farther south than the porter's lodge. The location of the Old or Convent Kitchen is noteworthy. In being immediately west of the Old Buttery (4:4, 6:20) and immediately south of the porter's lodge, it was in the best possible position for catering to the original refectory on the upper floor of the Old Buttery and to the guest houses on the upper floors of both buildings. Many years later Sir Henry Neville was to build another kitchen in the kitchen yard, still on the west side of the Old Buttery but farther south, with a stair leading out of it to his premises on the upper floor (15:4, 16:4). For the rest, the kitchen yard contained only a coal house and a common jakes or privy adjoining Cobham's garden on its southern side (10:4, 16:8), a woodyard adjoining Neville's kitchen (15:4, 16:4), and two larders whose location is not stated (14:2). A half century later, the kitchen yard was to be used for the arrival and turning of the playgoers' coaches.

The third and most southerly of the three yards lay on the west side of the Upper Frater. Its northeast corner was occupied by the Duchy Chamber, which is described as abutting east against the north end of the Frater and as being 50 feet long by 16 feet broad (4:10, 6:23), and three stories high. Hugh Losse, as bailiff and collector, listed it in 1540 in his schedule of Crown rents as "Chamber of the Duchy of Lancaster, called the *Douche Chambre*. Unoccupied."[49] Men notable in the national life knew that long narrow building, and at least two of them progressed from high office in the Duchy to the chancellorship of the realm. One was the great Sir Thomas More, who became Speaker of the Commons in

1523, Chancellor of the Duchy in 1525, and Lord Chancellor in 1529 upon Wolsey's fall. Another was Thomas Audeley, who, after being Attorney of the Duchy, was elected Speaker of the Commons in 1529 in succession to More, and Lord Chancellor three years later.[50]

The second important building in the southern yard was Sir John Portinary's house and parlor. Sir John was a Florentine by birth and an engineer by profession; he was one of Henry's gentlemen pensioners, and, as has already been related, was the man to whom the King entrusted the keys and the custody of the priory upon its suppression.[51] His house and parlor are mentioned frequently in the old documents as being abutted against or as abutting upon. The surveys say that his parlor abutted north on the kitchen yard, east on the Duchy Chamber, and west on Water Lane (4:3, 4:10, etc.); his house abutted south on the Little Kitchen and the Little Chamber (4:7, 4:8). Surprisingly, the parlor abutted upon the kitchen yard but the neighboring Duchy Chamber did not; and this suggests that the entry or passage may have blocked the Duchy Chamber from contact with the yard, but that the parlor may have bridged the passage so that it and the house together composed a sort of gatehouse. If so, one may suppose that Sir John Portinary, as custodian of the precinct, thought it prudent to have direct control of a principal avenue of approach, and so chose a gatehouse to live in. The dimensions of his house and parlor are not known.

Two other buildings in the southern yard are described in terms that seem to be irreconcilable. One is the Little Kitchen, which, according to the 1548 Survey, was only 23 feet long by 22 feet wide, but which nevertheless abutted west on Water Lane and east "towards"[52] the Blind Parlor—a distance great enough to contain the 50-foot length of the Duchy Chamber and therefore more than twice as great as the Little Kitchen could span. The other is the Little Chamber, described by the 1548 Survey as being 26 feet by 10, and yet as stretching from the Blind Parlor to Mr. Portinary's house some 50 feet away, and described further as abutting east to the Blind Parlor and west to the Little Kitchen (4:8), in spite of the fact that those two buildings abutted against each other. These specifications cancel each other out.

From other sources, however, we have reason to believe that the Little Kitchen was in fact near to or in abutment with the Blind Parlor. For one thing, it and the Little Chamber were associated with the Blind Parlor and the Paved Hall in being claimed by the Lord Warden. For another, the Burbage deed says that the Kitchen adjoined the Middle

Rooms or Middle Stories (19:8); and for a third, Lichfield testified that the Parlor stood handsome to the Kitchen.[53] The Little Kitchen's propinquity to the Blind Parlor is in fact the only dependable assumption that we have about the two little buildings.

A void room served as an entry to the Little Kitchen and to a coal house not elsewhere mentioned. The dimension of 30 feet by 17 feet may apply either to the coal house or to the entry (4:9, 6:22).

1. See p. 22 above.
2. See p. 89 below.
3. See p. 45 above.
4. The two men whose testimony will be quoted on pp. 97–98 below were testifying in 1572, and each said that he had known the friary for 40 years past.
5. Index Library, *Inquisitiones Post Mortem for London*, Tudor Period, Vol. I, p. 184.
6. Viz., the 1548 Survey (4:4), the 1550 Survey (6:20), certain copies of the Cawarden grant, the Cawarden-More deed to John Birch and others, the Cawarden *Inquisition*, etc.
7. The 52-foot length is probably an outside dimension and the 47-foot length an inside, but one is left in doubt as to the 21-foot width that accompanies both these measurements.
8. Cf. pp. 46–48 and 68, and Fig. 5.
9. See p. 114 below.
10. See p. 41 above.
11. See Feuillerat's introduction to Document XVI, *BR* p. 83.
12. A theatre was established in Apothecaries' Hall soon after the Restoration. Downes (*Roscius Anglicanus*, p. 20) says that Davenant's company acted there for a time before moving into the new "Opera" in Lincoln's Inn Fields in 1662. The Blackfriars theatre that Samuel Pepys attended on January 29, 1660/1661, can only have been that in Apothecaries' Hall. He wrote on that date that he "went to Blackfryers (the first time I was ever there since plays begun), and there after great patience and little expectation, from so poor beginning, I saw three acts of 'The Mayd in ye Mill,' acted to my great content."
13. As might be expected, the Dominican frater at Ipswich was an exception to the rule. Fr. Hinnebusch says (p. 158) that it was not on the main cloister, but in a

separate wing, which however was joined to the main group of buildings.
14. Cf. pp. 73–74 above.
15. Of the few Dominican fraters of which we have knowledge, two out of the six—Cardiff and Newcastle-on-Tyne—were in the south range, and three—Canterbury, Gloucester, and Bristol—were in the west. The sixth was Ipswich.
16. Sir Alfred was writing in 1912, at which time Union Street was still in existence. My inquiry about it brought the following reply from Philip D. Whitting, Esq., Honorary Secretary of the London Topographical Society: "The street was still there in 1918, but it has now disappeared. It ran from New Bridge Street (No. 38) eastward to Water Lane (i.e., Blackfriars Lane). It was thus very short, and if prolonged a little would hit Apothecaries' Hall in the middle." Harben, pp. 464 and 597, says that Union Street occupied the site formerly occupied by Paved Alley. The site is now occupied by Apothecary Street.
17. "On the Topography," p. 76. The dimensions of 42 feet in length and 14 feet in breadth are confirmed by the Blagrave-Bocher Survey of 1552, quoted in *BR* 109:13ff., and by an unidentified document quoted by Sir Walter Besant in *Mediaeval London*, Vol. II, Appendix IX.
18. This width agrees admirably with the inside width (29 feet within walls) of the structure that now occupies the site. Cf. Clapham, "On the Topography," p. 77.
19. *BR* 120:19.
20. When the Society of Apothecaries acquired the building in 1632, one of its first acts, after rough repairs had been completed, was to order the construction of a battlement, by way of ornamentation, "all along the west range of the roof of the hall and parlour" (Barrett, p. 43). The scars left by the removal of

the old gallery may still have been visible and have needed hiding.

21. Barrett, pp. 44–45.

22. The word "frater" does not derive from Latin *frater* as meaning a friar, brother, or comrade, but from Old French *fraitur*, short for *refreitor*, meaning refectory.

23. Cf. p. 20 above.

24. Cf. pp. 13–14 above.

25. The Cawarden lease of 1548 gives the length of the Old Buttery as 96 feet (*BR* 109:5–9); but since all other derivatives of the 1548 Survey give the figure as 95 feet, the 96-foot figure is doubtless a scrivener's error.

26. The figure given in the Farrant lease is actually $56\frac{1}{2}$ feet (16:2), but this is manifestly a clerical error. The Neville lease gives the length of the whole tenement as 157 feet $10\frac{1}{2}$ inches.

27. Since the Old Buttery abutted north upon the porter's lodge, no outer wall needs to be added at that end.

28. Four witnesses in the Poole-More arbitration proceedings testified that Joyner's fencing school on the lower floor of the Upper Frater building occupied a house "whereunto joineth an old buttery of the friars" (*BR* 47:18ff., 48:31ff., 49:32ff., 51:3ff.). On the face of it, the word "joineth" contradicts the theory of a passageway between the two buildings. I discount the testimony, however, on the grounds that the joining of which the witnesses speak did not necessarily imply actual contact, that contact or lack of it was not a point at issue and therefore did not demand exactness of expression, and that the four statements are too similar in phraseology to be acceptable as four independent opinions. A fifth witness said that the fencing school "stood near" the buttery (*BR* 42:27), and a sixth said that the two parcels "stood fast by" and

"handsome to" each other (*BR* 43:27ff.). I assume that it was the entry or passage, rather than the old buttery, which is described as abutting to the Blind Parlor in 4:4 and 6:20.

29. The relative importance of the middle floor is stressed in the Kingston lease also. The lease describes the infirmary as "all the house and edifice called the Firmary at the west end of the said [Inner] Cloister, and all the space over and under belonging to the same" (1:2).

30. 13:2, from *BR* 5:137–138.

31. Paragraph 19:8 contains a further specification that seems to be inexplicable as it stands. The difficulty lies in the word "westwards" in the description of the Middle Rooms or Middle Stories as "lying and being directly under part of those of the seven great upper rooms which lie westwards." Since the dimensions of 52 feet by 37 feet, as given in the same paragraph, suggest that the rooms stretched the whole width of the lower floor, I cannot account for the phrase.

32. Dr. Joseph Quincy Adams has a third interpretation. He relates the phrase to the parlor alone, taking it to mean that the parlor's length was the same as its breadth, and therefore that it was square (*Shakespearean Playhouses*, p. 188, and "Conventual Buildings," pp. 72–73).

33. *BR* 105:26–28.

34. *BR* 42:27–34.

35. *BR* 43:27–36. The buttery specified in both excerpts as standing near to the parlor was clearly the Old Buttery described as abutting to the Blind Parlor in 4:4, and the kitchen of the second excerpt was the Little Kitchen that abutted toward the said parlor in 4:7. The brewhouse of the second excerpt is mentioned nowhere else. It cannot have been the brewhouse described in the Kingston lease as adjoining the infirmary and stable (1:2).

36. *BR* 105:26–28. Professor Feuillerat, editor of *Blackfriars Records*, says that "the name might be 'ffrythis,' but the third and fifth letters are faded away." I have no hesitation in confirming his supposition that the word is "ffrythis" or "Frith's." Only on that basis can any part of the passage be explained.

37. Cf. p. 20 above.

38. Prof. Feuillerat, in commenting upon the description of the stairhead as "a hall place at the upper end of the stair and an entry there to the frater over the same buttery," says that it "means, of course, that the hall place and the entry to the frater were both over the buttery, and not that the frater was over the buttery. Still more impossible is it to suppose that there were two 'fraters'" (*BR* 110:21ff.). I have previously undertaken to prove that the original frater of the priory was in fact over the buttery and that there were in fact two fraters, though not simultaneously. But the Survey did not use the word "frater" with either of those fraters in mind, and Prof. Feuillerat is therefore perfectly correct in his interpretation of its meaning.

39. *BR* 119:3.

40. *BR* 119:7–13.

41. *BR* 118:39–42. See p. 124 below.

42. The earlier roofs of the Guildhall were of hammerbeam design. The present roof (the fifth to be supported by the ancient walls) is not. The Middle Temple roof is double hammerbeam. The roofs of Westminster Hall and the Great Hall at Hampton Court are single hammerbeam.

43. *Children of the Chapel*, p. 37, n. 12. It is a tribute to Professor Wallace's standing as an investigator and scholar

that both E. K. Chambers (*Elizabethan Stage*, Vol. II, p. 489) and Joseph Quincy Adams (*Shakespearean Playhouses*, p. 186) have followed him unquestioningly in calling the roof flat.

44. *BR* 124:3ff.

45. Cavendish, *Life of Wolsey*, Vol. I, p. 164. See p. 21 above.

46. *BR* 119:7–8.

47. As shown in Fig. 16, the line of Lord Cobham's garden wall accorded closely with that of the gallery over the Fleet both in position and in direction—so closely, in fact, as to suggest that the wall was built where the gallery had been.

48. The 1550 Survey gives this figure as 74 feet (6:19). The scribe has omitted the clause that gives the Old Buttery as the eastern boundary of the Kitchen Yard (cf. 4:3), but has nevertheless picked up the dimensions given in the missing clause.

49. Palmer, "London," p. 286.

50. Cf. p. 22 above.

51. Cf. p. 27 above.

52. The phrase "to abut towards" does not, as might be surmised, necessarily imply direction without actual contact. For instance, the Upper Frater is described as "abutting . . . west towards the said Duchy Chamber and Mr. Portinary's house" (4:5); and while it cannot have been in contact with the latter, it assuredly was with the former. As a matter of fact, of all the abutments specified with respect to the Little Kitchen and the Little Chamber, the only one that we can be reasonably sure of as involving contact is the Little Kitchen's abutment "towards" the Blind Parlor.

53. See p. 98 above.

❦ 5 ❦

Partition of the Blackfriars Precinct

THE SURRENDER of the Ludgate friary placed the precinct in the power of the King but left it still outside the jurisdiction of the City of London. As a religious community it had from the first been beyond the City's control. Its inhabitants had been subject to none but the King and the Prior. Its gates had been shut against the City at night by its own porters, and the sheriff had been powerless to serve writs or to make arrests within its walls. The most dramatic of its privileges had been that of sanctuary. By and large, sanctuary was a beneficent institution in those violent days: it gave the fugitive a breathing spell and a hope that lawful process might take the place of instant vengeance. But sanctuary had its seamy side as well. It permitted criminals to evade prosecution, debtors to elude their creditors, and swindlers to escape their gulls. It made the precinct a haven for felons who slept there during the day and emerged at night to commit new crimes.

The situation had long galled the City authorities, and when suppression put an end to the district's ecclesiastical character and privileges, the Mayor and his Council hoped that the time had come at last to take the area under their own control. They addressed a petition to Henry, praising him for having "extirped and extinct the orders of Freers to the great exaltacion of Crystes doctryne and the abolucion of Antecriste theyr first founder and begynner," and asking that the church and the rest of the precinct be granted to them for the use of nonparishioners and persons infected with the plague.[1] But Henry had no thought of surrendering so valuable a property. He is reported to have told the Mayor and the Common Council that "he was as well able to keep the Liberties, as the Friers were,"[2] and so the exemption from City jurisdiction that the district had first acquired as a cloistered community was continued

113

to it as a "Liberty" in royal tenure. In the course of time, as civil administration succeeded ecclesiastical, the inhabitants appointed their own justices to try petty offenders, their own porters and scavengers, and their own officers (of whom Sir William Kingston was to be one) to serve as civil magistrates.

The King's seizure of the friary had been merely one more step in a process of disintegration that had begun long before. The brotherhood of friars had already shrunk to a fifth of its former strength. Buildings that had once been busy and crowded now stood silent and empty; and this, in combination with the convent's straitened finances, had long since led the friars to rent some of their buildings and grounds to outsiders for residential purposes. Records fail to show when the brethren first admitted laymen and laywomen to their enclave as permanent residents. The earliest recorded rental is dated March 1, 1509/10, nearly thirty years before the Dissolution, but it was not the first to be made, for it concerned a property that had already been leased before; it gave to a certain Stephen Pecoke, or Peacock, the tenancy of a mansion, with shop, warehouses, cellars, solars, etc., that had previously been rented to Richard Snow.[3] The property lay south and west of the principal cloistral buildings, for the Peacock garden was later cited as the western boundary of a "way to the waterside" (1:1) and as "next the Thames."[4]

By 1522, when the Emperor Charles V was accommodated in the friary's guest house, the Blackfriars precinct had already become a favorite residential district for members of the aristocracy and gentry. In that year, and probably in preparation for the Emperor's visit, King Henry caused a list to be compiled of "them that hath lodgings within the Blak Freers."[5] It shows not merely that many of the Blackfriars residents were persons of title, but that they were persons in close association with the Court. The list includes the names of Lord Zouche of Harringworth; George Brooke Lord Cobham; Sir William Kingston, afterwards Comptroller of the Household and, as we have seen, Constable of the Tower of London; Sir Henry Wyatt, afterwards Treasurer of the Chamber; Sir William Parr, brother of Queen Catherine Parr;[6] Sir Thomas Cheyne or Cheyney, afterwards Treasurer of the Household and Lord Warden of the Cinque Ports; Jane, widow of Sir Richard Guildford, formerly Master of the Horse; Christopher More, clerk of the Exchequer, and several others.

Another early resident of the precinct was Dame Elizabeth Dentoney or Dentonys or Denton. She had been governess to Henry VIII and his sister when they were children, and in 1515 Henry had granted her a handsome annuity of £50 in recognition of her services to his royal father and mother.[7] She was a woman of great piety, with a special devotion for the altar of St. Thomas Aquinas in the priory church, and as early as 1518, eighteen years before she died, she had already erected for herself a notable tomb "before the image of St. Thomas of Aquine," where the faithful might pray for her during her life and for her soul after her death.[8] She was of the Jerningham family, and when she died in 1536 her property in the Blackfriars precinct was rerented by Prior Hilsey to her relatives by marriage, Sir William and Lady Mary Kingston and Lady Kingston's son by her previous marriage, Sir Henry Jerningham, a gentleman pensioner of the King.[9] The Kingston lease (1:1) shows that the property was just south of the Great Cloister and of considerable size; it probably included all the Inner Cloister and some neighboring buildings.

All these rentals, and many others to persons of less note, had been made by the friars themselves long before the priory became the property of the Crown. When the Crown took title the land rush began. Applicants for rentals, purchases, or grants flocked like shoppers to a bargain sale. Those who already held leases sought to have them confirmed by the Court of Augmentations; those who had none sought to get them; and now, for the first time, the records show ownership of property as being alienated by sale or grant. Only a few of the scores of transactions need be mentioned here.

On March 16, 1539/40, Sir Thomas Cheyne was granted "all and singular those our messuages, tenements, houses, buildings, gardens, curtilages and lands, with the appurtenances, now in the tenure and occupation of the said Thomas Cheyne, and formerly in the tenure and occupation of Jasper Filole, and recently in the tenure and occupation of Thomas Ferreby and William Lyllegrave."[10] The properties are identified in this fashion only; the houses and grounds are distinguished not by name or location or description, but by prior tenancy alone; and the lack of particulars inevitably gave rise to doubts as to the ownership of certain buildings that the Lord Warden claimed as having been granted to him—the hall and parlor on the lower floor of the Upper Frater block, and the Little Kitchen and Little Chamber nearby[11]—and to disputes still unresolved thirty years later. The depositions to which the controversy gave rise provide us with some important data.

In 1540 the Augmentations Office confirmed the Kingstons' lease of the properties that they already held; they now certainly had tenure of the Little Cloister, if they had not had it already, and many of the buildings fronting upon it, including all three floors of the Firmary at the south end of the Upper Frater block (1:2).

In 1544 it granted to Paul Gresham and Francis Boldero a parcel at the southeast corner of the Great Cloister (Document 2); and in 1548, after the death of Henry VIII, Edward VI made an extensive grant to Sir Francis Bryan as a reward for Bryan's services to the late King. Sir Francis had served Henry on embassies to France and to Rome; he was cousin to Anne Boleyn and one of Henry's favorites, "the chief companion of the King's amusements and the minister of his pleasures, . . . pointed out by common fame as more dissolute than all the rest."[12] The property granted to him covered an acre or more of ground at the east end of the church and on the east side of the Great Cloister, including a part of the chapter house, the prior's lodging, and many other ill-described chambers, kitchens, storerooms, and so on (Document 5).

These and other grants, sales, and leases accounted for most of the buildings and grounds in the east and south portions of the precinct. In the west, Portinary still had his house abutting on Water Lane, and Lord Cobham had his mansion on the upper floor of the porter's lodge, and other persons had minor holdings elsewhere; but for the most part the houses and yards on the north and west sides of the two cloisters still remained in the hands of the King. In 1550 King Edward VI presented them to Sir Thomas Cawarden. Cawarden got everything that had not already gone to someone else, including the Parliament Chamber. It was the last and greatest of the royal grants.

Sir Thomas Cawarden

Sir Thomas had been Master of the Revels since his appointment by Henry VIII in 1544. He was the first man to hold that office and to bear that title. Before his time there had been no official regularly charged with responsibility for royal diversions, but the King, "being disposed to pastime, would at one time appoint one person, at sometime another, . . . to set forth such devices as might be most agreeable to the Prince's expectation." Cawarden's immediate predecessor had been called Sergeant of the Revels, but Sir Thomas "did mislike to be termed a Sergeant because of his better countenance of room and place, being of the King's Majesty's Privy Chamber," and therefore was granted the more imposing title of *Magister Iocorum, Revelorum et Mascorum omnum et singulorum nostrorum, vulgariter nuncupatorum Revelles and Maskes.*[13] But even with this resounding title, the Master's jurisdiction still did not extend to the plays offered to the public by the professional companies; it covered only amateur entertainments staged at Court.

The Master of the Revels needed a place where costumes and properties could be stored, where tailors, carpenters, and painters could work, and where rehearsals could be held. During the latter years of Henry's reign the Parliament Chamber served this purpose, being the more suitable for it by reason of its nearness to the King's Wardrobe less than 200 yards away; and so useful was it in this employment that "the said chamber was not rented at the time of the [Kingston] grant nor long after to any person, but kept in the King's hands to the use of the Revels" (13:4). But within a decade after Henry's death the Revels Office was to move several times.

In 1548, two years before the grant, Cawarden had taken a lease for many of the houses and yards on the west sides of the Great and Inner Cloisters. The Survey of 1548 had been made in preparation for that lease; but already, before the survey was written, Cawarden had moved the Revels from the Parliament Chamber to a hall at the south end of the Old Buttery building, a hall designated in the survey as "a hall where the King's Revels lies at this present" (4:5). For two years Cawarden occupied the western buildings as lessee. After that he occupied them as owner; for on March 2, 1550, the Privy Council, as executors under the will of Henry VIII, made him a comprehensive gift of all that the Crown still held in the precinct. It gave him ownership of most of the property that he already held on lease, and again as much besides. Cawarden paid nothing for it. He subsequently explained the gift by saying that the property had been granted to him "only for and in recompense of a great sum of money by him disbursed upon warrant and commandment" (11:19), presumably in discharging the duties of his office as Master of the Revels. Be that as it may, all this property "the King's Majesty, by the advice of the lords his honorable Privy Council, [was] pleased and contented . . . to give and grant to Sir Thomas Cawarden, knight, and to his heirs, without anything yielding therefor" (6:24).[14]

The Survey of 1550 was made by Hugh Losse, the King's surveyor, for the purpose of defining and evaluating the properties about to be donated to Cawarden. It places a rental value of only £19 per year upon them (6:24), but gives them a capital value of £879 3s. 4d. (6:13).[15]

According to the Losse survey and the royal patent, Cawarden received the following parcels:

A] The Church (6:2, 7:1–2). This had not been included in the 1548 rental.

B] The Churchyard north of the Church (6:3, 7:3), again not a part of the rental.

c] The Great Cloister (6:4, 7:4), not a part of the rental.

D] The Chapter House (6:5, 7:5), or more properly a part of it, since another part had already been granted to Sir Francis Bryan (5:1). The Chapter House had not been included in the 1548 rental.

E] A plot of ground lying west of Water Lane, between it and the Fleet (6:18, 7:6; rental, 4:2).

F] The Old Kitchen and Kitchen Yard (6:19, 7:7; rental, 4:3).

G] The Upper Frater, exclusive of Lady Kingston's house (the Firmary), which is given as the boundary of the Upper Frater at the south (6:21, 7:8), and exclusive also of the two rooms (the Paved Hall and the Blind Parlor) that the Lord Warden claimed. Those rooms had not been included in the rental of 1548[17] nor in the survey of 1550, and they were not now included in the grant;[18] Cawarden proceeded to occupy them nevertheless, in spite of his cloudy title and the Lord Warden's claim. Actually, the only parts of the Upper Frater building to which Cawarden received a clear title were parts which the grant fails to specify —some cellars and the Parliament Chamber.

H] A void room or entry "towards the Little Kitchen and Coal House" (6:22, 7:9; rental, 4:9).

I] The Duchy Chamber (6:23, 7:10; rental, 4:10).

J] The Ankers House (7:11). This had not been included in either the 1548 rental or the 1550 survey.

K] Various messuages, tenements, houses, shops, cellars, solars, stables, gardens, etc. (7:11–12), each presumably too unimportant to warrant individual cataloguing and description.

L] Undoubtedly the Old Buttery building. It is not specified in *Patent Rolls*, 4 Edward VI, part 6, membrane 63, as one of the properties granted to Cawarden, but it had been included in the survey drawn up in preparation for the grant (6:20), and another version of the royal patent seems to have contained it.[19] In any event, Cawarden occupied the building, and his title to it seems never to have been challenged.[20]

These were the houses and grounds that Sir Thomas Cawarden received as a gift from his indulgent sovereign. His immediate concern was to make his properties "mansionable," and that meant dividing some of the larger structures into units of habitable size, and destroying others to recover their stone for use in new construction. He therefore proceeded forthwith to tear down the great priory church and to use its stone in erecting houses elsewhere on his land. In 1552, only two years after the property had come into his possession, the minster was already nothing more than "a vacant place which was the body of the church of the said Black Friars" (8:1); and according to his own story, by 1555 or 1556 he had built "above twenty mansion houses wherein are by estimation above eighty people" (11:20).[21] A few small structures abutting on the church—the Church Porch, the Ankers House, etc.—were left standing when the church itself was destroyed, for they were buildings of moderate size and could serve as dwellings with only minor alterations.

Cawarden's second major undertaking was the division of the great Parliament Chamber into apartments of residential size, as has already been briefly mentioned. If he had had a free choice, he would probably have split the Chamber into north and south halves by means of an east-west wall, with each half having the comfortable dimensions of 46 feet by about 50 feet; but this plan was ruled out by the lack of any stairs leading up to the Parliament Chamber at its southern end. He therefore split it in the opposite direction, dividing it into east and west halves by means of a wall running the long way of the hall, from north to south; and then, more probably as an afterthought than as part of his original plan, he joined the eastern half of the Parliament Chamber to the southern half of the Old Buttery's upper floor, to form a tenement 156½ feet long.

Its first occupant was no less a personage than Sir John Cheke. Sir John was a great classical scholar and unquestionably one of the most learned men of the age.[22] He had been tutor to Prince Edward, who retained him in that capacity after becoming king. Like Sir Thomas Cawarden, he sat in two Parliaments as member for Bletchingley, and in 1553 was made one of the Secretaries of State and a Privy Councillor. It is not known just when he leased the long apartment from Cawarden, but it cannot have been later than that year, as subsequent events prove.

Until then, Cawarden had been using a part of the tenement—the south end of the Old Buttery's upper floor—as a Revels office and storehouse for Revels equipment; but the Revels had to move out when Cheke moved in, so Cawarden carried the materials back to the Parliament

Chamber, whose west side still lay vacant. There they remained for a year or two. In 1553 Sir John served as Secretary of State for Lady Jane Grey during her nine days' reign, because of which, and because of his being a convinced and influential Protestant, Queen Mary threw him into the Tower and confiscated his wealth. At about the same time, Cawarden leased the western half of the Parliament Chamber to Richard Frith. Once again the Revels had to move; and although Cheke had prepaid the rent upon his lodging until 1557,[23] Cawarden moved the Revels effects back into the premises of his absentee tenant.

Mary kept Sir John in the Tower for more than a year, and then gave him leave to travel on the Continent. There he supported himself by lecturing and teaching Greek. But in the spring of 1556 he was treacherously seized in the Low Countries by order of Philip of Spain, was hustled back to England, and was again clapped into the Tower. He was threatened with the stake, and in terror he yielded, recanted his faith, and was received into the Church of Rome by Cardinal Pole; but "his apostasy or hypocrisy . . . so excessively dejected him that, . . . pining away with the shame and regret of what he had done, he died Sept. 13, 1557, aged 43."[24]

From the time of his first arrest in 1553, Sir John Cheke's home in the Blackfriars had no occupant except the Revels, until Sir Henry Neville rented it seven years later; and that is why the Neville lease of 1560 speaks of "Mr. Cheke's Lodging [as having been] sithence used by Sir Thomas Cawarden, knight, deceased, for the office of the Queen's Majesty's Revels" (12:2).[25] But by 1560 the Revels had recently been moved out of the lodging and out of the precinct, having been transferred by Sir Thomas Benger, Cawarden's successor as Master, to the Hospital of St. John of Jerusalem in Clerkenwell.

As we have seen, Sir Thomas Cawarden tore down the great minster of the friars as soon as it fell into his hands; and a few years later, motivated by Protestant zeal and prudent husbandry, he destroyed the little parish church of St. Anne also. The greater act of demolition seems to have aroused little interest; the lesser act, on the other hand, had perilous repercussions when the Catholic Queen Mary ascended the throne. The early part of the story is best told in the Bill of Complaint that the Blackfriars inhabitants addressed to the Lord Chanceller in late 1555. Greatly condensed, the story runs as follows:

An ancient parish church of St. Anne had stood within the Blackfriars precinct for as long as anyone could remember, and the priors of the convent had at their own costs provided it with successive curates to administer the sacraments, conduct divine services, and officiate at burials in the adjoining churchyard. When the parishioners had first learned that the friary was about to be dissolved, they had petitioned Henry VIII to spare their parish church, and he had consented; and after the Suppression the parishioners had themselves maintained a curate for seven or eight years and had paid for necessary repairs to the building. But after Henry's death Cawarden and other officials had erected brick walls to keep the parishioners out of their church, on the plea that the new King's pleasure was to have the church and churchyard for the storage of his Majesty's Pavilions, Tents, Masks, and Revels. The parishioners were, of course, forced to submit, but shortly thereafter they asked Edward VI to grant them some nearby place where they could worship, whereupon he gave them a room under an old gallery to use for a church and an adjoining piece of ground to use for a cemetery. There for two years they worshipped and buried their dead, until such time as the site and possessions of the Black Friars, amounting to the yearly value of £19,[26] came into the hands of Cawarden; and after that Cawarden unreverently defaced the parish church, used it for the stabling of horses, pulled down its roof and walls, leased its site and soil for tennis courts, converted its burial ground to a carpenter's yard, and even seized the room that the parishioners had been using as a makeshift church; and all this he did in spite of the fact that neither the parish church nor its churchyard had been granted to him by the late King.[27]

The complaint of the parishioners has the ring of truth. In its bare essentials it is confirmed by Stow and by several manuscripts in the Loseley archives.[28] In view of these facts, Cawarden's reply does him little credit. In it he has the impudence to deny that any parish church ever existed (11:1), to claim that his own efforts to provide a church were thwarted by certain evil-disposed persons (11:22), and to plead that if any church is now to be erected his own contributions to its cost should in right and conscience be little, his grant having been so small and his expenses so large (11:21). The whole affair reveals Cawarden in one of his less amiable aspects; doubtless it was the cause of his being "in Queen Mary's time . . . in disgrace and committed to the Fleet" (13:9). He lost out in the end, and was compelled to provide the parishioners with a chapel at his own cost; for "in Queen Mary's time, Sir Thomas Cawarden being in disgrace with her Majesty, and then not liked by the Lords of the Council, . . . seeing how hardly he was used in respect of his religion, he made a chapel in a part of his dwelling house."[29] Seemingly he built it at or near the east end of his mansion house, formerly the South Dorter, and on the upper floor.[30] Stow adds some later details in a brief account which says that the Parish Church of St. Anne

> was pulled downe with the *Fryers* Church, by Sir *Thomas Corden:* but in the raigne of Queen *Mary,* he being forced to finde a Church to the inhabitants, allowed them a lodging Chamber above a staire, which since that time, to wit, in the yeere, 1597, fell downe, and was againe (by collection therefore made) new builded and enlarged in the same yeere, and was dedicated on the eleventh of December.[31]

But Sir Thomas was not without honor in his own time. In 1553 and 1554 he represented the County of Surrey in Parliament as first knight of the shire, and before that he had twice sat for his borough of Bletchingley.[32] He served as Master of the Revels under Henry VIII, Edward VI, and Mary, and into the reign of Elizabeth.

Sir Thomas Cawarden died on August 25, 1559. His last will and testament placed the administration of his estate in the hands of his wife and William More of Loseley as joint executors, and named two men, of whom Thomas Blagrave[33] was one, to be its overseers (19:23). His widow and her coexecutor realized that it would be to their advantage to free themselves from their fiduciary relationship to the estate and from dependence upon the consent of the overseers, and to accomplish this objective they sold all the real property to three cardboard men and bought it back from them three days later. This devious transaction released them from their status as executors and enabled them to hold the property in fee simple. More goes out of his way to say that the proceeding was undertaken "by and with the assent, consent, agreement, and advice" of the overseers (19:23), and doubtless it was; but his protestations nevertheless suggest his awareness that such a procedure is open to suspicion of fraud. In the present instance, however, it was probably a legitimate device employed to accomplish a permissible end. It injured no one.

Dame Elizabeth Cawarden survived her husband by only six months. They had no children, and William More inherited as survivor. He automatically became the largest landowner in the Blackfriars district. He was thirty-nine years old at the time.

Sir William More

To William More, later Sir William, we owe much of our knowledge of the post-Dissolution history and topography of the Blackfriars precinct. He kept copies of many surveys and leases and deeds connected not only with the transactions to which he himself was a party, but those to which Cawarden had been. Among his own were the two of greatest present interest, the 1576 lease of the premises that housed the First Blackfriars Playhouse, and the 1596 sale of the premises that housed the Second. These and scores of other documents were found three and a half centuries later in the Muniment Room of his ancestral home at Loseley, near Guildford in Surrey. The most important of them are now in the Folger Shakespeare Library in Washington.

More was a remarkable man. He began his parliamentary career in 1547 at the age of twenty-seven, as member for the Surrey borough of Reigate, and ended it fifty years later at the age of seventy-seven, after having sat in twelve parliaments, sometimes for the county and sometimes for the borough. Professor J. E. Neale says of him that "he grew to be one of the most experienced parliamentarians of his age, and a local administrator of unrivalled influence and efficiency in the county."[34] He was the grandfather of the poet Donne's wife.

More's first recorded action, after taking possession of his property in the Blackfriars, was to lease the long upstairs apartment to Sir Henry Neville; the 1560 lease describes it as "all that his house and lodging containing four rooms, lately called or known by the name of Mr. Cheke's lodging" (12:2). During his tenure Neville divided the four rooms into six, of which two were in the Old Buttery or guest house portion of the premises, and four in the Parliament Chamber portion; and, as has already been related, he built a new kitchen with a service stair leading up to his apartment (16:4), and also other stairs described as "great stairs" (16:5). Eight years later More bought back the lease from Neville for £100. Presumably the payment was in recompense of Neville's expenses in improving the property.

After that More rented the property briefly to the Silk Dyers' Company,[35] and in 1571 to Sir William Brooke Lord Cobham, who had succeeded Cheyne as Lord Warden of the Cinque Ports. The lease now describes the premises as the "six upper chambers . . . lately (amongst others) in the tenure and occupation of Sir Henry Neville, knight"

(15:2); and in 1576 they were rented again, this time to Richard Farrant, under a lease that describes them as "six upper chambers . . . lately amongst others in the tenure and occupation of the right honorable Sir William Brooke, knight, Lord Cobham" (16:2). The story of Farrant's tenure will be told in the next chapter; but in the meantime it is necessary to bring the history of other parts of the western buildings up to the same important year of 1576.

By the time of the Farrant lease, the western half of the Parliament Chamber had already been occupied for twenty-two years by Richard Frith, who is described as a "scoellmastr" and the proprietor of a "dawn-synge Scole."[36] He had leased the property originally from Cawarden in 1554 (the lease being dated April 1555), and on December 24, 1559, he had obtained from More a renewal for an additional thirty-year term;[37] and it may well have been at this time, and in consideration of this long lease, that Sir William More gave Frith the exclusive use of the great winding stairs leading up to the Parliament Chamber.[38] Frith is not mentioned in any published Blackfriars records dated after 1561. Nevertheless, since his lease ran until Lady Day 1589, there is no reason to doubt that he still occupied the western half of the Parliament Chamber when Farrant took occupancy of the eastern half in 1576.

In that same year of 1576 the Firmary was probably the property of Anthony Kempe, who is described as "a buyer of titles." As we know, it had been granted to Lady Mary Kingston in 1545, two years after her husband had died. On her own death the property had passed to Sir Henry Jerningham, who is listed as its owner in the schedule of freeholders compiled for Cawarden's use in 1555 or 1556 (11:5). At some unknown date Sir Henry had sold it to Kempe, and Kempe had used his ownership of it as the basis of a claim to ownership of the Parliament Chamber also, thus provoking Sir William More's extraordinarily informative memorandum of *circa* 1562, here reprinted as Document 13.[39] The *Lay Subsidies* records show that Anthony Kempe was assessed in lands in Blackfriars in 1576,[40] and upon this rests the assumption that he still owned the Firmary fourteen years after making his abortive claim. Records do not tell who the tenant or tenants may have been.

The confused history of the Paved Hall and Blind Parlor beneath the Parliament Chamber, and the Little Kitchen and Little Chamber nearby, became a matter of legal record in 1572–1573, when a certain Henry Poole, or Pole, sued Sir William More for possession of the houses previously claimed by the Lord Warden. The parcels chiefly in dispute were the little house then occupied by Laurence Bywater, and a great room, paved, used by William Joyner for a fencing school; they were probably three of the four units listed in the Survey of 1548 as being subject to the claim of the then Lord Warden of the Cinque Ports, Sir Thomas Cheyne. He had long since died. His son and heir had predeceased him, and his son's widow had married Poole, who now claimed the houses in the right of his wife.

The validity or invalidity of Poole's claim rested upon the question of previous tenancy; if Cheyne had occupied the properties in 1539, or if Filole, Ferreby, or Lyllegrave had occupied them earlier, then they belonged to Poole as having been granted to Sir Thomas Cheyne by Henry VIII in 1539; if not, they belonged to More as having been granted to Cawarden by Edward VI in 1550. The contending parties submitted the dispute to arbitration in 1572; and since title hinged upon previous occupancy, occupancy played a large part in the testimony of witnesses.

The chamber occupied by Bywater is repeatedly described as "a little house having chalices and singing cakes painted in the window, and ceiled about with wainscot."[41] Before the Dissolution it had been a lodging for a friar that served as butler. After the grant to Cawarden, Thomas Phillips, Clerk of the Tents, occupied it for two years, until he was moved to the Ankers House; then Thomas Blagrave had it, but found it too little for him and his wife. Finally, about 1560, Laurence Bywater rented it, and still occupied it at the time of the arbitration proceedings. It seems probable that this little house was the Little Chamber claimed by Cheyne in 1548 (4:8). The Little Kitchen, if mentioned at all, was touched upon only incidentally, and not as a matter at issue.

The other and greater parcel in dispute was described in testimony as "a great room, paved, whereunto joineth an old buttery of the friars," and as "a great room, paved, wherein a school of fence is kept." In the days of the friary it had always been used by the friars themselves as "a parlor where commonly they did use to break their fast" or as "a parlor to dine and sup in," and it had never been let out or inhabited by any other persons until the house of friars was dissolved and surrendered.[42] When that happened the keys were delivered to Sir John Portinary to keep, and for a while the premises were vacant. Then Sir Thomas Cawarden made his lodging there, and about that time he invited Sir John and his wife to supper, "together with divers other gentlemen, and they all supped together" in the room that later became a fencing school, and

there saw a play.[43] After that Cawarden rented the place to one Woodman, who set up an ordinary table in a room nearby and did much hurt
to the property, and finally he rented it to William Joyner, who used it,
and was still using it, as a fencing school. Joyner's school occupied the
Blind Parlor, next to the entry or passage and near to the "olde Buttrye
of the Friars";[44] Woodman had previously put his ordinary "in theother
rome . . . and had his waye to the same through the said howse where
the said scole of fence ys kept."[45] The wall between Woodman's parlor
and ordinary, and later between Joyner's school and, perhaps, his domestic quarters, was still standing in 1596, when James Burbage bought
both rooms. At that time it divided the rooms occupied by Peter Johnson (19:15) from the Middle Rooms (19:8).

Eleven witnesses, testifying on behalf of More, said that neither
Cheyne nor the other persons named had ever occupied Bywater's little
house nor Joyner's great room, either before or after the Dissolution.
Witnesses for Poole, on the other hand, testified that Ferreby and Lyllegrave, but not Cheyne, had occupied one house or the other. But Poole's
strongest argument lay in the recognition of Cheyne's ownership by the
Court of Augmentations, in granting him, on March 1, 1549/50, a rental of £5 per year for the use of his premises for storage of the Tents.[46]

Apparently both sides were right: Henry VIII *had* granted the
properties to Cheyne in 1539, and Edward VI *had* granted them to Cawarden in 1550. The decision of the arbiters was a compromise, but substantially in More's favor. The Pooles were required to acknowledge
More's title to Joyner's great room, Bywater's house, and other minor
parcels. On the other hand, they were awarded title to certain other
properties, and More was ordered to lease the Bywater house to them,
for the nominal rental of 12 pence per year, for fifty years or for the
terms of their natural lives. (In 1601, nearly thirty years after the
award, Cuthbert and Richard Burbage were to purchase from More certain tenements and yards that were still subject to the life tenure of
Margaret Poole.)[47]

William Joyner was still living in Blackfriars in 1576,[48] and presumably was still teaching the art of fence in the hall beneath the Parliament Chamber. The lease was to change hands a few years later; some-
how or other it came into the possession of the poet John Lyly, who sold
it to another fencing master, Rocco Bonetti.[49] But these changes of ownership cannot have come much before 1584; in 1576 the lease undoubtedly
was still in Joyner's name.

126

Little is known of the 1576 status of the buildings in the western yards. Title to Sir John Portinary's house seems to have been in dispute between Poole and More in 1572, and to have been awarded to Poole.[50] The record of Portinary's testimony in the arbitration proceedings fails to identify him as a resident of Blackfriars, so he probably was not.

The Duchy Chamber had been listed as unoccupied two years after the Dissolution, but presumably was fully occupied in 1576. Nothing is known about its tenants.

The long apartment itself, the premises in which Farrant was to establish the First Blackfriars Playhouse, was occupied during early 1576 by Lord Cobham and his family; he had rented it from Sir William More in 1571, and for the next five years his lodging had included all the east side of the Parliament Chamber, all the upper story of the Old Buttery, and both floors of the porter's lodge—a tenement well over 230 feet long and never as much as 30 feet wide. The southernmost 46½ feet of the Old Buttery's upper floor, and the east side of the Parliament Chamber, he held on lease; he owned all the rest. In 1576 he was ready to relinquish the rented property, and at the same moment Richard Farrant was looking about for a place that could house a small private theatre. Farrant asked Sir Henry Neville, a former occupant of the long apartment, to bespeak Sir William More's good will for him as a prospective tenant. Sir Henry did so in a letter dated August 27, 1576.

1. Chambers, *Elizabethan Stage*, Vol. II, p. 477.

2. Strype's *Stow*, Vol. III, p. 179.

3. Palmer, "London," p. 279.

4. Palmer, "London," p. 286.

5. *Letters and Papers of Henry VIII*, Vol. III, Part 2, p. 1053, no. 2486.

6. Queen Catherine's father, Sir Thomas Parr, had already (1517) been buried in the Blackfriars church, and her mother was to be buried there later (Palmer, "London," pp. 267, 268).

7. *Letters and Papers of Henry VIII*, Vol. II, Part 1, p. 129, no. 454; dated Westminster, May 12, 1515.

8. Palmer, "London," p. 268; Clapham, "On the Topography," p. 66.

9. *Letters and Papers of Henry VIII*, Vol. IV, Part 1, p. 871; dated 1526.

10. *Patent Rolls*, 31 Henry VIII, Part 6, as printed in *BR* p. 104 and as translated from the original Latin by the author.

11. Cf. 4:6,7.

12. Brewer, Vol. II, pp. 161, 333.

13. Joseph Quincy Adams, ed., *Dramatic Records*, pp. 3–4.

14. Cf. 14:4, 19:23.

15. Of this total of £879 3s. 4d., Losse gives £709 11s. as the value of lead alone, leaving only about £170 as the value of all the other materials—stonework, woodwork, ironwork, slates, tiles, glass, etc.—in the buildings granted to Cawarden. In reading the Loseley documents and other similar papers, one is constantly reminded of the relatively high cost of lead in medieval times and of the concern that property owners felt for the safety of their lead roofs. As a matter of fact, the chief source of profit to the Crown in its plundering of the monasteries was the lead with which most of their roofs were covered. Roving bands of workmen stripped it ruthlessly from the roofs of even the finest churches, and melted it down at fires lighted in nave or chancel and fed with carved oak from stalls, screen, or rood. Cf. Gasquet, p. 430.

17. Cf. *BR* 109:9.

18. Nor were they subsequently listed as parts of Cawarden's estate in his *Inquisition Post Mortem*.

19. Wallace (*Evolution*, p. 143, n. 3) prints a digest of a patent that includes a paragraph about a *"vetus promptuarium,"* the description of which clearly identifies it with the Old Buttery.

20. It is listed as one of Cawarden's properties in the Inquisition of May 3, 1560, which catalogs it "by the name of all that old 'promptuarii' and the entry and passage thereof and of the great Stayer, the hall called the Halle place at the upper end of the said Stayers and the entry which led to the 'fratre' upon the same promptuar[ium], containing in length 95 feet and in breadth 36 feet, and abutting upon the said close on the east, the said kitchen on the west, the house of the said Lord Cobham on the north, and the parlor called the 'blynde parlour' on the south" (*Inquisitiones Post Mortem for London*, Part I, p. 193).

21. The Inquisition taken at the Guildhall on May 3, 1560, says that the lands granted to Cawarden had been built upon as follows at the time of his death: the soil and land of the church and belfry, nine messuages and shops; the cemetery or North Churchyard, nine messuages and shops; one piece of waste land, three tenements; and one gallery (probably between Water Lane and the Fleet), seven messuages. (*Inquisitiones Post Mortem for London*, Part I, pp. 191–92.)

22. Cf. *Encyclopaedia Britannica*, s.v. Cheke; *Dictionary of National Biography*; *Archaeologia* 38 (1860), pp. 98ff.

23. Loseley MS. 1390, as cited in *BR* 117:8.

24. Strype, *The Life of the Learned Sir*

John Cheke, Kt., London (1705), Oxford (1821), pp. 130–31.

25. Sir John Cheke's prepayment of rent on his lodging for the years 1553 to 1557 did not keep Cawarden from billing the Crown for the rent of the same premises during the same years for the use of the Revels. Cf. Wallace, *Evolution,* p. 140, n. 4, for the applicable Loseley manuscripts.

26. Cf. 6:24, which gives the same figure. The parishioners plainly were aware of Hugh Losse's survey.

27. *Chancery Proceedings, Miscellaneous, 3rd Series, 27th Part.* The document is printed in full by James Greenstreet in *The Athenaeum,* No. 3064, July 17, 1886, pp. 91–92.

28. *BR* 103:2ff. lists Loseley MSS. Nos. 417, 422, 427, and 428 as containing the bill of complaint, interrogatories administered to witnesses, and depositions and evidences.

29. A part of Loseley MS No. 425, as printed in *BR* 127:14ff.

30. *BR* 92:33ff., *BR* 117:36ff., *BR* 118:21ff., *BR* 125:39ff., *BR* 127:2ff. Strype's *Stow,* Book III, p. 180, describes the chapel as "an upper Room, of fifty Foot in length, and thirty Foot in breadth."

31. Stow, ed. 1618, p. 655.

32. Neale, p. 43.

33. Thomas Blagrave enters the Black-friars story in five different capacities: as overseer of Cawarden's estate, as Clerk of the Tents under Cawarden (*BR* 45:3), as author of the Survey of 1552 (Document 8), as witness in the Poole-More controversy (*BR* 52:26ff.), and as Acting Master of the Revels from 1573 to 1579 (*Shakespeare Companion,* p. 401).

34. PP. 43ff., 310.

35. *BR* 120:30ff.

36. *BR* 118:37, *BR* 119:28.

37. *BR* 118:39–42.

38. See p. 102 above.

39. The contents of the memorandum are discussed on pp. 99–100 above.

40. *BR* 124:17.

41. *Blackfriars Records* devotes nearly all of thirteen pages (pp. 40–53, 122) to the testimony of witnesses in the arbitration proceedings. Much of it is confused and repetitious. I omit all but a few highlights.

42. See pp. 97–98 above.

43. *BR* p. 52.

44. *BR* 48:32, *BR* 49:34, *BR* 51:5, etc.

45. *BR* 51:11ff.

46. *BR* 120:44–121:2.

47. *BR* pp. 70–71.

48. *BR* 121:6.

49. Cf. *BR* 56:22, *BR* 122:26, and Wallace, *Evolution,* pp. 186–87.

50. *BR* 38:28ff., *BR* 121:10ff.

☙ 6 ☙

The First Blackfriars Playhouse

T HE YEAR 1576 is doubly important in the history of the English stage. In that year Richard Farrant established the First Blackfriars Playhouse, and in that year James Burbage built the Theater. Farrant's Blackfriars was the first of the theatres later to be known as "private" houses.[1] Burbage's Theater was the first of those later to be called "public." The two types of playhouse came into existence simultaneously, and coexisted until the Puritan revolution.

The distinction between the two types was real, but was not based upon anything that the words "private" and "public" imply; both kinds were public in the sense that any person could enter either upon payment of the required admission fee. The origin of the term "private house" or "private playhouse" is not fully understood. W. J. Lawrence explained it as being an attempt by theatre managers to take advantage of a loophole in a 1574 Act of the Common Council, which, while seeking to restrict plays and acting, made an exception of

> any plays, interludes, comedies, tragedies or shows to be played or showed in the private house, dwelling or lodging of any nobleman, citizen, or gentleman, . . . without public or common collection of money of the auditory or beholders thereof.[2]

But this attractive theory fails to take account of certain relevant facts. For one thing, all the early private playhouses were established in Liberties, and thus had no need to fear the Common Council's restrictions. For another thing, they produced their plays under the pretense of readying them for performance before the Queen, and thus acquired an exemption more effective than either a Liberty or a private dwelling could provide. And finally, the term "private house," as designation for a play-

house, does not appear in print until thirty years after the Common Council's Act of 1574. It was first used by Webster in 1604, in his Induction
for the Globe performance of Marston's *Malcontent*, when he had Sly
say "Why, we may sit upon the stage at the private house." The term
"private playhouse" first appeared in 1606, in Dekker's *Seven Deadly
Sinnes of London.*[3]

But even though private playhouses were not distinguished from
public playhouses in respect of privacy, they were distinguished from
them in several other respects. Many of the private houses were located
in Liberties inside the City walls; all the public houses were built in
London's suburbs. The private houses were roofed over and probably
heated in winter; the public houses were open to the sky and the weather.
The private houses gave their performances by candlelight; the public
gave theirs by the light of the sun. The private houses were relatively
small; they charged admission fees ranging from sixpence to half a
crown, and they provided seats for all their patrons; the public playhouses had a far greater capacity, charged fees ranging from a penny to
a shilling, and furnished no seats in the pit. Finally, the first private
houses were occupied only by companies of child actors; all the public
playhouses were occupied by men.[4]

Elizabethans seem to have felt that this last difference was the essential distinction between the two types of playhouse. This is suggested
by the complaint against the Blackfriars Playhouse that some inhabitants
of the precinct addressed to the Lord Mayor and Aldermen of London
in 1619. In it they charged that "the owner of the said playhouse doth,
under the name of a private house, . . . convert the said house to a
public playhouse" (27:4). The City Corporation agreed that the conversion from private to public had taken place (29:2); but, as will be
seen later, the only important change that had in fact occurred was the
substitution of adult actors for children. After 1610, when that substitution took place, child actors were no longer a distinguishing mark of
the private theatre, but the cleavage between the two types persisted.
Thus *The Duchess of Malfi* was "Presented privately, at the Black-
Friers; and publiquely at the Globe," according to the title page of its
1623 Quarto; and the 1629 Quarto of *The Lovers' Melancholy* says of
that play that it was "Acted at the Private House in the Black Friers,
and publikely at the Globe."

As has been said, the distinction between the private playhouse and
the public was not recognized in print until the turn of the century.

Richard Farrant had no thought that he was creating a "private" house when he designed the First Blackfriars, nor James Burbage that he was building a "public" playhouse when he erected the Theater.[5]

Burbage's Theater was England's first building specifically designed for the presentation of plays; Farrant's Blackfriars was England's first indoor playhouse.[6] These two buildings for the first time gave players settled homes of their own, places permanently at their disposal both for rehearsals and for public performances, places equipped for the production of plays and the accommodation of audiences. They marked the emergence of the theatre as a business enterprise with something more at stake than the livelihood of strolling bands of adult players on the one hand, and occasional "rewards" to companies of child actors on the other. They were a long step toward permanency and professionalism—and commercialism—in the theatre.

Before the first permanent playhouses were built, troupes of adult players were nomads; they wandered about from village to village, putting on their shows in any suitable places that chanced to be available—in barns, town squares, in the mansions of nobles, in colleges and schools, and, most frequently of all, in the open yards of inns. Inn yards had served well as impromptu playhouses. They could quickly be equipped with platforms contrived out of planks laid across barrel heads or trestles; their galleries could be made to represent the walls of beleaguered towns, and nearby areas behind the stage could be used as dressing rooms. But as time went on the art of theatrical presentation became more complex, the audiences larger and more respectable, and the potential profits more tempting. James Burbage, an actor in one of the most important theatrical companies of the time, the Earl of Leicester's Men, saw the drift and decided to profit by it. His recognition of it led him to become, as his sons were later to call him, "the first builder of playehowses" (44:19).

He was well equipped for the task. He was originally "by occupation a joyner, and reaping but a small lyving by the same, gave it over and became a commen player of playes." As an actor he knew what sort of structure would best meet the needs of players and spectators, and as a joiner he knew how to create such a structure. And in addition to his technical qualifications, he had the ingenuity and audacity to tackle a job that no one had undertaken before.

Burbage well knew the hostility with which London's Lord Mayor and Common Council regarded all plays and players; only a patent

signed by the Queen herself had secured for Leicester's Men the right
to play within the City of London. His first task was therefore to find a
site that would make his playhouse easily available to London playgoers
and yet would place it outside the jurisdiction of the puritanical Common
Council. He found such a location in the Liberty of Holywell in Shoreditch, on the northern outskirts of the City. The tract was owned by a
certain Giles Alleyn, and from him Burbage leased it for a twenty-one
year term at a rental of £14 per year. He signed the indenture on April
13, 1576, and proceeded forthwith to erect a building which, with modest
ostentation and a right conferred by priority, he called simply The
Theater.

His venture demanded the more courage because the drama was still
dominated by the boy companies; the professional adult actors had not
yet achieved anything approaching the prestige enjoyed by the children
as purveyors of entertainment to polite audiences. It is easy to understand why this should have been so. While most of the adult troupes were
giving rough-and-tumble shows and dressing them with only such properties and costumes as they could carry with them on the road, the boys
were giving plays addressed to sophisticated and literate tastes, staging
them with costumes and properties drawn from the Revels Office or the
Great Wardrobe, and enriching them with music composed and directed
by accomplished musicians. In consequence of all these things, the boys
were summoned to play before the Queen nearly half again as often as
the men: during the eight-year period immediately before Burbage began
work on the Theater and Farrant on the First Blackfriars, the boy companies gave forty-six performances at Court, and all the adult companies
only thirty-two.[7]

The principal children's companies during this period were the Children of Paul's under Sebastian Westcott, the Children of Windsor under
Richard Farrant, and the Children of the Chapel Royal under William
Hunnis. Farrant had become a Gentleman of the Chapel Royal about
1553, and organist to the Queen at St. George's Chapel, Windsor. In
1564 he became Master of the Children of Windsor, and three years
later he took them to Court in the first of a series of plays that continued
for nearly a decade. In 1576 he seems to have become Deputy Master of
the Children of the Chapel Royal also, and in January of the next year
he presented *Mutius Scaevola* before the Queen with a cast composed of
the Children of Windsor and the Children of the Chapel jointly.

Farrant first heard of Burbage's plans at just about the time when he took both the chapel companies under his wing. The news stirred new ambitions. Why should not the Children capitalize their greater prestige by having a playhouse of their own? As things stood now, they would be at a grave disadvantage as compared with the men who would soon occupy the Theater. They could perform for profit only once or twice a year, when they were summoned to Court or to some noble house on a festive occasion, whereas the men would be able to play before audiences as often as they wished, and to charge admission fees for each performance. The Children, after weeks of rehearsal, could give each play only once or twice; the men could give theirs over and over again. But Farrant realized that any plan to create a playhouse for the Children must be handled discreetly. He must not give anyone an excuse for suggesting that he was using the royal choristers for his personal gain. He must manage affairs in such a way as to create the impression that the Children, even when playing before a paid audience, were merely rehearsing their roles so that they might act them the better when they were called upon to entertain the Queen.

Farrant was not well enough off to contemplate building a playhouse; his only chance was to rent a hall that might at moderate expense be converted into a theatre where the Children could play before small audiences. At just about this time he learned that the long apartment in the Blackfriars precinct was about to be vacated by its present tenant, Lord Cobham. He probably knew the place already. In its days as a Revels Office he may have visited it often for the purpose of selecting properties and costumes to be used by the Children in performances at Court, and he may have gone there later when it was the residence of his friend Sir Henry Neville. It would serve his purposes well as a small playhouse. It was within the City walls and in one of the most fashionable residential districts in London, and yet, as a Liberty subject only to the Crown, it was free from the jurisdiction of the City authorities; and it was even the more suitable because of its nearness to the Royal Wardrobe.

Farrant was not personally acquainted with Sir William More, the owner of the premises, so he asked Sir Henry Neville to introduce him. By prearrangement, both men wrote to More on the same day, August 27, 1576. Neither letter contained any hint that Farrant planned to use the premises for theatrical purposes.

Sir Henry Neville's letter was inscribed *in dorso* "To the right worshipful Sir William More, knight, at his house in Loseley," and read as follows:

SIR WILLIAM:

    After my hearty commendations unto you and to Mrs. More. I am to request your good friendship unto my very friend Mr. Farrant, who understanding that your house which I had of you is to be let, either presently or very shortly, that he may be your tenant thereof, giving unto you such rent as any others will. It may do him at this present great pleasure, and no man shall be readier to requite your friendship than he, I dare answer for him. If you may pleasure him without prejudice to yourself, I pray you certify your man that keeps your house of your pleasure, and accordingly he shall deal with you. . . . From Phyllyngber this 27th of August.

Yours to his power,
Henry Neville[8]

    Richard Farrant's letter carried an identical endorsement, and then continued as follows:

RIGHT WORSHIPFUL:

    My duty done, these are to signify unto you that where your Worship doth mind to let your house in the Blackfriars, late in the Lord Cobham's hands, I am earnestly to request your Worship if I may be your tenant there, if the Italian may be removed,[9] as it appeareth somewhat to me, it were easily done. If it be your pleasure so to accept me, though unacquainted unto you, I hope in God you will not mislike with me in any dealings concerning the rent or any other things to be performed. If it be my chance to have that favor at your hands, this yet farther am I to request: that I may pull down one partition and so make of two rooms—one; and will make it up again at my departure, or when my lease shall end. Thus craving your Worship's answer by this bringer, either to me, or your man the keeper of your said house. With my humble and hearty commendations. I commit you to the Almighty. From London this 27 of August.

Your Worship's to command,
Richard Farrant[10]

    More and Farrant reached an agreement by which the latter undertook to pay £14 per year—which, by coincidence, was the same amount as Burbage was paying for the rental of his plot of ground in Shoreditch—for the lease of the long apartment. The lease was signed on December 20, 1576, but was effective from the preceding September 29, the Feast of St. Michael the Archangel (16:10). It gave Farrant the occupancy of the following properties:

    A]   Six upper chambers with a total length of 156½ feet, two of which chambers were in the north end of the premises and were 46½ feet long[11] by 25 feet broad,[12] and the remaining four of which were 110 feet long by 22 feet broad (16:2);

B] The new kitchen lately built by Neville, with the stair leading out of it to the upstairs apartment (16:4);

C] The great stairs lately built by Neville (16:5);

D] Two rooms directly under part of the upper chambers (16:7); and

E] A little room (16:8) that Farrant had especially asked for by letter, and had described in that letter as "a little dark room . . . not past one yard and a half broad and two yards at the most in length."[13]

Farrant installed his playhouse in the north, or Old Buttery, portion of the premises. This confident assertion is based upon the following circumstances:

First, Farrant had to have stairs by which playgoers could reach his upstairs theatre, and the only stairs available to him led to the north end of the apartment, not to the south. For the reasons given on pages 101 to 102 above, it seems all but certain that he was debarred from using "that great pair of winding stairs" later to provide access to all the Seven Great Upper Rooms, but now providing access only to the Frith apartment. Farrant did, however, have the use of "the great stairs lately erected and made by the said Sir Henry Neville, . . . which said great stairs do serve and lead into the premises before demised" (16:5).[14] Neville had inevitably built the stairs on void ground to the west of the Old Buttery block, since void ground was available to him nowhere else: the empty plots to the east, the former Great Cloister and Inner Cloister, were in other hands, and Frith's apartment blocked any access to western yards at the south. The stairs leading to Farrant's theatre were thus necessarily at its northern, or Old Buttery, end.

Second, the northern end of the leased premises was wider than the southern end. Whether its width at the north be reckoned at 25 feet, at 26 feet 7½ inches, or at 27 feet, it was in any event wider than the southern end with its width of 22; and for the purposes of a playhouse, every additional foot of breadth would be a matter of importance.

Third, the only lower-level rooms leased to Farrant were beneath his premises at the Old Buttery end. This fact is established by the description of the two rooms as being located north of the entry leading from the void ground on the west to Sir William More's house (the former South Dorter) on the east (16:7). As will become clear a little later, lower-level rooms were indispensable to Farrant as areas from which actors or properties might begin their ascent by trap to the stage above; and the location of the two rooms not only joins with other considerations in indicating that the playhouse was installed on the upper floor of the Old Buttery block,[15] but indicates also that the stage was at the block's southern end.

The First Blackfriars Playhouse thus occupied the southern half of the hall that had been the original refectory of the friars and had later been the guest house in which Charles V was lodged.

Of the six rooms into which Farrant's premises were divided at the time when he signed the lease, two were in the northern section, with a wall between them; and undoubtedly this wall was the partition that Farrant asked and received permission to pull down in order to make two rooms into one. He pulled down other partitions as well, without More's consent (17:3), one of which was probably the wall at the south end of the hall that he was converting into a theatre. He would need to have a wall there, but it must be a wall of his own designing, a wall built to meet specific theatrical conditions rather than merely to separate one chamber from another.

Not one word survives to tell the design of the First Blackfriars Playhouse or its stage, to the extent that they can be reconstructed at all, they can be reconstructed only on the basis of what we know of Elizabethan playhouses and stages in general, together with what we can glean from the three extant plays known to have been acted there. Stephen Gosson wrote in 1582 that "a greate many Comedies" were played at the Blackfriars;[16] but out of the great many only seven are known by title, and out of the seven only three survive. All the plays presented during Farrant's managership—among them *A Game of the Cards, The History of Alucius, The History of Loyalty and Beauty,* and *Mutius Scaevola,* all by unknown authors—have perished. The only surviving plays are John Lyly's *Campaspe* and *Sapho and Phao,* and George Peele's *Arraignment of Paris.*[17]

The Stage

Before discussing the fragmentary information supplied by the three plays, however, it will be well to list some things common to all playhouses of the period, and therefore to be taken for granted. They are few and basic. We may assume without proof [A] that the First Blackfriars Playhouse had a platform raised above the floor of the auditorium; [B] that behind the platform was a backstage area called the "tiring-house"; [c] that the platform was separated from the tiring-house by a wall that served both as background for action on the platform and as a means of concealing behind-the-scenes activities; and [D] that doors pierced the wall, so that actors could go back and forth from one area to the other.

But perhaps the first thing to be taken for granted is that Farrant's Blackfriars was equipped simply and inexpensively. He lacked the means to furnish it as handsomely as he might have wished. As Master of the Children he probably received only a modest stipend; he had a family of ten children to support; he had no subsidy, and he was forced to borrow money to pay for equipping the playhouse, as evidenced by his widow's statement that he was "greatlie indebted" when he died four years later.[18] Furthermore, elaborate furnishings would have falsified his pretense of intending to use the house only for the teaching of the Children; and finally, the only specific alterations that Sir William More was later to complain of were the pulling down of partitions (17:3,7) and the spoiling of windows.[19]

The stage that Farrant built was probably elevated to a height of about 36 inches above the floor of the hall. This conjecture is based upon the supposition that the spectators at the First Blackfriars were seated on benches, and that they were not, like the groundlings at the Theater, expected to remain afoot from the play's beginning until its end. The playgoers whom Farrant hoped to attract were persons who had seen the Children in action at Court or in noble houses. There the auditors had been provided with seats, and they would expect the same accommodations in the playhouse. This assumption leads to the further assumption that the platform was 36 inches high, since that is the height best suited to an audience seated on benches on a level floor.

The wall at the back edge of the platform had two doors cut through it, one near each end. None of the extant plays bears testimony to two doors, but a single door would not have been enough. Two were necessary to permit the illusion that characters entering the stage were coming from different places, and that a character who departed was not necessarily returning to the place from which he had come. Abundant proof exists to show that the Second Blackfriars had two such doors, proof that usually takes the form of stage directions calling for the entrance of two or more characters through two different doors at the same time; and in spite of the lack of direct evidence, we may confidently assume that the First Blackfriars had two doors similarly arranged.

The existence of a tiring-house is taken for granted because such a backstage area was indispensable. It provided places where single actors or armies could stand, out of sight of the audience, until their turns came to enter. It provided a passageway by which actors could cross from one side of the stage to the other behind the scenes, and farther back it provided dressing or attiring rooms, and rooms where beards and costumes and properties could be stored; and, as will become clear presently, it also provided room for a disclosable inner stage immediately to the rear of the scenic wall and between the two stage doors.

Farrant's holdings, of course, stretched far to the south, beyond the reach of immediate theatrical needs, in the 110-foot-long eastern half of the Parliament Chamber. There he perhaps had living quarters for his wife and children when they came to London from their home in New Windsor, and dormitories and classrooms for the child actors. There too, presumably, was the part of the house that he subleased to some outsiders (17:3), in violation of his contract with Sir William More (16:15).

So much for the stage elements that may be taken for granted. When we pass on to those other elements whose existence and nature are evidenced by the plays themselves, we find that all three of the extant plays make use of an inner stage, and that two of the three require that the inner stage should at times be revealed to the audience by the opening of curtains, and at other times concealed. In their recurrent uses of the inner stage, the two Lyly plays display a freedom and flexibility surprising in plays that came so soon after the establishment of the first regular theatres.

Five times in *Sapho and Phao* the inner stage represents the bedchamber of the Princess Sapho, and the first four of those times—at III *iii* 1, III *iv* 36, IV *i* 1, and IV *iii* 1—the stage curtains open to reveal Sapho, lovesick for Phao, lying on her bed attended by six ladies of her court. The disclosure of the inner stage in III *iv* is preceded by a 35-line conversation between a waiting woman and Phao on the platform, ending with "Well, let us in," and with the opening of the curtains to admit them to the inner stage as to Sapho's bedchamber. Another disclosure, in IV *i*, is preceded by Phao's talk with Venus and Cupid on the platform, at the end of which Venus says "I must visit Sapho," and the action again moves from the platform to the inner stage. In both these sequences the platform serves as an anteroom to the bedchamber.[20]

The scenes in Apelles' studio, in *Campaspe*, make similar use of a discoverable inner stage. The first studio scene comes at III *iii*, when the stage curtains open to reveal Campaspe sitting for her portrait and Apelles at his easel. The second begins unexpectedly about midway of the next scene. The intervening action has been on the platform as in a market place. At III *iv* 57, Alexander of Macedon, who a moment before has been in the neighborhood of Diogenes' tub, calls out "Apelles?" and receives the answer "Here," and the curtains again open to reveal Apelles at his easel and Campaspe posing. Alexander enters the inner stage and addresses Campaspe: "Now Gentlewomanne, doeth not your beauty put the painter to his trump?" Hitherto the platform has been an open place upon which, as we now learn, Apelles' studio fronts. It regains that character as the interior scene comes to an end. At about line 116 Alexander and his companion leave the studio and come forward to the platform, and a few lines later Campaspe does so too, and exits to Alexander's admiring comment on "How stately she passeth by, yet how soberly." The stage curtains can have closed at any time after line 115, and they remain closed throughout the next four scenes. The studio is revealed again, and for the last time, in IV *iv*.

The inner stage was probably used also to represent or to contain Diana's bower in *The Arraignment of Paris*. The bower needed to be large enough to hold not fewer than eleven Olympian deities, with seats for at least some of them; it seems necessary, therefore, to assume that it was relegated to the rear stage, since a bower of the requisite size would have cluttered up the stage intolerably, especially during such episodes as the dance of the nine knights in armor, if it took the form of a property placed on the platform. But, even though the bower occupied the rear stage, we have no need to suppose that it was at any time concealed. It is mentioned as early as line 144 ("the entrance of the bowre") and line 381 ("Retire we to Dianaes bowre"), and it would at no time be incongruous to the play's pastoral setting; probably, therefore, it remained in sight from beginning to end. At line 915, when the deities assemble as a Council of the Gods for the arraignment of Paris, they are *"set in Dianaes bower,"* and there they remain until *"All they rise and goe forth"* at line 1172. A tree also is needed for Paris and Oenone to sit under together, and it too probably remains in place throughout the play.

The scenes just cited indicate that the First Blackfriars had an inner stage whose interior could be seen through an opening in the scenic wall. Both symmetry and the designs of other stages suggest that the opening was centered in the wall and that it was flanked at each side by one of the stage doors previously discussed. When we take up the matter of dimensions, the reader will recall that, as a compromise between irreconcilable figures, 26 feet was assumed to be the width of the hall containing the playhouse. The platform undoubtedly ran from one side of the hall to the other and was therefore 26 feet wide also, and so in consequence was the scenic wall. It seems necessary to suppose that each stage door was 4 feet wide, since the shepherds with their burden of Colin's hearse (*Arraignment*, III *v*) could not have passed through doors much narrower than that. Each door, of course, was suitably framed, and the central aperture was flanked on each side by a wall section wide enough to hide the stage curtains when they were fully opened. If reasonable allowances be made for these features and deducted from 26 feet, something in the neighborhood of 13 feet is left as the width of the inner-stage opening.

The inner stage presumably ran back to a depth of 7 or 8 feet at the rear of the scenic wall; surely no less depth than that, and no less width than 13 feet, could hold Sapho's tester bed and her six women-in-waiting, or a bower big enough to seat eleven deities.

The inner stage was necessarily closed off at the back with some sort of wall, if only to hide backstage areas and activities. The corresponding wall in the Second Blackfriars would later contain a door and window; we cannot know whether the wall at the First Blackfriars was similarly designed. The only possible reference to such a door comes in *Sapho and Phao*, v *ii*, when Sapho says "Come, Mileta, shut the doore," at the end of what is unmistakably an inner-stage scene. Perhaps she goes out at the back, with Mileta following and shutting the door, or perhaps she refers to an outer-stage door by which Venus has just departed. The only mention of any window is in *Campaspe*, III *i*, when Apelles says "Psyllus, stay you heere at the window, if anye enquire for me, aunswere, *Non lubet esse domi*." But the context makes it plain that Psyllus is on the platform, and the window therefore cannot have been at the back of the inner stage. It seems possible that Apelles refers to a wicket in one of the stage doors, but the question cannot be resolved, since the window is not again mentioned.

Platform Trap

Two scenes in *The Arraignment of Paris* show that the First Blackfriars Playhouse had a trap in the floor of the platform. At line 488 the stage direction reads *"Heereuppon did rise a Tree of gold laden with*

Diadems and Crownes of golde," followed at line 495 by *"The Tree sinketh";* and at line 902 *"Pluto ascendeth from below in his chaire. Neptune entreth at an other way."*

These two stage directions indicate not merely that a trap existed, but indicate also that it could be raised and lowered by mechanical means: the tree of gold did not rise by its own efforts, nor did Pluto in his chair. Clearly, therefore, some sort of apparatus, presumably a winch or wind-lass operated by stagehands, provided the power. The winch was neces-sarily located at some point below the platform; and this in turn, to-gether with the size of the objects brought up by the trap, suggests that it was not accommodated in the space between the floor of the hall and the underside of the platform, but in rooms below the hall.

This aspect of trap operation will be discussed more fully in con-nection with the platform trap at the Second Blackfriars, with respect to which far more data are available, but a digest of the argument must be inserted here. It amounts to this: the upper surface of the platform was probably not more than 36 inches high above the floor of the hall. It was composed of planks at least 2 inches thick, and the beams that supported the planking were oak joists which, as was usual in Tudor timber construction, were extravagantly thick by the standards of today. The space between the underbraces of the platform and the floor of the hall therefore cannot have been more than 26 inches high, and no such space could accommodate a golden tree or Pluto in his chair, and send them up in vertical position to the stage above; and even less could it accommodate a winch and stagehands to operate it. We must conse-quently assume that the ascents originated in a room or rooms beneath the hall, and that Pluto and the tree traveled upward through a hole cut through the intervening floor. As we know, the property rented by Far-rant did in fact include two lower rooms beneath the southern end of the 46½-foot hall; and this, it will be remembered, constitutes one of our reasons for assuming that the playhouse occupied that hall and that the stage was at its southern end. As I shall hope to show, the position of those rooms constitutes also a datum of the first importance in enabling us to estimate the respective sizes of the auditorium and the stage.

Farrant's lease describes the two lower rooms as being bounded on the south by the entry leading from the void ground on the west to Sir William More's house on the east (16:7); in other words, they were at the extreme south end of the Old Buttery block. An external wall, esti-mated to have been 3 feet thick, intervened between the rooms and the entry; and since the Old Buttery was 95 feet long, the north face of that wall was 92 feet south of the north end of the building. On the story above, Cobham had his mansion, which stretched southward 52 feet from the same north end, and then, after a 2-foot-thick intervening wall, Farrant had the rest. The south side of the intervening wall, and therefore the northernmost extent of Farrant's premises, was thus 54 feet south of the building's north end on the upper floor; on the lower floor, the southernmost extent of his premises was 92 feet south of the building's north end. If, therefore, the northern face of the lower-level wall should be projected upward to the floor above, it would be 38 feet away from the north end of Farrant's hall.

As we have seen, the platform trap was necessarily over some part of the lower rooms. Farrant would have wished to place it as far south as he could, so that the platform containing the trap could also be as far south as possible, and so that the auditorium could in consequence have the greatest possible depth and seating capacity. He would therefore have put the trap's southern edge directly over the northern face of the wall below.

We may suppose that the trap opening was 3 feet wide from north to south, since at least that width was necessary to permit the passage of a golden tree laden with diadems and crowns, and of Pluto in his chair; and we may assume further that some little distance, perhaps 2 feet or so, intervened between the front edge of the trap and the front edge of the platform. These figures lead to the conclusion that the front edge of the platform was 33 feet away from the north end of the hall and 13½ feet away from the southern end, and thus that the auditorium was 33 feet deep by 26 feet wide, and the platform 13½ feet deep by 26 feet wide.

Let me review this series of relationships for the sake of clarity: The south wall of the Old Buttery block determined the position of the two lower rooms; the position of those rooms determined the position of the trap; the position of the trap largely determined the position of the front edge of the platform, and the platform's front edge determined the depth of the auditorium. If, as seems unlikely, Farrant permitted the front edge of his platform to coincide with the front edge of the trap, he could have gained 2 feet of additional depth for his auditorium, but no more. The platform may, of course, have been deeper than the 13½ feet postulated above, but there is no reason to suppose that it was; a depth half as great as the width would have given Farrant a well-proportioned stage. In any event, the depth to which the platform extended southward of the trap would have no effect upon the size and capacity of the auditorium.

These reckonings have led to the conjecture that the platform at the First Blackfriars was 26 feet wide from east to west by 13½ feet deep from north to south; that it was closed off at the back with a scenic wall pierced by an inner-stage aperture perhaps 13 feet wide, and two doors each 4 feet wide; that the inner stage ran back from the scenic wall to a depth of perhaps 7 or 8 feet, and that behind the inner stage the tiring-house ran back for an indefinite distance.

We cannot know whether or not Farrant's playhouse had any acting areas on an upper level, such as the balconies and upstairs windows that were a part of the stage resources of virtually all playhouses of the Elizabethan and Jacobean eras. We cannot base a negative opinion upon the mere fact that none of the three extant plays makes use of an upper-level stage unit, since perhaps other lost plays did. If Farrant did decide against providing upper stages, he did so probably to save money or to avoid having his theatre seem overelaborate; he is not likely to have done so because of any lack of ceiling height in the great hall that had been the refectory of the friars and their hostelry for distinguished guests.

Nor can we be sure whether the playhouse was equipped with apparatus for staging flights of deities from the heavens. Again the surviving plays are silent, and again their silence is not conclusive. But it is noteworthy that, although two of the plays have a total of fifteen gods and goddesses in their casts, not one of the deities enters in flight.

A stage direction in *The Arraignment of Paris*, line 382—"*The storme being past of thunder & lightning*"—proves that the First Blackfriars had some sort of equipment for producing storm effects. In the public playhouses the sound of thunder would be simulated by bowling heavy balls of stone or iron along wooden troughs, supplemented by rolls on snare drums and kettle drums. The same methods were probably used in the private theatre. The effect of lightning was produced by some sort of pyrotechnical device not fully understood.

Methods of Production

The First Blackfriars Playhouse bridged the transition from the permanent multiple settings of the medieval stage to the successive settings of the Elizabethan. It retained vestiges of the medieval practice that permitted two or more different and distant places to be represented on the stage at the same time by the use of two or more "mansions" or "sedes," and it did so in spite of its having a disclosable inner stage that permitted different and distant places to follow one another, instead of occupying the stage simultaneously.

We have seen how the inner stage served recurrently to represent Sapho's bedchamber in *Sapho and Phao*, and Apelles' studio in *Campaspe*. The same two plays show survivals of the medieval practice. In the former play, v *ii*, Vulcan's forge is shown on the stage, with Venus waiting there for Cupid's return, and at the same moment the interior of Sapho's house is visible, with Cupid sitting on Sapho's lap. The situation develops in this manner:

Venus, infatuated with the beauty of Phao, visits Vulcan at his forge and begs him to make some special arrows that, when loosed by Cupid, will transfer Phao's love from Sapho to herself. Vulcan agrees, and his singing of "The Song, in making of the Arrowes," shows that he fashions the arrowheads, perhaps with hammer and anvil, while remaining on the stage (iv *iv*). The place is still Vulcan's forge in v *i*. Venus gives the arrows to Cupid and bids him shoot Phao with one and Sapho with another. She ends the scene by saying "But I will expect the event, and tarie for Cupid at the forge."

The next scene takes the action back to Sapho's house, where four previous scenes have been located, always with the inner stage serving as bedchamber. Sapho, having been shot with one of the arrows, is out of bed and fancy-free, but her room still unquestionably occupies the rear stage, for the sake of recognition if for no other reason. Cupid, with his task only half done, is persuaded by Sapho to shoot Phao with an arrow that will inspire him with loathing for Venus instead of love, on the promise of letting him sit in her lap and be rocked to sleep. He departs, carries out the new mission, and returns. Venus, all this time, has been waiting for Cupid at the forge, and at v *ii* 45 she has this startling line: "I mervaile Cupid commeth not all this while. How now, in Saphoes lap?" The subsequent conversation involves all three persons. In this scene we have two "mansions" occupied and functioning at the same time, with the inner stage serving for one and perhaps with an anvil symbolizing the other.

The scenes before Sybilla's cave constitute another series of recurring placements. In ii *i* Phao sees Sybilla in the mouth of her cave; in ii *iv* she bids him come in and he agrees, but there is no evidence that he does so; and in v *iii* he sees her sitting happily in her cave. The cave and Sapho's bedchamber are never in use concurrently, and the interior of the cave seems never to be revealed. Probably, therefore, the break between the stage curtains can serve as a "mansion" to symbolize the cave; all the necessary illusion can be conveyed by having the two halves of the curtains drawn a little apart in tentlike fashion, with Sybilla standing or sitting in the opening.

In *Campaspe* the rear stage, as representing Apelles' studio, serves as one "mansion," and Diogenes' tub serves as another. The tub is mentioned as being visible at II *ii* 119, III *iv* 45, and v *iii* 21; and although not specifically mentioned, it is probably on-stage also in I *iii*, IV *i,* v *i,* and v *iv,* to serve as a localizing symbol whenever Diogenes is involved in the action. It cannot occupy the rear stage, because of the juxtaposition of a tub episode and a studio episode in III *iv;* and if the tub serves in lieu of a "mansion" as often as seems likely, it probably remains permanently visible on the stage—merely ignored during the scenes to which it is incongruous—instead of being thrust out upon the platform by stagehands each time it is needed, and then being drawn back again afterwards.

No localization, by "mansion" or otherwise, is needed for the scenes in which Alexander appears. Their placement in Alexander's palace is a figment of editorial imagination,[21] based upon the fallacious notion that wherever Alexander is, there his palace must be also. All these scenes were probably played upon the platform as being unlocalized.

It seems probable that the First Blackfriars did not consistently have intermissions between the acts of a play, although the Second Blackfriars manifestly did. Twice in *Sapho and Phao,* and once in *Campaspe,* the action continues without interruption from one act into another; and this is the more surprising since the act divisions in both plays originate in their 1584 quartos, and are not editorial interpolations.

In the former play, Venus, Cupid, and Phao are in the anteroom to Sapho's bedchamber as Act III comes to an end. Venus, addressing Phao, says "Well, farewell for this time: for I must visit Sapho," and the act ends with the exit of Phao, and of Phao alone. Venus and Cupid remain on-stage; the curtains open to reveal the bedchamber, and without pause Venus enters the rear stage and begins Act IV with "Sapho, I have heard thy complaintes, and pittied thine agonies." At the end of Act IV Venus and Cupid are again on-stage, the place now being Vulcan's forge. Vulcan retires, and the action flows into Act v without a break, with the same two persons continuously visible, and again without change of place or lapse of time. *Campaspe* treats the division between Acts I and II similarly, with Diogenes remaining on the platform as one act ends and the next begins. Several philosophers have been interviewing him as Act II approaches its end. Then Plato says "Let us go," and, according to the stage direction, the philosophers exeunt; but Diogenes remains, and when Psyllus, Manes, and Granichus enter at the beginning of Act II they see him already there, "seeking either for bones for his dinner, or pinnes for his sleeves."

As might be expected, the First Blackfriars made copious use of song; this was a natural consequence of the boys' having been chosen in the first instance for the excellence of their singing voices and of their being trained in music by a choirmaster. *Campaspe* has four songs and *Sapho and Phao* has four, the last of them being Vulcan's song at the forge. *The Arraignment* has eleven or twelve, in addition to "*An artificiall charme of birdes*" and "*An Eccho to their song*," and "*A quier within and without.*"

The Arraignment has a dance of country gods and goddesses at line 190, and the stage direction at line 513 says that "*Hereuppon did enter .9. knights in armour, treading a warlike Almaine, by drome and fife*"; and *Campaspe*, in v i, presents a dancer and then a tumbler.

Earlier in this chapter I ventured the estimate that the auditorium or pit of the First Blackfriars was 33 feet in length by 26 feet in breadth. Some part of that space, of course, was given up to aisles—perhaps one aisle running down the center of the floor, and another at the rear end, leading to it from the external stairs. The rest of the pit was occupied by spectators seated on benches.

In modern theatres and stadia, the usual space allowance for each seated spectator is 18 to 22 inches from side to side by 30 inches from front to back. But the playgoer of Elizabethan times needed more breadth than that. His was the period of greatest extravagance in English dress. Both he and his lady wore elaborate and voluminous costumes; she wore a farthingale and puffed sleeves and a ruff, and he wore a slashed doublet and cape, and a sword at his side. Under these circumstances, a generous allowance of space per spectator is likely to be more realistic than a conservative one. I therefore base my estimates of seating capacity upon the supposition that each spectator occupied a space 2½ feet deep from front to back, and a full 2 feet wide. On this basis, after reasonable allowances have been made for aisles, a pit of the dimensions indicated would accommodate 120 to 130 persons.

It seems probable that the whole capacity of the playhouse was limited to the capacity of the pit. Some theatres would later have galleries for spectators, and some would permit fashionable gentlemen to sit on the stage, but it seems unlikely that the First Blackfriars made either of those provisions.

It had no galleries along the sides of the hall because the hall was too narrow to accommodate side-wall galleries with good sight lines to the stage. A gallery at the back end of the hall would avoid this difficulty but would incur others. Stairs would reduce the useful area both at floor level and at gallery level, and the space left for the seating of spectators might not be enough to justify the expense of construction. Besides, Sir William More had no complaints to make about a gallery when he repossessed the property eight years later.

The Second Blackfriars Playhouse would later permit gallants to sit upon the stage, and some vague references suggest that the practice antedated that playhouse;[22] none, however, connects it with the First Blackfriars, and Farrant is not likely to have tolerated it there. His stage was too small, in width more importantly than in depth or total area, for him to have been willing to sacrifice any part of it to stage-sitters; it was just over half as wide as the platform of the Second Blackfriars was later to be, and its area was only about one third as great. If Farrant had permitted gentlemen to sit on the stage, they could have sat only at the platform's ends, facing center. So seated, they would have obstructed the spectators' view of the entering doors at the two ends of the scenic wall. But Farrant could not have permitted that view to be obstructed, and to avoid it he would have had to move the doors inward toward the center of the stage; and by every foot that he moved them inward, by just so much would he have narrowed the aperture of the inner stage. In Farrant's time the custom of sitting on the stage had not yet been established as the recognized privilege of gentlemen of fashion, and he would have been unlikely to initiate a practice so disadvantageous to himself, for which no pressure of custom yet existed.

History of the First Blackfriars

Farrant's lease of the Blackfriars property stood in his name alone, and yet the playhouse seems to have been occupied both by his Children of Windsor and by Hunnis's Children of the Chapel. Both companies are designated in the Revels Accounts as having performed *Mutius Scaevola* at Court on January 7, 1577, the first play to be performed there after the Blackfriars Playhouse opened, and presumably the first play to be presented at Blackfriars. For the next four years Farrant continued to present plays at both places. None of the plays has survived.

Sir William More resented the situation in which Farrant had placed him. He said that Farrant had misrepresented his purpose in renting the property: he had given Sir William to understand that he would use the house only for the teaching of the Children of the Chapel, instead of which he had made it a continual house for plays, to the offense of the precinct (17:3); and doubtless the residents of the precinct, and those nearest to the playhouse in particular—Frith and Cobham and Joyner and Sir William himself—were inconvenienced by the arrival and departure of the playgoers' horses and coaches. But Sir William had no remedy; the lease contained no stipulation that the house should not be used for plays. It did, however, contain a stipulation that forbade Farrant to sublet any part of it to any person or persons without Sir William's prior consent in writing, the penalty being immediate forfeiture of the lease (16:15); and this provision was to cause years of wrangling in court and out, and was eventually to close the playhouse doors. Farrant started the long train of violations by letting two parcels of his premises to two different persons,[23] thus subjecting himself to the penalty of eviction. Sir William More immediately claimed that Farrant had forfeited his lease. The latter, manifestly at fault, offered some sort of settlement, but before an agreement could be arrived at, he died. To his widow he left ten small children, a load of debts, and the lease of the Blackfriars Playhouse.

Anne (or Annis or Agnes) Farrant could not herself operate the playhouse; she had heavy domestic responsibilities, little capital, no experience in producing plays, and no authority over the royal choristers. Since she could not operate the theatre herself, her only hope lay in persuading Sir William to let her sublease it to someone who could: that way the lease would be her greatest asset; any other way it could only be a crushing liability. She accordingly wrote to Sir William on Christmas Day of 1580, saying that she did not have the revenue of one groat any way coming in for the relief of her little ones, and begging him out of his abundant clemency and accustomed goodness to allow her to sublet the property.[24] More's reply is not in existence, and perhaps he never wrote one. He may have preferred not to commit himself in writing, but instead let her understand orally that he would wink at a transfer of the lease to her husband's former silent partner, William Hunnis.

Hunnis's relationship to Farrant is not entirely clear. He had been Master of the Children of the Chapel from 1566 until 1576, but from then until 1580, the years during which his Chapel Children were acting at Court in combination with the Children of Windsor, he seems either to have been succeeded by Farrant or to have made Farrant his deputy. But on Farrant's death Hunnis resumed the title of Master, and as Master he decided to continue taking the Children to Court and to continue rehearsing them before paid audiences at Blackfriars. He accordingly entered into a verbal agreement with the Widow Farrant for rental of the property. But Hunnis was unwilling that his tenure of the playhouse, and with it the success of the whole venture, should depend upon a mere verbal agreement with a lessee whose right to sublet was itself dependent upon an oral understanding. He therefore asked the Earl of Leicester to intervene with More on his behalf, and on September 19, 1581, the Earl wrote a letter introducing "my friend, Mr. Hunnis, this bearer," and recommending him to Sir William's favor.[25] The letter said that Hunnis wished to use the house as Farrant had done, "there to practice the Queen's Children of the Chapel . . . for the better training them to do her Majesty service." But by this time Sir William had learned what those phrases meant, and therefore was slow in consenting. Eventually, however, he must have given Hunnis enough reassurance to make him feel safe in going ahead with his project, for on December 20, 1581, Hunnis entered into a formal lease whereby he and a certain John Newman rented the property from Anne Farrant at an increase of £6 13s. 4d. over the amount that she had to pay to More. The joint lessees covenanted to pay the rent promptly and to keep the premises in repair, and Anne Farrant required of them a bond in the amount of £100 to guarantee their performance of all their commitments.

Hunnis seems to have occupied the playhouse in the meantime, without waiting for a formal lease. He took the Children of the Chapel to Court on February 5, 1581, December 31, 1581, February 27, 1582, and December 26, 1582, one of their plays being *A Game of the Cards* and another probably *The Arraignment of Paris*. But the undertaking seems not to have gone well financially. Hunnis and Newman neglected the repairs that they had promised to make, probably because they could not afford to make them, and they were tardy in their payments of rent to Mrs. Farrant, with the result that she was put to dire shifts to pay hers to More. On one occasion she was forced to make "humble and pitiful suit" to Lord Cobham, whose mansion adjoined her property at the north, to pay her rent for her. On another occasion she borrowed money from Mr. Henry Sackford of her Majesty's Privy Chamber, and at yet other times she pawned her plate and jewels or sold a dozen of gold buttons or a set of viols.[26] It goes without saying that she threatened Hunnis and Newman with the forfeiture of their bond, and perhaps she even commenced suit against them in early 1583; and it may have been this development that precipitated their decision to escape further obligations and the wrath of More by getting rid of their lease.

They transferred it to Henry Evans, a young Welsh scrivener who had acquired a love of the theatre through his friendship with Sebastian Westcott of St. Paul's. This unauthorized assignment of the sublease gave Sir William More the opportunity that he had been waiting for. He executed a fictitious lease "unto his own man, Thomas Smallpiece," and in the latter's name brought suit to have Evans ejected. But Evans "demurred in law upon it, . . . using many delays," and finally sold his sub-sublease to the Earl of Oxford, who made a gift of it to his secretary and protégé, John Lyly; "and," said Sir William, "the title thus was posted over from one to another from me, contrary to the said condition" (17:5).

Under these troublous circumstances a new company of boys was formed, with Henry Evans as manager, John Lyly as dramatist and proprietor of the playhouse, and the Earl of Oxford as patron. It was composed of the Children of the Chapel and the Children of Paul's, the latter group having been brought into the venture presumably in consequence of Westcott's death and Evans's prior association with him. This was the company that took *Campaspe* to Court on New Year's Day 1584, and *Sapho and Phao* on March 3rd, the payee for both performances being John Lyly. Once again the status of William Hunnis is unclear. He was still the Master of the Chapel Children, and on the title pages of the two Lyly plays his Children were listed before those of Paul's; on the other hand, he no longer had a financial interest in the lease of the playhouse, he was superseded by Lyly as payee for the performances at Court, and he was currently in such straitened circumstances that in November of 1583 he drafted a petition asking for an increased allowance for the food and keep of the Chapel Children, ending with the statement that he was not able upon so small an allowance any longer to bear so heavy a burden (Document 21).

In the meantime, the courts of law were busy with disputes arising out of the Blackfriars lease and its peregrinations. In Michaelmas Term of 1583 Anne Farrant brought two suits in the Court of Common Pleas for payment of the £100 bond, one against Hunnis and the other against

Newman, and they in turn sued her in the Court of Requests, asking for relief in equity against her suits at the common law. Sir William More pressed his suit for recovery of the premises through four terms of court. Having been put off by Evans's demurrer in Trinity Term (May–June) 1583 and again in Michaelmas Term (November), he demanded judgment in Hilary (January) 1584, but "the judges would not then give judgment, but required to have books of the whole proceeding delivered them."[27] Judgment was finally given in his favor at the end of Easter Term of 1584, and process was awarded to the sheriff to give him possession.[28] But even this did not close the matter for Anne Farrant. She appealed to the Privy Council, and it was this appeal that led Sir William to write his memorandum on the history of the Farrant lease (Document 17), presumably for the information of counsel. Nothing came of her appeal. The First Blackfriars Playhouse had come to an end after a stormy life of eight short years.

1. Perhaps the Children of Paul's had permitted paying customers to attend their rehearsals prior to 1576, but there is no clear evidence of plays at Paul's until Gosson speaks of them in 1582. In any event, their performances were probably given in their singing school, not in a theatre. Cf. Chambers, *Elizabethan Stage*, Vol. II, pp. 15–16.

2. *Those Nut-Cracking Elizabethans*, pp. 31–32. Chambers quotes the Act in full in *Elizabethan Stage*, Vol. IV, pp. 273–76. He cites Lawrence's theory, but does not endorse it.

3. *Cynthia's Revels* (1601), *Poetaster* (1602), and *Blurt Master Constable* (1601–02) have "privately acted" on their title pages, but do not speak of a private house.

4. In this discussion of private versus public playhouses, I have been greatly aided by William A. Armstrong's admirable pamphlet entitled *The Elizabethan Private Theatres: Facts and Problems*.

5. The private playhouses were the First Blackfriars of 1576, Second Blackfriars of 1600, Whitefriars of *circa* 1607, Porter's Hall of 1615, the Cockpit of Phoenix of 1616, and the Salisbury Court of 1629. The public playhouses were the Theater of 1576, the Curtain of 1577, the Rose of 1587, the Swan of *circa* 1595, the Globe of 1599, the Fortune of 1600, the Red Bull of *circa* 1604, the Hope of 1614, the Second Globe of 1614, and the Second Fortune of 1623.

6. Except for the tiny Trinity Hall, which was installed in a hall 35 feet long, 15 feet wide, and 17½ feet high, with a stage 15 feet wide by 7 feet 10½ inches deep, and which was used for plays from 1557 or earlier until 1568. See Professor Charles Tyler Prouty, "An Early Elizabethan Playhouse," *Shakespeare Survey 6* (1953), pp. 64–74.

7. Chambers, *Elizabethan Stage*, Vol. II, p. 4.

8. *Loseley MSS.*, Letters, II, no. 71, printed in its original spelling in Wallace, *Evolution*, p. 131, n. 1.

9. Chambers (*Elizabethan Stage*, Vol. II, p. 495) suggests that the Italian may have been one of the silk dyers; but the silk dyers had departed five years before, and it would be surprising if one of them had survived the Cobham tenancy.

10. Loseley MSS., Letters Undated, printed in its original spelling in Wallace, *Evolution*, p. 131, n. 2.

11. The indenture gives this dimension as 56½ feet, but this is clearly a typographical error, as proved both by the arithmetic of the paragraph and by the corresponding provision in the Cobham lease (15:2).

12. The Neville lease gives this width as 26 feet 7½ inches (12:2), and the Cobham deed gives the width of the north section of the same upper floor as 27 feet (10:2). In all my drawings of the upper story I use 26 feet as a compromise figure.

13. Loseley MSS., Letters Undated, printed in its original spelling in Wallace's *Evolution*, p. 132, n. 1. The reason for Farrant's eagerness to get the little room is not obvious.

14. The descriptions of Neville's stairs are confusing, and give cause for doubt as to whether he built one flight or two. Some descriptions speak of the stairs as leading out of a kitchen and/or as having their feet in a little void room (15:4, 16:4, 16:6, *BR* 89:10), and others speak of them as "great stairs" without reference to any kitchen or void room (16:5, 16:6). I assume, but without great confidence, that Neville built two flights of stairs, one of them being designed merely to get hot dishes from the kitchen to the upstairs dining chamber as quickly as possible, and the other being great stairs for the use of his family and their guests.

153

15. This location for the First Blackfriars Playhouse is accepted also by Joseph Quincy Adams, *Shakespearean Playhouses*, p. 101, n. 1; Thorndike, *Shakespeare's Theater*, p. 299; and Wallace, *Evolution*, pp. 145–46. On the other hand, the theatre is placed in the southern, or Parliament Chamber, portion of the premises by Chambers, *Elizabethan Stage*, Vol. II, p. 496, and by Harbage, *Shakespeare and the Rival Traditions*, pp. 42–43.

16. From *Playes Confuted in five Actions*, p. 188, as quoted by Chambers, *Elizabethan Stage*, Vol. IV, p. 216.

17. *The Wars of Cyrus* was published in 1594 with a title page that said it had been "played by the Children of her Majesties Chappell." W. J. Lawrence believes that Farrant's song, "Alas, you salt sea Gods," was written to be sung by Panthea in the fifth act of the play, and therefore attributes the play to Farrant and to the early years of the First Blackfriars (*Times Literary Supplement*, August 11, 1921). Chambers, on the contrary, thinks that the play is clearly post-*Tamburlaine*, though perhaps based on a lost play by Farrant (*Elizabethan Stage*, Vol. III, pp. 311–12). James Paul Brawner, in a long and scholarly introduction, agrees with Lawrence, but adduces no new evidence conclusive enough to clinch the matter (*The Wars of Cyrus*, Urbana, 1942). As a matter of fact, *Cyrus* adds nothing to, and subtracts nothing from, what we learn of First Blackfriars staging from the Lyly and Peele plays. It uses a discoverable inner stage (line 93), a trap into which Nicasia leaps as into the River Euphrates (line 1667), and a poplar tree under which two persons can sit (line 892). It does not necessarily involve the medieval principle of polyscenic setting.

18. Wallace, *Evolution*, p. 153, n. 2.

19. *Ibid.*, p. 175n.

20. Each time that the word "curteines" or "curtaines" occurs (at III iii 29, III iii 37 stage direction, and IV iii 95), it refers to bed curtains, not stage curtains. Lyly never specifies the opening or closing of stage curtains, but his intentions are unmistakable. Some beds in some plays are thrust out upon the platform, but Sapho's bed is not one of them. Her bed and bedchamber are consistently associated with the inner stage, never with the platform.

21. Cf. *Campaspe* as edited by R. Warwick Bond, in *The Complete Works of John Lyly*.

22. Spectators are mentioned as invading the stage of Gray's Inn in 1594, and Sir John Harington speaks of them in 1596 as being packed in together on the stage at Cambridge University. But both these incidents seem rather to have been encroachments upon the stage than orderly observances of a recognized privilege. Cf. Graves, p. 105. Except for these episodes, the only evidence of sixteenth-century stage-sitting resides in two epigrams by Sir John Davies, one of which has the line "Doth either to the stage himselfe transfer," and the other of which has "He that dares take Tobaco on the stage." They were printed in 1599, but were probably written earlier. See Baskervill, pp. 581–89.

23. Wallace, *Evolution*, p. 175n.

24. *Ibid.*, p. 153n.

25. *Ibid.*, p. 154n.

26. *Ibid.*, p. 164.

27. Wallace, *Evolution*, p. 176.

28. *Ibid.*, p. 175n.

7

The Years Between
the First Blackfriars and the Second

THE EIGHT YEARS in the life of the First Blackfriars, and the twelve that intervened between its end and the initial moves toward the establishment of the Second, were crucial years in the history of the English stage. The theatrical events of those years will be related shortly in their broadest outlines. But first I must clear up some of the loose ends left by the collapse of the Farrant Blackfriars, and fix the status of the west-range buildings as of the time when James Burbage opened negotiations with Sir William More for the purchase of the Seven Great Upper Rooms, the rooms on the floor below, and the rooms to the west in the Duchy Chamber.

As we have seen, John Lyly held the sublease to the First Blackfriars Playhouse during its final months. Sir William More started suit in 1583 to recover occupancy of the premises, and when it became obvious that he would sooner or later prevail, Lyly decided to make a last-minute profit by selling the unexpired term of his lease before More could regain possession by judicial decision. He sold it to Henry Carey Lord Hunsdon, who already was the occupant of More's mansion house and garden.[1] The Lyly-Hunsdon lease is not in existence, but it is alluded to in several documents, as for example a letter written by More to Hunsdon on April 8, 1586, which speaks of "the houses you had of Lyly,"[2] and Hunsdon's reply, with its reference to "the leases which I bought of Lyly."[3] Two letters written by Lord Hunsdon prove that one of his houses was at the northern, or Old Buttery, end of the premises leased by Farrant, and that the other was at the southern, or Parliament Chamber, end. The first letter mentions "a pipe of water which was wont to belong to one of those houses, which is now by your consent turned to my Lord Cobham's house,"[4] and in so doing identifies one of the houses with the Old Buttery

155

block; for of all More's houses that one alone, save for his own mansion house, was supplied with water (cf. 16:6). The second letter, written several years later, shows that another of the houses was about to be incorporated in Burbage's Second Blackfriars Playhouse,[5] and thus identifies it as a part of the Parliament Chamber.

Sir William More seems to have acquiesced for the time being in Lyly's sale of the lease to Hunsdon and in Hunsdon's occupancy of the premises. His financial records show that in 1584 he had received £20 and £8 from Oxford and Lyly respectively (twice the amount paid by Farrant for the same premises), plus £50 from Hunsdon for the mansion house, and that in 1585 he received the same three amounts, all from Hunsdon.[6] But from the beginning he warned his Lordship that he would not renew the leases when they expired: "The houses you had of Lyly, I determine that as soon as they both shall come into my hands, to keep them to the only use of me and my children,"[7] and he remained firm in his refusal when the leases terminated in 1590 or 1591, his excuse being that he had promised the houses to his daughter, the wife of Sir John Wooley, reserving in them certain rooms for his own use.[8] By that time Lord Hunsdon had become her Majesty's Lord Chamberlain, and he would shortly, from 1594 until his death in 1596, be the patron of the troupe of actors of which Shakespeare was a member.

Richard Frith's lease of the west half of the Parliament Chamber ended on Lady Day, 1589; Lord Hunsdon's lease of the east half ended a year or so later, at which time Sir William More, his promises to his daughter notwithstanding, rented both halves—all seven of the Great Upper Rooms—to William de Laune, Doctor of Physic (19:5).[9] The room to the north, the room that had been the playhouse, became the Pipe Office (19:5,7) after More's appointment as Chamberlain of the Exchequer on November 23, 1591.

Lord Oxford's prodigal gifts to Lyly had included not only the lease to the premises occupied by the playhouse, but also the lease to a room on the floor below, where William Joyner had kept his school of fence. At some unknown date the Earl had bought the unexpired term of Joyner's lease and presented it to Lyly, and Lyly had sold it to another and greater master of fence, Rocco Bonetti.

Bonetti had come to England from Italy about 1569. He first lived in Warwick Lane. Later he acquired several parcels of real estate in the Blackfriars precinct. In addition to the lease that he bought from Lyly, he purchased from Mrs. Poole her life interest in the butler's lodging, rented other rooms and yards from her and More (Document 18), and spent a fortune in repairing and improving them. His ambitions for his houses and grounds outran both his discretion and his funds, for he erected new buildings on More's land without More's consent, and in 1585 he owed his workmen £200.[10] When his leases approached expiration, disgruntled workmen petitioned More not to grant extensions until their claims were settled, and because of this and Bonetti's irresponsibility, More was reluctant to renew. But Bonetti enlisted the aid of influential men, among them Lord Peregrin Willoughby, Sir John North, and Sir Walter Raleigh, and eventually got More to extend the leases, but for shorter terms than Bonetti desired.

Bonetti was the most popular fencing master in Elizabethan England. George Silver, in his *Paradoxes of Defence* (1599), says that he was "so excellent in his fight, that he would have hit any English man with a thrust, just upon any button in his doublet, and this was much spoken of."[11] He was teaching the art of fence at Blackfriars at the time when Shakespeare presumably wrote *Romeo and Juliet,* and it was he in all probability whom the dramatist had in mind when he characterized Tybalt as "the very butcher of a silk button":

> *Mercutio.* . . . He fights as you sing pricksong—keeps time, distance, and proportion; rests me his minim rest, one, two, and the third in your bosom! the very butcher of a silk button, a duellist, a duellist! a gentleman of the very first house, of the first and second cause. Ah, the immortal passado! the punto reverso! the hay!
> *Benvolio.* The what?
> *Merc.* The pox of such antic, lisping, affecting fantasticoes—these new tuners of accent![12]

Bonetti's popularity drew down upon him the resentment of English fencing masters, one of whom, Austen Bagger by name, went to his house in Blackfriars and challenged him to come out and fight: "Signior Rocco, thou that art thought to be the only cunning man in the world with thy weapon, thou that takest upon thee to hit any Englishman with a thrust upon any button, thou that takest upon thee to come over the seas, to teach the valiant Noblemen and Gentlemen of England to fight, thou cowardly fellow, come out of thy house if thou dare for thy life, I am come to fight with thee."[13] Rocco came out and was badly chopped up, but his prestige seems not to have suffered, and he continued to teach.

Bonetti's fencing school at Blackfriars came to an end shortly before

1596. The rooms that housed his school are described in the Burbage indenture as "the Middle Rooms or Middle Stories, late being in the tenure or occupation of Rocco Bonetti, and now being in the tenure or occupation of Thomas Bruskett, gentleman" (19:8). The room immediately to the north, the Blind Parlor of the surveys, was occupied by one Peter Johnson (19:15), who is unknown apart from the Burbage deed.

The three-storied infirmary was tenanted by Sir George Carey at the time of the Burbage purchase (19:8,9). He presumably had bought it from Anthony Kempe.

In 1596 Lord Cobham still had his house on the upper floor of the Old Buttery, north of the Pipe Office, and his garden north of the brick wall (19:20). The lower rooms, beneath the Pipe Office and Cobham's mansion, had probably been kept by Sir William More for his own use.

As for the Duchy Chamber, Charles Bradshaw had two upper rooms or chambers (19:11), Edward Merry had two rooms or lofts on the floor above (19:12), and Peter Johnson had two ground-level rooms, adjoining his two others in what used to be the Blind Parlor (19:16).

To recapitulate: the Parliament Chamber was occupied by Dr. de Laune at the time of the Burbage purchase. The Paved Hall, having recently been vacated by Bonetti, was occupied by Thomas Bruskett. The infirmary was owned by Sir George Carey. Peter Johnson had the Blind Parlor and the lowest floor of the Duchy Chamber. Two other men divided the upper floors of the Duchy Chamber between them. The south end of the Old Buttery's upper floor had become Sir William More's Pipe Office, and the north end was occupied by William Brooke Lord Cobham, as was also the Porter's Lodge.

The two decades between the founding of the First Blackfriars and the founding of the Second were years of ferment and achievement for the English drama. The theatre became an institution. New playhouses were built. Acting and playwriting ceased to be the avocations of amateurs and became the vocations of professionals. The great traditions of the Elizabethan stage were established, and dramatic composition embarked upon the course which was to make it the wonder of succeeding generations.

Farrant's Blackfriars and Burbage's Theater were followed quickly by other playhouses. A second public playhouse, the Curtain, was built one year after the Theater and near it in the area of Finsbury Fields. Some sort of playhouse was in operation by 1580 at Newington Butts, a mile to the southwest of London Bridge, where the archery butts were located. The Rose was built in 1587 just south of the Thames in the suburb known as the Bankside, and by 1596 the building of playhouses had attained such momentum that the Swan and the Second Blackfriars would be built that year or the next, and the Globe and the Fortune three or four years later.

All these playhouses were intended to be used by adult actors, not by children. Child actors were in eclipse. Boys had performed at Court nearly half again as often as men during the eight years before 1576, but men played there more than twice as often as boys during the next seven years,[14] and in the last decade of the century children's companies virtually ceased to exist. Of the four that had played at the First Black-friars between 1576 and 1584, not one remained active into the nineties. The Children of Windsor stopped acting after Farrant's death in 1580,[15] and the Earl of Oxford's Boys after the closing of the playhouse in 1584.[16] The Children of Paul's acted at Court as late as the winter season of 1589–1590, but after that not again until about 1600.[17] The Children of the Chapel dropped out of sight immediately after 1584 as a company playing at Court, but did not wholly discontinue their theatrical activities; they played at Ipswich and Norwich in 1586–1587, and at Leicester before Michaelmas in 1591.[18] This, however, was their last known performance until their resurrection at the Second Blackfriars and their subsequent participation in the War of the Theatres. After a second eight-year spell of activity for the Children of the Chapel and the Children of Paul's, the phenomenon of children's theatrical companies in England would come to an end forever.

As for the adult players, as recently as 1572 an Act of Parliament had classed them as rogues, vagabonds, and sturdy beggars unless they were the licensed servants of some baron or personage of greater degree.[19] The need to secure noble patronage had eliminated the weaker companies but had strengthened those that remained, and from 1576 onwards the troupes of men increased in number, prestige, stability, and profession-alism. Before that date the only companies to achieve prominence were the Earl of Leicester's Men and the Duttons; after it many companies flourished for longer or shorter periods, including those of the Earls of Warwick, Sussex, Essex, and Pembroke, and others of lesser name. Queen Elizabeth herself sponsored a company of players for a time, and from 1583 until about 1592 the Queen's Men were the undisputed leaders of the London stage. Later they lost ground to the Lord Chamberlain's Men with Richard Burbage and Shakespeare, and the Lord Admiral's

Men with Edward Alleyn. In 1598 the Chamberlain's and the Admiral's had so far outstripped all the other companies that.an order of the Privy Council limited the London companies to those two.[20]

Most importantly of all, it was during these same two decades that men of genius began to turn to playwriting as a livelihood. Before 1576 the names of Nicholas Udall and George Gascoigne are alone conspicuous. The next few years brought the university wits: Robert Greene, Thomas Kyd, Thomas Lodge, John Lyly, Christopher Marlowe, Thomas Nashe, and George Peele. Shakespeare began writing in 1590 or 1591, and by the time that the Second Blackfriars opened he had written a third of all his plays. With him and after him came such others as Beaumont and Fletcher, George Chapman, Thomas Dekker, Thomas Heywood, Ben Jonson, John Marston, Philip Massinger, Thomas Middleton, and John Webster.

Of Shakespeare's early plays, *Henry VI, Part 1,* was probably first performed in 1592 by Lord Strange's Men at the Rose. *The True Tragedy* (Shakespeare's *Henry VI, Part 3*) was introduced before 1595 by the Earl of Pembroke's Servants at a playhouse not specified. *Richard III,* presumably the play that Henslowe refers to as "Buckingham" in his diary, was played by Sussex's Men in 1593, probably at the Rose. And *Titus Andronicus* was produced by at least four companies prior to 1594: those of the Earl of Derby, the Earl of Pembroke, the Earl of Sussex, and (at Newington Butts) either the Lord Chamberlain's Men or the Lord Admiral's.

The company that had been Lord Strange's in 1592 had become the Earl of Derby's in 1593, when Lord Strange succeeded to his father's title; and upon his own death in 1594 it passed to the patronage of Henry Carey Lord Hunsdon, and became the Lord Chamberlain's Men. Shakespeare joined the company at about this time, being then in his thirtieth year. From then on he acted and wrote for this company alone. Richard Burbage, four years younger than he, was its leading actor, and already one of the two greatest actors in a great theatrical age. Their principal associates were John Heminges, Augustine Phillips, William Kempe, Thomas Pope, George Bryan, Henry Condell, William Sly, and Richard Cowley. All were members of the company as early as 1594, and twenty-nine years later their names were to be the first ten of the twenty-six listed in the First Folio as "The Names of the Principall Actors in all these Playes."

The first playhouse known to have been occupied by the Lord

Chamberlain's Men was Newington Butts, which they shared with the Lord Admiral's Men for ten days in June of 1594. During their brief joint tenancy of the playhouse, one company or the other played *Titus* twice and *The Taming of a* (or *the*) *Shrew* once. When the companies separated, the Admiral's Men went to the Rose and the Chamberlain's Men to the Theater, with the Cross Keys Inn as their winter quarters. They performed *The Comedy of Errors* at Gray's Inn in December.

The Theater was the Chamberlains' regular playhouse for the next three years. It was now eighteen years old, and was still owned and managed by its builder, James Burbage, the father of Cuthbert and Richard. There Shakespeare acted, and there the company introduced his plays of the 1594–1597 period, they presumably being *The Two Gentlemen of Verona, Love's Labour's Lost, Romeo and Juliet, Richard II, A Midsummer Night's Dream, King John,* and *The Merchant of Venice.*[21]

As has been said, the elder Burbage had built the Theater upon rented land. The ground lease was due to expire in April of 1597. Long before that date—probably two or three years before—Burbage began his efforts to get the landlord, Giles Alleyn, to grant him the renewal that was stipulated as his right in the original contract. Alleyn did not refuse; on the contrary, he promised to renew, but perpetually found pretexts for putting it off. It was in his interest to keep Burbage dangling. The existing lease gave Burbage the right to pull down the building and remove its timbers at any time before the lease should expire, but not afterwards; if the building was still standing when the lease ran out, it automatically became the property of the landlord. After months of fruitless effort Burbage became convinced that Alleyn had no intention of renewing the lease, and, without waiting for the expiration date to draw near, he began to look about for a site for a new playhouse. His choice fell upon the Parliament Chamber in the Blackfriars precinct. He bought it more than a year before the ground lease expired, probably hoping to have it ready for the Lord Chamberlain's Men by the time that they had to vacate the Theater.

Burbage knew that a playhouse in the Blackfriars precinct would give the company unrivaled advantages and prestige. For the first time, a company of adult actors would have a playhouse within the City walls; for the first time, adult actors would play regularly in a "private" playhouse, with high entrance fees to exclude the rabble and a roof to exclude the rain. It would be in one of the most fashionable districts of London, close at hand for the courtly playgoer and far from the suburbs with their odium of stews. Under such conditions it would invite the attendance of the nobility and gentry, and perhaps even of royalty itself; and with all its other advantages, it would be exempt from the jurisdiction of the City authorities. James Burbage had built England's first outdoor playhouse; he now proposed to build England's first indoor playhouse for adult actors.

Our first intimation of his purpose is contained in a letter written to Sir William More on January 9, 1596, by Henry Carey Lord Hunsdon, who, as patron of the Lord Chamberlain's Men and as a former resident of the precinct, may have been consulted by Burbage in advance. Lord Hunsdon wrote in part:

> And understanding that you have already parted with part of your house to some that means to make a playhouse in it, and also hearing that you mean to let or sell your other house, which once I had also, these are heartily to pray and desire you that I may have it at your hand.[22]

The date of Hunsdon's letter suggests that Burbage approached More in late 1595. Seemingly the two men had little difficulty in reaching an agreement. The purchase was consummated on February 4, 1596, and Burbage took possession immediately.[23]

1. *BR* 124:12–14.
2. *BR* 123:14.
3. *BR* 123:22.
4. *BR* 123:19–21.
5. *BR* 123:35–40.
6. *BR* 123:9–12; Chambers, *Elizabethan Stage*, Vol. II, p. 497, n. 3.
7. *BR* 123:14–16.
8. *BR* 124:9–12; Wallace, *Evolution*, pp. 186–87.
9. William de Laune's son, Gideon de Laune, was to be one of the founders of the Society of Apothecaries, which later was to take over the Old Buttery building.
10. Wallace, *Evolution*, p. 190, n. 3.
11. P. 16.
12. *Romeo and Juliet*, II iv 21–30.
13. George Silver, *Paradoxes of Defence*, p. 65.
14. Chambers, *Elizabethan Stage*, Vol. II, p. 4.
15. *Ibid.*, Vol. II, p. 64.
16. *Ibid.*, Vol. II, p. 101.
17. *Ibid.*, Vol. II, pp. 16–23.
18. *Ibid.*, Vol. II, pp. 40–41.
19. *Ibid.*, Vol. IV, pp. 269–70, no. xxiv.
20. *Ibid.*, Vol. IV, p. 325, no. cxiv.
21. This list is based upon the chronology given by Chambers in *William Shakespeare*, Vol. 1, p. 270.
22. *BR* 123:37–40 (misdated 1595), and Wallace, *Evolution*, p. 195, n. 7. The "other house" was probably Sir William More's own mansion house, which Lord Hunsdon had occupied in 1584 and 1585 at an annual rental of £50 (*BR* 124:12–14). Sir William did not rerent the house to Lord Hunsdon; instead, he leased it to Ralph Bowes on March 3, 1596.

Lord Hunsdon died about six months after writing his letter to More, and his son Sir George Carey, who owned and occupied the former Blackfriars infirmary, succeeded to the title and to the patronage of the company of players. For a few months thereafter the actors were called Hunsdon's Men, but they regained their previous name when the son himself became Lord Chamberlain.
23. Wallace gives details of the financial aspects of the transaction in "The First London Theatre," pp. 23–24.

✠ 8 ✠

The Parliament Chamber
as Playhouse

BURBAGE'S PURCHASE included all the Upper Frater block except the
Firmary, and all the Duchy Chamber building. The indenture, with
Burbage's signature and seal attached, still exists as one of the documents
in the Loseley collection. It records that he acquired possession of the
following properties in exchange for £600 of lawful money of England:

A] The Parliament Chamber, now designated as "all those seven
great upper rooms as they are now divided, being all upon one floor and
sometime being one great and entire room" (19:2);

B] The lead roof over these upper rooms, together with the stairs
leading up to the roof (19:2,3);

C] The great stone walls that enclosed, divided, and belonged to
the seven great upper rooms, and all their wainscot, glass, doors, locks,
keys, and bolts (19:4,6);

D] The great pair of winding stairs leading up to the rooms out of
the yard next to the Pipe Office (19:5);

E] The use, but not the ownership, of a vault under the rooms or
under the entry between them and the Pipe Office (19:7);

F] The Paved Hall, now called the Middle Rooms or Middle
Stories, together with the door and entry at their southwest corner
(19:8,9), and the Blind Parlor, now described as the two lower rooms in
the occupation of Peter Johnson (19:15);

G] Two vaults or cellars under the Middle Rooms at their north
end (19:10);

H] The upper floor of the Duchy Chamber, now described as "two
upper rooms or chambers . . . at the north end of the said seven great
upper rooms and on the west side thereof," and also the floor below
(19:11,16);

ɪ] Other rooms, lofts, garrets, and stairs over the Duchy Chamber or over the entry next the Pipe Office (19:12–14);

ȷ] The Kitchen Yard (19:20), and also a little yard probably a part of the yard south of the Duchy Chamber (19:18).

We know, on the authority of Alexander Hawkins, that the great hall which contained the Second Blackfriars Playhouse was 66 feet long from north to south by 46 feet wide from east to west (40:3); and of the two houses bought by Burbage, only one was large enough to contain a hall of those dimensions. That one was the Upper Frater. The two scholars who have preceded me in examining the subject have believed that the playhouse occupied that building's lower floor. I contend, on the contrary, that it was installed in the Parliament Chamber. The following considerations support this theory:

First, the great hall that had housed parliaments and a legatine trial presumably was large and high enough, as well as handsome and accessible enough, to serve for an indoor theatre.

Second, the wording of Burbage's Deed of Purchase indicates his primary interest in the upper story; it mentions the upper floor first and oftenest. After the preliminaries of date, names of parties, and price, the first item to be specified is "all those seven great upper rooms" (19:2), and thereafter that cumbersome phrase is used fifteen times more in the course of the deed. Far less emphasis is placed upon the rooms on the floor below. The Middle Rooms or Middle Stories are not mentioned until the forty-seventh line of the document as printed in *Blackfriars Records*, pages 60 to 69, and are mentioned only five times in all; Peter Johnson's two rooms are not mentioned until the one-hundred-and-first line, and are mentioned only once. Similar evidence of special interest attaches to the staircase leading to the upper floor. It would be of great concern to Burbage if it were destined to carry playgoing crowds to the auditorium, of less concern if it were to lead only to a dormitory[1] or to storage lofts. Its actual importance is indicated by its being placed fourth in the list of items, after only some additional specifications relating to the seven great upper rooms.

Third, the lower story was unsuitable. It was called upon to support the weight of the Parliament Chamber above, and therefore was heavily vaulted and piered. Moreover, the unusual width of that great hall demanded that piers should rise from the center of the lower floor rather than merely from its edges, and such piers would interpose an intolerable barrier between spectators and stage. Furthermore, the ceiling of any such undercroft was in all probability far too low[2] to accommodate the galleries that are known to have existed, and to permit actors to make impressive descents from the stage heavens.

In locating the playhouse on the top floor with nothing over it but the roof, I am not forgetting the legal documents that describe it as "all that great hall or room, with the rooms over the same." That description probably originated in Richard Burbage's lost Indenture of Lease to Henry Evans, and thereafter, with trifling variations, it became the accepted terminology by which litigants designated the playhouse in their depositions. Robert Keysar, for instance, used the phrase in his complaint against Richard Burbage and others (41:1), and Burbage and his codefendants used it in their reply (41:7). Henry Evans used it in his Bill of Complaint against Edward Kirkham (42:1), and Kirkham used it in his Answer (42:8); and Alexander Hawkins used it in Latin translation— *"tocius illius magne aule vel loci anglice Roome cum locis anglice roomes super eadem"*—in his reply to the complaint brought against him by Rastall and Kirkham (40:3). One cannot doubt, therefore, that the great hall had rooms of some sort above it; and yet not one real estate document mentions any rooms at all as being over the Upper Frater, the Parliament Chamber, or the Seven Great Upper Rooms.[3]

I attach little importance to this omission; it does not, to my mind, indicate that no such rooms existed. After all, no single Blackfriars survey or lease or deed pretends to be complete and comprehensive. Each deals only with a particular part of the precinct at a particular time, and each omits many details. All must be correlated and integrated if an attempt is to be made to view the friary as a whole, and even then many items are wanting. For instance, no document mentions the stream of water that, as inevitably in all precincts, ran along the outskirts of the cloistral buildings to carry away the refuse of the kitchen and rere-dorter. None mentions the calefactory or warming house that adjoined the dorter in every monastery and friary. Only one real estate document alludes to the Parish Church of St. Anne, and that one does so only to deny that such a church ever existed; and yet, as we know, such a church is proved beyond peradventure to have stood within the friary walls.[4] And if items such as these were overlooked, why not rooms over the Parliament Chamber? They are not likely to have been rooms of any great importance, and the failure of the pre-Burbage documents to mention them does not prove that there were not, then or later, any "rooms over the same."

But perhaps the phrase is to be explained on a wholly different basis; perhaps the rooms did not exist when Burbage made his purchase, but were created by him in the process of converting his property to theatrical uses. This seems likelier than the other to be the true explanation, for the failure of the Burbage Indenture of Purchase to specify any such rooms cannot, like some of the omissions previously mentioned, be attributed to their lying outside the area under consideration or to mere casual oversight. The Burbage deed deals with only two buildings, and it lists their component parts with meticulous care. It itemizes between thirty and forty separate rooms, entries, stairs, yards, and so forth, and even goes so far as to stipulate "all the wainscot, glass, doors, locks, keys and bolts" (19:6). Not once, however, does it mention anything as being over the seven great upper rooms except "the roof over the same covered with lead" (19:2). As a result, one is probably justified in concluding that no such rooms existed when Burbage bought the building in 1596. Four years later, however, when he first used the troublesome phrase in his Indenture of Lease to Evans, they did exist. By that time the great hall had been converted to a theatre, and as a part of that conversion an enclosed platform had been built high above the stage to house the apparatus used in celestial flights.

We know that such apparatus had been provided because we know that the playhouse staged many flights during the Children's tenancy and afterwards; and we know that the apparatus necessary for their staging demanded an elevated room or rooms to contain the winches by which the actors were raised and lowered, the eagles and thrones upon which they rode, and the stagehands who cranked the windlasses. This enclosed platform, similar to the "huts" in the public theatres, perfectly fits the description of "rooms over the same"; and the supposition that Burbage had those rooms in mind when he first used the phrase is strengthened by our failure to find it in any document antedating the conversion of the hall into a playhouse, and by our finding it repeatedly in documents that deal with the hall not as a parcel of real estate, but as a theatrical property.

The problem of "the rooms over the same" presumably was the consideration that led Dr. Joseph Quincy Adams to reject the Parliament Chamber as the site of the playhouse. He felt that the playhouse could occupy no hall except one that had rooms above it, and he did not recognize any rooms as being over the Parliament Chamber; he therefore located the playhouse in the Blind Parlor and Paved Hall on the floor below, so that the Parliament Chamber itself could supply the need for "rooms over the same."[5]

Professor Charles W. Wallace also placed "the main body of the theatre" on the lower floor, but not for the same reason; the problem of rooms overhead gave him little pause; he dismissed it by asserting that "rooms, probably of the usual dormer sort, were built above the Great Hall."[6] His reason for basing the playhouse on the lower floor was the need to find height enough for a theatre. Wallace, it will be remembered, thought of the Parliament Chamber as having a flat roof[7] and therefore as being too low in itself to provide the necessary height; he consequently met the need for height by assuming that the floor of the Chamber was torn out so that the Parliament Chamber and the story below could combine to form one lofty hall.[8] Dr. Adams did not endorse this theory, but instead undertook to prove that the ceilings of the Paved Hall and Blind Parlor "must have been of unusual height."[9] He made heavy weather of this, for the probabilities were all against him.

The Second Blackfriars Playhouse, then, was installed in the Parliament Chamber, the top floor of the so-called Upper Frater, whose dimensions are given as 107 feet in length by 52 feet in breadth externally (4:5, 6:21), and whose internal dimensions were 101 feet by 46 feet within 3-foot walls. Entrance was at the north, by way of "all that great pair of winding stairs, with the staircase thereunto belonging, which leadeth up unto the same seven great upper rooms out of the great yard there which doth lie next unto the Pipe Office" (19:5). This great yard, the Kitchen Yard of the surveys, was to be used in the heyday of the playhouse for the arrival and turning of the playgoers' coaches; its site is commemorated by the name Playhouse Yard in the London of today. And since the entrance was at the north, the stage was toward the south.

But, in contrast with the inside dimensions of 101 by 46 feet as given above, the Hawkins deposition of 1609 gives the dimensions of the Great Hall as being 66 by 46 feet. Its Latin text describes the "magna aula" as

> continens per estimacionem in longitudine ab australe ad borealem partem eiusdem sexaginta et sex pedes assissae sit plus sive minus et in latitudine ab occidentale ad orientalem partem eiusdem quadraginta et sex pedes assissae sit plus sive minus (40:3).

The width agrees perfectly with the presumed interior width of the Parliament Chamber, but the length is 35 feet shorter.

I believe, however, that not all the playhouse was squeezed into the 66-foot length, but only those parts of it that lay in front of the scenic wall. Of necessity, a wall traversed the hall in an east-west direction; it separated those areas that were normally visible to spectators from those that were normally screened and reserved for behind-the-scenes activities. In front of it lay the auditorium and the platform; in back of it lay the inner stages, the dressing rooms, the corridors where actors awaited their cues, and the places where costumes and properties were stored. The wall formed a permanent background for action on the outer stage. Its structural features included the doors by which actors entered the platform from the backstage tiring-house, the window stages and balcony on the level above, and on each level the aperture of one of the inner stages.

I shall hope to demonstrate that the central section of the scenic wall was just 66 feet south of the north end of the Parliament Chamber, and thus that the wall itself was the terminus of the 66 feet specified by Hawkins as the north-to-south length of the Great Hall. But the playhouse as a whole did not stop there: its backstage elements stretched back beyond the wall into the remaining 35-foot depth of the Parliament Chamber.[10]

The wall had been built by James Burbage in the process of converting the Parliament Chamber into a playhouse. He had not had full freedom of choice in placing it; on the contrary, he had been forced to locate it with reference to a wall on the floor below. Burbage, it will be remembered, had bought the Middle Rooms or Middle Stories, but not Sir George Carey's house to the south of them (19:8). His holdings on the lower floor thus terminated at the wall that separated the former Paved Hall from the former Firmary, estimated to have been 70 feet south of the building's northern end.[11] This wall, therefore, the wall that divided Burbage's property from Carey's, was the southern limit of the space available to Burbage for theatrical purposes on the lower floor.

The Second Blackfriars had need of such space on a lower story, just as the First had had need of it, and for precisely the same reason. Burbage found that the space between the underbraces of the platform and the floor of the hall was inadequate for trapwork at the Second Blackfriars, just as Farrant had found it inadequate at the First. Both men, in consequence, were forced to make use of space on a lower floor as a point of origin for ascents by trap. I touched upon this matter briefly on an earlier page, and must develop it further at the present time.

The floor of any stage, whether medieval or modern, must be a few inches below the eye level of spectators seated at the front of the auditorium. In modern theatres this normally results in the stage's being raised about 3 feet 4 inches above the floor of the pit at Row A. But a flat floor like that at Blackfriars called for a lower stage than does the sloping floor of today, and the playgoer of 1600 was somewhat shorter than his successor of the nineteen-sixties. Probably, therefore, the platform at Blackfriars was not more than 36 inches above the floor of the hall.

It was undoubtedly like the stage of the Fortune in being built of "good and sufficyent newe deale bourdes of the whole thicknes," which means boards perhaps as much as 3 inches thick;[12] and, timber construction being what it was at that period, the stage floor was supported on beams that were perhaps 10 inches in scantling. Under such conditions the clearance between the beams and the floor is not likely to have been more than 24 or 26 inches.

As the discussion of trap work in later pages will show, the Second Blackfriars frequently had supernatural personages rise by trap from the netherworld to the stage. The allegorical figures of Envy and Echo did so, and Night and Neptune, and Proteus with other sea deities, and the God of the River with Amoret in his arms. Just as it was impossible to suppose that Pluto or a bejeweled tree could rise in an erect position from a 2-foot-high substage area at the First Blackfriars, so it is impossible to believe that Neptune could crawl out from so low a ceiling at the Second Blackfriars and still rise to the stage with the majesty befitting the God of the Sea, or that the God of the River, with the maid Amoret in his arms, could do so with majesty or without, or that Proteus and at least three other sea deities could descend simultaneously into so shallow a headroom without losing all their dignity on the way down. Necessarily, then, the ascents originated in a room beneath the Great Hall, and the descents ended there, passing in their transit through an opening cut through the floor of the hall under the trap. There, too, in a room beneath the hall, were the windlasses that raised and lowered the trap, and the stagehands that cranked them.

But the Second Blackfriars, unlike the First, had two traps. One was in the middle of the platform, and the other was farther back and farther south, behind the line of the scenic wall. Although it did not, as did the platform trap, have a raising-and-lowering mechanism and men to operate it, it did need enough space below the stage to permit actors to ascend and descend in an upright position. But the room that provided this vertical space could not have been farther south than the southern limit of the property that Burbage owned on the lower story, or 70 feet south of the building's northern end. This restriction determined the position of the southernmost of the two traps, the one that lay behind the scenic wall and within the inner stage. It demanded that the rear edge of that trap should not be farther south than the vertical projection of the south wall of the room below.

The rear-stage trap never needed to afford passage for large groups or large objects, but only for actors climbing up or down a ladder or stairs in single file. It therefore did not need to be more than 3 feet wide from north to south. But it did need to have some little space between it and the stage curtain, so that it could on occasion be equipped with properties, as in *Cynthia's Revels*, *The Isle of Gulls*, and *The Case Is Altered*; its front edge may thus have been a foot to the rear of the curtain line. By this reckoning, therefore, the curtain line was 66 feet distant from the north end of the Great Hall, and thus the curtain, the aperture in which the curtain was suspended, and the wall through which the aperture was cut, constituted the elements that terminated the 66-foot length specified by Hawkins.

Admittedly, there is one flaw in this identification: although Burbage could not have placed the scenic wall farther south, he could have placed it farther north. But he had everything to lose, and nothing to gain, by doing so, for space behind the wall was expendable, while space in front of it was at a premium. The space to the north of the wall held both the all-important platform and the spectators' seats; to sacrifice any part of that space was to forfeit revenue or to reduce the area of a stage that needed all the depth it could get. Space behind the scenic wall, on the other hand, was, after the first dozen feet or so, service space only, augmentable by space on the floor below. All considerations concurred in suggesting to Burbage that he place the wall as far to the south as he could, and nothing suggests that he failed to do so. It seems highly probable, therefore, that the playhouse as a whole was not limited to 66 feet in depth, but that it occupied the entire 101-foot interior length of the Parliament Chamber.

Stairs led down from the Parliament Chamber to the floor below. They are not mentioned in any known document, but they would have been indispensable; if they did not exist when Burbage bought the property, he must have built them; and in view of the special theatrical conditions that they had to meet, they probably were in fact built to his specifications. Those conditions demanded that actors should have a means of getting from one floor to the other out of sight of the audience;

an actor, for example, who was about to make an ascent by trap, must be able to get to the lower floor from which the ascent must start, and to do so without being seen by spectators. The stair must consequently have its head to the south or rear of the scenic wall, and its foot to the north of the downstairs wall between Burbage's property and Carey's. It was used also by actors, stagehands, and stage-sitters who entered the building by way of "the door and entry which do lie next unto the gate entering into the house of the said Sir George Carey, and used to and from the said Middle Rooms or Middle Stories out of a lane or way leading unto the house of the said Sir George Carey" (19:9), and who, being now on the lower floor, must mount to the Parliament Chamber on the level above. Since the door and entry gave access to Carey's premises as well as to Burbage's, they were at the southern end of Burbage's holdings on the lower floor.

Having consummated his purchase of the Seven Great Upper Rooms on February 4, 1596, James Burbage proceeded immediately to convert them into a playhouse; but his plans became known, and in November of that same year the inhabitants of the Blackfriars precinct addressed a petition to the Privy Council, humbly beseeching their Honors "to take order that the same rooms may be converted to some other use, and that no playhouse may be used or kept there" (22:3). They alleged that a "common playhouse" such as Burbage planned would "grow to be a very great annoyance and trouble . . . to all the inhabitants of the same precinct, both by reason of the great resort and gathering together of all manner of vagrant and lewd persons that, under color of resorting to the plays, will come thither and work all manner of mischief, and also to the great pestering and filling up of the same precinct, if it should please God to send any visitation of sickness as heretofore hath been, for that the same precinct is already grown very populous; and besides that the same playhouse is so near the church that the noise of the drums and trumpets will greatly disturb and hinder both the ministers and parishioners in time of divine service and sermons; . . . as also for that there hath not at any time heretofore been used any common playhouse within the same precinct, but that now, all players being banished by the Lord Mayor from playing within the City by reason of the great inconveniences and ill rule that followeth them, they now think to plant themselves in Liberties" (22:2–3).

The petition was signed by thirty-one residents of the precinct, including the redoubtable Lady Elizabeth Russell, dowager; Richard

Field, the printer of Shakespeare's poems; and George Carey Lord Hunsdon, who was the patron of the company of players at the time the petition was filed. The Privy Council promptly "forbad the use of the said house for plays."[13]

Whether or not his mounting troubles at the Theater and at Blackfriars were a contributing factor, James Burbage died soon after, in February 1597, at the age of sixty-seven. To his son Richard, the great tragedian, he left his costly and profitless investment in the Blackfriars; to his son Cuthbert he left the Theater, now tottering under a load of lawsuits and debts. The original lease for the Theater property still had two months to run, and Cuthbert tried, as his father had done before him, to have it renewed, but his efforts came to nothing. In July all the London playhouses were closed by order of the Privy Council as a result of the *Isle of Dogs* affair at the Swan; but when the ban was lifted in the autumn and all the other playhouses reopened, the Theater remained closed. Almost certainly the Chamberlain's Men moved at that time to the Curtain. Late the next year Cuthbert Burbage and his associates dismantled the Theater, ignoring the expiration of the lease and with it their legal right to do so, and carried the timbers across the Thames to Southwark, where they used them in building a new theater called the Globe. Thither the Lord Chamberlain's Men moved in 1599.

1. Joseph Quincy Adams, *Shakespearean Playhouses*, pp. 192, 197, says that the Parliament Chamber was kept as a lodging for residential purposes. He does not cite his authority for this statement.

2. We do not, of course, know the height of the rooms beneath the Parliament Chamber, but we do know that the Ludgate crypt or undercroft that was unearthed in 1900 was about 17½ feet high, and that, although it was only about 27 feet wide, its vaulted ceiling was supported by a row of marble shafts running down the middle of the floor. See p. 47 above. Such undercrofts as I have seen beneath great halls in other monasteries and friaries did not, by my estimate, in any instance exceed 24 to 26 feet in height.

3. I doubt that the chamber or loft that Richard Frith demised to John Austen in 1564–1565 would qualify as a room over the great hall. The indenture describes it as "all that one chamber or loft with a chimney therein, being next under the roof where the high gallery of William More . . . did stand, which said loft or story is the uppermost and highest story of the tenement or messuage now in the tenure and occupation of Thomas Hall, musician, the which said chamber or story amongst other the said Richard Frith hath." (*BR* 119:7–13).

4. See pp. 121-22 above.

5. *Shakespearean Playhouses*, p. 197.

6. *Children of the Chapel*, p. 40. Wallace cites no evidence in support of his assertion.

7. *Op. cit.*, p. 37. See comments on pp. 104–05 above.

8. *Op. cit.*, p. 49, and *Evolution*, p. 196. Wallace's theory ignores the formidable difficulties and risks that the removal of an intervening floor would entail. The Upper Frater was built of stone, and in such a building the elimination of a floor with its supporting piers and vaults might easily endanger the entire fabric.

9. *Shakespearean Playhouses*, pp. 195–97.

10. In thus making the 66-foot length of the "magna aula" include only the auditorium and platform, and exclude the rear stage and tiring-house, I am taking a position not shared by those who have preceded me in expressing opinions on the subject—Joseph Quincy Adams, Granville-Barker, and Wallace—all of whom assume that the 66-foot length contained the entire playhouse. For Adams, see *Shakespearean Playhouses*, p. 196 and plan on p. 187. For Granville-Barker, see *Prefaces to Shakespeare*, London ed., 2nd Series, p. 251, or Princeton ed., Vol. I, p. 471. For Wallace, see his "suggestive plat" in *Children of the Chapel*, pp. 50–51, or his floor plan in *Century Magazine*, Vol. LXXX No. 5 (September 1910), p. 748. Chambers is noncommittal (*Elizabethan Stage*, Vol. II, p. 513).

11. See pp. 96–97 above, and Fig. 15.

12. Cf. Smith, p. 216. The use of the word "deal" does not exclude the probability that the timber was oak. A deal board might be any thickness up to 3 inches. See *O.E.D.*, *s.v.* "deal."

13. Chambers, *Elizabethan Stage*, Vol. IV, p. 320, no. cvii.

⚔ 9 ⚔

The Little Eyases

IN THE MEANTIME, Richard Burbage had the Blackfriars property on his hands. It lay there unused, profiting no one. In spite of the Privy Council's ruling, he was still convinced that the premises must be used as a playhouse, for "if the said hall were converted from a playhouse to any other ordinary use, it would be of very little value" (43:9). The Privy Council, to be sure, had prohibited a common playhouse, but not necessarily a private one, and both the Council and the Blackfriars residents had previously tolerated the boy players under Farrant. Clearly, therefore, the answer to his problem lay in turning the theatre into a private playhouse tenanted by a company of children, in imitation of and in competition with the Children of Paul's, who a few months earlier had entered upon a new period of theatrical activity. With this in mind he approached Henry Evans, or else Evans, with the same thing in mind, approached him—the same Evans who had briefly managed the First Blackfriars more than twenty years earlier. Their discussions led to Burbage's renting the hall to Evans for twenty-one years at a rental of £40 per year. They signed the indenture on September 2, 1600. The lease became effective on the 29th of September following.

The Evans–Giles–Robinson Regime

The lease is no longer extant, but its essential provisions can be confidently reconstructed. Its terms were later recited no fewer than eleven times in various legal documents, including depositions by the two principals. The version here transcribed is the one that Henry Evans embodied in his Answer in the Kirkham *vs.* Paunton dispute; the others agree with it in all important respects, except for an obvious misdating by Burbage

175

in reporting it twelve years later (43:19). Evans recites its terms as follows:

> Richard Burbage, of the parish of St. Leonard's in Shoreditch in the County of Middlesex, gentleman, by his Indenture of Lease bearing date the second day of September in the two-and-fortieth year of the reign of our sovereign Lady Elizabeth, the Queen's Majesty that now is, hath leased and to farm letten unto . . . Henry Evans all that great hall or room, with the rooms over the same, in the said Indenture mentioned, situate in the precinct of the Blackfriars in London, to hold unto the said Henry Evans, his executors and assigns, from the feast of St. Michael the Archangel next ensuing after the date of said Indenture, unto the end and term of one-and-twenty years from thence next ensuing and fully to be complete and ended, yielding and paying therefor yearly during the said term unto the said Richard Burbage, his executors and assigns, forty pounds of lawful money of England, at four feasts or terms in the year; that is to say, at the feasts of the birth of our Lord God, the annunciation of the blessed Virgin Mary, the nativity of St. John Baptist, and St. Michael the Archangel, by even and equal portions to be paid.[1]

The Indenture also contained a stipulation that restrained Evans "from granting, assigning or putting away the premises, or any part thereof, for any term whatsoever, or unto any person whatsoever" (41:15), and another that bound him to keep the premises in good repair at his own expense (40:4, 41:8).

Richard Burbage was a shrewd businessman as well as a great actor, and he took no chances. He realized that the success of Evans's enterprise was not something that could be taken for granted. The playhouse might be prohibited, the danger of this being the greater in view of the Privy Council's action in June of that same year in repressing all playhouses except the Globe and the Fortune.[2] Furthermore, Evans might have difficulty in assembling a company of acting boys, the more so since children's companies had not been playing during the past ten years until Paul's reopened just a few months earlier; and even if both these obstacles should be surmounted, it might turn out that the vogue of child actors had passed. Burbage therefore exacted of Evans and his son-in-law, Alexander Hawkins, a joint bond in the huge amount of £400 as security for the payment of the rent and the performance of all the other convenants contained in the lease (cf. 43:19).

Evans had Nathaniel Giles and James Robinson as his associates in the project. Giles was the Master of the Children of the Chapel

Royal, having succeeded to that office upon the death of William Hunnis in 1597. He held his commission from the Queen. It cannot be supposed, therefore, that he flew in the face of the Privy Council's interdiction of 1596 without having received some intimation of her Majesty's acquiescence. If plays were to be given by the Children of her Chapel, that fact could not long remain unknown to her; and if they were given without her prior approval, the Queen would not be slow to make her displeasure felt. No evidence of her consent is upon record, but it is implied in her summoning the Children of the Chapel to play before her on January 6 and February 22, 1601, with Giles as payee. As things turned out, neither the Queen nor the Privy Council nor the precinct residents protested; the venture's great hazard lay in the qualities of the managers themselves.

Records fail to indicate just when the Children of the Chapel began to play at the Second Blackfriars. The following circumstances suggest that they cannot have begun before the last quarter of 1600:

A] The terms of the lease, as recited by Evans, indicate that his tenancy did not become effective until September 29, 1600, "the Feast of St. Michael the Archangel next ensuing after the date of the said Indenture."

B] Alexander Hawkins testified in 1609 that Evans entered into and took possession of the great hall "immediately after the said Feast of St. Michael the Archangel" (40:5).

c] Richard Burbage twice implied, and once stated categorically, that the organizing of the company of boy actors was still in the future at the time when he and Evans executed the lease of the playhouse. In his Answer in the Kirkham *vs.* Paunton dispute, he testified that at the date of the rental Evans "intended then presently to erect or set up a company of boys . . . in the same" (43:19), and that he (Burbage) had exacted a bond from Evans as security for payment of the rent, for fear that his tenant might be in arrears "except the said Evans could erect and keep a company of playing boys or others" (43:19). More definitely, he said that "*after* [the italics being mine] the making of the said lease unto the said Evans, he, the said Evans, did treat and deal with the complainant Kirkham and with one William Rastall and Thomas Kendall . . . about the setting and making up a company of boys and others to play plays and interludes in the said playhouse" (43:20).[3]

D] Of the plays known or believed to have been performed by the Children at Blackfriars, only one—*The Case Is Altered*—was supposedly written before 1600, and that not in the form in which it was later played by the Children. And finally,

E] Not until January 6 and February 22, 1601, did the Children appear at Court after their absence of seventeen years.

I have gone into the question of date the more fully because C. W. Wallace[4] and F. G. Fleay[5] have contended that the Children began to act at Blackfriars well before 1600, and also because the matter of date has a bearing upon the "little eyases" passage in *Hamlet*. Wallace believes that the Children began to act there "at a very early date," by which he seems to mean 1597. He bases his theory upon Evans's speaking of the great hall as having "then or late" been in his tenure or occupation at the time when the lease was signed (42:1); upon Richard Burbage's use of the word "beforetime" when he said that, in granting the lease to Evans, he had in mind that Evans would produce "plays and interludes in the said playhouse in such sort as beforetime had been there used" (43:19), and upon the fact that *The Case Is Altered*, whose title pages state that it was "sundry times Acted by the Children of the Blacke-friers," is mentioned in a book written before 1599.[6]

But "then or late" in the context of an Elizabethan legal document deserves no consideration at all; lawyers sprinkled it in their instruments liberally as a matter of routine, to guard against the eventuality that the condition under discussion, as for example a tenancy, might have begun or terminated before the date specified, without the writer's knowledge. "Beforetime" undoubtedly alludes to the First Blackfriars of twenty-odd years earlier. And *The Case Is Altered*, having first been produced before 1599 by some company unknown, was not played at Blackfriars nor published until several years later, and then in a version that seemingly had undergone extensive revision.[7]

If we believe, as evidently we must, that Evans did not take possession of the playhouse until September, 1600, then we must acknowledge that the Chapel Children and their managers achieved a surprising success in an astonishingly short time, since by 1603, when the spurious First Quarto of *Hamlet* was published—by which time, according to its title page, the play had already "beene diverse times acted by his Highnesse servants in the Cittie of London: as also in the two Universities of Cambridge and Oxford, and else-where"—the Children were so popular as to have thrown the Tragedians of the City into eclipse:

For the principall publike audience that
Came to them, are turned to private playes,
And to the humour of children (sig E3ʳ).

The "little eyases" passage, first printed in the Folio of 1623, tells of the Children's success in greater detail. It was presumably written in 1601 or 1602 at the latest, since the War of the Theatres was still being fought, though it was past its period of greatest frenzy. In two years at the outside, therefore, the company's managers had done these things: they had taken a never-used playhouse, a playhouse that had stood empty for three or four years, and had made it ready for public performances; they had gathered and trained a company of acting boys, none of whom had had any previous theatrical experience; they had commissioned plays and had had them written, delivered, and rehearsed; they had assembled properties and costumes; and after all these things had been done, they had still had time enough left for the Children to become the fashion and to force the adult actors to take to the road:

Hamlet.   How chances it they travel? Their residence, both in reputation and profit, was better both ways. . . . Do they hold the same estimation they did when I was in the city? Are they so follow'd?

Rosencrantz.   No indeed are they not.

Ham.   How comes it? Do they grow rusty?

Ros.   Nay, their endeavour keeps in the wonted pace; but there is, sir, an eyrie of children, little eyases, that cry out on the top of the question and are most tyrannically clapp'd for't. These are now the fashion, and so berattle the common stages (so they call them) that many wearing rapiers are afraid of goose-quills and dare scarce come thither.

Ham.   What, are they children? Who maintains 'em? How are they escoted? Will they pursue the quality no longer than they can sing? Will they not say afterwards, if they should grow themselves to common players (as it is most like, if their means are no better), their writers do them wrong to make them exclaim against their own succession?

Ros.   Faith, there has been much to do on both sides; and the nation holds it no sin to tarre them to controversy. There was, for a while, no money bid for argument unless the poet and the player went to cuffs in the question.

Ham.   Is't possible?

Guildenstern.   O, there has been much throwing about of brains.

Ham.   Do the boys carry it away?

Ros.   Ay, that they do, my lord—Hercules and his load too.[8]

179

I suggest that Shakespeare applied the name "little eyases" to the Children of the Chapel only, excluding the Children of Paul's, who at that time were the only other child actors. I base this opinion upon the following considerations:

First, Shakespeare used the singular noun, "an eyrie," rather than the plural "eyries."

Second, the Children of the Chapel could offer damaging competition to the Lord Chamberlain's Men; the Children of Paul's could not do so in any like degree. The Chapel Children occupied a great hall capable of accommodating several hundred persons;[9] the Paul's Boys occupied a playhouse that probably was much smaller, as evidenced by its being described as "S. Paules singing Schoole"[10] and as "behinde the Convocation-house in Pauls."[11]

Third, the prestige of the Chapel Boys was much greater than that of the Paul's Boys in the period with which we are concerned, and their drawing power was accordingly stronger. Their greater prestige is indicated by their playing at Court five times during the winters of 1600–01 and 1601–02, whereas during the same winters the Children of Paul's played there only once.[12]

Ben Jonson also bears testimony to the crippling effect of the competition presented by the Children. In *Poetaster*, acted in 1601, a character named Histrio, who serves as spokesman for the public theatres in general and perhaps for the Globe in particular, tells of a play that he plans to present: "O, it will get us a huge deale of money (Captaine) and wee have need on't; for this winter ha's made us all poorer, then so many starv'd snakes: No bodie comes at us; not a gentleman, nor a ----";[13] and since the winter of 1600–1601 was virtually free of plague, Histrio's complaint can be attributed only to the Children's rivalry.

In recruiting boys for their company, the managers of the troupe had made occasional use of a commission that the Queen had granted to Nathaniel Giles in his capacity as Master of the Children of the Chapel Royal. In effect, it gave him the right to kidnap children for her Majesty's service as chapel choristers. It is dated July 15, 1597, and it reads in part as follows:

> Elizabeth, by the grace of God, . . . & c., . . . to all mayors, sheriffs, bailiffs, constables, and all other our officers, greeting;
>
> For that it is meet that our Chapel Royal should be furnished with well-singing children from time to time, we have and by these presents do authorize our well-beloved servant, Nathaniel Giles, Master of our Children of our

said Chapel, or his deputy being by his bill subscribed and sealed so authorized, and having this our present commission with him, to take such and so many children as he or his sufficient deputy shall think meet, in all cathedral, collegiate, parish churches, chapels, or any other place or places, as well within Liberty as without, within this our realm of England, whatsoever they be; . . .

Wherefore we will and command you, and every of you to whom this our commission shall come, to be helping, aiding, and assisting to the uttermost of your powers, as you will answer at your uttermost perils.[14]

There was nothing unusual about the commission or its issuance. Giles's predecessors had held similar writs from the time of Edward IV on, and perhaps even earlier.[15] But Giles, or Evans and Robinson as his deputies, interpreted the commission more liberally than his predecessors had done; for whereas previous Masters had exercised the instrument only to recruit boys for her Majesty's service as choristers in the Chapel Royal, Giles and his colleagues exercised it to recruit boys for their own service as actors at Blackfriars.

Not all the Chapel boys, of course, were conscripted for service. Some joined the company voluntarily or on the initiative of their parents, like the Abell Cooke whose mother apprenticed him to one of the company's managers in 1606.[16] It seems probable that about twenty boys composed the troupe,[17] and of the twenty, seven are known to have been conscripted under the writ of impressment; the rest almost certainly had not been. The names of the conscripted boys were given by Henry Clifton as John Chappell, John Motteram, Nathaniel Field, Alvery Trussell, Philip Pykman, Thomas Grymes, and Salathiel or Salmon Pavey (24:4). Ben Jonson, in his lists of the principal actors in *Cynthia's Revels* and *Poetaster*, includes the names of two of the drafted boys—Field and Pavey —and of six others presumably not drafted: Robert Baxter, Thomas Day, John Frost, Thomas Marton, John Underwood, and William Ostler.

Generally speaking, the boys impressed for service were probably the better off for being taken into the company at Blackfriars; they were fed, lodged, clothed, trained in grammar and music and all the other accomplishments that went into the making of an actor, and they were brought into contact with the Court and courtiers. As to their training we have the testimony of the Duke of Stettin-Pomerania, whose Diary reports under the date of September 18, 1602, that the boys "have to apply themselves zealously to the art of singing, and to learn to play on various musical instruments, and at the same time to pursue their studies. These boys have special preceptors in all the different arts, and in particular very good instructors in music" (45:2).

Some of the boys liked the profession well enough to remain in it for the rest of their lives, as did three of those already named; John Underwood and William Ostler went from the Children's company to the King's Men in 1608, and Nathaniel Field probably about eight years later. They are the three of whom Cuthbert Burbage later said that "in process of time the boys growing up to be men, which were Underwood, Field, Ostler," they "were taken to strengthen the King's service" (44:20). Their names are grouped together in the list of "The Names of the Principall Actors in all these Playes" in the Shakespeare First Folio. Ostler and Underwood eventually became shareholders in both the Globe and the Blackfriars Playhouses. Field became a dramatist as well as an actor, the author of *A Woman Is a Weathercock* and *Amends for Ladies.*

One of the boys whom Giles and Evans impressed was Salathiel Pavey. He was drafted for service in 1600 when he was ten years old and "apprentice to one Peerce." He acted in *Cynthia's Revels* and *Poetaster* and other plays, specializing in the parts of old men. He died at thirteen, and Ben Jonson commemorated him in this gentle epitaph:

> Weep with me, all you that read
> This little story:
> And know, for whom a tear you shed
> Death's self is sorry.
> 'Twas a child that so did thrive
> In grace and feature,
> As heaven and nature seem'd to strive
> Which own'd the creature.
> Years he number'd scarce thirteen
> When fates turn'd cruel.
> Yet three fill'd zodiacs had he been
> The stage's jewel;
> And did act, what now we moan,
> Old men so duly,
> As sooth, the Parcae thought him one,
> He play'd so truly. . . .

The Clifton Affair

But at a time when the Giles-Evans-Robinson enterprise was as yet only about three months old, the members of the syndicate made the egregious blunder of picking up the thirteen-year-old son of an influen-

tial gentleman named Henry Clifton. As the father later told the story
in phrases that showed both his just indignation and his puritanical dislike of all plays and players, the confederates waylaid the boy as he was
on his way from his home to his school in Christ Church, London, and
forcibly hawled, pulled, dragged, and carried him away to the playhouse in the Blackfriars, and left him there "amongst a company of
lewd and dissolute mercenary players" (24:6). As soon as the father
learned of the outrage he repaired to the playhouse and demanded that
his son be released, but this the confederates utterly and scornfully refused to do, saying "that they had authority sufficient so to take any
nobleman's son in this land, and did then and there . . . deliver unto
his said son, in most scornful, disdainful, and despiteful manner, a scroll
of paper containing part of one of their said plays or interludes, and
him, the said Thomas Clifton, commanded to learn the same by heart"
on pain of being surely whipped (24:8). The boy was kept at Blackfriars for a day and a night, after which he was set at liberty by the
warrant of Sir John Fortescue, Master of the Wardrobe, Chancellor of
the Exchequer, and member of the Privy Council. But that did not end
the matter. Its repercussions were to be felt for several years to come.

I have previously made passing mention of another event of those
early years—an event to which, as we have seen, Shakespeare alluded
in *Hamlet,* and in which the Children at Blackfriars played a leading
part. I refer to the War of the Theatres, the Jonson-Marston-Dekker
feud that Dekker dignified with the name of the Poetomachia. Its first
tame skirmishes were fought in 1599 and 1600. The opening gun was
Histriomastix, refurbished by Marston and played at Paul's. Then came
Jonson's *Every Man Out of His Humour,* acted by the Chamberlain's
Men at the Globe, and in reply *Jack Drum's Entertainment,* again by
Marston and again at Paul's. Late in 1600 the Children of the Chapel
were installed at Blackfriars; Ben Jonson forthwith moved his big guns
to the Blackfriars stage, and the war was stepped up in heat and tempo.
Four attacks and counterattacks followed within the one year. Jonson
fired a broadside at Marston and Dekker from Blackfriars in *Cynthia's
Revels;* Marston answered with a salvo from Paul's in *What You Will;*
and then, as culminations of the quarrel, came *Poetaster* from Jonson,
and *Satiromastix* from Dekker, probably with Marston to help. The
quarrel was made up by 1604, when Marston dedicated his *Malcontent*
to Jonson; but in 1600 and 1601 "there was, for a while, no money bid
for argument unless the poet and the player went to cuffs in the question."

183

In the meantime, Henry Clifton was far from being appeased by the release of his son. He undertook an investigation of the Blackfriars management, collected evidence of other abuses of the Queen's commission, and on December 15, 1601, a year after the offense, he laid his complaint before her Majesty (Document 24). It was referred to her Court of Star Chamber for decision.

Giles took the Children of the Chapel to Court on January 6 and 10 and February 14, 1602, and this suggests that the Star Chamber did not begin its hearing of the case until after those dates, and therefore not until Hilary Term of that year. The decision has been lost, but a certain Edward Kirkham, with whom Evans was later to be associated as a partner in business and an opponent in litigation, reported ten years later that Evans "was censured by the right honorable Court of Star Chamber for his unorderly carriage and behavior in taking up gentlemen's children against their wills, and to employ them for players, and for other misdemeanors in the said decree contained; and further that all assurances made to the said Evans concerning the said house or plays or interludes should be utterly void and to be delivered up to be canceled" (43:43).

If we take Kirkham's biased deposition at its face value, Evans alone was censured, and Giles and Robinson went scot-free; but Kirkham's failure to mention the other two may well have been because Evans, alone of the three, was involved in the suit that Kirkham at that moment was prosecuting. That suit had nothing whatsoever to do with the Clifton affair, but it was one in which Kirkham and Evans were on opposite sides; and Kirkham seemingly dragged in the old decision against Evans for the purpose of discrediting his opponent. In view of these and other circumstances, it must be supposed that the Star Chamber's censure fell upon Giles and Robinson as well as Evans. Neither is heard of again in connection with the Blackfriars Playhouse. James Robinson disappears completely, and the name of Nathaniel Giles is conspicuously missing from the list of patentees to whom a license for the Children's company was issued two years later (26:2). Giles did retain his office as Master of the Children of the Chapel Royal, and he did retain his authorization to pick up well-singing children, but probably under a strict injunction to exercise the writ only for the impressment of choristers, not for the impressment of actors; and this dissociation of Chapel from playhouse was made explicit and mandatory in a new commission issued to Giles by King James I in 1606, which reaffirmed his right of impressment but made it subject to the following condition:

Provided always, and we do straitly charge and command, that none of the said Choristers or Children of the Chapel so to be taken by force of this commission, shall be used or employed as comedians or stage players or to exercise or act any . . . stage plays, interludes, comedies or tragedies, for that it is not fit or decent that such as should sing the praise of God Almighty should be trained up or employed in such lascivious and profane exercises.[18]

Evans was the only member of the Chapel syndicate whom we know to have been disciplined in connection with the Clifton affair,[19] and yet he was the only one of the three who survived in Blackfriars management; for Evans did survive, although his survival was for a time surreptitious.

At some unspecified date,[20] probably shortly before the Star Chamber's decree, Henry Evans conveyed "all his goods, chattels and leases, implements, household stuff, wares, commodities and all his goods" to his son-in-law Alexander Hawkins (43:37). He says that he did so to "save Hawkins harmless" under the £400 bond, and upon the earnest and importunate request of his (Evans's) wife. But he may well have had a more urgent and immediate motive. Evans may have learned of the Clifton complaint and have had some reason to fear its consequences, and he may have transferred his possessions to Hawkins, in advance of the Star Chamber's verdict, lest the Court should order them confiscated. If this was indeed his reason, he would have needed to make the transfer before the Court handed down its decision, for to alienate his possessions after the decree would be to render the transaction fraudulent and fruitless. But the Star Chamber did not, as far as we know, order the seizure of any of his properties; what it did do was to forbid him to take any future part in the management of the playhouse or of the Children.

Incidentally, Evans said that the Blackfriars lease was not among those that he conveyed to Hawkins; he said that he kept it in his own possession until 1608 (43:37). Others said that he did transfer it to his son-in-law (43:2, 43:14, 43:41, 43:44, etc.); and the issue of its transfer or nontransfer, and the conditions under which it was conveyed if it was conveyed at all, later became the subjects of legal controversy in the Chancery proceedings of Kirkham *vs.* Paunton (Document 43).

But whether or not the lease now nominally stood in Hawkins's name, Evans was still under bond to pay the rent as before, so he listened eagerly when three new men "earnestly labored with and entreated" him to let them have a share in the project (42:2). The new men were Edward Kirkham, Yeoman of the Revels, a merchant named William Rastall or Rastell, and a haberdasher named Thomas Kendall. Evans himself could not appear openly in the management of the enterprise, but he still wanted a share of the profits; and since he controlled the indispensable lease to the playhouse property, he was able to negotiate a partnership with the three men whereby they were to have the ostensible management and one half of the profits, and he was to have the other half.

The partnership was ratified on April 20, 1602, presumably not much more than two months after the Star Chamber had rendered its decision. The agreements entered into by the partners were evidenced by three documents destined to be matters at issue in legal embroilments extending over several years. The documents were signed by Evans and Hawkins as parties of the first part, and by Kirkham, Rastall, and Kendall as parties of the second part.

The first document, which I shall call the Condition of the £200 Bond (Document 36), provided that the parties of each part should have "the joint use, occupation, and profit . . . of and in the said great hall or room and other the premises" leased to Evans by Richard Burbage, without interference by the parties of the other part, and that each party should pay one half of the rent and one half of the costs of repairs to the premises; and for their observance of these conditions Evans and Hawkins gave their £200 bond to the parties of the second part. Kirkham and his colleagues presumably thought that such a guarantee was necessary because the lease stood in the name or names of one or both of the parties of the other part, and the whole enterprise could be wrecked if they should make the playhouse unavailable.

The second document, which I shall call the Condition of the £50 Bond, bound Kirkham and his associates to pay 8 shillings to Henry Evans, weekly on Saturdays, for each week that the Children should play; and as security for such payment they gave Evans their bond in the amount of £50 (Document 37). Nowhere is there any clear statement of the purpose for which the weekly payment was to be made. Evans, in a deposition made ten years later, spoke of the £50 bond as being "conditioned for payment of the said sum of 8 shillings weekly unto this defendant, because after the said agreements [were] made, the complainant and his said partners would at their directions have the dieting and ordering of the boys used about the plays there, which before the said complainant had, and for the which he had weekly before that disbursed and allowed great sums of money" (43:36). Evans was a defendant in the current lawsuit; it was he who previously had had direction of the dieting and ordering of the boys; the second "complainant" must therefore be assumed to be an error for "defendant." But having made that correction, we now have the defendant (Evans) receiving 8 shillings weekly from the complainant (Kirkham) because the defendant (Evans) is now relieved of a heavy expense that he previously had to meet, but that the complainant (Kirkham) would have to meet in the future. The logic of this arrangement is not entirely clear. Besides, if the payments relate to the subsistence of the boys, for which they seem wholly inadequate, it is unreasonable that they should be paid only "when and so often as any interludes, plays or shows shall be played, used, showed, or published in the great hall . . . in the Blackfriars" (37:1), since the boys needed feeding whether they were acting or not.

Kirkham was later to state that the weekly payments were made in consideration of the reassignment of the Blackfriars lease to him and his partners (42:19), but this statement was contradicted by Evans (43:36), Burbage, and Heminges (43:25). Still another explanation was given by a man named Percival Golding. Testifying in the 1609 Chancery suit of Kirkham and Anne Kendall *vs.* Evans and Hawkins, he said that the partners had agreed to pay 8 shillings per week to Evans on condition that he "should no further intermeddle with the affairs of the Playhouse of Blackfriars, but should leave them to be managed by the said Alexander Hawkins."[21] Evans did in fact depart from London soon after the £50 Bond was signed, and did in fact leave Hawkins to deal for him, and these circumstances give some support to Golding's allegation. But Evans himself said that he had left the country on orders of the Lord Chamberlain (42:20), and both he and Kirkham subsequently spoke of his absence without relating it to the £50 Bond or the 8-shilling payments (42:3, 42:10); and, whether or not he was paid for not intermeddling, Evans was back in the Blackfriars management within one or two years. He was later to sue Kendall for failure to keep up the 8-shilling payments, but neither his complaints nor Kendall's answers throw any light upon the reasons for which the payments were to be made (Document 38). Lacking the Articles of Agreement, we shall probably never know the true reason.[22]

The third document was the Articles of Agreement. It has been lost, because Evans later thought it "long and tedious" and therefore not meet to be inserted in his Answer in the suit of Kirkham *vs.* Paunton *et al.* in 1612 (43:31). It may have dealt with the sharing of profits after expenses had been met, and perhaps also with expenses of theatrical production not covered in the two extant documents—items such as the purchase of costumes and properties and the commissioning of plays. Besides, it may have thrown needed light upon the reasons for which the parties of the second part paid, or alleged that they paid, certain sums of money variously stated as £300,[23] £400,[24] and £600,[25] and loosely described as money to be spent "about the premises" and "for divers employments."[26] It seems probable that this was the consideration by which the new partners bought their way into the enterprise. Evans, it must be remembered, had something to sell. The Children were then at the peak of their popularity, the profits were potentially great (although reduced at the moment by a visitation of the plague), and Evans held or controlled the lease that made the whole venture possible—the lease, furthermore, of the most desirable theatrical property in London. Under these circumstances he would have been reluctant to admit Kirkham and his associates to actual partnership and nominal control without receiving something substantial in return, and the £300 or £400 may have been that something. But Kirkham was later to explain the expenditure very differently.[27]

Within a month after the partnership came into being, Evans left London. He first implied that he had done so out of sheer good-heartedness, and that he had given his new associates the free run of the premises "to their use and dispose as best liked them at their free wills and pleasures for a long space and time, to their great benefit and profit" (42:3). Later he told the true story. Lord Hunsdon, who was both Lord Chamberlain and a near neighbor of the playhouse, had made a personal investigation of the affairs of the Children, presumably to assure himself that the Star Chamber's decree was being obeyed. He probably had learned from Kirkham that Evans still held a half interest in the business and an undercover share in its management, whereupon Evans was "commanded by his Lordship to avoid and leave the same, for fear of whose displeasure [Evans] was forced to leave the country" (42:20). He claims that he lost near £300 as a result, but Kirkham says that "he left the said Alexander Hawkins to deal for him and to take such benefit of the said house as should belong unto him in his absence, which the said Alexander Hawkins did accordingly, so as the said [Evans] lost nothing" (42:10). Just when he felt it to be safe to return to London is not known, but Richard Burbage intimates that he had returned by 1603 or 1604 (43:21), perhaps emboldened by the appointment of a new Lord Chamberlain under James I in 1603. Be that as it may, he was certainly back in open participation in the management of the company not later than New Year's Day of 1605, at which time he was one of two payees for performances given by the Children at Court.

Evans and Kirkham seem to have been at loggerheads from the start, and to have remained so to the end. Within the first month of their partnership, according to Evans, Kirkham gave false information against him to the Lord Chamberlain, of purpose to prejudice him (42:20); and Evans, according to Kirkham, had violated one of their agreements by January 1604 (42:5), and by 1608 he had violated all the rest. Certainly a more litigious quintet of partners never joined in any enterprise. Out of their six years of association were to spring nine intra-partnership lawsuits and six others involving outsiders; and of the fifteen Kirkham was to be a party to nine, either as plaintiff or as defendant. The muddy details of their misbegotten partnership became matters of record in 1608 to 1612, as testimony in divers legal controversies that must be discussed later. Unfortunately, the claims and counterclaims yield almost as much confusion as they do clarification, largely because nearly every statement made under oath is categorically contradicted under oath. One cannot know whom to believe, or whether to believe anybody.

In 1603 London suffered one of its worst visitations of the plague. One sixth of the city's population perished during the year the epidemic raged.[28] The theatres were closed on May 26, and not until April 9 of the next year were the public playhouses permitted to reopen. With his income from the theatre reduced to nothing, Henry Evans "grew weary and out of liking" with his commitment to a twenty-one-year lease, the more so in view of "the importunity and earnest entreaty of the said Alexander Hawkins . . . to the intent that he might be freed and discharged of the said bond of £400, wherein he was and stood bound for the payment of the said rent of £40" (43:21). Evans had some talk with Richard Burbage about canceling the lease, but nothing came of it at that time.

The Children of the Queen's Revels

In 1603 Queen Elizabeth died and King James ascended the throne. The managers of the Children thought it prudent to have the company officially recognized by the new sovereign, and at their request, perhaps supported by the solicitation of the poet Samuel Daniel, the King issued a royal patent on February 4, 1604, that entitled the Children thenceforth to call themselves the Children of the Revels to the Queen, and that thus broke their last link with the Chapel Royal—their name. The license designated Kirkham, Hawkins, Kendall, and Robert Payne as patentees (Document 26). Evans's name does not appear; either it was not submitted or it was found unacceptable; but Evans was still, of course, a member of the syndicate in financial control. Rastall's name disappears for unknown reasons. Of Robert Payne nothing whatsoever is known; his name occurs nowhere else.

To the patent the King attached a proviso that named Samuel Daniel as censor and licenser of all the Queen's Revels plays:

> . . . provided always that no such plays or shows shall be presented before the said Queen our wife by the said Children, or by them anywhere publicly acted, but by the approbation and allowance of Samuel Daniel, whom her pleasure is to appoint for that purpose (26:4).

This strange provision, which ostensibly gave Daniel some of the powers normally exercised by the Master of the Revels, is not easy to understand; the most likely explanation is that the King inserted it at the suggestion of Daniel's friends at Court in order to provide him with a pension payable by the Blackfriars syndicate, not by the Crown. The royal patent itself says nothing about any payment, but a deposition filed by Kirkham and Anne Kendall in 1609 reveals that the Blackfriars managers were obligated to pay Daniel £10 per year, and that they gave him their bond in the amount of £100 as security for the due performance of their obligation (39:1); and since they can hardly have expected that Daniel would render them services commensurate with any such expense, it must be supposed that they gave their promise and their bond on orders from the King. Daniel seems to have thought of his office as being a sinecure: according to him, the annuity was payable not for present or future services, but "for and in consideration of his great pains and travel therein formerly taken" in inducing his Majesty to grant the patent of February 4, 1604 (39:3).

The Master of the Revels was still presumably responsible for the actual licensing of plays, but Daniel's anomalous appointment may have led him to relax his vigilance as censor, with the result that some plays may have gotten into production without the approbation and allowance of either man. If Daniel did act as censor, he made a notably poor job of it, for during the next four years the Children produced one play after another, including one written by Daniel himself, which were painfully indiscreet and offensive to royal sensibilities.

Long before this time the Children had already achieved the popularity that made them serious rivals of the adult companies. Many things contributed to their success—the availability and comfort of their playhouse, their excellent dramatists, including nearly all the best men of the day except Shakespeare himself, their sophisticated plays, and the copious interspersion of their plays with spectacular effects, instrumental music, dance, and song. But the popularity of the Children was in part due also to their audacity in skirting close to the danger line in political indiscretion. Nearly every play produced by the Children during the years 1600 to 1608 satirized the government and the Court, and often ridiculed the King himself, with an impudence and persistence that eventually sent some of them to jail and closed the playhouse. A few of the dramatists—Jonson, and perhaps Chapman and even Marston—may be credited with moral aims in attacking James and his corrupt Court, but certainly not the managers of the company. Their motives were wholly commercial. Personal satire bred sensationalism, and sensationalism attracted crowds; and the greater the risks they took, the greater the notoriety they achieved.

To be sure, the adult companies themselves occasionally ran into difficulties with the authorities, as did the King's Men when they produced Middleton's *Game at Chess* in 1624; but they did not deliberately invite official disfavor for the sake of publicity, as the Children seem to have done. For the men, the consequences of such action would have been disastrous; for the Children, on the other hand, a certain degree of impunity was conferred by the mere fact of their being children; and the irresponsibility of their managers in thus trading upon and capitalizing a privilege conferred by youth, is deplored by Thomas Heywood in his *Apology for Actors*, probably written in 1608:

> Now, to speak of some abuse lately crept into the quality, as an inveighing against the state, the court, the law, the city, and their governments, with the particularizing of private men's humors (yet alive) noblemen, and others: I know it distastes many; neither do I any way approve it, nor dare I by any means excuse it. The liberty which some arrogate to themselves, committing their bitterness and liberal invectives against all estates to the mouths of children, supposing their juniority to be a privilege for any railing, be it never so violent, I could advise all such to curb and limit this presumed liberty within the bands of discretion and government.[29]

Before the days of the Kirkham regime and the Daniel censorship, Ben Jonson's *Poetaster* had already incensed the military and legal professions, and Chapman's *Sir Giles Goosecap* had contained scurrilous scenes that needed to be expunged when the play was published. After 1603, every year produced its contretemps.

In 1604 the company gave serious offense by acting *Philotas*, written by Samuel Daniel himself, which was considered to be a commentary upon the career of the Earl of Essex, as it undoubtedly was, and therefore upon affairs of state in a particularly sensitive area. Its performance brought Daniel a summons to appear before the Privy Council. He presumably cleared himself by disclaiming any sympathy with the Essex rebellion, but the play was accompanied by a printed apology when it was published the next year.

In 1605 the company gave still more grievous offense by acting *Eastward Ho!*, which enraged the King by its slighting allusion to his Scottish countrymen who had followed him to London, and by its ridicule of his "thirty-pound knights" in particular. Of the play's three authors, Jonson and Chapman were jailed and in imminent danger of having their noses slit and their ears cropped; but Marston, said by his collaborators to be the principal offender, escaped punishment by going into hiding. After this, the Children of the Queen's Revels did not again appear at Court.

Early in 1606 the company produced Day's *Isle of Gulls*, with its many jibes at courtly scandals. By this time the King was in no mood to be lenient. "Sundry were committed to Bridewell," which had now become a prison. Kirkham was driven from the management of the troupe, the playhouse was closed for a time, and the Queen's patronage was withdrawn. Thereafter the Children were called simply the Children of the Revels, or the Children of Blackfriars.[30]

The Keysar Regime

Under the King's mandate the control of the troupe shifted once again. A London goldsmith named Robert Keysar bought a share in the assets and revenues of the company and assumed its active management. For the first year or two Keysar steered clear of offense, but in March of 1608 he enraged the Court by producing Chapman's two-part play, *The Conspiracy and the Tragedy of Charles, Duke of Byron,* which dealt with the domestic affairs of the King of France, and which in one scene (deleted in the printed version), showed the French Queen and Mlle. de Verneuil engaging in an indecorous quarrel that culminated in the Queen's boxing of the lady's ears. The performance immediately brought a furious protest from the French ambassador, to which King James listened the more sympathetically because his own royal person had been the object of ridicule in another play, now lost, only a day or two before—a play that lampooned the King's favorites and his Scotch mines, and represented him as drunken, irascible, and foul-mouthed. The accumulation of offenses had gone too far. His Majesty promptly gave orders for the imprisonment of some of the players, the disbanding of the troupe, and the closing of the playhouse. These events were reported in a letter written to Lord Salisbury on March 11, 1608, by Sir Thomas Lake, Clerk of the Signet:

> His Majesty was well pleased with that which your Lordship advertiseth concerning the committing of the players that have offended in the matters of France, and commanded me to signify to your Lordship that for the others[31] who have offended in the matter of the mines and other lewd words, which is the Children of the Blackfriars, that though he had signified his mind to your Lordship by my Lord of Montgomery, yet I should repeat it again, that his Grace had vowed they should never play more, but should first beg their bread, and he would have his vow performed; and therefore my Lord Chamberlain by himself, or your Lordships at the table, should take order to dissolve them, and to punish the maker besides.[32]

The King's action put an end to child actors at Blackfriars. It put an end, too, to any profits that Evans or Kirkham might hope to derive therefrom. According to Evans, Kirkham was in an understandably sullen mood, and took the initiative in terminating a partnership that had become profitless and burdensome; and with what he believed to be Kirkham's consent, Evans thereupon reopened negotiations with Burbage for the surrender of the lease. This time they came to terms. Burbage took back the lease, gave Evans the £400 bond for cancellation, and in August 1608 took over the playhouse for the occupancy of the King's Men (42:22–23, 43:38–39).[33]

Although the subsequent fortunes of the Children are not strictly a part of the Blackfriars story, they will be dealt with briefly so as to leave fewer loose ends.

Keysar did not give up easily; in spite of the King's command and the closing of the playhouse, he kept the Children together. He later claimed that Richard Burbage and his associates had promised him that they would come to no agreement with Evans that would prevent the Children's returning to Blackfriars after the cessation of the plague (41:3–4); and even after he knew that Burbage had accepted Evans's surrender of the lease and that the King's Men would occupy the playhouse themselves, he maintained the Children at his own expense and perhaps took them on the road. Later that same year, the King's anger having abated in the meantime, he brought them back to London for the Christmas season of 1608–09 under the name of the Children of Blackfriars, and they gave three performances at Court, with Keysar as payee. The next autumn they moved to Whitefriars, and it was as the Children of Whitefriars that they performed at Court during the winter of 1609–10.

At about this time Keysar brought in a new partner named Philip Rosseter, through whose influence the Children received a patent on January 4, 1610, that permitted them once again to call themselves the Children of the Queen's Revels.[34] Keysar is not named in the patent, but he was still one of the sharers.[35]

For two years Keysar nursed his resentment against Evans and Burbage for having reached an agreement in 1608 that prevented his use of the Blackfriars Playhouse, and in 1610 he brought suit against them and others in the Court of Requests, charging breach of agreement and other offenses. As defendants he named Evans, the two Burbages, Heminges, Condell, "and others," the others presumably being the rest of the Blackfriars housekeepers, including Shakespeare. Keysar seems to have been a man with a persecution complex of extraordinary dimensions, and many of his statements must be regarded with caution; but his charges, and the answers of the defendants, nevertheless have much of interest to tell about the last days of the Children at Blackfriars and the first days of the King's Men. Without this suit we should not know, for instance, about the action taken jointly by the Children of Whitefriars and the King's Men of Blackfriars in buying off the competition of the Children of Paul's.

In 1609 and 1610 London had three "private" playhouses—Whitefriars, then in the hands of Keysar and Rosseter; Blackfriars, then in the hands of the King's Men but not yet restored to active use; and Paul's, then in the hands of Edward Pearce. Pearce had produced a distinguished series of plays at Paul's from 1600 until 1605 or 1606, but then he seems to have stopped. Four years later he presumably was on the point of starting again, but Rosseter bought him off. Rosseter did not want to face the competition of another private playhouse and another children's company, so he offered Pearce a "dead rent" to keep the playhouse closed, and the two men reached an understanding that provided for "a cessation of playing and plays to be acted in the said house near St. Paul's Church aforesaid, for which the said Rosseter compounded with the said Pearce to give him . . . £20 per annum" (41:18). At about this time Blackfriars was ready to reopen, and Rosseter had no difficulty in convincing the managers of the King's Men that his deal with Pearce had been as much to their advantage as to his own, and in persuading them to pay half the cost of the dead rent (41:19).

These facts were brought out by Richard Burbage and his associates in their Rejoinder to Keysar's Bill of Complaint. In that complaint Keysar had charged, with an astonishing disregard for both truth and logic, that the defendants had contrived the whole plot with the sole purpose of injuring him (41:12). What it did accomplish was to put an end to the Children of Paul's.

Keysar's complaint about the dead rent was merely incidental; his basic grievance was that the defendants had fraudulently deprived him of his right to a one-sixth interest in the remaining term of the Blackfriars lease, a one-sixth share in certain goods, and a one-sixth part of the profits of the playhouse; he valued the goods at £600 in the whole, including costumes, properties, and play scripts, and he estimated the profits at £1,500. He said that he had bought these one-sixth shares from John Marston, the dramatist, who had previously bought them from Evans (41:2, 41:4).[36] But after having opened negotiations with

195

Marston, he had heard humors to the effect that Burbage and Evans were plotting some chicanery prejudicial to him. He had therefore gone to Burbage and his partners before consummating the deal, had told them of his intended purchase, and had asked for their assurance that they would do nothing harmful to his interests (41:3), whereupon they had given him their faithful promise that they would take no action without first seeing to it that the rights of all parties were fully protected. Thus encouraged, Keysar had paid his £100 to Marston, the more confidently since Burbage and his fellows had offered to buy his sixth part for £400 under certain conditions (41:4). But in spite of their promises, he said, they had bribed Evans to surrender his lease, and were now themselves occupying the premises and taking profits to the value of £1,500, in disregard of his rights to a sixth part thereof (41:5).

The defendants denied everything. They denied that Keysar had ever told them of his intended purchase, that they had ever made him any promises, that they had offered to pay him £400 or any other sum (41:7), that the Blackfriars goods were worth £600, or that the profits amounted to £1,500 (41:10); they doubted that Keysar had in fact ever bought any rights to the playhouse lease from Marston, especially since they knew of no deed or writing evidencing the transaction, and they said that Evans could not have sold any portion of the lease to Marston if he had wanted to, since the terms of the original lease forbade his assigning any part of it for any term whatsoever to any person whatsoever (41:15).[37] Finally, Cuthbert Burbage said that the defendants would support their denials by calling as witnesses John Marston, Henry Evans and his wife, Nathaniel Field, John Underwood, William Ostler, William Baxstead, Philip Rosseter, and Margaret Hawkins, widow.[38] Since the testimony of these witnesses is not upon record, it seems probable that the case was settled out of court.

The Porter's Hall Playhouse

At the time when Keysar launched his suit, he and Rosseter and the Children of the Queen's Revels were still at Whitefriars; but the Whitefriars lease ran out in 1614, and upon its expiration Rosseter took the troupe to a new playhouse that he had fitted out in the Blackfriars precinct. Its construction had been authorized by King James in a license granted under the Great Seal of England on June 3, 1615, which empowered Rosseter and his partners to erect, build, and set up, on the

premises described as "situate and being within the precinct of the Blackfriars, near Puddle Wharf in the suburbs of London, called by the name
of the Lady Saunders' house, or otherwise Porter's Hall, . . . one convenient playhouse for the said Children of the Revels, the same playhouse to be used by the Children of the Revels for the time being of
the Queen's Majesty, and for the Prince's Players, and for the Lady
Elizabeth's Players."[39]

By this time, however, the Blackfriars precinct had come within the
jurisdiction of the City of London, and the Lord Mayor and Aldermen
wanted a second playhouse in the precinct even less than they had wanted
a first. They addressed a protest to the Privy Council, reciting that Rosseter and his partners had already "pulled down a great messuage in
Puddle Wharf, which was sometimes the house of the Lady Saunders
within the precinct of the Blackfriars," and were "now erecting a new
playhouse in that place, to the great prejudice and inconvenience of the
government of that City." The Privy Council found itself faced with a
dilemma whose horns were a royal patent on the one side and a City protest on the other, and in its predicament it sought the advice of the Lord
Chief Justice, Sir Edward Coke. His Lordship found an escape from the
difficulty in the phrase "in the suburbs of London" in the King's patent;
for the Blackfriars precinct, since it was at last under the City's jurisdiction, was no longer "in the suburbs of London," but in the City itself.
In spite, therefore, of the patent's specification of the Blackfriars precinct and of a particular building within that precinct, "the Lord Chief
Justice did deliver to their Lordships that the license granted to the said
Rosseter did extend to the building of a playhouse without the liberties
of London, and not within the City." Fortified by this astonishing quibble,
the Privy Council on September 26, 1615, ordered that "there shall be
no playhouse erected in that place."[40] But whether the King intervened
in Rosseter's favor or whether Rosseter simply ignored an order based on
so flimsy a pretext, he went on with his building. He finished the playhouse and produced plays there, two of which—*The Scornful Lady* and
Amends for Ladies—were later published with title pages that mis-
leadingly mentioned Blackfriars only, and not Porter's Hall.

The King himself put an end to the Porter's Hall playhouse early
in 1617. He had his Privy Council address a letter to the Lord Mayor
of London on January 27 directing that the playhouse be destroyed. It
contained no reference to the license that he had issued less than two
years earlier. Instead, it said merely that "whereas . . . there be cer-

tain persons that go about to set up a playhouse in the Blackfriars near unto his Majesty's Wardrobe, and for that purpose have lately erected and made fit a building which is almost if not fully finished, you shall understand that his Majesty hath this day expressly signified his pleasure that the same shall be pulled down so as to be made unfit for any such use."[41]

Probably as a result of this formidable setback, the Children of the Queen's Revels were disbanded. With their end came the end of children's theatrical companies in England. Nathan Field, who had remained with the troupe ever since his impressment in 1600, now joined the King's Men.

Litigation, 1608–1612

I return to the Blackfriars Playhouse and to the year 1608. The King's summary action in closing the playhouse after the *Byron* offense had put an end to all revenue from plays to be produced there, but not to the financial obligations of some of the former syndicate members. Evans and Hawkins were still under a £400 bond to pay £40 per year rent to Richard Burbage. Kirkham, Rastall, and Kendall were still under a £200 bond to pay £20 per year to Evans and Hawkins; and Kirkham and others were under a £100 bond to pay a salary of £10 per year to Samuel Daniel. With the playhouse closed down and profitless, the strains growing out of the old obligations made themselves increasingly felt, and led to the spate of lawsuits that began almost before the doors of the playhouse were shut, and that lasted until 1612.

The first was a suit brought by Henry Evans against Thomas Kendall, alleging violation of the conditions of the £50 bond. Those conditions were no longer operative, since the Children were no longer playing at Blackfriars, but the violations of which Evans complained had occurred several years earlier, and over a period of time. Evans charged that the arrearages were great in the stipulated payments of 8 shillings weekly for each week that the Children should play, and therefore he brought suit in Easter Term of 1608 to have the £50 bond declared forfeit (38:1). Kendall answered that he himself had well and truly paid to Henry Evans the sum of 8 shillings for each week that plays were presented by the Children at Blackfriars, beginning with Saturday, April 24, 1602, and continuing until the day when Evans commenced his suit. Evans replied that Kendall had made no payment on June 16, 1604, and Kendall rejoined that there had been no play on that day. The Court's decision is not upon record; but from Evans's Answer in the Kirkham *vs*. Paunton dispute, it appears that Kirkham and Kendall gave Hawkins a new bond in the adjusted amount of £54 (43:36). On this new obligation Evans sued again, a year later.[42] Eventually the controversy seems to have been settled by Kirkham's payment of an amount that he gives as £52 10s. (43:3) but that Evans gives as £48 10s. (43:36). Incidentally, it seems strange that Evans should have brought his first suit against Kendall only, without naming Kendall's more active partner, Kirkham, as codefendant. By this time Rastall had presumably died.

While the Evans *vs*. Kendall case was still pending, a man named John Gerrard brought suit against Kirkham in Samuel Daniel's name. Daniel had sold his £100 bond, and all future benefits under it, to Gerrard, and he, claiming that he had not been paid according to contract since the assignment, put the bond in suit (39:3). Kirkham and Anne Kendall, the widow of the last of Kirkham's partners, thereupon sued in the Court of Chancery for the purpose of staying the suit brought against them by Gerrard in the King's Bench. They sought to reduce their liability by arguing that the salary was not payable to Daniel for services previously rendered, but only "in regard of the pains to be taken by the said Samuel Daniel about the approbation and allowance of such plays," and that it was to be paid at the full rate of £10 per year only "if the said Children should play or make any shows . . . the full time six months in every year"; if the season should be shorter, payment was to be made at the rate of 16s. 8d. per month (39:1). They went on to say that the original commitment had been superseded by a later one under which Daniel was to receive 5 shillings per week for each week that the Children should play, and that this new commitment, by Daniel's own admission, was now fully satisfied and discharged; but instead of returning the bond for cancellation as he had promised to do, Daniel had kept it and commenced suit upon it in the Court of King's Bench. They therefore asked the Lord Chancellor to issue a writ of injunction, commanding Daniel and his attorneys to proceed no further in their suit (39:2). The outcome of this case is not known.

In 1611 Kirkham launched the first of his "multiplicity of suits and vexations," as Evans called them, and continued them through much of 1612. By this time the King's Men were installed at Blackfriars, and the playhouse was prospering again; Evans, either directly or through a nominee in the King's Men's syndicate, was probably sharing in the profits, and Kirkham wanted to get his hands on whatever Blackfriars money he could. He made two great efforts. First he demanded forfeiture of the £200 bond on the plea that Evans had violated its conditions, and after that he demanded a half of all present and future Blackfriars profits on the plea that he was entitled to a moiety by reason of his ownership of one half of the Blackfriars lease. By the deaths of his erstwhile partners in the Revels venture, he was now the sole survivor of the three original parties of the second part, and the only claimant of any continuing interest that they singly or jointly might have had in Blackfriars assets and revenues. By their deaths he was also left without witnesses who could either support or refute his claims.

He began his attacks in Trinity Term of 1611 by having Evans arrested "by writ out of the King's Bench upon several actions of £1,000 damage" and forcing him to put up bail (42:3, 42:11). Next he commenced three several new actions against him, demanding forfeiture of the £200 bond on the grounds that Evans had severed from the great hall a certain room called the Schoolhouse, and the chamber over it,[43] and had used the two rooms as private apartments to dine and sup in (42:5, 42:15), thus violating the guarantee that Kirkham and his partners should at all times have the joint use, occupation, and profit, together with Evans and Hawkins, of and in the great hall and all the rest of the premises demised by Burbage to Evans. Evans replied that he had furnished the rooms at his own expense, that they could contribute nothing to the earning capacity of the premises, that he had been ready at all times to open them to Kirkham and his friends upon request, and that in any case it had been understood from the beginning that he was to have for his own use the one or two rooms wherein he was then inhabiting (42:2, 42:6). Kirkham admitted that Evans had fitted up the rooms at his own proper costs and charges to dine and sup in, but denied that the doors were always opened at request, that he and his partners had suffered no loss by the doors being shut (42:15), or that they had ever agreed to an exception in respect of Evans's dwelling or inhabiting in part of the demised premises (42:9). Faced by Kirkham's renewed assertion that the doors were not always ready to be opened, Evans revised his statement of the open-door policy by saying that the doors were always ready to be unlocked and left open at the "public request" of Kirkham and his associates, "upon notice given that they . . . meant to make any joint use, occupation and profit thereof" (42:17). On Evans's own showing, therefore, Kirkham probably had little enough use of the schoolhouse and the chamber over it; but even so it seems a trivial pretext on which to base a legal claim, ten years later, for the forfeiture of a substantial bond.

All these charges and countercharges came to light when Evans petitioned the court to cancel the bond as a means of relieving him from the vexations and jeopardies caused by Kirkham's efforts to collect damages from him "upon no or very small occasions" (42:5). The result of Evans's complaint is not known, but it may be surmised that he did secure himself from further persecution arising out of petty breaches of agreement; for by the time that Evans filed his Bill of Complaint, Kirkham's suit against him on the £200 bond had already come to trial before the Lord Chief Justice at Easter Term of 1612, and Kirkham had been nonsuited (42:18, 42:24, 43:33); and a decision adverse to Kirkham is further indicated by his failure to mention the rooms or the bond in later litigation.

Probably without waiting for the Court's decision on the Evans complaint, Kirkham started a new suit, this time against a certain Edward Paunton, naming Henry Evans, Richard Burbage, and John Heminges as codefendants. In it he sought to prove [A] that Evans had surrendered the Blackfriars lease to Burbage with the fraudulent intention of excluding him, Kirkham, from the share of the profits to which he was entitled under the agreements of 1602; [B] that because the surrender had been fraudulent, he was still the rightful owner of one half of the lease; and [C] that as its rightful owner, he was entitled to a half of all the Blackfriars profits that had accrued since the surrender, or that might accrue during the remaining years that the lease had to run. Evans countered by saying that the lease, far from having been surrendered fraudulently, had been surrendered with Kirkham's implied consent and even on his initiative; Burbage and Heminges testified that it had been surrendered openly and honestly; and Paunton claimed that whether the lease had been surrendered fraudulently or honestly or not at all, it was entirely his property, and his alone.

Alexander Hawkins, Evans's son-in-law and business partner, had died in 1610. His widow had married Paunton (or Painton or Paynton), who claimed that the Blackfriars lease, and all profits deriving from it, were wholly and absolutely his in the right of his wife (43:13, 43:14). Kirkham was willing to concede that Paunton was entitled to a half interest in the lease by inheritance from Hawkins (43:5), but not to the entirety. He therefore petitioned the Court of Chancery in July of 1612 to disallow Paunton's claim to the second moiety, and to allow his own.

Kirkham's claim to the second half rested upon the following elaborate system of allegations:

That when Evans had transferred the lease to Hawkins in 1601, he had done so subject to the stipulation that Hawkins should hold only one half of it in his own right, and that he should hold the other half in trust for Kirkham, Rastall, and Kendall, to be reassigned to them at any time that they might request it (43:1, 43:2, 43:44);

That with the deaths of Rastall and Kendall, their interests in the lease had descended to him by right of survivorship, and that he now therefore held a full moiety (43:5, 43:41);

That his rightful ownership of it had not been voided by the surrender of the lease to Burbage in 1608, since the surrender had been made without Hawkins's knowledge and consent (43:4), nor had it been voided by Hawkins's death before having reassured the lease to the three partners (43:6);

And that, since Hawkins at his death had held no more than one half in his own right, it had not been in his power to bequeath more than that half to his widow, under whom Paunton laid his claim.

Evans flatly denied having transferred the lease to Hawkins subject to reassignment of a moiety thereof to the parties of the second part upon request (43:34); Paunton denied it for reasons of his own (43:13, 43:18), and Burbage and Heminges said that there had been no such stipulation to their knowledge (43:25). Quite apart from their denials, one may doubt that such an understanding ever existed. For one thing, the transfer of the lease, according to Paunton, took place on October 21, 1601 (43:14), six months before the partnership came into existence on April 20, 1602. For another, the two extant partnership documents—the Conditions of the £200 Bond and of the £50 Bond—give no evidence of it, and Kirkham's failure to cite the lost Articles of Agreement in support of his claim is proof enough that that document did not. Kirkham's claim, therefore, rests solely upon his unsupported allegation, and his frantic efforts to bolster that allegation actually tend to break it down. At one point, for instance, he says that the 8 shillings that he and his associates were bound to pay weekly to Evans was a consideration for the reassurance of the lease, and so was the £52 10s. paid by Hawkins to Evans (43:3); but the 8-shilling payment was tied up with the £50 Bond, whose conditions say nothing about the reassignment of the lease (Document 37); and as for the payment of £52 10s., Kirkham's assertion would make it appear that one party of the first part paid a sum of money to another party of the first part in order to secure an advantage for the parties of the second part; and this makes no sense at all. At another point Kirkham says that the payment of £400, four times mentioned vaguely as money spent "about the premises," was made in consideration of the assignment (43:1, 43:41), but he himself had previously spoken of the payment without attaching any such connotation to it (42:11). But the most convincing disproof of Kirkham's claim lies in his having failed to take advantage of his alleged rights. Kirkham being Kirkham, he would assuredly have gotten the moiety of the lease into his own hands long before 1612 if it had been in his power to do so for the mere asking. This he did not do nor claim to have done.

In support of his charge that the surrender of the lease was fraudulent, Kirkham alleged that Mrs. Evans had stolen the document while it was in Hawkins's keeping as trustee, that she had delivered it to Burbage for cancellation, and that she, Evans, Burbage, and Heminges had entered into a conspiracy to cheat Kirkham and his partners out of the profits that were rightfully theirs (43:4). Evans admitted that his wife was the person who had delivered the lease to Burbage, but said that she had done so with his and Hawkins's knowledge and consent (43:39). Burbage and Heminges denied that she had been the emissary (43:26). All, of course, united in denying that they had been parties to any conspiracy.

Evans insisted that he had surrendered the lease to Burbage with Kirkham's knowledge and indeed upon his initiative, and he went into considerable detail in support of his assertion. He said that after the King's inhibition had closed the playhouse and brought its profits to an end, Kirkham seemed to be ready to forgo the house, for "the moiety of the said rent was yearly to be paid by [Kirkham], and he was also tied by the articles of agreement to perform many other matters of charge, and, . . . as it seemed to [Evans], was willing to free himself from the same; and in pursuing his said purpose, first caused the apparels, properties and goods belonging to the copartners and masters of the Queen's Majesty's Children of the Revels (for so it was often called) to be indifferently [ap]praised, and upon such praisement the same to be divided" (43:38); "after which partition so made, . . . [Kirkham] said he would deal no more with it, 'for,' quoth he, 'it is a base thing,' or used words to such or very like effect, . . . and . . . delivered up their commission, which he had under the Great Seal, authorizing them to play, and discharged divers of the partners and poets" (42:23). Believing Kirkham thus to have taken the first step toward voiding the 1602 agreement and dissolving the partnership, Evans had felt completely justified in coming to terms with Burbage.

Kirkham said that he had suffered heavy financial loss in consequence of being dispossessed through the complots of Evans, Heminges, and Burbage. He based his estimates of that loss upon the profit that he and his partners had received before their alleged eviction, and upon what he supposed the King's Men to have been earning since then. Prior to 1608, he said, he and his colleagues "have had and received the sum of £100 per annum for their part and moiety in the premises, without any manner of charges whatsoever," and under the Keysar administration they received "above the sum of £150 per annum only for the use of the said great hall, without all manner of charges" (43:45). After he had been turned out, Evans and Burbage and Heminges had received profits of eightscore pounds by the year, besides rents, during the years 1608 to 1612 (43:4), and he estimated his own personal loss during those four years at threescore pounds per annum (42:14). As for the profits currently being earned by the King's Men, Kirkham said that "during such time as the said defendants, Heminges and Burbage and their company, continued plays and interludes in the said great hall in the Friars, that they got, and as yet doth, more in one winter in the said great hall, by a thousand pounds, than they were used to get in the Bankside" (43:42). In this last statement certainly,[44] and in all the others probably, Kirkham was exaggerating; he magnified the profits as a means of magnifying his own losses.

When the case of Kirkham vs. Paunton came before the Court of Chancery for decision, the Court did not undertake to say whether or not an agreement had in fact existed for the conveyance of the lease by Hawkins to Kirkham and his partners, but it did say that no such conveyance had ever been perfected and sealed. It ruled in effect that the lease in controversy was no longer a factor, for the reason that "the defendant Evans hath surrendered the lease of the whole playhouse unto the defendant Burbage, of whom he had formerly purchased the same, and that the said plaintiff [Kirkham], nor the said Evans, under whom he claimeth, had ever paid any rent unto the said Burbage since the said surrender"; and "it is therefore ordered by this Court that the matter of the

plaintiff's Bill be clearly and absolutely dismissed out of this Court"
(43:46).

End of the Child Actors

The success of the Little Eyases in the period from 1600 to 1608 is
harder to explain than the success of their predecessors a quarter of a
century earlier. Playgoers had flocked to the First Blackfriars between
1576 and 1584 because the children had better playwrights and plays than
the adult actors, better costumes and properties, better music, and a more
accessible and comfortable playhouse. But by the turn of the century the
men had caught up with the children in nearly all these respects. Their
dramatists and plays were at least as good. Their actors—Richard Burbage
and Edward Alleyn being the two greatest actors of the age—were better.
Their costumes and properties were no longer inferior. Only in music
and in the accessibility of their playhouse did the boys still outrank the
men. And to counterbalance these superiorities, the children had inherent
disabilities. By definition, they could not have served long apprenticeships
to their profession, nor could they continue in it long after having started.
Neither visually nor vocally could they express maturity in the male
characters that they portrayed, and their piping voices could not sound
the heavy notes of passion or tragedy.

Yet all the greatest dramatists of the day, barring Shakespeare,
wrote for the Children at Blackfriars, and did so without making obvious
allowances for deficiencies in power or in skill. The Little Eyases became
the fashion and beat the Lord Chamberlain's Men at their own game;
and when finally their career was ended by royal mandate, they bequeathed to their elders a group of traditions that lasted as long as the
Blackfriars lasted, and that even left their impress upon the final plays of
Shakespeare. These things they accomplished in spite of being managed
by shifting syndicates made up of men of quarrelsome habits, money-
grabbing propensities, and (except for Evans and perhaps Kirkham) a
total lack of previous theatrical experience.

By the time that King James ordered the Porter's Hall pulled down,
the phenomenon of child actors had spent its vitality. It has had no important rebirths since.

1. Kirkham vs. Paunton *et al.*, *Chancery Proceedings*, James I, K 5, No. 25, printed in its original spelling in Fleay, pp. 240-41. Cf. 43:30.

2. Chambers, *Elizabethan Stage*, Vol. IV, pp. 329–31, no. cxxiv.

3. Burbage seems to have forgotten that Evans's first partners were Giles and Robinson, and that Kirkham, Rastall, and Kendall did not come into the venture until 1602. But he is explicit in saying that the setting up of the company of boys came *after* the making of the lease.

4. *Children of the Chapel*, pp. 56–58.

5. Pp. 125, 153.

6. Viz., Nashe's *Lenten Stuff*, which was entered in the Stationers' Register on January 11, 1599.

7. Cf. Chambers, *Elizabethan Stage*, Vol II, p. 42, and Vol. III, pp. 357–58. On p. 358 Chambers says that "with the assumption that C[ase Is] A[ltered] was a Chapel play disappears the assumption that the Chapel themselves began their renewed dramatic activities at a date earlier than the end of 1600."

8. *Hamlet*, ed. Kittredge, II ii 343–379.

9. See p. 297 below.

10. Edmund Howes, *Annales, or A Generall Chronicle of England*, 1631, sig. iiii, verso.

11. Flecknoe.

12. Chambers, *Elizabethan Stage*, Vol. IV, pp. 166–67.

13. III iv 373.

14. Document 23, transcribed from Wallace, *Children of the Chapel*, p. 61, n. 1. Wallace's whole conception of the Children of the Chapel is based upon the assumption that they enjoyed the special favor of Queen Elizabeth and that they were fed, clothed, housed, and trained at the Queen's expense. He interprets the Giles commission as being merely one

manifestation of that special interest (pp. 58–72), and finds other indications in the following circumstances:

(a) That the Queen attended a play at Blackfriars on December 29, 1601, as evidenced by a letter written to John Chamberlain by Sir Dudley Carleton: "The Q: dined this day privately at my Ld Chamberlains; I came even now from the blackfriers where I saw her at the play wth all her candidae auditrices." But it is highly improbable that her Majesty went to the Blackfriars Playhouse, as Wallace assumes (pp. 95–97). At the end of 1601 the Lord Chamberlain was George Carey Lord Hunsdon, who had a mansion in the precinct and was patron of the Lord Chamberlain's Men. Probably, therefore, the play was given in his great hall by his company of actors. The Queen was not in the habit of going to a playhouse when she wished to see a play: she had the play brought to her; and even if she did make an exception on this occasion, that fact still fails to demonstrate that she was financing the Children.

(b) That the Duke of Stettin-Pomerania says in his Diary that "the Queen has established for them a special theatre and has provided them with a superabundance of rich apparel" (*op. cit.*, pp. 105–14). But the Duke was certainly mistaken in saying that the Queen had provided the Children with a theater, and was probably equally mistaken in saying that she had provided them with costumes. After all, a traveling foreigner should not be expected to be an expert witness as to the internal affairs of a playhouse that he visited only once.

(c) That Evans gave testimony in 1612 which Wallace takes to mean that Edward Kirkham, as Yeoman of the Revels, had "disbursed and allowed great sums of money" out of the Queen's purse for the dieting of the boys (pp. 98–104). This question is discussed on page 187 above.

15. Both Chambers (*Elizabethan Stage*, Vol. II, pp. 33–34) and Wallace (*Children of the Chapel*, p. 65, n. 1) recite the almost identical commission issued to Richard Edwardes in 1561, and Wallace (*op. cit.*, p. 66, n. 2) also recites the commission issued to William Hunnis in 1567.

16. This is evidenced by a King's Bench suit discovered by Professor Hillebrand, in which Thomas Kendall, who from 1602 until 1607 was one of the managers of the Children's company, demanded forfeiture of an indenture given to him by Alice Cooke. Mrs. Cooke had apprenticed her son Abell to him on November 14, 1606, under an obligation that bound the boy to remain with Kendall for three years as an actor in the company; but the boy had left after six months, whereupon Kendall sued the mother. See *The Child Actors*, pp. 197–98.

17. Most of the Chapel plays contain from twenty to thirty roles, of which the less important were of course played by substitutes or doubled. Keysar said in 1610 that during his regime the company consisted of "the most expert and skillful actors within the realm of England, to the number of eighteen or twenty persons" (41:12).

18. *Public Record Office Patent Roll*, 4 James I, Part 18, dorso, here reprinted with modernized spelling from *Malone Society Collections*, Vol. I, pp. 362–63. Incidentally, the commission issued by King James on February 4, 1604 does not confer the right of impressment upon the patentees of the Children of the Queen's Revels (Document 26).

19. Wallace's affection for Giles leads him astray. He contends that Evans was the only malefactor and the only one punished, and says that the Star Chamber decision did not "in any way affect Gyles in his official position, which he continued to hold for the rest of his life. The Queen's Court seems to have found no fault in him" (*Children of the Chapel*, p. 83; cf. p. 58, n. 3). As has been said, Giles did indeed continue to hold the office of Master of the Children of the Chapel for the rest of his life; but even Wallace, who, as he says of the Queen's Court, finds no fault in him, fails to associate him even once with any Blackfriars event or activity postdating the decree.

20. Evans says that he transferred "all his goods, chattels, and leases" to Hawkins "long time before any communication [was] had" between himself and Hawkins on the one party, and Kirkham and his colleagues on the other (43:37); in other words, long before April 20, 1602. He says that he did not transfer the Blackfriars lease to Hawkins at the same time (43:37). According to Paunton, the transfer of the lease took place on or about October 21, 1601 (43:14).

21. Mark Eccles, "Martin Peerson and the Blackfriars," *Shakespeare Survey 11*, pp. 103–104.

22. Hillebrand, p. 167, suggests that the money was paid "as a kind of interest on the money Evans had spent in getting the company going, paid to him in view of his interests in the Blackfriars and his withdrawal from active management." But this still fails to explain why payments were to be made only when plays were being given.

Wallace, *Children of the Chapel*, pp. 98ff., refusing to substitute "defendant" for "complainant," believes that Kirkham, as Yeoman of the Revels, acted as the Queen's deputy in supplying funds out of the royal treasury for the Children's maintenance. But why should Kirkham pay Evans a weekly stipend because he (Kirkham) had previously maintained the boys out of funds supplied by the Queen? This is a part of Wallace's ill-advised theory of royal subvention for the Children of the Chapel.

23. 42:11, 42:21.

24. 43:1, 43:2, 43:25, 43:34, 43:41.

25. 43:42.

26. 42:11. This word is spelled "ymploiments" in Fleay's transcription of the document in its original spelling (*Chronicle History*, p. 217). In the parallel passage at 42:21, the corresponding word is spelled "Implements" (*ibid.*, p. 221).

27. See p. 203 above.

28. Murray, *English Dramatic Companies*, Vol. I, pp. 147–48.

29. Quoted from Chambers, *Elizabethan Stage*, Vol. IV, p. 253.

30. But the various titles were sometimes carelessly used, and those that had been discarded were apt to be revived for the prestige that they gave to the title pages of printed plays.

31. Sir Thomas Lake seems to imply that the play dealing with the Scotch mines was played by the Children of Blackfriars, but that the "matters of France" were played by some other company. If so, he is mistaken. Both the title page of *Byron* and a letter by M. de la Boderie, the French ambassador, make it clear that *Byron*, like the play about the mines, was presented at Blackfriars.

32. Printed in its original spelling in Chambers, *Elizabethan Stage*, Vol. II, pp. 53–54, and in Hillebrand, p. 200.

33. Hillebrand, p. 203, says that agreement for surrender of the lease was concluded on August 10, 1609. He names this date because the defendants in the Keysar suit, in their plea dated February 12, 1610, said that "the said surrender . . . was about the tenth of August last past" (41:9). But the defendants were speaking carelessly and erroneously. The surrender actually took place a year earlier, as proved by the following sequence of events: the King closed the playhouse in March, 1608, after the *Byron* incident; Kirkham had the costumes, etc., appraised on July 26, 1608, in preparation for dissolution of the partnership (42:22); Burbage and Heminges said that they reached agreement with Evans for surrender of the lease "about August in the sixth year of his Majesty's reign" (43:22), and Richard Burbage's indentures of lease to his six partners were executed on August 9, 1608 (see p. 246 below). Kirkham's testimony, for whatever it was worth, also pointed to 1608 when he said on July 1, 1612, that Evans had shared the profits of the playhouse with Burbage and Heminges "for the space of these four years last past" (43:4).

34. *Patent Roll*, 7 James I, part 13, printed in *Malone Society Collections*, Vol. I, pp. 271–72.

35. The first edition of *The Knight of the Burning Pestle*, 1613, is dedicated by Walter Burre, the publisher, "To his many ways endeared friend, Master Robert Keysar," in gratitude to Keysar for having preserved the play and sent it to Burre for printing.

36. Marston was not the only outsider to whom the patentees had sold a share in the enterprise. Another one-sixth share was held in 1604 by William Strachey, who later was to survive the Bermuda shipwreck and write an account of it that supplied material for Shakespeare's description of the storm in *The Tempest*. Still another share was owned in 1606 by a musician named Martin Peerson, who sold it back to Thomas Kendall for £45. See Eccles, pp. 100–103.

37. But this stipulation almost certainly had not kept Evans from reassigning the lease to Hawkins. See pp. 201–04 above.

38. Court of Requests, Affidavits, 6–9 James I, Miscellaneous Books, 127.

39. *Patent Roll*, 13 James I, part 20, printed in full in *Malone Society Collections*, Vol. I, pp. 277–79.

40. *Privy Council Register*, James I, Vol. II, p. 74; printed in full in *Malone Society Collections*, Vol. I, pp. 373–74.

41. *Privy Council Register*, James I, Vol. II, p. 516; printed in full in *Malone Society Collections*, Vol. I, p. 374.

42. *King's Bench, Coram Rege Rolls*, Easter 7 James I, m. 265b. See Hillebrand, p. 189, n. 40. Percival Golding, testifying in Chancery in 1609, said that Kirkham and Kendall had given the new bond to Hawkins on condition that their disputes should be referred to arbiters, and on the further condition that Hawkins, not Evans, should manage the affairs of the playhouse. See Eccles, p. 104.

43. The Schoolhouse was probably the middle story of the Duchy Chamber. This conjecture is based upon the following facts: (a) that story was on the same level as the great hall; (b) it had a chamber over it; (c) it could be severed from the great hall by locking of a door; and (d) it was in point of fact of no monetary importance to the playhouse as playhouse.

44. Earlier in the same suit Kirkham estimated "the profits of the said premises [as] being worth eightscore pounds by the year, besides the rents reserved thereupon" (43:4).

❧ 10 ❧

Blackfriars Repertories

No CONTEMPORARY drawing or description of the Blackfriars stage is known to exist. In the absence of any direct information as to its design and equipment, we can reconstruct it only by analyzing the demands made upon the stage by the plays performed upon it, and so recognizing the physical resources that enabled the stage to meet those demands.

This short chapter lists the titles of 133 plays admitted in evidence for this purpose, and gives the reasons for accepting them and rejecting others. The lists do not include all the plays known or believed to have been presented at the Second Blackfriars by the Chapel-Revels Children and the King's Men. On the contrary, they include only those extant plays that presumably were written specifically for performance on the Blackfriars stage. They exclude all plays, among others, that were revived at Blackfriars after having first been performed elsewhere, on the theory that such plays are likely to reflect the conditions of the stages for which they were originally written, rather than those of the stage on which they were later revived. The lists therefore exclude all plays of the King's Men that had their first performances in any public playhouse, including the Globe; and this means that they exclude all of Shakespeare's plays except the last three that he wrote alone, and the two that he wrote with Fletcher.

Subject to this blanket exclusion of all plays that were initially produced elsewhere than at Blackfriars, the lists include plays that fall into one or both of the following categories: first, plays specifically known to have been performed at Blackfriars; and second, plays known to have been acquired by the Chapel-Revels Children or the King's Men during their respective tenancies of that playhouse, and thus presumed to have been presented originally upon its stage. Each category has its special exceptions.

Direct Evidence of Performance at Blackfriars

Information that points directly to a play's having been performed at Blackfriars may take one or more of several forms. Sometimes it resides in the play itself, either on the title page of the play as printed in quarto, or in dialogue, or in an address to spectators or readers. At other times it is found in contemporary letters or diaries, or in the Office Book of the Master of the Revels, or in the schedules of plays allotted to Davenant or Killigrew after the Restoration.

Of the 133 plays in the two lists that follow, 68,[1] or just over one half, have quarto title pages that make the claim that the play was acted at Blackfriars. Nearly all such claims may be accepted without reservation, but a few are subject to mistrust. The Blackfriars name on a title page had sales appeal; it carried weight with the gentry and literati of the time, and its prestige led some stationers to make improper use of it to promote the sale of their wares. Thus the title pages of two King's Men's plays make Blackfriars claims that their prefaces refute,[2] and those of two Children's plays apply the Blackfriars name to a playhouse not entitled to bear it.[3]

Conversely, the name of the Globe alone, on the title page of a King's Men's play printed after 1609, is cause for doubt that the play was acted at Blackfriars; its lesser value as an inducement to buy is evidenced by its being cited alone only five times on the title pages of the company's plays, as against ten times for the Blackfriars and the Globe together, and forty-nine times for the Blackfriars alone. If, therefore, the five plays that mention only the Globe had been acted at both houses, Blackfriars would in all probability have been specified in addition to, or instead of, the Globe; and since it was not, the five plays are excluded from the Blackfriars list in spite of their having clearly been the property of the King's Men.[4]

The Davenant and Killigrew warrants give the names of 121 plays as having been the property of the King's Men and as having been performed at Blackfriars (Documents 33 and 34). Of that total, 115 plays are otherwise known or believed to have been owned by that company, and 44 are otherwise known to have been presented at Blackfriars. It is difficult to know just how much authority should be granted to the warrants' assertion that the remaining 77 plays also were presented there. On the one hand, the warrants give some evidence of having been carefully compiled; the plays of a given dramatist tend to be grouped together, and the lists even show an unexpected approach toward alphabetical arrangement; on the other hand, the Davenant schedule was made up eighteen years after the playhouse had been closed and the company disbanded, and the Killigrew schedule twenty-six years after; and in those intervals records could be lost and memories could fail. I therefore cite the testimony of the warrants when it is supported by evidence from other sources, but I omit from the list any play as to which the presumption of performance at Blackfriars rests upon the authority of the allotment warrants alone.

Presumption Based on Ownership

The King's Men's occupancy of two playhouses after 1609 removes any hope of achieving complete accuracy in compiling a list of the plays written specifically for performance at Blackfriars; five plays have already been mentioned as being excluded from the present list on the theory that they were presented only at the Globe. In general, however, the King's Men's ownership of any given play is sufficient reason for assuming that they acted it at Blackfriars. Both with respect to revenue and with respect to prestige, Blackfriars quickly became the company's leading playhouse, and the Globe slipped into second place: the company therefore purchased or commissioned plays primarily with a view to their performance at Blackfriars; it did not buy them for presentation at the Globe alone. It is thus more realistic to include a play in the Blackfriars list merely on the basis of ownership—barring special reasons for rejection—than to exclude it for lack of direct evidence that it was performed at Blackfriars.

Such direct evidence would exist for more of the King's Men's plays if more of them had been printed in quarto before being published in folio. This is particularly true of the plays written by Beaumont and Fletcher, the most prolific of the company's dramatists. Forty-four of their plays are listed by Professor Bentley as having been the property of the King's Men and as having been printed during the seventeenth century;[5] of the forty-four, thirty-one were first published in the Folio of 1647, and therefore lacked individual title pages on which statements of Blackfriars performance could have been printed; of the thirteen plays first printed in quarto, nine have title pages that claim performance at Blackfriars. Of Ben Jonson's plays, only five offer proof, aside from the Davenant-Killigrew warrants, of Blackfriars performance; four others are included in my list because they belonged to the King's Men, and because that company would not have failed to present them to Black-friars audiences. Of Shakespeare's final plays, only *The Two Noble Kinsmen* bears documentary evidence of having been played at Black-friars; for *Cymbeline, The Winter's Tale, The Tempest,* and *Henry VIII,* the presumption that they were played there rests solely upon the fact of their being the property of the King's Men.

By these processes of inclusion and exclusion, we arrive at a list of 133 plays accepted as Blackfriars plays for the purposes stated at the beginning of this chapter. Of the 133, 25 were in the repertory of the Children,[6] 112 in that of the King's Men,[7] and 4 plays were in both.[8]

In the lists that follow, the title of the play is given first, the name of the author second, and the date third. Dates up to 1616 are those of Chambers;[9] after 1616, those of Bentley.[10] Capital letters within square brackets refer to the index letters below, and indicate the nature of the evidence that justifies the play's inclusion in the list. Letters at the be-ginning of the alphabet, A through E, relate to direct evidence that the play was performed at Blackfriars. Letter X indicates a presumption of Blackfriars performance, based upon the play's having been in the reper-tory of one or the other of the two companies during its tenure of that playhouse.

Key

[A] A statement on the title page of the printed play, to the effect that the play was acted at Blackfriars.

[B] Internal evidence of Blackfriars performance, in dialogue, ad-dresses to spectators or readers, etc.

[C] Notation in the Office Book of the Master of the Revels, showing that the play was licensed for performance, or was performed, at Blackfriars.

[D] Mention in contemporary diaries, letters, laudatory poems, etc., of the play's having been performed there.

[E] Inclusion in the Davenant or Killigrew allotment warrants.

[X] Inclusion in the repertory of the Chapel-Revels Children or of the King's Men during their respective tenancies of the Blackfriars Playhouse.

1. *All Fools* : George Chapman : 1604? : [A]
   Byron's Conspiracy. See *The Conspiracy of Charles Duke of Byron*
   Byron's Tragedy. See *The Tragedy of Charles Duke of Byron*
2. *The Case Is Altered*: Ben Jonson : 1597?–1609 : [A,x]
3. *The Conspiracy of Charles Duke of Byron* : George Chapman : 1608 : [A]
4. *Cupid's Revenge* : Beaumont and Fletcher : 1607–1608[11] : [x]
5. *Cynthia's Revels* : Ben Jonson : 1600–1601 : [A,x]
6. *The Dutch Courtesan* : John Marston : 1603–1604 : [A,x]
7. *Eastward Ho!* : Chapman, Jonson, and Marston : 1605 : [A,x]
8. *The Faithful Shepherdess* : Beaumont and Fletcher : 1608–1609 : [x]
9. *The Fawn (Parasitaster)* : John Marston : 1604–1606 : [A,x]
10. *The Fleir* : Edward Sharpham : 1606 : [A,x]
11. *The Gentleman Usher* : George Chapman : 1602? : [x]
12. *The Isle of Gulls* : John Day : 1606 : [A,D,x]
13. *The Knight of the Burning Pestle* : Beaumont and Fletcher : 1607 : [x]
14. *Law Tricks, or Who Would Have Thought It* : John Day : 1604 : [x]
15. *The Malcontent* : John Marston : 1604 : [B,x]
16. *May Day* : George Chapman : *circa* 1609 : [A]
17. *Monsieur D'Olive* : George Chapman : 1604 : [A,x]
    Parasitaster. See *The Fawn*
18. *Philotas* : Samuel Daniel : 1604 : [x]
19. *Poetaster* : Ben Jonson : 1601 : [A,x]
20. *Sir Giles Goosecap* : Anonymous : 1601–1603 : [x]
    Sophonisba. See *The Wonder of Women*
21. *The Tragedy of Charles Duke of Byron* : George Chapman : 1608 : [A]
22. *A Trick to Catch the Old One* : Thomas Middleton : 1604–1606? : [A]
23. *The Widow's Tears* : George Chapman : 1603–1609 : [A]
24. *The Wonder of Women, or Sophonisba* : John Marston : 1606 : [A]
25. *Your Five Gallants* : Thomas Middleton : 1607 : [A]

1. *Aglaura* : John Suckling : 1637 : [A,D,E,X]
2. *The Alchemist* : Ben Jonson : 1610 : [E,X]
3. *Alphonsus, Emperor of Germany* : Anonymous : > 1604?, > 1630? : [A,B,E,X]
4. *Anything for a Quiet Life* : Thomas Middleton : *circa* 1621 : [A,X]
5-6. *Arviragus and Philicia, Parts 1 and 2* : Lodowick Carlell : 1635–1636 : [A,E,X]
   Barnavelt. See *Sir John van Olden Barnavelt*
7. *The Bashful Lover* : Philip Massinger : 1636–1637 : [A,E,X]
8. *The Beggars' Bush* : Beaumont and Fletcher : > 1622 : [E,X]
9. *Believe As You List* : Philip Massinger : 1631 : [X]
10. *The Bloody Brother (Rollo Duke of Normandy)* : Beaumont and Fletcher : 1617? : [E,X]
11. *Bonduca* : Beaumont and Fletcher : 1609–1614 : [E,X]
12. *Brennoralt (The Discontented Colonel)* : John Suckling : 1639–1641 : [A,E,X]
13. *The Broken Heart* : John Ford : *circa* 1627–1631? : [A,X]
14. *The Brothers* : James Shirley : 1641? : [A,E,X]
   Byron's Conspiracy. See *The Conspiracy of Charles Duke of Byron*
   Byron's Tragedy. See *The Tragedy of Charles Duke of Byron*
15. *Caesar and Pompey* : George Chapman : *circa* 1613? : [A]
16. *The Captain* : Beaumont and Fletcher : 1609–1612 : [E,X]
17. *The Cardinal* : James Shirley : 1641 : [A,E]
18. *Catiline his Conspiracy* : Ben Jonson : 1611 : [E,X]
19. *A Challenge for Beauty* : Thomas Heywood : 1634–1635? : [A,X]
20. *The Chances* : Beaumont and Fletcher : *circa* 1617? and *circa* 1627? : [E,X]
21. *The City Madam* : Philip Massinger : 1632? : [A,X]
22. *The City Match* : Jasper Mayne : 1637–1638? : [A,X]
23. *The Conspiracy (Pallantus and Eudora)* : Henry Killigrew : 1634–1635 : [B,D]
24. *The Conspiracy of Charles Duke of Byron* : George Chapman : 1608 : [A]
25. *The Country Captain* : William Cavendish : 1639–1641 : [A,E,X]

26. *The Coxcomb* : Beaumont and Fletcher : 1608–1610 : [E,X]
27. *The Cruel Brother* : William Davenant : 1626–1627 : [A,X]
28. *The Custom of the Country* : Beaumont and Fletcher : *circa* 1619–1620, and 1638? : [D,E,X]
29. *Cymbeline* : William Shakespeare : 1609? : [E,X]
30. *The Deserving Favorite* : Lodowick Carlell : *circa* 1622–1629 : [A,E,X]
31. *The Devil Is an Ass* : Ben Jonson : 1616 : [B,E,X]
    The Discontented Colonel. See *Brennoralt*
32. *The Distresses (The Spanish Lovers?)* : William Davenant : 1639 : [X]
33. *The Double Marriage* : Beaumont and Fletcher : *circa* 1621 : [E,X]
34. *The Duchess of Malfi* : John Webster : 1613–1614 : [A,E,X]
35. *The Duke of Milan* : Philip Massinger : 1621–1622 : [A,E,X]
36. *The Elder Brother* : Beaumont and Fletcher : 1625? : [A,D,E,X]
37. *The Emperor of the East* : Philip Massinger : 1630–1631 : [A,B,E,X]
38. *The Fair Favorite* : William Davenant : 1638 : [X]
39. *The Fair Maid of the Inn* : Beaumont and Fletcher : 1625–1626 : [C,E]
40. *The Faithful Shepherdess* : Beaumont and Fletcher : 1608–1609 : [A,E,X]
41. *The False One* : Beaumont and Fletcher : *circa* 1620 : [E,X]
42. *The Fatal Dowry* : Philip Massinger : 1616–1619 : [A,E,X]
43. *The Goblins* : John Suckling : 1637?–1641 : [A,E,X]
44. *The Guardian* : Philip Massinger : 1633 : [A,E,X]
    Hengist King of Kent. See *The Mayor of Quinborough*
45. *Henry VIII* : Shakespeare and Fletcher : 1613? : [E,X]
46. *The Honest Man's Fortune* : Beaumont and Fletcher : 1613 : [X]
47. *The Humorous Lieutenant* : Beaumont and Fletcher : 1619? : [E,X]
    Humours Reconciled. See *The Magnetic Lady*
48. *The Imposture* : James Shirley : 1640 : [A,E,X]
49. *The Inconstant Lady* : Arthur Wilson : > 1630 : [B,X]
50. *The Island Princess* : Beaumont and Fletcher : 1619–1621 : [E,X]
51. *The Just Italian* : William Davenant : 1629 : [A,X]
52. *The Knight of Malta* : Beaumont and Fletcher : 1616–1618 : [E,X]

216

53. *The Laws of Candy* : Beaumont and Fletcher : 1619? : [E,X]
54. *The Little French Lawyer* : Beaumont and Fletcher : 1619–1623 : [E,X]
55. *The Lost Lady* : William Berkeley : 1637–1638 : [D,E,X]
56. *Love and Honour* : William Davenant : 1634 : [A,X]
57. *The Lover's Melancholy* : John Ford : 1628 : [A,C,X]
58. *The Lover's Progress* (*The Wandering Lovers*) : Beaumont and Fletcher : 1623, 1634 : [E,X]
59. *Love's Cure, or The Martial Maid* : Beaumont and Fletcher : ? and 1625 : [E,X]
60. *Love's Pilgrimage* : Beaumont and Fletcher : 1616?, 1635 : [E,X]
61. *The Loyal Subject* : Beaumont and Fletcher : 1618, 1633 : [E,X]
62. *The Mad Lover* : Beaumont and Fletcher : 1616? : [E,X]
63. *The Magnetic Lady, or Humours Reconciled* : Ben Jonson : 1632 : [D,E,X]
64. *The Maid in the Mill* : Beaumont and Fletcher : 1623 : [E,X]
65. *The Maid's Tragedy* : Beaumont and Fletcher : > 1611 : [A,E,X]
66. *The Malcontent* : John Marston : 1604 : [B,X]
The Martial Maid. See *Love's Cure*
67. *The Mayor of Quinborough, or Hengist King of Kent* : Thomas Middleton : 1616–1620? : [A,E,X]
68. *Monsieur Thomas* : Beaumont and Fletcher : 1610–1616 : [A]
69. *More Dissemblers Besides Women* : Thomas Middleton : *circa* 1615? : [E,X]
70. *The New Inn* : Ben Jonson : 1628–1629 : [E,X]
71. *News from Plymouth* : William Davenant : 1635 : [X]
72. *The Noble Gentleman* : Beaumont and Fletcher : 1625–1626? : [C,E,X]
73. *The Northern Lass* : Richard Brome : 1629 : [A,E,X]
74. *The Novella* : Richard Brome : 1632 : [A,E,X]
75. *Osmond the Great Turk* : Lodowick Carlell : 1622? : [E,X]
Pallantus and Eudora. See *The Conspiracy*
76. *The Parson's Wedding* : Thomas Killigrew : 1639–1640 : [B]
77–78. *The Passionate Lovers, Parts 1 and 2* : Lodowick Carlell : 1638 : [A,X]
79. *Philaster* : Beaumont and Fletcher : > 1610 : [E,X]
80. *The Picture* : Philip Massinger : 1629 : [A,X]
81. *The Pilgrim* : Beaumont and Fletcher : 1621? : [E,X]
82. *The Platonic Lovers* : William Davenant : 1635 : [A,X]

83. *The Prophetess* : Beaumont and Fletcher : 1622 : [E,X]
84. *The Queen of Aragon* : William Habington : 1640 : [B]
85. *The Queen of Corinth* : Beaumont and Fletcher : 1616–1617 : [E,X]

Rollo Duke of Normandy. See *The Bloody Brother*

86. *The Roman Actor* : Philip Massinger : 1626 : [A,E,X]
87. *The Royal Slave* : William Cartwright : 1636–1637 : [E,X]
88. *Rule a Wife and Have a Wife* : Beaumont and Fletcher : 1624 : [D,E,X]
89. *The Sea Voyage* : Beaumont and Fletcher : 1622 : [E,X]
90. *The Second Maiden's Tragedy* : Anonymous : 1611 : [X]
91. *Sir John van Olden Barnavelt* : Beaumont and Fletcher : 1619 : [X]
92. *The Sisters* : James Shirley : 1642 : [A,E]
93. *The Soddered Citizen* : John Clavell : *circa* 1630 : [X]
94. *The Sophy* : John Denham : 1641? : [A,E,X]
95. *The Spanish Curate* : Beaumont and Fletcher : 1622 : [C,E,X]

The Spanish Lovers. See *The Distresses*

96. *The Staple of News* : Ben Jonson : 1625–1626 : [E,X]
97. *The Swisser* : Arthur Wilson : 1631 : [B,X]
98. *The Tempest* : William Shakespeare : 1611 : [E,X]
99. *Thierry and Theodoret* : Beaumont and Fletcher : date? : [A,E,X]
100. *The Tragedy of Charles Duke of Byron* : George Chapman : 1608 : [A]
101. *The Two Noble Kinsmen* : Shakespeare and Fletcher : 1613 : [A,X]
102. *The Unfortunate Lovers* : William Davenant : 1638 : [A,D,X]
103. *Valentinian* : Beaumont and Fletcher : 1610–1614 : [E,X]
104. *The Variety* : William Cavendish : 1641–1642? : [A,E,X]
105. *A Very Woman* : Philip Massinger : ? and 1634 : [A,X]

The Wandering Lovers. See *The Lover's Progress*

106. *The Widow* : Thomas Middleton : *circa* 1616 : [A,E,X]
107. *A Wife for a Month* : Beaumont and Fletcher : 1624 : [E,X]
108. *The Wild-Goose Chase* : Beaumont and Fletcher : 1621? : [A,E,X]
109. *The Winter's Tale* : William Shakespeare : 1610? : [E,X]
110. *The Witch* : Thomas Middleton : *circa* 1610–1616? : [A,X]
111. *The Wits* : William Davenant : 1633–1634 : [A,D,X]
112. *Women Pleased* : Beaumont and Fletcher : 1619–1623 : [X]

1. In this total, the two *Byron* plays count as two, and so do the two parts of *Arviragus and Philicia* and of *The Passionate Lovers*.

2. The 1652 title page of *The Doubtful Heir* says that the play was acted at Blackfriars, but the author, James Shirley, says in his Prologue that it was acted at the Globe instead. Similarly, the 1657 title page of *The Queen's Exchange*, by Richard Brome, claims performance at Blackfriars, but the author of the preface says of the play that "when 'twas written, or where acted, I know not."

3. Both the 1618 title page of *Amends for Ladies*, and the 1616 title page of *The Scornful Lady*, lay claim to performance at Blackfriars; but theirs was the short-lived Porter's Hall Playhouse established by Rosseter within the Blackfriars precinct. See pp. 197-198 above.

4. Viz., *Albertus Wallenstein*, by Henry Glapthorne; *A Game at Chess*, by Thomas Middleton; *The Late Lancashire Witches*, by Heywood and Brome; *The Merry Devil of Edmonton*, by an unknown author; and *The Unnatural Combat*, by Philip Massinger.

5. *Jacobean and Caroline Stage*, Vol. I, pp. 109–15.

6. Repertories of the Chapel-Revels Children are given by Chambers, *Elizabethan Stage*, Vol. III, p. 145, n. 2; Harbage, *Shakespeare and the Rival Traditions*, pp. 347, 350; Hillebrand, pp. 205–06; and Thorndike, *Shakespeare's Theater*, p. 327. Wallace, *Children of the Chapel*, p. 75, gives a list for the Chapel Children only,

excluding the Revels. None of the lists agrees completely with any other, and none agrees completely with mine.

7. Repertories of the King's Men are given by Bentley, *Jacobean and Caroline Stage*, Vol. I, pp. 108–34, and by Harbage, *Annals of English Drama, cursim*. For our present purposes, these lists have the disadvantage of including plays performed either at the Blackfriars or at the Globe.

8. Viz., *The Conspiracy* and *The Tragedy of Charles Duke of Byron*, *The Faithful Shepherdess*, and *The Malcontent*.

9. For plays up to 1616, Chambers gives all the applicable data in *Elizabethan Stage*, Vols. III and IV, under the titles of the individual plays.

10. For plays after 1616, Bentley summarizes the essential data in *Jacobean and Caroline Stage*, Vol. I, pp. 108–34, and gives it in more extended form in Vols. III to V of the same work.

11. Chambers (*Elizabethan Stage*, Vol. III, p. 225) gives 1612 as a terminal date for this play, and says that no close inferior limit can be fixed. But James E. Savage shows that allusions to contemporary events suggest a date of 1607 or early 1608. See his "Beaumont and Fletcher's *Philaster* and Sidney's *Arcadia*," *Journal of English Literary History*, Vol. XIV, No. 3, pp. 194–206, and "The Date of Beaumont and Fletcher's *Cupid's Revenge*," *idem*, Vol. XV, No. 4, pp. 286–94.

☙ II ❧

Blackfriars Conventions

I N THEIR EIGHT YEARS as tenants of the Blackfriars Playhouse, the Chapel-Revels Children developed certain stage practices most of which had their origin in practices at Court, and all of which throve because they answered to the tastes of courtly audiences. When the Children left Blackfriars, they bequeathed their customs to the King's Men; and so valid were they for the Blackfriars and its audiences that, as the event proves, they lasted until both Court and stage came to an end under Oliver Cromwell. Some indeed were revived after the Restoration. I shall trace this acceptance of the Children's practices as it is reflected in the plays of Blackfriars dramatists generally, and particularly in the final plays of Shakespeare.

Sitting on the Stage

For one thing, the Blackfriars Playhouse permitted gallants to sit upon the stage during performances, in spite of the actors' and the dramatists' dislike of the practice. The Globe did not. Several of the Children's plays mention this dubious privilege accorded to fashionable gentlemen. The earliest of them is *Cynthia's Revels*, which probably was first acted in 1600 or 1601. In the Induction to that play, the First and Second Children represent members of the playhouse staff. The Third Child impersonates an inexperienced playgoer, and his fictional ignorance of his prerogative of sitting on the stage suggests that the practice was still something new.

> *3 Child.* . . . And here I enter.
> *1 Child.* What? upon the stage, too?

2 *Child.*   Yes: and I step forth like one of the children, and aske you, Would you have a stoole, sir?

3.   A stoole, boy?

2.   I, sir, if youle give me six pence, Ile fetch you one.

3.   For what I pray thee? what shall I doe with it?

2.   O lord, sir! will you betraie your ignorance so much? why throne your selfe in state on the stage, as other gentlemen use, sir.

Marston's *Malcontent* declares stage sitting to be the settled privilege of gallants at the Blackfriars, and expressly denies it for the Globe. The play was acted at both playhouses, first at Blackfriars by the Children and later at the Globe by the King's Men. In the special Induction that Webster wrote for the Globe performance, William Sly enters in the role of a gentleman who knows his rights. The passage runs thus:

Enter W. Sly, a Tyre-man following him with a stoole.

Tyre.   Sir, the Gentlemen will be angry if you sit heare.

Sly.   Why? we may sit upon the stage at the private house. . . . Where's Harry Cundale, D: Burbidge, and W: Sly, let me speake with some of them.

Tyre.   An't please you to go in sir, you may.

Sly.   I tell you no. . . .

Lowin.   Good sir will you leave the stage, Ile helpe you to a private roome.

The Knight of the Burning Pestle clearly has several gentlemen sitting on stools on the stage as the Induction begins. No authentic stage direction proves their presence, but several scraps of dialogue do. For instance, when the Citizen's Wife tries to climb from the auditorium to the stage, her husband addresses one of them with "I pray you, sir, lend me your hand to help up my wife: I thank you sir. So. . . . Boy, let my wife and I have a couple stools, and then begin"; and a few lines later the delightful Wife settles herself among them with "Sit you merry all Gentlemen, I'm bold to sit amongst you for my ease." Throughout the rest of the play she distributes green ginger, sugar candy, and kisses, and helps to direct the action of the play from her place of vantage on the stage.

The fullest dissertation on the subject of stage sitting is to be found in Chapter 6 of *The Guls Hornbook*, by Thomas Dekker.[1] This mordant treatise on contemporary manners was published in 1609, but its allusions are to conditions that prevailed a few years earlier.[2] Nearly all of Chapter 6 is devoted to expounding the advantages of sitting on the stage and to instructing gallants in the fine points of indecorum that the practice encouraged. It sets forth the benefits of stage sitting as giving the gallant "a conspicuous Eminence" and the right to gird and to rail at the author. It admonishes him to time his appearance upon the stage so that he will "creepe from behind the Arras" just as the quaking Prologue is upon the point of entering; "to laugh alowd in the middest of the most serious and saddest scene of the terriblest Tragedy"; to "mewe at passionate speeches, blare at merrie, finde fault with the musicke, whew at the childrens Action, whistle at the songs"; and "in the middle of the play [to] rise with a screwd and discontented face from your stoole to be gone: no matter whether the Scenes be good or no; the better they are the worse do you distast them; and, beeing on your feet, sneake not away like a coward, but salute all your gentle acquaintance, that are spred either on the rushes, or on stooles about you, and draw what troop you can from the Stage after you." This last cynical admonition was not needed; gallants were already in the habit of making ostentatious departures from the stage while the play was in progress, and their doing so was an eventuality that dramatists dreaded. George Chapman alludes to it in the Prologue to his *All Fools* of 1603:

> . . . for if our other audience see
> You on the stage depart before we end,
> Our wits go with you all, and we are fools;

and Ben Jonson does so in *The Devil Is an Ass*, iii v, when Fitzdottrel pleads to be permitted to go to "the Black-fryers Play-house," desiring less to see the play than

> But to be seene to rise, and goe away,
> To vex the Players, and to punish their Poet—
> Keepe him in awe!

In the Prologue to the same play Jonson complains of another of the nuisances that the custom involved: the crowding of the stage by grandees to the extent of "allowing us no place" and forcing us to act "in compasse of a cheese-trencher." In spite of everything, however, the King's Men found it necessary or expedient to continue the privilege after they took over. Later allusions to the custom are, of course, less frequent than in the earlier years, for by then it was taken for granted.[3] The final proof of its acceptance at Blackfriars is to be found in the Shakespeare First Folio, in the address "To the Great Variety of Readers"; and here again the stage-sitter's license to censure plays is recognized:

> And though you be a Magistrate of wit, and sit on the Stage at *Black-Friers,* or the *Cock-pit,* to arraigne Playes dailie, know, these Playes haue had their triall alreadie, and stood out all Appeales; and do now come forth quitted rather by a Decree of Court, then any purchas'd Letters of commendation.

The strange custom of sitting on the stage was revived when the theatres reopened upon Charles II's accession to the throne, and lasted for almost another hundred years. On one occasion a formidable riot broke out when an actor remonstrated with a nobleman for crossing the stage in front of the actors to speak to a friend, while a principal scene of *Macbeth* was playing, and was struck across the face for his pains.[4] David Garrick is credited with having put an end to the practice.

Act Intermissions

The King's Men found, too, that the Children's usage at Blackfriars differed from their own at the Globe in the matter of intermissions between the acts of a play. Plays were still not divided into acts in performance at the Globe and other public playhouses. There the action was continuous; such act divisions as were indicated in the texts of their printed plays did not represent actual practice in the theatre, but were a literary convention merely, designed to give the play an added respectability by suggesting that it had been constructed in accordance with the classical five-act form. Even in the printing house the divisions were often ignored, as evidenced by their absence in all of Shakespeare's plays as published during his lifetime. At the Blackfriars, on the other hand, acts were units of theatrical presentation, with intermissions between; and this difference, as will presently be seen, led to differences both in the structure of plays and in the techniques of production.

One evidence of act intermissions at Blackfriars during the Children's regime lies in the directions for music, and sometimes dancing, between the acts; and more often than not, the word "act" in such directions means the intermission itself, rather than a fifth part of the play.[5]

The most elaborate sequence of directions is to be found in Marston's *Wonder of Women, or Sophonisba,* in which the meticulous specification of instruments shows that the dramatist thought of the entr'acte music not merely as filling a break in the action, but as setting the mood for the action to come. The directions read as follows:

At the end of Act i, ". . . *the Cornets and Organs playing loud full Musicke for the Act"*; at the beginning of Act ii, *"Whil'st the Musicke for the first Act soundes . . ."*; between Acts ii and iii, *"Organ mixt with Recorders for this Act"*; between iii and iv, *"Organs Violls and Voices play for this Act"*; and between Acts iv and v, *"A bass Lute and a Treble Violl play for the Act."*

In the same author's *Dutch Courtesan* the indications of entr'acte music are given in dialogue rather than by stage direction. At the end of Act ii occurs this exchange:

Mulligrub. . . . Is there any Fidlers in the house?
Mrs. Mul. Yes, M. Creakes noyse.
Mul. Bid 'em play, laugh, make merry.

At the end of Act iii:

Mul. Come, lets goe heare some musicke, I will never more say my praiers. Lets goe heare some dolefull musicke.

And at the end of Act iv:

Cockledemoy. Tis time to take a nap, untill half an hour hence: God give your Worship Musicke, content, and rest.

The Knight of the Burning Pestle has, after Act i, *"Boy danceth. Musicke. Finis Actus primi"*; after Act ii, *"Musicke. Finis Actus secundi"*; and after Act iii, *"Finis Actus tertii. Musicke. Actus quartus, scoena prima. Boy daunceth."* On each of these occasions the Citizen and his Wife, seated upon the stage, comment upon the music. As the music strikes up at the end of Act i, the Wife says "Hark, hark Husband, hark, Fiddles, Fiddles; now surely they go finely. They say 'tis present death for these Fidlers to tune their Rebecks before the great Turks grace." And at the end of Act ii, in a passage that perhaps indicates that patrons of the theatre were permitted to ask for tunes that they fancied, we find the Citizen calling out "Musicians, play 'Baloo'." "No, good George," begs his Wife, "let's ha 'Lachrymae'." "Why, this *is* it, Cunny," he replies.

Other brief indications of entr'acte music are scattered through the plays in the Children's repertory, but so irregularly and casually as to create the impression that the practice was a matter of routine that needed mention only when it was tied up with other business on the stage. For instance, *The Fawn* introduces Act v with *"Whilest the Act is a playing, Hercules and Tiberio enters."* *The Gentleman Usher* begins Act iii with *"Medice after the song whispers alone with his servant."* *The Malcontent* heads Act ii with *"whilst the Act is playing: Enter* [Farneze] *unbraced, 2 Pages before him with lights";* and *A Trick to Catch the Old One* has a peremptory *"Music"* between Acts i and ii, and again between ii and iii.

Dances between the acts, twice alluded to in *The Knight of the Burning Pestle* in the stage directions already quoted, and twice in the Wife's comments, seem also to have been customary. Beaumont makes passing mention of them in his poem "To my Friend Master John Fletcher upon his Faithfull Shepherdess," in which he condemns the critics who presume to censure a play without having any knowledge of the dramatic art. His poem contains these lines:

> Nor want there those, who as the Boy doth dance
> Between the Acts, will censure the whole Play;
> Some if the Wax-lights be not new that day;
> But multitudes there are whose judgement goes
> Headlong according to the Actors cloathes.

All the foregoing allusions to entr'acte music and dance have come from the Children's plays. Like references to sitting on the stage, and presumably for the same reason, such allusions are less frequent in the plays of the King's Men. I find only the following: *The City Madam* closes Act iv with *"Whilst the Act Plays, the Footstep, little Table, and Arras hung up for the Musicians,"* and *The Fatal Dowry* ends Act ii with *"Here a passage over the stage, while the act is playing for the marriage of Charalois with Beaumelle, &c."* But the scarcity of later directions for entr'acte music does not mean that the custom fell into disuse. We have abundant evidence that both act intermissions and orchestral music persisted at Blackfriars until the end.

A second indication of act intermissions at Blackfriars lies in the frequency with which characters in plays, after having been on-stage until the end of an act, reenter at the beginning of the act that follows. Such reentrances were possible at Blackfriars because, and only because, entr'-actes provided intervals of time that separated returns from departures.

225

An actor or actors left the stage at the end of an act; the musicians struck up a tune and a boy danced, and as they did so some minutes or days or years of dramatic time slipped by, or the actor made an imaginary journey from the place of the earlier act to the place of the act that followed. Reentry at the beginning of the next act was wholly acceptable under such conditions, as much to be taken for granted as it is on the modern stage.

At the Globe and other public playhouses such reentrances were avoided; and the difference between the public and the private theatres in this respect constitutes a hitherto unexplored indication that act intermissions were customary in the private playhouses but not in the public. Because of the significance of reentrances as evidence bearing upon a question still not completely resolved, I here give the relevant data more fully than might otherwise be necessary.

Twelve plays of the Chapel-Revels Children contain twenty-two reentrances of one or more persons. The list is as follows:

Cynthia's Revels: Mercury is on-stage both at the end of Act IV and at the beginning of Act V.

The Dutch Courtesan: I–II, Freevile.

Eastward Ho!: I–II, Touchstone; II–III, Sir Petronel, Quicksilver, Security.

The Fawn: II–III, III–IV, and IV–V, Hercules.

The Fleir: II–III, Florida and Felecia; III–IV, Sparke, Ruffell, Petoune, Fleir; IV–V, Petoune.

The Gentleman Usher: II–III, Medice.

Law Tricks: III–IV, Horatio.

May Day: II–III, Lodovico; III–IV, Quintiliano, Leonoro, Innocentio, Lionello, Fannio.

Sir Giles Goosecap: I–II, Clarence; IV–V, Momford.

The Tragedy of Byron: I–II, the King; III–IV, Byron.

The Widow's Tears: II–III and III–IV, Tharsalio.

The Wonder of Women: I–II, Hanno, Bytheas, Carthalon, Gelosso; IV–V, Syphax, Erichtho.

But at the very time when the Children's dramatists were making use of reentrances at the Blackfriars whenever it suited their convenience to do so, the dramatists of the Chamberlain's-King's Men were avoiding them at the Globe. There the action was continuous; scene followed hard upon scene, and act upon act, with no breaks between. If, under such conditions, an actor should depart at the close of one act and return at the very beginning of the next, his return would be immediate; his action could only seem purposeless, awkward, and confusing, and could convey no implication that he had journeyed from one place to another or that dramatic time had elapsed. The lack of such pauses created a problem for Globe dramatists, and led them to devise the convention which has been called the Law of Reentry. It operated as follows:

> If any character appears in two consecutive acts or scenes whose action is presumed to be separated by an interval of time or to occur at places distant from each other, he must, in order to make the interval or change of place seem credible in a scheme of dramatic time, either make his exit from the stage at least ten lines before the close of the earlier scene, or delay his entrance to the later scene by at least ten lines.[6]

The Law of Reentry, though not formulated until three centuries later, was consistently observed by the public playhouse dramatists after 1595. Evidences of Shakespeare's compliance are to be found in nearly all his plays. Of his few seeming lapses from strict observance,[7] none, probably, involved an immediate reentrance as the play was presented on the public stage; nearly all, as printed, can perhaps be explained by the omission of an internal exit in the earlier scene or of a delayed entrance in the scene that follows, or by the character's actually remaining upon the stage continuously, instead of reentering.

When the King's Men took over the Blackfriars, however, they took over with it the Children's device of exits and reentrances separated by act intermissions. Of their Blackfriars plays, sixty-two contain ninety-four reentries of one or more characters. The sixty-two plays[8] cover the whole thirty-odd years of tenancy by the King's Men, and include plays by all the more important of the company's dramatists. Among them is a play by Shakespeare. In *The Tempest*, Prospero and Ariel remain on the stage to speak the last lines of Act IV, and return after a brief lapse of dramatic time to speak the first lines of Act V. As it stands, the reentry seems to be of Shakespeare's authorship and to be intentional; but in this play, which so clearly has been disfigured by other hands, the possibility exists that intervening matter has been deleted or displaced.

Incidentally, the King's Men presumably were forced to make some sort of an adjustment whenever they transferred one of the sixty-two plays from the stage of the Blackfriars to the stage of the Globe. Either the Globe was called upon to provide an unaccustomed act intermission, or the play was modified so as to make an intermission unnecessary. We have no information on this point.

Act intermissions at Blackfriars not merely permitted the reentrances which are one of the evidences of their existence, but they made another important difference in the techniques of production. They enabled one inner stage at Blackfriars to do much of the work that two did at the Globe.

This is a matter that will be more easily understood later, when the inner stages come up for discussion, but a word or two about it is desirable here, in connection with the subject of breaks between the acts. The Globe had a deep inner stage at platform level, and a corresponding inner stage on the level above. Both stages could be concealed from the audience by the closing of front curtains, and while thus concealed could be set with properties in preparation for a scene to come; and since the Globe had two inner stages, action could proceed in one while the arranging of properties proceeded in the other. At Blackfriars, on the contrary, this was impossible. Blackfriars did, to be sure, have inner stages on both levels, but that on the upper level had inadequate visibility for patrons seated in the pit, and therefore was seldom used. Act intermissions, however, largely removed the need for a second inner stage; they allowed the inner stage on the lower level to serve as the place of action in a given act, to have its properties changed during the next intermission, and to serve as a different place in the act that followed.

Reentrances and music—not merely music between the acts, but music scattered throughout the plays as an enrichment of the drama—were recognized in their own time as being characteristic of the private stage and contrary to the usages of the public playhouses. Marston makes this clear in a note at the end of his *Wonder of Women, or Sophonisba:*

> After all, let me intreat my Reader not to taxe me, for the fashion of the Entrances and Musique of this Tragidy, for know it is printed onely as it was presented by youths, & after the fashion of the private stage.

As was said a few pages back, act divisions in public theatre plays were largely meaningless; if they existed at all, they existed only in print, not in performance. Except for Ben Jonson, dramatists divided their plays arbitrarily, or permitted their printers to do so, with little regard for intervals of time, for changes of place, or for the development of the plot. But with the recognition of act divisions in actual performance on the stage at Blackfriars, the five-act structure took on an importance that it had not hitherto had. Dramatists now began to conform their intermissions to time or place or plot, or to conform time and place and plot to the intermissions. Most often the entr'actes serve to cover the passage of dramatic time. The interval may be long or short. In *The Parson's Wedding*, II–III, it is as long as the time needed for the eating of an off-stage dinner. In *Valentinian*, II–III, it covers the time during which the Emperor ravishes Lucina. In *The Duchess of Malfi*, II–III, it is a period long enough for the Duchess to conceive and bear two children; and in *The Winter's Tale*, III–IV, it is sixteen years. Sometimes, on the other hand, it represents almost no interval at all; the action stops in its tracks and then resumes with a heightening of tension. Thus in *The Alchemist*, the rogues who have abused Lovewit's house for four acts look out of the window and see the dreaded approach of the owner as Act IV comes to an end. He enters at the beginning of Act V.

It is not surprising that the act divisions inserted in the print shop in Shakespeare's pre–Blackfriars plays, since they were not of his authorship and were not observed in performance, should correspond very little to the time-distribution or place-distribution of the plays. As printed in the First Folio, most of the plays are divided acceptably enough, even though there is often nothing inevitable about the division and another would serve as well. But sometimes a major shift of dramatic place is unaccompanied by an act division, as when the action moves from London to Wales within the second act of *Richard II* and returns within the fourth, or when it moves from Rome to Corioli in the middle of Act I of *Coriolanus* and to Antium in the middle of Act IV; or when, in *Antony and Cleopatra*, a comparatively long interval of time falls within each of the first four acts, but none at a point where an act division has been inserted.

But it is interesting to find that in the matter of act divisions, as in some other respects, Shakespeare still did not change his habits in response to the changed conditions at Blackfriars; he continued to divide his plays, or not to divide them, as he had done or had not done in writing for the Globe. The act divisions still show little correspondence to dramatic place or time. The move from Sicilia to Bohemia comes in the middle of Act III of *The Winter's Tale*, and in *Cymbeline* the action moves from Britain to Wales (and after that remains there, except for three parenthetical scenes) in the midst of Act III. Only in the sixteen-year interval between Acts III and IV of *The Winter's Tale,* and in the reentrance of Prospero and Ariel, if indeed in that, does Shakespeare show any awareness, for theatrical purposes, of the existence of breaks between the acts.

Shakespeare's seeming indifference to act divisions may have been caused by his realization that the splitting up of a play into five parts was an unmitigated nuisance in actual performance; it robbed the plot of continuity, diverted the thoughts of the spectators from the drama to extraneous trivia, and forced the actors to recapture the audience's attention when the next act began. Nevertheless, frequent intermissions were unavoidable in the private playhouses because their auditoriums were lighted by candles, and because candles needed frequent tending; in the sunlit auditoriums of the public playhouses, on the other hand, that need did not exist, and plays could be presented there without a pause. This relationship between candles and act breaks was pointed out to me by Dr. John Cranford Adams in conversation. The matter of candles is further discussed on pages 301–302 below.

Masques

The masque was another Blackfriars convention that the King's Men inherited and made their own.

In its primitive nontheatrical form, a masque was merely a dance in masquerade. Its participants were persons who visited a neighboring house unexpectedly, wearing masks and carrying torches; they danced before the host and his company, then invited the spectators to take part, and finally departed. But masques of another sort, related to their predecessors only in having dancing as an essential feature, increasingly became a favorite form of royal entertainment after the accession of James I. At his Court they eventually achieved their fullest development, with poetry by Ben Jonson, music by Ferrabosco or Lanier, and scenery and costumes by Inigo Jones. Jonson's first experiment with the courtly masque came in 1605, midway in the Children's occupation of the Blackfriars. By that time the Children had already presented masques in several plays, in modest imitation of the regally expensive masques at Court, and Jonson had gained experience for his *Mask of Blackness* by providing masques in two plays produced by the Children.

In their eight years at Blackfriars, the Little Eyases staged thirteen masques or masquelike episodes in eleven plays. Sometimes the masques took the simple early form, at other times the artificial form of the classical masques at Court. Sometimes they had a relationship to the plot, at other times none. The list is as follows:

Cynthia's Revels, v *vii–x*, had two masques, the one presented by Cupid and the other by Mercury, with a final dance of the two combined. *The Dutch Courtesan*, iv *i*, had an informal masque that was broken off by a pretended duel. *The Fawn*, v *i*, had a "sporte" or "shew" supervised by Cupid. *The Gentleman Usher*, ii *i*, had a farcical masque acted by stage-frightened amateurs. *The Malcontent* had two, the first of which (iv *ii–iii*) was interrupted by news of the Duke's death, and the second of which (v *iv*) brought the plot to a climax. *May Day*, v *i*, had a masked ball. *Poetaster*, Act v, had a "prettie fiction [of] a heavenly banquet" in which the guests were dressed as classical deities, presided over by Mercury. *Sir Giles Goosecap* closed with a dance in honor of Hymen. *The Tragedy of Byron*, ii *i*, had a masque in which ladies danced before the King, with Cupid as presenter. *The Widow's Tears*, iii *i*, had a nuptial dance during which Hymen descended from the heavens; and *Your Five Gallants*, v *ii*, had a dance of maskers, torch-bearers and shield-boys.

The King's Men, on the other hand, had not yet made masques a part of their stock in trade. During the years when the Children at Blackfriars were presenting masques in nearly half their plays, the adult actors at the Globe were presenting only two, one in *The Revenger's Tragedy* and the other in *Timon of Athens*.

Shakespeare had previously called for masques in three of his plays. All were of the older and simpler form. The first was the disguising arranged by the King of Navarre and his friends for the entertainment of the French Princess in *Love's Nabour's Lost*, v *ii*, a play known to have been revived at Blackfriars later. The second was the masked ball in *Romeo and Juliet*, i *v*, led up to by the entrance of "*Romeo, Mercutio, Benvolio, with five or sixe other Maskers, Torch-bearers*," who invaded the Capulet house as uninvited guests and danced with the company there assembled. The third came in *Much Ado About Nothing*, ii *i*, when Don Pedro and his nobles entered as "Maskers with a drum" and joined in the revels of Leonato's guests. These three are the only masques in the thirty-one plays that Shakespeare wrote before writing *Timon* in 1607 or 1608.[9] All are closely related to the plots of their plays.

But the incidence of masques in King's Men's plays increased markedly after the company occupied Blackfriars; as a matter of fact, that coming event seems to have cast its shadow before, and to have influenced Shakespeare in his writing of *Timon of Athens*. He presumably wrote it at a date late enough for the company to have thought it probable, even if not yet inevitable, that they would take over the Blackfriars Playhouse for their own use; and in this and one other respect[10] he seems to have written *Timon* with Blackfriars performance in mind. Now, for the first time, he has a masque of the formal mythological kind, and, as with three of the Children's plays just cited, he has Cupid act as presenter; and now, for the first time, he has a masque that serves merely as a divertissement, with no essential relationship to the plot.

The masque in *Timon* is the last of those that can confidently be attributed to Shakespeare; the four masques or quasi-masques in the final plays are believed by some scholars to be by other hands than his. The informal masque in Cardinal Wolsey's palace in *Henry VIII*, I *iv*, with its "*Enter King and others as Maskers, habited like Shepheards,*" occurs in a scene commonly ascribed to Fletcher; so too does the masquelike vision that appears to the dying Queen Katharine in IV *ii*.[11] The vision in *Cymbeline*, V *iv*, is almost certainly interpolated and spurious.[12] The majestic vision conjured up by Prospero in *The Tempest*, IV *i*, may be by Shakespeare or may not, but in either event it probably was not a part of the play as originally written.[13] But the presence of these masques, whether or not they were interpolated—and especially if they were— underscores the importance attached to such diversions in plays performed at Blackfriars.

Having introduced only five masques in their pre-Blackfriars plays, the King's Men now have many. Beaumont and Fletcher alone furnish eight. *The False One*, III *iv*, has a masque arranged by Ptolemy in the hope of diverting Caesar's attention from Cleopatra. *The Mad Lover*, IV *i*, has a Masque of Beasts, designed as a cure for Memnon's madness. *The Maid in the Mill*, II *ii*, has an amateur masque described as a country revel. *The Maid's Tragedy*, I *ii*, has an allegorical masque in which Night rises from below in mists, and in which Neptune rises and descends. *The Prophetess*, V *iii*, has a dance of shepherds and shepherdesses, with Pan leading the men and Ceres the maids. *Valentinian*, V *vii*, has a masque in honor of the Emperor's coronation, during which a boy descends from above with a wreath for the imperial brow. *A Wife for a Month*, II *vi*, has a masque in which "*Cupid descends, the Graces sitting by him*"; and *Women Pleased*, V *iii*, has a "Masquerado of several Shapes."

Of the other Blackfriars dramatists, Brome, in *The Northern Lass*, II *vi*, has a masque of the primitive form. Carlell, in *Osmond the Great Turk*, Act II, has a masque that is indicated only by the word "[*Masque*]" in italics and square brackets. Clavell, in *The Soddered Citizen*, IV *ii*, has a dance of "7 *Maskers all in Shrowdes*." Ford, in *Lover's Melancholy*, III *iii*, has a morbid affair in which dancers impersonate diseases. Both of Massinger's masques—that in *The Picture*, II *ii*, and that in *The City Madam*, V *iii*—make use of mythological figures. Middleton's *More Dissemblers Besides Women*, I *iii*, has a street masque with a boy descending, and Shirley's *Cardinal*, III *ii*, has a dance that reaches its climax when four masquers bring in a still-bleeding corpse.

Masques at Blackfriars lost much of their popularity after the sixteen-twenties, probably in sympathy with their loss of popularity at Court after the death of King James I in 1625. The years 1630 to 1642 produced only three.

Dances

Ben Jonson, always an exception to all the rules, deplored the current fondness for dancing on the stage; he said that "the Concupiscence of Daunces and Antickes so raigneth as to runne away from Nature."[14] The stage dances of 1610 did, of course, run away from nature, just as do the ballets of today, but they were not enjoyed the less for that fact. Ben seems to have felt compelled to yield to the demand for dances when he wrote *Cynthia's Revels*, in which, in addition to the masque, he has Asotus sing and dance in III *v*; but he resisted it in the "prettie fiction" in *Poetaster*, Act V, which, of all the masques or near-masques mentioned in the last few pages, is the only one that bears no evidence of dancing.

Dancing in masques, and dancing between the acts, were not enough to satisfy Elizabethan and Jacobean tastes; the popular appetite for dancing seems to have grown by what it fed on. As a result, many of the Children's plays provide interpolated dances quite apart from any masques they may contain. Thus in *Cupid's Revenge*, I *ii*, four young men and maids dance a ceremonial measure before the Temple of Cupid. Francischina dances in *The Dutch Courtesan*, V *i*. Zoya sings and dances in *The Fawn*, II *i*, and in V *i* the courtiers address themselves to dancing while the Duke enters and takes his state. *Law Tricks*, III *i*, has dancing to a fiddler's playing. *May Day* opens with a chorus of youths dancing, and Quintiliano skips about in IV *i*. In *Sir Giles Goosecap*, II *i*, a character "daunceth speaking," and provokes the comment that "your lord is very dancitive, methinks." And in *The Wonder of Women*, I *ii*, four boys, antiquely attired with bows and quivers, dance a fantastic measure to the music of cornets. And all this, be it noted, is in addition to the masked dances that all but two of the plays contain.

The custom of interpolated dances was one that the public play-houses did not share to any great degree. We find some evidence of dancing after plays, but little more. The infrequency of dances in public-theatre plays generally is suggested by their infrequency in Shakespeare's earlier plays. Apart from the dances in the masques already mentioned, his pre-Blackfriars plays contain only the dance of the fairies in Theseus' palace in *A Midsummer Night's Dream*, v *i*, the dance of the make-believe fairies around Herne's oak in *The Merry Wives of Windsor*, v *v*, and the terminal dances in *As You Like It* and *Much Ado*.[15] In short, in the thirty-three plays that Shakespeare wrote before the King's Men began to act at Blackfriars, one finds only four dances apart from masques.

The ratio rose after that. Instead of four dances in thirty-three plays, one now finds five in the five Blackfriars plays associated with Shake-speare's name; but of the five he himself may have been responsible for only one or two. He undoubtedly specified the Dance of the Strange Shapes in *The Tempest*, III *iii*, since it occurs in a scene of his author-ship and is essential to the plot; he may or may not have called for the Dance of the Reapers and Nymphs in IV *i* of the same play. But it seems unnecessary to assume that he inserted the Dance of the Shepherds and Shepherdesses or the Dance of the Twelve Satyrs in *The Winter's Tale*, IV *iv*, or the Morris Dance in *The Two Noble Kinsmen*, which comes in a scene (III *v*) believed to have been written by Fletcher.

Other dramatists for the King's Men were more zealous than Shake-speare in continuing the tradition of dances apart from masques. Each of the following plays contains at least one: *Alphonsus of Germany*, *Barnavelt*, *The Broken Heart*, *The City Madam*, *The Custom of the Country*, *The Duchess of Malfi*, *The Fair Maid of the Inn*, *The Gob-lins*, *The Guardian*, *The Little French Lawyer*, *Love and Honour*, *More Dissemblers Besides Women*, *The Novella*, *The Parson's Wed-ding*, *The Prophetess*, *The Queen of Corinth*, *The Royal Slave*, *The Soddered Citizen*, *Thierry and Theodoret*, *Valentinian*, *The Variety*, *The Wild-Goose Chase*, *The Witch*, and *Women Pleased*. The dates of these plays indicate that dances did not, as did masques, suffer a tapering off in popularity. There were about as many in the Blackfriars' final decade as in the decade before.

Theoretically, the Little Eyases were songsters before they were actors. The commission granted by Queen Elizabeth to Nathaniel Giles had authorized him to pick up "well-singing children" wherever he might find them, "in all cathedral, collegiate, parish churches, chapels, or any other place or places . . . within this our realm of England," and to take them into her service as choristers in her Chapel Royal (23:2). We know that Evans and his colleagues abused the commission and picked up some "children no way able or fit for singing" (24:4), but, by and large, the boys were probably endowed with good voices to begin with, and thereafter were trained in song by competent masters. The likelihood is that they were as fine a group of boys' voices as could be assembled in all England.

Under such circumstances, it was inevitable that the Children's plays should make much use of music. Their twenty-five extant plays contain between sixty and seventy indications of song, sometimes with the words supplied, sometimes with no other indication than a mere "*cantat.*" The only plays that provide no evidence of song are *The Tragedy of Byron* and *The Isle of Gulls.*

The King's Men continued the tradition. Seventy-six of their non-Shakespearean plays call for songs approximately two hundred and forty times. Among the songs are the still lovely "Why so pale and wan, fond lover?" in John Suckling's *Aglaura,* two songs from Middleton's *Witch* (later intruded into *Macbeth*), and "Take, O, take those lips away," which Beaumont and Fletcher lifted bodily from *Measure for Measure,* IV i, and, with a new second verse, inserted in *The Bloody Brother,* v ii.

Songs are scattered liberally through most of Shakespeare's earlier comedies, and the lyrics that he wrote for them are some of the loveliest in the language. But there were almost no songs in the histories, and those in the tragedies—the snatches sung by the Gravedigger in *Hamlet* and the Fool in *King Lear,* the pathetically salacious ballads of the mad Ophelia, Iago's Drinking Song and Desdemona's Willow Song—were introduced rather for their dramatic impact than for their lyric quality. But after five or six years of relative disuse, the song *qua* song reappears in Shakespeare's Blackfriars plays. In *Cymbeline* he has "Hark, hark, the lark" and "Fear no more the heat o' th' sun"; in *The Winter's Tale* he has "When daffodils begin to peer," and "Lawn as white as driven snow" and three others; and in *The Tempest* he has nine in all, including "Come unto these yellow sands," "Full fadom five thy father lies," and "Where the bee sucks, there suck I." Of the Shakespeare-Fletcher plays, *Henry VIII* has one song, "Orpheus with his lute made trees," which comes in a scene ascribed to Fletcher, and *The Two Noble Kinsmen* has three, of which "Roses, their sharp spines being gone" is probably Shakespeare's. The ratio of songs per play is decidedly higher in the five Blackfriars plays than in the preceding twelve.

During the regime of the Chapel-Revels Children, the Blackfriars Playhouse not only had songs and entr'acte music, but it also had hour-long concerts before the plays began. The diary of the Duke of Stettin-Pomerania, in recounting his visit to Blackfriars on September 18, 1602, says that "for a whole hour before the play begins, one listens to a delightful instrumental concert played on organs, lutes, pandorins, mandolins, violins, and flutes, as on the present occasion" (45:4).

Furthermore, the Children made much use of mood music to increase the emotional effect of action on the stage. We find such stage directions as these in the Children's plays:

From *The Fawn*, IV *i*:

Enter Zoya supported by a gentleman ussher followed by Herod and Nympha-dora with much state, soft music playing.

From *Law Tricks*, IV *iii*:

Solemnpe Musique to a funerall song the Herse borne over the stage.

And from *The Wonder of Women*, IV *iii*:

Infernall Musicke plaies softly, whilst Erichtho enters and when she speakes ceaseth. . . . A treble Violl and a base Lute play softly within the Canopy. . . . A short song to soft musick above. . . . Orgaine and Recorders play to a single voice.

The Chamberlain's-King's Men at the Globe made less use of music. As to this we have the word of Richard Burbage himself. Standing on the stage of the Globe *in propria persona* in Webster's Induction to Marston's *Malcontent*, he explained that the play, upon being transferred from the Blackfriars to the Globe, had needed to be padded to make up for "the not received custome of musicke in our Theater."

There is no possibility of measuring the extent to which the use of atmospheric music increased after the King's Men occupied the Blackfriars, but directions such as the following are now found in their plays in greater profusion than before: "*soft musick*"; "*very solemn music*"; "*a dismal kind of music*"; "*a horrid noise of musique*"; "*dreadful music,*" and "*still music above.*" In Shakespeare's later plays, "*solemn Musick*" is called for in *Cymbeline,* IV *ii,* just before Arviragus enters with the supposedly dead Imogen in his arms, and again at V *iv,* when the Apparitions enter. "*Sad and solemne Musicke*" accompanies the dancers in the Vision in *Henry VIII,* IV *ii.* "*Solemne Musicke*" lulls the courtiers to sleep in *The Tempest,* II *i,* and "*solemne and strange Musicke*" precedes Prospero's entrance "*on the top (invisible),*" in III *iii;* "*soft Musicke*" accompanies the return of the Strange Shapes later in the same scene, and introduces the masque in IV *i.* In *The Winter's Tale,* V *iii,* Paulina summons music to awaken Hermione, and "*a sudden twang of instruments*" marks the fall of the rose from the tree in *The Two Noble Kinsmen,* V *i.*

The Blackfriars orchestra under the King's Men came to be "esteemed the best of common musitians in London." We have this on the authority of Bulstrode Whitelocke, who was at the same time a diplomat, a parliamentarian, and an amateur musician of some standing.[16] He took a pardonable pride in the compliment that the orchestra paid him by playing a certain musical composition of his whenever he came to the theatre; and their doing so perhaps suggests that the concert before the play, inaugurated by the Children, was being continued thirty years later by the King's Men. He wrote as follows in 1633 or 1634:

> I was so conversant with the musitians, and so willing to gaine their favour, especially at this time, that I composed an Aier myselfe, with the assistance of Mr. Ives, and called it *Whitelocke's Coranto;* which being cried up, was first played publiquely, by the Blackefryar's Musicke, who were then esteemed the best of common musitians in London. Whenever I came to that house (as I did sometimes in those dayes), though not often, to see a play, the musitians would presently play *Whitelocke's Coranto,* and it was so often called for, that they would have it played twice or thrice in an afternoon.[17]

Flights

The Chapel-Revels Children at Blackfriars had machinery for flights, but they used it in only two plays. Cupid made three descents from the heavens in *Cupid's Revenge,* each time to the accompaniment of cornets, and Hymen flew part way down in *The Widow's Tears,* III *ii,* and remained hovering in midair while six Sylvans entered beneath, carrying torches.

During the same years, the Chamberlain's-King's Men staged no descents at the Globe, so far as we know. We assume that the Globe had the apparatus necessary for flights, but we assume it merely because we know that other public playhouses had such equipment, and because we believe the Globe to have been at least as well-equipped as the best of them. Later, however, when the company was acting at Blackfriars, it staged flights in *Cymbeline* and *The Tempest* and the following non-Shakespearean plays: *The Mad Lover,* v *iii; More Dissemblers Besides Women,* i *iii; The Prophetess,* ii *iii; Valentinian,* v *viii; The Variety,* iv *iv; A Wife for a Month,* ii *vi,* and *The Witch,* iii *iii.* Probably most of these plays were presented at the Globe as well.

Shakespeare did not call for a flight in any pre-Blackfriars play, whether performed at the Globe or elsewhere: even when he had Hymen enter in *As You Like It*[18] and Diana in *Pericles,* he had them enter on foot like mortals, not in flight like deities.[19] Of the three celestial descents in his final plays, he probably was responsible for only one, the entrance of Ariel like a harpy in *The Tempest,* iii *iii.*[20] As has been said, someone other than Shakespeare interpolated the Vision in *Cymbeline,* v *iv,* in which "*Jupiter descends in Thunder and Lightning, sitting uppon an Eagle: hee throwes a Thunder-bolt,*" and someone other than he doubtless supplied the marginal direction "*Juno descends*" in *The Tempest,* iv *i,* opposite lines 72–73. Some of these descents will be examined in detail on a later page.

When we come to the second category of mechanical effects—the use of floor traps—we find that the children had little to teach their elders; the men were already as far advanced as they, probably because trapwork is one of the oldest of stage sciences. During their eight-year tenancy of Blackfriars, the Chapel-Revels Children made skillful and imaginative use of floor traps in seven plays.[21] But during the same years the Chamberlain's-King's Men were making equal use of traps at the Globe, and they made no increased use of them when they followed the children at Blackfriars. Several of the trap scenes of both companies are analyzed on pages 313–317 and 358–365 below.

As this chapter has demonstrated, the children were in several respects fathers to the men; when they left Blackfriars and the men took over, they left behind them a bequest of traditions and conventions that the King's Men gladly accepted and perpetuated.

Shakespeare as an individual dramatist responded to the Blackfriars innovations less readily than the King's Men and their dramatists as a group seem to have done. Although his plays as presented at Blackfriars now had intermissions between the acts, he still seems to have shown little interest in making the divisions accord with the distribution of either time or place. He did not yield to the demand for more masques and dances; all the masques in his final plays, and all but one or two of the dances, were intruded by other men. But he did provide more songs, and this may have been partly a concession to Blackfriars tastes and partly a consequence of his having, in all probability, better voices to sing his songs, and better accompaniments, than ever before. And if he did for the first time introduce a flight from the heavens, he introduced only one.

All these things, however, were mere extrinsicalities, things so superficial that when Shakespeare himself failed to supply as many masques or dances or flights as the playgoers wanted, other men could supply them for him. But in the basic character of the plays he does seem to have tried to conform to the expectations of Blackfriars audiences; in consequence, his last plays show a change in general tenor that all scholars recognize, whether they call them his romances, his tragicomedies, or merely the plays of his final period. Now, for the first time, he is writing for a courtly and sophisticated audience in a private playhouse. He now has no farces like *The Comedy of Errors* and *The Taming of the Shrew*, no lighthearted comedies like *As You Like It* and *Twelfth Night*, no tragedies or "bitter comedies," and only the one historical pageant. Instead, he has plays with improbable plots in which tragic scenes alternate with idyllic to furnish emotional variety and contrast, in which startling and ingenious situations follow one another in rapid succession, and in which, after being involved in all sorts of perils and entanglements, the virtuous emerge at the end triumphantly happy. Of necessity, he often sacrifices rational motivation to the vagaries of the plot, and gives less play than before to his immense power of characterization.

1. Chapter 6 seems to relate to the Blackfriars specifically, for the following reasons: boy actors are mentioned twice, and "infants" once; lords, knights, and inns-of-court men are spoken of as habitual patrons; and Dekker advises his reader to "provide yourself a lodging by the water-side, for . . . it adds a kind of state unto you, to be carried from thence to the stairs of your Playhouse." This would seem to be applicable only to the Blackfriars, since the Blackfriars was probably the only private playhouse that had water stairs of its own at the time when *The Guls Hornbook* was written.

2. In his address "To the Reader," prefixed to the text, Dekker says that "This Tree of Guls was planted long since, but not taking roote, could never beare till now."

3. The custom of sitting on the stage is alluded to in these other Blackfriars plays also: *City Madam*, II *ii*; *Isle of Gulls*, Prologue; *Magnetic Lady*, Induction, and Chorus between Acts II and III; *New Inn*, Dedication to the Reader; and *Staple of News*, Induction. Fitzgeffrey alludes to the custom in "Notes from Black-Fryers" (1617), sig. F8.

4. Mander and Mitchenson, pp. 32–33.

5. Cf. *Midsummer Night's Dream*, III *ii* 463 (F₁), "They sleepe all the Act." Cotgrave's *Dictionary*, 1611, has "Acte . . . also, an Act, or Pause in a Comedie, or Tragedie."

6. Cf. John Cranford Adams, "The Original Staging of *King Lear*," *Joseph Quincy Adams: Memorial Studies* (1948), p. 323. The so-called Law was first stated by R. Prölss in his *Von den ältesten Drucken der Dramen Shakespeares* in 1905. It has been discussed by several writers, including W. J. Lawrence, *Shakespeare's Workshop* (1928),

pp. 17–18, and C. M. Haines, "The 'Law of Re-Entry' in Shakespeare," *Review of English Studies*, Vol. I (1925), pp. 449–51.

7. C. M. Haines, *op. cit.*, finds that immediate reentrances occur fourteen times in Shakespeare, including *The Tempest*, V *i*, and *A Midsummer Night's Dream*, IV *i* (following the stage direction "They sleepe all the Act"), but not including reentrances in battle scenes nor in scenes misdivided in modern texts, where Shakespeare intended no clearance of the stage.

8. *Aglaura*, IV–V; *Alchemist*, III–IV; *Bashful Lover*, I–II; *Beggars' Bush*, III–IV, IV–V; *Bonduca*, III–IV; *Brennoralt*, III–IV, IV–V; *Challenge for Beauty*, IV–V; *Chances*, III–IV, IV–V; *Conspiracy*, II–III, IV–V; *Country Captain*, II–III; *Custom of the Country*, IV–V; *Deserving Favorite*, I–II, II–III, III–IV; *Devil Is an Ass*; I–II, IV–V; *Distresses*, II–III; *Duchess of Malfi*, III–IV; *Duke of Milan*, III–IV; *Emperor of the East*, I–II, II–III, III–IV; *Fair Favorite*, I–II; *False One*, III–IV; *Goblins*, I–II, IV–V; *Honest Man's Fortune*, IV–V; *Imposture*, I–II, III–IV; *Island Princess*, II–III; *Knight of Malta*, II–III; *Laws of Candy*, II–III, IV–V; *Little French Lawyer*, IV–V; *Lost Lady*, IV–V; *Love and Honour*, I–II, II–III; *Lovers' Progress*, II–III; *Love's Cure*, IV–V; *Loyal Subject*, I–II, IV–V; *Mayor of Quinboro*, I–II, II–III, III–IV; *Monsieur Thomas*, I–II; *New Inn*, IV–V; *News from Plymouth*, I–II; *Noble Gentleman*, IV–V; *Northern Lass*, I–II, II–III; *Novella*, II–III; *Osmond the Great Turk*, II–III; *Parson's Wedding*, II–III, IV–V; *2 Passionate Lovers*, II–III, IV–V; *Philaster*, II–III, III–IV, IV–V; *Pilgrim*, I–II, II–III, III–IV; *Platonic Lovers*, I–II, II–III, IV–V; *Prophetess*, I–II; *Queen of Corinth*, I–II, IV–V; *Roman Actor*, III–IV; *Royal Slave*, III–IV; *Rule a Wife*, II–III,

IV–V; *Sea Voyage*, IV–V; *Sisters*, IV–V; *Soddered Citizen*, II–III; *Sophy*, I–II, II–III, IV–V; *Swisser*, III–IV; *Tempest*, IV–V; *Thierry and Theodoret*, III–IV; *Unfortunate Lovers*, I–II, IV–V; *Valentinian*, I–II, IV–V; *Variety*, I–II; *Wild-Goose Chase*, I–II, IV–V; *Witch*, IV–V; *Wits*, IV–V.

9. It seems probable that Shakespeare originally intended to have a masque in *The Merchant of Venice*. A supper or masque at Bassanio's house is forecast thirteen times in five consecutive scenes, II *ii* to II *vi*, before the plan is abandoned at II *vi* 64. The first two scenes mention a supper or feast only, but beginning with II *iv* the masque comes increasingly to the fore. It seems unlikely that Shakespeare would have alluded to it so often as a coming event, and have led his audience to expect it, if he had intended to let it fall through at the end. It need not have been lacking in dramatic interest. It might have shown the leave-taking of Bassanio and Antonio, Shylock's discomfort in the house of a Christian, and his recognition or nonrecognition of his daughter in her disguise as a boy.

10. That is, Timon's description of the heavens as "the marbled mansion all above" (v *iii* 191). See page 418 below. *Pericles* too seems to show the approach of the Blackfriars influence in the Gower choruses that introduce the acts, and in the vision of Diana.

11. The orthodox view, as formulated by Spedding and Hickson in 1850, assigns both the revels scene (I *iv*) and the vision scene (IV *ii*) to Fletcher. Chambers agrees doubtfully (*William Shakespeare*, Vol. I, p. 497) and Kittredge unreservedly (*Complete Works*, p. 837). But R. A. Foakes, editor of the New Arden *Henry VIII*, after citing all the arguments for and against Fletcher's collabora-

tion (pp. xvii–xxvi), shows a guarded preference for Shakespeare as sole author.

12. Many editors, including Pope, Johnson and Steevens, have rejected the vision (v *iv*) as being spurious, and the majority of present-day critics endorse their view. Kittredge (*Complete Works*, p. 1331) thinks that a part of the vision may be genuine, but Chambers (*William Shakespeare*, Vol. I, p. 486) rejects it altogether.

13. Frank Kermode, editor of the New Arden *Tempest*, says that many scholars, including Fleay, the old Cambridge editors, W. J. Lawrence, Dover Wilson, and W. W. Greg, have held some variety of the opinion that the masque is a later interpolation. He himself believes it to be an integral part of the play as Shakespeare wrote it (p. xxiv). Chambers (*William Shakespeare*, Vol. I, pp. 492–93) and Kittredge (*Complete Works*, p. 3) think that some spectacular and musical elements may have been adapted or expanded, but that the masque as a whole is fully Shakespearean. Be that as it may, I find strong evidence that it was inserted as an afterthought. See my article entitled "Ariel as Ceres," *Shakespeare Quarterly*, Vol. IX No. 3 (Summer 1958), pp. 430–32.

14. The Address to the Reader, prefacing *The Alchemist*. Some copies have "Jigges and Daunces" instead of "Daunces and Antickes."

15. I exclude the Dance of the Witches in *Macbeth*, IV *i* 132, as not being Shakespeare's and as not being pre-Blackfriars. At some unknown date, probably after Shakespeare's retirement and certainly before the First Folio of 1623, the King's Men presumably decided to revive *Macbeth* at Blackfriars, but felt that it needed the addition of music and spectacle to make it palatable to Blackfriars audiences.

They gave the job to Thomas Middleton, one of their regular dramatists, who had already written a play called *The Witch*. Middleton interpolated two songs from that play—"Come away, come away" at III *v* 33, and "Black spirits and white" at IV *i* 43—and the Dance of the Witches, and the flight of Hecate at III *v* 35 ("I am for th' air. . . . My little spirit, see, / Sits in a foggy cloud and stays for me.") All are spurious.

16. Whitelocke (1605–1675) was a lawyer, and later became keeper of the Great Seal, ambassador to Sweden, and a member of the Long Parliament. He served in various official capacities under Charles I, Cromwell, and Charles II. In 1633, when the four Inns of Court jointly gave a masque before the King and Queen, Whitelocke had "the whole care and charge of all the music for this great masque, which was so performed that it excelled any music that ever before that time had been heard in England" (this being taken from a quotation in *D.N.B.*).

17. Quoted from Charles Burney, *General History of Music* (1789), Vol. III, p. 377.

18. Some scholars have felt that Hymen is a non-Shakespearean interpolation. Chambers (*William Shakespeare*, Vol. I, p. 404) thinks this "quite possible," but Kittredge, in his introduction to the play, says that "Hymen is no interloper."

19. Middleton is responsible for the flight of Hecate in *Macbeth*, III *v*. He probably inserted it in preparation for a revival of the play at Blackfriars. See footnote 15 above.

20. See the article by John Cranford Adams, "The Staging of *The Tempest*, III *iii*," in *The Review of English Studies*, Vol. XIV, No. 56 (October 1938), pp. 1–16.

21. *Case Is Altered*, III *v* and IV *viii–ix*; *Cynthia's Revels*, I *ii*; *Faithful Shepherdess*, II *i*; *Isle of Gulls*, sig. G2ᵛ; *Law Tricks*, III *i* and V *ii*; *Poetaster*, Induction; and *Wonder of Women*, III, IV, and V.

✄ 12 ✄

Blackfriars under the King's Men

JAMES BURBAGE had built the Theater on rented land in 1576. Twenty years later, alarmed by the landlord's reluctance to renew the ground lease as its expiration approached, he had bought the Parliament Chamber for conversion into a playhouse for the Lord Chamberlain's Men. Fourteen years were to elapse between the time of his purchase and the time when that company first acted on the Blackfriars stage. Within the first of those years, his plan to install an adult company in a playhouse within the City walls had been wrecked by a protest from the precinct residents and a veto from the Privy Council. Within the second year, Burbage had died and the Theater's ground lease had expired. Within the third year, Burbage's two sons, in association with some of their colleagues in the Lord Chamberlain's Men, had rented a plot of ground on the Bankside in Southwark, had dismantled the Theater, and had ferried its timbers across the Thames for use in building a new playhouse called the Globe. Within the fourth year, the Globe had been built and the company had moved into it; and within the fifth year, Richard Burbage, owner of the Blackfriars Playhouse since his father's death, had leased it to Henry Evans for the use of the Children.

The Globe was the only London playhouse of the Chamberlain's-King's Men from 1599 until 1609 or 1610. It had been erected at the expense of a syndicate in which a half interest was held by the two Burbage brothers, and the other half divided between William Shakespeare, John Heminges, Augustine Phillips, Thomas Pope, and William Kempe. All the expenses of leasing a site, erecting a building upon it, and subsequently operating the building as a theatre, were paid by the members of the syndicate in proportion to their respective holdings, and all the profits that accrued were distributed on the same basis. The members

243

of the syndicate were thus the owners and proprietors of the Globe, and were called by the technical name of "housekeepers." The syndicate was a new idea in theatrical management. Actors had previously shared in the ownership of dramatic scripts, costumes, and properties, but never before had they participated in the ownership of a playhouse.

In the perspective of three and a half centuries, it can be said unhesitatingly that the supreme decade in the history of the English drama was the decade during which the Lord Chamberlain's Men played at the Globe alone. The Globe staged the first performances of many of Shakespeare's greatest comedies, of all his tragedies except *Romeo and Juliet*, and of all his Greek and Roman plays except *Titus Andronicus*. The plays of those years were *Julius Caesar, As You Like It, Twelfth Night, Hamlet, The Merry Wives of Windsor, Troilus and Cressida, All's Well That Ends Well, Measure for Measure, Othello, King Lear, Macbeth, Antony and Cleopatra, Coriolanus, Timon of Athens*, and *Pericles*.[1] The Globe's repertory of that decade doubtless also included revivals of most of Shakespeare's earlier plays, and new plays by Dekker, Jonson, and Middleton, and potboilers that did scant honor to the stage on which Richard Burbage created the roles of Hamlet and Lear.

The Lord Chamberlain's Men performed at Court during the Christmas seasons of 1599–1600 and 1600–1601. They revived *Richard II* at the Globe on February 7, 1601, the day before the Essex rebellion, and, since Elizabethan imaginations saw analogies between the reigns of Richard and of Elizabeth herself, they were suspected in some quarters of having done so with seditious intent. But they proved their innocence and escaped punishment. They played at Court four times during the holiday season of 1601–1602, and twice during the next winter. These were their last performances before Queen Elizabeth.

Upon the Queen's death all playing in London immediately ceased. James ascended the throne in March of 1603, and two months later he issued a commission that entitled "these our servants, Lawrence Fletcher, William Shakespeare, Richard Burbage, Augustine Phillips, John Heminges, Henry Condell, William Sly, Robert Armin, Richard Cowley, and the rest of their associates" (25:2) to be known thereafter as the King's Men. From then on, they overtopped all other companies in the number of performances staged at Court.

They probably saw new opportunities opening up before them when King James evicted the Children from Blackfriars in 1608 and closed the playhouse doors; it was then, presumably, that they again began seriously to entertain the idea of taking Blackfriars over for their own use. Five months went by before they did so, for the venture needed careful thought. Tradition was against them, since no adult company had ever hitherto acted in a roofed "private" theatre, and none had ever hitherto occupied a playhouse within the City walls. Proscription was against them, since the Privy Council had forbidden that particular company to occupy that particular playhouse twelve years before, and its veto had not been rescinded. But they believed that events had moved in their favor in the intervening years, and that the tolerance which had been denied to the elder Burbage in 1596 would not now be denied to the son. Many things contributed to their optimism. For one thing, the Little Eyases had occupied the playhouse for eight years without protest from the precinct inhabitants; and although the King had finally expelled them, he had done so not because he objected to the theatre as a theatre, but because he objected to it as one whose managers persisted in producing objectionable plays. Even more importantly, the company was now under the patronage, and wore the liveries, of the King himself. Shakespeare was now recognized as being rivaled only by Jonson and Fletcher, and Richard Burbage, ever since Edward Alleyn's retirement in 1604, as being rivaled by no one; and the company as a whole had an easy supremacy over all others in the land.

With these reasons for confidence, Richard Burbage took the lease back from Evans in August, 1608. Within a few weeks of his doing so a new hazard arose, for on September 20 the jurisdiction of the City was extended to include various Liberties, including the Blackfriars.[2] But, as things turned out, the King's Men's occupancy of the playhouse was secure. Protests there were from time to time, but all were ineffective, and the Privy Council now winked at the playhouse that it had frowned upon before. The King's Men could not hope for the approbation of the City authorities, but they could hope—and the event proved that they were justified in hoping—that if the City should attempt to suppress the playhouse, great command would o'ersway the order.

The Blackfriars Syndicate

As soon as the occupancy of the playhouse was his again, Richard Burbage proceeded to organize a syndicate to hold and administer it, just as his brother Cuthbert had done for the Globe nine years before. The syndicate was made up of seven equal partners: Richard Burbage him-

245

self, John Heminges, William Shakespeare, Cuthbert Burbage, Henry Condell, William Sly,[3] and a new man named Thomas Evans. Except for the newcomer and Cuthbert Burbage, all were members of the King's Men; and except for the newcomer alone, all were members of the similar syndicate that operated the Globe.[4] On August 9, 1608, Richard Burbage executed six leases, one to each of his partners. Each lease conveyed to its holder a one-seventh share in the Blackfriars Playhouse for a term of one-and-twenty years, and each bound the shareholder to pay a one-seventh part of the rent, which, as under the previous lease to Evans, stood at £40 per annum. Richard Burbage kept the seventh share for himself.

The names of the seven Blackfriars partners, as listed above, are known from a deposition filed in a case set for trial in February, 1616; it was a plea at the Common Law that Thomasina Ostler, widow and administratrix of the estate of William Ostler, the actor, filed against her father, John Heminges, complaining of his handling of shares in the Globe and Blackfriars.[5] Thomas Evans's name is to be found only in that one document, and it is to be found there only once. Perhaps, and even probably, "Thomas" is an error for "Henry." Such slips of the quill are not hard to find in the records of the period. For instance, Edward Kirkham's name is erroneously given as Richard in Henry Evans's recital of the Condition of the £200 Bond,[6] and Margaret Paunton's name is given as Anne in two depositions in the Kirkham vs. Paunton dispute (43:5-6, 43:28). If the name Thomas is not a similar erratum, then presumably the newcomer was a nominee of and agent for Henry Evans. But whether Thomas was Thomas or Thomas was Henry, one wonders why Richard Burbage and his colleagues should have admitted him to their syndicate of housekeepers. It cannot be supposed that they were eager to bring into their closely-knit professional group an outsider with no known experience as an actor, and to make him an equal sharer in their profits. The fact that they did so suggests that Henry Evans was able to exert some pressure, either on his own behalf or on behalf of his nominee, and raises questions as to the conditions under which Richard Burbage sought or accepted the surrender of the lease.

He was later to say that he took back the unexpired portion of the lease "upon labor and much importunity of the said Evans and other his special friends" (43:22). But his brother Cuthbert told a different story; he said that "it was considered that house would be as fit for ourselves, and so [we] purchased the lease remaining from Evans with our money"

(46:20); and the money thus given to Evans in return for his surrender of the lease was presumably a remittance quite apart from any
money that may have been paid him "in recompense of his, the said
Evans's, charge formerly bestowed in buildings in and about the premises"
(41:8). This purchase of the lease, taken in combination with the inclusion of an Evans as a member of the syndicate, suggests that Evans
had a commodity to sell, and that Burbage was willing to pay a price for
it.[7] That commodity can only have been the thirteen-year period that the
lease still had to run. Merely by sitting pat, Evans could hold the lease,
take the King's Men as his subtenants, and look forward to a substantial
and stable profit without efforts of his own. He may have made such a
suggestion to Burbage, but Burbage would hardly have welcomed the
anomalous situation that it entailed: an owner renting to a tenant who
rented back to the owner and who absorbed some of the owner's profits
on the way. Evans therefore was able to stipulate that he or his agent
should be given a place in the syndicate and a one-seventh share in the
profits; and this, in all probability, was one of the "private agreements
between [Evans] and the said Richard Burbage" (43:15) that preceded
the surrender of the lease.

Beginning of the King's Men's Occupancy

Although Burbage recaptured the Blackfriars Playhouse in August
of 1608,[8] it is unlikely that the King's Men began to produce plays there,
or to derive any profit therefrom, until late in 1609 or early in 1610.
Two things combined to delay them. One was the need to make repairs,
and the other was the plague.

As far back as July 1, 1604, according to Hawkins, "the said tenements . . . were then dilapidated in various parts and unrepaired, namely
in the flooring lying on the eastern side of the same hall, and in the
flooring at the eastern end of . . . the stage in the said hall, and in the
wall there above the steps, . . . and in the window glass, and in the
wooden windows, . . . and in the wall at each end of the said hall, and
in the leaden gutters, . . . and in the roof of the premises" (40:6).
Evans had laid out £10 in repairs in the following December, but Kirkham had refused to bear his part (40:7). For the next three years, during the regimes of Kirkham and Keysar, little enough reconditioning
in all probability had been done, and during most of 1608 the premises
had lain empty and unused. As a result of this neglect, the playhouse "ran

247

far into decay for want of reparations" by the time Burbage took it back (41:8).

And in that year and the next the city was plague-ridden. Fifty plague deaths were recorded for the week ending July 28, 1608, and more than forty for each week during the rest of the year, with a maximum of 147 on September 29. Theatres, of course, were closed, and the King's Men for a time took to the road; they were at Coventry on October 29, and at Marlborough on an unspecified date. Having returned to London, they rehearsed in private for their holiday appearances before the King, and gave twelve plays at Court during the following winter; and early in 1609 they received a special payment of £40 "by way of his Majesty's reward for their private practice in the time of infection, that thereby they might be enabled to perform their service before his Majesty in Christmas holidays 1609."[9] The plague was even worse the next year. Dekker, writing in 1609, said that

> Play-houses stand (like Tavernes that have cast out their Maisters) the dores locked up, the Flagges (like their Bushes) taken down; or rather like Houses lately infected, from whence the affrighted dwellers are fled, in hope to live better in the Country.[10]

That year the King's Men went on tour early. In May they performed at Ipswich, Hythe, and New Romney. All that summer and fall their playhouses remained closed. Again they rehearsed before empty benches for their appearances at Court, and during the winter of 1609–10, "before Christmas and in the time of the holidays and afterwards," they gave thirteen plays before the King. For this John Heminges, as payee, received £130, and later he received an additional £30 "for himself and the rest of his company being restrained from public playing within the City of London in the time of infection during the space of six weeks, in which time they practiced privately for his Majesty's service."[11]

Records on theatre closings are lacking for some parts of the period, but comparison with inhibitions in other plague years suggests that the London playhouses remained closed from July, 1608, until December, 1609, and that the King's Men cannot have begun to play at Blackfriars until the last days of 1609 or the first days of 1610. The first sixteen months of their tenancy of the playhouse were therefore lean indeed. Not merely did the housekeepers have to meet the heavy costs of repairs, but the company as a whole probably had little revenue beyond its takings on the road and its receipts from the royal purse.[12]

But to say that the King's Men did not begin to act at Blackfriars until the winter of 1609–1610 is not to say that it was not until then that the playhouse began to make its influence felt by them and by their chief dramatist, Shakespeare. For several years they must have faced the possibility that they would eventually occupy it themselves. As we know, Henry Evans had approached Burbage as early as 1603 or 1604 with a plea to be relieved of responsibility for the lease (43:21), and from that time on, what with plagues and internal squabbles and political indiscretions, the continuing occupancy of the playhouse by the Children had never been something that could be taken for granted.

The physical playhouse was no stranger to the King's Men when they took it over. The elder Burbage had planned it for their use in the first place, and in its designing he had probably consulted—if not the group as a whole, its industrious and versatile nucleus at least—his two sons, and Shakespeare, Heminges, and Condell. Three years later, the same company had built the Globe, and in the designing of its stage they had inevitably been influenced by their experience in designing the stage at Blackfriars. Of their own knowledge, they knew all the respects in which the two stages were alike, and those in which they differed.

They knew also about the unfamiliar usages that had been developed by the Children at Blackfriars. Doubtless they had acquired some of the information by attending the Children's performances and watching the boys at their work; they had learned other things from John Underwood and William Ostler, who had been members of the Children's company since its beginning, and had now joined the King's Men. As a result of all these contacts, they knew that Blackfriars permitted gentlemen to sit on the stage, as the Globe did not. They knew that Blackfriars had the "received custome of musicke," as the Globe did not, and that to compensate for the time devoted to music, plays at Blackfriars tended to be shorter than plays at the Globe; and they knew that Blackfriars had intermissions between the acts, as the Globe did not. They learned that the enclosed candlelit hall at Blackfriars permitted and demanded subtler and gentler speaking than the open Globe, and new delicacies of expression; more elaborate plots and more diffuse writing; the same violence, perhaps, but less noise; fewer of the old clattering battles, but finer processions than ever, and apparitions twice as effective as ever before. Rhetoric would lose a little, and sentiment would become as telling as passion. Humor might be less brisk, and the pace of acting would slow down.[13]

The months between August of 1608 and the winter of 1609–1610 were busy ones for the King's Men. To meet the demand for new plays, they secured the services of Ben Jonson and of Beaumont and Fletcher to supplement the output of their own man, Shakespeare. Jonson had already written four plays for the Children at Blackfriars—*Cynthia's Revels, Poetaster, The Case Is Altered,* and (in collaboration) *Eastward Ho!*—and Beaumont and Fletcher had written three—*Cupid's Revenge, The Faithful Shepherdess,* and *The Knight of the Burning Pestle.* All three of the new men, therefore, were thoroughly conversant with the requirements of the Blackfriars stage and the preferences of Blackfriars audiences. Jonson had written plays for the Lord Chamberlain's Men at the Globe, but not recently; Beaumont and Fletcher, never; but after 1610, all Jonson's plays except two, and all Beaumont and Fletcher's except perhaps two or three, were written for Blackfriars and the King's Men. From then until 1616, Blackfriars had all the greatest dramatists in one of the greatest periods of dramatic history.[14]

The King's Men gave fifteen plays at Court during the winter season of 1610–11, and were paid at the rate of £10 per play.[15]

They gave twenty-two plays before their Majesties between October 31, 1611, and April 26, 1612, an average of almost one a week. For their services they received £166 13s. 4d., John Heminges being the payee. The plays included *The Tempest* and *The Winter's Tale.*[16]

On June 8, 1612, they presented Shakespeare's lost *Cardenio* before the ambassadors of the Duke of Savoy, and during the holiday season of 1612–1613 they gave twenty plays at Court, including *Much Ado About Nothing* twice, "Sir John Falstaffe," "Hotspur," "Caesar's Tragedy," *Othello,* and again *The Tempest, The Winter's Tale,* and *Cardenio.* Payments totaled £153 6s. 8d., and Heminges was again the payee.[17]

The King's Men gave sixteen plays at Court during the winter of 1613–1614, and eight during the next winter. Between November 1, 1615, and April 1, 1616, they gave fourteen plays before the King and Queen.[18]

Shakespeare's Gatehouse

On March 10, 1613, Shakespeare bought a lodging and a plot of ground inside the Blackfriars precinct. The lodging was the upper floor of a gatehouse that straddled one of the entrances to the precinct on its eastern side. It was at or near the place where the way called Ireland Yard met the highway called St. Andrew's Hill. The deed describes the property as follows:

> All that dwelling-house or tenement, with the appurtenances, situate and being within the precinct, circuit and compass of the late Black Fryers, London, . . . and now or late being in the tenure or occupation of one William Ireland, . . . abutting upon a street leading down to Puddle Wharf on the east part, right against the King's Majesty's Wardrobe, part of which said tenement is erected over a great gate leading to a capital messuage; . . . and also all that plot of ground on the west side of the same tenement, . . . which said plot of ground was sometime parcel and taken out of a great piece of void ground lately used for a garden.[19]

Shakespeare bought the property from a musician named Henry Walker. The purchase was a complicated transaction. Title went to Shakespeare and to three trustees, one of whom, inevitably, was his trusted friend John Heminges of the King's Men, and the other two of whom were a vintner named John Jackson and William Johnson of the Mermaid Tavern. The price was £140, of which Shakespeare paid £80 in cash and £60 by mortgage. He undertook to liquidate the debt at the following Michaelmas, and as security he and the trustees leased the property back to the vendor, Walker, for a rental of one peppercorn per year. Whether by intention or not, the effect of the trusteeship was to deprive Shakespeare's wife of her dower rights to the property.

It cannot now be known whether Shakespeare bought the gatehouse as an investment or as a place where he could lodge on his trips to London. By 1613 he was probably spending most of his time in Stratford. Two years earlier he had written the last of the plays that he was to write alone, and doubtless he had long since ceased to act; but perhaps he foresaw that his affairs would still necessarily take him to London now and then, and that it would be advantageous to have a place where he could live and work. He was now collaborating with Fletcher—Beaumont having retired upon making a wealthy marriage—and the first of the plays upon which he was working with Fletcher would be produced in June. Two things in particular suggest that he bought the gatehouse for his own use: its nearness to the playhouse, only a hundred yards away, and his payment of a price high enough to have discouraged his buying the property merely as an investment; for he paid Walker forty percent more than Walker had paid for the same property only nine years before.

But if Shakespeare did intend to pay off the mortgage promptly and to use the gatehouse as his own residence, he seems to have been disappointed on both counts. His plans may have been upset by the heavy financial obligation that devolved upon him as a result of the grievous mischance of June 29.

Second Globe ✓

On that day the Globe Playhouse burned to the ground during a performance of *Henry VIII*. The housekeepers immediately decided to rebuild. At that time Shakespeare held a one-fourteenth interest in the Globe, and was therefore liable for a fourteenth part of the cost of rebuilding, amounting to £50 or £60.[20] That levy, coming less than four months after his disbursement of £80 for the gatehouse, may have strained his cash resources, and either of two things may have followed as a result: he may have sold his Globe shares rather than pay the assessment levied against him for the rebuilding after the fire, or he may have allowed the gatehouse mortgage to remain unpaid. The former alternative seems the more probable, since his will makes no mention of any shares in the Globe[21] nor of any encumbrance upon the gatehouse property. He bequeathed the gatehouse to his daughter Susanna Hall, describing it in his will as "all that messuage or tenement, with the appurtenances, wherein one John Robinson dwelleth, situate, lying and being in the Blackfriars in London, near the Wardrobe."[22] John Robinson may have been the same person as the John Robbinson who signed the petition against James Burbage's Blackfriars Playhouse in 1596 (cf. 22:3).

As for the Globe, the rebuilding went forward without delay, and "the next spring it was new builded in far fairer manner than before." It was ready by June 30, 1614, and was reputed to be "the fairest that ever was in England."[23]

William Shakespeare died on April 23, 1616.

By the time of his death, the company of the Chamberlain's-King's Men was nearing the midpoint in its history. It had been in existence for twenty-two years, and during most of that time its preeminence had been unchallenged; it would exist for twenty-six years more before coming to an end under Oliver Cromwell. Its membership was remarkably stable. Of the ten actors who presumably were members of the Lord Chamberlain's Men when the company was formed in 1594,[24] eight remained with the company as long as they lived, and had an average term of service of more than twenty-one years; one of the remaining two resigned only when he left the profession, and only one—Kempe—left the company to pursue his calling elsewhere. Of the original Globe housekeepers, all, with the same two exceptions, stayed with the troupe until they died. Of the King's Men who held Blackfriars shares, all did so; and of the twenty-six "Principall Actors in all these Playes" in the First Folio, all stayed with the company until they died or until the company itself disbanded, except the two already mentioned and three others besides.

Such a record argues a remarkable degree of congeniality and loyalty. Other indications point in the same direction, as for instance the will of Augustine Phillips, who bequeathed "to my Fellowe William Shakespeare a thirty shillings peece in gould," and who left other legacies to his "fellows" Condell, Fletcher, Armin, Cowley, Cooke, and Tooley, and to the company's hired men. Similarly, Nicholas Tooley left the sum of £10 "unto Mrs. Burbage, the wife of my good friend Mr. Cuthbert Burbage (in whose house I do now lodge) as a remembrance of my love in respect of her motherlie care over me," and left other bequests to Richard Burbage and Henry Condell and their families, and to Joseph Taylor, John Underwood, and William Ecclestone. But the most convincing indication of harmony lies in the absence of legal disputes. The age was one of hot-tempered individualism, when any difference of interest or opinion might lead to a duel or a quick resort to the courts, and we have seen how the eight years of the Chapel-Revels Children engendered a multiplicity of suits at law; and yet not one lawsuit arose from among the original members of the company, or from among the original housekeepers of the Globe or the Blackfriars. Disputes were to come later—a total of three in forty-eight years—but they were to originate with latecomers or outsiders. Truman, in *Historia Histrionica*, was later to speak of the men of Blackfriars as being "Men of grave and sober Behaviour." As a matter of fact, this very lack of internal strife accounts in large measure for the meagerness of the records that have come down to us about the Blackfriars as a functioning playhouse.

All the disputes, when they did come, grew out of the ownership of shares in the two playhouses. The first was brought against John Heminges by his daughter, Thomasina Ostler, widow of the actor William Ostler, in an effort to recover the shares that her deceased husband had formerly held. The second was brought by John Witter for recovery of his share in the Globe. The third was a petition addressed to the Lord Chamberlain by three actors of whom only one had been a member of the company before Shakespeare's death. They complained that an unfairly large portion of the profits of the business went to the housekeepers, and therefore they sought to become housekeepers themselves.

The reader will recall that the Globe syndicate, as originally set up, gave the two Burbage brothers a half interest in the playhouse, and that the other half interest was equally divided between Shakespeare, Phillips, Pope, Heminges, and Kempe. Kempe withdrew soon afterwards, and his interest was distributed among the other four, so that each of them for a time held a fourth part of the moiety. Pope died before February 13, 1604, and left his share to Basil Nicoll and to John Edmonds and Mary his wife. Phillips died in May 1605, and his interest went to another outsider, a man named John Witter; and between 1605 and 1608 the moiety was redivided into six parts, so as to provide shares for Condell and Sly. Sly died in 1608, and Heminges and Condell bought his sixth part between them; and on February 20, 1612, the moiety was again divided, this time from six parts into seven, in order to provide a share for William Ostler. After this transaction, the seven parts of the second moiety were distributed as follows: one part each to Shakespeare, Witter, and Ostler, one and a half parts each to Heminges and Condell, and one part split between Edmonds and his wife, and Basil Nicoll.

As for Blackfriars, its housekeepers' shares were originally seven, divided equally between the two Burbages, Shakespeare, Heminges, Condell, Sly, and Evans. Sly died only five days after the syndicate was set up. His share was for a time divided among the six surviving shareholders, but on May 20, 1611, it was transferred to William Ostler. At the time of his death in 1614, therefore, Ostler had a one-seventh interest in each of the two playhouses. Two years later his widow brought suit against her father for recovery of the two shares.[25]

Taken at their face value, Thomasina's charges tarnish the character of John Heminges both as a man of probity and as a father. He was, as far as we know, a man against whom no other accusations have been brought. He seems to have been regarded with exceptional affection, trust, and respect by his fellows in the King's Men. Shakespeare made him a legatee under his will and a trustee for his Blackfriars gatehouse, and at least three of his associates made him the overseer or executor of their estates. He was the regular payee for the company's performances at Court, was its treasurer and business manager as long as he lived, and on occasion he seems even to have represented all the London theatrical companies in their relations with government officials.[26] In judging Thomasina's damaging charges, one must remember that her side of the story is the only side we have. It runs as follows:

William Ostler died intestate on December 16, 1614, and the administration of his estate was entrusted to his widow. His shares in the two playhouses should have descended to her as beneficiary, but when the indentures came into the hands of John Heminges for safekeeping, there they stayed; he withheld all the interest arising from the two shares, leaving her nothing on which to live and with which to pay her husband's debts. He told her that her late husband had made an assignment in his favor before he died, but she had never heard of it and doubted its existence. Seeking to recover the indentures and the profit arising under them, she caused her learned counsel to draw up a bill returnable in the Court of Chancery, whereupon Heminges promised to satisfy her if she would stay her suit and submit herself to him and her mother. This she did with all reverence and humility, but he, caring nothing for his promise, kept the shares of the two playhouses for himself, thus defrauding her of £600 as the value of the two shares. As a last resort, she brought suit in February 1616. The court's decision is not upon record. Seemingly she lost, since Heminges kept the shares.

The second lawsuit came three years later, in 1619. It was brought by John Witter for recovery of a share in the Globe. Augustine Phillips had died in 1605, and his widow had married Witter. By doing so she had forfeited her interest in her late husband's estate, but Heminges, as executor under Phillips's will, had leased a share, at that time one sixth of a moiety, to the Witters for a term of eighteen years. But Witter fell behind in his payments of ground rent and was unable to pay the amount assessed against him for the rebuilding of the Globe after the fire. Heminges therefore cancelled the Witters' lease, resumed possession of their share, and gave half of it to Condell gratis. In 1619 Witter brought an action against Heminges and Condell in the Court of Requests for recovery of his share, which now, in consequence of the admission of Ostler, had become a seventh part instead of a sixth. On November 29, 1620, the Court dismissed his suit.[27]

These, presumably, were the cases that Cuthbert Burbage had in mind when he said later that "making the leases for twenty-one years hath been the destruction of ourselves and others; for they dying at the expiration of three or four years of their lease, the subsequent years be-

255

came dissolved to strangers, as by marrying with their widows, and the like by their children" (46:19). The third complaint arose many years later.

The Petition of 1619

In January of 1618/19 a group of churchmen and precinct officers petitioned the Lord Mayor and Aldermen of London to put an end to the inconveniences that the playhouse occasioned, and by implication to put an end to the playhouse itself. The first signature was that of William Gouge, the Puritan minister of St. Anne's, Blackfriars. After him, two churchwardens and two sidemen signed the petition because "We find this house a great annoyance to the church," two constables signed it because "We find this house a great occasion for the breach of the peace," two collectors because "We find this house a great hindrance to our poor," and two scavengers because "We find this house a great annoyance for the cleansing of the streets." In addition to their individual causes for complaint, they had a common ground for grievance because

> there is daily such resort of people, and such multitudes of coaches (where-of many are hackney coaches, bringing people of all sorts) that sometimes all our streets cannot contain them, but that they clog up Ludgate also, in such sort that both they endanger the one the other, break down stalls, throw down men's goods from their shops, and the inhabitants there cannot come to their houses nor bring in their necessary provisions of beer, wood, coal, or hay, nor the tradesmen or shopkeepers utter their wares, nor the passenger go to the common water stairs, without danger of their lives and limbs. . . . These inconveniences falling out almost every day in the winter time (not forbearing the time of Lent) from one or two of the clock till six at night, which being the time also most usual for christenings and burials and after-noons service, we cannot have passage to the church for the performance of those necessary duties, the ordinary passage for a great part of the precinct aforesaid being close by the playhouse door (27:4–5).

The complaint of the churchmen and officers was endorsed in a supplementary petition filed by twenty-four other residents of the precinct, including seven women (Document 28).

The Common Council acted quickly. On January 21, 1619, it issued an order which said in part that this Court doth think fit, and so order, that the said playhouse be suppressed, and that the players shall from henceforth forbear and desist from playing in that house, in respect of the manifold abuses and disorders complained of as aforesaid (29:3).

The King's Men promptly countered by asking his Majesty to intervene in their favor, and on March 27, 1619, he issued a new license that authorized "these our well-beloved servants . . . freely to use and exercise the art and faculty of playing comedies, tragedies, histories, interludes, morals, pastorals, stage plays, and other such like, . . . within their two their now usual houses called the Globe within our County of Surrey, and their private house situate in the precincts of the Blackfriars within our City of London" (30:2–3). That settled the matter until 1633.

"*Exit Burbage*"

Between the time when the Common Council ordered the Blackfriars Playhouse closed, and the time when the King countermanded the order, Richard Burbage died.[28] His death came on March 13, 1619, at the age of fifty-one. He had been Shakespeare's associate and friend from 1594 or earlier until the poet's death, and as a token of his affection Shakespeare had left him a sum of money by will to buy a memorial ring. He was the undisputed leader of the English stage in his later years, and he had been privileged beyond all other men in his profession, then or since, in being permitted to create the greatest roles that the language affords, and to be coached in their interpretation by Shakespeare himself. Of the many elegies that his death inspired, one said that

> No more young Hamlett, ould Heironymoe,
> Kind Leer, the greved Moore, and more beside,
> That lived in him, have now for ever dy'de.

The shortest of them all said merely "Exit Burbage."

Times of Playing at Blackfriars

The 1619 complaint of the churchmen and precinct officers testified eloquently to the popularity of the Blackfriars Playhouse and to its attraction for what was later to be called the carriage trade; the Common

Council, in its order to suppress the playhouse, agreed. The precinct residents and the Council agreed also that the inconveniences occasioned by the congestion of playgoers and coaches occurred "almost every day in the winter time . . . from one or two of the clock till six at night" (27:5). The sentence raises several questions: When did the company begin and end its winter season at Blackfriars, and when its summer season at the Globe? How frequently did the company play? Were its plays given in the afternoon or at night? And how long did the average performance last?

On slight evidence, it seems probable that the King's Men habitually made the shift from Blackfriars to the Globe about the middle of May, but not on a constant date; for Sir Humphrey Mildmay's diary and account book show that he attended performances at the Globe as early as the sixteenth day of May, and at Blackfriars as late as May 19th. He did not go to Blackfriars during any June, July, August, or September, nor, so far as his records go, to the Globe except during May, June, and July. His earliest visit to Blackfriars in the fall was on the twenty-seventh of October,[29] but the transfer from the Globe to Blackfriars had probably been made earlier than that.

If we assume that the Globe was used from the middle of May until the middle of October, then it was open for five months of each year, and Blackfriars for seven months. On this basis, the Blackfriars season in the days of the King's Men was a month longer than it had been in the days of the Little Eyases, when, under ideal conditions, the Children were expected to play "the full time six months in every year" (39:1).

Probably, too, the King's Men gave performances more often in each week than the Children had done. Two documents suggest that the Children had acted only once a week, on Saturdays. One is the diary of Philip-Julius, Duke of Stettin-Pomerania, who saw them play at Blackfriars on Saturday, September 18, 1602, and who afterwards wrote that they presented their plays "*wöchentlich*" (45:3). The second is another document of the same year, the Condition of the £50 Bond, which contains the stipulation that Kirkham and his associates should pay Evans the sum of 8 shillings "every week, weekly on Saturday, . . . when and so often as any interludes, plays, or shows shall be played . . . in the great hall and other the rooms situate in the Blackfriars, London . . . by the Children" (37:1). Such infrequency was appropriate for growing boys who had lessons to learn as well as plays to rehearse and act. But we have no need to suppose that the King's Men played so seldom. The statement that they acted "almost every day in the winter time" may be slightly exaggerated for effect, but probably not greatly; the ability of the King's Men to give plays in close sequence is indicated, for instance, by their schedule of plays at Court during the winter season of 1607–1608, when they gave performances on December 26, 27, 28, and January 2, 6 (two plays), 7, 9, 17 (two plays), 26, and February 2 and 7,[30] presumably in addition to performances at Blackfriars; and Heminges and Condell, in their address "To the great Variety of Readers" in the Shakespeare First Folio, speak of those who "sit on the Stage at Black-Friers, or the Cock-pit, to arraigne Playes dailie."

The King's Men sometimes gave their plays in the afternoon, sometimes at night, and sometimes, as when they gave two plays at Court on January 6th, 1608, and two on the 17th, both in the afternoon and in the evening. Afternoon performances are referred to in the 1619 complaint and in *The Devil Is an Ass*, III v, when Fitzdottrel identifies the time "after dinner" with "just play-time"; and Sir Humphrey Mildmay testifies to afternoon performances by noting in his diary and account book that he went to plays at Blackfriars "after dynner" on April 25, 1635, October 27, 1638, and May 15, 1640.[31] On the other hand, performances at night are alluded to in the following Blackfriars plays:

> *The Chances*, Prologue:
>> Aptness for Mirth to all, this instant Night
>> Thalia hath prepar'd for your delight,
>> Her Choice and curious Viands, in each part
>> Season'd with rarities of Wit and Art.

> *The Custom of the Country*, "Another Prologue":
>> We wish, if it were possible, you knew
>> What we would give for this nights look, if new.

> *The Elder Brother*, Prologue:
>> You will expect what we present to night
>> Should be judg'd worthy of your ears and sight.

> And *Love's Pilgrimage*, Prologue:
>> . . . This night
>> No mighty matter, nor no light,
>> We must intreat you look for.

259

When the authors of the 1619 complaint spoke of the "inconveniences" as lasting "from one or two of the clock till six at night," they did
not, of course, mean that a Blackfriars play lasted for four or five hours,
but that the precinct roads were clogged with pedestrians and coaches for
that long a time. The playgoer came early to the playhouse to hear the
preliminary concert. His coach dropped him at the door and then sought
some place where it could stand until the play was over. At the play's
end it could hardly come back to the door, the roads being so narrow and
congested; instead, it probably had to stand where it was until a linkman
found it in the dark and led its passengers to it; and after that the coach
had to thread its slow way through the tortuous streets into the clear.
Under such conditions, the inconveniences of which the inhabitants complained might well last "till six at night."

Eight plays and one eulogistic poem mention two hours as the duration of a Blackfriars performance. The plays include the two written
by Shakespeare and Fletcher in collaboration. Thus the Prologue to
Henry VIII has this:

> Those that come to see
> Only a show or two and so agree
> The play may pass—if they be still and willing,
> I'll undertake may see away their shilling
> Richly in two short hours.

and the prologue of *The Two Noble Kinsmen* has

> You shall hear
> Scenes, though below his[32] art, may yet appear
> Worth two hours' travail.

Durations of two hours are mentioned also in the Prologues to *The Alchemist, The Brothers, Love's Pilgrimage,* and *The Unfortunate Lovers,*
in the first scene of *The Mayor of Quinborough,* and in the Epilogue to
The Platonic Lovers; and Robert Stapylton specifies two hours in his
laudatory poem prefacing the Beaumont and Fletcher First Folio.

On the contrary, a duration of three hours is mentioned in the Prologue to *The Lover's Progress* and the Epilogue to *The Loyal Subject,*
and in James Shirley's Preface to the works of Beaumont and Fletcher,
in which he speaks of

the Authentick witt that made Blackfriars an academy, where the three howers spectacle while Beaumont and Fletcher were presented, were usually of more advantage to the hopeful young Heire, than . . . forraigne Travell.

It would be profitless to attempt to reconcile these discrepant figures; both the two hours and the three were specified by poets writing with a poet's accustomed license. It would be equally fruitless to attempt to estimate the length of a Blackfriars play by reference to the careful studies made by Alfred Hart,[33] who has counted the lines in 144 Elizabethan and Jacobean plays and has found that they averaged 2,626, and who says that 2,420 lines at the most could be acted in two hours. His calculations are inapplicable on the one hand because performances at Blackfriars were lengthened by concerts before the plays began, and by instrumental music, sometimes with songs and dances, between the acts. They are inapplicable on the other hand because the texts of plays as printed often include passages that were omitted in performance. This cutting of plays is evidenced by a statement on the title page of the first edition of *The Duchess of Malfi* (1623), which describes the printed text as being "The perfect and exact Coppy, with diverse things Printed, that the length of the Play would not beare in the Presentment," and by an assertion by the publisher of the First Folio of Beaumont and Fletcher, to the effect that "When these Comedies and Tragedies were presented on the Stage, the actours omitted some Scenes and Passages (with the Authour's consent) as occasion led them.[34]

The year 1623 was notable for the publication of the First Folio of Shakespeare's plays. The plays had been "collected & publish'd" by John Heminges and Henry Condell, the last of the original band of Lord Chamberlain's Men. They were the other two of the three King's Men to whom Shakespeare left legacies for the purchase of memorial rings.

In that same year the Blackfriars precinct was the scene of a tragic occurrence that Stow has chronicled under the title of "The fatall Vesper, or dismall Evensong." On the afternoon of Sunday, October 26, 1623, more than three hundred persons were assembled in a chamber near the French ambassador's house to hear a sermon. A gentlewoman told the minister, Father Drury, that she feared that the crowd was more than the building could bear, but he, "being led on by a divine and fatal necessity," told her that he meant to go forward with his intended service. "The sermon inclining toward the middest and the day declining towards an end," the floor of the chamber gave way under the overbearing weight of the multitude, and the floor below gave way in turn, until the worshipers fell at last upon the lowest chamber of the edifice, where ninety-five persons or thereabout perished, besides those that were bruised or maimed.[35]

In 1624, for the first time since it presented *Richard II* on the eve of the Essex rebellion twenty-three years before, the company found itself in difficulties with the Court over the production of an objectionable play. The play was Middleton's *Game at Chess*. It contained attacks on the King of Spain, on Count Gondomar, the former Spanish ambassador, and on the Spanish party in England. It was produced at a time when anti-Spanish feeling was running high, and it had a phenomenal success: contrary to all precedent, it was acted at the Globe "nine days together." The current Spanish ambassador protested emphatically to James, and the King ordered his Privy Council to summon the dramatist and the players for examination. The actors were able to prove that the play had been duly licensed and therefore that they were not at fault; nevertheless, they were reprimanded and restrained from playing for several days and were forbidden to present the play again. For this reason it was never acted upon the Blackfriars stage.

The King's Men were in trouble again before the end of the year over the production of *The Spanish Viceroy*, a play no longer extant. The offense this time was their performance of a play that had not been licensed by the Master of the Revels. But the leaders of the company appeased Sir Henry Herbert by making an humble submission and apology and promising that they would not again offend by producing a play that he had not approved.

King James died on March 27, 1625, and liveries were issued to fifteen members of the King's Men to enable them to participate in the funeral procession. His son, upon succeeding to the throne as Charles I, transferred his patronage from his own company, the Prince's Men, to the company of which his late father had been patron, and issued a new patent that continued the company's right to be called the King's Servants and to act "within these two theire most usuall Houses called the Globe within Our County of Surrey, and their private Houses scituate within the Precinct of the Black Fryers within Our Citty of London."[36] John Heminges and Henry Condell headed the list of players as named in the patent, but neither had acted for several years past.

That year the plague struck London with savage violence. Plague deaths rose steadily from the time of King James's death until they reached the staggering total of 4,463 during the week ending August 18; according to one historian, the plague of that year was more deadly than any other that London had known since the days of the Black Death.[37] All the playhouses, having originally been closed on account of the death of King James, remained closed until the end of November on account of the plague; and during the last part of that period, as during the winters of 1608–1609 and 1609–1610, the company probably rehearsed before bare benches in preparation for its appearances at Court. It gave ten plays before his Majesty in his first Christmas season as King.

In 1628 the King's Men agreed to give Sir Henry Herbert two benefit performances each year, with both the actors and the housekeepers contributing their shares after deducting £2 5s. for expenses. He records the agreement as follows:

> The kinges company with a generall consent and alacritye have given mee the benefitt of too dayes in the yeare, the one in summer, thother in winter, to be taken out of the second daye of a revived playe, at my owne choyse. The housekeepers have likewyse given their shares, their dayly charge only deducted, which comes to some £2 5s. this 25 May 1628.[38]

During the next five years Sir Henry kept a record of his receipts under this agreement. He fails to specify Blackfriars or Globe, but the dates make such specifications unnecessary. In the table below, the figures are arranged in two columns to facilitate comparison, and in each instance the £2 5s. deduction has been restored. The figures thus show gross receipts.

WINTER *(Blackfriars)*				SUMMER *(Globe)*			
Nov. 22, 1628	£19	15s.	0d.	May 25, 1628	£7	0s.	0d.
Nov. 22, 1629	12	1	0	July 21, 1629	8	12	0
Feb. 18, 1630/31	14	9	0	June 12, 1631	7	11	6
Dec. 1, 1631	15	5	0	Summer, 1632	3	10	0
Nov. 6, 1632	17	5	0	June 6, 1633	6	15	0
Totals	78	15	0		33	8	6
Averages	15	15	0		6	13	8

These figures show that in the period indicated, the earning capacity of Blackfriars was nearly two and a half times as great as that of the Globe. Taken in combination with other figures previously cited, which show that the Blackfriars name was mentioned on the title pages of

King's Men's plays nearly ten times as often as the name of the Globe,[39] they suggest that by 1628, and probably long before, Blackfriars had superseded the Globe as the principal theatre of the King's Men.

Visiting French actors, and, to make matters vastly worse, visiting French actresses, appeared at Blackfriars in November, 1629. The occasion may have been the first on which a woman appeared upon an English stage. The innovation was not well received. The reception accorded to the visitors is thus reported in a letter written on November 8, 1629, by Thomas Brande:

> Furthermore you should know, that last daye certain vagrant French players, who had beene expelled from their owne countrey, *and those women,* did attempt, thereby giving just offence to all vertuous and well-disposed persons in this town, to act a certain lacivious and unchaste comedye, in the French tonge at the Blackfryers. Glad I am to saye they were hissed, hooted, and pippin-pelted from the stage, so as I do not thinke they will soone be ready to trie the same againe. — Whether they had license for so doing I know not; but I do know that, if they had licence, it were fit that the Master [of the Revels] be called to account for the same.[40]

John Heminges died in 1630. Henry Condell, the friend and colleague with whose name his had been linked so long and so often, had died three years before. Together they had sponsored the Shakespeare First Folio, a task for which they were uniquely fitted by their long acquaintance with the poet as dramatist, actor, and friend; and in seeking thus "to keepe the memory of so worthy a Friend, & Fellow alive, as was our Shakespeare," they made their own memories imperishable. Heminges's age at the time of his death is not known, but he had already been called "old" in lines written on the burning of the Globe seventeen years earlier:

> Then with swolne eyes, like druncken Flemminges,
> Distressed stood old stuttering Heminges.

He was succeeded as business manager and treasurer by John Lowin and Joseph Taylor, acting jointly.

The year 1631 brought new agitation for the suppression of the Blackfriars Playhouse. This time the agitation took the form of a petition which the churchwardens and constables of the precinct addressed to William Laud, then Lord Bishop of London and a member of his

Majesty's Privy Council. It told, even more graphically than the petition of 1619 had done, of the perils arising from the great recourse of people and coaches at playtime, and it reminded his Lordship of the Council's action of June 22, 1600, in limiting the number of playhouses to two, and those without the City.[41] Bishop Laud endorsed the petition "To the Coun. Table" and sent it to the Privy Council. So far as is known, the Council took no action.

The matter came up again two years later, and this time with such urgency that the Privy Council felt compelled to act. At its meeting of October 9, 1633, "Their Lordships, calling to mind that formerly, upon complaint hereof made, the Board was of opinion that the said playhouse was fit to be removed from thence, and that an indifferent recompense and allowance should be given them [i.e., the housekeepers] for their interests in the said house and the buildings thereunto belonging" (31:2), appointed a committee to interview the property's owners and arrive at an impartial estimate of its value, with a view to buying them out. The report was brought in six weeks later. It said that the players valued the property at £21,000 and the commissioners at just under £3,000, and that the only offer toward a compensation fund was one of £100 from the St. Anne's parishioners.[42] In view of these figures, all thoughts of buying out the players were of course allowed to drop, and the question resolved itself again to one of traffic control. Finally, in "consideration of the great inconveniences that grow by reason of the resort to the playhouse of the Blackfriars in coaches," their Lordships voiced the ingenuous hope "that those which go thither should go thither by water, or else on foot" (31:4), and then decreed

> that if any person, man or woman, of what condition soever, repair to the aforesaid playhouse in coach, so soon as they are gone out of their coaches, the coachmen shall depart thence, and not return till the end of the play, nor shall stay or return to fetch those whom they carried, any nearer with their coaches than the farther part of St. Paul's Churchyard on the one side, and Fleet Conduit on the other side (31:5).

The order had no chance of succeeding. Mr. Garrard, in a letter dated January 9, 1633/34, says:

> Here hath been an Order of the Lords of the Council hung up in a Table near Paul's and the Black-Fryars, to command all that Resort to the Play-House there to send away their Coaches, and to disperse Abroad in Paul's

Church-Yard, Carter-Lane, the Conduit in Fleet-street, and other Places, and not to return to fetch their Company, but they must trot afoot to find their Coaches; 'twas kept very strictly for two or three Weeks, but now I think it is disorder'd again.[43]

It was not merely disordered, but by the time Garrard's letter was written, the order had in effect been rescinded. The Council had quickly been made aware of "the discommodity that divers persons of great quality, especially ladies and gentlewomen, did receive in going to the playhouse of Blackfriars, by reason that no coaches may stand within the Blackfriars Gate or return thither during the play" (31:8); and consequently, at a meeting which his Majesty himself attended, the Board

did think fit to explain the said Order in such manner: that as many coaches as may stand within the Blackfriars Gate may enter and stay there, or return thither at the end of the play" (31:9).

But the order was rescinded not merely because it caused discommodity to persons of great quality, but also because it worked to "the prejudice of the players, his Majesty's servants" (31:8); and this consideration, in all probability, had been urged by his Majesty himself. There are many indications that the King's Men enjoyed the special favor of King Charles and his Queen. During the King's first year on the throne, when the players had been hard hit by closings caused by the plague and therefore had been unable to purchase the new costumes needed for their approaching appearances at Court, he had come to their relief by ordering his exchequer to pay them 100 marks as of his free gift and princely bounty.[44] In 1633, noting that the company's ranks had been depleted by sickness, he had caused his Lord Chamberlain to give John Lowin and Joseph Taylor an unprecedented warrant that empowered them to commandeer the services of any actor or actors belonging to any licensed company in London;[45] and three years later, when both the King's Men's playhouses were again closed by the plague, he gave his players a subsidy of £20 per week.[46]

Queen Henrietta Maria had already showed her own partiality by making them a gift of the clothes that she and her ladies had worn in her own pastoral—clothes that the players subsequently used in a special performance of *The Faithful Shepherdess*.[47] More than that, she had done them the signal honor of attending plays presented at the Blackfriars Playhouse. Sir Henry Herbert records that on "the 13 May, 1634, the Queene was at Blackfriars to see Messengers playe." She went again sometime between November 1635 and May 1636 to see the Second Part of *Arviragus and Philicia*. On May 5, 1636, she went to Blackfriars to see *Alphonsus, Emperor of Germany*, with the Prince Elector, and on April 23, 1638, she went there to see *The Unfortunate Lovers*.[48] Presumably the Queen reserved the entire playhouse on each occasion for herself and her invited guests, since for the last two performances certainly, and probably for the first two as well, the King's Men were paid as for performances at Court.

Year after year, of course, the King's Men performed at Court more often than did any other company. As has been said, they gave ten plays before Charles in the first holiday season of his reign. They gave ten again in 1627–1628, sixteen in 1628–1629, twelve in 1629–1630, nineteen or twenty in 1630–1631, eleven in 1631–1632, and twenty-three in 1632–1633. In 1633–1634 they gave eleven plays, and twenty in 1634–1635.[49]

Sir Anthony Vandyke chose the Blackfriars precinct for his home when he came from Flanders in 1632 at the desire of the King. He painted the portraits of Charles and Henrietta Maria a dozen times during his first year in London, and was rewarded with a knighthood, an annuity of £200, and the title of Painter in Ordinary. The King frequently visited Vandyke at his studio, and to make his visits the easier and safer, he had new landing stairs built at the river's edge, and a new causeway:

> Allowed the said Accomptante for Money by him yssued and paid for Workes and Reparacons donne and performed within the tyme of this Accompt at the Blackfryers in making a new Causey Way and a new paire of Staires for the King's Majesty to land to goe to Sr Anthoney Vandike's house there to see his Paintings, in the months of June and July 1635.[50]

Sir Anthony's daughter Justiniana Anna was born in the precinct on December 1, 1641, and baptised in St. Anne's on December 9, the day of her father's death.

The Blackfriars precinct was already a favorite headquarters for painters long before Vandyke arrived. Ben Jonson alludes to their presence in *The Devil Is an Ass*, 1 *vi*, written in 1616:

> I'll goe bespeake me straight a guilt caroch,
> For her and you to take the ayre in. Yes,
> Into Hyde-parke, and thence into Black-Fryers,
> Visit the painters, where you may see pictures,
> And note the properest limbs, and how to make 'hem.

Isaac Oliver, the miniature painter, was one of the earlier residents. He died there in 1617, and was buried in St. Anne's.

Incidentally, Ben Jonson was himself a resident of the precinct at the time when he wrote some of his greatest plays. He dated the dedication of *Volpone* "From my House in the Black-Friars, this 11th day of February, 1607," and he laid the scene of *The Alchemist* "here, in the friers" (1 *i*).

By some strange quirk of chance, the aristocratic Blackfriars precinct, and particularly the Pilgrim Street neighborhood at its north end, became the headquarters for the London feather merchants, and remained so for many years; allusions to their residence in Blackfriars begin in 1604, and continue until 1630 or afterwards. The feather merchants were Puritans; and Bird, in *The Muses' Looking-glass*, himself both a feather merchant and a Puritan, was well aware of the inconsistency between his frivolous trade and his religious convictions:

> *Enter Bird a Featherman, and Mrs. Flowrdew wife to a Haberdasher of small wares; the one having brought feathers to the [Blackfriars] Play-house, and the other Pins and Looking-glasses; two of the sanctified fraternity of Black-Friers ...*
>   *Mrs. Flowerdew.*   Indeed it sometimes pricks my conscience,
>   I come to sell 'em pins and looking-glasses.
>   *Bird.*   I have their custom too for all their feathers:
>   'Tis fit that we, which are sincere professors,
>   Should gain by infidels.

Ben Jonson alludes to the feather merchants in *The Alchemist*, 1 *i*:

> A whoreson, upstart, apochryphal captain,
> Whom not a Puritan in Blackfriars will trust,
> So much as for a feather.

Other references to the Blackfriars feather merchants are to be found in *Bartholomew Fair*, v *iii*, the Induction to *The Malcontent*, and *Monsieur Thomas*, II *ii*.

Twice in October of 1633 the Master of the Revels censored King's Men's plays. On October 19 Sir Henry Herbert sent peremptory orders to the company not to present *The Tamer Tamed* that afternoon, but to do some other play instead. He found fault with it not because it was politically or diplomatically indiscreet, but because it contained "oaths, prophaness, and publique ribaldry, wh[ch] for the future I doe absolutely forbid." Five days later he took similar exception to Ben Jonson's *Magnetic Lady.*[51]

Theatrical Scenery

The King's Men acted *The Faithful Shepherdess* at Denmark House on January 6, 1633/34. Sir Henry Herbert recorded the event as follows:

> On Monday night, the sixth of January and the Twelfe Night, was presented at Denmark-house, before the King and Queene, Fletchers pastorall called *The Faithfull Shepheardesse,* in the clothes the Queen had given Taylor the year before of her own pastorall. The scenes were fitted to the pastorall, and made by Mr. Inigo Jones, in the great chamber, 1633.[52]

The occasion was more important than Sir Henry's laconic last sentence indicates, for this was probably the first time that professional English actors had performed a play with painted scenery as background. Scenery had been used before, but not by professional actors, and not for a play.

Changeable painted scenery had made its first appearance early in the century in amateur masques presented in the great banqueting halls of royal palaces. A generation later it was used in plays similarly presented at Court, the performance of *The Faithful Shepherdess* at Denmark House presumably being the first. Still another generation was to pass before it was used in plays presented in commercial theatres.

The name of Inigo Jones was the first to be associated with the art of scenic design in England, and it remained the outstanding name in that field until the Rebellion. Beginning with *The Mask of Blackness* in 1605 and ending with *Salmacida Spolia* in 1640, he designed the scenery for perhaps twenty-seven masques at Court, and a few plays. His system of scenic decoration, as he ultimately developed it, consisted of "shutters" or "shuts" at the back of the stage, painted with distant vistas, and at the sides narrower shutters, later called wings, arranged so that they produced an illusion of solid structures in perspective. The shutters slid in horizontal grooves that permitted them to be retracted laterally; and to effect a change of scene, a shutter on each side was drawn back out of sight, so that the shutter next behind it was revealed. Inigo Jones also sometimes made use of a contrivance based on a wholly different principle: a *machina versatilis* that revolved so as to display successively the different faces of the structure placed upon it. Eventually he developed the "picture stage," framed by a painted proscenium arch appropriate to the poetical theme, behind which the scene was set and initially concealed by a curtain. With these devices, Jones staged masques that involved as many as five changes of scene.[53]

On August 29, 1636, the students of Christ Church, Oxford, presented William Strode's *Floating Island* before Charles I and his Queen and the two Princes of the Palatinate. Anthony à Wood, in his account of the performance, says that the stage

> had on it three or four openings on each side thereof, and partitions between them, . . . out of which the Actors issued forth. The said partitions they could draw in and out at their pleasure upon a sudden, and thrust out new in their places according to the nature of the Screen, whereon were represented Churches, Dwelling-houses, Palaces, etc. which for its variety bred very great admiration. Over all was delicate painting, resembling the Sky, Clouds, etc. At the upper end a great fair shut of two leaves that opened and shut without any visible help. . . . All these representations being the first (as I have been informed) that were used on the English stage.

On the following day their Majesties and the Princes saw another play produced with scenery in Christ Church Hall. The second play was Cartwright's *Royal Slave*. Anthony à Wood again describes the scenery:

> Within the shuts were seen a curious Temple, and the Sun shining over it, delightful forests also, and other prospects. Within the great shuts mentioned before, were seen villages, and men visibly appearing in them, going up and down, here and there, about their business. The Interludes thereof were represented with as much variety of scenes and motions as the great wit of Inigo Jones (well skilled in setting out a Court Maske to the best advantage) could extend unto.[54]

Her Majesty was so favorably impressed by *The Royal Slave* and its scenery that, having seen it performed by amateur actors, she wished to see it presented by a professional company. She therefore asked Archbishop Laud, now Chancellor of the University, to send the scenery and costumes to Hampton Court for a performance by the King's Men. According to the Archbishop,

> I caused the University to send both the clothes, and the perspectives of the stage; and the Play was acted at Hampton Court. . . . Then I humbly desired of the King and Queen, that neither the Play, nor clothes, nor stage, might come into the hands and use of the common players abroad, which was graciously granted.[55]

The text of *The Royal Slave* preserves a list of the play's eight scenes or "appearances," at least one of which, the Castle, must have been a practicable three-dimensional structure rather than a perspective flat, since it had battlements capable of holding several persons. The list is as follows:

> The first Appearance a Temple of the Sun.
> The second Appearance, a City in the front, and a Prison on the side.
> 3rd Appearance a stately Palace.
> 4th Appearance, a Wood.
> 5th Appearance, A Castle.
> 6th Appearance, the Court again.
> 7th Appearance, the Temple again discover'd, an Altar, and one busie placing fire thereon.
> 8th Appearance, the Sun eclipsed and a showr of rain dashing out the fire.

The next year, on February 7, 1637/38, the King's Men acted Sir John Suckling's *Aglaura* at Court, with painted scenery presumably designed by Inigo Jones. In reporting the event, Aubrey said of Sir John that

> When his *Aglaura* was [acted], he bought all the cloathes himselfe, which were very rich; no tinsill, all the lace pure gold and silver, which cost him — I have now forgot. He had some scaenes to it, which in those dayes were only used at masques;[56]

and Garrard, in one of his letters to the Earl of Strafforde, said that "Sutlin's Play cost three or four hundred Pounds setting out, eight or ten Suits of new Cloaths he gave the Players; an unheard of Prodigality.[57]

In 1638 *The Conspiracy (Pallantus and Eudora)* was presented before the King and Queen at York House on the occasion of the marriage of Lady Mary Villiers and Lord Charles Herbert. The company of actors is not named. A statement at the end of the play, presumably by the author, says that the drama

> had Scenes fitted to every Passage of it throughout, and the last in this place was a Funerall Pile, bearing on the top the body of the Dead Tyrant, and set out with all the Pomp the Ancients us'd in those Ceremonies. This Scene consisted onely of Musick and Shew; on the one side of the Pile stands a Consort of Musitians, representing the Priests of the Land, and on the other side of it another, representing the People. . . . About the middle of the last Stanzo, Timeus puts a lighted Torch to the bottome of the Pile which gives fire to some Perfumes laid there on purpose; the which wraps the Pile in smoak, and smells ore all the Roome. At the End of the Song the Curtain falls, and shuts both the Scene and Actors from the Beholders Sight.

In 1638 the King's Men presented Carlell's *Passionate Lovers* before the King and Queen at Somerset House, with scenes and costumes by Inigo Jones.[58]

And finally, Habington's *Queen of Aragon, or Cleodora*, was played before their Majesties at Whitehall on April 9, 1640. Its scenery and costumes were designed by Jones, and were described as being "very riche and curious." Three of the scenery designs are preserved in the collection of the Duke of Devonshire. They are entitled "first sceane a shutter of a fortified Towne & a Campe a farr off"; "Cleodora / 2 sceane of Releive"; and "3 sceane. A shutter with statues & figures a farr off."[59]

The seven plays just mentioned are believed to be the only plays—as distinct from masques—to have been acted with changeable painted scenery prior to the Puritan revolution. They show that scenery was used as a setting for plays during at least the last seven years of the sixteen-thirties, and that its use was known to professional acting companies. These facts have led some writers to assume that scenery was used in theatres, as well as at Court, during that decade. Thus Professor Lily B. Campbell, in commenting upon Archbishop Laud's request that the scenery for *The Royal Slave* should not be relinquished to the common players, says:

> Why the chancellor should fear that the "stage" or scenes, as well as the play and costumes, might fall into the hands of the common players, is not

apparent unless they were at that time presenting plays with scenes and presumably presenting court plays with the scenes used at court after they were discarded there. . . . That the possibility of using scenes in these playhouses was accepted in 1636 seems the inevitable conclusion from the request of the chancellor.[60]

W. J. Lawrence, while denying that successive scenery was regularly employed in the English theatre before the Civil War, nevertheless says that "there are sound reasons for believing that some tentative use had been made of movable scenery in the private theatres about the period of 1637–40."[61] F. E. Halliday says that "it is reasonable to assume that . . . before the closing of the theatres in 1642 something of Inigo Jones's methods was applied to the common stage."[62] And F. G. Fleay, the earliest of them all to take this position, said that "*The Conspiracy* was acted by the King's Men at Blackfriars, and had scenes fitted to it throughout, being the first English *play* publicly acted with scenery."[63]

Fleay was jumping to conclusions. He knew that *The Conspiracy* was performed with scenery on the occasion of the Villiers-Herbert wedding, and he knew that the play was in the repertory of the King's Men, so he assumed that the King's Men produced it with scenery at Blackfriars. But the record says nothing to justify his assumption, nor do the records of any other of the scenery-equipped plays give the slightest support to the theory that scenery was used in any professional theatre prior to the Restoration; on the contrary, all the information available to us, including the accounts of the three contemporary historians of the Caroline stage—Downes, Wright, and Flecknoe—indicates that scenery made its first appearance in playhouses during the first years of the reign of Charles II. For example, John Downes writes as follows in *Roscius Anglicanus:*

> Sir William [Davenant] in order to prepare Plays to Open his Theatre, it being then a Building in Lincoln's-Inn Field, His Company Rehears'd the First and Second Part of the Siege of Rhodes; and the Wits at Pothecaries-Hall; And in Spring 1662, Open'd his House with the said Plays, having new Scenes and Decorations, being the first that e're were Introduc'd in England.[64]

In *Historia Histrionica*, James Wright gives the lack of scenery in pre-Rebellion theatres as part of the reason why London "could then maintain Five Companies, and yet now Two can hardly Subsist." Speaking through the character of Truman, he says that

Tho' the Town was then, perhaps, not much more than half so Populous as now, yet then the Prices were small (there being no Scenes). . . . It is an Argument of the worth of the Plays and Actors, of the last Age, and easily inferr'd, that they were much beyond ours in this, to consider that they cou'd support themselves meerly from their own Merit; the weight of the Matter, and goodness of the Action, without Scenes and Machines.

Later in the same dialogue, Wright has Lovewit give the following account of the first use of scenery by the King's Men:

Presently after the Restoration, the King's Players Acted publickly at the Red Bull for some time, and then Removed to a New-built Playhouse in Vere Street, by Claremarket. There they continued for a Year or two, and then removed to the Theater Royal in Drury-lane, where they first made use of Scenes, which had been a little before introduced upon the publick Stage by Sir William Davenant, at the Duke's Old Theater in Lincolns-Inn-fields.

Wright, still speaking through Lovewit, relates the date of the first appearance of scenery to that of actresses:

About the same time that Scenes first enter'd upon the Stage at London, Women were taught to Act their own Parts;[65]

and the first appearance of a professional actress upon the London stage seems to have been that of Mrs. Margaret Hughes, who played Desdemona under Killigrew's management in early December, 1660, her presence in the cast being announced to the audience in a "Prologue to introduce the first woman that came to act on the stage."[66] A month later, on January 3, 1660/61, that inveterate playgoer, Samuel Pepys, wrote this in his *Diary*:

To the theatre, where was acted "Beggars' Bush," it being very well done; and here the first time that ever I saw women come upon the stage.

Richard Flecknoe's dating of the advent of scenery is presumably the same as that of Downes in *Roscius Anglicanus* and Wright in *Historia Histrionica*, but he is unfortunately less specific. His *Short Discourse of the English Stage* was published in 1664, and was probably written about 1660. In it he has this to say about the theatres of "former times":

274

Now, for the difference betwixt our Theaters and those of former times, they were but plain and simple, with no other Scenes, nor Decorations of the Stage, but onely old Tapestry, . . . whereas ours now for cost and ornament are arriv'd to the heighth of Magnificence. . . . For Scenes and Machines they are no new invention, our Masks and some of our Playes in former times (though not so ordinary) having had as good or rather better then any we have now. . . . Of this curious Art the Italians (this latter age) are the greatest masters, the French good proficients, and we in England onely Schollars and Learners yet, having proceeded no further then to bare painting, and not arriv'd to the stupendious wonders of your great Ingeniers.[67]

Finally, it will be recalled that Aubrey, in speaking of Sir John Suckling's production of *Aglaura* in 1637–1638, said that "scaenes . . . in those dayes were only used at masques."

Scenes in those days were only used at masques, and only in great royal banqueting halls. The public and private playhouses of pre-Commonwealth times could not compete with the Court in the use of scenery. They might have made a feeble attempt at its use if the function of scenery had been merely to provide appropriate backgrounds for action in two or three places, but that would not have been scenery as the word was then understood. Scenery was spectacle. Scenery was eye-filling vistas and frequent changes. It needed lofty unencumbered spaces such as none of the commercial theatres could provide. As for Blackfriars in particular, its stage was wholly unsuitable, what with its permanent structures and its modest dimensions. Its lower stage is believed to have been only 9 feet high,[68] 2 feet less than the 11 feet that Sir William Davenant deplored as being grotesquely inadequate when he staged *The Siege of Rhodes* at Rutland House in 1656:

It has been often wisht that our Scenes (we have oblig'd our selves to the variety of Five Changes, according to the Ancient Drammatick distinctions made for time) had not been confin'd to eleven foot in height, and about fifteen in depth, including the places of passage reserv'd for the Musick. This is so narrow an allowance for the Fleet of Solyman the Magnificent, his Army, the Island of Rhodes, and the varieties attending the Siege of the City; that I fear you will think, we invite you to such a contracted Trifle as that of the Caesars carv'd upon a Nut.

The absence of scenery at Blackfriars is suggested also by the Prologue to *The Country Captain*, written by the Duke of Newcastle and acted at Blackfriars in 1640 by the King's Men. If the playhouse had had scenery, it would have made the most of that fact; it would have boasted of it, pointed to it with pride; but not having it, Blackfriars permitted the noble Duke to disparage scenery as being nothing more than a substitute for good playwriting:

> Gallants, I'le tell you what we doe not meane
> To shew you here, a glorious painted Scene,
> With various doores, to stand instead of wit,
> Or richer cloathes with lace, for lines well writ;
> Taylors and Paynters thus, your deare delight,
> May prove your Poets onely for your sight.

The Sharers' Papers

Three junior members of the King's company addressed a petition to the Lord Chamberlain in 1635, asking him to compel shareholders in the Globe and Blackfriars to sell them some of their shares. The three actors were Robert Benfield, Eliard Swanston, and Thomas Pollard; the Lord Chamberlain at the time was Philip Herbert, Earl of Pembroke and Montgomery, one of the two brothers to whom Heminges and Condell had dedicated the First Folio of Shakespeare in 1623, and the one to whom the suppressed King's Men would dedicate the Folio of Beaumont and Fletcher in 1647. The petitions and answers are now usually referred to collectively as the Sharers' Papers.

The petitioners complained that the shareholders took too large a part of the profits of the enterprise, and that the players got too little. The housekeepers, they said, took half the receipts from the boxes and galleries in both houses, and from the tiring-house door at the Globe;[69] the actors got the receipts from the outer doors, and the other half of the receipts from the galleries and boxes (46:2,8,19). Out of their share the actors had to pay the wages of the hired men and boys, and the costs of apparel, lights, music, playwrights, and other expenses, amounting to £900 or £1,000 per annum or thereabouts, being £3 a day, one day with another (46:2,8). The housekeepers, on the other hand, had to pay nothing except rent and repairs for the two houses; and the rent, said the petitioners, amounted to no more than £65 per annum for both houses, and towards that they raised £20 to £30 per annum from the tap houses and a tenement and garden belonging to the premises (46:8). In consequence of this inequality, "when some of the housekeepers share 12s.

a day at the Globe, the actors share not above 3*s.*" (44:9). But the petitioners did not seek to have the inequality remedied; what they sought was to become capitalistic housekeepers themselves:

> The petitioners have a long time, with much patience, expected to be admitted sharers in the playhouses of the Globe and the Blackfriars, whereby they might reap some better fruit of their labors than hitherto they have done, and be encouraged to proceed therein with cheerfulness (46:2);

and they therefore hoped that his Lordship would be nobly pleased

> to call all the said housekeepers before you, and to use your Lordship's power with them to conform themselves thereunto, the rather considering that some of the said housekeepers who have the greatest shares are neither actors nor his Majesty's Servants as aforesaid, and yet reap most or the chiefest benefit of the sweat of their brows, and live upon the bread of their labors, without taking any pains themselves (46:7).

John Shank argued against them. He was himself one of the King's Men, and, having bought all Heminges's shares after Heminges died, he was the largest single shareholder in the Blackfriars, and one of the three largest in the Globe. He disputed the petitioners' statement that the housekeepers paid no more than £65 per annum rent; he said that the amount was £100 yearly, besides reparations (46:14). He said further that each of the three petitioners had earned £180 during the past year, and that Swanston was already the owner of a third part of a share in the Blackfriars (46:13), a detail that the petitioners had not thought needful to mention. He said that he was "an old man in this quality, . . . and having in this long time made no provision for himself in his age, . . . did at dear rates purchase these parts . . . and hopeth he shall not be hindered in the enjoying the profit thereof; . . . all which being considered, your suppliant hopeth that your Lordship will not enforce your suppliant against his will to depart with what is his own, and what he hath dearly paid for, unto them that can claim no lawful interest thereunto" (46:12,16).

The petitioners' request was opposed also by Cuthbert Burbage and by Richard Burbage's widow, now Mrs. Robinson. Cuthbert confirmed Shank's statements as to the earnings of the three actors during the previous year and as to Swanston's ownership of a third part of a Blackfriars share (46:22); but his answer is interesting primarily for its chronicle of early theatrical history and of the part the Burbages played in it:

The father of us, Cuthbert and Richard Burbage, was the first builder of playhouses, and was himself in his younger days a player. The Theater he built with many hundred pounds taken up at interest. . . . He built this house upon leased ground, by which means the landlord and he had a great suit in law, and by his death the like troubles fell on us, his sons. We then bethought us of altering from thence, and at like expense built the Globe, with more sums of money taken up at interest, which lay heavy on us many years; and to ourselves we joined those deserving men, Shakespeare, Heminges, Condell, Phillips, and others, partners in the profits of that we call the House. . . .

Now for the Blackfriars, that is our inheritance. Our father purchased it at extreme rates, and made it into a playhouse with great charge and trouble; which after was leased out to one Evans, that first set up the boys commonly called the Queen's Majesty's Children of the Chapel. In process of time the boys growing up to be men, which were Underwood, Field, Ostler, and were taken to strengthen the King's service; and the more to strengthen the service, the boys daily wearing out, it was considered that house would be as fit for ourselves, and so purchased the lease remaining from Evans with our money, and placed men players, which were Heminges, Condell, Shakespeare, etc. (46:19–20).

With this history as background, Cuthbert contended that those who had given their whole lives to the profession "ought not, in all charity, to be disabled of [their] livelihoods by men so soon shot up, since it hath been the custom that they [i.e., the shareholders] should come to it by far more antiquity and desert than those can justly attribute to themselves" (46:17).

In the course of their petition, the three actors said that the shares in the two playhouses were then distributed as follows:

	Globe	Blackfriars
Cuthbert Burbage	3½	1
Mrs. Robinson	3½	1
Mrs. Condell	2	1
John Shank	3	2
Joseph Taylor	2	1
John Lowin	2	1
Underwood's heirs[70]		1
	16	8

Specifically, they asked the Lord Chamberlain to order Cuthbert Burbage and Mrs. Robinson each to sell them one Globe share out of their three and a half shares apiece, keeping two and a half shares apiece for themselves, and to order Shank to sell them one of his three Globe shares, keeping two (46:4,9), and one of his two Blackfriars shares to be divided between them, keeping one (46:6,9). Each of the petitioners would thus have one Globe share and a third part of a Blackfriars share.

The Lord Chamberlain ruled in their favor. He ordered the three housekeepers to sell the petitioners the shares that they requested, under penalty of being suspended from the stage or otherwise punished if they should fail to comply (46:25). Presumably Cuthbert Burbage and Mrs. Robinson obeyed the order, but not Shank; the likelihood is that he evaded compliance by putting exorbitant prices on his shares. He later said that "according to his Lordship's order, he did make a proposition to his fellows for satisfaction, but they not only refused to give satisfaction, but restrained him from the Stage." Thereupon his Lordship appointed a committee of three, of whom Sir Henry Herbert was one, to look into the matter thoroughly and to set a fair price upon Shank's two shares. But all three of his Globe shares, and his two in Blackfriars, were still in his possession when he died a few months later.

The Witter-Heminges case,[71] the Thomasina Ostler plea, and the Sharers' Papers, are our principle sources of information with respect to the distribution and perambulations of Globe and Blackfriars shares. But a gap of several years intervenes between the first two documents and the third, and in that gap we lose sight of the shares held by Shakespeare. We know from Thomasina's deposition that he held shares in both playhouses when Ostler made his purchases in 1611 and 1612, and we know that those shares are not recognizably mentioned in his will nor in the transactions of his heirs. Presumably he disposed of them between February 20, 1612, and March 25, 1616.

I have previously traced the history of the Globe shares up to the time when Heminges acquired the Ostler share, and when he and Condell divided the Witter share between them. After these proceedings, Heminges had three parts out of the seven into which the second Globe moiety was divided, and Condell had two. The sixth presumably still stood in Shakespeare's name, and the seventh was either halved by Nicoll and the Edmondses, or had already gone from them to Underwood. All the shares in the first moiety were owned by the Burbage family.

Not until 1635 do we have another inventory of Globe shares. By that time several things have happened. The fourteen shares in the two moieties have been divided into sixteen. The names of Shakespeare and

Underwood have disappeared, and the name of Nathaniel Field has come and gone. Heminges has acquired another share, and Condell has acquired two; and Condell has died, leaving his four shares to his widow. After his death, therefore, and until about 1631, Heminges and Mrs. Condell were the only shareholders, and were equal shareholders, in the second moiety, and Cuthbert Burbage and Mrs. Robinson were equal shareholders in the first. Each of the four persons thus held four parts of a moiety or a quarter of the whole (46:3).

Between 1631 and 1635, Taylor and Lowin were permitted to buy two shares apiece, one from Heminges, two from Mrs. Condell, and half shares from Cuthbert Burbage and Mrs. Robinson (44:3); after that, for the first time, the Burbage family held less than a moiety of the Globe. Heminges died in 1630, and his son William sold his three remaining shares to John Shank (44:3). This accounting accords with the schedule printed on page 278.

Of the seven Blackfriars shares, Heminges had been the owner of two after he took over the Ostler share, and Richard Burbage, Cuthbert Burbage, and Henry Condell had each been the owner of one. As far as we know, Shakespeare had one of the remaining two, and Evans had the other. At some uncertain date, probably in 1616 and probably to provide a share for Field, the seven shares were increased to eight. Fifteen years later, the relative holdings of the Burbages, Heminges, and Condell were unchanged in quantity: they were still two, two and one; but Richard Burbage's and Henry Condell's shares had descended to their widows, and Heminges's two shares had been sold to Shank. Cuthbert Burbage still had his one. Three old names—Shakespeare, Evans, and Field—had disappeared from the list of shareholders, and three new names—Lowin, Taylor, and Underwood—had entered it, each as the owner of a single share. This accounting is in agreement with the inventory embodied in the Sharers' Papers and printed above, but it fails to allow for the third part of a share said to have been owned by Swanston (46:13,22).

Cuthbert Burbage, the last survivor of the original shareholders, died in 1636 at the age of seventy.

Fear of the plague was never out of mind in those days. In 1636 and 1637 the Blackfriars Playhouse was closed for seventeen consecutive months, barring only one week, and in September of the latter year the King's Men addressed a petition to the Privy Council praying that the inhibition might be removed and that they might be permitted to act again, having by reason of the plague "been for a long time restrained, and having now spent what they got in many yeares before and soe not able any longer to subsist & mainteine their families."[72] Three years later the plague forced the closing of all the theatres for about two months in the early autumn, and in 1641 it closed them for about four months. By the time that all the playhouses were suppressed in 1642, nearly two years had passed since London had had a week free of deaths from the plague.[73] Since the plague was normally at its worst during the warm months, it of course affected the King's Men's receipts at the Globe more than it did their receipts at Blackfriars.

During all these years, however, the King's Men were still producing plays at Court, and doing so far more often than any other company. They presented twenty-two plays before the King and Queen in late 1636 and early 1637, fourteen in 1637–1638, and twenty-three at Court and one at Blackfriars for the Queen in 1638–1639. Speaking of this latter group of twenty-four plays, Professor Bentley says that

> It is interesting to note how many old plays the King's company was producing at this time. More than half those presented at court in 1638 were over five years old, and about one-third of the twenty-four performances were productions of plays which we still think of as Elizabethan classics.[74]

The company played at Court twenty-one times during the last half of 1639 and the early part of 1640, and probably sixteen times in late 1640 and early 1641.

In February of 1641 the inhabitants of the Blackfriars precinct petitioned again for the suppression of the playhouse, and this time their petition was addressed not to the royalist Privy Council, but to the House of Commons, where the Puritan influence was beginning to make itself strongly felt; and the Commons listened to the petition sympathetically not merely for the practical reason that the playhouse clogged the streets and thus hindered trade, but also for the moralistic reason that the devil's house should not be so near God's house. Because of the changing political situation, this 1641 threat to the playhouse was more serious than those of 1619, 1631, and 1633 had been, and only an interruption of their procedure prevented the Commons from taking action that might have put an end to the playhouse eighteen months earlier than that end was actually to come. Sir Simonds D'Ewes records the event as follows in his journal for February 26, 1904/41:

> Then a petition preferred by the inhabitants of Blacke Friers and others against the play howse ther etc. hinderance of trade, by Alderman Pennington. Hee spake to further it. I etc. A good petition. Gods howse not so neare Divils. This a particular greivance this and the other a generall. All the objection men without them could not tell how to imploy them themselves etc. Others spake against this playhowse and others.
>
> Then Sir Henry Fane being returned his reporting that the Lords would give us a present meeting brake offe our agitation.[75]

This may have been one of the straws in the wind that led the King's Men to seek official protection for their plays. They had presumably received intimations that some of the plays were about to be published by certain unscrupulous printers, so they appealed to the Lord Chamberlain, now the Earl of Essex, to forbid the printing of any play belonging to the King's Men without the company's consent. He did so in a letter addressed to the Masters and Wardens of the Stationers' Company on August 7, 1641. His letter was accompanied by a list of sixty-one King's Men's plays, and it forbade the unauthorized printing of any of them, whether under the titles named or under fraudulent titles. The list naturally did not include any plays that had been printed already; it therefore included no plays by Shakespeare or Ben Jonson. But it did contain the titles of twenty-seven plays by Beaumont and Fletcher, and it was doubtless the Lord Chamberlain's restraint of piracy that enabled the King's Men to publish the Beaumont and Fletcher Folio, containing thirty-four plays and one masque, in 1647.

On January 6, 1642, the King's Men played at Court for the last time. Sir Henry Herbert's chronicle of the event is an omen of what lay ahead:

> On Twelfe Night, 1641–[1642], the prince had a play called *The Scornful Lady*, at the Cockpitt, but the kinge and queene were not there; and it was the only play acted at courte in the whole Christmas.[76]

One month later, on February 4, 1641/42, the matter of closing the playhouse came up in Parliament again; and this time, significantly, the complaint was not against the Blackfriars Playhouse in particular, but against playhouses in general. *The True Diurnal Occurrances* reports that on that day "there was a great complaint made against the Play-houses, and a motion made for the suppressing of them."[77]

The end came on September 2, 1642, when the Commons adopted this resolution and the Lords concurred:

> Whereas the distressed Estate of Ireland, steeped in her own Blood, and the distracted Estate of England, threatned with a Cloud of Blood, by a Civill Warre, call for all possible meanes to appease and avert the Wrath of God appearing in these Judgements; amongst which, Fasting and Prayer having bin often tryed to be very effectuall, have bin lately, and are still enjoyned; and whereas publike Sports doe not well agree with publike Calamities, nor publike Stage-playes with the Seasons of Humiliation, this being an Exercise of sad and pious solemnity, and the other being Spectacles of pleasure, too commonly expressing lacivious Mirth and Levitie: It is therefore thought fit, and Ordeined by the Lords and Commons in this Parliament Assembled, that while these sad Causes and set times of Humiliation doe continue, publike Stage-Playes shall cease, and bee forborne.[78]

The ordinance of September 2, 1642, closed the Blackfriars Play-house and dispersed the King's Men. Wright says that "most of 'em, except Lowin, Tayler and Pollard (who were superannuated) went into the King's Army, and like good Men and true, Serv'd their Old Master, tho' in a different, yet more honourable, Capacity. . . . I have not heard of one of these Players of any Note that sided with the other Party, but only Swanston."[79] The assets of the company may have been liquidated at the same time. An actor named Theophilus Bird testified several years later that Michael Bowyer and Thomas Pollard and others of the company who were in London immediately after the suppression of the playhouses in 1642, "seized upon all the said apparel, hangings, books, and other goods . . . and sold and converted the same to their own uses."[80] If Bird's biased testimony is trustworthy, it suggests that the King's players had little hope of returning to their craft and their play-house after the wars.

A few playhouses gave surreptitious performances from time to time in defiance of the law. Four of them—the Fortune, Red Bull, Cock-pit, and Salisbury Court—responded to the public's love for plays and the actors' need for money by giving plays occasionally in spite of raids by Roundhead soldiers and the confiscation of their theatrical costumes. En-forcement of the ordinance lost some of its energy and effectiveness over

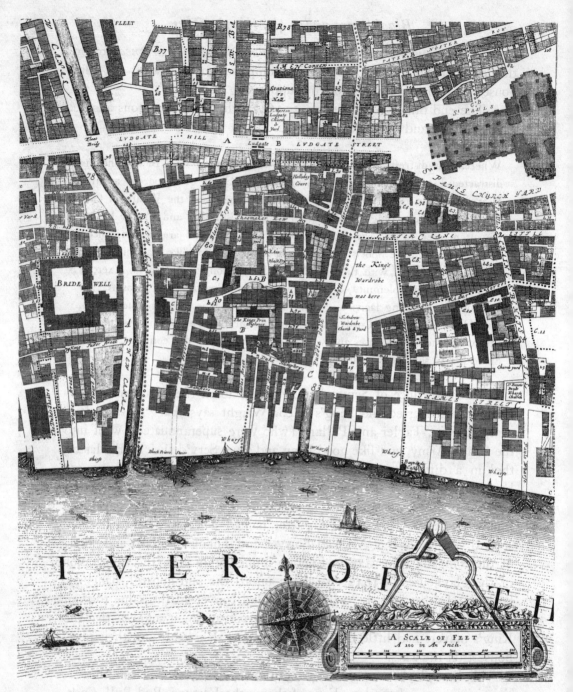

Figure 19. A part of the Ogilby and Morgan Map of 1677, here reprinted by courtesy of the London Topographical Society.

the years, with the result that plays were being performed openly by 1647 and the Blackfriars company began to have hopes of acting again. This is frankly acknowledged in the Parliament newsbook called *The Perfect Weekly Account,* in its issue of October 6–13, 1647:

> Plays begin to be set up apace neverthelesse not without disturbance yet they give out that it shall go forward at three houses, and blacke Fryars is repairing to the end that may be one.[81]

But Parliament enacted a new measure that provided penalties harsher than any that had gone before, and Blackfriars remained closed. The next year those that were left of the company "petitioned for leave to set up their old trade againe,"[82] but nothing came of their appeal. They made another attempt in 1650 or thereabouts, when "diverse poor and distressed men, heretofore the Actors of Black-Friers and the Cock-pit," joined in a petition for relief, saying that they had "long suffered in extream want,

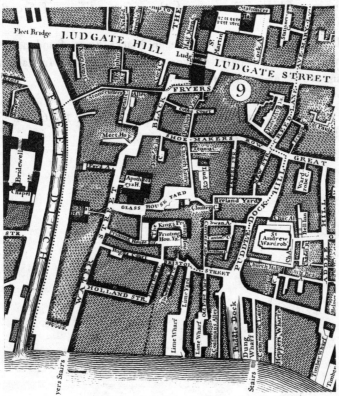

Figure 20. A portion of John Rocque's Survey of London, etc., 1746, reprinted by courtesy of the London Topographical Society.

by being prohibited the use of their qualitie of Acting, in which they were trained up from their childhood, whereby they are uncapable of any other way to get a subsistance, and are now fallen into such lamentable povertie, that they know not how to provide food for themselves, their wives and children."[83] The second appeal, like the first, was fruitless.

Richard Flecknoe made this eye-witness report in 1653:

> Passing on to Black-fryers, and seeing never a Play-bil on the Gate, no Coaches on the place, nor Doorkeeper at the Play-house door, with his Boxe like a Church-warden, desiring you to remember the poor Players, I cannot but say for Epilogue to all the Playes were ever Acted there (that the Puritans)
>> Have made with their Raylings the Players as poore
>> As were the Fryers and Poets before.[84]

The building lasted only two years more. According to a note written in Sir Thomas Phillipps's copy of the 1631 edition of Stow's *Annals*,

> The Blacke Friers players play house, in Blacke Friers London, which had stood many yeares, was pulled downe to the ground on Munday the 6 day of August .1655. and tenements built in the rome.[85]

The last trace of it perished in the Great Fire of 1666. Its site is now occupied by the offices of *The Times*.

1. This list is based upon the chronology published by Chambers in *William Shakespeare*, Vol. I, pp. 270–71.

2. Cf. Chambers, *Elizabethan Stage*, Vol. II, pp. 480, 511.

3. William Sly died within a week after the syndicate was formed, and was buried on August 16, 1608.

4. The two Burbages between them had one half of the Globe and two sevenths of the Blackfriars, and John Heminges and William Shakespeare each had one tenth of the Globe and one seventh of the Blackfriars. Condell and Sly had not been members of the Globe syndicate originally, but they had acquired small holdings prior to August 16, 1608. Cf. Chambers, *Elizabethan Stage*, Vol. II, p. 418.

5. C. W. Wallace prints the Latin text of a portion of the plea in a 16-page pamphlet entitled *Advance Sheets from Shakespeare, the Globe, and Blackfriars.* Chambers reprints it in *William Shakespeare*, Vol. II, pp. 58–64.

6. Cf. Fleay, p. 241. The error is corrected in Document 36 in the present volume.

7. Keysar said that Evans had received "some small piece of money . . . to the end that he would surrender up the original lease to the said Richard Burbage" (41:5). I accept Keysar's testimony in the present instance because Cuthbert Burbage confirms it.

8. See footnote 33, p. 208, above.

9. Chambers, *Elizabethan Stage*, Vol. IV, p. 175.

10. *Work for Armorours* (*Works*, 1609, Vol. IV, p. 96).

11. Chambers, *Elizabethan Stage*, Vol. IV, pp. 175–76.

12. Keysar was clearly far out in his reckoning when he said on February 6, 1610, that Richard Burbage and his colleagues "have entered in and upon the said playhouse . . . and made profit thereof to themselves to the full value at the least of £1,500" (41:5).

13. The last half-dozen lines are based upon Sir Harley Granville-Barker's appraisal of the new conditions that would confront the King's Men at Blackfriars, and their response to those new conditions. See his *Prefaces to Shakespeare*, London ed., 2nd Series, pp. 248–50, or Princeton ed., Vol. I, p. 470.

14. Professor Gerald E. Bentley has discussed the Blackfriars influence upon Shakespeare and the King's Men in a masterly article entitled "Shakespeare and the Blackfriars Theatre," *Shakespeare Survey 1* (1948), pp. 38–56.

15. Chambers, *Elizabethan Stage*, Vol. IV, p. 176.

16. *Ibid.*, Vol. IV, pp. 177–78.

17. *Ibid.*, Vol. IV, pp. 179–80.

18. *Ibid.*, Vol. IV, pp. 181–83.

19. Halliwell-Phillipps, Vol. II, pp. 31ff.; see also Vol. I, pp. 238ff.; Vol. II, pp. 34ff. and 345–56. The gatehouse purchase is also discussed in Chambers, *William Shakespeare*, Vol. II, pp. 154–169.

20. This is the amount assessed against John Witter, who, like Shakespeare, had a one-fourteenth interest in the Globe. See Chambers, *William Shakespeare*, Vol. II, p. 56.

21. Chambers says that it is not known that Shakespeare held his Globe shares to the end of his life, and that he may have sold them in 1613 rather than pay the assessment (*William Shakespeare*, Vol. II, pp. 67–68; cf. Vol. I, p. 82).

22. Chambers, *William Shakespeare*, Vol. II, pp. 172–73. Halliwell-Phillipps, Vol. II, p. 345, says that "in all probability the mortgage was paid off by the Halls."

23. Birch, *James I*, Vol. I, p. 329, as quoted by Chambers, *Elizabethan Stage*, Vol. II, p. 423.

24. I.e., Shakespeare, Richard Burbage, Heminges, Phillips, Kempe, Pope, Bryan, Condell, Sly, and Cowley.

25. The Plea of Thomasina Ostler in the suit of Ostler *vs.* Heminges (*Coram Rege Roll* 1454, 13 Jac. 1, Hilary Term, m. 692), discovered by C. W. Wallace and printed in *Advance Sheets from Shakespeare, the Globe, and Blackfriars*; reprinted by Chambers, *William Shakespeare*, Vol. II, pp. 58–64.

26. Cf. Bentley, *Jacobean and Caroline Stage*, Vol. I, pp. 21–22; Vol. II, pp. 465ff.

27. Witter *vs.* Heminges and Condell, Court of Requests, printed in full by C. W. Wallace in "Shakespeare and His London Associates," and reprinted in part by Chambers in *William Shakespeare*, Vol. II, pp. 52–57.

28. The royal patent of March 27, 1619 had already been drafted by the date of Burbage's death, but not yet published. He is thus listed as one of the King's Men, although the patent was not issued until two weeks after his death.

29. Cf. Bentley, *Jacobean and Caroline Stage*, Vol. II, pp. 674–80.

30. Chambers, *Elizabethan Stage*, Vol. IV, p. 174.

31. Bentley, *Jacobean and Caroline Stage*, Vol. II, pp. 677–79.

32. I.e., Chaucer's.

33. "The Length of Elizabethan and Jacobean Plays," and "The Time Allotted for Representation of Elizabethan and Jacobean Plays."

34. *Comedies and Tragedies*, A3r.

35. Stow, ed. 1633, pp. 380–87.

36. *Foedera*, tom. xviii, pp. 120–21, printed in full in *Jacobean and Caroline Stage*, Vol. I, pp. 17–18.

37. *Jacobean and Caroline Stage*, Vol. II, p. 654.

38. *Herbert*, p. 43.

39. Page 211 above.

40. Collier, Vol. I, pp. 452–53, as quoted in *Jacobean and Caroline Stage*, Vol. I, p. 25. The French players had in fact been licensed by the office of the Master of the Revels on November 4, 1629 (*Herbert*, p. 59).

41. Collier, Vol. I, p. 455, reprinted in full by Joseph Quincy Adams in *Shakespearean Playhouses*, pp. 228–30.

42. Cf. Chambers, *Elizabethan Stage*, Vol. II, pp. 511–12, and Bentley, *Jacobean and Caroline Stage*, Vol. I, pp. 32–33.

43. *Strafforde's Letters*, Vol. I, pp. 175–76, quoted in Joseph Quincy Adams, *Shakespearean Playhouses*, p. 231, and in Bentley, *Jacobean and Caroline Stage*, Vol. I, pp. 33–34.

44. *Jacobean and Caroline Stage*, Vol. I, p. 20.

45. *Ibid.*, Vol. I, p. 34.

46. *Ibid.*, Vol. I, p. 53.

47. *Ibid.*, Vol. I, pp. 38–39.

48. Ibid., Vol. I, p. 48 and 48n.; *Shakespearean Playhouses*, p. 232.

49. *Jacobean and Caroline Stage*, Vol. I, pp. 96–98.

50. *Audit Office Records*, xx. li. ii., as quoted in Wheatley, Vol. I, p. 196.

51. *Jacobean and Caroline Stage*, Vol. I, pp. 37–38.

52. *Herbert*, pp. 53, 55n.

53. Cf. Chambers, *Elizabethan Stage*, Vol. I, pp. 178–84.

54. Wood, *History and Antiquities of Oxford*, Vol. II, Book I, pp. 409 and 411–12, as quoted in *Jacobean and Caroline Stage*, Vol. III, p. 137.

55. *Autobiography*, pp. 207–208.

56. *Brief Lives*, Vol. II, pp. 244–45.

57. *Strafforde's Letters*, Vol. II, p. 150, as quoted in Bentley, *Jacobean and Caroline*

Stage, Vol. I, p. 58, and Vol. V, p. 1202.

58. Bentley, *Jacobean and Caroline Stage*, Vol. III, p. 123.

59. *Ibid.*, Vol. IV, p. 524.

60. *Scenes and Machines*, pp. 190–91, p. 210.

61. *Elizabethan Playhouse*, Second Series, p. 121.

62. *Shakespeare Companion*, p. 477.

63. *Biographical Chronicle of the English Stage*, Vol. II, p. 23.

64. P. 20. As has been said, Apothecaries' Hall was the former Porter's Lodge and Old Buttery in the Blackfriars precinct.

65. The quotations from *Historia Histrionica* are from pp. 5–6 and 10–11.

66. Cf. *Shakespeare Companion*, *s.v.* "Actresses," and Mander and Mitchenson, p. 21. The debut of the French actresses at Blackfriars had been followed by a few random appearances of women on the London stage, but the role of Desdemona was probably the first to be performed by a professional actress.

67. Published in *Love's Kingdom*, 1664, sig. G6ᵛ.

68. See pp. 411–12 below.

69. I fail to understand how there could have been receipts at the tiring-house door of the Globe. At the Blackfriars, yes; Blackfriars permitted gentlemen to enter by the tiring-house door for the purpose of sitting on the stage, and collected fees from them for admission and for stools. But the Globe did not. I therefore suspect that "Globe" was written in error for "Blackfriars."

70. The schedule lists Underwood, not Underwood's heirs; but Underwood had died in 1624.

71. Wallace, "Shakespeare and His London Associates," pp. 47ff., reprinted by Chambers, *William Shakespeare*, Vol. II, pp. 51–57. My brief account of shares and shareholders is based largely upon the detailed study by Professor T. W. Baldwin in *Organization and Personnel of the Shakespearean Company*, pp. 90–117.

72. *Malone Society Collections*, Vol. I, p. 394.

73. Cf. Bentley, *Jacobean and Caroline Stage*, Vol. II, pp. 670–71.

74. *Ibid.*, Vol. I, p. 62. For the numbers of plays presented at Court, see Vol. I, pp. 98–100.

75. *The Journal of Sir Simonds D'Ewes*, p. 412, as quoted by Bentley, *Jacobean and Caroline Stage*, Vol. I, p. 64.

76. *Herbert*, p. 58.

77. Hotson, p. 5.

78. Bentley, *Jacobean and Caroline Stage*, Vol. I, pp. 68–69.

79. *Historia Histrionica*, as quoted by Bentley, *op. cit.*, Vol. II, pp. 694–95.

80. Hotson, pp. 31–33.

81. *Ibid.*, p. 27.

82. *Ibid.*, p. 29.

83. *Ibid.*, pp. 43–44.

84. As quoted by Hotson, *ibid.*, p. 54.

85. Phillipps MS 11613, p. 16, now removed from Stow and catalogued as V.b. 275 in the Folger Shakespeare Library. But Dr. McManaway says that there is good reason to suspect this of being a Collier forgery.

❧ 13 ❧

The Playhouse:
THE AUDITORIUM

T HE BLACKFRIARS PLAYHOUSE provided accommodations for its patrons in the pit, in boxes, in two upper galleries, and on the stage
itself. It did not, as did the public playhouses, make provision for
standees.

The Galleries

Four contemporary legal documents mention the galleries at Blackfriars. The Hawkins deposition of 1609, written in Latin interspersed
with English translations of technical terms, says that the great hall was
furnished *"cum . . . porticibus Anglice Galleries"* (40:3). Keysar's bill
of complaint, 1610, speaks of "galleries and seats" (41:1), and so does
the answer of the defendants (41:7); and the petition of the complainants in the so-called Sharers' Papers of 1635 links the galleries at Blackfriars with those at the Globe by speaking of "the galleries and boxes in
both houses" (44:8). All the documents speak of the galleries in the
plural, but none says how many there were nor how they were disposed.

Professor Wallace, who discovered the first of the documents quoted
above, believes that the galleries were arranged in three tiers along the
end of the hall and along both its sides. He bases his theory upon the
plural "galleries," which implies at least two, and upon the phrase "the
middle region" in Marston's *Dutch Courtesan*, v *iii*—"And now, my very
fine Heliconian gallants, and you, my worshipful friends in the middle
region"—which he takes to mean the middle gallery of three.[1] Chambers
challenges Wallace's theory by pointing out that "the middle region" is
not necessarily any gallery at all; it may just as probably be the space
between the end galleries and the stage. Furthermore, two galleries

constitute a plural as well as three; and whether two or three, the galleries are not necessarily superimposed: one along each wall would satisfy the specification as fully as would triple tiers.[2] Nevertheless, Wallace may have been right in his interpretation of the phrase, especially since Henry Fitzgeffrey speaks of "the middle Region" in a context that includes the word "Ranke" and thus almost certainly has reference to spectators' accommodations in a gallery. He uses the phrase in "Notes from Black-Fryers" (London, 1617), sig. E7[v]:

> See *(Captaine Martio)* he ith' *Renounce me* Band,
> That in the middle Region doth stand
> Woth' reputation steele! Faith! lets remove,
> Into his *Ranke,* (if such discourse you Love).

But whether or not "the middle region" meant the middle gallery of three arranged in vertical sequence, Blackfriars probably had three galleries so arranged. I base this opinion upon the triple tiers in every Elizabethan playhouse of which we have knowledge in this respect—the Fortune and (as prototype of the Fortune) the Globe, and the Swan and (as replica of the Swan) the Hope, and upon the triple tiers, presumably representing an inherited tradition, in nearly all Restoration theaters.

The contract for building the Fortune Playhouse specifies three "stories" or galleries, and gives their dimensions; it is the only document that gives the dimensions of the galleries in any playhouse. It is dated January 8, 1599/1600, just four years after James Burbage undertook to convert the Parliament Chamber to theatrical purposes, and one year after Cuthbert Burbage began to build the Globe; and since the Fortune was admittedly modeled upon the Globe, which in turn may in some respects have been modeled upon the Blackfriars, it is the best guide we have to the proportions of the Blackfriars galleries. The relative section reads as follows:

And the said Frame to contain Three Stories in height. The first or lower Story to contain Twelve foot of lawful assize in height, the second Story Eleven foot of lawful assize in height, and the Third or upper Story to contain Nine foot of lawful assize in height; All which Stories shall contain Twelve foot and a half of lawful assize in breadth throughout, besides a Jutty forwards in either of the said Two upper stories of Ten Inches of lawful assize.[3]

The figures given as the heights of the three galleries were presumably specified as their measurements from the floor of one gallery to the floor of the gallery next overhead. The floor of the second gallery was then 12 feet above the floor of the first, and the floor of the third was 23 feet above. The 9 feet specified as the height of the third gallery was probably its measurement from floor to roof. All these dimensions, except the last, may be transferred to Blackfriars. The final figure must be ignored, since the narrow roofs over the galleries at the Fortune were not comparable to the great roof, four times as wide, that covered the Parliament Chamber.

The Parliament Chamber could easily accommodate three tiers of galleries of these heights. For the reasons given on page 102 above, we may assume that its vertical walls were 38 to 40 feet high, more than high enough to hold three galleries with a total height of 23 feet to the topmost gallery's floor.

So much for the galleries' vertical dimensions. As for their horizontal dimensions, the builder's contract provided that the lowest "story" at the Fortune should "contain twelve foot and a half of lawful assize in breadth throughout." But this included the thickness of an exterior wall, since "the frame of the said house . . . [was] to contain fourscore foot of lawful assize every way square without, and fifty-five foot of like assize square every way within"; and since the lowest gallery was to be "fenced with strong iron pikes" to prevent its being invaded from the yard, the 12½-foot breadth also necessarily included the width of a passageway so that playgoers could reach their gallery seats from the rear. The Fortune was of timber construction, with walls thinner than the stone walls of conventual buildings. If, therefore, we estimate the wall's thickness and the passageway's width at a combined total of 5 feet and deduct that figure from 12½, we are left with 7½ feet as the depth of the area provided for the seating of spectators in the first gallery at the Fortune.

Unlike the Fortune's lowest gallery, that at Blackfriars could probably be entered from the floor of the hall; it could thus dispense with a rear passageway and devote all its depth to spectators' benches; and if we may suppose that the lowest gallery at Blackfriars provided the same depth for spectators as did that at the Fortune, we arrive at 7½ feet as its depth inside the exterior wall.

On page 147 I suggested that a seated spectator at the First Blackfriars needed a front-to-back depth of 2½ feet and a width of 2 feet. I make the same assumption for spectators at the Second Blackfriars. On this basis, a gallery 7½ feet wide would hold three rows of seats. The floor of the lowest gallery, as of the others also, was stepped up in "degrees" or lifts, to provide a better view of the stage for persons seated in the rear. Figures 18, 21 and 25 show the lowest degree as being 1 foot high, the second 2, and the third 3, and thus show the third as being on a level with the floor of the platform, which presumably, like that at the First Blackfriars, was 3 feet high.[4]

Each of the upper galleries at the Fortune overhung the gallery beneath it by a distance of 10 inches, the overhangs serving the practical purpose of protecting the sills and walls from wet by causing rainwater to drip free of foundations and frame, and so preventing it from seeping into timber joints and rotting them. But this need did not exist in the roofed-over Blackfriars. We may therefore suppose that all the Blackfriars galleries were of the same width, and that their supports were post-over-post.

The posts are alluded to in *The Isle of Gulls*, sig. G3ᵛ, in these lines:

> As they [the playwrights] stand gaping to receive their merrit,
> Insted of plaudities, their chiefest blisses,
> Let their desarts be crownd with mewes and hisses:
> Behinde each post and at the gallery corners,
> Sit empty guls, slight fooles and false informers.

Stairs to the upper galleries were perhaps constructed in the back corners of the auditorium. So placed, they would have the double advantage of utilizing space of little value for spectators and of being near the entrance door. A passageway ran along the rear of each upper gallery, to enable patrons to get to their seats; it reduced the gallery's capacity from three rows of seats to two.

In the Swan certainly, and doubtless in all the other public playhouses as well, the galleries did not stop at the front edge of the stage, as galleries must do in modern proscenium-arch theatres. Instead, they continued back at each side, past the platform, until they made contact with the tiring-house. The lowest gallery at Blackfriars, since it was no higher than the platform itself, necessarily stopped at the platform's front edge, but the upper galleries swept on toward the rear. The middle gallery spanned the areas occupied by stage-sitters at the two sides, and abutted upon the down-stage walls of the window stages; parts of them—

the parts that stretched over the platform—were often used as acting areas, as will be explained presently.[5] The top gallery presumably continued on around all four sides of the auditorium, virtually without a break.

The architectural device of extending the galleries over the stage had enough appeal to survive the Puritan revolution; it persisted in the playhouses built after the Restoration, as one more instance of the continuity of theatrical traditions. Eventually the custom of sitting on the stage was abolished, and the ends of the stage where the gallants had sat were converted into boxes at platform level, which thus corresponded to the lowest galleries of the traditional three; and boxes on all three levels ran back beyond the forward edge of the platform for a distance equivalent to the width of two boxes or more, with the upper galleries overriding the proscenium entering doors. This extraordinary arrangement survived at Covent Garden and Drury Lane until well after the middle of the eighteenth century.[6]

Boxes or Lords' Rooms

A few plays and other contemporary records allude to boxes at Blackfriars and indicate that they could be reserved in advance. Thus the Captain in *The Parson's Wedding*, v i, says that "there's a new play at the Friars today, and I have bespoke a box for Mr. Wild and his bride." Anne Frugal, in *The City Madam*, ii ii, makes it a condition of her marrying Sir Maurice Lacy that she shall have "the private box ta'en up at a new play, For me and my retinue." Fitzgeffrey's "Notes from Black-Fryers," F[v], tells of a courtesan who disappoints two gentlemen's expectations and leads them to assume that, since "she'l not come ore,/ Sure shee's bespoken for a box before." And finally, a letter written by George Garrard in 1635 shows that the boxes had keys and could be locked:

A little Pique happened betwixt the Duke of Lenox and the Lord Chamberlain about a Box at a new Play in the Black Fryars, of which the Duke had got the Key: Which if it had come to be debated betwixt them, as it was once intended, some Heat or perhaps other Inconvenience might have happen'd. His Majesty hearing of it, sent the Earl of Holland to commend them both not to dispute it, but before him, so he heard it and made them Friends.[7]

Lords' rooms at Blackfriars are mentioned only once: Dekker uses that term in *Satiromastix*, v ii 350, when, in satirizing Blackfriars conditions and personnel, he twits Ben Jonson upon his amiable habit of venturing on the stage when his play was ended, "to exchange curtezies and complements with gallants in the lordes roomes." Presumably "boxes" and "lords' rooms" were two names for the same thing, and both were names for small compartments in the lowest of the three tiers of galleries running along the three sides of the auditorium. As being in the lowest tier, their position at Blackfriars corresponded with that of the boxes in the Hope Playhouse, described in the builder's contract as "Two Boxes in the lowermost storie fitt and decent for gentlemen to sitt in," and with that of the gallery labeled "orchestra" in the DeWitt sketch of the Swan;[8] for "orchestra," as defined by the playwright Thomas Heywood in 1624, meant "a place in the Theatre onely for the Nobilitie."[9] Their position corresponded too with the position of the boxes that would later circle the pit at about platform level in nearly all Restoration theatres.

The boxes were probably entered from the front, since entrance from the back would demand that valuable space be sacrificed to rear corridors serving the boxes alone; entrance from the front, on the other hand, would utilize corridors that served both the boxes and the pit. On this theory, the boxes were guarded along their front edges by balustrades or railings broken at intervals by gates that could be locked, and were separated from each other by low partitions. The upper galleries necessarily had their front edges guarded by railings.

The Pit

The Hawkins Latin document of 1609 speaks of the playhouse as being equipped with "seats to the amount specified in the schedule thereto attached" (40:3), but the schedule, alas, has vanished. Davenant speaks of benches in the Prologue to his *Unfortunate Lovers*, and implies that in the later days of the playhouse the benches were "adorn'd with Mats." Thomas Carew also speaks of benches in his lines to Davenant on *The Just Italian*.

One cannot say categorically that either the First or the Second Blackfriars originated the seated pit, but in all probability one of them did. The seating of the entire audience worked a revolution in theatrical practice. Unlike the restless standing pits of the public playhouses, the Blackfriars pit was quiet. The audience was more comfortable, more stable, more attentive. It followed the dramatist's lines more easily and with greater reward, and thus encouraged both the dramatist and the actor to greater sophistication and subtlety.

The nature of the audience changed in response to the new conditions. The seated pit reduced the capacity of the house, and in so doing it both compelled and justified higher admission fees. The general atmosphere of the playhouse was more formal, more dignified. And as for the pit itself, instead of being the least desirable part of the house, it became the best.

Capacity

As was said a few pages back in discussing the dimensions of the spectator galleries, I assume that each seated spectator at Blackfriars occupied a space 2 feet wide from side to side by 2½ feet deep from front to back. I am aware that this module of 5 square feet is greater than is allowed in some modern theatres and stadia, and greater than some writers feel to be necessary in calculating the capacity of Elizabethan playhouses. But the costumes worn by Elizabethan and Jacobean playgoers were more voluminous than those worn by playgoers of today, and those worn at Blackfriars were bulkier than those worn at the Globe or the Swan. I therefore base my estimate of seating capacity upon an allowance of 5 square feet for each spectator.

We know the Blackfriars auditorium to have been 46 feet wide from east to west; for reasons that will be given in the next chapter, I assume it to have been 44 feet long from north to south. Galleries or boxes, each of them 7½ feet deep, ran along nearly all of the north, east, and west sides, fronted by corridors perhaps 3 feet wide or a little more; and another corridor probably ran down the center of the floor. Allowances having been made for these galleries and corridors, an area of about 650 square feet is left for the seating of spectators, enough to accommodate thirteen rows of benches, each row being able to seat ten persons. Figure 22, on page 310, thus shows the pit as having a capacity of 130 spectators.

The lowest gallery necessarily sacrificed some of its space to the entrance corridor leading into the auditorium from the great winding stairs, and to lesser stairs leading to galleries above. Figure 22 shows the side galleries as being divided into eight boxes capable of seating twelve persons apiece, and the rear gallery as being divided into two boxes with a joint capacity of thirty persons.

The middle gallery bridged the entrance corridor, and, as has been said, extended over the ends of the platform also. It lost some space to the stairs that mounted to it from the pit, and to other stairs that continued up to the topmost gallery. It had only two rows of seats, the third giving place to a rear passageway. Figure 23 shows it as being able to seat 112 persons.

The top gallery could accommodate a few persons more than the middle gallery, since it had no need to make allowance for stairs to a gallery overhead. I estimate its capacity at 120.

Again anticipating explanations to be given in the next chapter, I assume that the platform provided seats for about twenty-eight stage-sitters.

As indicated in the table below, the seating capacity of the Second Blackfriars thus seems to have been about 516 persons. Because of my 5-foot module, my estimate is smaller than those of other persons who have written on the subject.[10]

Area	*Number of Spectators*
The Pit	130
The Lowest Gallery	126
The Middle Gallery	112
The Top Gallery	120
Stage-Sitters	28
	516

Prices of Admission

Information about prices of admission at Blackfriars is fragmentary and confused. The only statement that can be made with assurance is that sixpence was the price of a stool on the stage. Three sources agree in showing this to have been the price. The first is the Induction to *Cynthia's Revels*, in which two boys, one impersonating a playhouse attendant and the other a playgoer, have this conversation:

2 *Child.* . . . Would you have a stoole, sir?
3 *Child.* A stoole, boy?
2 *Child.* I, sir, if youle give me sixpence, Ile fetch you one.

297

Dekker, in *The Guls Hornbook*, Chapter 6, says:

> By sitting on the stage, you may (with small cost) purchase the deere acquaintance of the boys: have a good stoole for sixpence;

and Ralph Brideoake, in his lament upon the death of Master Ben Jonson in *Jonsonus Virbius*, says:

> And though thy Phancies were too high for those
> That but aspire to Cockepit-flight, or prose,
> Though the fine Plush and Velvets of the age
> Did oft for sixpence damne thee from the Stage . . .

Two shillings seems to have been the whole cost of a seat on the stage, with eighteen pence as the price of admission and sixpence as the supplementary price of a stool. In each of the passages that follow, the license to gird at the play and the poet is recognized; and since that license was the special prerogative of stage-sitters, it becomes clear that the passages relate to seats on the stage. Jasper Mayne, in the "Epilogue at Black-friars" to his play *The City Match*, says that his play is not for those

> Who, if they speak not ill o' th' poet, doubt
> They lose by the play, nor have their two shillings out;

and his subsequent reference to those "Who singly make a box, and fill the pit," shows that it was not they whom he had in mind as occupants of the two-shilling seats. In *The Magnetic Lady*, the censorious Damplay, who is known from the Induction to have been sitting on the stage, has this to say in the chorus between Acts II and III:

> I see no reason, if I come here, and give my eighteene pence, or two shillings for my Seat, but I should take it out in censure, on the Stage.

And William Habington, in his "Prologue at the Fryers" to *The Queen of Aragon*, says

> Ere we begin, that no man may repent
> Two shillings and his time, the Author sent

1. The East Range at Cleeve Abbey, Somerset.

The dorter occupies the upper floor. On the lower level, the first door from the left is probably that of the sacristy. Then comes the entrance to the chapter house, with a window on either side, and then the day stairs to the dorter. The building at the right is the frater. Attachments for the cloister roofs are visible along both walls.

11. The Dominican Preaching Cross at Hereford.

This outdoor pulpit is the only one of its kind left in England. It presumably is similar to the cross that once stood in the Blackfriars churchyard at Ludgate, described in Piers the Plowman's Creed *as "a curious cross, craftily built,/With tabernacles encircled, facing all sides."*

III. The Night Stairs at Hexham Priory.

This deeply-worn staircase is the finest example of a night stair·surviving in England. It led down from the priory's dorter to the church's south transept. The friars, awakened at midnight by the ringing of a bell, filed down these stairs into the choir for the first and longest office of the conventual day.

IV. The Novices' House at Battle Abbey.

Pillars and vaults of this sort normally served to support a principal chamber above, and thus almost inevitably supported the great hall that contained the Second Blackfriars Playhouse.

v. The Lavatory in the Cloister of Gloucester Cathedral.

This is the best-preserved medieval lavatorium in England. It is 47 feet long, and projects into the garth by some 8 feet. The flat upper shelf originally supported a leaden cistern with a row of taps. The monks washed their hands in the trough below before filing into the frater for their meals.

VI. The Abbot's Kitchen at Glastonbury Abbey.

Two medieval monastic kitchens remain in England, one at Glastonbury and the other at Durham. The Glastonbury kitchen was built outside the cloister, near the frater. It is square on plan, with fireplaces in the corners as to create an octagonal interior, with arches above supporting intricate vaulting, and with a central louvre for the escape of smoke.

VII. The Prior's Lodging at Ely Cathedral Priory.

The lodging communicates with a magnificent series of halls and chambers that once made it possible for the prior to give appropriate entertainment to any number of guests of whatever rank. Prior Crauden's beautiful chapel, over an undercroft, adjoins the lodging at the left.

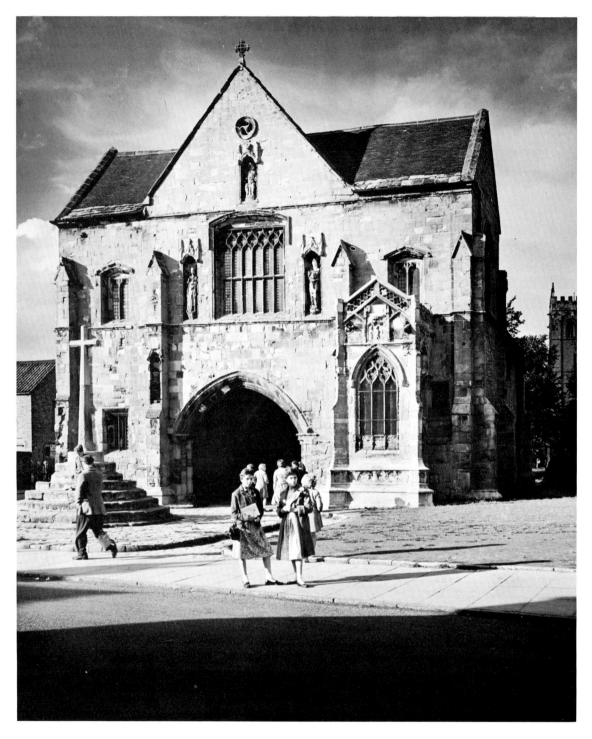

VIII. The Worksop Priory Gatehouse.

This gatehouse, dating from the fourteenth century, is one of the less pretentious structures of its kind. The projection to the right of the gateway is the porch of a former oratory, behind which was the porter's lodge. The upper floor originally served as the priory's guest house, and now serves as a school.

The Prologue, with the errors of his play,
That who will may take his money and away.

Sir Humphrey Mildmay's diary and account book show that he paid eighteen pence or its multiples for admission to Blackfriars on various occasions, and twelve pence at other times. His records include the following items:

22 Jan.	1632/33	"To a play att the bla: ffryers"	1s. 0d.
21 Jan.	1633/34	"To a playe att Bla: fryers"	1s. 6d.
22 Jan.	1633/34	"To a playe att the fryers, the Witts"	1s. 0d.
12 Dec.	1634	"To a play of Love & honnor wth the :2: Southlandes	4s. 6d.
25 Apr.	1635	" . . . to the Elder Brother att the bla: ffryers".	1s. 0d.
28 Apr.	1635	"Expended att the bla: fryers . . . wth good Company"	3s. 0d.
6 May	1635	" . . . att the bla: ffryers & a play this day Called the More of Venice" (but the amount disbursed includes "other Expenses")	7s. 2d.
16 Dec.	1635	"To a playe at bla: fryers wth good Company"	3s. 6d.
3 Nov.	1637	"To my Exp. att the play . . . the fryers blacke to a play"	2s. 6d.
27 Oct.	1638	" . . . to the fox playe att bl: fryers wth my Cozen fra. Wortley & my Brother Anth."	4s. 6d.
15 May	1640	" . . . to the Newe play att Bla: fryers . . . wth my wife & Company"	11s. 0d.
19 May	1641	"To the play att Blacke fryers"	1s. 6d.[11]

The entries of January 21, 1633/34, 12 December 1634 (three persons), October 27, 1638 (three persons), and May 19, 1641, suggest that eighteen pence was the price of admission to seats in some part of the auditorium, perhaps the pit. Similarly, the items of January 22, 1632/33, January 22, 1633/34, and April 25, 1635, suggest that one shilling also was a price of admission.[12] This is confirmed by the following extracts from Blackfriars plays:

From *The Captain,* Prologue:

> . . . and those that think
> Twelve pence goes farther this way than in drink,
> Or Damsels, if they mark the matter through,
> May stumble on a foolish toy, or two.

From *The Goblins,* Epilogue:

> O, what a monster-wit must that man have,
> That could please all which now their twelvepence gave!

From *Henry VIII,* Prologue:

> Those that come to see
> Only a show or two and so agree
> The play may pass — if they be still and willing,
> I'll undertake may see away their shilling
> Richly in two short hours.

and from *The Mad Lover,* Prologue:

> Remember, ye're all venturers; and in this Play
> How many twelve-pences ye have 'stow'd this day.

Jasper Mayne gives half a crown as the price of a box, in the line "They who possest a Box, and halfe Crowne spent," in his commendatory verses in the Beaumont and Fletcher First Folio; and Fletcher's *Wit Without Money,* produced in another private playhouse, the Cockpit, speaks of "the halfe crowne boxes." We have no explicit assurance that these prices apply to boxes at the Blackfriars, but they probably do.

Ben Jonson twice refers to seats priced at sixpence each. In the Induction to *The Magnetic Lady,* he speaks of

> the faeces, or grounds of your people, that sit in the oblique caves and wedges
> of your house, your sinful sixe-penny Mechanicks,

and in his lines to Fletcher on his *Faithful Shepherdess,* he catalogs some of the members of the "many headed bench, that sits / Upon the Life and Death of Playes," and among them he includes

> the shops Foreman, or some such brave spark,
> That may judge for his six-pence.

And Jasper Mayne, in the epilogue to his *City Match,* denies that he, as author,

> feares his name can suffer wrack
> From them who six-pence pay, and six-pence crack.
> To such he wrote not.

The six-penny price applied to "the oblique caves and wedges" of the house, the least desirable seats that the playhouse afforded.

As has been mentioned already,[13] we know the total amounts that Blackfriars took in at each of five benefit performances tendered to Sir Henry Herbert during the years 1628 to 1632. The largest amount was £19 15s. 0d., and the smallest was £12 1s. 0d. The average was £15 15s. 0d.

Light and Darkness

Blackfriars presented its plays by artificial light. Evidence of this is derived from four sources. The diary of the Duke of Stettin-Pomerania, in describing a performance of the Children of the Chapel in 1602, says that "*Alle bey Lichte agiret, welches ein gross Ansehen macht*" (45:4). Francis Beaumont refers to "wax-lights" in his poem to John Fletcher on his *Faithful Shepherdess,* and the Induction to *The Staple of News* contains an episode in which the book-holder calls to the tiremen to "Mend your lights, gentlemen," and a moment later "*The Tiremen enter to mend the lights.*" Finally, Wright's *Historia Histrionica,* in describing the London playhouses before the wars, says that "the Black-friers, Cockpit, and Salisbury-court, were called Private Houses. . . . Here they had Pits for the Gentry, and Acted by Candle-light."[14]

Presumably the candles were held in branched candelabra similar to those shown in the frontispiece to *The Wits;*[15] like them, they were suspended from above, necessarily by cords or wires running over pulleys, so that they could be lowered for "mending," lighting, and extinguishing. Miss Elizabeth Burton, in writing of the furnishings of Elizabethan homes, says that

Candles, with their thick wicks curling over until the hot charred end dipped into the melted wax of the gutter, needed constant care and attention, and a servant or several servants were employed whose sole duty was to see to the candles;[16]

and the need to "mend" the candles frequently, as related on page 230 above, was a compelling reason for intermissions between the acts of plays presented in the private playhouses, in contrast with those in the public playhouses, where no such need existed. The auditorium and the stage were lighted equally, and by the same means; not for many years was the auditorium to be lighted less brightly than the stage during a performance.

Footlights were as yet unknown. The earliest evidence of their use comes after the Restoration, in the frontispiece to *The Wits, or Sport upon Sport,* first published in 1672.[17] It shows an improvised stage of the sort used in performances of Drolls "when the publique Theatres were shut up," and bears no relationship to the stages of public or private playhouses before the Puritan revolution.

Dekker, in *The Seven Deadly Sinnes of London,* implies that the private playhouses had some means of shuttering their windows so as to darken their interiors; he speaks of "all the Citty [as looking] like a private Play-house, when the windowes are clapt downe, as if some Nocturnal, or dismall Tragedy were presently to be acted . . . "[18] The clapping down of the windows would, of course, be effective only in the afternoon, not at night; and, since the windows in the Parliament Chamber were doubtless many and large, the process would take too long, both in the original clapping down and in the subsequent unclapping, to be resorted to for temporary theatrical effect during the course of a play. Presumably the windows were darkened so that afternoon plays could be given by candlelight, and they were clapped down, as Dekker implies, before the plays began, and remained so until the end.

Two contemporary documents contain allusions that may have a bearing upon the shuttering of the windows. One is a memorandum written by Sir William More, in which he complains that during Farrant's tenure of the premises in the days of the First Blackfriars, "the wyndows [were] spoyled."[19] The other is Hawkins's deposition to the effect that in 1604 the great hall of the Second Blackfriars was "dilapidated in various parts and unrepaired, namely in . . . the wooden windows as well above as below on each side of the premises" (40:6). The "wooden windows" to which Hawkins alludes were probably shutters of some sort, since the window frames themselves were almost certainly of stone.

When Blackfriars staged episodes that were presumed to take place at night, it created an illusion of darkness just as the public playhouses did, by verbal suggestion and by the use of symbolic costumes and properties. Thus in *Caesar and Pompey,* II *iv,* Demetrius tells of the coming of nightfall:

> What sudden shade is this? Observe, my lords,
> The night, methinks, comes on before her hour;

and in *The Deserving Favorite,* at about line 870, Lysander and Clarinda have this exchange:

> *Lys.*   Had you not sent me word, I had not come to night,
>   It is so darke.
> *Clar.*   It is darke indeed, the fitter for one orecharged
>   With griefe in heart as I am.[20]

Even more frequently, darkness is suggested by having the actors wear night garments or carry lights, as in *Alphonsus of Germany,* I *i,* which has the stage direction *"Enter Alphonsus the Emperor in his nightgown and his shirt, and a torch in his hand,"* and in *The Duchess of Malfi,* II *iii,* which has both *"Enter Bosola, with a dark lantern,"* and *"Enter Antonio with a Candle, his Sword drawn."*[21]

In *Catiline,* I *i,* Ben Jonson vividly dramatizes the approach of an unnatural darkness:

> *Var[gunteius].*   Feele you nothing?
> *Lon[ginus].*   A strange un-wonted horror doth invade me,
>   I know not what it is!
> *Lec[ca].*   The day goes back,
>   Or else my senses!
> *Cur[ius].*   As at Atreus feast!
> *Ful[vius].*   Darknesse growes more, and more!
> *Len[tulus].*   The vestall flame,
>   I thinke, be out.

And directly opposite these lines, at the right-hand side of the page, Jonson has placed the marginal stage direction *"A darkenesse comes over the place."* In all the Blackfriars plays, this is the only direction suggesting that darkness was visibly realized upon the stage;[22] but since the playhouse did not, to the best of our knowledge, have any means of darkening the stage suddenly or briefly, it seems probable that the dramatist inserted the sentence in his *Works* as a literary aid to readers, not as a direction to actors.

1. *Children of the Chapel*, pp. 42, 50–51. W. J. Lawrence agrees with Wallace in assuming that "the house had the regulation three galleries, running along three sides of a rectangle" (*Elizabethan Playhouse*, First Series, p. 17). Joseph Quincy Adams interprets Wallace's data as indicating that the playhouse had only two tiers (*Shakespearean Playhouses*, p. 197 n.). E. K. Chambers finds no evidence for more than one (*Elizabethan Stage*, Vol. II, p. 514).

2. *Elizabethan Stage*, Vol. II, p. 514.

3. The contract is printed in Smith, pp. 215–18. For the three galleries at the Swan, see Plate XVII in the same book.

4. See p. 138 above.

5. See pp. 387–394 below.

6. For Covent Garden, see Mander and Mitchenson, Plates XCII, CXVIII, CXIX, CCXXXI, and Lawrence, *Elizabethan Playhouse*, Second Series, opposite p. 147. For Drury Lane, see Mander and Mitchenson, Plates XXXIII, CXX, CXXX, CXLVII, CCXLIX, and Lawrence, *Elizabethan Playhouse*, Second Series, frontispiece. For the Haymarket, see Lawrence, *Elizabethan Playhouse*, Second Series, opposite p. 143.

7. *Strafforde's Letters*, Vol. I, p. 511.

8. Cf. Smith, p. 220, and Plate XVII.

9. *History of Women*, p. 449, as quoted by John Cranford Adams, *Globe Playhouse*, p. 71. Dekker, in *The Guls Hornbook*, warns the gallant not to go "into the Lords roome (which is now but the Stages Suburbs): No, those boxes, by the iniquity of custome, conspiracy of waiting-women and Gentlemen-Ushers, that there sweat together, and the covetousnes of Sharers, are contemptibly thrust into the reare, and much new Satten is there dambd, by being smothred to death in darknesse." Although I have previously sought to relate Dekker's dissertation on stage-sitting to the Blackfriars in particular, I suggest that the foregoing paragraph is rather to be related to a public playhouse. Dekker specifically makes it apply to either "the publique or private Play-house," and boxes such as he describes are not such as Mr. Wild would take his bride to, nor Anne Frugal her retinue, nor such as the Duke of Lenox and the Lord Chamberlain would quarrel over. Besides, the prices of boxes at Blackfriars were not scaled to the purses of waiting-women and gentlemen-ushers.

10. Wallace, *Children of the Chapel*, p. 52, estimates the capacity of the playhouse at 558 to 608, depending upon the number of stage-sitters, which he reckons at 30 to 80. Lawrence, *Elizabethan Playhouse*, First Series, p. 17, believes that it was incapable of accommodating more than 600. Harbage, *Shakespeare and the Rival Traditions*, p. 43, gives the total seating capacity as "certainly less than 900 and possibly less than 700," but at another point (*ibid.*, p. 340) he gives 955 as the maximum if the playhouse had three galleries, and 696 if, as he thinks more probable, it had two.

11. Abstracted from Bentley, *Jacobean and Caroline Stage*, Vol. II, pp. 647–80. *Love and Honour*, which Mildmay saw on December 12, 1634, is known to have been a King's Men's play and to have been performed at Blackfriars. The December date suggests that he saw this particular performance at Blackfriars rather than at the Globe.

12. The Duke of Stettin-Pomerania, speaking of conditions under the Children of the Chapel in 1602, says in his diary that the price of admission was 8 shillings of Pomeranian coinage (45:3), the equivalent, according to Wallace, of 12 English pence (*Children of the Chapel*, p. 107 n.).

13. See p. 263 above.
14. As quoted by Bentley, *Jacobean and Caroline Stage*, Vol. II, p. 694.
15. Reproduced in Smith, Plate XX.
16. *The Pageant of Elizabethan England*, p. 115.
17. Reproduced in Smith, Plate XX.
18. *The Seven Deadly Sinnes of London*, p. 19.
19. *Evolution*, p. 175n.
20. See also *Cruel Brother*, v i; *Guardian*, Act III; *Thierry and Theodoret*, Act V; *Widow*, III ii; etc.
21. Lights are carried also in *Country Cap-*

tain, IV iii; *Dutch Courtesan*, II i and IV i; *Henry VIII*, V i; *Law Tricks*, V i; *Novella*, I i; *Picture*, III iv; *Platonic Lovers*, II ii; etc.
22. Cartwright's *Royal Slave*, v ii, has a stage direction that says *"the Sun appeares eclipsed, &c."* But the text of this play, as it has come down to us, is that of its performance at Oxford or Hampton Court, with scenery that included a Temple of the Sun (cf. p. 271 above). Certainly the scenery was not in evidence when the play was performed at Blackfriars, and probably the eclipse was not.

⚔ 14 ⚔

The Playhouse:
THE PLATFORM

As used in this book, the word "stage" means the aggregate of diverse elements that comprised the acting area of an Elizabethan playhouse. It includes the platform and the rear or inner stage behind it, the windows and balcony and inner stage on the level above, and any other areas regularly or occasionally used by actors in the presentation of plays. Shakespeare and his fellow dramatists, however, invariably used the word in a narrower sense. To them "stage" meant the platform alone. It is used with this meaning three times in the play of *Henry VIII*: at II *iv* in the stage direction "*The rest of the Attendants stand in convenient order about the Stage*," at IV *i* in the direction "*Exeunt, first passing over the Stage in Order and State, and then, A great Flourish of Trumpets*," and at v *v* in the direction "*The Troope passe once about the Stage, and Garter speakes*." The word is used in the same limited sense in many other Blackfriars plays, usually in directions specifying that such and such persons pass over the stage, and thus removing any doubt as to the word's meaning.[1]

The Platform

The platform at Blackfriars needed to be large; it had to contain such crowded spectacles as the battles in *Cymbeline* and *Caesar and Pompey*, the marching of armies in *The Bashful Lover* and *The Roman Actor*, the processions and pageants in *Henry VIII*, and the masques and dances in *The Maid's Tragedy* and many another play; and, in addition, it needed to accommodate an unknown number of stage-sitters. Information as to its size is lacking. An estimate of its dimensions can be arrived at only indirectly.

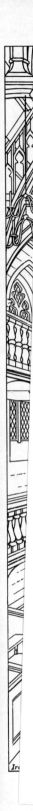

... imaginative reconstruction of the Blackfriars auditorium and ... gure 18, the design of the roof is based upon that of Westminster Hall.

We have reason to believe that the forward edge of the platform in an Elizabethan playhouse tended to lie at or near the center of the playhouse yard, and that the platform was therefore half as deep as the yard was long. This is certainly true of the Fortune; the contract for building that playhouse specifies that the stage should "extende to the middle of the yarde of the saide house"; and since the yard was 55 feet square, the platform was $27\frac{1}{2}$ feet deep. Similarly, the stage of the Globe is believed to have extended to the middle of a yard 58 feet across, and the stages of both the Cockpit-in-Court[2] and of the Swan[3] seem to have reached to about the middles of their respective yards. But if we wish to apply this middle-of-the-yard rule to the Blackfriars stage, we must first arrive at a Blackfriars "yard" that corresponds in meaning to the yards in the other playhouses. Those other yards did not have spectator galleries contained within them at the ends opposite the stages; the galleries were outside the yards, and therefore did not encroach upon the yards' dimensions. The spectator galleries at Blackfriars, on the contrary, did lie within the 66-foot length of the "magna aula," and their presumed depth must therefore be deducted from that length if we are to find the depth of a Blackfriars "yard" inside the gallery enclosures. If we take the front-to-back depth of the lowest rear gallery to have been $7\frac{1}{2}$ feet—that being the depth that seems to be indicated for the reasons given on pages 292 and 293 above—we are left with $58\frac{1}{2}$ feet as the depth of a hypothetical "yard" and with $29\frac{1}{4}$ feet as one half of that figure and thus as the theoretical depth of the Blackfriars platform if the middle-of-the-yard rule should be strictly applied.

But other considerations suggest that the pit at Blackfriars may have been somewhat deeper, and the platform in consequence somewhat shallower, than that rule would prescribe. For one thing, all the public playhouses mentioned—Fortune, Globe and Swan—had spectator galleries far more commodious than we can suppose those at Blackfriars to have been; those playhouses could therefore sacrifice space in the yard and make up for it in the galleries. For another, their galleries, not their yards, were the places of greatest prestige and price; at Blackfriars, on the other hand, the floor of the hall offered the preferred accommodations and brought the higher fees. Finally, the yards in the public playhouses made provision only for standees, whereas the pit at Blackfriars provided seats, and therefore needed to be nearly twice as large to accommodate an equal number of spectators. All these dissimilarities combine to suggest that the yard at Blackfriars was relatively larger, and the platform correspondingly smaller, than those in the public playhouses. Instead of taking 29 feet as the depth of the platform from front to back, therefore, I take 22, thus leaving 44 feet for the north-south depth of the auditorium; and these dimensions, since they are one third and two thirds of 66, have the advantage of seeming to be more probable than they probably are. I further assume that the platform stretched from one side wall to the other, a distance of 46 feet. I shall hope to justify these assumptions as our examination of the evidence proceeds.

The established custom of stage sitting must be taken into account at the outset of any attempt to reconstruct the Blackfriars stage. It implies that the platform, in its size and in its arrangements, could accommodate the gallants without permitting them to obstruct the traffic of the stage or to "wrong the generall eye."[4] No information exists as to the number of stage-sitters nor as to the amount of space that they occupied. If either figure can be approximated, it must be by indirection.

Presumably the gallants sat in two groups at opposite ends of the platform, facing toward the center and toward each other: they could sit nowhere else without blocking a view of the stage for playgoers seated in the pit. They sat on individual stools, not on long benches shared with other spectators; their seats, therefore, were more casually and loosely arranged than those in the auditorium. Besides, the fashionable gentleman's chief reason for sitting on the stage was to display his finery to public view, and this forbade crowding; it demanded, on the contrary, that he follow Dekker's instructions in *The Guls Hornbook*, to put himself into "true scaenical authority . . . by spreading [his] body on the stage." It thus seems probable that the fop on the platform occupied more space than the man in the pit: perhaps he needed three feet of front-to-back space, instead of two feet and a half. On this assumption, two rows of stage-sitters at each side of the platform would occupy a depth of 6 feet, or 12 feet for the two sides together; and this, deducted from 46, would leave a usable platform width of 34 feet. Three rows at each side would occupy 18 feet in all, leaving a stage 28 feet wide in the clear; but this, for reasons that will appear shortly, would narrow the stage unduly; a width of 34 feet would seem to be the irreducible minimum. We therefore go back to two rows of stools at each end of the platform.

As will be explained in connection with the position of the stage doors (pages 330 to 332 below), we have reason to believe that the scenic wall angled forward at its ends and so reduced the depth of the platform from 22 feet to 16 at the ends where the gallants sat. If we

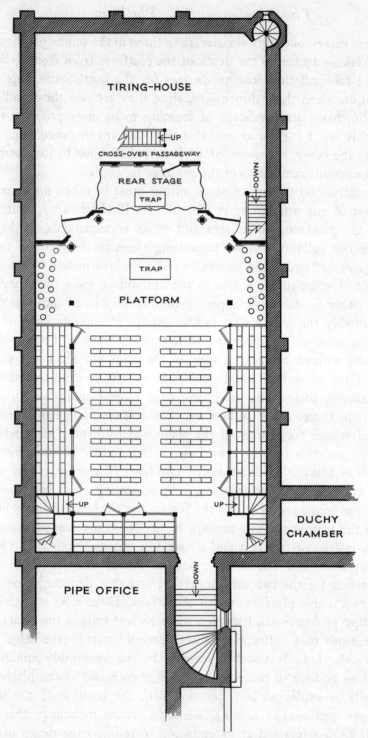

TIRING-HOUSE

UP

CROSS-OVER PASSAGEWAY

REAR STAGE

TRAP

DOWN

TRAP

PLATFORM

UP

UP

DUCHY
CHAMBER

PIPE OFFICE

DOWN

*Figure 22. A conjectural plan of the Blackfriars Playhouse
at the level of the pit and platform.*

allow each man a width of 24 to 27 inches, we arrive at an estimate of seven or eight sitters in each of four rows, for a total of perhaps twenty-eight or thirty in all.

Probably no stairs led up from the floor of the auditorium to the floor of the stage. If such stairs had been provided, stage-sitters and the Citizen's Wife would have used them in mounting to the platform, but neither they nor she did so. Stage-sitters seem always to have entered the platform from the rear, by way of the tiring-house. Dekker, in his *Guls Hornbook*, takes this for granted. In telling the gallant how to make his entrance upon the stage as offensive as possible to good manners, he advises him to delay his appearance until the prompter is "upon point to enter: for then it is time, as though you were one of the properties, or that you dropt out of ye Hangings, to creepe from behind the Arras, with your Tripos or three-footed stoole in one hand, and a teston mounted betweene a forefinger and a thumbe in the other." And W. Sly, in the 1604 Induction to *The Malcontent*, assuredly enters from the tiring-house, since the tireman who follows him with a stool would necessarily have come from there.

The rest of the evidence is less specific, and most of it is negative, but it all points in the direction of entrance from the rear and thus removes any likelihood that stairs led to the platform from the floor of the hall. It amounts to little more than this, that whenever certain actors impersonate stage-sitters and others impersonate members of the playhouse staff, they seem always to enter together. Not once does an attendant on the platform address an arriving stage-sitter as a person threading his way through the audience, mounting stairs to the platform, or otherwise as being upon the point of entering. Always the stage-sitter is already on the platform, and his concern is merely to get a stool.[5]

The Citizen's Wife, in the Induction to *The Knight of the Burning Pestle*, clearly has to scramble to the stage without benefit of stairs. The passage has already been briefly quoted. In more extended form, it runs as follows:

> *Wife.*   Husband, Husband.
> > *Wife below, Ralph below. . .*
> *Ralph.*   Peace, Mistriss.
> *Wife.*   Hold thy peace Ralph,
> > I know what I do,

I warrant ye. . . . Husband,
Shall I come up Husband?
Citizen. I Cony.
Ralph, help your Mistriss this way:
Pray Gentlemen make her a little room,
I pray you sir
Lend me your hand to help up my Wife.
I thank you sir.
So.
Wife. By your leave Gentlemen all,
I'm something troublesome.

After the Restoration, King Charles II turned his royal attention to the twin subjects of entering a theatre by way of the tiring-house, and of sitting on the stage, and forbade them both. His prohibitions did not apply directly to the Blackfriars: they came too late for that; but in view of the often-noticed persistence of theatrical customs, those to which his Majesty took exception may well have originated there. The King's order of 1664–1665 said, in part, that

> Our will and pleasure is that no person, of what quality soever, do presume to enter at the door of the attiring-house, but such only as do belong to the company and are employed by them;[6]

and the order of 1673–1674 said that

> Our will and command is that no person of what quality soever presume to stand or sit on the stages or to come within any part of the scenes before the play begins, while 'tis acting, or after 'tis ended.[7]

For the reasons given on page 170 above, I assume that the floor of the platform was elevated to a height of 3 feet above the floor of the hall. As with the stage of the Fortune, its front face was probably "paled in belowe wth good stronge and sufficyent newe oken bourdes"; but whereas the paling at the Fortune was merely one of smooth boards set vertically, with no recesses or moldings that would afford toeholds for groundlings who might be tempted to clamber to the stage, the vertical face of the Blackfriars platform may well have been handsomely wainscoted.

Perhaps the front edge of the platform was guarded by a low balustrade; more probably it was not. On this subject we have no information applicable to the Blackfriars in particular, and theatrical practice seems to have varied. Stage rails are shown in the *Roxana* and *Messallina* vignettes and the plans for the Cockpit-in-Court, but not in the DeWitt sketch of the Swan and the frontispiece to *The Wits*.[8] Where balustrades existed, they existed primarily to keep spectators from invading the stage, a need that would have been less urgent at the decorous Blackfriars than in the rowdier public playhouses.

The Platform Trap

The Blackfriars stage had a floor trap in the middle of the platform. Ben Jonson is helpfully specific as to its location. In calling for the ascent of Envy at the beginning of *Poetaster*, he provides a stage direction that says *"Envie. Arising in the midst of the stage."* The ascent comes immediately after the second of the three trumpet calls that always announced the start of any play. Upon that signal, the trap cover, with Envy standing on it, rises to platform level. Envy spits out a venomous tirade for fifty-eight lines, and then asks to be lowered: "downe, sinke again." While Envy speaks his next three lines, the stage-hands who operate the winches lower the actor at the rate of about a foot and a half per line:

> This travaile is all lost with my dead hopes.
> If in such bosomes, spight have left to dwell,
> Envie is not on earth, nor scarse in hell.

As he finishes speaking, Envy's chin is about level with the floor of the stage. Then comes the third sounding. The descent is halted. The Prologue enters, advances to the middle of the platform, and puts his foot on Envy's head:

> Stay, Monster, ere thou sinke, thus on thy head
> Set we our bolder foot; with which we tread
> Thy malice into earth: So spight should die,
> Despis'd and scorn'd by noble industrie.

And having been trodden into earth, Envy continues the downward journey and disappears.

313

This example of trap operation is informative in more respects than one. Not only does it locate the trap as being in the middle of the platform, but it shows that the rate of ascent or descent could be controlled with some accuracy, and that the motion could be arrested at a predetermined level. It also illustrates the use of sound signals as cues for the men stationed at the windlasses below the stage.

The unpredictable Ben Jonson disliked descents from the heavens, and had none in any of his plays. But he had no objection to ascents from the lower regions. He was willing that otherworld creatures should make their entrances by rising from below the stage, but not by coming down from above. Before he wrote the *Poetaster* passage just quoted, he had already called for an ascent in *Cynthia's Revels*, another of the plays that he wrote for the Children of her Majesty's Chapel. In this play he has an actor on the stage give the sound cue to the trap operators below by striking the stage with his rod, and he has another actor speak from beneath the stage before ascending. Mercury is calling to Echo as the episode begins (1 *i*):

> *Mercury.*   Eccho, faire Eccho, speake,
> Tis Mercurie, that calls thee, sorrowfull Nymph,
> Salute me with thy repercussive voice,
> That I may know what caverne of the earth
> Contained thy airye spirit, how, or where
> I may direct my speech, that thou maist heare.
> *Echo.*   Here.
> *Merc.*   So nigh?
> *Echo.*   I....
> *Merc.*   Make haste, sad Nymph, thrice shall my winged rod
> Strike th' obsequious earth, to give thee way.
> Arise, and speake thy sorrows, Eccho, rise,
> Here, by this fountayne, where thy love did pine....
> *Echo.*   His name revives, and lifts me up from earth.
>
> *Ascendit.*

The elaborate masque in *The Maid's Tragedy*, 1 *i*, makes frequent use of the platform trap. It begins with the stage direction "*Night rises in mists.*" Later "*Neptune rises,*" and still later "*Proteus and other Sea-deities enter,*" probably by trap, since it is by trap that they subsequently depart. As the masque approaches its end, "*Neptune descends and the Sea-gods,*" and Night vanishes into mists.

314

Chapman's *Caesar and Pompey*, II *i*, has a spectacular ascent that calls for

Thunder, and the gulf opens, flames issuing, and Ophioneus ascending, with the face, wings and tail of a dragon; a skin coat all speckled on the throat.

And in the first scene of *Catiline his Conspiracy*, the platform trap presumably serves for the entrance of the Ghost of Sylla, in spite of the absence of a stage direction specifying ascent.

Episodes such as these—episodes in which supernatural creatures rise from subterranean caverns of the earth—were the special province of the platform trap. But that trap could on occasion serve other purposes also. In *The Double Marriage*, II *i*, it is a hatchway in the deck of a ship, down which the Boatswain shouts "Ho, in the hold!"; and in *The Tempest*, I *i*, it may again be a hatchway leading up to the deck from the leaking hold, from which the mariners enter wet. In these incidents, however, the trap mechanism is not used; instead, the ship's boy and the mariners climb to the deck by way of a ladder that serves as companionway.

On pages 170 and 171 I spoke of a second trap as piercing the floor of the rear stage behind the line of the scenic wall, and as being an important factor in enabling us to fix the wall's position. The nature and uses of that trap will be examined on a later page; I mention it now merely for the purpose of acknowledging that in some scenes there is real cause to be unsure whether the platform trap or the rear-stage trap is used in a given ascent or descent. No doubt exists, however, with respect to the ascents just mentioned. We know that Envy rises by the trap in the middle of the platform because Ben Jonson tells us so. We know that Echo uses that trap because, as will later become clear, the other is at the same moment serving as the fountain to which Mercury alludes. Night and Neptune use the platform trap because the rear stage is occupied by the King, Evadne, Aspatia, and other lords and ladies as audience for the masque. Ophioneus as a dragon ascends by way of the outer-stage trap because his ascent comes within a scene that could be staged only on the platform; and Sylla's Ghost uses it because the rear stage is not revealed until fifteen lines later, and then probably by the Ghost's agency. The shipboard scenes use the platform trap because the other would be inappropriate. Fortunately, these undoubted instances of forestage trapwork illustrate all the points basic to discussion, and remove the need for citing other instances as to which there may be cause for doubt.

My brief preliminary discussion of trapwork, on page 170, showed that ascents, whether by platform trap or by rear-stage trap, could not originate in the cramped space between the floor of the hall and the underbraces of the platform; they necessarily originated in rooms beneath the Parliament Chamber, and traveled through holes that had been cut through the floor to permit the passage of the lifts with their burdens. This assumption receives collateral support from another source: to wit, from the absence of any need for thunder or other loud sounds to drown out the noise of trap operation. The lack of such disguise sounds at Blackfriars is in significant contrast with their regular employment as an accompaniment for trapwork in the public playhouses.[9] There the raising-and-lowering apparatus was probably not more than 8 or 10 feet below the level of the stage, and only a paling of boards intervened between the substage machinery and the ears of the auditors; and since in their operation the windlass and trap inevitably voiced the creaks of strained ropes and chafed timbers, public-playhouse dramatists commonly called for loud sounds of some sort—thunder or "hellish musicke" or trumpet blasts—to drown out the clatter of the trap mechanism. At Blackfriars, on the contrary, Envy, Echo, Night, and Neptune were able to rise and sink silently; and this silence suggests that the platform trap at Blackfriars could be operated without causing the spectators to be disenchanted by mechanical creaks and groans. It thus reinforces the assumption otherwise arrived at, that the windlass at Blackfriars was more remote than those in the public playhouses, and was separated from the audience by distance, massive vaulting, and a floor of stone. The thunder that accompanies Ophioneus's ascent is an exception to the rule of silence, but not a disproof; it cannot prove that disguise sounds were needed, because other plays demonstrate that they were not. With two exceptions, of which Ophioneus is one, all trap ascents at Blackfriars, by whichever trap they may have been made, were either made silently or to an accompaniment of music played so softly that it cannot have been intended to drown out mechanical noises: music such as the "*Musick below, . . . strange Musick* [that] stirs and joys me" in *The Prophetess*, v *iii*; or the "*Infernall Musicke* [*that*] *plaies softly*" in *The Wonder of Women*, IV *i*; or the song in *The Humorous Lieutenant*, IV *iii*. Ophioneus's thunder, and the "dreadfull Musicke" that accompanied the entrance of the

316

ghosts of Junius Rusticus and Palphurius Sura in *The Roman Actor,*
v *i,* therefore served some purpose other than the merely utilitarian one
of overriding mechanical noises. They may have been signals to the
stagehands below, or they may have been designed to intensify the in-
fernal atmosphere of the scene. They may even have been specified with
the needs of the Globe in mind.

Two of the ascents just discussed were accompanied by pyrotechnic
effects: Night rose in mists, and Ophioneus had flames issuing. The
mists, of course, were smoke, probably produced by the burning of
resin; they and the flames served the double purpose of suggesting the
supernatural character of the entrants and of hiding mechanical devices
destructive of illusion.

The platform trap and its cover were undoubtedly rectangular in
shape; their long axis ran parallel to the front edge of the platform,[10]
this being the arrangement that permitted objects or groups of persons
to be disposed upon the trap cover with maximum visibility for the
audience. It was large enough to carry four persons or more at a time,
as evidenced by the descent of at least that number near the end of the
masque in *The Maid's Tragedy;* for when Proteus and other Sea-deities
entered earlier they cannot have been fewer than three, and when Neptune joined them in their descent they were at least four, and perhaps
several more than that. (The ascent of Ophioneus, in spite of his dragon-
like wings and tail, tells us nothing about the size of the trap, since we
have no means of knowing whether he traveled upright or on all fours.)
Dr. John Cranford Adams estimates that the platform trap at the Globe
needed to be at least 8 feet in length by 4 feet in width, basing his conjecture upon the size of objects that public-playhouse traps were called
upon to raise or lower—objects as large as "a brave Arbour" in *A
Looking Glass for London and England,* line 522, and Pluto's brass-
shod wagon drawn by devils in *The Silver Age,* III *iv.*[11] I fail to find
that the trap at Blackfriars needed to carry objects as big as these, but
this does not necessarily imply that the trap at Blackfriars was smaller
than that at the Globe. Figure 22 therefore shows the platform trap as
being 8 feet long by 4 feet wide.

Blackfriars plays provide a few scenes in which sounds emanate
from the areas beneath the stage, and in which those areas have a dramatic character of their own. In *Believe As You List,* IV *ii,* the substage area is the dungeon in which Antiochus is imprisoned, and from
which he talks with his jailer above. In *Catiline,* I *i,* "*A grone of many*

people is heard under ground." In *Cynthia's Revels,* as has already been mentioned, the nymph Echo answers Mercury from her subterranean cavern of the earth. In *The Duchess of Malfi,* v iii, one hears an *"Eccho, (from the Dutchesse Grave.)." The Prophetess,* v iii, has *"Musick below."* And *Rule a Wife and Have a Wife,* v v, makes the substage area serve as a wine cellar whence Cacafogo's voice can be heard by those on the stage above. Inasmuch as all these sounds were intended to be heard by the audience, the speakers doubtless were raised by the trap mechanism to a height that permitted their voices to be heard with whatever degree of clarity was thought desirable.

Rushes on the Platform

The floor of the Blackfriars stage, like the floors of contemporary cottages and palaces all over England, was strewn with rushes. In Elizabethan and Jacobean homes, moist green rushes served primarily to lay the dust; on the stage they served that purpose and others. In outdoor scenes they suggested the greensward, in indoor scenes they represented an accustomed item of domestic furnishing, and in both they protected theatrical costumes. Nearly every play of the period had scenes in which actors sat, lay, struggled, or died upon the floor; and since costumes were extravagantly elaborate and costly, actors preferred to die on clean rushes rather than on the dusty boards. This last use of rushes is commented upon in the pre-Blackfriars play *Summer's Last Will and Testament,* in which Summer says to the bookkeeper:

> You might have writ in the margent of your play-booke, Let there be a fewe rushes laide in the place where *Back-winter* shall tumble, for feare of raying his cloathes: or set downe, Enter *Back-winter,* with his boy bringing a brush after him, to take off the dust if need require.

Rushes were spread both on the platform and on the rear stage. Without attempting to distinguish between the two, I cite the following lines from Blackfriars plays as indicating that rushes in each instance were within sight and reach of the speaker:[12]

From *The Cruel Brother,* IV *iv*:

> *Borachio.*   O, Sir! I would not a' given this Rush,
> t'have been assur'd all th' offices in's gift.

From *Cymbeline,* II *ii:*

> *Iachimo.*   Our Tarquin thus
> Did softly press the rushes ere he waken'd
> The chastity he wounded.

From *The Duchess of Malfi,* v *v:*

> *Cardinal.*   Look to my brother:
> He gave us these large wounds as we were struggling
> Here i' the rushes. And now, I pray, let me
> Be laid by and never thought of.   [*Dies.*]

From *Love's Cure,* III *iii:*

> *Malroda.*   You are marrying: . . . And who of all the world
> But the virago, your great Arch-foes daughter?
> But on: I care not, this poor rush.

And this stage direction from *The Fair Favorite,* IV *ii:*

> *Enter Second Lady, who curtsies to all, but Saladine, they to her; then she sits on the Rushes, and takes out a Book to read.*

Rushes on the platform are mentioned twice in Chapter 6 of *The Guls Hornbook,* the chapter that instructs gallants in the niceties of sitting on the stage. Dekker speaks of "the very Rushes where the Comedy is to daunce," and later of the gentlemen "that are spred either on the rushes, or on stooles about you."

Although the stage was customarily strewn with rushes as a matter of routine, the plot of a play sometimes demanded that it be restrewn in the course of the action, as for instance in compliment to a distinguished guest upon his arrival. This strewing of fresh rushes is illustrated in the following Blackfriars plays:

In *Valentinian,* II *iv:*

> *Phorba.*   Where is this stranger? rushes, Ladys, rushes,
> Rushes as green as Summer for this stranger.

In *The Widow's Tears,* III *ii:*

> *Argus.*   Rushes and seats instantly!

And in *The Gentleman Usher,* II *i:*

> *Bassiolo.*   Come, strew this room afresh; . . . lay me 'em thus,
> In fine smooth threaves; look you, sir, thus, in threaves.
> Perhaps some tender lady will squat here,
> And if some standing rush should chance to prick her,
> She'd squeak, and spoil the songs that must be sung. . . .
> Nay, see if thou canst lay 'em thus, in threaves.
> *Vincentio.*   In threaves, d'ye call it?
> *Bass.*   Ay, my lord, in threaves.
> *Vin.*   A pretty term!

In well-to-do houses, loose rushes tended in the course of time to be displaced by braided mats made of broad-leaved rushes coarsely plaited. Mats of this sort constituted "the matting of the stage" that Sir Henry Wotton singled out for special mention as the most extraordinary of all the "many extraordinary circumstances of pomp and majesty" that characterized the King's Men's presentation of *Henry VIII* at the Globe on the sorry afternoon of June 29, 1613. A few Blackfriars plays allude to mats, but none does so in such terms as necessarily imply that the mats are in evidence on the stage.[13]

When loose rushes represented grass in outdoor scenes, they were not, of course, referred to in dialogue as rushes; but it can only have been rushes that lent verisimilitude to Iris' description in *The Tempest,* IV *i,* when on behalf of Juno she bade Ceres

> Here on this grass-plot, in this very place,
> To come and sport,

and to Ceres' when she asked

> why hath thy queen
> Summon'd me hither to this short-grass'd green?

and again to Iris' when she bade the Naiades to

320

Leave your crisp channels, and on this green land
Answer your summons.

Two Blackfriars plays contain allusions to carpets; and although at that period carpets normally served as coverings for tables and chests rather than for floors, these particular carpets were spread upon the stage.

From *The Gentleman Usher*, II *i*:

> *Enter Bassiolo with Servants, with rushes and a carpet. . . .*
> *Bas.*   Spread here this carpet.
> Nay, quickly, man, I pray thee; this way, fool;
> Lay me it smooth, and even; look if he will!
> This way a little more; a little there.

And from *The Conspiracy of Byron*, I *i*:

> *Enter Picoté, with two others, spreading a carpet.*
> *Pic.*   Spread here this history of Catiline,
> That earth may seem to bring forth Roman spirits
> Even to his genial feet, and her dark breast
> Be made the clear glass of his shining graces;
> We'll make his feet so tender they shall gall
> In all paths but to empire; and therein
> I'll make the sweet steps of his state begin. . . .
> *Byron.*   They hide the earth from me with coverings rich.

The platform lacked any front curtain, and therefore could not be hidden from the spectators' eyes. This fact has left its mark upon every pre-Restoration play. For want of a curtain, a dramatist could not begin a platform scene by revealing a group already assembled, nor could he end it suddenly at a climactic point; instead, he had to make his characters walk on at the beginning of every outer-stage scene, and walk off, with a lessening of tension as an inevitable consequence, at the end; and if a character had died or been killed during the course of the scene, as they had a way of doing in the plays of the period, the playwright was compelled to devise some means of having the corpse removed from the stage.

The Stage Doors

As has been said, a wall stood at the rear of the platform; it provided a background for action on the forestage, and concealment for backstage activities. Two doors cut through the wall, one at each side of the wide central aperture of the inner stage. They were used by actors in going from the tiring-house to the outer stage and back again.

Blackfriars plays contain abundant references to the doors, and abundant proofs that two doors existed. The references usually take the form of stage directions that specify the simultaneous entrance or departure of two or more actors through separate doors. Sometimes the directions read *"Enter A at one door and B at the other,"* or *"Exeunt A and B at both doors."* Such directions limit the doors to two.[14] But other directions permit the idea of more than two doors. They may take such forms as these: *"Enter A at one door and B at another,"* or *"Exeunt A and B at several [i.e., separate] doors,"* or *"Exeunt divers ways,"* or *"Enter A and B, meeting one another."*[15] As a matter of fact, however, the differences in phraseology imply no differences in meaning; no stage direction intends to suggest the existence of more than two doors, in the usual meaning of the word "door." This is indicated by the many plays that contain stage directions in both categories. One of them is *Henry VIII*, which has these:

In Act I Scene *i*:

> *Enter the Duke of Norfolke at one doore. At the other, the Duke of Buckingham, and the Lord Aburgavenny.*

In Act I Scene *v*:

> *Then Enter Anne Bullen, and divers other Ladies, & Gentlemen, as Guests at one Doore; at an other Doore enter Sir Henry Guilford.*

In Act II Scene *i*:

> *Enter two Gentlemen at severall Doores.*

In Act IV Scene *i*:

> *Enter two Gentlemen, meeting one another.*[16]

But occasionally a stage direction crops up that unmistakably calls for a third or middle door, as for instance this from *Eastward Ho!*, I i:

> *Enter Maister Touchstone and Quick-silver at several dores. . . . At the middle dore, Enter Golding, discovering a Gold-smiths shoppe, and walking short turnes before it.*

or this from *The Parson's Wedding*, I iii:

> *Enter Wild, Careless, and the Captain, going in haste; he comes in at the middle door.*

When this happens, the third or middle means of entrance is either the break in the curtains that conceal the inner stage, or, if that stage is exposed, the door in its back wall. Such entrances will be examined more fully when the rear stage is under consideration.

The two main doors were at opposite sides of the stage; if they had not been, they would have failed of their purpose in being two, which was to permit actors to enter through two opposed doors as from two different rooms or houses or towns or countries. The opposition of the doors is illustrated in these stage directions:

The Duchess of Malfi, II i:

> *Exeunt Duchess and Ladies.—Exit, on the other side, Bosola.*

The Guardian, v iv:

> *Enter at different sides, various parties of the Banditti.*

The Imposture, I i:

> *Enter Duke, Honorio, and Flaviano, at opposite doors.*

The Malcontent, v i:

> *Enter Malevole and Maquarelle, at several doores opposite, singing.*

Sir Giles Goosecap, IV *ii*:

> *Enter Jacke and Will on the other side.*

In specifying entrances by way of two doors at the same time, dramatists did not hesitate to use the word "door" in scenes as to which any sort of door would be grossly incongruous. Thus Chapman, in *Caesar and Pompey*, IV *ii*, uses it in describing the action on the battlefield of Pharsalia:

> *At the door enter again the five Kings. . . . The fight nearer; and enter Crassinius, a sword as thrust through his face; he falls. To him Pompey and Caesar fighting: Pompey gives way. Caesar follows, and enters at another door.*

Shakespeare has "doors" on the field of battle in *Cymbeline*, V *ii*:

> *Enter Lucius, Iachimo, and the Romane Army at one doore: and the Britaine Army at another: Leonatus Posthumus following like a poore Souldier.*

Other doors in unlikely places are to be found in *The Lover's Progress*, II *iii* (a dueling field), *Sir Giles Goosecap*, III *i* (a road near Barnet), and *The Wonder of Women*, V *iii* (a battlefield). In this respect, as also in the use of the word "stage" previously noticed, the dramatists are employing a theatrical idiom; they are speaking not in terms of the dramatic environment, but in terms of the theatre; they speak not of the forest or the field, but of the stage.

The plays produced at Blackfriars indicate that the stage doors were of considerable width and height; for not only did they admit the Roman and British armies in *Cymbeline*, V *ii*, and the Strange Shapes bringing in a banquet table in *The Tempest*, III *iii*, but they were called upon also to permit the passage of the persons and objects described in these stage directions:

From *The Bashful Lover*, IV *iii*:

> *Loud music. Enter Soldiers unarmed, bearing olive branches, Captains, Lorenzo, Matilda crowned with a wreath of laurel, and seated in a chariot drawn by Soldiers.*

324

From *The Roman Actor*, I *iv*:

Enter Captains with laurels, Domitian in his triumphant chariot, Parthenius, Paris, Latinus, and Aesopus, met by Aretinus, Sura, Lamia, Rusticus, Fulcinius, Soldiers, and Captives.

From *The Fatal Dowry*, I *ii*:

Solemn music. Enter the Funeral Procession. The Coffin borne by four, preceded by a Priest, Captains, Lieutenants, Ensigns, and Soldiers; Mourners, Scutcheons, & c., and very good order.

From *Henry VIII*, IV *i*, the coronation procession of Queen Anne:

A Canopy, borne by foure of the Cinque-Ports, under it the Queene in her Robe. . . . On each side her, the Bishops of London and Winchester.

And again from *Henry VIII*, the christening procession of the infant Elizabeth (v *v*), with its

foure Noblemen bearing a Canopy, under which the Dutchesse of Norfolke, Godmother, bearing the Childe richly habited in a Mantle, & c. Traine borne by a Lady.

Doors capable of admitting these processions, with their chariots, coffins, and canopies, can hardly have been less than 5 feet wide by 8 feet high.

A few Blackfriars plays provide evidence that at least one of the stage doors had a wicket, or small grated window, cut through its upper half. The evidence is to be found in scenes in which a character speaks or looks through a door that is closed and presumed to be locked. *Catiline*, III *v*, is such a scene. It requires that the Porter, off-stage and behind a door that remains closed, should converse with men on the platform, and should be heard both by them and by the audience. The place of action is Rome, on a street before Cicero's house; the time is before dawn. Vargunteius and Cornelius, with other armed men, enter the platform by way of an outer-stage door and cross the stage to the opposite door as to the door of Cicero's dwelling.

Vargunteius.   The dore's not open, yet.
Cornelius.   You'were best to knocke. . . .
Porter.   Who's there?

Var.   A friend, or more.
Por.   I may not let
Any man in, till day.
Var.   No?   why?
Cor.   Thy reason?
Por.   I am commanded so.
Var.   By whom? . . .
Pray thee, good slave, who has commanded thee?
Por.   He that may best, the Consul.
Var.   We are his friends.
Por.   All's one.
Cor.   Best give your name.
Var.   Do'st thou heare, fellow?
I have some instant business with the Consul.
My name is Vargunteius.

The Humorous Lieutenant, IV iv, refers to the wicket as a window, and proves that characters could look through it as well as speak through it. Demetrius, distracted when he hears the false report of the death of his beloved Celia, shuts himself away in his own chamber and admits no one. The Lieutenant volunteers to try to get to him.

Enter Leontius, Lieutenant, Gent.

1 Gent.   There's the door, Lieutenant, if you dare do anything. . . .
Dare ye go forward?
Lieutenant.   Let me put on my Skull first.
My head's almost beaten into th' pap of an Apple.
Are there no Guns i' th' door?
Leontius.   The Rogue will do it.
And yet I know he has no Stomach to't.
Lieu.   What loop-holes are there when I knock for stones,
For those may pepper me? I can perceive none.
Leo.   How he views the Fortification. . . .
Lieu.   Stay, stay,
Here is a window, I will see, stand wide.
By ——— he's charging of a Gun.
Leo.   There's no such matter.
There's no body in this room.
Lieu.   O 'twas a fire-shovel.
Now I'll knock louder. . . .

326

But Demetrius does not answer. About twenty lines later he comes out with a pistol and frightens the Lieutenant into a swoon. The "window" is used again in iv *viii*. The place is the same, outside the door of Demetrius' chamber. Leontius is already onstage as the scene begins; Celia enters later.

> *Leon.*   She goes to knock at's door. . . .
> *Celia.*   Are ye within Sir? . . . pray Heaven he be here!
>   Master, my royal Sir: do you hear who calls ye?
>   Love, my Demetrius. . . .
>   Can ye be drowsie,
>   When I call at your Window?[17]

In *Monsieur Thomas,* iii *iii*, Mary pretends willingness to yield to Thomas's importunities, but then gives him the slip by darting into her house and locking the door behind her, leaving him outside:

> *Tom.*   How now? the door lock't, and she in before?
>   Am I so trim'd?
> *Mary.*   One parting word sweet Thomas,
>   Though to save your credit, I discharg'd your Fidler,
>   I must not satisfie your follie too Sir.

In *The Novella,* iv *i,* the situation is reversed: now someone inside a house wants to get out, and is heard on the far side of the door, asking for the key:

> *Guadagni.*   Nanulo!   The Key to let me forth.   *Within.*
>   . . . The Key I saw.
>   . . . Villaine, slave!   come open the dore.
>   *Enter Guadagni, Nanulo.*

The wicket in a stage door is presumably "your old spy-hole yonder" in *Your Five Gallants,* ii *i.*

As Dr. John Cranford Adams has pointed out,[18] the wicket also served the practical purpose of providing a place where the prompter or book-holder could take his stand off-stage, unseen by the audience but in a position to see and hear everything that occurred on the platform, and to make himself heard there if the need should arise. The presence of a book-holder, though not his station, is attested in three Blackfriars plays. The Induction to *The Staple of News* has the book-holder, off-stage, give the order "Mend your lights, gentlemen. — Master Prologue, beginne," whereupon the tiremen enter to trim the candles. In another of Ben Jonson's plays, *Cynthia's Revels*, three boys are squabbling as to which of them shall speak the Prologue, and the prompter or book-holder within calls out "Why, children! are you not ashamed? Come in there." And in *The Maid in the Mill*, II *ii*, an amateur masque is interrupted by a woman's screams of "Help, help, help!" from within, whereupon Bustopha, knowing that something is amiss but not knowing what, says "They are out of their parts sure: it may be 'tis the book-holder's fault; I'll go see."

These incidents show that the prompter at Blackfriars was off-stage, but in a position to hear and to be heard. The conjecture that he stood behind a stage-door wicket is confidently based upon the wicket's suitability for this purpose and upon the lack of any other vantage point equally convenient.[19]

No play, whether performed at the Blackfriars or elsewhere, demands wickets in both the outer-stage doors; if wickets existed in both, it was as a matter of convenience and symmetry rather than necessity.

All the scenes just cited as proof of the existence of wickets, and many more besides,[20] have demanded that one of the outer-stage doors should be locked or should seem to be locked. In each of the scenes, furthermore, the business of locking was probably a matter of pretense rather than of actuality, for the rattling of a make-believe key in a counterfeit lock would carry all the conviction needed, and would avoid the difficulties—the loss of a key among the rushes on the stage, or a failure to unlock the door when the scene comes to an end—that might attend an actual locking; and this conjecture receives strong support from a stage direction in *The Platonic Lovers*, III *i*, which reads "*Exit [Ariola]. Theander seems to lock her in.*" As will be seen later, the business of locking a door involves the door in the back wall of the rear stage at least as often as it does one of the outer-stage doors, and probably more often.[21]

A free-standing post or pillar stood at each side of each outer-stage door, in imitation of those that framed many a street doorway in Shakespeare's time[22] and gave added dignity to houses of the better sort. On the stage they served the practical purpose of providing support for the projecting bay windows over the doors, and the theatrical purpose of furnishing a semblance of concealment for characters who were called upon to hide themselves during the course of action on the outer stage. Two non-Blackfriars plays allude to posts in terms that prove their presence on two contemporary stages.[23] The only Blackfriars play that does so—if indeed it does—is *The Maid in the Mill*, I *iii*, in which Antonio says

> I wait still,
> And will do so till I grow another Pillar,
> To prop this house, so it please you.

The substantial evidence for the existence of doorposts at Blackfriars rests upon the presumed similarity of the Blackfriars stage to the stages of other playhouses, and upon the episodes in which persons find a means of concealment on the outer stage in the immediate vicinity of the doors or of the windows over the doors. The hiding usually follows a command to "stand close."

A part of one such episode has been quoted just a few pages back in another connection. It occurs in *Catiline*, III *v*. Vargunteius and Cornelius have come to Cicero's door and have found it locked. Vargunteius is about to knock, but wants first to make sure that the Porter, when he opens the door, will not see the armed ruffians whom he has brought with him. He therefore orders them to stand close. The applicable lines run thus:

Vargunteius.   The dore's not open, yet.
Cornelius.   You'were best to knocke.
Var.   Let them stand close, then: And, when we are in,
    Rush after us.

Another example occurs in *Monsieur D'Olive*, v *i*. The Countess Marcellina, with her sister Eurione as her sole companion, has shut herself away from all society through grief at the causeless jealousy of her husband, the Count Vaumont. Vandome, brother to the two sisters, undertakes to bring Marcellina out of her self-imposed confinement, and with this in mind he stands at night at Vaumont's door and under the ladies' window. The Count accompanies him. He is permitted to see and to overhear, but not to make his presence known to his estranged wife and her sister.

Vandome. Stand close, my lord. . . .

　Page? Who's above? Are you all dead here? . . .

Enter Eurione above.

Eurione. What's the matter, who's there? Brother Vandome! . . .

　What tempest drives you hither at such an hour? . . .

Enter Marcellina above . . . .

Van. O mistress, come down with all speed possible, and leave that mournful
　cell of yours; I'll show you another place worthy of your mourning . . . .
　If you please to come down, I'll impart what I know; if not, I'll leave you.

Eur. Why stand you so at gaze, sister? Go down to him.
　Stay, b[r]other, she comes to you.

Exeunt Marcellina and Eurione . . . .

Van. Stand close, my lord.

Vaumont. 　I warrant you; proceed.

Yet another example occurs in *The Novella*, 1 *i*. Piso and Fabritio
are standing at night in front of the house of Victoria. Divers gentlemen
cross the stage, and Piso, unwilling to be discovered, bids his friend
"peace, and stand close." Later, when Horatio and Francisco enter and
prepare to sing a serenade under Victoria's window, Piso says "O here
they pitch, stand close, wee'l heare their Musick."

It is noteworthy that nearly all the outdoor concealment scenes take
place at night. A doorpost would hardly pass for an adequate means of
concealment during the daytime, and dramatists did not ask their audiences to accept it as such; but at night, with the fiction of darkness to
help, they could ask the spectators to accept it as a matter of theatrical
convention.

So much for what we know, or think we know, about the stage doors
at Blackfriars; when we go beyond these few facts, we pass from the
area of reasonable assurance into that of mere probability. This is especially true when we try to determine the location of the doors.

Three possibilities demand to be examined in this connection: first,
that one door was in each of the two side walls; second, that both doors
were in a flat back wall; and third, that one door was in each of two
oblique walls that cut across the angles from the side walls to the back.
The stage-sitters must be taken into account in considering each of these
possibilities, for the doors cannot have been so placed as to permit the
gallants on the stage to obstruct the audience's view of actors who were
entering or departing. We have assumed that the gallants were seated in
double rows at each side of the platform, and that they occupied a depth

330

of 6 feet on each side. Obviously, then, if the stage doors were in the side walls, they would have to be downstage of the sitters. If they were in a flat back wall, they would have to be at least 6 feet in from the corners; and if they were in oblique walls, they would again have to be 6 feet nearer to the center line of the stage than would be necessary if stage-sitters did not complicate the problem.

Doors in the side walls would have some advantages.[24] They would face each other, and therefore would facilitate the across-the-stage march of processions, and the excursions and retreats of armies in battle. They would be opposite each other, and therefore could not be mistaken for two doors belonging to the same house; instead, they would obviously be doors that led to and from different houses or different parts of the world. But the disadvantages would seem to be insuperable. They arise primarily from the necessity that the doors should be downstage of the groups of stage-sitters; and since they must be downstage, an enclosed passageway must lead down each side of the stage from the tiring-house to the door, so that an actor might remain concealed until the moment of his entrance. We have estimated that the doors needed to be 5 feet wide in order to permit large objects and groups of persons to pass through them. The same objects and groups would have to go through the passageways also in order to reach the doors, so the passageways too would need to be 5 feet wide. Another 10 feet must therefore be subtracted from the usable width of the platform; and this, added to the 12 feet already allotted to stage-sitters, would reduce the platform's effective width to 24 feet. More importantly, each passageway must end in a right-angle turn when its stage door is reached: an awkward means of entrance under many conditions, and especially so for Strange Shapes bringing in a banquet table, or for Four of the Cinque Ports bearing a canopy under which walks the Queen with a Bishop on each side. Finally, the theory of down-stage doors conflicts with what we believe to have been the rule on the Elizabethan stage, that actors entered at the rear and then came forward.[25] The theory of doors in the side walls must therefore be discarded.

Doors in the flat back wall of the platform would have the recommendation of conforming to those on the stage of the Swan and to the single door pictured in the frontispiece to *The Wits*,[26] but they would have the counterbalancing disadvantage of not conforming to those at the Globe and the Cockpit-in-Court.[27] They would be an improvement upon side-wall doors in two important respects: they would permit direct entrance instead of a long approach through a side passageway with a right-angle turn at the end, and they would be fully visible to spectators, whereas side-wall doors could be viewed only obliquely. But their avoidance of passageways would add nothing to the width available for the rear-stage opening, since the doors themselves would occupy as much lateral space as the passageways would do. Their full visibility might actually be a disadvantage, since the doors, unless they were kept closed, would permit glimpses of behind-the-scenes activities and of actors awaiting their cues. In threshold scenes, of which there are many in Blackfriars plays, they would force an actor, when knocking at a door for entrance, to do so with his back to the audience, and in processional scenes they would compel marchers to make a U-turn upon the stage. In consequence of their being in a single continuous wall, they would suggest that they were two doors in the same house, leading to the same interior: a concept that no Blackfriars play involves. And finally, they would violate the idea of oppositeness that is specifically stated in the stage directions quoted on page 323, and that, even if not stated, is implicit in the action of many scenes.

The third possibility is that the doors were set in oblique walls that closed in the upstage corners of the platform at, let us say, a 45-degree angle. Doors so placed would seem to have all the advantages of either side-wall doors or back-wall doors, and the disadvantages of neither. They would face each other at a 90-degree angle, and so would meet the requirement that they be opposite. They would permit armies and processions to march across the platform from door to door with a downstage swing, but without an awkward loop. They would be fully visible and yet would not cause spectators to be distracted by back-stage activities, for door shutters, hinged at their upstage edges and swinging toward the rear, would block any view into the tiring-house. and finally, they would permit the aperture of the rear stage to be wider by about 3 feet, for a 5-foot door set in such a wall preempts only about 3½ feet of lateral space.

We therefore assume that the scenic wall of the Blackfriars stage did not lie in a straight line. The central section, almost wholly occupied by the aperture of the rear stage, was parallel with the platform's forward edge. On each side of it, a flanking section, perhaps 7 feet wide so as to accommodate a 5-foot door and its frame, slanted forward at an angle of, or approximating, 45 degrees; and the remainder of the wall, beyond the oblique sections, returned to its parallel course, since nothing was to be gained, and some platform space was to be lost, by continuing it at the 45-degree angle. And having arrived at this conclusion as a result of our inquiry into the placement of the outer-stage doors, we shall presently find it confirmed by the probable arrangement of the architectural elements on the level above.

With these as its limits, the platform appears to have had a usable acting area of 22 feet from front to back by 34 feet from side to side, less the two triangles cut off by the oblique walls at the upstage corners. Its total of 712 square feet is approximately 230 square feet less than the platform at the Globe is believed to have contained.

After this digression to consider the placement of the doors and its effect upon the size of the acting area, I return briefly to the subject of the doors as they were used in actual performance. They served in two different capacities. Sometimes, in unlocalized scenes or scenes in which doors of any sort would be incongruous (battlefields, forests, and so forth), they were mere points of entrance or departure; at other times, in threshold scenes, they represented the veritable doors of cottages, castles, or palaces.

When serving in the first capacity, the doors were ignored: actors walked through them from tiring-house to platform without recognizing their existence. In the second capacity, however, they were treated as doors: they were knocked upon by persons who sought admission to the house; they were opened from within by persons who were departing from the house, and then closed again.

Blackfriars plays contain many such threshold scenes; several have already been mentioned in connection with wickets, locks, and posts, and fifty more could be listed. I cite one more as a threshold scene pure and simple, to show the extent to which the door itself might be involved in the action.

In Beaumont and Fletcher's *Philaster*, Prince Pharamond of Spain is visiting the court of the King of Sicily to make arrangements for his marriage to the King's daughter, Arethusa. The King has been informed that his guest, in spite of his protestations of love for the Princess, is entertaining a Court lady, Megra, in his bedchamber. To find out for himself whether or not the charge is true, the King goes with a guard to the door of Pharamond's lodging (II *iii*):

> *King.*   You o' th' guard,
> Wait at the back door of the prince's lodging,

And see that none pass thence, upon your lives.
Knock, gentlemen; knock louder; louder yet.
What, has their pleasure taken off their hearing? —
I'll break your meditations. — Knock again! —
Not yet? I do not think he sleeps, having this
Larum by him. — Once more. — Pharamond! Prince!

Pharamond appears at a window above. The King orders him to come down, whereupon he descends, throws the door open, and stands within the doorway with his sword in his hand.

Pharamond.   Nay, press not forward, gentlemen; he must come
Through my life that comes here.
King.   Sir, be resolved I must and will come. — Enter!
Pha.   I will not be dishonored.
He that enters, enters upon his death.
Sir, 'tis a sign you make no stranger of me,
To bring these renegadoes to my chamber
At these unseasoned hours.
King.   Why do you
Chafe yourself so? You are not wronged nor shall be;
Only I'll search your lodging, for some cause
To ourself known. — Enter, I say.
Pha.   I say, no.

The argument is interrupted by the appearance of Megra herself at an upstairs window.

With respect to Shakespeare's plays in particular, it seems probable that there are far more threshold scenes than are recognized as such in modern locality notes. Sir Edmund K. Chambers has stated this theory admirably:

I do not think that it has been fully realized how large a proportion of the action of Elizabethan plays passes at the doors of houses; and as a result the problem of staging, difficult enough anyhow, has been rendered unnecessarily difficult. Here we have probably to thank the editors of plays, who have freely interspersed their texts with notes of locality, which are not in the original stage-directions, and, with eighteenth-century models before them, have tended to assume that action at a house is action in some room within that house. The playwrights, on the other hand, followed the neo-classic Italian tradition, and for them action at a house was most naturally action before the door of that house. If a man visited his friend he was almost certain to meet him on the doorstep; and here domestic discussions, even on matters of delicacy, commonly took place. Here too, of course, meals might be served.[28]

Many Shakespearean scenes which the editorial locality notes allocate to interior rooms were, I strongly suspect, intended to be enacted under the sky rather than under a roof, at the threshold rather than within the house, and therefore on the platform rather than in an inner stage.

The Platform in Use

The platform was "the stage." It was an elevated area upon which actors could stand and be seen, and from which they could speak and be heard. For much of the time it was nothing more than that. Sometimes it became a specific locality—a battlefield, a forest, a street—but localization of the outer stage was probably less frequent, and of shorter duration, than is generally supposed; the dramatist evoked a sense of locality when and for as long as he needed it in the telling of his story, and for the rest of the time he permitted the platform to be nowhere in particular. Thus *Othello* opens upon the platform with no suggestion of place whatsoever; for the first seventy-three lines of the first scene the stage is merely a place where two men are talking together; not until line 74 is it revealed that the men are standing before Brabantio's house, nor, for that matter, on a street, or in Venice, or in Italy. The second scene follows upon the platform with no hint that the place has changed, if indeed it has; forty-seven lines pass before one learns that the action now is before Othello's door. In both scenes Shakespeare has created a sense of dramatic place when he needed it, and not before; until then he has permitted the stage to be as unlocalized as a lecture platform. In these and scores of other scenes, editors have belied his intention by pinning down the action to a particular place in their locality notes, when Shakespeare intended nothing of the kind.

No great harm, one may say. With respect to these two particular scenes, no, no great harm; but in giving a local habitation and a name to every one of the 750 scenes in the Shakespearean canon, editors have misrepresented Shakespeare's dramaturgy and indirectly the dramaturgy of nearly every other Elizabethan and Jacobean playwright. It is too late now to seek to delocalize those of Shakespeare's scenes that need de-

335

localization; the traditional locality notes get in our way. Even if we are reading an edition that omits them, we remember them almost as well as we do the verse itself, and they color our conception of each new scene as we begin to read it. But in the plays of some of the minor dramatists one can often read act after act without finding that the idea of dramatic place makes itself felt.

The unlocalized scene was necessarily played upon the platform, since the platform alone, of all the stage elements, permitted an actor to walk far enough forward to free himself from association with the localizing features of the scenic wall and to stand on neutral ground. When the platform did represent some particular locality, it was normally a place under the open sky.

Change of Place

Change of dramatic place between scenes was usually indicated on the Blackfriars stage, and was best indicated, by having one group of actors depart from a given unit of the multiple stage when the earlier scene came to an end, and by having another group of actors enter a different unit of the stage to begin the next scene. Sometimes, however, it became necessary for the platform to represent two or more different places in two or more successive scenes or episodes. When this need arose, one actor or group of actors left the platform by one outer-stage door, and the second actor or group entered a moment later by the other door; the stage was the same, but the place of action had changed. Sometimes the same actors reentered. After departing, they crossed the stage from side to side behind the scenes, and returned to the platform by the opposite door as to a different place. The following scenes illustrate both these uses.

In *Aglaura*, Act v, Ziriff and Ariaspes, rivals for Orbella's love and enemies for other reasons as well, agree to settle their differences on the field of honor. Ziriff has gotten possession of Ariaspes' sword.

> *Ziriff.*   Orbella is our quarrel;
> And I do hold it fit, that love should have
> A nobler way of justice than revenge
> Or treason. Follow me out of the wood,
> And thou shalt be master of this again:
> And then best arm and title take.

336

The Playhouse: The Platform

They go out and enter again.

There!   *Gives him his sword.*

Ariaspes.   Extremely good! Nature took pains, I swear;
The villain and the brave are mingled handsomely . . . .

Fight.

In the undivided third act of *Brennoralt*, the place is the castle of the Governor, father to Francelia. Brennoralt is waiting impatiently for Raguelin to arrive with the keys to the garden, the privy walks, and the back stairs leading to Francelia's chamber.

Brennoralt.   He comes not.
   One wise thought more, and I return:
   I cannot in this act separate the foolish
   From the bold so far, but it still tastes o' th' rash.
   Why, let it taste! it tastes of love too,
   And to all actions 't gives a pretty relish, that —
                        Enter Raguelin.
Raguelin.   My lord?
Bren.   O, here!
Rag.   'Sfoot, you're upon our sentries;
   Move on this hand.   *Exeunt.*
                 Enter again Brennoralt and Raguelin.
Bren.   Where are we now?
Rag.   Entering part of the fort,
   Your lordship must be wet a little.   *Exeunt.*
                     They enter again.
Bren.   Why, are there here no guards?
Rag.   There needs none:
   You presently must pass a place,
   Where one's an army in defence,
   It is so steep and strait.
Bren.   'Tis well.
Rag.   These are the steps of danger.   Look to your way,
   My lord.
Bren.   I do not find such difficulty . . . .
   Wait me hereabouts.   *Exit Raguelin.*

In *1 Passionate Lovers*, IV *ii*, Cleon has dragged the lovely Clorinda into a forest. Fortunately for her, Agenor is pursuing a boar near by.

337

Cleon.   Your beauty, and my love, both plead against you;
But you may think me cold to talk thus long,
We must remove into a thicker place.

Clorinda.   Help, help you Gods! murder, treason, help.   *Exeunt.*
Enter Agenor.

Agenor.   It is impossible this Bore can scape,
Having so many wounds; sure I shall track him
By his blood.

Within, Clo.   Help, oh help! Traitor!

Age.   Ha! 'tis a womans voice.   *Exit.*
Enter Agenor, Cleon, Clorinda.

Age.   Rude slave, how canst thou injure so much sweetness?

In *Catiline*, v *vi*, a group of Roman senators, led by Cicero, has been commissioned to arrest three known conspirators and deliver them up to execution. The action moves through Roman streets to three different houses in which the traitors are being held in custody, but the actors never leave the platform:

Cicero.   Leade on:
Where are the publike executioners?
Bid 'hem wait on us. On, to Spinther's house.
Bring Lentulus forth. Here, you, the sad revengers
Of capitall crimes, against the publike, take
This man unto your justice: strangle him.
. . . Leade on, to Quintus Cornificius house.
Bring forth Cethegus. Take him to the due
Death, that he hath deserv'd: and let it be
Said, He was once.
. . . Leade
To Caius Caesar, for Statilius.
Bring him, and rude Gabinius, out. Here, take 'hem
To your cold hands, and let 'hem feele death from you.

In *Bonduca*, the platform is the Roman position on the battlefield in III *ii*, the British position in III *iii*, the Roman again in III *iv*, and in III *v* it is alternately three times the British position and three times the Roman.

Similarly, the platform is Gonzaga's camp in *The Bashful Lover*, II *ii*; Lorenzo's camp in II *iii*; various parts of a forest in II *iv, v,* and *vi*; Lorenzo's camp again in II *vii*; and fields or woods in III *i, ii,* and *iii*.[29]

1. *1 Arviragus and Philicia*, Act I; *Brennoralt*, Act II; *Broken Heart*, III *ii*; *Brothers*, IV *iv*; *Caesar and Pompey*, II *i*, IV *ii*, V *ii*; *Cardinal*, IV *i*; *Conspiracy*, III *ii*; *Cupid's Revenge*, I *i*, IV *i*; *Cynthia's Revels*, Induction, V *iv*; *Goblins*, Act III; *Honest Man's Fortune*, II *iv*; *Imposture*, IV *ii*; *Isle of Gulls*, sig. G¹, G², G²ᵛ; *Law Tricks*, IV *iii*; *Little French Lawyer*, III *iii*, V *i*; *Lover's Melancholy*, I *ii*; *Loyal Subject*, IV *ii* (twice); *Mad Lover*, I *iv?*; *Magnetic Lady*, III *iii*; *Monsieur Thomas*, II *ii*; *New Inn*, III *ii*; *Novella*, II *ii*; *Osmond the Great Turk*, I *i*; *Poetaster*, Induction; *Royal Slave*, V *vii*; *Second Maiden's Tragedy*, II *ii*; *Sisters*, I *ii*; *Valentinian*, IV *iv*; *Wonder of Women*, Prologue.

2. Smith, Plate XXII.

3. Smith, Plate XVII.

4. The phrase is wholly appropriate to the present discussion. It comes from Marston's *What You Will*, 1601, which probably was performed by the Children of Paul's. In the Induction, Atticus says "Let's place our selves within the Curtaines, for good faith the Stage is so very little we shall wrong the generall eye els very much."

5. Cf. the Inductions to *Cynthia's Revels*, *Magnetic Lady*, *Isle of Gulls*, and *Staple of News*.

6. Percy Fitzgerald, *A New History of the English Stage*, Vol. I, p. 96.

7. *Bibliotheca Lindesiana*, Vol. VI, No. 3588.

8. Smith, Plates XVII to XX, and XXII.

9. Cf. John Cranford Adams, *Globe Playhouse*, pp. 120–21.

10. Cf. the *Messallina* sketch, reproduced in Smith, Plate XIX.

11. John Cranford Adams, *op. cit.*, pp. 114–16.

12. Cf. also *Alchemist*, IV *ii*; *Anything for a Quiet Life*, II *i*; *Deserving Favorite*, line 2537; *Knight of Malta*, IV *i*; *New Inn*, III *ii*, V *iii*; *Mayor of Quinboro*, I *ii*; and *Your Five Gallants*, V *ii*.

13. *Broken Heart*, III *ii*; *Coxcomb*, IV *iii*; *Fair Favorite*, III *i*; and *Variety*, V *i*.

14. Stage directions that limit the doors to two occur 57 times in 33 Blackfriars plays.

15. Stage directions that permit the idea of more than two doors occur 124 times in 72 Blackfriars plays.

16. These other plays contain stage directions of both kinds: *Cardinal*, *Cruel Brother*, *Distresses*, *Double Marriage*, *Just Italian*, *Malcontent*, *Mayor of Quinboro*, *Northern Lass*, *Sir Giles Goosecap*, *Sophy*, *Trick to Catch the Old One*, and *Wits*.

17. Sir Edmund K. Chambers notwithstanding (*William Shakespeare*, Vol. I, p. 107, n. 3), the two uses of the word "window" in this scene are not to be interpreted as meaning that the stage had a window, apart from the wicket in the door, on the lower level. As our examination of the scenic wall proceeds, it will become clear that no space for such a window existed. If there had been a window fronting the platform, it would have been used many times in many plays, but no such episode is to be found in plays produced at the Blackfriars or elsewhere. The identification of this window with the door seems to be established by the Lieutenant's question about "Guns i' th' door" and by his knocking, and by Celia's knocking "at's door."

18. *Globe Playhouse*, pp. 161–62.

19. Amateur prompting is called for in *Gentleman Usher*, II *i*, and *Roman Actor*, IV *ii*.

20. As for instance *Conspiracy*, Act I;

Guardian, III *v*; *Novella*, IV *i*; *Spanish Curate*, IV *vii*; *Wife for a Month*, II *vi*, etc.

21. W. J. Lawrence was inclined to believe that "where only one door was locked, it was invariably the rear-stage door. . . . To have locked only a single front-stage door would have been foolishness" (*Physical Conditions*, p. 21). But Lawrence was overlooking the large number of scenes in which one of the front-stage doors serves as the street door of a house. See pp. 333–335 above.

22. Cf. photographs in Lloyd, pp. 317–22.

23. *The Puritan*, sig. E2ᵛ, and *The English Traveller*, IV *i*. The former play was acted by the Children of Paul's, and the latter, in which Reginald praises the "brave carv'd poasts" at the entrance to Ricot's house, was acted by the Queen's Majesty's Servants at the Cockpit or Phoenix in Drury Lane. Incidentally, the floor plan and elevation of the stage of that other Cockpit, the Cockpit-in-Court (Smith, Plate XXII) show door posts as framing the outer-stage doors. They were not free standing, however.

24. Sir Edmund K. Chambers says that "the Blackfriars was a rectangular room. . . . And it is quite conceivable that there may have been side-doors in the planes of these [side] walls, and at right angles to the middle door. Whether this was so or not, and if so how far forward the side-doors stood, there is certainly nothing in the formulae of the stage directions to tell us." (*Elizabethan Stage*, Vol. III, p. 134).

25. Actors clearly entered at the rear of the four Elizabethan or Jacobean stages of which we have contemporary drawings. See Smith, Plates XVII to XX.

26. *Ibid.*, Plates XVII and XX. The *Roxana* and *Messallina* vignettes (Plates XVIII and XIX) show curtains at the rear of the platform, but no doors.

27. *Ibid.*, Plate XXII.

28. *Elizabethan Stage*, Vol. III, pp. 59–60.

29. The platform serves as two or more different places in immediate sequence in the following plays also: *Goblins*, final scene of Act I (a street, and then a walled garden); *Humorous Lieutenant*, III *vi* (two parts of a battlefield); *Love's Pilgrimage*, II *i* and II *ii* (before Leonardo's house, and then a woody thicket); *Loyal Subject*, V *v* (different parts of a battlefield); etc.

♔ 15 ♔

The Playhouse:
THE REAR STAGE

THERE IS A tendency nowadays for writers on the Elizabethan drama to refer to the rear stage as "the study." They have much justification for doing so, since pre-Restoration dramatists, on at least the twenty-nine occasions of which I have knowledge, wrote *"Enter So-and-so in his study,"* or other phrases incorporating that word, when they had the rear stage in mind. But it is noteworthy that the old playwrights did not use "study" in a theatrical sense, as a synonym for "the rear stage"; instead, they used it in a dramatic sense, as an equivalent for a small private room belonging to some character in the drama. This relationship of the room to the person is indicated by the use of possessive nouns or pronouns (i.e., his, my, my master's, etc.) as attributives to "study," on twenty-four out of the twenty-nine times that I have found the word used with this connotation in Elizabethan and Jacobean plays, as for example in these stage directions from plays in the Blackfriars repertory: *"Enter Barnavelt (in his studdy),"* *"Discovers Catiline in his study,"* and [*Pellegrin speaks*] *"As out of his study."*[1] On two of the remaining five occasions, the use of "his" is avoided because the occupant of the study is not its owner, but a woman guest.[2]

If the dramatists had thought of "study" as being a synonym for "the rear stage," they would have used it without regard to dramatic congruity, just as they used the word "door" with no such regard (as, for instance, did Shakespeare when he wrote *"Enter the King of Fairies at one doore with his traine, and the Queene at another with hers,"* in a scene located in a wood near Athens). But this they did not do. They used "study" in stage directions only when the rear stage represented a domestic interior, and when, therefore, the word was wholly appropriate; never once did they use it when, as happened even more often, the rear stage represented some entirely different kind of place—perhaps a part of a great hall, a shop, a cave, a tomb, an arbor—with respect to which the word would be incongruous.

Shakespeare presumably used the word "study" in accordance with the theatrical convention in the First Quarto of *Hamlet*, Scene *vi;* there the word seems to mean a private room, and Corambis probably had the rear stage in mind when he used it. But whenever else Shakespeare used the word, the study occupied some place other than the rear stage. Titus' study is on an upper level in *Titus Andronicus*, v *ii;* Friar Laurence's study is off-stage in *Romeo and Juliet*, III *ii*, and so is Brutus' study in *Julius Caesar*, II *i*. Because Shakespeare normally used "study" with reference to some place other than the rear stage, and because the word tends to suggest that the rear stage was limited to the representation of a small room in a home, I prefer to avoid the word altogether, and instead to use the nonrestrictive title "the rear stage."

The rear stage lay in back of the scenic wall, communicating with the platform by way of a broad aperture between the outer-stage doors. Curtains hung in the aperture; they could be opened to reveal the rear stage, or closed to conceal it.

"Curtains" is one of five words used by the old dramatists to designate textiles used as furnishings on the Elizabethan stage, the others being "hangings," "arras," "traverses," and "canopies." The words were not used indiscriminately.[3] "Curtains" always meant suspended cloths that could be drawn back. It was the name most often given to the draperies at the front edge of the rear stage[4] and to the corresponding draperies on the upper level.[5] In a few plays it meant smaller withdrawable draperies within the rear stage,[6] and in a few others it meant bed curtains.[7]

"Hangings" were the cloths that composed the side walls of the rear stage.[8] Unlike curtains, they could not be drawn back; instead, they were lifted if a person had to pass through them. This is evidenced by a stage direction in *The Conspiracy*, v *iv*, when Pallantus is ushering Eudora into the presence of a brother whom she believes to have been killed: "*Pallantus goes out, and returns presently again, and holds up the Hanging for Eudora.*" In only one Blackfriars play does the word clearly mean anything other than side-wall draperies. That one is *The Unfortunate Lovers*, a play that came late in Blackfriars history. In the Prologue, Davenant speaks of the "half dress'd Player, as he still / Through th' hangings peep'd to see how th' house did fill," in which context "hangings" can only have meant the curtains at the front edge of the rear stage. He may have used the word with the same meaning in two stage directions in v v—"*Draws the hangings. . . . Draws the Hangings.*"—but, whether or not he meant those particular draperies, nowhere else in Elizabethan dramatic literature are "hangings" spoken of as being "drawn."

"Arras" says merely that the cloths are of tapestry weave; it tells nothing about their position or use. It is used both for curtains and for hangings, but it means the hangings within the rear stage[9] more than three times as often as it means the curtains in the forward aperture.[10]

"Traverse" means a screen that hides a small area within a larger room, and perhaps also a screen that divides a room into parts. The word is used in only one Blackfriars play (*The Duchess of Malfi*, iv i), and in only three other plays in the whole body of pre-Restoration drama.[11]

"Canopy" properly means a covering suspended over a throne or bed, or carried over the head of a dignitary as he marches in a procession. The canopy in *The Fair Favorite*, ii iii, presumably covers a chair of state, and so does that in *The Just Italian*, iv ii; that in *The Picture*, i ii, is carried over the head of Honoria. The canopy in *The Wits*, iv ii, and that in *The Parson's Wedding*, v ii, are testers over beds, but the word seems to mean the side curtains of a bed in *The Platonic Lovers*, ii i, and in *The Wonder of Women* at the end of Act iv. I have no idea what it means in iv i of the latter play, when "*A treble Violl and a base Lute play softly within the Canopy.*"

The Stage Curtains

The Citizen's Wife said that the curtains hanging in front of the rear stage at Blackfriars were of painted cloth. While she sat looking at the closed curtains during the intermission between the second and third acts of *The Knight of the Burning Pestle*, she asked her husband "Now, sweet lamb, what story is that painted upon the cloth? The Confutation of St. Paul?" And he replied "No, lamb; that's Rafe and Lucrece." She may have been mistaken with respect to the fabric as well as the story, for painted cloth would seem to have been out of character for Blackfriars; it was the poor relation of arras or tapestry. Besides, one of the boys in the Induction to *Cynthia's Revels* called the curtain a "silke cortaine, come to hang the stage here," and several dramatists called it "arras."

As we shall see presently, the aperture of the rear stage was just under 20 feet wide, and presumably two pieces of cloth were used to close it, with an overlap in the middle; and this central break between the two halves probably constituted the "middle door" mentioned in *East-ward Ho!*, I *i*, and *The Parson's Wedding*, I *iii*.

Through the use of the curtains, the rear stage could at will be either hidden or revealed. The curtains thus were a central factor in the method of successive staging that superseded the medieval system of multiple settings and preceded the advent of scenery. They made these things possible:

A] When closed, the curtains concealed the interior of the rear stage and permitted it to be dressed with properties and hangings in preparation for a scene to come, while at the same time the action continued on the outer stage.

B] When the curtains were opened, the rear stage could merge with the platform to compose a single great stage representing one locality, or the two stages could be used in combination to represent two distinct but logically related places, or the rear stage could serve alone as a room or other enclosure in its own right, free of association with the platform.

c] The curtains permitted the rear stage to be used, as the platform could not be, for the disclosure of groups already assembled, or for the revelation of persons whose condition or situation prevented their walking out upon the stage, as for example persons confined to their beds, shackled in prison, or engaged in a game of chess. Similarly, the curtains permitted a scene to come to an end with actors still on the stage.

Disclosures effected by the opening of the rear-stage curtains were technically known as discoveries. The word occurs frequently in Black-friars stage directions such as the following:

From *The Case Is Altered*, I *i*:

> *Sound : after a flourish, Juniper a Cobler is discovered, sitting at worke in his shoppe and singing.*

From *The Goblins*, Act IV:

> *Orsabrin discovered in prison, bound.*

From *The Knight of Malta*, V *ii*:

> *An Altar discover'd, with Tapers, and a Book on it. The two Bishops stand on each side of it; Mountferrat, as the Song is singing, ascends up the Altar.*

344

From *The Second Maiden's Tragedy*, IV *iii*:

> *Enter the Tirant agen at a farder dore, which opened, brings hym to the Toombe wher the Lady lies buried; The Toombe here discovered ritchly set forthe.*

And from *Your Five Gallants*, I *i*:

> *A Room in Frippery's House. Frippery discovered summing up his pawns, one Fellow standing by him.*

Other discoveries are listed in the notes.[12]

A few stage directions make it clear that the discovery is effected by the opening of curtains. In the three that follow, as in all those hitherto cited, the curtains are presumably opened by stagehands who remain out of sight of the audience.

From *The Faithful Shepherdess*, V *i*:

> *The Curtayne is drawn. Clorin appeares sitting in the Cabin, Amoret sitting on the one side of her, Alexis and Cloe on the other, the Satyr standing by.*

From *The Parson's Wedding*, V *ii*:

> *The fiddlers play in the tiring-room; and the stage curtains are drawn, and discover a chamber, as it were, with two beds, and the ladies asleep in them; Mr. Wild being at Mrs. Pleasant's bed-side, and Mr. Careless at the Widow's.*

And this from *A Wife for a Month*, Act II:

> *A Curtaine drawne. The King, Queene, Valerio, Evanthe, Ladies, Attendants, Camillo, Cleanthes, Sorano, Menallo.*

The last two directions show that the discoverable area was large enough to contain two beds in the first instance, and twelve persons at the lowest possible count in the second.

Some stage directions differ from those previously cited in showing that the curtains might on occasion be opened by an actor in view of the audience, as an incident in the dramatic story. Such a direction is that in *The Tempest*, v *i*, in which, for the only time in all his plays, Shakespeare uses the word "discovers" in its technical sense:

> *Here Prospero discovers Ferdinand and Miranda, playing at Chesse.*

In the following scenes, too, the curtains are opened by visible agents:

From *The Distresses*, IV *v*:

> *He [Leonte] steps to the Arras softly, draws it. Claramante is discovered sleeping on her Book, her Glass by.*

From *The Mad Lover*, v *iii*:

> *Enter Nun, she opens the Curtain to Calis. Calis at the Oracle.*

And from *News from Plymouth*, IV *ii*:

> *A Curtain drawn by Dash (his Clerk) Trifle discover'd in his Study, Papers, Taper, Seale and Wax before him, Bell.*

Other discoveries of the same sort are listed in the notes.[13]

Many disclosures fail to be labeled with the word "discovery," and even more fail to mention the opening of curtains. Some even speak of an actor as entering rather than as being revealed. But the word "enter," like the word "door," is often a theatrical technicality; it may mean merely that the enterer becomes visible to the spectators, not necessarily by locomotion, and "entrance" therefore does not rule out the possibility of discovery. The actor is almost certainly discovered, as a matter of fact, if his "entrance" is made under circumstances that in real life would prevent his striding out upon the platform. The following stage directions illustrate this point:

From *Cymbeline*, II *ii*:

> *Enter Imogen, in her Bed, and a Lady.*[14]

346

From *The Deserving Favorite*, line 867:

Enter Clarinda and Lysander, (as in an Arbour), in the night.

From *The Fleir*, Act iv:

Enter Signior Alunio the Apothecarie in his shop with his wares about him.

From *Love's Pilgrimage*, i *ii:*

Enter Theodosia and Phillipo on several beds.

And from *Valentinian*, ii *i:*

Enter the Emperour, Maximus, Licinius, Proculus, Chilax, as at dice.[15]

A few discoveries are evidenced in dialogue rather than by stage direction, as for instance this from *The Sea Voyage*, iv *iii:*

> *Aminta.*   O blind fortune;
>   Yet happy thus far, I shall live to see him,
>   In what strange desolation lives he here now?
>   Sure this Curtain will reveale.
> > *Enter Albert.*
> *Albert.*   Who's that? ha!
>   Some gentle hand, I hope, to bring me comfort.
>   Or if it be my death, 'tis sweetly shadowed.
> *Amin.*   Have ye forgot me, Sir?
> *Alb.*   My Aminta?

Similarly, dialogue shows that chess players are discovered in *Sir Giles Goosecap*, iv *i*, and that Hermione as a statue is discovered in *The Winter's Tale*, v *i.*

Just as "enter" might mean that the actor was revealed in the rear stage without motion on his part, so "exit" might mean that he was concealed while still on-stage, when the curtains closed. Iachimo's exit at the end of the scene in Imogen's bedchamber (*Cymbeline*, ii *ii*) was into a trunk, but he was still on the stage, as was Imogen herself, when the curtains closed and the scene ended.

The rear-stage curtains placed it within the power of dramatists to end a scene suddenly upon a note of tension, but they seldom took advantage of the opportunity; because of the long outer-stage tradition with its inescapable dispersing of actors, the dramatists clung to the "soft" ending, and made little use of the curtain as a means of cutting a scene off abruptly or arresting the action. The final scene of *The Tragedy of Byron* is a notable exception.

Byron has been convicted of treason and sentenced to the block. A scaffold for his execution is revealed when the curtains open. Vitry, addressing the condemned man, says "My lord, 'tis late; will't please you to go up?" and Byron replies "Up? 'Tis a fair preferment. . . . Come, since we must." He ascends the steps of the scaffold, blindfolds himself, speaks his farewell to the world while kneeling at the block, and then bids the executioner strike:

> Strike, strike, O strike; fly, fly, commanding soul,
> And on thy wings for this thy body's breath,
> Bear the eternal victory of Death!

The executioner raises his axe, and at that moment the rear-stage curtains close upon the tableau. The play ends with *"Finis"* instead of with the usual *"Exeunt."*

Sometimes the plot required that the curtains be closed by actors on the stage, and this probably happened far more often than the stage directions indicate. Only three such incidents are explicit in Blackfriars plays. In *The Mad Lover*, v *i*, the Nun closes the curtain upon Calis; in *The Widow's Tears*, IV *ii*, Cynthia, the widow, shuts up the tomb; and in *The Faithful Shepherdess*, v *i*, Clorin, having taken the wounded Alexis to her cabin, leaves him within and closes the curtain:

> Soon again he ease shall find,
> If I can but still his mind.
> This curtain thus I do display,
> To keep the piercing air away.

The stage directions already quoted, showing as they do the discovery of elaborate inner-stage settings of many sorts, lead to the conclusion that all the more intricate settings were as a matter of course set up in the rear stage and later revealed to the audience by the opening of the curtains. To say this is not to overlook the many occasions on which properties were carried or shoved out upon the platform, either by actors as incidents in the dramatic action or by stagehands as matters of convenience. But whenever a full setting was involved—a cobbler's shop, or a presence chamber for a king, or a grove with a fountain in it—we may assume that the rear stage served the purpose.

A few pages back I spoke of the relationships that might exist between the rear stage and the platform when the curtains were opened and the rear stage was called into play: they might jointly represent one place, or they might represent two different but related places, or the rear stage might represent an enclosed area in its own right, ignoring the platform. Shakespeare's Blackfriars plays illustrate all these relationships.

The two stages combined to represent a single great hall in *Henry VIII*, ii *iv*, the scene that reenacted the historical event that had taken place in the same chamber eighty-four years earlier. The stage direction at the head of the scene specifies the setting in greater detail than does any other direction in the canon. It indicates that the stagehands, working behind closed curtains while an unlocalized and unpropertied scene (ii *iii*) was proceeding on the platform, were required to set up in the rear stage a throne with a cloth of state over it for the King, seats under him for the two Cardinals as judges, seats for the Bishops on each side in manner of a consistory, seats for the Lords next the Bishops, and below the Bishops seats for the Scribes. The Queen, since she sat at some distance from the King, occupied a chair that perhaps was carried to the outer stage after the curtains opened. The Attendants who stood "in convenient order about the Stage" were by specification upon the platform.

An earlier scene in the same play (i *iv*) had similarly used the two stages to represent a single great chamber. This time the place was the presence chamber of Cardinal Wolsey in York Palace, and the setting in the rear stage included a small table under a state for the Cardinal and a longer table for the guests. Entrances were by way of the outer-stage doors, with Anne Boleyn and divers other ladies and gentlemen entering as guests at one door, and with Sir Henry Guilford, as spokesman for the Cardinal, entering at another. The tables were carried away when the masquers approached, and the combined stages provided space for the dance that followed.

The two stages merged to represent a single place of a different kind in *The Two Noble Kinsmen*, v *i*. Here the scene was an open field near Athens, with three altars in the rear stage, to Mars, Venus, and Diana.

There were of course other similar scenes that need not be specified here, for the combined stages, as representing a single place, served in a large proportion of the "big" scenes in Blackfriars plays—scenes that called for properties, several points of entrance and departure, and space enough for free movement and a full company of actors.

The second relationship—that in which the two stages represent two separate but related places—is exemplified in *The Tempest*, v i. In that scene the platform is the ground before Prospero's cell and the rear stage is the cell itself, whose interior Prospero reveals when he draws the curtains and discovers Ferdinand and Miranda playing at chess. It is exemplified also in *The Winter's Tale*, v iii, with the platform serving as the chapel in Paulina's house to which King Leontes has come to see the statue of his dead queen, and with the rear stage serving as the place lonely, apart, where Hermione stands behind a curtain like a statue, waiting to be discovered.[16]

Henry VIII, v ii-iii, uses the two stages together in a relationship that illustrates the extraordinary flexibility which was characteristic of the Elizabethan stage. The two scenes are one in the First Folio, the break between them having been intruded by modern editors. In the earlier scene the platform is the lobby before the Council Chamber. Cranmer, Archbishop of Canterbury, enters by one of the stage doors and crosses to the other as to the door leading into the Chamber. He expects to be admitted to a meeting of the Council of which he is a member, but his entrance is barred by a Keeper on orders of the Council, and he is left standing outside the door amongst pursuivants, pages, and footboys. His humiliation is witnessed by the King, who looks down upon the lobby from an upstairs window. Presently his Majesty leaves the window, and at the same moment the stage curtains open to reveal the rear stage as the interior of the Council Chamber, with a stage set up in readiness for the King's arrival. Cranmer and the Keeper have not left the stage; they are still, presumably, near the door, but for the moment they are forgotten in the commotion of having attendants bring in a council table with chairs and stools, and then having the Lord Chancellor and other members of the Council enter and take their seats. Although the two stages have now merged, Cranmer is still technically "without" the Chamber (v iii 5). The Lord Chancellor tells the Keeper to let him come in; the Keeper says "Your Grace may enter now," and *"Cranmer approaches the Council table."* From now on the platform is merely a forward extension of the rear stage; its former character as the lobby is forgotten.

The two-place relationship is exhibited also in many non-Shakespearean plays. In all the following scenes the two stages represent two separate but related places, and the action moves from one to the other within the course of a single scene, while characters remain continuously upon the stage. Thus in *The Captain*, IV *iv*, the platform represents a street before Lelia's house, and the rear stage a room within it. In *Catiline*, V *vi*, the rear stage is the interior of a public building in Rome, and the platform is the street outside. In *The Faithful Shepherdess*, V *ii*, the platform is a forest glade and the inner stage is Clorin's cottage. In *The Goblins*, Act V, the action begins on the platform as some indefinite place outside Sabrina's chamber, and moves thence to its interior. In *Law Tricks*, IV *ii*, the rear stage is Polymetes' study and the platform is a street upon which a funeral procession passes. In *The Novella*, II *i*, the platform is a street and the rear stage the interior of a gentleman's lodging, with a table and seats and wine. In *The Queen of Corinth*, IV *iv*, the action moves uninterruptedly from a street to the inside of a wine shop. And in *The Widow's Tears*, during a sequence beginning at IV *ii* and ending with V *iii*, the platform is a churchyard and the inner stage is the interior of a mausoleum in which Lysander is supposedly entombed.

Scenes in the third category—scenes in which the rear stage serves as a room or other enclosure in its own right, free of association with the platform—occur less frequently. The scene is Imogen's bedchamber (*Cymbeline*, II *ii*) is the perfect example of such a scene, and its action is, I think, confined to that one stage more strictly than is that of any other scene in Shakespeare; except for the departure of the gentlewoman, the action never moves outside the walls of the inner stage. The scene begins with a discovery. Discovery is not specified, but it is inevitable; the opening of the curtains reveals Imogen in her bed, reading the tale of Tereus by the light of a taper at her bedside. Thereafter the action is continuously related to the inner stage by the bed, the taper, and Iachimo's trunk. The scene can end only by having the curtains close.

But in speaking of the action as being continuously related to the inner stage, I have no thought of intimating that it was at all times necessarily confined to that stage. In all such scenes, the dividing line between the rear stage and the platform ceased to exist as soon as the curtains were thrown wide; the platform became merely a forward extension of the rear stage, and took its character from it; and actors felt completely free to overrun the imaginary line and to move toward the front of the stage, into closer contact with the audience. Probably, however, the actors in such a scene were initially discovered within the rear stage or made their first entrances to it, so as to establish that stage as the

351

setting for the action, and at the end they either departed through the rear-stage exits or were concealed there when the curtains closed.

The Rear-Stage Walls

The rear stage was closed off at the back by a rigid partition, presumably of oak, with a window and door cut through it. The door often served as the means by which a person could enter a house (the rear stage) as from a street or garden at the back (the back passageway); and when it served in this capacity, the window sometimes provided the means by which persons inside the house could observe the approach of those about to enter. The following episodes illustrate these uses:

In *The Alchemist*, I *i*, Lovewit, the master of a house in the Blackfriars district of London, has moved to the country to escape the plague. Face, his housekeeper, has taken advantage of his master's absence by permitting a cozener named Subtle, and his punk Doll Common, to put the house to outrageous misuse. A bell rings off-stage.

> *Subtle.* Who's that? one rings. To the windo', Dol.
>   Pray heav'n
> The master doe not trouble us, this quarter.
> *Face.* O, feare not him . . .
> *Sub.* Who is it, Dol?
> *Doll.*   A fine young quodling.
> *Fac.*   O,
> My Lawyers clarke, I lighted on, last night,
> In Hol'bourne, at the dagger. . . .
> *Doll.* O, let him in.

Later in the same play, in III *ii*, Ananias hears a knocking without, and recognizes Face and admits him, and in III *iii* Dapper knocks and is admitted.

An analogous situation occurs in *The Humorous Lieutenant*, II *iii*. Leucippe, the madam of a brothel in need of recruits, is discovered reading, with her two maids sitting at a table writing. She hears a knock within.

> *Leucippe.* Who's that? look out, to your business, Maid,
> There's nothing got by idleness. . . .
> How now, who is't?

1 Maid.   An ancient woman, with a maid attending,
      A pretty Girl, but out of Cloaths; for a little money,
      It seems she would put her to your bringing up, Madam.
                Enter Woman and Phebe.

In each of these episodes, the door admits the arrivals after they
have sought admittance by ringing or knocking. The timing of the knocks
thus often serves to distinguish a rear-stage scene from a scene acted on
the platform. If the person knocks first and is admitted afterwards, then
his entrance is by way of the back door, and he enters the rear stage.[17]
But if the person knocks *after* entering, the implication is that he has
entered the platform through an outer-stage door as from a distant
point, has crossed the stage to the other door as to the street door of a
house, and that he now knocks upon it and is admitted to the house or
greeted at the threshold.[18]

Sometimes, instead of being treated as leading to the outdoors, the
back door is treated as leading to other parts of the house, and in particular
to the stairs and so to the upper floor. It is used so in *The Maid in the
Mill*, I *iii.* Ismena and Aminta, on the ground floor of their house, are
awaiting the arrival, under Ismena's window, of her admirer Antonio.

> *Ismena.*   Look out, 'tis darkish.
> *Aminta.*   I see nothing yet. . . .
>   Hark, I hear something: up to th' Chamber, Cosin,
>   You may spoil all else.
> *Ism.*   Let me see, they are Gentlemen;
>   It may be they.
> *Am.*   They are they: get ye up,
>   And like a Land-star draw him.

The two girls scurry upstairs and reappear at a window fronting the platform and the audience, and Antonio and his friend, having come around
the house, enter the outer stage.

The back door could be locked, as evidenced by two scenes in *The
Fatal Dowry*, both of them readily identifiable as rear-stage scenes. In
III *i,* Romont says:

> Lose not, sir, yourself,
> And I will venture: — so, the door is fast.
>   *Locks the door.*

353

and in IV *i* he says:

> Your boy's gone,   *Locks the door.*
> And your door's lock'd; yet for no hurt to you,
> But privacy.

It is locked also in *The Captain*, IV *iv*, a scene to be quoted at length later, when, as we shall see, the Father locks the door before making his identity known to his daughter, unlocks it to permit Angelo to enter from upstairs, and locks it again after Angelo's entrance.[19]

Three times in Blackfriars plays the back door serves as the door of a small room in which a person is hidden. In *The Maid in the Mill*, V *ii*, Otrante hopes to conceal Florimell, a young girl who loves him, from the King, Don Philippo.

> Go, lock her up;
> Lock her up where the courtiers may not see her;
> Lock her up closely, sirrah, in my closet.

The King enters and immediately begins a systematic search of the premises: first the gallery, and then some lodging-chambers o'er a homely garden, and then some rooms that lead to the other side of the house; and finally—

> *Philippo.*   This little Room?
> *Otrante.*   'Tis mean: a place for trash Sir,
>   For rubbish of the house.
> *Phil.*   I would see this too:
>   I will see all.
> *Otr.*   I beseech your Majesty!

Otrante offers one excuse after another for not opening the door: the savor of the place would be offensive; he does not have the key. But the King, his curiosity now thoroughly aroused, is insistent:

> But I will see it: force the lock (my Lords)
> There be smiths enough to mend it: I perceive
> You keep some rare things here, you would not show Sir.
>   *Florimel discover'd.*

The second such scene occurs in *The Goblins*. Orsabrin, fleeing from pursuers, has sought refuge in Sabrina's house. As Act II nears its end, Sabrina says:

> Hark! A noise, sir!
> The tread's too loud to be my Samorat's.
> > *Enter the Searchers to them.*
> *Searchers.* Which way? which way?
> *Sabrina.* Some villany is in hand. Step in here, sir:
> quick, quick.   [*Locks him in her closet.*]

Philatel enters with the Guard, threatens to kill his sister unless she tells him where she has hidden her brother's murderer, and Orsabrin, upon hearing the threat, "*bounces thrice at the door: it flies open.*"

In *The Laws of Candy*, IV i, the closet is used for eavesdropping.

> *Hyp[archa]*. The Lord Gonzalo
> Attends you, Madam.
> *Er[ota]*. Comes as we could wish,
> Withdraw, Antinous, here's a Closet, where
> You may partake his errand; let him enter.

A few Blackfriars plays contain stage directions calling for So-and-so to enter "behind." Such directions do not, I think, necessarily mean that the character enters by way of the back door. He may do so, but the important thing is that he enters the rear stage to eavesdrop on action that usually is taking place on the platform. He remains in the rear, with his presence known to the audience but not to those upon whom he is spying, until the story requires him to come forward. Such entrances "behind" are to be found in *The Brothers*, II i and v iii; *The Duchess of Malfi*, III ii; *The Fatal Dowry*, III i (twice); *The Imposture*, IV ii, IV iii, and v i; and *The Inconstant Lady*, II ii.

Sometimes the back window serves as a pretext for enabling persons on the stage to pretend that they can see things that cannot in actuality be shown. A conspicuous instance of this occurs in *Catiline*, I i, a scene whose placement in the rear stage is removed from doubt by an initial stage direction saying that Catiline is discovered in his study. His fellow-conspirators have assembled at his home in the early morning, and suddenly "*A fiery light appeares.*"

355

Var[*gunteius*].   What light is that?
Cur[*ius.*]   Looke forth.
Len[*tulus*].   It still growes greater!
Lec[*ca*].   From whence comes it?
Lon[*ginus*].   A bloudy arme it is, that holds a pine
   Lighted, above the Capitoll! and, now,
   It waves unto us!
Cat[*iline*].   Brave, and omenous!
   Our enterprise is seal'd.
Cet[*hegus*].   In spight of darkeness,
   That would discountenance it. Looke no more;
   We loose time, and our selves.

The back window serves a similar purpose in *The Alchemist*, iv *v*, when Face says that he sees a coach standing at the door, and in iv *vii*, when Doll sees the master of the house approaching, with forty of his neighbors about him talking. In *The Widow*, iii *iv*, Violetta watches the disguised Martia gallop away on her horse, and in *The Wits*, ii *iv*, Pert, having heard "*a noise within*," reports that "old Snare / The Constable, his wife, a Regiment of Halberds, / and Mistress Queasie too, . . . / are at the door."

The window in the rear stage was listed by Iachimo in his inventory of the articles in Imogen's bedchamber:

                 I will write all down:
Such and such pictures; there the window; such
Th' adornment of her bed.

Directly in back of the rear stage, a crossover passageway ran from side to side out of sight of the audience. Its primary purpose was to make back-stage circulation possible when the inner stage was in use and when the curtains therefore were open. But, as we have seen, it occasionally served as a street or garden from which persons entered the rear stage by way of the back door, and sometimes, as will be discussed in the next chapter, it became an indoor corridor leading to the stairs. The costumes of the period being what they were, the passageway and stairs together probably needed to be at least 6 feet wide.

As has already been intimated, the side walls of the rear stage were composed of hangings. They thus looked to Tudor eyes like the

walls of Tudor chambers, where cloth of arras served the triple purposes of conserving heat, reducing drafts, and contributing beauty.
Domestic hangings were supported along their top edges by tenterhooks
fastened over rods or wooden frames, and they hung several inches out
from the wall, to prevent their taking stain or mildew from the wall's
dampness. On the stage, however, the arras did not hang in front of a
wall; it *was* the wall. It concealed off-stage activities, enclosed the rear
stage with a flexible screen through which actors could pass and stagehands could carry properties, and presented a stage picture at once
familiar, colorful, and alterable.

The hangings were, of course, decorated with inwoven pictorial subjects. Imogen's bedchamber

> was hang'd
> With tapestry of silk and silver; the story
> Proud Cleopatra, when she met her Roman
> And Cydnus swell'd above the banks, or for
> The press of boats or pride: a piece of work
> So bravely done, so rich, that it did strive
> In workmanship and value; which I wonder'd
> Could be so rarely and exactly wrought.

The hangings in Count Lurdo's house in *Law Tricks*, III *i*, were decorated
with "the Poeticall fiction of Venus kissing Adonis in the violet bed,"
and those in *The City Match*, II *iii*, presumably dealt with the Trojan
War and showed at least "one of them Trojans."

On the stage, as in the homes of the period, wall hangings were
removable and interchangeable. They were often changed in expectation
of the arrival of a guest or guests. Leon, in *Rule a Wife and Have a
Wife*, III *i*, has this custom in mind when he asks

> Are all the chambers
> Deck't and adorn'd thus for my Ladies pleasure?
> New hangings every hour for entertainment . . . ?

and so does Sciolto in *The Platonic Lovers*, I *i*, when he is told reassur-
ingly that "The inner room's new hung." In *Love's Cure*, I *ii*, Eugenia,
as a part of her preparation for welcoming her husband back home after
an exile of several years, orders her servant to

Haste, and take down those Blacks with which my chamber
Hath like a widow, her sad Mistriss mourn'd,
And hang up for it, the rich Persian arras,
Us'd on my wedding night, for this to me
Shall be a second marriage.

In *The Custom of the Country*, I *ii*, the hangings are changed in view of the audience, when Charino enters with servants in blacks, "*covering the place with blacks*" in token of mourning for the imminent loss of Zenocia's honor. Black hangings are used again later in the same play, when in v *ii* Donna Guiomar's room is hung in sable colors as a sign of true sorrow for the supposed death of her son.[20]

Apart from their primary function of concealing back-stage activities, the side-wall hangings at Blackfriars were sometimes used by characters in the drama for hiding or eavesdropping. I quote two instances from among several:[21]

From *The Duchess of Malfi*, I *ii*:

Duchess: Good dear soul,
Leave me; but place thyself behind the arras,
Where thou mayst overhear us.
        Cariola goes behind the arras.

And from *The Noble Gentleman*, III *iv*:

Shattillion: I will not speak
Before these witnesses.
Duke. Depart the room, for none shall stay,
No, not my dearest Duchess.
Wife. We'll stand behind the Arras and hear all.
       Exeunt.

The Rear-Stage Trap

The trap in the floor of the rear stage was used more often, and under more varied guises, than that in the floor of the platform. Because it could be concealed from the view of spectators by the rear-stage curtains, it could be set in advance with properties, as the platform trap could not be. It could acquire an indoor character, as being an opening in the floor of a room or cave, from the mere fact of being within the rear stage. It could be opened or closed from above, and perhaps from below also, whereas the platform trap could presumably be operated only from beneath; and it did not suffer from that trap's disadvantage of being looked down into, when it was open, by spectators in the galleries. On the other hand, it did not, as the platform trap did, have a lifting-and-lowering mechanism; it had only a ladder or stairs to enable actors to go up or down.

In *The Isle of Gulls*, sig. G2ᵛ, the rear-stage trap is the hole in the ground where Dametas digs for treasure, and it has accordingly been supplied in advance with stones and gravel for Dametas to remove. There he digs with mattock and spade for the treasure that he believes to have been buried under Diana's oak, but in the end he finds nothing but a coxcomb, a bell, and a writing. Four persons watch his digging and comment upon it; they therefore are nearer to the audience than he, presumably on the platform.

The trap serves similarly as a hole in the ground in *The Case Is Altered*. In III *v* Jaques buries his gold beneath a scuttleful of horse-dung. In IV *iii* he disinters it for a few minutes of gloating and then restores it to its grave; and in the next scene Onion scrapes away the dung and shows the gold to Juniper.

Two traps are in use at the same time in *Cynthia's Revels*, Act I. The rear-stage trap serves throughout the act as the spring called the Fountain of Self-Love, and while it does so, Echo rises from her cavern of the earth by way of the platform trap. In preparation for its role as a spring, the opening in the floor of the rear stage has perhaps been edged with rushes or flowers to disguise the trap itself and the basin of water suspended in it. Although the Fountain of Self-Love is mentioned often during Act I, it is involved in the action only once, when Amorphus dips up some water with his hand.

In *The Wonder of Women*, III *i*, the rear-stage trap serves as the indoor end of an underground passageway whose other end is in far-off Belos Forest. Sophonisba elicits these facts by her questioning of Vangue.

> *Sophonisba.* To what use gentle Negro serves this cave
> Whose mouth thus opens so familliarly,
> Even in the Kings bedchamber?
> *Vangue.* O my Queene
> This vault with hideous darkness and much length

> Stretcheth beneath the earth into a grove
> One league from Cirta.

Sophonisba decides to investigate. She says to her handmaid

> Deere Zanthia close the vault when I am sunk
> And whilst he slips to bed escape, . . .

after which *"Shee descends."* A few moments later Zanthia *"descends after Sophonisba,"* and still later Syphax *"descends through the vault."* Incidentally, both Vangue's earlier line—"Close the vaults mouth least we do slip in drinke"—and Sophonisba's admonition to Zanthia to "close the vault when I am sunk," prove that the trap could be closed by an actor on the stage. It is also characteristic of the rear-stage trap that Sophonisba, Zanthia, and Syphax descend in single file, presumably going down unseen steps.

Aglaura has a similar underground passageway, "a vault that has his passage under the little river" from a lodging on one side to a cypress grove on the other. This play does not show the departure of persons from the household end of the tunnel, as does *The Wonder of Women*, but it does show the return of two of them. Aglaura has been warned that the King will come through the tunnel that night with intent to ravish her, so in Act v she stands at the vault's mouth with a torch in one hand and a dagger in the other, awaiting his arrival. But the Prince her husband comes instead. *"Enter Prince rising from the vault, shee stabs him two or three times, hee falls, shee goes back to her chamber. . . . [Ziriff] brings up the bodie, shee swounes and dies."*

In both plays one might have expected the platform trap to be used as the distant end of the vault; perhaps it was, but the evidence is unclear. In the earlier play, iv *i*, the emergence of the characters in the forest is described thus: *"Enter Sophonisba and Zanthia as out of a caves mouth,"* and *"Through the vautes mouth in his night gowne, torch in his hand, Syphax enters just behind Sophon[isba]."* No ascent is indicated, but the words "cave," "mouth," and "vault" were all applied to the bedchamber end of the tunnel in iii *i*, with descents three times specified. "Cave" and "mouth" are similarly used to designate the forest end of the vault in the latter play, again with no clear indication of trap use; but here there is special reason for doubt, for *Aglaura* is a late Blackfriars play for which its extravagant author, Sir John Suckling, provided scenery.

The Wonder of Women calls for trapwork twice again: in v *i* "*Erichtho slips into the ground as Syphax offers his sword to her,*" and "*Out of the Aultar the ghost of Asdruball ariseth*" in the same scene; but this involves a trapped altar rather than a floor trap. This play, as a matter of fact, makes more use of traps, as also of music, than any other play in the Blackfriars repertory.

In *Thierry and Theodoret*, III *ii*, the rear trap is the mouth of a vault that opens into the throne room of the royal palace, just behind the state. Protaldy, suborned by Queen Brunhalt to murder her son, "*behind the State stabs Theodoret,*" and hides in the vault until the Queen addresses him as her good faithful servant, and bids him rise.

In *The Two Noble Kinsmen*, v *i*, the business of the hind, the altar, and the rose tree undoubtedly involves manipulation by one or two stagehands standing in the rear-stage trap: "*Here the Hind vanishes under the Altar: and in the place ascends a Rose-Tree, having one Rose upon it. . . . Here is heard a sodain twang of Instruments, and the Rose falls from the Tree,*" and after the flower is fallen the tree descends.

Ghosts and spirits almost invariably made their entrances by rising through traps; their doing so was a theatrical convention so generally recognized that dramatists seldom troubled to specify ascent if real ghosts were involved. But they made a point of doing so if the apparitions were humbugs, as half the Blackfriars apparitions were. Whenever a charlatan summoned a bogus spirit to appear, he invariably ordered it to rise, since only by its rising could he convince his gulls that it was an honest ghost that they had seen. Paulo, in *A Very Woman*, IV *ii*, boasts of his duplicity in this respect:

> For these, I have
> Prepared my instruments, fitting his chamber
> With trapdoors, and descents; sometimes presenting
> Good spirits of the air, bad of the earth,
> To pull down or advance his fair intentions.
> He's of a noble nature, yet sometimes
> Thinks that which, by confederacy, I do,
> Is by some skill in magic.

In *The Chances*, v *iii*, Vecchio, a necromancer, gives the order "Ascend, Asteroth," to a counterfeit devil impersonated by Don John. The magician in *The Humorous Lieutenant*, IV *iii*, "seems to Conjure" some spirits to help him in preparing a love potion for the King, directing them to

> Rise from the Shades below,
> All you that prove
> The helps of looser love;

and Milesia in *The Lost Lady*, who is believed to be dead and buried but who is actually posing as a Moorish sorceress behind a burnt-cork complexion, tells her mourning lover that

> if this night you'll come
> Unto her tomb, you there shall see her;

and when he does come to the tomb in IV *i*, "*Milesia riseth like a ghost*," and later "*Sinks*."

These spurious ghost scenes are even more persuasive than veritable ghost scenes could be in indicating the potency of the tradition that spirits must ascend and descend. They justify one in supposing that ascent is intended in spectral scenes even when it is not prescribed, as when the ghosts of Posthumus's father and mother and brothers enter, as in an apparition, in *Cymbeline*, v *iv*; or when Satan enters in *The Devil Is an Ass*, v *iv*; or when the Countess enters in *Law Tricks*, v *ii*, after having been dismissed "from those shades / Where pleasure springs and never fades"; or when Delphia conjures a she-devil in III *ii* of *The Prophetess*, and a Spirit enters from a well in v *iii* of the same play; or when the ghosts of Junius Rusticus and Palphurius Sura enter in *The Roman Actor*, v *i*.

In these ghostly scenes the ascent would seem to have been made by way of the rear-stage trap more often than not, partly because that trap was more remote, and therefore more obscure, than the platform trap. But Sylla's Ghost certainly entered by the platform trap in *Catiline his Conspiracy*, I *i*, since Catiline's study had not yet been discovered; and the Ghosts of Posthumus' parents and brothers may have done so too, since the action was outdoors and the rear-stage curtains were probably closed.

The trap scenes discussed in the last few pages, when contrasted with those examined on pages 313–317, suggest that recognizable differences existed between the platform trap and the rear-stage trap in their natures and their uses. The platform trap was characteristically—but not uniformly—a nondescript opening in the crust of the earth, leading up from some obscure region in the netherworld. It was seldom used by mortals; those who rose or sank by it were for the most part allegorical or mythological creatures such as those previously mentioned—Envy, Echo, Night, Neptune, and so on—who ascended without effort of their own and who commonly made their first appearances by rising through the floor of the stage. The rear-stage trap, on the other hand, was customarily—but again not always—used by human beings who provided their own motive power and who made their first appearances by door rather than by trap. More often than not it represented an opening or depression of a sort within the scope of human experience: a hole where a man might dig, or a vault into which he might descend, or a tunnel through which he might travel from one familiar place to another. Sometimes, as we have seen, it was a place from which ghosts or spirits might rise, and in being so it violated its usual human associations only slightly; for ghosts had once been mortals even if they were no longer so, and ghosts in the days of King James were more domesticated than they have since become. The corresponding rear-stage traps in the public playhouses often served as graves—Ophelia's grave, for instance—but no play provides evidence that the rear-stage trap at Blackfriars was put to that use.

The trap sequences in two plays present special difficulties; they cross the boundaries just drawn, and refuse to be pigeonholed. One is the sequence that centers around the magic well or fountain in *The Faithful Shepherdess*, Act III. The well is involved in much that happens in that act. First the Sullen Shepherd lowers Amarillis into it at the end of a hempen cord and draws her up wet, transformed into the shape of Amoret. Later in the same scene he tries to drown the true Amoret by flinging her into the well, but *"the God of the River riseth with Amoret in his arms,"* heals her wounds, and then himself sinks again. The trap is thus traversed both by human beings and by mythological. The identification of the well with the rear-stage trap is suggested by Amarillis' description of it as having

> About the sides, all herbs which witches use,
> All simples good for medicine or abuse,
> All sweets that crown the happy nuptial day,
> With all their colours,

which sounds like a trap that has been bedecked by stagehands behind closed curtains. Besides, use of the rear-stage trap would have the advantage of making it impossible for gallery occupants to look down into a well that could only show itself to be dry, and its use is furthermore indicated by the fact that the well or fountain appears only in Act III, the one act in which the rear stage is not preempted by Clorin's bower. On the other hand, use of the platform trap is suggested by the well's involvement in the action, which seems to call for a trap more centrally located, and perhaps larger, than we can suppose the rear trap to have been, and by the desirability of having the God of the River rise by lift, rather than walk up stairs, with Amoret in his arms. As for the argument that only the rear trap could serve because only it could be rimmed with herbs to answer Amarillis' description, it need carry little weight; for Amarillis told of the herb-bordered sides of the well in II *iii*, and not until the next act was the well revealed; and in the interim the audience would have forgotten the herbs and simples. The alternatives are too evenly balanced to permit a confident solution.

Love and Honour contains a trap sequence that presents other difficulties. The Princess Evandra of Milan is a prisoner of war; her captor, Count Prospero, falls in love with her and conceals her in a "cave" to save her from the sworn vengeance of her enemy, the Duke of Savoy. In II *ii* Prospero and his friend Alvaro, son to the Duke, visit the cave.

> *Enter Alvaro, Prospero, with a Key and Lights. . . .*
> *Alvaro.*   With soft and gentle summons, call.
> *Prospero.*   Evandra! speak! ascend to us! I am
> Your penitential Enemy, who come
> To weep away my trespass at your feet.
> *Alv.*   Evandra! rise! break from this thick
> And silent darkness, like the first fair light.
> *The Stage opens, Prospero lifts Evandra up.*

Later "*They put Evandra down into the Cave,*" and both depart. But the vengeful Duke, unable to find the Princess, threatens death to Prospero and to his own son unless she is delivered to him. Wishing to save them, she tricks the two young men into going down into the cave so as to give her time to devise some plan. Alvaro is the first to go. In III *iv* he says "Give me the Light," and "*He descends the Cave.*"

> *Evandra.*   Lock safe the door, Melora, with this Key.
> *Pros.*   What's your design? Will you imprison him?

But later he too goes. "*Pros. takes from behind the Arras a Bottle and a Basket: they open the Cave. . . .* [*Prospero*] *descends the Cave,*" and again Evandra tells Melora to "lock the door; now they are both secure."

Which trap is used in this sequence? "*The Stage opens*" suggests the platform trap: not only does "stage" normally mean platform, but the phrase as a whole reminds one of the scene in *Caesar and Pompey* in which "*the gulf opens*" for the ascent of Ophioneus; it intimates, too, that the stage opens of itself without the aid of human hands. But why should the stage open to let Evandra climb out of a cave? It was proper enough that it should do so for Envy and Echo and Night and Neptune, but why for a mortal who might be expected to climb a ladder or stairs and emerge through the lockable door that is later mentioned twice? And what were Alvaro and Prospero doing before the stage opened? Were they addressing their invocation to a floor in which no rift had as yet appeared? In spite of the reference to "the stage,"[22] the locking of a door after each descent makes it seem probable that the rear-stage trap is used, and so does the taking of a bottle and basket from behind the arras. But any theory leaves as many questions unanswered as those that it solves.

Properties Thrust Out

On pages 348 and 349 I alluded briefly to the occasions on which properties were carried or thrust out on the platform in full view of the audience. Such properties include chairs, chests, couches or litters, bars, and even such large articles as a scaffold, tables, and beds.[23] Most of the episodes can be dismissed as being incidental to the plot or as reflecting the conditions of a day when domestic furnishings were scarcer than they are now, and when pieces of furniture were carried about from place to place as they were currently needed. But beds are in a special category. For one thing, the beds that are pushed out on the platform are always occupied:

From *Aglaura*, alternate Act v:

A bed put out: Thersames and Aglaura on it, Andrages by. . . . Draw in the bed.

From *The Cruel Brother*, v vi:

The Duke (on his Bed) is drawn forth.

365

From *The Lost Lady*, v *i:*

> *Enter the Moor on her bed, Hermione, Phillida, and Irene. The bed thrust out. . . . Exeunt. Draw in the bed.*

From *Monsieur Thomas*, v *i:*

> *A Bed discovered with a Black-moore in it.* . . . "Draw in the Bed, Maids, / And see it made again."

From *The Spanish Curate*, IV *v:*

> *Bed thrust out [with Diego on it].*

And from *The Wild-Goose Chase*, IV *iii:*

> *Enter Oriana on a Bed.*

The beds are necessarily thrust out *from somewhere*, and probably that place is the rear stage, since beds could be thrust through its wide forward aperture more easily than through a stage door. It thus seems probable that the beds and their occupants are initially discovered (as is stated specifically with respect to the bed in *Monsieur Thomas*) and that afterwards they are dragged forward on the platform so that the persons in them—who in all instances are central figures in the ensuing action—can the better be seen and heard. Thus the turning point in *The Lost Lady* comes when the dark-skinned Moor on the bed, fainting from the poison given her by Lysicles, is revealed as his beloved Milesia when her face is bathed; and Oriana, after entering on a bed in *The Wild-Goose Chase*, proceeds to enact an Ophelia-like mad scene in hopes of snaring a husband. This activity of the bed's occupant after being trundled in is an essential condition of all such scenes, and it is this consideration that removes any likelihood that Imogen's bed is thrust out. The scene in her bedchamber begins with the stage direction "*Enter Imogen, in her Bed, and a Lady,*" which parallels the "*enters*" in the two scenes just cited. But there the similarity ends, for Imogen has nothing to say or do after line 10.

Similarly, large properties are sometimes carried off the stage when the episode ends. According to the stage directions, the beds in *Aglaura*, *The Lost Lady*, and *Monsieur Thomas* are "drawn in," and probably, for the reason previously given, they are drawn into the rear stage. In *The Tempest*, III *iii*, the Strange Shapes carry out the banquet table in the course of their dance, and in *Henry VIII*, I *iv*, the tables in Cardinal Wolsey's palace are removed to make way for the dance, when the banquet is interrupted by the arrival of the King and his fellow maskers.

The articles that are thrust out are usually single pieces, or at the most a table and stools. When elaborate arrangements are involved, as for instance a goldsmith's or cobbler's shop or a presence chamber with a royal state, we may assume that they are set up in the rear stage and discovered. Incidentally, I find no Blackfriars play in which a state is thrust forward.

Dimensions of the Rear Stage

The rear stage at Blackfriars was called upon not merely to contain, but to make visible to the audience, such large properties and groups of actors as these: in *Love's Pilgrimage*, I *ii*, two beds, which at that period were of formidable size, and two in *The Parson's Wedding*, IV *vi* and V *ii*; in *Cymbeline*, II *ii*, a bed for Imogen, a table for her book and taper, and a trunk for Iachimo; in *Caesar and Pompey*, I *ii*, seats for the Roman consuls and senators, arranged on ascending tiers or "degrees"; in *The Knight of Malta*, V *ii*, an altar with steps leading up to it; in *A Wife for a Month*, II *vi*, a king and queen and at least ten courtiers and attendants, most of them presumably seated; and in *Henry VIII*, II *iv*, a throne for the King under a cloth of state, seats under him for the cardinals as judges, and other seats for bishops, lords, and scribes.

Under such circumstances, the rear stage needed all the width it could get; and that maximum width, as measured across the front aperture of the inner stage, was probably about 19 feet. This figure is arrived at by deducting the allowances previously discussed, for stage-sitters, for two oblique doors and their frames, and 3 feet more for the frame at the two sides of the rear-stage aperture itself, from 46 feet as the whole width of the stage. The 19-foot width is 4 feet narrower than that at the Globe is conjectured to have been, but Blackfriars had compensating advantages. The inner stage at the Globe was viewed from three sides over an angle of about 120 degrees, and therefore needed a wide aperture to permit spectators to see into its interior. The rear stage at Blackfriars, on the other hand, was viewed by spectators spread over a relatively narrow arc, and thus needed to make less allowance for divergent sight lines.

The rear stage stretched back for an uncertain distance behind the scenic wall, occupying the first few feet of a back-stage area whose whole depth was 35 feet. With so deep a space at his disposal, James Burbage was not, like the builders of the public playhouses, forced to restrict his rear stage to a depth of about 7 or 8 feet, and the crossover passageway behind it to a width of about 5;[24] and both because he was subject to no such limitations and because the Blackfriars sight lines were more favorable, he may have made his rear stage 9 feet deep, and his passageway, a part of whose width was necessarily sacrificed to a staircase, 6 feet wide. On this basis, the two elements together would have the same depth as Sir William Davenant had at his disposal when he produced *The Siege of Rhodes* at Rutland House in 1656;[25] and although Sid William deplored a depth of 15 feet as being like "Caesars carv'd upon a Nut" in comparison with what he needed for his elaborate scenery, it probably was adequate for the unsceneried productions at Blackfriars.

For reasons that will be given later,[26] the floor of the upper stage is believed to have been 9 feet above the surface of the platform. After making allowances for the thickness of the upper-stage's floor-planking and its supporting beams, one may therefore suppose that the ceiling of the lower inner stage was a few inches more than 8 feet high.

The Tiring-House

The backstage area of an Elizabethan playhouse was called the tiring-house. Shakespeare uses the word in *A Midsummer Night's Dream*, III *i*. When the Athenian rustics are about to begin their outdoor rehearsal of *Pyramus and Thisby*, Quince says

> Here's a marvail's convenient place for our rehearsal. This green plot shall be our stage, this hawthorn brake our tiring house.

Ben Jonson uses the term in three of his Blackfriars plays. In *The Magnetic Lady*, IV *vii*, he has Chaire say

> Wee shall marre all, if once we ope the mysteries
> O' the Tyring-house, and tell what's done within.

In the Induction to *The Staple of News*, Mirth, in speaking of the poet, says

> Yonder he is within (I was i' the Tiring-house a while to see the Actors drest) rowling himselfe up and down like a tun.

And in the Induction to *Cynthia's Revels*, the Third Child, impersonating a playgoer, asks where he can find the play's author, and receives this reply:

> Not this way, I assure you, sir: wee are not so officiously befriended by him, as to have his presence in the tiring-house, to prompt us aloud, stampe at the booke-holder, sweare for our properties, curse the poore tire-man, raile the musicke out of tune, and sweat for everie veniall trespasse we commit.

The tiring-house at Blackfriars lay just behind the rear stage and the crossover alleyway; from there it probably stretched back to the far end of the Parliament Chamber. It was thus roughly 20 feet deep from north to south, by the full 46 feet wide. It provided attiring or dressing rooms, wardrobes for costumes, closets for wigs and beards, lockers for play scripts, and storage space for properties. It had rooms where actors could wait between their scenes, and corridors where armies and processions could form their ranks. Seldom-used properties could be stored in rooms beneath the Parliament Chamber, and brought up to the stage by means of the platform trap.

1. These three stage directions are to be found in *Barnavelt*, IV *iii*; *Catiline*, I *i*; and *Goblins*, Act V, all of which are Blackfriars plays. Possessive attributives are used also in connection with "study" in all the following plays (Blackfriars plays being distinguished by asterisks): **Aglaura*, Act I; *Devil's Charter*, I *iv* and IV *i* (twice); *Doctor Faustus*, I *i*; **Fair Maid of the Inn*, IV *ii*; *Histriomastix*, Act I (twice) and Act V; **Law Tricks*, IV *ii* and V *ii*; *Massacre at Paris*, line 438; **News from Plymouth*, IV *ii*; **Novella*, I *ii*; *Ram Alley*, sig. B3ᵛ; *Thomas Lord Cromwell*, III *ii* (dialogue); *Tragedy of Sforza*, V *iii*, *Two Noble Ladies*, line 82; and *Woman Hater*, V *i* (three times).

2. I.e., the gentlewoman Pecunia in *Staple of News*, II *v* (a Blackfriars play). "Study" is preceded by "the" in *Hamlet*, Q¹, Scene *vi*, and in *Thomas Lord Cromwell*, III *ii* (stage direction). It is preceded by "a" in *Satiromastix*, I *ii*.

3. In saying so I am taking issue with the late W. J. Lawrence, who said that the five words had precisely the same significance (*Physical Conditions*, pp. 29–30).

4. *Brennoralt*, Act V (twice); *City Match*, III *ii* and V *vii*; *Cynthia's Revels*, Induction; *Dutch Courtesan*, V *i*; *Faithful Shepherdess*, V *i* (twice); *Guardian*, III *vi* (three times); *Henry VIII*, II *ii*; *Lover's Progress*, III *iii* (three times); *Mad Lover*, V *i* and V *iii* (twice); *News from Plymouth*, IV *ii*; *Parson's Wedding*, IV *vi* and V *ii* (three times); *Sea Voyage*, IV *iii*; *Sir Giles Goosecap*, V *ii* (four times); *Wife for a Month*, Act II; etc. In this meaning, the word "curtain" (singular) is used about twice as often as "curtains" (plural). Only once does a dramatist use the full phrase, "the stage curtains." This is in *Parson's Wedding*, V *ii*.

5. *Emperor of the East*, I *ii*; *Goblins*, Act V.

6. *City Match*, III *ii*; *Fatal Dowry*, II *ii*; *Valentinian*, II *iv*; and perhaps *Winter's Tale*, V *iii*; but I think it more likely that the curtain that conceals Hermione as a statue is the curtain at the front edge of the rear stage.

7. *Parson's Wedding*, V *ii*; *Trick to Catch*, IV *v*; *Wonder of Women*, I *ii* (three times), III *i*, V *i*.

8. *Anything for a Quiet Life*, IV *i*; *City Match*, II *iii*, III *ii*, and V *vii* (three times); *Custom of the Country*, II *iv*; *Law Tricks*, III *i*; *Lover's Progress*, III *iii* (twice); *New Inn*, Dedication; *News from Plymouth*, IV *v*; *Northern Lass*, IV *iii*; *Philaster*, II *i* (twice); *Rule a Wife*, III *i*, IV *iii* (twice); *Swisser*, IV *ii*; *Variety*, IV *iv*; *Wits*, I *i*, II *ii*, II *iv*; etc.

9. *Anything for a Quiet Life*, II *i*, V *i*; *Cymbeline*, II *ii*; *Duchess of Malfi*, I *ii* (three times); *Honest Man's Fortune*, III *iii* (twice); *Law Tricks*, III *i* (three times); *Love and Honour*, III *iv*; *New Inn*, Dedication; *Noble Gentleman*, III *iv*; *Platonic Lovers*, V *i*, V *vi*; *Swisser*, I *ii* (three times); *Trick to Catch*, II *i*; *Unfortunate Lovers*, IV *vi*; *Women Pleased*, IV *iii*; etc.

10. *Believe As You List*, IV *ii*; *Cruel Brother*, III *i* and V *i*; *Distresses*, IV *v*; *Lover's Melancholy*, II *ii*; *Maid in the Mill*, I–II; etc.

11. *Godly Queen Hester* (?1525–1529), twice; *Volpone*; *White Devil*. Cf. Chambers, *Elizabethan Stage*, Vol. III, pp. 25–26.

12. *Anything for a Quiet Life*, II *ii*; *Broken Heart*, III *ii*; *Catiline*, I *i*; *Eastward Ho!*, I *i*; *Imposture*, I *iii*; *Knight of Malta*, IV *i*; *Lost Lady*, I *ii*; *Mayor of Quinboro*, I *ii*; *Monsieur Thomas*, V *i*; *Parson's Wedding*, IV *i*; *Wife for a Month*, III *i*; *Your Five Gallants*, II *iii*, etc. In *The Widow's Tears*, the rear stage, as representing the interior of a mauso-

leum, is revealed in IV *ii*, IV *iii*, V *i*, V *ii*, and V *iii*.

13. Curtains are opened by visible agents in *Brennoralt*, Acts III and V; *City Match*, III *ii* and V *vii*; *Guardian*, III *vi*; *Henry VIII*, II *ii*; *Lover's Melancholy*, II *ii*; *Sir Giles Goosecap*, V *ii*; *Unfortunate Lovers*, V *v* (twice); *Wife for a Month*, III *i*; etc. Discoveries are effected by visible agents, but without specific mention of curtains, in *Caesar and Pompey*, IV *v*, and *Double Marriage*, II *iii*.

14. Beds were sometimes pushed out upon the stage, but I am convinced that Imogen's was not. The question of "beds thrust out" is discussed on pp. 365 to 366 above.

15. Similar "entrances" occur in *2 Arviragus and Philicia*, Act III; *Brennoralt*, Acts I, II, and III; *Guardian*, III *ix*; *Humorous Lieutenant*, II *iii*; *Inconstant Lady*, V *iii*; *Knight of the Burning Pestle*, I *ii*; *Lost Lady*, V *i*; *Lover's Progress*, III *v*; *Maid's Tragedy*, V *i*; *Pilgrim*, V *vi*; *Trick to Catch the Old One*, IV *v*; *Women Pleased*, I *ii*; etc.

16. Two writers on the Elizabethan stage have suggested that Hermione, in her role as statue, may have been concealed by a temporary curtain or "traverse" within the rear stage, rather than by the ordinary curtains in the line of the scenic wall (John Cranford Adams, *Globe Playhouse*, pp. 187–88, and R. Crompton Rhodes, *Stagery of Shakespeare*, p. 39). I base my contrary opinion upon the assumption that the regular curtains were available and wholly adequate, that special curtains would inevitably have attracted the attention of Leontes, who up to the moment of discovery remains innocent of any suspicion as to the whereabouts of the statue for which he has been searching, and that in this critical scene the actors would have wished to have the statue stand as far to the front as the curtain line would permit.

17. Characters enter after knocking in the following scenes also: *Barnavelt*, V *iii*; *Duchess of Malfi*, III *iii*; *Fair Favorite*, III *ii*; *Love and Honour*, II *ii*; *Mad Lover*, III *vi*; *Parson's Wedding*, IV *iv*; *Witch*, IV *ii*; *Wits*, II *i*; etc. The back window is not involved in any of these episodes. In scenes that require a character to leave the stage in order to see who is knocking or to open the door, the door is obviously an imaginary one off-stage.

18. *The Coxcomb*, II *i*, seems to be an exception to my generalization about knocking before entrance. Viola knocks, is "at the street door," and speaks "within," and yet she probably is not standing outside the back door. That door must serve three times as an interior door leading to the stairs, and it could not, without causing confusion, serve also in the same scene as an exterior door leading to the street. Besides, Viola speaks "within" four times, and she would need a wicket to make herself heard. Presumably she stands outside one of the outer-stage doors as on the street, and the platform serves as a hall in Antonio's house.

19. The back door is locked also in *Duke of Milan*, V *ii*; *Fair Favorite*, III *ii*; *Island Princess*, III *iii*; *Knight of Malta*, IV *ii*; *Novella*, I *ii*; etc. *Alchemist*, IV *v*, contains the stage direction "*He speakes through the key-hole, the other knocking.*"

20. See also *Anything for a Quiet Life*, IV *i*; *City Madam*, IV *iv*; *Rule a Wife*, IV *iii*, etc.

21. See also *Anything for a Quiet Life*, V *i*; *Custom of the Country*, II *iv*; *Law Tricks*, III *i*; *Honest Man's Fortune*, III *iii*; *Lover's Progress*, III *iii*; *News from Plymouth*, IV *i*; *Northern Lass*, IV *iii*; *Philaster*, II *i*; *Platonic Lovers*, V *i* and V *vi*; *Swisser*, I *ii* and IV *ii*; *Unfortunate Lovers*, IV *vi*; etc. In all these

episodes, the means of concealment is called "the arras" or "the hangings." Only once is it called "the curtain," in *Dutch Courtesan*, V *i*, on which occasion I believe the curtains at the front edge of the rear stage to have been used.

22. On p. 343 I said that Davenant was the only Blackfriars dramatist who speaks of "hangings" as being "drawn." Here he may be using "stage" as meaning some place other than the platform, in which event he is again the only Blackfriars dramatist that does so.

23. Tables are brought on in *Henry VIII*, V *iii*; *Imposture*, V *i*; *Love and Honour*, III *iv*; *Love's Pilgrimage*, I *i*; *Platonic Lovers*, II *ii*; *Swisser*, I *ii*; *Variety*, II *i*, IV *iv*, V *i*; etc. Bars are brought on in *Queen of Corinth*, I *iv*, and *Barnavelt*, IV *v*. A scaffold is set out in *Barnavelt*, V *iii*.

24. John Cranford Adams, *Globe Playhouse*, pp. 171–72.

25. See p. 275 above.

26. See pp. 411–412 below.

⚔ 16 ⚔

The Playhouse:
THE UPPER STAGES

BY MY COUNT, 102 stage directions in fifty-four Blackfriars plays embody the word *"above"* as an indication that the dramatist intended to have the specified action occupy some part or parts of an upper stage.[1] Those parts were as follows:

> Two windows, one above each of the outer-stage doors;
> A balcony or "tarras" which stretched across the façade
>   of the scenic wall from one window to the other;
> An upper inner stage behind the tarras;
> And, as has already been mentioned, a gallery over each end of the platform,
>   forming a continuation of the spectator galleries and abutting upon one of
>   the window stages.

Action on the upper level was almost invariably related to action on the level below, and this relationship determined the distinctive use or uses of each of the upper stages. Thus when a person inside a house had occasion to talk with a person outside, a window was appropriately used. When both persons were supposedly outdoors, the tarras was used in combination with the platform, serving perhaps as the battlement of a castle, the balcony outside a palace, the quarterdeck of a ship, or any other elevated surface under the open sky. When both persons were supposedly indoors, the tarras was sometimes used, serving then as a balcony inside a hall; but sometimes, under special conditions, a side-wall gallery was called into service as a place from which persons above could spy upon persons below. In the infrequent scenes that involved discoveries on the upper level or action within an upstairs room inside

373

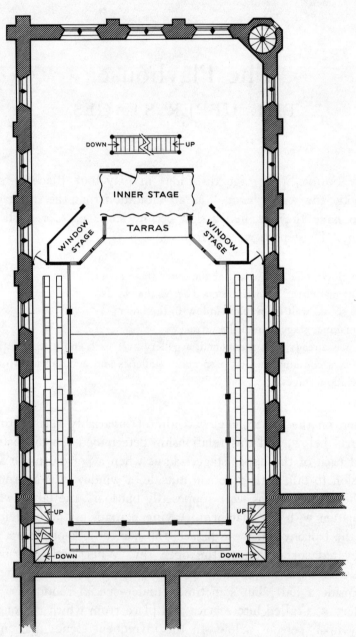

*Figure 23. A conjectural plan of the Blackfriars Playhouse
at the level of the middle gallery and the upper stage.*

a house, the upper inner stage was used. Each of these relationships will be examined in the pages that follow.

The Window Stages

Of the 102 stage directions just mentioned as incorporating the word *"above,"* 22 directions in twenty plays use it with reference to action that takes place at an upstairs window. The upper-level position of the windows is stated repeatedly, as for instance in these stage directions from Blackfriars plays:

From *The Duke of Milan,* ii *i*:

Marcelia appears at a Window above, in black.

From *Henry VIII,* v *ii*:

Enter the King, and Buts, at a Windowe above.

And from *The Poetaster,* iv *ix*:

Shee appeareth above, as at her chamber window.

Windows are also mentioned in stage directions or dialogue as a place of action, and their upper-level situation specifically stated or unambiguously implied, in the Blackfriars plays listed in the footnote.[2]

Under all normal circumstances, the windows were the means by which a person inside a house could talk with a person outside, and, except for the few scenes in which persons talked through the wicket in an outer-stage door, they provided the only means by which an indoor-to-outdoor conversation could be conducted. Whenever, therefore, an actor indoors and "above" exchanges words with someone in a street or garden outside, it may be taken for granted that he does so by way of a window, even though no window is specified. One may thus confidently suppose that Cicero speaks to Vargunteius and Cornelius from an upstairs window in *Catiline,* iii *v;* that Pharamond and Megra speak so to the King in *Philaster,* ii *iii;* that Franceschina does so to the chimneysweep in *May Day,* iii *ii;* Eurione to Vandome in *Monsieur D'Olive,* v *i;* Shattillion to his Love in *The Noble Gentleman,* iv *iii,* and so on.[3]

Students of the pre-Restoration drama have generally assumed that a window surmounted each of the outer-stage doors. This assumption is not based upon any quotable line in stage direction or in dialogue, but upon the many scenes in which a window and a door are presumed to be parts of the same house. A door and window serve together in this relationship in each of the plays mentioned in the last paragraph, and in many more besides; and the close association between them could, of course, best be made obvious to spectators by placing them in the same wall. This window-over-door relationship implies that two windows existed, and implies also that they were as far apart as the doors themselves were. Both these propositions are confirmed by *The Picture*, IV *ii*, a scene that will be discussed shortly.

The windows projected from the scenic wall as three-sided bay windows, which again was characteristic of Tudor domestic architecture. They are described as bay windows in *Love and Honour*, v *i*, when Altesto says "Come Boys, lift up your voices to yon bay Window," and in an episode in *The Parson's Wedding*, I *iii*, that begins with the stage direction "*Widow and Pleasant looking out at a window*," and that has the Widow say "I shall love this bay-window."

Like their prototypes in real life, the windows could be opened and closed. In *Love and Honour*, v *ii*, Alvaro says "The Casement now is open," and in *The Widow*, I *i*, Philippa says "Open not the window, an' you love me." Frank, in *The Captain*, II *ii*, bids Clora "Shut the window," and Ismena, in *The Maid in the Mill*, I *iii*, brings the scene to an end with "Pluck to the windows." Elizabethan windows were glazed with rectangular or diamond-shaped panes of thick glass called "quarries," held together by lead strips called "cames." They had little transparency, and any actor who appeared in a window stage must always open the casements so that he might be seen and heard.

On occasion, but perhaps not all the time, the windows were fitted with curtains. In *Monsieur D'Olive*, I *i*, Vandome has the lines

> And see, methinks, through the encurtain'd windows
> (In this high time of day) I see light tapers.
> This is exceeding strange!

In *The Parson's Wedding*, I *iii*, a stage direction says "*Widow shuts the curtain*." In *The Picture*, IV *ii*, Ubaldo and Ricardo are in two different windows, and at the end of the scene "*They draw the Curtains*"; and in

Henry VIII, v *ii*, the King, having witnessed Cranmer's rebuff from an upper window, tells Dr. Butts to "Let 'em alone, and draw the curtain close."

Probably a substantial perpendicular mullion ran down the central face of each window and divided it into two lights. This division of a window into two casements was a commonplace of the household architecture of the time,[4] and may account for an occasional plural "windows" in Blackfriars plays where one would expect a singular "window." Thus only one window can be intended, in spite of the plural, in *The Parson's Wedding*, II *vii*. The stage direction says "*Enter (at the windows) the Widow and Master Careless, Mistress Pleasant and Master Wild, Captain, Master Sad, Constant, Jolly, Secret: a table and knives ready for oysters.*" But everything that happens in the course of this long scene indicates that the nine persons compose one group in one window. Only one table is specified, and when the oysters are served only one person serves them. If the plural "windows" is not a misprint, it implies that a single window, divided into two halves by a mullion, is here spoken of as being two.[5]

I mention the matter not because it is important in itself, but because it provides a clue to the original staging of the difficult prison sequence in *The Two Noble Kinsmen*. In II *i* of that play, the Jailer and his Daughter stand on the platform as in a garden outside the castle in which Palamon and Arcite are imprisoned. At line 58 comes the stage direction "*Enter Palamon and Arcite above.*" Their being at a window is not immediately stated, but is implied in their being visible to the Jailer and his Daughter:

Jailer.   Look, yonder they are! That's Arcite looks out.
Daughter.   No, sir, no; that's Palamon. Arcite is the lower of the twain; you may perceive a part of him.
Jailer.   Go to, leave your pointing. They would not make us their object. Out of their sight!
Daugh.   It is a holiday to look on them. Lord, the difference of men!

The next scene begins with the stage direction "*Enter Palamon and Arcite in prison.*" There has been no change of place or stage. The platform is still the garden beneath the castle walls. Emilia will soon walk in it with her woman, and the kinsmen will watch her from their window or windows above. The word "window" is first used when the cousins' former love changes to bitter enmity out of rivalry for Emilia. Their frantic threats show that they can strike each others' heads if the heads are out of the window, but that otherwise neither can reach the other. Lines 212 to 219 can be explained only on the assumption that the men are at two windows, or two halves of a single window—Palamon uses the singular noun at line 212 and the Keeper the plural at 262—which are immediately adjacent to each other. Inside the castle walls, however, the kinsmen occupy separate cells with a partition between.

> *Palamon.* Put but thy head out of this window more,
>   And, as I have a soul, I'll nail thy life to't!
> *Arcite.* Thou dar'st not, fool; thou canst not; thou art feeble.
>   Put my head out? I'll throw my body out,
>   And leap the garden, when I see her next, . . .
>   And pitch between her arms to anger thee.
> *Pal.* No more! the keeper's coming. I shall live
>   To knock thy brains out with my shackles.

As for the Keeper, he necessarily enters above, since he is on the same level as the kinsmen; and since he sees and speaks to both of them and they to him, he probably enters by way of the tarras.

In contrast with this prison scene, that in *The Picture*, IV *ii*, requires two windows several feet apart. The episode deals with two courtiers, Ubaldo and Ricardo, who are laying siege to the honor of the chaste Sophia. She lets each of them think that she is ready to yield:

> *Ubald.* But when?
> *Sophia.* Why, presently; follow my woman,
>   She knows where to conduct you, and will serve
>   To night for a page.

Ubaldo departs under the conduct of Corisca, and then Ricardo in his turn is dismissed with a servant to guide him. Sophia is alone for a few lines, and then comes this stage direction:

> *A noise of clapping a door; Ubaldo appears above, in his shirt.*
> *Ubald.* What dost thou mean, wench?
>   Why dost thou shut the door upon me? Ha!
>   My clothes are ta'en away too! shall I starve here?
>   Is this my lodging? . . .

> 'Slight, 'tis a prison, or a pigsty. Ha!
> The windows grated with iron! I cannot force them,
> And if I leap down here, I break my neck. . . .
> *Soph.* Let him rave, he's fast;
> I'll parley with him at leisure.
>> *Ricardo entering with a great noise above, as fallen.*
> *Ricardo.* Zounds! have you trapdoors?
> *Soph.* The other bird's i' the cage too, let him flutter.
> *Ric.* Whither am I fallen? into hell!
> *Ubald.* Who makes that noise, there?
> Help me, if thou art a friend.
> *Ric.* A friend! I am where
> I cannot help myself; let me see thy face.
> *Ubald.* How, Ricardo! Prithee, throw me
> Thy cloak, if thou canst, to cover me; I am almost
> Frozen to death.
> *Ric.* My cloak! I have no breeches;
> I am in my shirt, as thou art; and here's nothing
> For myself but a clown's cast suit.

Ubaldo is imprisoned behind a window "grated with iron"; and although the text fails to say that Ricardo is imprisoned similarly, he undoubtedly is: both men are *"above,"* and both are treated alike in the sequel by those on the stage below. But they are in separate cells, and so far apart that Ubaldo's plea is not that Ricardo should hand him his cloak, but that he should throw it to him "if thou canst."

In *Eastward Ho!*, Security's place of confinement is identifiable as a window stage through its similarity to the two scenes just described. Here the platform serves as the lobby or common room of a jail. Bramble enters (v *iii*) and is met by the keeper, Holdfast:

> *Holdfast.* Who would you speak with, sir?
> *Bramble.* I would speak with one Security, that is prisoner here.
> *Hold.* You are welcome, sir! Stay there, I'll call him to you.
> Master Security!
> *Security.* Who calls?
> *Hold.* Here's a gentleman would speak with you.
> *Sec.* What is he?

A few lines later he recognizes Bramble. At lines 19–20 he says "My case, Master Bramble, is stone walls and iron grates; you see it, this is the weakest part on't. And for getting me forth, no means but hang myself, and so be carried forth, from which they have bound me in intolerable bands." Although Security is able to talk with persons on the platform, he cannot, on account of his bands, walk out upon the stage, and his off-stage position is confirmed by Quicksilver's plea to Bramble, "Good sir, go in and talk with him. The light does him harm." A window stage, and only a window stage, satisfies all the conditions.

As was said a few pages back, the window casements could be opened and closed; and doubtless, like those in contemporary homes, they could also be removed from their frames. A writer on the domestic architecture of the period says that

> the detachable butt was an invention inspired by necessity or, at least, convenience. For in the reign of the first Tudors glazed window sash were a luxury, and your nobleman, when he traveled from one of his country seats to another, not only carried his bed and other furniture, but, with his tapestries to keep out the drafts, he unhinged his windows and brought those along.[6]

And another writer says that, until Lord Coke ruled otherwise in 1597, casements were considered to be removable pieces of furniture, and not integral parts of a house:

> In 1597 a legal decision was given on the point whether glass in removable frames was furniture or a fixture. As a previous decision was reversed, it has a special interest: "Glass fixed by nails to windows or in any other manner cannot be moved, for without glass is no perfect house."[7]

The removability of windows is also testified to in a play produced by the King's Men at Blackfriars. In *Anything for a Quiet Life*, I i, Chamlet speaks of "the taking down and setting up again of my Glass-windows."

Two of the prison scenes just cited make specific mention of iron grates. Ubaldo, in *The Picture*, says "The windows grated with iron! I cannot force them"; and Security, in *Eastward Ho!*, speaks of "stone walls and iron grates." In view of the ease with which window sash could be removed from its frame, it seems likely that the audience at Blackfriars was not asked to imagine iron grates in prison scenes; instead, casements fitted with grating were substituted for the usual casements fitted with leaded glass.

Nine persons appear at a window in *The Parson's Wedding*, IV vii. Even though it is not necessary to suppose that all nine persons are visible at the window all the time, the size of the group still suggests that the bay windows on the Blackfriars stage were of considerable size. Figure 23 therefore shows each window as being 7 feet wide across its central face, and as being 12 or 13 feet wide at its greatest span.

The Tarras

Two Blackfriars plays use the word "tarras" to designate an element of the upper stage or the place it represents. *The Knight of Malta* uses the word once, and spells it "tarrase." *May Day* uses it seven times, and spells it "tarrasse." Four other Blackfriars plays use it in dialogue, but not as referring to places on-stage.[8]

In the *The Knight of Malta*, Zanthia brings 1 *ii* to a close with "Hist, wenches: my Lady calls, she's entring / The Tarrase, to see the show," the show being the ceremony by which two gentlemen will be invested with the badge of the Order of Knights of Malta. The next scene is in the great hall of the Grand Master of the Order, with the tarras serving as an indoor balcony; it begins with the stage direction "*Enter (above) Oriana, Zanthia, two Gentlewomen, (beneath) Valetta, Mountferrat, Astorius, Castriot, Gomera, Miranda, Attendants of knights, etc.*"

Although the tarras is not named, it is unquestionably the unit of the stage upon which ten persons enter "*above*" in *The False One*, III *iv*, to watch the masque and other diversions on the stage below. The stage directions read "*Enter Caesar, Antony, Dolabella, Sceva, above. . . . Enter Cleopatra. . . . Enter Ptolemy, Achoreus, Achillas, Photinus, Apollodorus,*" all of them also undoubtedly above; and presently "*Music. Enter below, in a Masque, Isis, and three Labourers.*"

The tarras serves the same purpose, as a place for the observation of events on the platform, in other plays also. In *The Maid's Tragedy*, 1 *ii*, Melantius seeks a place for his Lady from which she will be able to watch the masque soon to be presented.

Melantius.   Open the door.
Diagoras.   Who's there?
Mel.   Melantius.
Diag.   I hope your Lordship brings no troop with you, for if you do, I must
return them.   *Enter Melantius.*
Mel.   None but this Lady Sir.
Diag.   The Ladies are all plac'd above, save those that come in the Kings
Troop, the best of Rhodes sit there, and there's room.

Again, before the King enters his throne room in *The Humorous Lieutenant*, ɪ *i*, the First Usher says "Madams, the best way is the upper lodgings, / There you may see at ease."

All the foregoing scenes presumably take place within the walls of a palace or castle, and under such conditions the tarras automatically assumes the character of a balcony within a great hall. In *A Trick to Catch the Old One*, ɪv *iv*, it serves in humbler circumstances as an indoor balcony from which the Niece drops her note to Master Witgood:

> *Niece.* Master Witgood!
> *Witgood.* My life!
> *Niece.* Meet me presently; that note directs you. [*Drops him a paper.*]
>   I would not be suspected. Our happiness attends us. Farewell!
> *Witg.* A word's enough.

May Day treats the tarras as a balcony projecting from the outer wall of a building, and proves that a man could climb up to it by means of a rope ladder, and could climb from it into a bedchamber by way of a window. The incident develops as follows: Aurelio, a Venetian gentleman, is in love with Æmilia and she with him, but they have never told their love to each other. Lodovico, cousin to Æmilia, offers to bring Aurelio to her, and in Act ɪɪ Scene *i* he asks her where the interview can be held.

> *Æmilia.* There is the mischief, and we shall hardly avoid it; my father plies my haunts so closely, and uses means by our maid to entrap us, so that this tarras[9] at our back gate is the only place we may safely meet at, from whence I can stand and talk to you. But, sweet coz, you shall swear to keep this my kindness from Aurelio, and not intimate by any means that I am anything acquainted with his coming.
> *Lodovico.* 'Slife, dost think I am an ass? To what end should I tell him? He and I'll come wandering that way to take the air, or so, and I'll discover thee.
> *Æem.* By mere chance, as 'twere.
> *Lod.* By chance, by chance; and you shall at no hand see him at first, when I bring him, for all this kindness you bear him.
> *Æem.* By no means, coz. . . .
> *Lod.* Well, dame, leave your superfluous nicety in earnest, and within this hour I will bring him to this tarras.
> *Æem.* But, good coz, if you chance to see my chamber window open, that is upon the tarras, do not let him come in at it in any case.

Lod. 'Sblood, how can he? Can he come over the wall, think'st?

Æm. O sir, you men have not devices with ladders of ropes to scale such walls at your pleasure, and abuse us poor wenches.

Lod. Now a plague of your simplicity! Would you discourage him with prompting him? Well, dame, I'll provide for you.

Æm. As you love me, coz, no words of [any] kindness from me to him.

Lod. Go to, no more ado! *Exeunt.*

Act III Scene *iii* begins with the stage direction "*Enter Lodovico with a ladder of ropes, Aurelio; Æmilia above.*"

Lod. Here's thy ladder, and there's thy gallows; thy mistress is thy hangman, and must take thee down. This is the tarras where thy sweetheart tarries. . . .

Æm. Cousin Lodovic!

Lod. Who calls Lodovic?

Æm. What tempest hath cast you on this solitary shore? Is the party come?

Lod. The party? Now a plague of your modesty, are your lips too nice to name Aurelio?

Æm. Well, is he come then?

Lod. He? Which he? 'Sfoot, name your man with a mischief to you! I understand you not.

Æm. Was there ever such a wild-brain? Aurelio!

Lod. Aurelio? Lord, how loath you are to let any sound of him come out on you, you hold him so dear within. . . . Hold you, fasten the end of this ladder, I pray!

Æm. Now Jesus bless us! Why cousin, are you mad? . . .

Lod. Go to, tell me, will you fasten the ladder or no?

Æm. I know not what I should say t'ye. I will fasten it, so only yourself will come up.

Lod. Only myself will come up, then.

Æm. Nay, sweet coz, swear it!

Lod. If I should swear, thou wouldst curse me; take my word, in a halter's name, and make the ladder as fast to the tarras as thou wouldst be to Aurelio. . . .

Æm. Well, coz, here I have fastened it for your pleasure. . . .

Lod. Come, sir, mount!

Æm. O cousin Lodovic, do you thus cozen and betray me? . . . What does he know?

Lod. Why, all that thou told'st me, that thou lov'st him more than he can love thee, that thou hast set up thy resolution, in despite of friends or foes, weals or woes, to let him possess thee wholly, and that thou didst woo

383

me to bring him hither to thee; all this he knows — that it was thy device to prepare this ladder, and, in a word, all the speech that passed betwixt thee and me, he knows. . . . Mount, I say!

Aurelio mounts, and he and Æmilia exeunt into the house. A later scene (v i) tells of his having had "the help of a ladder to creep in at a wench's chamber-window."

The foregoing sequence shows that the tarras abutted upon one window stage. The sequence that follows shows that it abutted upon the other as well, and thus that it spanned the façade of the tiring-house from one window to the other. Act ii of *The Devil Is an Ass* treats the windows as being those of two neighboring houses, one the home of Mrs. Fitzdottrel and the other the home of Eustace Manly, and it treats the tarras as being a gallery upon which both windows open. A gallant named Wittipol desires closer acquaintance with Mrs. Fitzdottrel, and has sent her a message suggesting a meeting. She is not unwilling to respond to his advances, but she mistrusts the messenger, whom she suspects of having been hired by her husband to spy upon her. Her reply to Wittipol is therefore couched in equivocal terms:

> Bid him put off his hopes of straw. . . . I am no such foule,
> Nor faire one, tell him, will be had with stalking,
> And wish him to for-beare his acting to mee,
> At the Gentlemans chamber-window in Lincolnes-Inne there,
> That opens to my gallery.

Wittipol interprets her message correctly and forthwith betakes himself to the chamber of Manly, who happens to be his friend:

> This was a fortune, happy above thought,
> That this should prove thy chamber; which I fear'd
> Would be my greatest trouble! this must be
> The very window, and that the roome.

A moment later Mrs. Fitzdottrel comes upstairs to her own window. At first she fails to see Wittipol, and fears that her message has been misdelivered or misunderstood; but then she hears singing and catches sight of him standing in the chamber window that opens to her gallery. As their courtship progresses, they are close enough together for Wittipol to be able to say that

Love hath the honour to approach
These sister-swelling brests; and touch this soft
And rosie hand.

The probability is, therefore, that he has climbed from Manly's chamber window to Mrs. Fitzdottrel's gallery (the tarras), has walked the length of the gallery, and that he now stands at its end, close to Mrs. Fitzdottrel's open window and its occupant.[10] The supposition that he has crossed to her window, rather than she to his, is strengthened by later stage directions which say that *"Her husband appeares at her back. . . . Hee speakes out of his wives window."* This reconstruction of the stage business conflicts with a marginal note in the 1640 Folio, stating that *"This Scene is acted at two windo's, as out of two contiguous buildings"*; but this note in turn fails to accord with Mrs. Fitzdottrel's allusion to the chamber window that opens to her gallery. Probably the marginal note just quoted, like another marginal direction mentioned on page 303 above, was added by Ben Jonson for the information of readers when he was editing the play for the press, long after its first performances at Blackfriars.

Shakespeare's only use of the word "tarras" comes in *2 Henry VI*, the play presumed to have been the first that he wrote. In IV *ix* of that play he has the stage direction *"Enter King, Queene, and Somerset on the Tarras,"* with the tarras serving as the battlements of Killingworth Castle. After that he used the tarras similarly, but without naming it specifically, to represent the ramparts of beleaguered castles or towns in nearly all his historical plays. It is so used by other dramatists in eight plays written for production at Blackfriars. Thus in *Bonduca*, IV *iv*, the Queen and her daughters appear upon the tarras as upon the parapets of a fortress that the Roman legions are besieging. The stage direction reads thus: *"Enter Swetonius, Junius, Decius, Demetrius, Curius, and Souldiers: Bonduca, two Daughters, and Nennius, above. Drum and Colours."*

> *Swetonius.* Bring up the Catapults and shake the wall,
>   We will not be [out-brav'd] thus.
> *Nennius.* Shake the earth,
>   Ye cannot shake our souls. Bring up your Rams,
>   And with their armed heads, make the Fort totter;
>   Ye do but rock us into death.
> *Junius.* See, Sir,

385

> See the Icenian Queen in all her glory
> From the strong battlements proudly appearing,
> As if she meant to give us lashes.

The tarras represents walls, ramparts, or battlements in seven other Blackfriars plays, none of which mentions it by name. *The Mayor of Quinborough*, v *ii*, has *"above"* in the main stage direction, and *"on ye walls"* in a marginal note. Three other plays make similar use of the word *"above"* in stage directions,[11] and four say *"on the walls."*[12]

On at least three occasions the tarras becomes a hill. In *Bonduca*, III *v*, the direction *"Enter Drusus and Penyus above"* is followed by these lines of dialogue:

> *Drusus.*   Here ye may see 'em all, Sir; from this hill
>   The Country shews off levell.
> *Penyus.*   Gods defend me,
>   What multitudes they are, what infinities.[13]

In *The Sea Voyage*, I *iii*, *"Aminta above"* is on a hill whence she calls down warnings that the ship is floating away, and about ten lines later *"La-mure and Franville goes up to see the ship."* In II *i* of the same play, Albert says

> Follow me, my Aminta: my good genius,
> Shew me the way still; still we are directed;
> When we gain the top of this near rising hill,
> We shall know further.   *Exit, and Enter above.*

In *The Wonder of Women*, v *ii*, a scene difficult to envision on any hypothesis, *"Cornets sound a march Scipio leads his traine up to the mount."*

Probably, also, the tarras serves for a steep rock in *Bonduca*, Act v, in the touching sequence of the valiant old general and the boy. The act begins with the stage direction *"Enter Caratach upon a rock, and Hengo by him, sleeping."* The only alternative to the use of the tarras is the thrusting out or discovery of an enormous property rock with two persons already upon it.

Finally, the versatile tarras serves sometimes as the quarterdeck of a ship. The Londoners of Blackfriars days were a sea-conscious lot: every time they crossed London Bridge or ferried the Thames, they saw vessels riding at anchor or setting forth on hazardous voyages to distant seas.

They knew that a ship's quarterdeck was the domain of the Master and of passengers of exalted station, and that commoners and sailors belonged in the waist. They therefore would expect that Rodorigo, the General of the Spanish Gallies, should *"Enter . . . above"* in *Love's Pilgrimage,* IV *i*, and that he should sit there with his noble guest Markantonio in II *iii* of the same play. Similarly, in one of the shipboard scenes in *The Double Marriage,* the stage direction has *"Enter Duke of Sesse above, and his daughter Martia like an Amazon."* In spite of the lack of any *"above,"* one may thus suppose that the Master enters on the tarras in *The Sea Voyage,* I *i*, and that in *The Tempest,* I *i*, both the Master and the Boatswain, and King Alonso and his courtiers, enter initially on the upper stage.

As seen from below, the tarras was a shelf-like projection beneath which a man could stand. Twice in Shakespeare's plays the corresponding tarras at the Globe was called a penthouse and was so used, in one instance as a shelter from the rain.[14] The tarras at Blackfriars is similarly called a penthouse in *The Distresses,* II *ii*. Musicians have arrived to accompany a serenade, and one of them says:

> This is the place . . . . Stand all close beneath
> The Penthouse; there's a certain Chamber-maid
> From yond' Casement, will dash us else.

Probably the overhang of the tarras, instead of a doorpost, was used for concealment when the eyes to be guarded against were those of a person at an upstairs window or on an upstairs gallery, rather than those of a person about to emerge from a door. Thus Lodovico supposedly wants Aurelio to stand beneath the tarras in *May Day,* III *iii*, to prevent his being seen by Æmilia, who has already entered *"above"*: "Stand up close, for she must not see you yet, though she knows you are here."

We have no direct information as to the front-to-back depth of the tarras. The ten persons of high station who watched a masque from the tarras in *The False One,* III *iv*, were undoubtedly seated, some of them on thrones. This would imply a depth of perhaps 4 feet.

The Side-Wall Galleries

Several Blackfriars plays contain scenes in which persons described as being *"above"* spy upon the actions of persons on the lower stage. When the victims of the spying occupy the platform as a place outdoors, the spiers, if they are within a house, naturally look down from an upstairs window; if they too are outdoors, they stand upon the tarras as perhaps upon an exterior gallery or hill. If the objects of the spying occupy the platform as a room inside a house and if the watchers also are within, the spying again is done from the tarras, with the tarras now serving as an indoor balcony inside a great hall. But if those who are being watched occupy the rear stage on the lower level, the watchers can no longer stand either upon the tarras or at a window. The tarras is unsuitable because the floor beneath the observers' feet would block all sight of action in the inner stage below, and a window is unsuitable both because it would yield only a shallow view into the rear stage and because it would be inappropriate as a means of looking from one room into another in the same house. In such scenes the eavesdroppers must stand in one of the side-wall galleries; they must enter the middle gallery from the tiring-house at the rear, and walk forward until they reach a point from which they can look back into the interior of the lower rear stage. Only a side-wall gallery can provide a position from which such a view is possible.

One cannot be certain that the action of any given scene passes wholly within the confines of the rear stage on the lower level; even if it begins there with a discovery, it may move forward as the scene progresses. But in any eavesdropping scene of the sort about to be described, the persons spied upon probably occupy the lower rear stage, for at least a part of the scene, if the scene begins with a discovery, if it requires large immovable properties, if it involves the use of the back door or stairs, or if the persons below believe that they are in a room where they can talk confidentially and if those above are conscious of invading their privacy. Any illusion of privacy would be minimized if the platform should be used.

The scenes in this category have a recognizable similarity. The would-be eavesdroppers usually appear first upon the lower stage and announce their intention of watching the ensuing action from above. They depart, and after a brief interval during which they mount the stairs, they appear on the upper level. The persons to be spied upon then enter below; with only one exception, they know nothing of the observers above, and hear none of their comments. The observers commonly descend and re-enter below before the scene closes.

The Captain, by Beaumont and Fletcher, illustrates these conditions more fully than any other play in the Blackfriars repertory. As IV *iv* begins, Angelo, a Venetian gentleman, stands on the platform as on a street before Lelia's door, irresistibly drawn thither by her beauty.

Angelo.   This is the door, and the short is,
   I must see her again.   *He knocks.*
           Enter Maid.
Maid.   Who's there?
Ang.   'Tis I, and I would speak with your Mistriss.

The Maid holds him off for about forty lines, but weakens when he offers her a bribe to hide him where he can watch Lelia.

Ang.   . . . But take it,
   And let me see her; bring me to a place
   Where, undiscerned of herself, I may
   Feed my desiring eyes but half-an-hour.
Maid.   . . . If you will swear,
   As you are gentle, not to stir or speak,
   Whatever you shall see or hear, now or hereafter—
   Give me your gold: I'll plant you.
Ang.   Why, as I am a gentleman,
   I will not.
Maid.   Enough. Quick! Follow me. *Ex. Angelo and Maid.*
       . . . *Enter Angelo above.*

Meanwhile the curtains have opened to reveal the rear stage as a room in Lelia's house, with servants setting forth a banquet for their mistress and an expected guest. The guest arrives; he is Lelia's father in disguise.

Father.   What, all wide open? 'Tis the way to sin
   Doubtless; but I must on; the gates of Hell
   Are not more passable than these. . . .
   What's here? a Banquet? and no mouth to eat
   Or bid me do it?

Lelia enters, and Angelo, from his perch above, watches the long distasteful scene that follows. He breaks his silence when the father threatens to kill his daughter.

Father draws his sword, Angelo discovers himself. . . .
Ang.   Hold, Reverend Sir, for honour of your Age. . . .
Fath.   Who's that?
Ang.   For safety of your Soul, and of the Soul
   Of that too wicked woman yet to dye.
Fath.   What art thou? and how cam'st thou to that place?

Ang. I am a man so strangely hither come,
That I have broke an Oath in speaking this. . . .
And I desire your patience: let me in,
And I protest I will not hinder you
In any act you wish, more than by word;
If so I can perswade you, that I will not
Use violence, I'll throw my Sword down to you;
This house holds none but I, only a Maid
Whom I will lock fast in as I come down.
Fath. I do not know thee, but thy tongue doth seem
To be acquainted with the truth so well,
That I will let thee in: throw down thy Sword.
Ang. There 'tis.
Lel. How came he there? I am betray'd to shame.
The fear of sudden death struck me all over
So violently, that I scarce have breath
    He [*Father*] *lets in Angelo, and locks the Door.*
To speak yet.

This scene is of special value in the present discussion because it shows clearly that the spied-upon action occupies the rear stage. Initially the platform was no part of Lelia's house; it was the street before her door; the interior of her house was not revealed until the curtains opened to discover the inner stage—a discovery not specified by stage direction, but clearly indicated nevertheless. There, in the rear stage, the servants are setting forth the banquet, and through the wide-open curtains the father enters his daughter's house. The door in the back wall of the rear stage, as being the one that leads to and from the stairs, is the door the father unlocks to admit Angelo, and locks again afterwards to secure himself from interruption.

Since Lelia and her father are in the inner stage, Angelo cannot watch them from the tarras, as he might do if they were on the platform; nor, for the reasons previously given, can he watch them from a window. As I reconstruct the Blackfriars stage, the only place from which he can watch them, since by specification he is *"above,"* is one of the side-wall galleries. In that position he is nearer to the audience than the persons he spies upon, and therefore his comments can be heard by the audience while by convention remaining inaudible to Lelia and her father; and if he were accompanied by a dozen other eavesdroppers instead of being alone, the gallery would have room enough for them all.[15]

All the scenes in which eavesdroppers conceal themselves *"above"* follow a similar routine, and thus suggest that they conform to an established theatrical convention. Some fail to indicate the use of the lower inner stage as clearly as does the scene just cited, but in many its use is highly probable and in none would it be out of place. All show most of the distinguishing marks just mentioned, and all would gain some advantage from having the spiers located nearer to the audience than the persons spied upon. For these reasons I suggest that the same procedure is followed in all scenes in which the observers are explicitly *"above"* and in a few others in which that direction is lacking, and that in all such scenes the observers occupy a side-wall gallery and the persons observed occupy the lower rear stage. I have the following scenes in mind:

In *The Bashful Lover*, v *iii*, Beatrice leads four noblemen to a place whence they can hear Hortensio's conversation with the Princess Matilda, who is at that moment arriving.

> *Beatrice.*   She's come; there are others I must place to hear
>   The Conference.   *Aside, and exit.*
>   *Enter Matilda.*
> *1st Woman.*   Is't your excellency's pleasure
>   That we attend you?
> *Matilda.*   No; wait me in the gallery. . . .
> *Re-enter above Beatrice with Lorenzo, Gonzaga, Uberti, and Farnese.*

In the conference that follows, Hortensio protests his unworthiness for Matilda's hand and by doing so wins her love, and during it the listeners above comment among themselves in hushed voices. Finally they *"Exeunt above"* and *"Re-enter below"* after a ten-line interval that gives them time to descend the off-stage stairs.

In *Bonduca*, II *iii*, five soldiers of the invading Roman legions have been captured, and are dragged before the Queen and her two daughters with starvation in their cheeks and halters about their necks. The three women condemn them to lashing and hanging, but the British general, Caratach, orders them released and fed.

> *2nd Daughter.*   Let's up and view his entertainment of ['em.]
>   I am glad they are shifted any way, their tongues else
>   Would still have murdred us.
> *1st Daughter.*   Let's up and see it.   *Exeunt.* . . .
> *Caratach.*   Sit down poor knaves: why where's this Wine and Victuals?

391

Who waits there?
Swet. within.   Sir, 'tis coming. . . .

Daughters above.

1 Daugh.   Here's a strange entertainment: how the thieves drink.
2 Daugh.   Danger is dry, they look'd for colder liquor.

In *The Custom of the Country*, Arnoldo and Zenocia have fled from their home immediately after their wedding, to avoid submitting to the custom that permits the Governor to take the maidenhead of a bride on the night of her marriage. They are separated when their boat is attacked by pirates, and Zenocia is given in service to the beautiful and lewd Hippolyta. Arnoldo catches a glimpse of his wife in Hippolyta's house and returns thither in hopes of seeing her again; and in ɪv *iii* Hippolyta, summoned by her servant Zabulon, watches from above as her handmaid is reunited with her husband, the man whom she herself desires:

Enter above Hippolyta and Zabulon. . . .

Arnoldo.   'Tis she again: the same,
   The same Zenocia.
Zabulon.   There are they together;
   Now you may mark.
Hippolyta.   Peace; let 'em parley.
Arn.   That you are well, Zenocia, and once more
   Bless my despairing eyes with your wish'd presence,
   I thank the gods! . . .
Hip.   They are acquainted.
Zab.   I found that secret, madam,
   When you commanded her to go home. Pray hear 'em.

And so it goes on for many lines more, while Hippolyta watches from above with mounting rage. Finally, determined to have Arnoldo for herself and to give Zenocia to the Governor, she orders Zabulon to descend and seize them both.

In *The Double Marriage*, v *i*, the make-believe king, dressed in royal robes, sits down in state to a banquet he is forbidden to eat, while four persons watch delightedly from above.

In *The Inconstant Lady*, ɪv *iv*, Pantarbo, having entered above, looks on as his father is entertained by two or three wenches in a brothel.

In *Love's Cure*, ɪv *ii*, Clara, the Martial Maid, watches from above as her love Vitelli dallies with a strumpet named Malroda, and then descends, sword in hand, fights off some bravoes who have engaged Vitelli in a brawl, and rescues her repentant cavalier.

In *The Novella*, v *i*, two men eavesdrop from above as Victoria rejects the advances of a wealthy suitor, and are afterwards chidden for having done so, as having exceeded the privileges of guests.

In *The Picture*, IV *iv*, the King and a few of his courtiers appear above to witness an interview between Mathias and the Queen. They do so at the Queen's invitation; and this, I think, is the only play in which a person below is aware of the presence of listeners above.

Other scenes of spying from above are to be found in *Believe as You List*, IV *ii*; *The Gentleman Usher*, v *i*; *The Just Italian*, III *iii*; *The Little French Lawyer*, v *i*; *The Roman Actor*, IV *ii*; and *Your Five Gallants*, v *i*.[16]

The fifteen scenes just mentioned permit one to assume that the upper level is used for eavesdropping in a few other plays in which the word *"above"* is lacking. Such a scene is v *ii* of *Sir Giles Goosecap*, in which twelve persons, including Momford and Furnifall, eavesdrop upon Clarence and the Doctor.

> *Momford.*   Bring hither the key of the gallery;
>   Methought I heard the Doctor and my friend.
> *Furnifall.*   I did so, sure.
> *Mom.*   Peace, then, awhile, my lord!
>   We will be bold to eavesdrop, for I know
>   My friend is as respective in his chamber,
>   And by himself, of anything he does,
>   As in a critic synod's curious eyes.

A later stage direction says that Clarence *"draws [i.e., closes] the curtains and sits within them,"* thus indicating that he has been in the discoverable rear stage, and so creating the presumption that the eavesdroppers have been above.

Act I Scene *ii* of *The Widow's Tears* is probably another such scene. Lysander wishes to spy upon his brother's wooing of the wealthy and noble widow Eudora, and asks his friend Lycus to favor him so much as to make him a spectator of the scene. When Eudora is about to enter, Lycus says "Well, her ladyship is at hand, y'are best take you to your stand," and Lysander exits, presumably to ascend the stairs. The next scene begins with the stage direction *"Lysander, from his stand."*

393

In *The Conspiracy of Byron*, i *ii*, the place to which Byron and Picoté go is probably also above, since it is so remote that "no stranger knows this way." Chapman provides nineteen lines for Byron to get to his hiding place, and fifteen for his return.

I have no thought of suggesting that Blackfriars dramatists had a side-wall gallery in mind when they used the word "gallery" in Blackfriars plays. In Jacobean times, as at present, the word was ambiguous. Sometimes it implied elevation in the area to which it referred,[17] just as it does today when one speaks of a gallery in a modern theatre; far more often it did not,[18] just as it does not now when it refers to a picture gallery or a shooting gallery. Nearly all allusions to galleries in the Blackfriars drama are to places off-stage;[19] the only galleries unmistakably on-stage are that to which Eustace Manly's chamber window opens (*Devil Is an Ass*, Act II), that in which Ferdinand is instantly to take the air (*Duchess of Malfi*, v *ii*), that which the King tells Lovell to avoid (*Henry VIII*, v *i*), and that to which Leonella takes her love Bellarius (*Second Maiden's Tragedy*, v *i*).

On page 294 I said that the prolongation of the spectator galleries over the stage had survived the Commonwealth and had lasted at Covent Garden and Drury Lane until well after the middle of the eighteenth century. In these later years, as at Blackfriars a hundred years earlier, actors sometimes ousted the spectators and used the galleries as parts of the acting area. *The City Ramble*, acted at Drury Lane in 1711, shows this survival of an old theatrical custom. One of its stage directions reads thus:

> *In the Middle Gallery Side-Box are seated the Common Councilman, his Wife, and Jenny their Daughter, as Spectators. The Common Councilman calls to the Speaker of the Prologue;*

and thereafter they are the principals in the play's secondary plot, until the very end.

Gallery Posts

Three Blackfriars plays call for trees or posts that could be climbed, and six call for posts or trees to which captives could be bound. The trees needed to be firmly enough planted, and sturdy enough in girth, to enable a man to climb them. They therefore were probably not temporary property trees, but structural posts that rose permanently from the platform to support the galleries.

Ben Jonson's *Case Is Altered*, IV *iii*, provides one instance of climbing. Jacques comes to the courtyard in back of his house to investigate noises that he supposes to have been made by thieves, and *"Onion gets up into a tree"* to avoid being discovered. He remains *"above"* during eighty-one lines of dialogue.

The Prophetess, I *iii*, has an episode in which Geta climbs some unidentified object out of fear of a dead boar. The incident seemingly takes place on a street, and runs thus:

> *Diocles.*   Go, take it [the boar] up, and carry it in, 'tis a huge one,
>   We never kill'd so large a Swine, so fierce too,
>   I never met with yet.
> *Maximinian.*   Take heed, it stirs again;
>   How nimbly the Rogue runs up! he climbs like a Squirrel.
> *Dio.*   Come down, ye Dunce, is it not dead?
> *Geta.*   I know not.
> *Dio.*   His throat is cut, and his bowels out.
> *Get.*   That's all one,
>   I am sure his teeth are in.

In *The Fawn*, Act V, a tree is the means by which Prince Tiberio climbs to the Princess Dulcimel's window. He has come to the court of the Duke Gonzago to sue for her hand on behalf of his father, the Duke of Ferrara. He and the Princess have fallen in love; but because of the ambassadorial relationship existing between father and son, Gonzago has ordered Dulcimel to have nothing to do with the Prince. So she puts her pretty head to work and devises a plan. She tells her father that Tiberio hopes to find his way into her bed by climbing "a well growne plain tree [that] spreads his happie armes" near to her chamber window; and by inducing her father to tell the Prince that he must not seek to enter her chamber by climbing the tree, she contrives to have him tell the Prince precisely how he can. Near the end of Act IV Gonzago gives the Prince this warning:

> Sir sir this plaine tree was not planted here
> To get into my daughters chamber: and so she praide me tell you.
> What though the maine armes spread into her window?
> And easie labour climes it.

Dulcimel's plan works. After an intermission, Act v begins with this stage direction:

> *Whilest the Act is a playing, Hercules and Tiberio enters, Tiberio climes the tree, and is received above by Dulcimel, Philocalia and a Preist: Hercules staies beneath.*

This last scene suggests that the posts-alias-trees were near the window stages but not under them. Twice it goes out of its way to assert that Dulcimel's window was reachable, not by way of the tree's trunk, but rather by way of "his happie armes," "the maine armes [that] spreade into her window." It therefore seems probable that Tiberio climbs a post that stands a few feet away from the window stage, and then clambers along the gallery's railing until he reaches the window.

As for the tying of captives to trees, examples of it occur in *The Bashful Lover*, III *iii*; *The Beggars' Bush*, III *iii*; *The Distresses*, III *iv*; *The Imposture*, v *iv*; *The Pilgrim*, IV *ii*; *The Sea Voyage*, last scene of Act IV, and probably *Cymbeline*, v *iv–v*.

The Inner Stage on the Upper Level

Four scenes in four Blackfriars plays indicate that the playhouse had a discoverable area on the upper level. Eleven scenes in ten other plays, although failing to specify discovery, nevertheless suggest that the playhouse had an upper inner stage comparable in some respects to the rear stage on the level below. Like that stage, it had a back wall containing a door and a window. It was neither the tarras nor a window stage, and yet it was immediately available to them both, and to the stairs leading up from the lower level.

The following stage directions testify to the existence of a discoverable unit on the upper level, and two of them testify to the use of curtains as the means of effecting discoveries:

From *Eastward Ho!*, IV *i*:

> *Enter Slitgut, with a pair of ox-horns, discovering Cuckold's Haven above.*

From *The Emperor of the East*, I *ii*:

> *The Curtains drawn above: Theo[dosius] and his eunuchs discovered.*

From *The Fawn*, v *i*:

> *Tiberio and Dulcimel above are discovered, hand in hand.*

And from *The Goblins*, Act v:

> *A curtain drawn; Prince, Philatel, with others, appear above.*

Except for two doubtful references to the drawing of curtains in *The Parson's Wedding*, iv *vi* and v *ii*,[20] these are the only allusions to upper-level discoveries at Blackfriars.[21] Probably, however, the curtains were opened whenever the upper inner stage was called into play, and at all other times were kept closed.

The upper-level curtains are necessarily opened when Anabel enters in her bed in *The Little French Lawyer*, III *iii*. The place is the home of Champernel. Two gallants, Dinant and Cleremont, have come thither in hopes of enjoying the favors of Lamira, Champernel's wife. She, intent only on making gulls of the two men, tells them that her husband is abed and asleep; but, she says, he sometimes reaches out his hand to feel if she is at his side, and therefore Cleremont must take her place, lest he awake and find himself alone. Cleremont reluctantly agrees and goes up the stairs. But Champernel is not in his bed; his place has been taken by his pretty niece, Anabel, a substitution that Cleremont fails to discover. In the meantime, "*Enter Champernel privately*," probably to a side gallery as to a place whence he can watch all that happens on the stage below. He knows that his wife and Dinant are somewhere downstairs, and he sees the nurse and a waiting-woman enter and "*pass over the Stage with Pillows, Night cloaths, and such things.*"

> *Champernel.*   What can this Woman do, preserving her honour?
>   I have given her all the liberty that may be,
>   I will not be far off though, nor I will not be jealous,
>   Nor trust too much: I think she is virtuous. . . .
> *Stands private.*
>   She may be, and she may not, now to my observation.
> *Enter Dinant, and Lamira.*
> *Dinant.*   Why do you make me stay so? if you love me—
> *Lamira.*   You are too hot and violent.
> *Din.*   Why do you shift thus
>   From one Chamber to another?

Lam. A little delay, Sir,
Like fire, a little sprinkled o'er with water
Makes the desires burn clear, and ten times hotter.
Din. Why do you speak so loud? I pray'e go in,
Sweet Mistris, I am mad, time steals away,
And when we would enjoy—

The Nurse creates a new delay by entering with wine that Lamira insists upon drinking with Dinant, and then music starts to play so loudly that he is afraid the whole house will be aroused. It brings Cleremont from the bedchamber to the tarras.

Enter Cleremont above.

Cleremont. What a Devil ail you?
How cold I sweat! a hogs pox stop your pipes, [*Musick.*
The thing will 'wake; now, now, methinks I find
His Sword just gliding through my throat. What's that?
A vengeance choak your pipes. Are you there, Lady?
Stop, stop those Rascals; do you bring me hither
To be cut into minced meat? . . .
Lam. 'Twas but an over-sight, they have done, lye down. . . .
'Tis nothing but your fear, he sleeps still soundly,
Lie gently down.
Cler. 'Pray make an end.
Din. Come, Madam.
Lam. These Chambers are too near. *Ex*[*eunt*] *Din. Lam.*

And all this time Champernel is watching privately, delighting in his wife's adroitness in outwitting Dinant.

Well, go thy wayes, I'le trust thee through the world,
Deal how thou wilt.

Cleremont enters above for a second time, learns from Dinant that Lamira has duped them both, and instantly decides to revenge himself on Champernel, whom he supposes to be in the bed that he has just left:

You shall pay for't grey-beard.
Up, up, you sleep your last else!

398

At this point, I take it, the upper-stage curtains open to reveal Anabel in her bed; the stage direction reads "*Lights above, two Servants and Anabel.*"

> *1 Serv.*   No, not yet, Sir,
>   Lady, look up; would you have wrong'd this Beauty?
>   Wake so tender a Virgin with rough terms?
>   You wear a Sword, we must entreat you leave it.
> *2 Serv.*   Fye Sir, so sweet a Lady?
> *Cler.*   Was this my bed-fellow, pray give me leave to look,
>   I am not mad yet, I may be by and by.
>   Did this lye by me?
>   Did I fear this? is this a Cause to shake at?
>   Away with me for shame, I am a Rascal.

This scene makes use of all the elements of the upper and lower stages except the windows. On the lower level, Lamira leads Dinant from platform to rear stage and back again, and to imaginary rooms off-stage. On the upper level, the tarras is an indoor balcony whence Cleremont can talk with Lamira and Dinant on the stage below; a side-wall gallery is a private place whence Champernel can see everything that happens on either level, and can comment upon it without being overheard; and an inner stage, presumably directly behind the tarras and connected with it, is discoverable as Anabel's bedchamber.

A scene in *Alphonsus, Emperor of Germany*, agrees with that just cited in indicating that the upper inner stage was large enough to hold a bed.[22] It seems to indicate also that the stage had a wall rigid enough to support a door that could be locked. In 1 *i*, the Emperor orders his page to give him the master key of all the doors in the Court, and with it he goes to the bedchamber of the learned Lorenzo.

> *He opens the door and finds Lorenzo asleep aloft.*
> *Alph.*   Nay, sleep, Lorenzo, I will walk awhile. . . .
>   And now, methinks, he wakes.
> *Lorenzo riseth and snatches at his sword, which hung by his bedside.*
> *Lor.*   What, are there thieves within the Emperor's Court?
>   Villain, thou diest! What mak'st thou in my chamber?
> *Alph.*   How now, Lorenzo, wilt thou slay thy lord?

> *Lor.* I do beseech your sacred Majesty
>   To pardon me, I did not know your Grace.
> *Alph.* Lie down, Lorenzo, I will sit by thee.

After which Lorenzo dozes off again, and the Emperor murders him in his sleep.

The door, like that in the rear stage on the floor below, was probably in the back wall. Although the text of this scene makes no mention of upper-stage curtains, curtains were presumably opened at or before the time that the Emperor unlocked the door, and were necessarily closed at the end of the scene to conceal the bed and the body.

The Chances, II *i* and II *iii,* makes much use of a door in a wall of the upper inner stage. Constantia, protesting that she is in grave danger, has induced Frederick to hide her in his own chamber. In II *i* he tells his friend Don John about the lady whom he has taken under his protection, but at the same time tells him that he may not see her.

> *John.* But let me see her though: leave the door open
>   As ye go in.
> *Frederick.* I dare not.
> *John.* Not wide open,
>   But just so, as a jealous husband
>   Would level at his wanton wife through.

The next scene identifies Frederick's chamber as being above by having his servant Anthony speak of the sound of a lute as coming from "Above, in my master's chamber." Scene *iii* has Constantia enter first, and then *"Enter Frederick and Don John, peeping."* Frederick joins Constantia, leaving John at the door, fuming with frustration:

> *John.* Pox upon ye,
>   Stand out o'th' light. . . . Would she would turn:
>   See, and that spightful puppy be not got
>   Between me and my light again. . . .
> *Fred.* Pull in your head and be hang'd. . . .
> *Constantia.* Nay let him enter. . . .
> *Fred.* Shall he enter?
>   Who e're he be?
> *Con.* With all my heart.
> *Fred.* Come in then.
>   *Enter Don John.*

400

The Captain, v *ii*, shows that the upper inner stage had a window in its back wall. Although no stage direction employs the word *"above"* in connection with this scene, the nature of the central episode demands that it be enacted at a rear window on the upper level. The situation is this: Frank (a girl) is in love with the woman-shy Jacomo, and wants to lure him into the house so that she can confess her love to him; but he thinks that she mocks him, and refuses to come. To get him into the house, her friends hit upon the unconventional plan of infuriating him by emptying a chamber pot on his head as he stands on the street below. The window is specifically mentioned: "He [Jacomo] walks below for me / Under the window." The offensive incident is not shown; Jacomo never enters; he is ostensibly on a street at the far side of the house, and his furious reprisals are made known to the audience only as the maid reports them. And since Jacomo is off-stage at the back, the window is necessarily in the back wall of the inner stage on the upper level.

The Novella, iv *i*, treats the upper curtained stage as an upstairs chamber and treats a window stage as part of the same room, with Astutta passing from one to the other so readily that not a line of dialogue is needed to cover the time of her passage. The place is Flavia's chamber, she and her maid Astutta being present. Guadagni, Flavia's father, is on his way upstairs in search of a lost paper, and she has therefore locked the half-dressed Francisco into a "presse" or wardrobe to hide him.

> *Enter Flavia, and Astutta above.*
>
> *Flavia.* Our hast and feares could not find time to dress him
> But I have lock'd him up into that presse.
>
> *Astutta.* Your Father's coming up to seek a writing,
> Pray Love it be not there.
>
> *Fla.* I am undone then.
>
> *Ast.* Well hold you peace, looke bold and chearfully,
> And be you silent, youth. . . .
>
> *Guadagni.* Where are you Flavia?   *Within.*
>
> *Fla.* O me he comes! . . .
>
> *Enter Guadagni above.*
>
> *Gua.* Tis here that I would have thee Flavia.
> Give me the Key of this presse here.
>
> *Fla.* O Father, Father—   *Shee falls.*
>
> *Gua.* What's the matter? ha! . . .
>
> *Ast.* Shee thinks shee has lost it, but I saw her lock it

> Togither with a writing which you dropt
> Out of this presse this morning, safe enough
> Here in her Cabinet.
>
> *Gua.*   Tis like I let it fall.
>
> *Ast.*   Where is your Key of this? Give mee't, give mee't.
>   How hast and feare perplexes her! I could
>   Have pickt it open.
>
> *Gua.*   Doe, or break it open.
>
> *She lets the Cabinet fall out of the Window.*
>
> *Ast.*   Ay me the fruits of rashness? See, tis fallen
>   With all her Jewells and your writing too
>   Into the street. O my unlucky hand!
>
> *Gua.*   Peace giddy headed harlot, watch that none
>   Take it away, while I runne to recover't.

Since the cabinet falls to the platform and Guadagni's recovery of it is enacted there, the window from which it has fallen, unlike that in *The Captain*, is manifestly a front window.

The following scenes also may have been enacted in the upper inner stage. Some perhaps are more doubtful than those already discussed, but if the preceding scenes could be accommodated in that stage, so could all those that follow.

In *The Elder Brother*, the upper rear stage probably serves in two scenes (II *iv* and III *iv*) as the library of the studious Charles, and the tarras as the balcony from which he observes the arrival of the beauteous Angellina.

In *The Loyal Subject*, II v, it perhaps serves as an upper story in Archas's house, where the Duke insists upon seeing the inside of an off-stage room of which Archas says he has lost the key.

In *The Wits*, IV *iii*, six or seven persons are on-stage at the same time in a room presumably upstairs, together with a chest large enough to hold a man.

And in *Women Pleased*, II *vi*, Isabella conceals one admirer by directing him to "Step here behind this hanging," and when she learns that her husband is coming upstairs, she tells another how to pass him on the stairs without arousing his suspicions:

> Draw your sword quickly, and go down inrag'd,
> As if you had pursu'd some foe up hither,
> And grumble to your self extreamly, terribly,
> But not a word to him, and so pass by him.

The foregoing scenes indicate that the upper inner stage was discoverable by the opening of curtains, that it had a back wall pierced by a door and window, that it had a hanging behind which a man could hide, that it was readily accessible to the head of the stairs, the tarras, and a stage window, and that it was large enough to contain a bed. The greatest number of persons present in it at any one time may have been six or seven in *The Wits* and eight in *The Loyal Subject*.

Nothing in any scene tells the position of the curtains that were opened to effect discoveries. Probably, however, they were in the line of the scenic wall, as were those on the level below. So placed, they would permit the tarras to serve as a balcony, battlement, or hill without requiring that it be discovered, and, since the curtains would be closed behind it, would permit it to serve in those capacities with no disturbing vision of an inner stage beyond. When the curtains were opened, the discovered space to the rear merged with the tarras to form a single stage. The two stages had no separate identities at such a time, as the platform and the rear stage on the lower level sometimes had. Instead, they combined to represent a single place, and that place was always an upper room in a house.

The fourteen scenes just discussed are the only ones that can be assigned to the upper inner stage with any degree of confidence.[23] They constitute an extremely small percentage of all the scenes presented upon the Blackfriars stage; for if we assume that 133 Blackfriars plays had an average of four scenes in each of five acts, the total is 2,660 scenes; and fourteen scenes in 2,660 is the equivalent of one in 190, or one scene in nine and a half plays. The disproportion is so great as to cause one to doubt whether even those fourteen scenes were actually performed upon the upper stage. Under any interpretation, the ratio shows a precipitous falling off in the use of that stage at Blackfriars, as compared with the use of its counterpart at the Globe.

Differences in the use of the upper stages in the two playhouses were undoubtedly caused by differences in the distribution of their patrons. Vertical sight lines into the upper inner stage were unfavorable for the man in the pit in both houses. If he stood or sat immediately in front of the forward edge of the platform in either house, he had to look upward at an angle of 20-odd degrees in order to see into the interior of the upper stage. He could see none of its floor, and he could see an actor only from the waist up if the actor stood a few feet back from the front edge of the tarras, and progressively less as the actor moved farther to the rear. Differences existed between the two houses with relation to angles of vision from the pit into the upper stage, but in themselves they were unimportant; perhaps, indeed, they may even have been slightly more favorable for the lordling in the pit at Blackfriars than for the groundling in the yard at the Globe. Yet Blackfriars made far less use of its upper inner stage. It did so because of differences between corresponding parts of the two auditoriums with respect to revenue, capacity, and prestige.

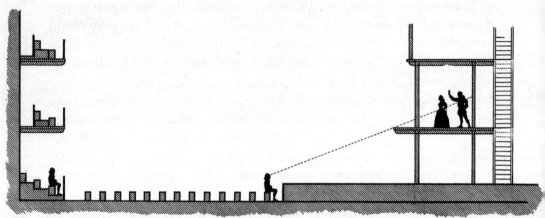

Figure 24. Diagram showing the angle of vision from the pit into the upper stage.

At the Globe, the playgoers in the yard were those of least importance. They were the one-penny men, the standees. Socially, financially, and numerically, they were outranked by the gallery patrons, those who paid a supplementary fee to get the better seats, those who constituted more than two thirds of the Globe's total audience.[24] For persons in the galleries, the interior of the upper stage was adequately visible. Adequate visibility was less important for those in the yard.

But at Blackfriars the conditions were reversed. There the more prominent and profitable personages sat at floor level, as in the theatres of today; the social eligibility of seats probably reflected that of seats at Court, where the sovereign had his dais on the floor, with his family and favorites seated around him. Furthermore, the pit and lowest gallery at Blackfriars seem to have held about half of the whole audience.[25] Under these conditions, a stage not adequately visible to patrons at floor level was a stage not worth using.

Sir Edmund Chambers has commented as follows upon the lesser use of the upper stage at Blackfriars:

Neither at Paul's nor at the Blackfriars was there an upper stage capable of holding the action of a complete scene, such as we found at the sixteenth-century theatres, and apparently on a still larger scale at the Globe and the Fortune. . . . Although there is action "above" in many private house plays, it is generally a very slight action, amounting to little more than the use by one or two persons of a window or balcony. Bedchamber scenes or tavern scenes are provided for below; the public theatre, as often as not, put them above. I may recall, in confirmation, that the importance of the upper stage in the plays of the King's men sensibly diminishes after their occupation of the Blackfriars.[26]

Nevertheless, it seems necessary to assume that the fourteen scenes were enacted in the upper inner stage at Blackfriars, since half the plays in question are known from their title pages to have been performed there,[27] and the rest are confidently believed to have been. But I assume at the same time that Lorenzo's and Anabel's beds were shoved forward to the curtain line, that the rear wall of the inner stage was no farther back than the width of a bed made necessary, and that the actors left the inner stage behind them and moved forward to the tarras as soon as they were free to do so.

The Stage Stairs

All the upper-level scenes mentioned in this chapter, and many more besides, imply the existence of stairs by which actors could go from one stage level to the other. Pharamond, in *Philaster*, II *iii*, used such stairs when he came storming down to the door of his lodging, sword in hand, to keep the King's guard from invading his bedchamber. Ismena and Aminta, in *The Maid in the Mill*, I *iii*, used them when they scampered upstairs to await the arrival of Antonio and Martine beneath their chamber window. Angelo, in *The Captain*, IV *iv*, used them when he rushed downstairs to prevent the outraged Father from killing his daughter; and Drusus and Penyus, in *Bonduca*, III *v*, used off-stage stairs to gain the top of a hill from which they could survey the field of battle. Many other plays imply the existence of stairs by calling for ascents or descents or both,[28] and even more do so by the mere fact of having characters appear on two levels of the stage.

It is noteworthy, however, that no ascent or descent in any Blackfriars play is made within sight of the audience; the actor always leaves the stage when he takes to the stairs.[29] Sometimes his brief absence is marked by stage directions calling for his exit and reentrance, as when Albert, in *The Sea Voyage*, II *i*, is given an "*Exit. And Enter above*" when he climbs the hill, or as when the five noblemen "*Exeunt above*" in *The Bashful Lover*, V *iii*, and ten lines later "*Re-enter below.*" But whether or not stage directions are provided, the ascent and descent, and therefore the stairs themselves, are invariably off-stage and out of sight. This is true even when the stage curtains are open and the rear stage revealed. It was necessary that the stairs should be out of sight under all conditions, since actors needed to be able to get from one level of the stage to the other in preparation for a scene to come, and to do so without being seen, whether or not the inner stage was exposed.

But the stairs were near at hand, near enough for their position to be indicated by a word and a wave of the hand. Thus *Brennoralt*, IV *i*, contains the line "This was the entry, these the stairs." *The Lover's Melancholy*, III *ii*, has Kala say:

> Walk up these stairs; and take this key, it opens
> A chamber door, where, at that window yonder,
> You may see all their courtship.

The Second Maiden's Tragedy, II *ii*, has this:

> *Anselmo.*   Which way took the villain,—
>   That marriage felon, one that robs the mind
>   Twenty times worse than any highway-striker—
>   Speak, which way took he?
> *Votarius.*   Marry, my lord, I think—
>   Let me see, which way was't now?—up yon stairs.

And the Drawer, in *A Trick to Catch the Old One*, III *iii*, tells the arriving guests to go "Up those stairs, gentlemen."

I have previously said (pages 352 to 356 above) that the back wall of the lower rear stage contained a door and a window. The foot of the stairs was probably just outside that door. This supposition conforms not only to the requirement that the stairs should be near at hand and yet invisible, but also to the stage direction that immediately follows Angelo's descent of the stairs in *The Captain*, IV *iv*: "*He [Father] lets in Angelo, and locks the Door.*"[30] Presumably the head of the stairs had a similar position on the upper level, just outside the chamber door alluded to by Kala in the lines just quoted from *The Lover's Melancholy*.

A trip up or down the stairs normally took as long a time as the speaking of about nine lines of verse; in other words, just under half a minute. When, as in *The Noble Gentleman,* IV *iii,* only two lines were spoken, or no lines at all in *Philaster,* II *iii,* the time was presumably extended by stage business; and when, as in *Bonduca,* II *iii,* fifty-five lines were spoken, the Daughters were idling off-stage.

With this as background, I approach the difficult "up the stairs" scene (II *iv*) in Fletcher's *Valentinian.* The Emperor has lured the beautiful and virtuous Lucina to his palace by sending her a summons that purports to come from her husband, and to his well-trained panders he has entrusted the task of breaking down her resistance by every means known to their profession—flattery, music, perfumes, jewels, and ropes of pearl laid in the way she passes. Knowing the Emperor's wont with women, she comes in fear. At the palace door she asks for her husband. Chilax, one of the Emperor's men, offers to lead her to him. She mistrusts him, but she has no choice; she departs under his guidance, and for a moment the stage is empty. Then three more of the Emperor's procurers enter.

> *Licinius.*   She is coming up the stairs; Now the Musick;
>   And as that stirs her, let's set on: perfumes there.
> *Proculus.*   Discover all the Jewels.
> *Lici.*   Peace.   [*Musick.*

At this point two songs are inserted, labeled respectively "SONG" and "SECOND," each of them twenty lines long. At their close Lucina reenters with her women, led by Chilax. The jewels are displayed, but she has no interest in them:

> Nay, ye may draw the Curtain, I have seen 'em,
> But none worth half my honesty.

Two bawds enter, Phorba and Ardelia.

> *Phorba.*   Where is this stranger? rushes, Ladys, rushes,
>   Rushes as green as Summer for this stranger.
> *Luc.*   ... Where's my Lord?
>   For there's the business that I came for Ladies.
> *Phor.*   We'l lead ye to him, he's i'th' Gallery.
> *Ardelia.*   We'l shew ye all the Court too.

Luci. Shew me him,
  And ye have shew'd me all I come to look on.

A few moments later the Emperor joins her.

Luci. Good your Grace,
  Where are my women Sir?
Emperor. They are wise, beholding
  What you think scorn to look on, the Courts bravery.

One line in this scene—"She is coming up the stairs"—and that line alone, suggests that the later action occupies an upper room in the palace and an upper level of the stage. If that assumption be justified with respect to the upper stage at Blackfriars, then that stage is proved to have been large enough to contain at least nine persons at the same time, together with a display of jewels behind a curtain, and still to have been so uncrowded that the ladies could strew rushes on the floor in honor of the stranger. But all my studies of the upper stage at Blackfriars indicate that it had no such capacity, and indicate also that it was seldom used for sustained action in important scenes.[31] Furthermore, the forty lines of song strengthen the presumption that Lucina did not go up the stairs; if she had done so, ten lines of dialogue would have been more than enough to cover her ascent. The "SONG" and the "SECOND" therefore served some other purpose, and that purpose may have been to provide a break that would permit the illusion of a change of place without change of stage, as discussed on pages 336 to 338 above. Or perhaps the "up the stairs" line was omitted in performance at Blackfriars; and this is the more likely since no change of place seems to be necessary to the development of the plot.

The Music Room

The Music Room at Blackfriars was on an upper level. This is indicated by the many stage directions that allude to the music as being "above." Thus *The Cruel Brother*, v *ii*, has "*Still Musick above.*" *The Picture*, II *v*, has "*Musick above, a song of pleasure.*" *The Roman Actor*, II *i*, has "*Musicke above, and a song by Domitia.*" *The Unfortunate Lovers*, v *v*, has "*Strange Musick is heard above,*" and *The Wonder of Women*, IV *i*, has "*A short song to soft Musique above.*" *The Prophetess*, II *iii*, and *The Variety*, IV *iv*, speak of the music as being of or from the spheres, and *The Tempest* has these two passages. From I *ii*:

> *Ferdinand.*   Where should this music be? I' th' air, or th' earth? . . .
> This is no mortal business, nor no sound
> That the earth owes. I hear it now above me.

and from v *i*:

> *Prospero.*   . . . But this rough magic
> I here abjure; and when I have requir'd
> Some heavenly music (which even now I do) . . .
> I'll break my staff.

And Massinger indicates the normal position of the musicians as being above by providing in *The City Madam*, III *i*, a marginal stage direction reading "*Musicke come down*," and another at v *i* reading "*Musicians come down to make ready for the Song at Arras.*"

Jasper Mayne and Thomas Killigrew suggest that the room was on the level next above the platform, and that it occupied the tarras or the space immediately behind it. Mayne, in *Jonsonus Virbius*, commends Ben Jonson for avoiding absurdities in his plays, and among other things he praises him because "Thou laidst no sieges to the Musique-Roome." As we have seen, sieges are laid to castles whose defenders stand on the tarras; Mayne thus in effect says that the music room and the tarras are the same. Killigrew is less definite: his music room may be either the tarras or the space behind it. In *The Parson's Wedding*, I *ii*, he calls for the presence on stage of Mistress Pleasant, Widow Wild her aunt, and Secret her woman, together with a glass and a table, and he specifies that all these things shall be "*above in the music room.*" But whether the musicians occupied the tarras or the inner stage to its rear, they necessarily moved elsewhere on the rare occasions when the plot called for the use of those stages. At such times they may have moved to one of the side-wall galleries.

Their position on a level so short a distance above the platform enabled the musicians to hear dialogue on the main stage and to pick up their cues without needing to have them relayed. On a few occasions actors on the platform addressed the musicians directly, as when Calantha, in *The Broken Heart*, Act v, told them to "Strike up more sprightly," or when the Citizen, after Act II of *The Knight of the Burning Pestle*, called out "You Musicians, play 'Baloo'," or when Lillia-Bianca, in *The Wild-Goose Chase*, II *ii*, bade them "Strike up again." Normally they began and ended their music without the need for signals or direct address.

Passages in three Blackfriars plays indicate that the musicians were audible, but not visible, to the person speaking.

In *The Prophetess*, II *iii*, Geta says:

> would I could hire
> These fine invisible Fidlers to play for me
> At my instalment.

In *The Fatal Dowry*, IV *ii*, Aymer calls to the musicians "Begin the last new ayre," and this exchange follows:

> *Charalois.*   Shall we not see them?
> *Aymer.*   This little distance from the instruments
> Will to your eares convey the harmony
> With more delight. . . .   *Song above.*

And in *The Knight of the Burning Pestle*, the Citizen suspects that the wrong musicians have been fobbed off on him, but he cannot see them to make sure. He has paid money to be used in hiring "the waits of Southwark," and as he and his Wife sit on the stage in the intermission between Acts II and III, he expects to hear the plaintive tone of shawms. Instead of that, he hears fiddles.

> *Wife.*   The Fidlers go again Husband.
> *Citizen.*   I Nell, but this is scurvy Musick: I gave the whoreson gallows money, and I think he has not got me the Waits of Southwark, if I hear him not anon, I'll twinge him by the ears.

Probably, therefore, the musicians were hidden from sight by thin curtains. Concealment would not merely lend an ethereal quality to music of the spheres, but it would enable the musicians to come downstairs without being seen, when they had occasion to accompany singers or dancers on the lower stage—as when, for example, they played the accompaniment for "Hark, hark! the lark" outside Imogen's chamber door in *Cymbeline*, II *iii*.[32]

The prototype of the music room at Blackfriars was the music gal-

lery in a Tudor banqueting hall; and in placing its musicians on an upper
level, the playhouse thus conformed to an ancient convention and at the
same time conserved space on the lower stage. G. H. Cowling believes
that the number of musicians need not have exceeded eight or ten, some
of whom presumably played more than one instrument.[33]

Height of the Upper Stages

It seems reasonable to suppose that all the elements of the upper
stage had their floors on the same level, and two Blackfriars plays suggest
that that level was about 9 feet above the surface of the platform. The
first of these plays is *The Picture*. In IV *ii*, as has already been related,
Sophia has imprisoned Ubaldo and Ricardo in two upper-level cells
fronted by grated windows. She now tells them that they will have to
work to earn a spare diet, and, speaking of Ubaldo first, she bids her
servant to

> Reach him up that distaff
> With the flax upon it. . . .
> As you spin well at my command, and please me,
> Your wages, in the coarsest bread and water,
> Shall be proportionable. . . .
> Deliver him his materials. Now you know
> Your penance, fall to work; hunger will teach you.

As the upshot proves, the distaff was reached up to Ubaldo and he
was able to grasp it. Now a distaff, according to the *New Oxford Dictionary*, was about 3 feet long, and the boy who played the part of Corisca,
standing on tiptoe and reaching as high as he could, would have been able
to raise its tip to a height of about 9 feet. Ubaldo, for his part, could
have leaned down from his grated window and grasped the distaff at
about the level of the floor upon which he stood. The floor of the window
stage was thus presumably about 9 feet higher than the floor of the platform.

The second play is *Monsieur Thomas*. In III *iii*, Thomas is standing
under Mary's window at night, accompanied by his man Launcelot. Mary
tells her maid to get rid of him. "Then have at him," says the maid; and,
impersonating her mistress, she comes to the window and sings this song:

> Come up to my window love, come, come, come,
> Come up to my window my dear,
> The wind, nor the rain shall trouble thee again,
> But thou shalt be lodged here.

Launcelot offers by gesture to help his master climb up to the window.

> *Thomas.*   And art thou strong enough?
> *Launcelot.*   Up, up, I warrant ye.

With Launcelot's hands to lift him and with the door posts to steady him, Thomas probably clambers up on Launcelot's shoulders, clutches the window ledge, and raises his face toward the lady in the window; whereupon

> *Madge with a Devils vizard roaring, offers to kiss him,*
> *and he falls down.*

As Thomas stands on Launcelot's shoulders, straining upward, his upturned face is perhaps 10½ or 11 feet above the platform floor; Madge, leaning out from the window, can "offer to kiss him" at that height. This scene thus agrees with that in *The Picture* in suggesting that the persons in the windows were standing on floors about 9 feet above the level of the platform; and if the floors of the window stages were at that height, then so presumably were those of the tarras, the upper inner stage, and the side-wall galleries also.[34]

I have previously suggested that the middle spectator galleries were 12 feet above the floor of the auditorium,[35] and that the platform was 3 feet high.[36] The floors of the upper-level stages were thus on the same level as the floors of the spectator galleries.

"The Top"

The Blackfriars stage had acting areas on three levels. The first was that of the platform. The second was that of the tarras and the window stages. The third, high above the tarras, was called "the top" in theatrical parlance. It was used in two Blackfriars plays certainly, and possibly in three.

The most informative of the plays is *The Double Marriage*, II *i*, in which the top serves as the maintop of a ship at sea, and in which all three levels of the stage are concurrently in use. A Boy is sent aloft to

412

search the horizon for enemy ships, and while he is *"a top"* as in the crow's nest, the tarras serves as the quarterdeck (*"Enter Duke of Sesse above, and his daughter Martia like an Amazon"*), and the platform serves as the main deck (*"Enter below the Master and Sailors"*). Perhaps the trap in the middle of the platform is a companionway leading up from the hold.

> *Boatswain.* Ho, in the hold.
> *Enter a Boy.*
> *Boy.* Here, here.
> *Boats.* To th' Main top, Boy.
>   And thou kenst a ship that dares defie us,
>   Here's Gold.
> *Boy.* I am gone.   *Exit Boy.*
>   . . .   *Boy a top.*
>
> *Boy above.* A Sail, a Sail.
> *Master.* A cheerful sound.
> *Boy.* A sail.
> *Boats.* Of whence? of whence boy?
> *Boy.* A lusty Sail.
> *Daughter.* Look right, and look again.
> *Boy.* She plows the Sea before her,
>   And fomes i' th' mouth.
> *Boats.* Of whence?
> *Boy.* I ken not yet sir.
> *Ses.* Oh may she prove of Naples. . . .
> *Boy.* Hoy.
> *Mast.* Brave boy.
> *Boy.* Of Naples, Naples, I think of Naples Master,
>   Methinks I see the arms.
> *Mast.* Up, up another,
>   And give more certain signs.   *Exit Sailor.* . . .
> *Sayl. above.* Ho.
> *Ses.* Of whence now?
> *Sail.* Of Naples, Naples, Naples.
>   I see her top-Flag, how she quarters Naples.
>   I hear her Trumpets.
> *Ses.* Down, she's welcome to us.

Shakespeare uses the top in *The Tempest*, III *iii*, when, to an accompaniment of *"solemne and strange Musicke,"* Prospero appears *"on the top (invisible)*." From this position, high above the stage, he is able to dominate the creatures of the earth, the underworld, and the air, theoretically invisible to them but fully visible to the audience; and it is interesting to note that the phrase *"on the top,"* here used by Shakespeare in one of the last of his plays, is the same phrase as he used twenty years before in one of his earliest, when he had Joan of Arc climb to a high turret from which she could flash a beacon to her friends—"*Enter Pucell on the top, thrusting out a Torch burning*"—in *1 Henry VI*, III *ii*.

In *The Gentleman Usher*, v *iii*, Margaret is distracted with grief over the supposed death of her lover, and threatens to cast herself down headlong from a tower. A window stage could hardly provide the necessary illusion of great height, and therefore the top, though not specified by stage direction, is presumably used:

> *Enter Cortezza and Margaret above.*
> *Margaret.* I'll cast myself down headlong from this tower. . . .
> *Cortezza.* Oh, 'tis the easiest death that ever was;
>   Look, niece, it is so far hence to the ground
>   You should be quite dead long before you felt it.
>   Yet do not leap, niece.

We have no knowledge that the top was used in any Blackfriars plays other than these three. In none did it need to hold more than two actors. It may therefore have been nothing more than a high alcove or opening in the scenic wall, guarded by a rail along its forward edge.

The Heavens

In two plays of the Chapel-Revels Children, and in nine plays of the King's Men, actors flew down to the platform at the end of a rope or wire. Their flights were controlled from an enclosed scaffold which, as in the public playhouses, was perhaps divided into two or more huts. As stated on pages 166 to 167 above, the huts may have been "the rooms over the same" mentioned so often in legal documents growing out of the controversies of the Children's managers. They were called "the heavens."[37]

Gods or mortals descended from the heavens in the following Blackfriars plays:

In *Cupid's Revenge*, Cupid descends and ascends in three different scenes, always to an accompaniment of cornets.

In *Cymbeline*, v *iv*, "*Jupiter descends in Thunder and Lightning, sitting uppon an Eagle.*" He remains hovering in midair for twenty lines, with the eagle's talons approaching, but not touching, the heads of the Apparitions on the platform. His return into the heavens needs six lines, from the time he gives the command to rise—"Mount, eagle, to my palace crystalline"—until "The marble pavement closes; he is enter'd / His radiant roof."

In *The Mad Lover*, v *iii*, Venus, presumably impersonated by Chilax, descends to music, recites a spurious prophecy, and ascends.

In *More Dissemblers Besides Women*, I *iii*, "*A Cupid, descending, sings,*" and then "*Ascends,*" in the course of a masque designed to welcome Andrugio on his return home from his victorious military campaign.

In *The Prophetess*, II *iii*, Delphia and Drusilla enter in flight "*in a Throne drawn by Dragons.*" Delphia tells the dragons to

> Fix here, and rest a while your Sail-stretch'd wings
> That have out-stript the winds,

and she bids her niece to

> Look down, Drusilla, on these lofty Towers,
> These spacious streets, where every private house
> Appears a Palace to receive a King:
> The site, the wealth, the beauty of the place,
> Will soon inform thee 'tis imperious Rome.

The dragon-drawn throne remains in midair for 176 lines, after which Delphia says "Mount up, my birds," and "*Ascends Throne.*"

In *Valentinian*, v *viii*, a masque is presented to celebrate the coronation of the new emperor, and in it a boy, habited like one of the Graces, descends with a song and a wreath for Caesar.

In *The Variety*, III *iii*, Formall explains that Newman has fitted up a room as a theatre in the tavern he frequents, and "o're the great Roome he uses to be drunk in, they say, he has built a heaven, a Players heaven, and thence a Throne's let down, in which, well heated, successively they are drawn up to the clouds to drink their Mistris health"; and in IV *iv* a throne descends to music with a boy in it, and Formall and a Wench are put in the throne and sent up to heaven, with glasses of wine in their hands for sceptres.

In *The Widow's Tears*, III *ii*, a nuptial masque includes the descent of the bridegroom's nephew in the role of Hymen. Sixty-six lines before he descends, a man on the stage below says "And there's your young nephew too, he hangs in the clouds deified with Hymen's shape," thus indicating that the boy is visible aloft long before his descent begins. He does not alight upon the stage; instead, his descent is halted at such a level that *"six Sylvans enter beneath, with torches."*

In *A Wife for a Month*, Act II, *"Cupid descends, the Graces sitting by him, Cupid being bound the Graces unbind him,"* and after a dance by maskers, *"Cupid and the Graces ascend in the Chariot."*

In *The Witch*, III *iii*, *"A Spirit like a Cat descends,"* and afterwards both Hecate and the Spirit depart in flight.

In *The Tempest*, III *iii*, Ariel probably enters in flight in the guise of a harpy, in spite of the stage direction's failure to specify descent: *"Thunder and Lightning. Enter Ariell (like a Harpey) claps his wings upon the Table . . .,"* and later *"He vanishes in Thunder."* Here the "like a Harpey," the "wings," and the alighting upon the table, all suggest that he makes his entrance by flying down from the heavens and his departure by flying back again. Conversely, Juno probably does not enter in flight in IV *i*, in spite of the marginal note opposite lines 72–73 saying that *"Juno descends."* Some editors, following Collier, assume that her car appears in the sky at about line 72, that she makes a slow descent, and that she alights from the car at 101. But so prolonged a descent would leave Juno in full view for some thirty lines while Iris and Ceres remain unaware of her approach. It would keep her suspended aloft for all that time without her uttering a word, and it would let her and her celestial car vie for attention with the masque on the stage below. Her car, having come to earth and discharged its passenger, must then either return to heaven empty (which is unexampled in the stagecraft of the period) or remain on the ground, to the inconvenience of the reapers and nymphs in their dance. And finally, a descent from heaven conflicts with Ceres' announcement of Juno's approach at lines 101–102, which makes it clear that she is afoot:

> Highest queen of state,
> Great Juno, comes; I know her by her gait.

In this greatly mutilated scene, one cannot be sure that any stage direction is original. Perhaps Juno descended in flight when *The Tempest*

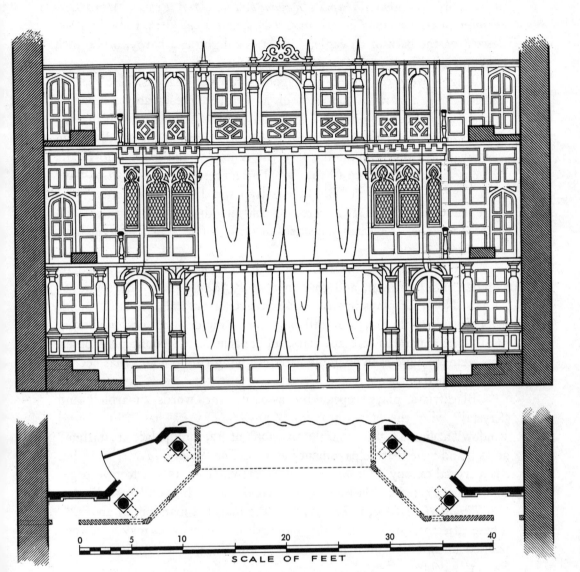

Figure 25. The three levels of the Blackfriars stage.

was presented at Court during the winter of 1612–1613 to grace the betrothal of the Princess Elizabeth and the Elector Palatine. It seems unlikely, however, that she did so at the Blackfriars or the Globe.

A car, throne,[38] or chariot was the vehicle normally used in celestial flights. A throne is specified in *The Prophetess* and *The Variety*, and a chariot in *A Wife for a Month*; and one or another of the three was

417

presumably used also in *Cupid's Revenge, The Mad Lover, More Dissemblers, Valentinian, The Widow's Tears,* and *The Witch.* Both Jupiter's descent on the back of an eagle, and Ariel's flight as a harpy, broke with tradition in failing to use a car.

Flights were controlled by stagehands in the heavens. The raising-and-lowering apparatus consisted of a windlass presumably similar to that shown by Inigo Jones in his design for the staging of the masque *Salmacida Spolia,*[39] and a rope or wire that originated at the windlass, ran from it over a pulley located above the center of the great trap in the heavens floor, and thence to the car. The largest object known to have been lowered through the Blackfriars trap was Delphia's throne (itself large enough to hold two persons) and its dragons with their sail-stretched wings. It probably needed an orifice at least 9 feet long by 5 feet wide.

The descents in *Cymbeline* and *The Tempest* are accompanied by thunder and lightning, and that in *Cupid's Revenge* by the sound of cornets. No other plays in the Blackfriars repertory call for loud sounds as obbligatos to flights; they call only for music or song, or for nothing at all. The apparatus at Blackfriars, unlike that in the public playhouses, thus seems to have been operable without giving rise to noises that needed to be drowned out.

Blackfriars plays repeatedly associate the words "marble" and "crystal" with the stage heavens. *Cymbeline,* v *iv,* has "thy crystal window" at line 81, "thy marble mansion" at 87, "my palace crystalline" at 113, and "the marble pavement" at 120. *The Roman Actor,* III *ii,* has "yon crystal canopy." *Othello,* which is known from its quarto title pages to have been acted at Blackfriars, has "yond marble heaven" at III *iii* 460, and *Timon of Athens,* IV *iii* 191, has "the marbled mansion all above."[40] These adjectives suggest that the underside of the heavens may have been painted in imitation of marble, as we know the wooden columns at the Swan to have been.[41]

The heavens huts at the Globe held cannons or "chambers" that could be shot off in battle scenes or as salutes; the wadding from one of them set fire to the Globe's thatched roof on June 29, 1613, and caused the building to burn to the ground. But probably Blackfriars had no such cannon, partly because its battle scenes were few,[42] and partly because lighter artillery sufficed. In the roofless public playhouses, the din of heavy guns was doubtless needed in battle scenes, but in the roofed

Blackfriars their noise would have been excessive and their smoke unpleasant; Blackfriars thus seems to have made do with nothing heavier than a pistol. This is evidenced by a scene in *Love's Pilgrimage*. In IV *i*, the platform is the waterside in Barcelona and the tarras is the quarterdeck of a moored galley. Markantonio, having gone ashore, has outraged the citizens by insisting on seeing the face of a veiled lady, and a riot has broken out; and Rodorigo, still on the galley, seeks to protect his friend by ordering the ship's gunner to "make a shot into the Town." The shot is supposedly fired from one of the galley's mounted guns; but eighty lines before the gun is discharged, the First Folio has this prompt warning: "*Joh. Bacon ready to shoot off a Pistol.*"

Just as Blackfriars made less use of cannon fire than did the public playhouses, so it also made less use of fireworks, presumably for a similar reason. Aside from a few specifications of lightning,[43] only three plays call for fire or smoke, and two call for mists. In *1 Arviragus and Philicia*, Act IV, two men attempt to enter a witch's cave, whereupon "*Fire flashes out of the Cave, and hideous noyse.*" In *Bonduca*, III *i*, the Queen and her daughters beg their gods to give victory to the British arms, and after an anxious interval they see "*A smoak from the Altar*," and presently "*A flame arises.*" And, as previously mentioned, *Caesar and Pompey*, II *i*, has Ophioneus ascend through the platform trap to an accompaniment of "*flames issuing.*" Mists, simulated by smoke, are called for in *The Maid's Tragedy*, I *i*, when "*Night rises in mists*," and in *The Prophetess*, in the dumb show preceding Act IV, when Delphia raises "a foggy mist" to hide the Persians from their pursuers. In all the plays produced at Blackfriars over a period of 42 years,[44] these five, I think, are the only ones that make use of pyrotechnical devices. The reason for their avoidance at the roofed-over Blackfriars is probably that which the Page sets forth in *The Fawn*, I *ii*:

> *Page.* There be squibs sir, which squibs running upon lines like some of our gawdie Gallants sir, keepe a smother sir, and in the end sir, they do sir—
> *Nymphadoro.* What sir?
> *Page.* Stink sir.

The playhouse had a great bell that served as an alarm bell in *Alphonsus of Germany*, III *i*; *The Cardinal*, V *iii*; *The Island Princess*, I *i* and II *iii*; and *A Wife for a Month*, V *i*. In *Cymbeline*, II *ii*, it marked the hours—"One, two, three. Time, time!"—and in *The Mayor of Quinborough,* v *i,* it rang to celebrate a victory:

> *Simon.* Fates, I thank you for this victorious day!
>   Bon-fires of pease-straw burn, let the bells ring.
> *Glover.* There's two in mending, and you know they cannot.
> *Simon.* 'Las the tenor's broken! ring out the treble.

The bell probably did not hang inside the heavens huts, for there its clangor would have been distressing to those inside and muffled to those below. More probably it was mounted among the roof rafters, and operated by a rope that fell behind the scenes to platform level.[45]

The playhouse inevitably had the customary apparatus for imitating thunder—heavy balls of stone or iron bowled along a wooden "run" or trough, accompanied by rolls on snare drums and kettle drums.[46] Since the thunder would sound most convincing if coming from aloft, it seems probable that the thunder balls were kept in the heavens.

We have no clue to the size of the heavens huts; we merely know that they needed to be large enough to have a trap, estimated at 9 feet long by 5 feet wide, cut through their floor, and still to have enough floor space left to hold the winch and the men who operated it, and to provide storage for the thrones, chariots, dragons, and eagles not at the moment in use. James Burbage, when he built the huts, would naturally have lodged them upon the timbers that composed the framework of the roof, and therefore the size of the huts may have depended upon the distances between those timbers more directly than upon anything else: the size of the floor may have been determined by the spacing of the beams upon which it rested, and the position of the side walls by that of the queen posts.

Stagehands needed some way to get up to the heavens, and so did actors who were about to make descents. Either of two ways may have been available. The first was the stone staircase, presumably spiral, that we know to have led up from the Parliament Chamber to the roof (19:3). Those stairs are the second item specified in James Burbage's deed of purchase, preceded only by the seven great upper rooms themselves. This perhaps indicates that Burbage looked upon the stairs as being important; and if he foresaw a theatrical need for them, it is hard to imagine what that need can have been unless to get actors and stagehands up to the heavens. On this theory, the stairs were probably at the southern or stage end of the great hall, not at the northern or audience end; and on this theory, too, actors mounted the spiral stairs to the walkway just inside the parapet, climbed through a trap door cut through the roof, and mounted a flight of internal stairs to the door of the huts. The second possibility is that a ladder led up to the heavens from "the top."

1. "Above" is the customary theatrical idiom for the upper stage. Only once is any other word used in a stage direction in a Blackfriars play. It occurs in *Alphonsus of Germany*, I *i*, in the direction "*He opens the door and finds Lorenzo asleep aloft.*"

2. *Captain*, II *ii*; *Chances*, IV *iii*; *Devil Is an Ass*, II *vi–vii*; *Distresses*, II *ii*; *Dutch Courtesan*, II *i*; *Fawn*, IV *i*; *Island Princess*, IV *ii–iii*; *Lost Lady*, III *i*; *Love and Honour*, V *ii*; *Maid in the Mill*, I *iii*; *Monsieur Thomas*, III *iii*; *Novella*, II *ii* and IV *i*; *Picture*, IV *ii*; *Roman Actor*, II *i*; *Swisser*, III *i*; *Two Noble Kinsmen*, II *i–ii*; *Widow*, III *i*.

In only one Blackfriars play does the word "window" occur in a context that places the "window" on the lower level, facing the platform. The word is so used in *The Humorous Lieutenant*, IV *iv* and IV *viii*, in both which scenes the so-called window is probably the wicket in an outer-stage door. See pp. 326 to 327 above.

3. Other scenes that presumably employ a window, though none is specified, are *Barnavelt*, IV *iv*; *Chances*, V *i*; *Distresses*, II *iii*; *Eastward Ho!*, II *ii*; *Knight of the Burning Pestle*, III *v*; *Novella*, II *ii*; *Osmond the Great Turk*, II *ii*; *Wild-Goose Chase*, V *iv*; etc.

4. Cf. Lloyd, pp. 327–43.

5. Plurals are similarly used in *Maid in the Mill*, I *iii* ("Pluck to the windows"), *Monsieur D'Olive*, I *i* ("the encurtained windows"), *Picture*, IV *ii* ("the windows grated with iron"), and *Two Noble Kinsmen*, II *ii* ("the windows are too open").

6. Allen W. Jackson, *The Half-Timber House*, p. 90.

7. Lloyd, p. 71, quoting Lord Coke's Reports, 41–42 Elizabeth, 1597, p. 36b.

8. Viz., *Distresses*, IV *ii*; *Fair Favorite*,

II *ii*; *Platonic Lovers*, I *i*; and *Spanish Curate*, II *ii*.

9. By permission of Routledge & Kegan Paul, Ltd., publishers of *The Plays and Poems of George Chapman*, I here quote the text edited by Thomas Marc Parrott; but I follow Chapman in his use of the word "tarrasse" rather than Parrott in his use of "terrace."

10. The similar relationship of the tarras to the window stages at the Globe, as evidenced in these two plays, is discussed by John Cranford Adams, *Globe Playhouse*, pp. 250–52.

11. *Alphonsus of Germany*, IV *i*; *Double Marriage*, V *iii*; and *Queen of Corinth*, IV *iii*.

12. *Alphonsus of Germany*, IV *iii*; *Barnavelt*, II *iv*; *Maid's Tragedy*, V *ii*; and *Royal Slave*, V *i*. With respect to this last item, see footnote 22 on page 305.

13. Perhaps the tarras has previously served as a hill in *Bonduca*, III *iii*. Nennius speaks of "yond' hill's brow" and Caratach says "Let's thither," but it is not wholly clear that they enter above.

14. *Much Ado*, III *iii*; see also *Merchant of Venice*, II *vi*.

15. John Cranford Adams, *Globe Playhouse*, pp. 222–27, finds that the Globe had a trap that pierced the floor of the upper inner stage and the ceiling of the rear stage on the level below, and he reconstructs this scene, and all others in the same category, by having the eavesdropper stand in the upper stage and peer down through the trap at his feet. I find no evidence for the existence of such a trap at Blackfriars.

16. I suggest that the following scenes do *not* belong in the category just discussed: *Duchess of Malfi*, V *v*, since the four men above are in a position to hear, but not to see, what is happening on the stage

below; *Emperor of the East*, I *ii*, since the stage direction ("*The Curtains drawn above, Theodosius and his eunuchs discovered*") proves that the eavesdroppers above are revealed in the discoverable stage behind the tarras; *Love's Cure*, V *iii*, since the scene is probably not indoors and the presence of those above is not surreptitious; and *More Dissemblers Besides Women*, I *iii*, since the action is manifestly on a street. In the last two plays, the persons above are probably on the tarras.

17. *Second Maiden's Tragedy*, v *i*.

18. *Bashful Lover*, V *iii*; *Cruel Brother*, V *iii*; *Duchess of Malfi*, I *i* and V *ii*; *Duke of Milan*, III *ii*; *Maid's Tragedy*, IV *i*; *Sir Giles Goosecap*, IV *i* and V *ii*; *Valentinian*, II *iv*; *Variety*, II *ii* and III *iv*; *Winter's Tale*, V *iii*; etc.

19. All those in the above footnote except *Duchess of Malfi*, V *ii*, and perhaps *Sir Giles Goosecap*, V *ii*.

20. A stage direction in IV *vi* says "*curtains drawn*," and one in V *ii* says "*the stage curtains are drawn, and discover a chamber*." But the dramatist was admittedly not sure whether the upper stage was capable of containing the first of these scenes. Probably both scenes were performed on the lower stage.

21. A stage direction in *The Royal Slave*, V *i*, says that several persons are "discover'd on the Castle walls." But the play's author, Cartwright, sometimes uses the word "discover" informally, as meaning merely to come into view, rather than technically, as meaning to be revealed by the opening of curtains. Thus in III *iii* of the same play he has "*Cratander is discover'd over-hearing them*," and in IV *iii* he has "*C[ratander] is discover'd walking toward them*."

22. Probably the stage was not large enough to contain two beds. Thomas Killigrew, when he wrote *The Parson's Wedding* in exile, wished to have Wild's chamber (IV *vi*) staged on the upper level, but he was not sure that the upper stage was large enough to hold two beds and two tables. He therefore ended his stage direction with the proviso "*all above if the scene can be so ordered*."

23. In *The Witch*, IV *iii*, the stage direction ("*Enter Francisca, in her Chamber*") points to the use of the upper inner stage, but her actions suggest that she is on the tarras.

24. Cf. John Cranford Adams, *Globe Playhouse*, p. 88; Smith, p. 64.

25. See p. 297 above.

26. E. K. Chambers, *Elizabethan Stage*, Vol. III, p. 153.

27. Viz., *Alphonsus*, *Elder Brother*, *Novella*, *Witch*, and *Wits*.

28. The following plays, in addition to those already mentioned, call for actors to ascend or descend the stairs within the course of a scene: *Bashful Lover*, V *iii* (five noblemen); *Bonduca*, II *iii* (two daughters); *Custom of the Country*, IV *iii* (Zabulon, Hippolyta); *Devil Is an Ass*, II *vii* (Fitzdottrel and his wife); *Distresses*, II *iii* (Amiana); *Gentleman Usher*, V *i* (Alphonso, Medice, and two others); *Goblins*, V (Prince and Philatel); *Island Princess*, V *v* (Syana, Bakam, etc.); *Love's Cure*, IV *ii* (Clara); *Monsieur D'Olive*, V *i* (Marcellina and Eurione); *Noble Gentleman*, IV *iii* (Shattillion); *Novella*, II *ii* (Paulo), IV *i* (Astutta, Guadagni, Nanulo), V *i* (Piso, Horatio, Jacconetta); *Picture*, IV *ii* (Ubaldo, Ricardo), IV *iv* (Ladislaus, Ferdinand, etc.); *Roman Actor*, IV *ii* (Caesar); *Sea Voyage*, I *iii* (Lamure and Franvile); etc.

29. W. J. Lawrence, in *Pre-Restoration Stage Studies*, pp. 16–23, argues that

"an outer visible staircase" existed, in addition to the backstage staircase. John Cranford Adams has refuted his arguments convincingly in *Globe Playhouse*, pp. 398–401.

30. The stairs at the Globe were similarly off-stage and near the door in the back wall. Cf. John Cranford Adams, *Globe Playhouse*, pp. 229–40.

31. See pp. 403 to 405 above.

32. Musicians take part in action on the lower stage in the following scenes also: *City Madam*, III *i*; *Custom of the Country*, III *ii*; *Cymbeline*, V *iv*; *Distresses*, II *ii*; *Duke of Milan*, II *i*; *Guardian*, IV *ii*; *Love and Honour*, III *iii* and IV *ii*; *Monsieur Thomas*, III *iii*; *News from Plymouth*, III *iii*; *Parson's Wedding*, V *iv*; *Wits*, III *v* and V *iii*; etc.

33. *Music on the Shakespearean Stage*, pp. 81–82.

34. I am indebted to Professor John McCabe of New York University for calling my attention to the importance of these two scenes in suggesting the height of the window stages.

35. See pp. 291 to 292 above.

36. See pp. 169 to 170 above.

37. Thomas Heywood, in his *Apology for Actors*, published 1612, speaks of "the covering of the stage, which we call the heavens." Higgins, in his *Nomenclator*, published 1584, defines "Machina" as "The skies or counterfet heaven over the stage, from whence some god appeared or spake." Cotgrave's *French-English Dictionary* of 1611 defines "volerie" as "a place over the stage which we call the Heaven"; and William Cavendish, in the Blackfriars play *The Variety*, III *iii*, speaks of "a Players heaven, and thence a Throne's let down." Nicola Sabbatini has this description of the heavens in the Italian theatre (1638): "When it is

necessary for machines to ascend to the sky or descend thence to the stage, one must have a 'cut' heaven, both for convenience and for the delight and wonder which audiences take in it, since they cannot see how the machines which rise from the earth disappear, or how they descend from the heavens to the stage." For the Higgins and Cotgrave items I am indebted to Lawrence, *Physical Conditions*, p. III; for the Sabbatini item, to Halliday, *Shakespeare Companion*, p. 269.

38. As used in connection with flights, the word "throne" of course has no association with a royal throne, which, in any event, was usually called a "state." Flying apparatus used in an Italian theatre in the seventeenth century, including both a car and the rigging for "free" flights, is pictured in Smith, Plate XXIII.

39. Reproduced by Reyher from Lansdowne MS. 1171, and reprinted by Ashley H. Thorndike, p. 188.

40. We have no assurance that *Timon* was acted at Blackfriars, but its presumed date (1607–1608) and its Masque of the Amazons suggest that it may have been written with Blackfriars performance in mind.

41. DeWitt described the Swan's wooden columns in 1595 as being "painted in such excellent imitation of marble that it is able to deceive even the most cunning." Cf. Joseph Quincy Adams, *Shakespearean Playhouses*, p. 168.

42. Only two other Blackfriars scenes require heavy arms. They are II *i* of *Double Marriage*, with "*Charge Trumpets and shot within. . . . Charge Trumpets, Pieces go off*," and III *iii* of *Conspiracy* (*Pallantus and Eudora*), with "*A vollie of Great Shot interrupts their discourse. . . . Great Shot still.*"

43. Viz., *Caesar and Pompey*, II *iv*; *Catiline*, III *v*; *Cymbeline*, V *iv*; *Prophetess*,

II *iii* and V *iii*; *Sea Voyage*, I *i*; *Tempest*, I *i* and III *iii*, etc.

44. I exclude *Conspiracy* (*Pallantus and Eudora*), V *iv*, with its perfumed smoke, and *Royal Slave*, V *ii*, with its sacrificial fire, since both these effects undoubtedly had to do only with the elaborate sceneried production of the plays before Charles I and his Queen at Oxford and York House respectively. See pp. 270–272 above.

45. Bells at off-stage doors are called for in *Novella*, I *ii*, IV *i* and V *i*, and in *Bloody Brother*, IV *ii*. "*Musicke of Bels*" is called for in *Isle of Gulls*, II *v*. Hand bells are used in several plays.

46. Cf. *Othello*, V *ii* ("Are there no stones in heaven / But what serves for the thunder?") and *Every Man in His Humour*, Prologue (" . . . roll'd bullet heard / To say, it thunders."). For the drums, cf. John Melton, *Astrologaster, or The Figure Caster* ("Drummers make Thunder in the Tyring-house."). For a fuller discussion, see John Cranford Adams, *Globe Playhouse*, p. 320, n. 15.

⚔ APPENDIX ⚔

Document I

⟦ The Kingston Property

SEPTEMBER 20, 1536

The following paragraph describes the property that John Hilsey, Prior of the convent, leased to Sir William Kingston, Lady Mary Kingston, and Sir Henry Jerningham[1] in 1536, two years before the Suppression. (*Aug. Off. Book* 216, f. 52, printed in *Blackfriars Records*, p. 104.)

§1 . . . All the messuage, tenements [and] garden which of late was in the hands of Dame Elizabeth Dentonys, with a way to the waterside between the garden of my Lady Peacock of the west part, and the garden of Richard Trice of the east part; and also two chambers and a cellar underneath the library, which sometime was the under-library adjoined to the hill garden.

MAY 6, 1540

Having taken possession of the precinct on November 12, 1538, King Henry VIII leased the following additional parcels to Sir Henry Kingston. (*Aug. Off. Book* 212, f. 134^v, or *Loseley MS* 332 (30), printed in the original Latin in *Blackfriars Records*, p. 104, and here translated by the author.)

§2 . . . All the former cloister called the Inner Cloister, being now a garden; and all the houses and edifices under the dormitory; and all the hall, storehouse and cellar on the north part of the said cloister; and all the house and edifice called the Library on the east part of the said cloister; and all that part of the dormitory not assigned nor demised to the Lady Anne Gray, widow, on the north part of the said cloister; and also all the space beneath, within the aforesaid cloister; and also all the house and edifice called the Firmary at the west end of the said cloister, and all the space over and under belonging to the same, and all the mill and brewhouse adjacent to the said firmary, and one stable situated next to the said brewhouse, together with all ways, footpaths, entrances and exits.

426

Document 1

SEPTEMBER 5, 1545

After the death of her husband, Lady Mary Kingston was granted the reversion and rent reserved on the messuage described in paragraph 1 above, and ownership of the parcels specified in paragraph 2 and redescribed below. (*Rec. Off. Patent Roll*, 37 Henry VIII, part 1, or copy in *Loseley MS.* No. 1396, f. 72ᵛ–73ᵛ. The ellipses in this paragraph occur in the Latin text as printed in *Blackfriars Records*, p. 105. The present translation is by the author.

§3 . . . All that our cloister, land, ground and garden called the Inner Cloister-yard, and our hereditament commonly called the Inner Cloister, with the appurtenances, formerly in the tenure of the said William Kingston, knight, and now in the tenure of the said Lady Mary Kingston . . . [and] all that our house and all the houses . . . called the Library, situated and being on the east part of the said cloister, land, ground and hereditament called the Inner Cloister . . . and also all that house . . . called the Firmary, situated and being at the west end of the said cloister . . . and all our space, land, ground, edifice and hereditament being over and under the same firmary and belonging or appertaining to the same firmary . . . and also all that our mill and brewhouse adjacent to the said firmary . . . and all that our stable with the appurtenances, next adjacent to the said brewhouse.[2]

1. Sir Henry Jerningham was the son of Lady Mary Kingston and the stepson of Sir William.

2. Paragraph 2 lists the [south] dorter, but paragraph 3 omits it. So does 11:5, which inventories the property after it had passed to Sir Henry Jerningham.

Document 2

⟪Grant to Paul Gresham and Francis Boldero

SEPTEMBER 7, 1544

Aug. Off. Particulars for Grants, 524, 36 Henry VIII. This document is printed in Latin in *Archaeologia,* Vol. 63, p. 70, n. I, and is here translated by the author. *Blackfriars Records,* p. 106, lists four additional unpublished documents as giving the particulars of the grant.

§1 The rent of all that entrance called "le entree," adjacent and annexed to "le gallorye" of Lady Anne Gray towards the south, containing by estimation 16 feet in length to the door leading to the cloister, and in width by estimation 8 feet, leading to the door in the east side of the dorter; and from the same dormitory 20 feet in length from the south wall to the first beam towards the north, and so leading to the entrance which leads to a certain small chamber commonly called "the provincyalles Chamber" over the garden;

§2 And also the rent of a certain ruinous chamber called "le comon Jakes Chamber" next to the said chamber called "the provyncyalles chamber," and of one pair of stairs called "le payer of Stayers" leading by the stone wall south of the said dormitory to the said chamber called "the provyncyall Chamber";

§3 And also the rent of three rooms, with two fireplaces in the same;

§4 And also of one chamber called "le Scolehouse," standing at the east end of the great cloister; and also of one small garden lying in front of the windows of the same house called "le Scolehouse," at the present time demised to the said Lady Ann Gray, widow, her executors and assigns.

Document 3

❲ Lord Cobham's Original Purchase in the Blackfriars

AUGUST 29, 1545[1]

Loseley MS. No. 1396, f. 75[v], printed in Latin in *Blackfriars Records*, p. 13, and here translated by Miss A. L. D. Kennedy-Skipton of the staff of the Folger Shakespeare Library. This document describes the mansion that King Henry VIII sold to George Lord Cobham.

The Lord Cobham's particular of his purchase in the Blackfriars

§1 A parcel of the lands and possessions lately the house of the Friars Preachers within the City of London.

§2 The farm[2] of one tenement or mansion there, with a certain window called the Closet Window looking into the church there, together with all the rooms, kitchens, storerooms, larders, cellars, solars, and all other the houses and buildings, with a conduit of water in the said kitchen garden, and other the places there belonging to the same tenement or mansion, which formerly were in the tenure of Lady Jane Guildford, and now demised to the honorable gentleman George Cobham, by his Indenture dated the tenth day of April in the 27th year of the reign of King Henry VIII [1536], for a term of 80 years from then next ensuing and fully to be completed, yielding therefor, at the feasts of the Annunciation of the blessed Virgin Mary and of St. Michael the Archangel, in two equal portions every year —— £5 6s. 8d., at nine years £48.

Parcel of the site or said precinct lately the house of the Friars Preachers

These been the first particulars.

Examined by me, Thomas Mildmay, auditor.

The 29th day of August in the 37th year of the reign of King Henry VIII for George Lord Cobham

§3 The farm of one tenement and other the premises within the precinct of the late Blackfriars in London, by year 106s. 8d., which rented at nine years' purchase is —— £48.

John Baker   Richard Southwell   Edward North
ENROLLED BY JOHN HAWBY

1. *Blackfriars Records*, p. 12, gives the date of this document as 1546, but 1545 would seem to be more probable. The reign of Henry VIII began on April 22, 1509, and August 29 in the 37th year of his reign (paragraph 3) would therefore fall in 1545. Furthermore, nine years had elapsed since Cobham acquired the premises on April 10 in the twenty-seventh year of the same reign (1536).

2. The noun "fferme" (here in Latin "ffirma"), occurs repeatedly in these documents, especially as embodied in the phrases "to fferme lett," "to fferme hath letten," etc. In all such contexts it is an obsolete term equivalent to "rent." See *O.E.D.*, *s.v.* "Farm."

Document 4

⟨The Survey of 1548

Loseley MS. No. 393, printed in type facsimile in *Blackfriars Records,* pp. 6–8. This document enumerates the buildings and parcels of ground which were leased to Sir Thomas Cawarden on April 4, 1548.

At the Black Friars besides Ludgate in London

§1 A Survey of certain edifices, buildings and void ground, there taken the 18th day of March in the second year of the reign of King Edward the Sixth, by [name omitted]:

§2 A void ground with a decayed gallery therein, with void rooms thereunder wherein old timber and cart-wheels lieth, containing in length 98 foot; abutting against Bridewell Ditch on the west side, being in breadth at that end 74 foot; abutting to the common highway and lane that guideth to the common highway and stair to the Thames-side on the east side, being in breadth at that end 94 foot; abutting to the Lady or Mistress Harper's garden, and also Francis's garden, on the north side; and to Sir Christopher More's garden on the south side;

§3 A kitchen yard, an old kitchen, an entry or passage joining to the same, containing in length 84 foot; abutting to the lane aforesaid on the west side, being in breadth at that end 68 foot; abutting against an old buttery on the east side, being in breadth at that end 74 foot; abutting to Mr. Portinary's parlor, next the lane, on the south side; and to my Lord Cobham's brick wall and garden on the north side;

§4 An old buttery and an entry or passage with a great stair therein, with cellars thereunder, with a hall place at the upper end of the stair and an entry there to the frater over the same buttery, all which contain in length 36 foot and in breadth 95 foot; abutting to the cloister on the east side, the kitchen on the west side, to the Lord Cobham's house on the north side, and on the south side to a blind parlor that my Lord Warden[1] did claim;

§5 A house called the Upper Frater, containing in length 107 foot and in breadth 52 foot, abutting south and east to my Lady Kingston's house and garden, north to a hall where the King's Revels lies at this present, and west towards the said Duchy Chamber and Mr. Portinary's house;

§6 A hall and a parlor under the said frater of the same length and breadth;

Memorandum:
my Lord Warden
claimeth the said
hall, parlor, kitchen,
and chamber

§7 A little kitchen containing in length 23 foot and in breadth 22 foot, abutting to the aforesaid lane on the west, towards the said parlor on the east, to Mr. Portinary's house on the north, and to a way leading to my Lady Kingston's house on the south;

§8 A little chamber with a void room thereunder, containing in length 26 foot, in breadth 10 foot, abutting west to the kitchen, east to the parlor, north to Mr. Portinary's house, and the said way to my Lady Kingston's house south, with four small cellars or dark holes thereunder;

§9 A void room being an entry towards the little kitchen and coalhouse, containing in length 30 foot and in breadth 17 foot;

§10 A chamber called the Duchy Chamber, with a dark lodging thereunder, containing in length 50 foot and in breadth 16 foot, abutting east against the north end of the said frater, abutting west on Mr. Portinary's parlor —— 66s. 8d.

Document 5

❬ Grant by King Edward VI to Sir Francis Bryan

DECEMBER 12, 1548

Rec. Off. Patent Roll, 2 Edward VI, part 7; a copy in *Loseley MS*. No. 1396, f.63ᵛ–64ᵛ; also No. 392. Printed in Latin in *Blackfriars Records*, pp. 103–104, and here translated by the author. The ellipses in the first two paragraphs occur in the Latin text as printed.

§1 All that our hall . . . a parcel of the chapter house there, and adjoining the cloister there on the east side;

§2 And all that site . . . formerly called the Prior's Lodging, now in the tenure or occupation of the said Francis [Bryan], as well as all that our chamber under the dorter, adjacent to the said cloister on the east side aforesaid;

§3 And all that our other chamber, and the partition in front of the cellar called a Buttery, adjacent to the same cloister;

§4 And all that our house there called a Storehouse, under the dorter aforesaid, adjacent to the cellar called the Buttery on the north side;

§5 And all that our house with a fireplace, adjacent to the same house called the Storehouse, and also all that our kitchen, with a certain curtilage adjacent to the storehouse on the east side;

§6 And also all that our house there called a Larderhouse, adjacent to the kitchen on the north side;

§7 And all that our cellar there, adjacent to the said house called the Larderhouse and the kitchen, on the east side;

§8 And all that our little chamber, adjacent to the church of the Blackfriars aforesaid on the south side;

§9 And all that our chapel there, adjacent to the said church formerly the house of the Friars Preachers, on the south side;

§10 And all that our cenacle called a Parlor, under the house and building called the Gallery there, adjacent to the said chapel on the south side aforesaid;

§11 And all that our great chamber called a Great Dining Chamber, over the cellar there;

§12 And also all that our chamber there called a Bedchamber, with a little

433

chamber over the same, and adjacent to the said great chamber there on the north side;

§13 And all that other chamber, adjacent over the west end of the said great chamber called the Great Chamber;

§14 And all that our building and house called the Gallery, over the cenacle there, adjacent to the east end of the said chamber called the Great Chamber;

§15 And also all that our house and building called the Little Gallery, with two little chambers above the same, adjacent to the said great chamber on the south side aforesaid;

§16 And all that our chamber over the hall aforesaid, with divers partitions within the same, adjacent to the said little gallery on the south side aforesaid;

§17 And also those our two gardens there, adjacent to the said hospice called the Prior's Lodging on the east side, and over the great royal wardrobe there commonly called the King's Great Wardrobe on the west side, containing by estimation one acre of land, with all and singular their appurtenances.

Document 6

⟪Hugh Losse's Survey of 1550

Loseley MS. No. 1396, f.49ᵛ, printed in type facsimile in *Blackfriars Records*, pp. 8–12.[1] This survey was undoubtedly made in preparation for the grant of houses and lands by King Edward VI to Sir Thomas Cawarden on March 12, 1550 (Document 7). In paragraphs 18 through 23 it parallels paragraphs 2, 3, 4, 5, 9, and 10 of the 1548 Survey (Document 4), but it excludes the parcels claimed by the Lord Warden (4:6, 4:7 and 4:8).

Sir Thomas
Cawarden's
particular of the
Black Friars

§1 A Survey there taken by me, Hugh Losse, esquire, the King's Majesty's surveyor, . . . the 4th of January . . . [1550], by virtue of a warrant from the right worshipful Sir Richard Sackville, knight, Chancellor of the King's Majesty's Court of the Augmentations and Revenues: . . .

§2 The site or soil of the said late church called the Black Friars, within the City of London, with the two aisles, chancel and chapel to the same belonging, containing in breadth from the north churchyard to the south cloister[2] 66 foot, and in length from the lodging of John Barne[tt],[3] gentleman, on the west end of the same church to the garden belonging to the mansion or tenement belonging to Sir Anthony Ager, knight, on the east end of the same church, 220 foot;

§3 The churchyard on the north side of the body of the said church containeth in breadth from the said church unto a certain brick wall [and][4] the houses, tenements and gardens in the tenure of Peter Hosier and Mr. Holt on the north side of the same churchyard 90 foot, and in length from the houses and tenements of Mrs. Partridge, Mr. Southcote and the Ankers House [i.e., the house of the Anchoress] on the west end, unto a certain wall adjoining to the King's highway on the east end, 200 foot;

§4 The soil of the cloister, being on the south side of the body of the said church, containeth in breadth from the body of the said church to the lodging of the Lady Kingston on the south side of the same cloister 110 foot, and in length from the wall belonging to the lodgings sometime [of] Sir Francis Bryan and now

435

[of] Sir Anthony Ager, knight, and Mr. Walsingham on the east part, to the lodging of the Lord Cobham and John Barnett on the west part, 110 foot;

§5 The chapter house being on the west end[5] of the said cloister, containeth in length 44 foot and in breadth 22 foot;

§6 Which all said soil or ground is valued in the whole to be worth by the year —— £8.

§7 The stones of the arches of the body of the said church, with the windows, walls, buttresses and tombs of the same church, and the stones of the choir and of one chapel on the north side of the said church, and also the paving and free stone of the south cloister, valued at in the whole / sum —— £66 6s. 8d.

§8 The slates and tiles of the east dorter and of the south dorter, with the tiles that covereth the roof of a piece of a chamber now in the tenure of Sir Thomas Cawarden over the old kitchen in the south end of the Lord Cobham['s] lodging, valued in the whole at / sum —— £11.

§9 The glass of the same church, as well within the body of the said church as also within the choir, chapel and cloister, valued in the whole at / sum —— 46s. 8d.

§10. The iron of the same church, as well within the body of the same as also within the choir, chapel and cloister, valued in the whole at / sum —— £8.

§11 The timber of the whole body of the same church, with the timber of the choir, both aisles, and also the timber of the whole cloister, and with the timber of the south and east dorters, is valued in the whole at / sum —— £63.

§12 The contents of the whole lead of the body of the said church, and the lead of the two aisles, with the lead of the roof of a vestry on the north side on the east end of the said church, and the lead of a little roof covering the stairs coming out of the church to the dorter, and also the lead of the whole south cloister, with a cistern of lead in the old kitchen, containeth 112½ fothers. The whole contents of the lead that covereth the frater parcel of the said Black Friars, and the lead that covereth a shed adjoining to the said frater, amounteth to 16½ fothers. Every fother of the said lead, valued and rated at £5 10s.,[6] amounteth in the whole to —— £709 11s.

§13 Sum totals —— £879 3s. 4d.

§14 The rent or farm of a certain tenement within the precinct of the said late Black Friars, called the Ankers House, late in the tenure of Sir Morisse Griffith, clerk and archdeacon of Rochester, and renteth yearly —— 40s.

§15 The rent or farm of a certain tenement, with all and singular the appurtenances, within the precinct of the said late Black Friars, in the tenure and occupation of John Barnett, gentleman, and renteth yearly —— £4.

§16 The rent or farm of two gardens within the precinct of the said late Black Friars in the tenure of Sir Philip Hoby, knight, and renteth yearly —— 13s. 4d.

§17 The rent or farm of a little tenement within the precinct of the said late Black Friars, situate and being over against the tenement of Sir Thomas Cheyne,

knight and Lord Warden of the Cinque Ports, in the tenure of Sir Robert Kyrkham, knight, and renteth yearly —— 20*s.*

§18 One void ground with a decayed gallery therein, with void rooms thereunder wherein old timber and cart-wheels lieth, containing in length 98 foot;
abutting against Bridewell Ditch on the west side, being in breadth at that end 74
foot; abutting to the common highway and lane that goeth to the common stairs to
the Thames-side on the east side, being in breadth at that end 94 foot; abutting
to Mr. Harper['s] garden and also Francis his garden on the north side, and to
Sir Christopher More's garden on the south side;

§19 One kitchen yard, an old kitchen, an entry or passage joining to the same,
containing in length 84 foot, abutting to the lane aforesaid on the west side, being in
breadth at that end 74 foot;[7] abutting to Mr. Portinary's parlor next the lane on
the south side, and to the Lord Cobham['s] brick wall and garden on the north
side;

§20 One old buttery, and a entry or passage with a great stair therein, with cellars thereunder, with a hall place at the upper end of the stairs and a entry there
to the frater over the same buttery, which all containeth in length 95 foot and in
breadth 36 foot, abutting to the cloister on the east side, the kitchen on the west
side, to the Lord Cobham['s] house on the north side, and on the south side to a
blind parlor that my Lord Warden did claim;

§21 One house called the Upper Frater containeth in length 107 foot and in
breadth 52 foot, abutting south and east to the Lady Kingston['s] house and garden, north to a hall where the King's Revels lieth at these presents, and west
towards the Duchy Chamber and Mr. Portinary's house;

§22 A void room, being an entry towards the little kitchen and coalhouse, containing in length 30 foot and in breadth 17 foot;

§23 One chamber called the Duchy Chamber, with a dark lodging thereunder,
containing in length 50 foot and in breadth 16 foot, abutting east against the north
end of the said frater, and abutting west upon Mr. Portinary's parlor; all which
premises be valued to be worth by year —— £3 6*s.* 8*d.*

by me, *Hugo Losse*

§24 . . . The clear yearly value of the premises —— £19; which the King's
Majesty, by the advice of the lords his honorable Privy Council, is pleased and contented, together with the lead, stone, timber, glass, iron and other the premises above
mentioned, to give and grant to Sir Thomas Cawarden, knight, and to his heirs,
without anything yielding therefor, as by a letter from the lords of the King's most
honorable Privy Council, dated the 16th of February last, to me directed, appeareth.

The tenure in free burgage.

To have the issues from Michaelmas last.

Richard Sackville

1. Chambers prints paragraphs 18 to 23 of this document in *Elizabethan Stage*, Vol. II, p. 487, n. 2, and Wallace prints the same paragraphs, but less accurately, in *Evolution*, p. 143, n. 2.

2. "South cloister," as used in this document, refers to the cloister immediately to the south of the church, and not to the southernmost of the two cloisters.

3. The original documents spell this name variously as Barne, Barnet, Barnett, and Barnard. All spellings clearly apply to the same man.

4. In the manuscript, "brickwall" ends a line, and "The" is capitalized. But Hosier's and Holt's houses and the brick wall were all on the north boundary of the churchyard, and both sentence structure and sense demand a connective "and." The parallel passage in the Cawarden grant (7:3) supplies the "and," and so does the Cawarden Inquisition.

5. "West end" is an error. Chapter houses in monasteries and friaries of all orders were uniformly sited on the east side of the cloister. The eastern site of the chapter house is correctly stated in the Bryan grant (5:1).

6. The manuscript gives the price of a "foder" of lead as "Cv^{li} x^s," which is wildly excessive. A fother of lead weighed about 19½ cwt., or nearly a ton; and at the end of the 16th century a ton of lead still sold for just under £8 (cf. W. H. Pulsifer, *History of Lead*, p. 56). The initial "C" of the price per fother is therefore clearly an error and must be disregarded, and the price must be read as £5 10*s*. This, when multiplied by 129 fothers, gives the product £709 10*s*., which is just one shilling less than the amount given in paragraph 12 as the total value of the lead.

7. The 1548 Survey gives this dimension as 68 feet (4:3). The scribe has omitted the clause that gives the old buttery as the eastern boundary of the kitchen yard, but seems nevertheless to have picked up the dimension given in the clause which he omitted. The royal patent of 1550 repeats the error (7:7).

Document 7

❨ The Royal Grant to Sir Thomas Cawarden

MARCH 12, 1550

Patent Rolls, 4 Edward VI, part 6, membrane 63. The original document is in Latin. It is printed in translation in *The Site of the Office of* The Times, pp. 116–17, and is here reprinted by courtesy of that newspaper.

The Patent is based upon the 1550 Survey (Document 6), differences in phraseology being accounted for by the Survey's having been translated into Latin and the Patent's having been translated back into English.

§1 All that house and site of the Friars Preachers in London, the church, steeple, churchyard and cloister of the same, the house called the Chapter House, and all buildings, yards, orchards, gardens, curtilages, stables, ponds, stews and ground within the same site;

§2 And the two "les isles" [= aisles], chancel and chapel pertaining to the said church, containing in width from the churchyard called "le North churchyard" to the south cloister 66 feet, and in length from the house of John Barnett, gentleman, on the west side of the said late church, to the garden belonging to the dwelling of Anthony Ager, knight, on the east of that church, 220 feet;

§3 Which churchyard on the north side of the said church contains in width, from the church to "le brickewall" and the tenement and garden in the tenure of Peter Hosier and [John] Holt 90 feet, and in length from the houses of [Anne] Partridge and [*blank*] Southcote and le Ankeres House on the west, to the partition wall adjoining the King's highway on the east, 200 feet;

§4 And the ground of the said cloister lying on the south side of the said church contains in width, from the church to the dwelling of "le lodging" of Lady Kingston on the same south side of the said cloister 110 feet, and in length from the partition wall belonging to "le lodginges" formerly of Francis Bryan, knight, and now of Anthony Ager, knight, and [Thomas] Walsingham, on the east, to "le lodgyng" of Lord Cobham and John Barnett on the west, 110 feet;

§5 And the said "le Chapiter House" lying at the western end of the said cloister contains in length 44 feet and in width 22 feet;

§6 Also the void plot of land with a ruined "le galerie," and also other void

439

places called "voyde rowmes" within the said site of Friars Preachers, containing in length 98 feet, and abutting against Bridewell Ditch on the west, and in width at that end 74 feet; abutting on the common way and lane which leads to "le commen stayres" at the Thames on the eastern side, being in width at that end 94 feet; and abutting on the garden of Lucy Harper and Francis Gardiner on the north, and the garden of Christopher More, knight, on the south;

§7 Also the old kitchen and "le kychyn yerde" and the entry and passage adjacent to it within the said site of the Friars Preachers, containing 84 feet; abutting upon the lane aforesaid on the west, and being in width at that end 74 feet;[1] and abutting upon the inner room ["intrale"] or "le parlor" of John Portinary next the lane on the south, and upon "le Brickewall" and the garden of Lord Cobham on the north;

§8 Also the house called "le Upper Frater," 107 feet long by 52 feet wide, abutting on the house and garden of Lady Kingston on the south and east, and on the hall where "lez revelles" of the King are now laid up on the north; against "le Dutchie Chamber" and the house of John Portinary on the west;

§9 Also a void plot or entry against the little kitchen and "le coole house," in length 30 feet and in width 17 feet;

§10 Also a grant of "le Dutchie Chamber" aforesaid and "le lodging" beneath it, 50 feet long by 16 feet wide, abutting eastwards against the north end of the said "le frater" and westwards upon the said "le parlor" of John Portinary;

§11 Also the messuage called "le Ankeres House" within the aforesaid site, in the tenure of Morisse Griffith, clerk; the messuage within the said site in the tenure of John Barnett, gentleman; the two gardens in the tenure of Philip Hoby, knight; and the little tenement lying against the tenement of Thomas Cheyne, knight, lord of "lez Cinque Portes," in the tenure of Robert Kyrkham.

§12 And all houses, buildings, shops, cellars, solars, stables, curtilages, and other profits, commodities and easements whatsoever to the same messuages and tenements or any one of them belonging or appertaining, or with the same or any of them being demised or leased, lying within the said site, enclosure, circuit, ambit or precinct of the said late house formerly of the Friars Preachers of London.

§13 We give and grant also, by our special grace and of our sure knowledge and mere motion, and by the advice aforesaid, by these presents, to the aforenamed Thomas Cawarden, knight, all the stones, tiles, "le slates," glass, iron, timber, lead roofing, and lead of the said late house formerly of the Friars Preachers aforesaid of London, or of, in or upon the church, cloister, dormitory, frater, chapel and chancel, and other the premises or any parcel thereof, being of the said late house formerly of the Friars Preachers aforesaid of London, as well as all and singular the messuages, houses, buildings, solars, cellars, curtilages, gardens, void ground, alleys, ways, gates, bridges, staithes of water conduits, and free conduits of water, easements, commodities, profits and hereditaments whatsoever, of whatever kind, nature or species they may be, or by whatever names they are known, called or acknowledged, situate, lying or being within the site, circuit, enclosure, ambit and precinct of the said late house formerly of the Friars Preachers of London.

The foregoing Patent — or this particular transcript of it — omits any mention of the Old Buttery (cf. 4:4 and 6:20) as being included in the grant to Cawarden. But its omission is undoubtedly a mere clerical error.[2] The Cawarden *Inquisition Post Mortem* lists the Old Buttery as having been granted to Cawarden by King Edward VI,[3] and Wallace quotes a patent or Loseley manuscript that includes the "yetus Promptuarium" in the schedule of properties granted:

All that "vetus promptuarium" [promptorium] with entrance or passage, and the great stair, with cellar; with hall called "the hall place" at upper end of stair, and an entry there leading to the "frater" over the "promptuarium," all in length 95 ft., and in breadth, 36 ft., abutting on cloisters on east, kitchen on west, Cobham on north, and "ad quoddam intrale seu le parlor vocat le blinde parlor" on south.[4]

1. See footnote to 6:19.
2. Both times that the Old Buttery is described in a survey, it is preceded by an item that ends with "Lord Cobham's brick wall and garden on the north side" (4:3, 6:19), and the Old Buttery item itself has "Lord Cobham's house on the north side" near its end (4:4, 6:20). The similarity of the two phrases seems to have trapped the scribe into skipping from the first Cobham allusion to the second, omitting everything between.
3. Inquisition taken at the Guildhall on May 3, 1560, printed in *Inquisitiones Post Morten for London*, pp. 191–95.
4. *Evolution*, p. 143, n. 3. Wallace identifies the document as "*Loseley MSS.*, also in *Patent Rolls*, 12 March, 4 Edw. VI (1550)."

Document 8

⟨Thomas Blagrave's Survey of 1552

Loseley MS. No. 401, printed in *Blackfriars Records*, pp. 115–16. A preceding section of the same survey, not reprinted here, is given in *Blackfriars Records*, pp. 109–10.

§1 [*Blank*] Scryven, gentleman, **holdeth** a tenement abutting north upon the High Street (leading from the Gate Street to the Water Lane) in length 30 foot; west upon Water Lane (leading from the High Street to the Thames-side and bridge of the Black Friars) in length 50 foot; south upon a tenement in the tenure of Jane Freemount, widow, in length 24 foot; and east upon a vacant place which was the body of the church of the said Black Friars, in length 62 foot, and upon the yard of a house in the tenure of Thomas Phillips 15 foot: in the whole on that side 77 foot;

§2 With a loft sailing over [the entry of][1] the tenement of the said Jane Freemount, being in length 28 foot and in breadth 12 foot, abutting north upon his own said tenement, west upon the said Water Lane and certain lodgings in the tenure of Mr. Harper, south upon certain lodgings in the tenure of the Lord Cobham, and east upon the late west cloister. . . .

§3*a* Jane Freemount, widow, holdeth a tenement whereof the entry is under the said tenement of [*blank*] Scryven, and the other rooms under the lodgings of the Lord Cobham; the whole abutting east upon the late body of the church of the Black Friars, in length by estimation 28 foot, and upon the late cloister of the same church 21 foot by estimation, in the whole on that side by estimation 49 foot; [b] west upon certain housing in the tenure of Mr. Harper 49 foot, and upon the said highway called Water Lane 4 foot, being the room of the door of her said entry and way into her house: in the whole on that side 53 foot; [c] north upon the said tenement of [*blank*] Scryven 24 foot; upon the wall of the said late body of the church towards the east side 20 foot,[2] and upon the said housing in the tenure of Mr. Harper towards the west side 15 foot: in the whole on that side (deducting 7 foot of the butt against Mr. Harper's housing, which is also a parcel of the 24 foot abutted against Mr. Scryven's tenement, so that the body of this tenement abutteth more and farther out towards the west side, against the said houses of Mr.

Harper, than the entry and butt against Mr. Scryven's tenement is, but only by 8 foot), 52 foot; [d] and south upon certain houses in the tenure of the Lord Cobham, in length 52 foot. . . .

1. The bracketed words are from the corresponding passage in *Loseley MS.* No. 429 (*BR* 116:12). They accord with the first two lines of paragraph 3.

2. The excavations of 1915 verified the overlap reported by Blagrave; they showed that the house whose lower floor was occupied by Jane Freemount, and whose upper floor was occupied by Lord Cobham, overlapped the south wall of the nave by approximately 20 feet. The buildings' sharing of a common wall made it possible for Cobham's lodging to have a window looking into the church. See pp. 85 and 86 above.

Document 9

([Sir Thomas Cawarden's Lease to Ninyan Sawnders

APRIL 16, 1553

Loseley MS. No. 1396, f.42, or 332 (36); printed in type facsimile in *Blackfriars Records*, pp. 110–12.

The Indenture witnesses that Sir Thomas Cawarden has let to Ninyan Sawnders, citizen and vintner of London:

§1 "All that his parcel of ground within the late Blackfriars[1] . . . whereupon is or was lately situate and included the late chancel, a part of the late belfry, at the north end; that is to say, to the breadth of the south end of the said chancel, the chapel, and a vestry at the end there belonging to the same chapel . . . the late chapel sometime annexed to the same;

§2a "And a piece of the churchyard, which said parcel of ground abutteth east-north-east upon a garden sometime in the tenure of Sir Francis Bryan, knight . . . that is to say, the east end of the said vestry, taking 22 foot, and the end of the said chancel 43 foot, in the whole at that end from north to south 65 foot;

§2b "Abutting south upon certain houses and ground sometime the said Sir Francis Bryan's and the same Sir Thomas Cawarden's, not letten to the same Ninyan, in length 94 foot, and upon a stair going up, not letten, into the late east dorter of the said late Black Friars, and a way, not letten, leading between the south end of the said belfry and the north end and side of the late cloister adjoining to the said dorter, 40 foot, in the whole on that side from east to west 134 foot;

§2c "Abutting west upon the said late east dorter, being the breadth of the buttress of the south wall of the chancel 3 foot, upon the late body of the church of the said late Black Friars, not letten to the same Ninyan Sawnders, 56 foot, and running into the aforenamed churchyard, and abutting upon the east end of a parcel of the same churchyard, reserved with the rest not letten, and not letten to the said Ninyan Sawnders nor comprised in this grant, 20 foot, in the whole at that end from the south to the north fourscore foot;

§2d "And abutting north upon a common highway parting the said churchyard, and leading enlongs and through the same into Carter Lane, and containing in

444

length on that side from the west to the east as the way goeth, 222 foot, together with all the pillars, arches, buttresses and walls now defaced and standing in and upon the said demised ground or any part or parcel thereof.

§3*a* "And also all that his parcel of ground, sometime parcel of the said late churchyard, and at the making of these indentures severed and appointed and marked out to be enclosed from the foresaid part of the said churchyard reserved and not letten nor comprised in this grant, which parcel of ground abutteth east upon Carter Lane end, containing in length from north to south 12 foot;

§3*b* "Abutteth south upon the said common highway, not letten unto the same Ninyan otherwise than before, leading enlongs and through the said churchyard into Carter Lane, and containeth in length on that side from east to west 222 foot;

§3*c* "Abutteth west upon the foresaid part of the churchyard reserved and not demised nor comprised in this grant 78 foot, and upon a parcel of the same reserved part of the said churchyard, letten unto John Holt at the will and pleasure of the said Sir Thomas Cawarden, and wherethrough the said John Holt and his family do pass and have recourse to and from the tenement of the said John Holt into the aforesaid reserved part of the churchyard by the sufferance of the said Sir Thomas Cawarden and at his will and pleasure, 9 foot, being in the whole at that end from the south to the north 87 foot;

§3*d* "And abutteth north upon the said way of sufferance for the passage of the said John Holt 24 foot, and upon a brick wall including the yard of the tenement of Henry Codnam now in the tenure of Ninyan Sawnders, and certain houses and ground in the tenure of Doctor Arnsted, and containeth in length alongs that way, and in compass as the wall showeth and goeth 234 foot, being in the whole on that side from the west to the east in compass as the wall showeth and goeth, 258 foot;

§4 "And also the south end of the said late belfry, reserved and not letten to the said Ninyan Sawnders, to build only upon and above the walls, so that the nether floor of the same be at the least 14 foot in height from the ground, except and always reserved the nether parts and room of the same from under the said building to the ground, which reserved parcel of ground containeth in length from east to west 20 foot, and in breadth from north to south 13 foot. . . .

§5 "And the said Sir Thomas Cawarden covenanteth and granteth to and with the said Ninyan Sawnders that he, the said Sir Thomas Cawarden, shall permit and suffer one common way for the said Ninyan Sawnders, his family, and all other people having occasion of access, to have recourse and pass with foot, pack, and horse through the way made, made out of the said reserved part of the churchyard between the tenement in the tenure of Thomas Phillips and the tenement in the tenure of [*blank*] Southcote, and so alongs and through the said made way into Carter Lane, in and upon the said part of the churchyard reserved and not letten to the said Ninyan nor comprised in this grant, and upon so much of the same reserved ground as lieth between the two parcels of ground

445

above demised to the said Ninyan, the said common way to be 10 foot broad, and at the east end thereof a gate for carters to come into and go out of the said church-yard into and from Carter Lane, to be kept and shut with lock, by and at the appointment of the said Sir Thomas Cawarden. . . .

1. Ellipses in this transcript are confined to those that occur in the text as printed in *Blackfriars Records*.

Document 10

⟨ Sir Thomas Cawarden's Sale to Lord Cobham

APRIL 25, 1554

Loseley MS. No. 1396, f.71^v, printed in type facsimile in *Blackfriars Records*, pp. 15–19.

The Lord Cobham's purchase of Sir Thomas Cawarden in the Blackfriars

§1 THIS INDENTURE, made the 25th day of the month of April in the first year of the reign of our sovereign Lady Mary, . . . between Sir Thomas Cawarden of Bletchingley in the County of Surrey, knight, of the one party, and George Brooke, of the right honorable Order of the Garter knight, Lord Cobham, of the other party, WITNESSETH that the said Sir Thomas Cawarden, knight, as well for and in consideration of the sum of £60 of good and lawful money of England to the said Sir Thomas Cawarden by the said Lord Cobham well and truly . . . paid, . . . as for other good and especial considerations, . . . by these presents giveth, granteth, bargaineth and selleth unto the said Lord Cobham:

§2 All that his hall and hereditament with the appurtenances, set, lying and being within the late site, circuit, ambit and precinct of the late Blackfriars, London, adjoining to the house of the said Lord Cobham, [a]butting upon the south on the house now in the tenure or occupation of Sir John Cheke, knight, . . . and on the north butting upon the stairs leading up into the house wherein the said Lord Cobham now dwelleth, and on the east butting upon the late cloister yard of the said late Blackfriars, and on the west butting upon the garden of the said Lord Cobham; which said hall . . . containeth in length from the north end to the south end 52 foot, and in breadth from the east part to the west part thereof 27 foot;

§3 And further the said Sir Thomas Cawarden . . . selleth unto the said Lord Cobham all that his nether room, ground, soil and hereditament . . . under the chambers of the said Lord Cobham, containing in length from the east part to the west part thereof 47 foot, and in breadth from the north part to the south part 21 foot, butting upon the late cloister-yard end of the said late Blackfriars on the east, and on the west butting on the yard of Sir George Harper, knight; . . .

447

§4 In consideration of which bargain and sale, the said Lord Cobham . . . by these presents doth for him and his heirs remit, release and quit claim to the said Sir Thomas Cawarden and his heirs, all that his right, title, claim, estate and interest . . . to or in all and singular those tenements, houses, edifices, buildings and hereditaments . . . lying on the west side of the highway leading from the great gate of the said late Friars near Ludgate to the stairs called the Blackfriars Stairs, and also . . . all that his right, title, claim, state and interest . . . in or to all that void ground, soil and hereditament called the Kitchen Yard, and of, to or in one coal house and one common jakes, . . . on the south side adjoining to the garden of the said Lord Cobham. . . .

§5 IN WITNESS WHEREOF, as well the said Sir Thomas Cawarden as the said Lord Cobham interchangeably have set their seals the day and year above written. . . .

Document 11

([Survey of Freeholders in the Blackfriars Precinct

CIRCA 1555—1556

Loseley MS. No. 390, printed in type facsimile in *Blackfriars Records,* pp. 2—6. This document is Sir Thomas Cawarden's reply to a petition addressed to the Lord Chancellor by the inhabitants of the Blackfriars precinct, in which they asked that a parish church be erected to replace the Church of St. Anne, which Cawarden had destroyed. The petition and reply are discussed on pp. 120—22 above.

The document contains a valuable list of the persons who held lands and grounds in the dissolved priory. The list serves to limit the property that went to Cawarden and from him to More, and later, in part, from More to James Burbage.

Concerning the foundation and erection of a parish church within the precinct of the late Black Friars near London, and what freeholders within the ambit and circuit thereof ought by their inheritance and fee simple of the late possessions of the same house to be contributory thereto

§1 A view of the inheritance and possessions of the same house and within that precinct purchased by divers persons, briefly declaring the parties' names with the places and parcels purchased; compiled upon complaint and suggestion of certain the inhabitants that there was a parish church within the said precinct and Friars, and for that upon denial and manifest disproof of the same, not only because the complainants could not verify it by the approof of any parson, vicar, curate, or incumbent clerk or sexton, . . . or any common bell to call the parish together, or other circumstances incident to a parish church, . . . but also for that the contrary is upon search of the records of the first fruits and tenths and other precedents in the exchequer to be found apparent, and by other due proof to be justified, upon further trial it falleth out that any such church as needfully behooveth to be there erected, must be builded and founded by the inhabitants within that precinct, and at their costs and charges which will be parishioners of the same and enjoy any benefit of the divine service there ministered; . . . so that for the more equal division of the charges of the erection and edifying of the church, hereunder is by estimation set out what

449

proportion of fee simple hath been purchased and now is in the several tenures of the freeholders there for approbation and appearance, who ought to be contributory to the burden thereof; videlicet:

§2 The Bishop of Ely, in the right of him Mr. Blackwell, hath the prior's lodging, the convent garden, with other lands and tenements there, with the upper part of the choir, part of the dorter, part of the chapter house, the vestry, and other houses of office, worth by year [blank];[1]

§3 The Lord Cobham hath his house and gardens, with many fair edifices and certain lands and tenements; . . .

§4 The Lord Warden hath his house and garden, with certain lands and tenements; . . .

The possessions of the said late Friars, purchased of King Henry and King Edward before the remain of the whole precinct was granted to Sir Thomas Cawarden; videlicet:

§5 Sir Mr. Jerningham, Fee Chamberlain to the Queen's Highness, hath his house, the great and upper library, the half of the nether library, the south cloister and cloister-yard, the firmary, the brewhouses, the bakehouse, and the stable, with certain gardens, . . . besides other edifices which he holdeth are not granted by any letters patents;

§6 The Lady Gray hath, by the right and purchase of one [Robert] Harris and Paul Gresham, a part of the under library, a part of the dorter, the common schoolhouse, the provincial's lodging, the great stone house being a storehouse, the common privy, and the hill gardens, with divers other lands, rents and tenements; . . .

§7 The Lady Perrin hath her house and garden, with other tenements; . . .

§8 Sir Philip Hoby hath a house and a garden; . . .

§9 Sir George Harper hath his house and garden and other tenements; . . .

§10 Mr. Tate hath a house and certain gardens; . . .

§11 Mr. Parris hath a house and garden; . . .

§12 Parson Allyn, priest, hath lands and tenements; . . .

§13 Mr. William More hath a house and garden; . . .

§14 Mr. Kirkham holdeth a house and certain gardens; . . .

§15 Mrs. Lewcas, alias Knight, holdeth a house and garden; . . .

§16 Francis Gardiner[2] hath a house and a garden; . . .

§17 Peter Hosier hath a house and gardens, with divers lands, rents and tenements; . . .

§18 Nicholas Crotcher, extronomer, hath divers lands, rents and tenements; . . .

Over and besides their freedom of the privilege enjoyed thereby.

§19 Sir Thomas Cawarden hath but the remain that was left unsold by the said late Kings, with the liberties and royalties of the precinct of the said Friars, which also he had only for and in recompense of a great sum of money by him disbursed upon warrant and commandment, of all which portion to him so granted (when it came to his hands) was mansionable but only one house in the tenure of John

The remain left
unsold by the said
Kings was granted
to Sir Thomas
Cawarden

Barnett, whereof during Barnett's life he had no benefit; and one house in the tenure of Thomas Phillips, for which he never had rent and yet was fain to purchase prior quondam's estate therein; two little tenements, old and ruinous, worth by year 40s; and the residue waste ground or not mansionable, the whole worth then by the year, as was delivered by valuer, £19;

§20 Upon which parcels are built, to his great costs and charges, besides his own lodgings, above twenty mansion houses wherein are by estimation above eighty people, the building whereof hath cost and doth stand him in one way and other in above £1,300; and whatsoever he hath of yearly revenue at this presents was by reason of his own building, only Barnett's house and two little tenements except[ed]; whereas the other possessions in the tenures of the freeholders were for the most part ready builded to their hands, or else they found them in such sort as the alteration of any part thereof stood them in little charges.

§21 So by comparison and conferment of the premises, [it] appeareth that the possessions first purchased of the said late kings, and before their Majesties' grant of the whole precinct and liberties to Sir Thomas Cawarden, is more than four times so much in space and quantity than the portion of the said Sir Thomas Cawarden, notwithstanding that the chief substance of the same he hath builded almost from the ground, and most upon vacant places; so that in right and conscience he ought to be contributory but to a small piece of that burden in respect of the rest.

§22 Nevertheless, the said Sir Thomas Cawarden, of his own mere motion, about four years past went about at his own proper costs and charges to erect a church sufficient for the inhabitants, and had appointed ground for the church and church-yard in place convenient, and prepared his stuff in areadiness for the same; and then certain evil-disposed persons, more of malice to molest him than of any devotion or towardness to accomplish any good act, . . . occasioned him to leave his good purpose and stand to the answering of their slanderous reports before the Queen's most honorable Council at divers and sundry times, whereby the burthen fell in their own necks as aforesaid.

§23 All which notwithstanding, the said Sir Thomas Cawarden, being since then called before the said most honorable Council, by their gentle usage of him, and in respect that the patronage should be in his gift, granted to the late Lord Chancellor, Bishop of Winchester, with the rest of the honorable Council, to give the ground for a church and churchyard, with also roof timber for the same, so that these foresaid freeholders, with the inhabitants, would rear up the walls; to the which grant Mr. Vice-Chamberlain was called, and then there granted that he, with the Lord Cobham, would undertake that the freeholders and the inhabitants should do it, and so parted with thanks; and to this time [Cawarden] hath expected the same and prepared the roof thereof, and doth stand and agree to the same if it will be taken, which he thinketh reasonable for his part. Thus the time on their behalf is [pro]-

451

tracted, and nothing done to the walls as promise was made, and yet he beareth the burthen of their fault.

1. Each of the items here numbered 2 to 18 is followed by the phrase "worth by year," and then by a blank instead of the figure that one is led to expect. Since the unfinished phrases have nothing to contribute, they are here omitted.

2. Here the reading seems to be "Francis Gardiner." The original document has "ffrauncs gardin[er]", the bracketed letters being supplied from an upward loop that serves as a symbol of abbreviation (*BR* 4:11). But at 4:2 and 6:18 the reading seems to be "Francis's garden," the originals being respectively "ffrauncs garden" (*BR* 7:2) and "ffrauncis his gardeine" (*BR* 11:22).

Document 12

[William More's Lease to Sir Henry Neville

JUNE 10, 1560

Loseley MS, Parcel 348; printed in type facsimile in *Blackfriars Records*, pp. 19–26.

§1 THIS INDENTURE, made the 10th day of June in the second year of the reign of our sovereign Lady Elizabeth, by the grace of God Queen of England, France and Ireland, Defender of the Faith, etc., between William More of the City of London, esquire, on the one party, and Sir Henry Neville of the same City of London, knight, on the other party, WITNESSETH that the said William More hath demised, granted and to farm letten, and by these presents doth demise, grant and to farm let unto the said Sir Henry Neville:

§2 All that his house and lodging containing four rooms, lately called or known by the name of Mr. Cheke's Lodging, and sithence used by Sir Thomas Cawarden, knight, deceased, for the office of the Queen's Majesty's Revels, containing in length fifty-and-two yards and a half and a half quarter of a yard, and every yard Friars, near Ludgate within the City of London, between the tenements of Sir thereof containing three foot of assize [157 feet 10½ inches],[1] and in breadth at the south end thereof . . . [21 feet 9 inches], and in breadth at the north end thereof . . . [26 feet 7½ inches]; which said house and lodging is set, lying and being within the precinct of the late Friars Preachers, commonly called the Black Henry Jerningham, knight, and of the said William More, on the east part; and a tenement of the said William More, now in the tenure or occupation of Richard Frith, and the way leading from the house and garden of the said William More now in his manurance or occupation, and a vacant or void piece of ground of the said William More adjoining unto the said way, on the west part; and a tenement of the Lord Cobham on the north part;

§3 And also so much of his said piece of vacant or void ground above recited as containeth in length . . . [72 feet 9 inches] and in breadth . . . [18 feet 9 inches],[2] and lieth . . . between the said tenement of the said Lord Cobham on the north part, and the way aforesaid leading from the same house and garden of the said William More towards the Water Lane on the south part, and the same lane called

Water Lane on the west part, and the said house and lodging called Mr. Cheke's Lodging . . . on the east part;

§4 And also all that his cellar, lying and being . . . part under the said house and lodging called Mr. Cheke's Lodging . . . and part under the said tenement of the said William More, . . . which said cellar containeth in length . . . [25 feet 6 inches] and in breadth . . . [24 feet], with a mud wall cross over the midst of the same cellar;

§5 And also all that and those his two other rooms called the Buttery and Pantry, with a little entry leading between them, lying and being . . . under the said house and lodging above granted, called Mr. Cheke's Lodging; and part of the same two rooms is over the cellar above granted and demised, between the way or entry leading from the said house and garden of the said William More . . . towards the Water Lane, on the north part, and the entry leading into that end of the house of the said William More wherein John Horley, his servant, doth lodge, on the south part; and the same two rooms and entry above granted do contain in length . . . [28 feet 10½ inches] and in breadth . . . [25 feet 1½ inches];

§6 And also all that his great room in manner of a great cellar, having a chimney in it, containing in length . . . [57 feet] and in breadth . . . [25 feet 1½ inches], and lieth . . . under the said tenement of the said William More . . . between certain lodgings called Lygon's Lodging, now in the manurance or occupation of the said William More on the east part, the cellar aforesaid above granted on the west part, the tenement of the said Sir Henry Jerningham on the south part, and the said garden of the said William More on the north part.

§7 Except and always reserved to the said William More, his heirs and assigns, the residue of the said piece of vacant or void ground above recited, which said residue now lieth between the way leading from the said Water Lane to the tenement now in the tenure or occupation of Richard Frith on the south part, and the said parcel of the said void or vacant ground, before by these presents demised, on the north part, and containeth in length . . . [83 feet 3 inches] and in breadth . . . [11 feet 3 inches], and the east end thereof spreadeth to greater breadth to serve towards two entries.

§8 And also except one entry leading under parcel of the premises before by these presents demised, from the said garden of the said William More to the said residue of the said piece of void or vacant ground before excepted;

§9 Except also, and reserved to the said William More, . . . as well one other entry leading under parcel of the premises before by these presents demised, from that end of the said house of the said William More wherein the said John Horley, his servant, doth lodge, to the said residue of the said piece of void or vacant ground before excepted, as also such rooms and places adjoining to the said entry as be now in the manurance or occupation of the said William More or John Horley.

§10 And also the said William More doth demise and grant unto the said Sir Henry Neville . . . free egress and regress into . . . and out of and from all and singular the premises above demised and granted, into the said Water Lane, in, by and through all usual ways, entries, gates and passages, . . . other than by or through the said house and garden of the said William More. . . .

§11 To have, hold, occupy and enjoy the said lodging lately called Mr. Cheke's Lodging, and all other the premises above by these presents demised and granted . . . to the said Sir Henry Neville, . . . from the feast of the nativity of St. John the Baptist next coming after the date hereof, unto the end and term of threescore years from thence next ensuing fully to be complete, ended and determined; yielding and paying therefor yearly unto the said William More . . . £6 of current money of England, at four terms in the year: that is to say, at the feasts of St. Michael the Archangel, the birth of our Lord God, the annunciation of our blessed Lady, and the nativity of St. John Baptist, by even portions during the said term of 60 years.

§12 And if it fortune the said yearly rent of £6 to be behind or unpaid . . . by the space of 28 days, . . . that then . . . the said Sir Henry Neville . . . shall forfeit and pay to the said William More . . . £3 for and in the name of a pain or penalty; . . . and also if it shall fortune the said yearly rent of £6 or the said pain or penalty to be behind unpaid . . . by the space of 50 days, . . . that then . . . it shall be lawful to the said William More . . . into all and singular the premises . . . to reenter, and the same to repossess. . . .

§13 And the said Sir Henry Neville doth further covenant and grant . . . that he . . . shall well and sufficiently keep, uphold, sustain, repair and maintain all the buildings, edifices, houses, walls, and all and singular other the premises, with the appurtenances, before by these presents demised and granted, . . . notwithstanding . . . any manner of ruin or fall of a certain high gallery of stone that is situate and over the foresaid buildings, houses, edifices or walls; . . . provided always that if the said Sir Henry Neville . . . shall in any wise remove, take up or new-cast any part or parcel of any lead or leads, . . . to any other intent or purpose than to solder and amend such faults and reparations as shall fortune to be in the same leads or any of them, or in the timber or roof under . . . them, . . . that then this present demise, lease, and grant shall utterly cease and be void; . . . provided also . . . that it shall be lawful at all times hereafter only for the said William More and his wife for the time being . . . to have, use and take their free entry, egress, and regress . . . into and upon all such leads . . . and other the leads next adjoining, to the intent and purpose only to view, solder, repair, or amend the leads. . . .

§14 And where a certain spring of water is conveyed by a conduit pipe into the said garden of the said William More, the most part of which water and spring is there employed and taken for the use of the said William More, . . . and where the residue of the said water . . . is now conveyed out of the said garden by a conduit pipe into the said residue of the said piece of void or vacant ground before excepted, the said William More . . . shall permit and suffer the said Sir Henry Neville . . . to have and take out of the said pipe or conduit . . . so much of the residue of the said water . . . as will serve for the use and occupation of the said Sir Henry Neville, . . . to convey the same water . . . by a pipe to be laid either above the ground or under, unto such parts and places of the premises . . . afore demised, as to him, the said Sir Henry, . . . shall be thought meet and convenient. . . .

§15 IN WITNESS WHEREOF, the parties abovesaid to these Indentures interchangeably have set their seals: given[3] the day and year above written.

1. In the original document, all dimensions are stated in terms of yards and diminishing fractions of a yard. Hereafter they are transposed into terms of feet and inches, enclosed in square brackets.

2. This piece of ground, 72 feet 9 inches long by 18 feet 9 inches wide, seems to have been a strip lying immediately to the west of the Old Buttery block. Presumably it was leased to Neville so that he could build his kitchen and great stairs upon it.

3. The word here translated as "given" is spelled "yeven" in the original document, "yeve" at 16:61, and "Yeouen" at 20:8. Cf. *O.E.D.*, *s.v.* "Give," 19.

Document 13

(Sir William More's Answer to Kempe's Claim

CIRCA 1562

A portion of *Loseley MS.* No. 424, printed in *Blackfriars Records,* pp. 105–106. In or about the year 1562, a certain Mr. Kempe bought Sir Henry Jerningham's title to the infirmary and to the rooms above and below it, and "by color of this grant of the firmary and of the building, &c., above and beneath," he laid claim also to "a great room called the parliament chamber." Sir William More contested Kempe's claim, "for answer whereunto" he said:

§1 First, the firmary had a room above the same which was a lodging for those that were sick, and also one other room beneath the firmary, all which Mr. Kempe hath.

§2 Also the parliament chamber [whereof part is over the room above the firmary][1] did never pertain to the firmary, and is three times as big as the said firmary.

§3 Also there never was any way or passage to go out of the firmary to the said chamber.

§4 Also the said chamber was not rented at the time of the grant nor long after to any person, but kept in the King's hands to the use of the Revels.

§5 Also it was never in the tenure of Sir William Kingston.

§6 Also King Henry VIII possessed it during his life.

§7 Also King Edward did the like until the second year of his reign, at which time he let it by lease to Sir Thomas Cawarden.

§8 Also the chamber is covered all with lead, being more worth than all the money he paid for the purchase.

§9 Also Sir Thomas Cawarden, having the same granted unto him and his heirs by King Edward in the fourth year of his reign, did quietly enjoy the same during his life, as I have done ever since until this present, so that almost these fourteen years, and since the Lady Kingston's grant, there was never any title made to the same. If Sir Henry Jerningham had thought he had had any interest in it, he would in Queen Mary's time have sought the same, being then Vice-Chamberlain

457

and of the Privy Council, and Sir Thomas Cawarden in disgrace and committed to the Fleet, and afterwards committed to his house.

1. The bracketed insert is a variant found in another copy of Sir William More's answer to Kempe's demands (*Loseley MS.* No. 426 (2), cf. *BR* 106:13–16). In all other respects *MS.* No. 426 is a duplicate of *MS.* No. 424.

Document 14

⟨Lord Cobham's Arrears

AUGUST 5, 1566

Loseley MS. No. 1396, f. 120ᵛ; printed in type facsimile in *Blackfriars Records*, pp. and here translated by Miss A. L. D. Kennedy-Skipton of the staff of the Folger Shakespeare Library.

Court of the City of §1 In the Book of Arrearages there of the Lady
Exchequer London Elizabeth, now Queen, for divers debtors for the several years ending at the Feast of St. Michael the Archangel in the seventh year of the reign of the same Queen, amongst other things the following is contained; viz.:

§2 By William Lord Cobham, for the farm of the same great hall lying right next to the house of the said Lord Cobham, and of one hall lying next to the said great hall; and also of one kitchen called the Convent Kitchen, of two houses called Larders, together with a void plot of ground lying next to the west part of the said kitchen, and also of one gallery containing in length 40 feet and in breadth 10 feet, lying on the east part of the said kitchen; and of one

Lately the house small garden[1] leading from the said kitchen to the great
of the Friars cloister in the tenure of the said Lord Cobham: at 103s.
Preachers in the 4d. per year, owing and unpaid for the nineteen years
City of London ending at the feast of St. Michael the Archangel in this seventh year of Elizabeth, now Queen, from which the arrearages [amount to] —— £98 3s. 4d.

§3 In addition to this sum, he is charged with £36 3s. 4d. for the said farm of the buildings above written, which was owing for the seven years ending at the feast of St. Michael the Archangel in the thirty-eighth year of the late King Henry VIII, as this was the charge for a fourth of the said possessions for the same year. And then he owed £134 6s. 8d., from which he has be excused from [paying] £82 13s. 4d., for the farm of all and singular the said buildings, owing for the sixteen years ending at the feast of St. Michael the Archangel in the seventh year of the said Elizabeth, now Queen;

§4 The reason being that the late lord King Edward VI, by his letters patents

459

given at Westminster on the twelfth day of March in the fourth year of his late reign, amongst other things gave and granted all and singular the above-mentioned buildings and the rest of the premises to Thomas Cawarden, knight, his heirs and assigns forever, without his yielding anything therefor, together with the revenues [arising] from them, from the feast of St. Michael the Archangel then last past, as appears in the same letters patents, which were shown to the auditor this fifth day of August in the year 1566. And so he owed the further sum of £51 13s. 4d.

Examined by William Fuller, auditor

5th August 1566

1. The Latin text has "p[ar]vi gardini," but it seems unlikely that a garden should lead from the kitchen to the cloister. Two earlier documents say stairs ("p[ar]vi Grad[?]" and "paris graduu[m]") rather than a garden. Cf. *BR* 116:31-32.

Document 15

⟨William More's Lease to Lord Cobham

FEBRUARY 6, 1571

Loseley MS. No. 332 (53); printed in part in *Blackfriars Records*, pp. 27–28. This Indenture deals with the premises that had been leased to Sir Henry Neville in 1560 (Document 12) and to the Silk Dyers after Sir Henry's surrender of the lease in 1568, and that would be leased to Richard Farrant in 1576. Many of its provisions are later repeated in the Farrant lease (Document 16), and are therefore omitted here.

§1 THIS INDENTURE, made the sixth day of February in the thirteenth year of the reign of our sovereign Lady Elizabeth . . . between William More . . . and the right honorable Sir William Brooke, knight, Lord Cobham and Lord Warden of the Cinque Ports . . . WITNESSETH that the said William More . . . doth demise, grant and to farm let unto the said William Lord Cobham:

§2 All those his six upper chambers, lofts, lodgings or rooms . . . lately (amongst others) in the tenure and occupation of Sir Henry Neville, knight, and do contain in length, from the north end thereof to the south end of the same, 156½ foot of assize; whereof two of the said six upper chambers, lofts, lodgings, or rooms in the north end of the premises, together with the breadth of the little room under excepted and reserved, do contain in length 46½ foot, and from the east to the west part thereof in breadth 25 foot of assize; and the four other chambers or rooms, residue of the said six upper chambers, do contain in length 110 foot, and in breadth from the east to the west part thereof 22 foot of assize; of which four chambers last recited, one of them is ceiled with wainscot on the east part, south part, and a part of the west, with a great round portal contained within the same chamber and ceiling, which ceiling, over and besides the said portal, doth contain fourscore and fourteen yards; and the north end of the premises before letten doth abut upon the south part of the now dwelling house of the said William Lord Cobham;

§3 Except, and always reserved to the said William More and to his heirs, one little room lying within the limits and bounds or contents above expressed, which little room was sometime used for a withdraught or privy; . . .

§4 And also all that his new kitchen lately builded by the said Sir Henry Neville, with the stair leading out of the same kitchen up into the premises before letten, with the little void room wherein the foot of the said stairs standeth, and the wood-yard to the same kitchen adjoining; . . .

§5 And also the use and commodity of one quill of conduit water; . . .

§6 Except, and always reserved unto the said William More . . . all the leads covering the premises before demised, and the use of them, and the cellars and rooms directly under the said upper chambers, lodgings or rooms. . . .

§7 And the said William More doth covenant and grant . . . that it shall and may be lawful unto the said William Lord Cobham, his executors and assigns, at his and their own proper costs and charges, to break the walls within the premises above letten, and there to make and set up such convenient doors, in such convenient places of the same walls, as shall be thought meet and convenient by the said William Lord Cobham . . . to lead out of his said dwelling house into the said chambers, rooms, lodgings and premises above demised by this Indenture during the said term.

Document 16

⟨Sir William More's Lease to Richard Farrant

DECEMBER 20, 1576

Loseley MS. No. 1396, f. 120ᵛ; printed in type facsimile in *Blackfriars Records,* pp. 28–35.¹

§1 THIS INDENTURE, made the twentieth day of December in the nineteenth year of the reign of our sovereign Lady Elizabeth, . . . between Sir William More of Loseley in the County of Surrey, knight, on the one party, and Richard Farrant of New Windsor in the County of Berk[s.], gentleman, on the other party, WITNESSETH that the said Sir William More hath demised, granted and to farm letten, and by these presents doth demise, grant and to farm let unto the said Richard Farrant:

§2 All those his six upper chambers, lofts, lodgings, or rooms lying together within the precinct of the late dissolved house or priory of the Blackfriars, otherwise called the Friars Preachers in London, which said six upper chambers, lofts, lodgings, or rooms were lately amongst others in the tenure and occupation of the right honorable Sir William Brooke, knight, Lord Cobham, and do contain in length, from the north end thereof to the south end of the same, 156½ foot of assize, whereof two of the said six upper chambers, lofts, lodgings, or rooms in the north end of the premises, together with the breadth of the little room under granted, do contain in length 56½ foot,² and from the east to the west part thereof in breadth 25 foot of assize; and the four other chambers or rooms, residue of the said six upper chambers, do contain in length 110 foot, and in breadth from the east to the west part thereof 22 foot of assize;

§3 Of which four chambers last recited, one of them is ceiled with wainscot on the east part, south part, and a part of the west, with a great round portal contained within the same chamber and ceiling, which ceiling, over and besides the said portal, doth contain fourscore and fourteen yards; and the north end of the premises before letten doth abut upon the south part of the now dwelling house of the said William Lord Cobham; and also the said Sir William More . . . by these presents doth demise, grant and to farm let unto the said Richard Farrant all the said wainscot and round portal contained within the said chamber above demised;

463

§4 And also all that his new kitchen lately builded by Sir Henry Neville, knight, with the stair leading out of the same kitchen up into the premises before letten, with the little void room wherein the foot of the said stairs standeth, and the wood-yard to the same kitchen adjoining, situate . . . under part of the premises above demised on the east part, and a certain way called Water Lane, leading to the Blackfriars bridge at the Thames-side, on the west part, and the said dwelling house of the said Lord Cobham on the north part, and a certain void ground, and a way of the said Sir William More, leading from the said Water Lane towards and unto the dwelling house or tenement and garden of the said Sir William More . . . on the south part;

§5 And also . . . the great stairs lately erected and made by the said Sir Henry Neville upon part of the said void ground and way last above expressed, with the little void room under the same great stairs, which said great stairs do serve and lead into the premises before demised;

§6 And also the use and commodity of one quill of conduit water issuing and running from the conduit and water of the said Sir William More, together with the cocks thereof, set, lying, and being in the little void room at the said stair-foot before mentioned, for the only use of the said Richard Farrant and his family; . . . and also free ingress, egress, and regress to and from the said new stairs lately erected and made by the said Sir Henry Neville in and upon the said void ground and way leading from the said way called Water Lane unto the said great new stairs; . . .

§7 And also . . . all those two rooms with the two cellars, and directly under part of the upper chambers, lodgings, or rooms above demised, which said two rooms and two cellars . . . do lie between the said void ground on the west part, and an entry leading from the said void ground into the garden of the said Sir William More on the north part, and an entry leading from the said void ground into the said dwelling house or tenement of the said Sir William More of the south part, and the garden of the said Sir William More on the east part, with free and quiet ingress, egress and regress into and from the said two rooms and two cellars; . . .

§8 And also . . . one little room, sometime two little rooms, . . . whereof one part was sometime used for a withdraught or privy, and the other part thereof was lately used for a coal house;

§9 Except and always reserved unto the said Sir William More . . . all that great room now used for a washing-house, being directly under parcel of the premises first above demised and adjoining unto the said two rooms last above [demised], bounden on the east part of the same two rooms; and also except . . . all the leads covering the premises before demised, and the use of them, saving that it shall and may be good and lawful for the said Richard Farrant . . . to have free ingress, egress, and regress to and from the said leads to repair, maintain and amend the same; . . .

§10 To have and to hold all and singular the premises before demised . . . with their appurtenances (except before excepted) unto the said Richard Farrant . . . from the feast of St. Michael the Archangel last past . . . unto the end and term of twenty-and-one years; . . . yielding and paying therefor yearly . . . unto the said Sir William More . . . £14 of lawful money of England at four usual terms of the year . . . or within fifteen days next after every of the same feasts, by even portions yearly to be paid;

§11 And the said Richard Farrant doth promise, covenant and grant . . . that he . . . shall well and sufficiently repair . . . all manner of reparations whatsoever to the premises above demised, . . . and also shall repair . . . all such defaults and reparations as shall at any time hereafter be in the leads above excepted, and in the timber-work and roof that beareth the same leads, . . . together with the said wainscot and great round portal;

§12 And also the said Richard Farrant doth covenant and grant . . . that he . . . shall at all times hereafter . . . bear and pay all manner of charges and payments from henceforth due to be paid unto the church and scavenger, . . . and also shall scour, cleanse and make clean the privy or withdraught; . . .

§13 And if it shall happen the said yearly rent of £14 to be behind unpaid . . . by the space of fifteen days, that then it shall be lawful unto the said Sir William More . . . into all the said chambers . . . to enter and distrain, and the distress thereof taken lawfully to lead, drive, bear, and carry away; . . . and if it shall happen the said yearly rent of £14 by the year to be behind unpaid . . . by the space of twenty days, . . . it shall be lawful unto the said Sir William More . . . into all and singular the premises . . . to reenter, and all the same . . . to have again, repossess and enjoy; . . .

§14 Provided alway . . . that it shall and may be lawful unto the said Sir William More . . . to shut, lock, bar or open the gate joining upon the said way called Water Lane from time to time, at such convenient hours of the night and of the morning as . . . shall seem meet and convenient; . . . provided also that the said Richard Farrant . . . shall not alter nor cut the pipe of the said conduit or water, nor . . . employ any the water aforesaid but only to the use of the said Richard Farrant and his family, . . . nor shall suffer the same water to run to waste; . . .

§15 Provided also that the said Richard Farrant, his executors or assigns, . . . shall not in any wise demise, let, grant, assign, set over, or by any ways or means put away, his or their interest or term of years, or any part of the same years of or in the said premises . . . to any person or persons . . . without the especial license, consent and agreement of the said Sir William More . . . first had and obtained in writing, . . . but only by the last will and testament of the said Richard Farrant in writing to the wife of the said Richard or to his children; . . . and that the said wife or child . . . shall or may . . . have the use and commodity of the said quill of water; . . . and further it is agreed . . . that the said

Richard Farrant . . . shall and may . . . open and unlock the said gate joining upon the said way called Water Lane, so often as occasion shall serve. . . .

§16 IN WITNESS whereof, the parties abovesaid to these Indentures interchangeably have set their seals: given the day and year first above written.

1. Another copy of this lease, from *Loseley MSS* "Deeds, Elizabeth," Bundle 348, is printed in Wallace, *Evolution*, pp. 132-36.

2. This dimension, given as "fyftye and syxe foote and a half" in the manuscript, is incorrect. It should be 46½ feet, as proved both by the arithmetic of the paragraph and by the parallel passage in the Cobham lease (15:2).

Document 17

(Sir William More's Comments on the Farrant Lease

CIRCA 1585–1586

Loseley MSS. Bundle 425, printed in Wallace, *Evolution*, pp. 175–76. The notes were written by Sir William More in the first person, and copied by a clerk.

Touching the matter in variance between me and Anne Farrant, widow, for an house in the Blackfriars

§1 First I let the said house to Sir Henry Neville for a term of one-and-twenty years, and took of him no fine for the same. Sir Henry Neville added a new kitchen and set up [*blank*] partitions in the house. Afterward Sir Henry Neville sold me his lease thereof for an hundred pounds, which I paid him at one payment, besides forbearing of two or three years' rent, so far as I remember.

§2 Afterward Sir Henry Neville desired me by his letter to let the said house to Farrant, which I did upon condition that he should not let nor set the same, nor any part thereof, to any person without my consent had and obtained in writing under my hand and seal.

§3 Farrant pretended unto me to use the house only for the teaching of the Children of the Chapel, but made it a continual house for plays, to the offense of the precinct, and pulled down partitions to make that place apt for that purpose, which Sir Henry Neville had set up; and contrary to the condition let out part of the said house, for the which I charged him with the forfeiture of his lease, whereunto he yielded and offered composition; but before I could take remedy against him he died.

§4 After whose death I entered upon the said house, and refused to receive any rent but conditionally, nevertheless offering Farrant's widow that if she would commit the cause to two lawyers indifferently chosen, or to any two judges, I would yield to whatsoever they should determine therein; which she utterly refused.

§5 Immediately after, she let the house to one Hunnis, and afterward to one Newman or Sutton, as far as I remember, and then to Evans, who sold his interest to the Earl of Oxford, who gave his interest to Lyly; and the title thus was posted over from one to another from me, contrary to the said condition.

467

§6 At what time Evans was so possessed of it, I brought my action against him for the same, and when it came to be tried he demurred in law upon it, which was done in Trinity Term.[1] The demurrer being drawn, the said Evans kept the same in his hands all Michaelmas Term next following, using many delays. After the demurrer had, I caused my learned counsel in Hilary Term to demand judgment, arguing the case at the usual place, but the recorder argued against me. The judges would not then give judgment, but required to have books of the whole proceeding delivered to them, whereof I delivered one to every of them. At the end of Easter Term following I had judgment against Evans, and process awarded to the sheriff to give me possession.

§7 In all which time of my suit I never heard of Farrant's widow, but only by her said means I was put to this great charges of suit, very injuriously. My charges in following the said suit and lying in London for that business, stand me in not less than forty pounds. The house is much impaired by the pulling down the partitions thereof. She had of the said Newman or Sutton thirty pounds in money at his entry into the said house, as he told me.

1. The terms of court were as follows: Hilary, January 11 to 31; Easter, April 5 to May 8; Trinity, May 22 to June 2; Michaelmas, November 2 to 25.

Document 18

《 Sir William More's Lease to Rocco Bonetti

MARCH 20, 1585

Loseley MS. No. 1396, f. 134ʳ; printed in type facsimile in *Blackfriars Records,* pp. 55–60.

§1 THIS INDENTURE, made the twentieth day of March in the 27th year of the reign of our sovereign Lady Elizabeth, . . . between Sir William More of Loseley, in the County of Surrey, knight, of the one party, and Rocco Bonetti of the Blackfriars, London, gentleman, on the other party, WITNESSETH: that the said Sir William More . . . doth demise, grant and to farm let and set unto the said Rocco Bonetti:

§2 All that his messuage or tenement containing these particular rooms hereafter expressed and mentioned, as the same are lately demised by one Margaret Poole, widow; viz., a hall, a chamber above the hall, a little room under the said hall, a yard, a little chamber or vault within the said yard, a cellar adjoining to the said yard under the fence-school under the south end of the same, being the tenement now in the tenure of the said Rocco Bonetti; an entry, a kitchen adjoining to the said hall and a small rowne [?] within the said kitchen; all which chambers and rooms of the demise of the said Margaret Poole do contain in length from north to south twenty foot and eight inches, and four foot and a half by the present demise of the said Sir William More; and from east to west in breadth twenty foot and a half of the demise of the said Margaret Poole, and two foot over and beside by this present Indenture of the demise of the said Sir William More;

§3 All which six foot and a half in length and breadth of the demise of the said Sir William More, and now taken in and adjoined as part and belonging to the aforesaid messuage or tenement, do belong to the tenement late in the tenure of John Lyly, gentleman, and now in the tenure of the said Rocco Bonetti; containing, between the yard of Sir William More on the north, to the lane leading to the house of Sir George Carey, knight, on the south, 33 foot; and between the tenement of Margaret Poole on the south and west, and the tenement and yard of the said Sir William More, in the tenure of the said Rocco Bonetti, 39 foot and 8 inches; . . . all which premises (except the foresaid six foot and a half) the said

Margaret Poole now holdeth for and during the term of her natural life, and after her decease to descend and come to the said Sir William More, his heirs and assigns;

§4 To have, hold, occupy and enjoy the said messuage or tenement . . . from and after the decease of the said Margaret Poole . . . unto the full end and term of ten years from thence next and immediately ensuing; . . . yielding and paying therefor every year . . . unto the said Sir William More . . . the full sum of £6 of lawful money of England, at four feasts or terms in the year. . . .

§5 Provided always . . . that the said Rocco Bonetti . . . shall not at any time hereafter use or keep . . . any manner [of] victualling-house or tippling-house in and upon the said tenement and messuage . . . without the privity, consent and good will of the said Sir William More. . . .

§6 IN WITNESS whereof the parties aforesaid to this present Indenture interchangeably have put their hands and seals, the day and year first above written.

Document 19

❮[Sir William More's Sale to James Burbage

FEBRUARY 4, 1596

Loseley MS. No. 348, printed in type facsimile in *Blackfriars Records*, pp. 60–69. The Loseley MS is the original counterpart of the Indenture, and bears James Burbage's signature and seal.

§1 THIS INDENTURE, made the fourth day of February in the eight-and-thirtieth year of the reign of our sovereign Lady Elizabeth, . . . between Sir William More of Loseley in the County of Surrey, knight, of the one party, and James Burbage of Hollowell in the County of Middlesex, gentleman, of the other party, WITNESSETH that the said Sir William More, for and in consideration of the sum of £600 of lawful money of England, to him by the said James Burbage . . . truly paid, . . . by these presents doth fully and clearly bargain, sell, alien, enfeoff and confirm to the said James Burbage, his heirs and assigns, forever:

§2 All those seven great upper rooms as they are now divided, being all upon one floor and sometime being one great and entire room, with the roof over the same covered with lead, together also with all the lead that doth cover the same seven great upper rooms;

§3 And also all the stone stairs leading up unto the leads or roof over the said seven great upper rooms out of the said seven great upper rooms;

§4 And also all the great stone walls and other walls which do enclose, divide and belong to the same seven great upper rooms;

§5 And also all that great pair of winding stairs, with the staircase thereunto belonging, which leadeth up unto the same seven great upper rooms out of the great yard there which doth lie next unto the Pipe Office; which said seven great upper rooms were late in the tenure or occupation of William de Laune, Doctor of Physic, or of his assigns, and are situate, lying and being within the precinct of the late Blackfriars Preachers near Ludgate in London;

§6 Together also with all the wainscot, glass, doors, locks, keys and bolts to the same seven great upper rooms and other the premises by these presents bargained and sold; . . .

§7 Together also with the easement and commodity of a vault, being under

471

some part of the said seven great upper rooms, or under the entry or void room lying between those seven great upper rooms and the said Pipe Office, by a stool and tunnel to be made into the same vault in and out of the great stone wall in the inner side thereof, next and adjoining to the said entry or void room being towards the south;

§8 And also all those rooms and lodgings, with the kitchen thereunto adjoining, called the Middle Rooms or Middle Stories, late being in the tenure or occupation of Rocco Bonetti, and now being in the tenure or occupation of Thomas Bruskett, gentleman, or of his assigns, containing in length 52 foot of assize more or less, and in breadth 37 foot of assize more or less, lying and being directly under part of those of the said seven great upper rooms which lie westwards; which said Middle Rooms or Middle Stories do extend in length southwards to a part of the house of Sir George Carey, knight;

§9 And also all the stone walls and other walls which do enclose, divide and belong to the same Middle Rooms or Middle Stories, together also with the door and entry which do lie next unto the gate entering into the house of the said Sir George Carey, and used to and from the said Middle Rooms or Middle Stories out of a lane or way leading unto the house of the said Sir George Carey; . . .

§10 And also all those two vaults or cellars late being in the occupation of the said Rocco Bonetti, lying under part of the said Middle Rooms or Middle Stories at the north end thereof as they are now divided, and are now in the tenure or occupation of the said Thomas Bruskett and of John Favor, and are adjoining to the two little yards now in the occupations of Peter Johnson and of the said John Favor, together also with the stairs leading into the same vaults or cellars out of the foresaid kitchen in the occupation of the said Thomas Bruskett;

§11 And also all those two upper rooms or chambers, with a little buttery, at the north end of the said seven great upper rooms and on the west side thereof, now being in the occupation of Charles Bradshaw, together with the void room, way and passage now thereunto used from the said seven great upper rooms;

§12 And also all those two rooms or lofts now in the occupation of Edward Merry, the one of them lying and being above or over the said two upper rooms or chambers in the occupation of the said Charles Bradshaw and on the east and north part thereof, and having a chimney in it, and the other of them lying over part of the said entry or void room next the foresaid Pipe Office; together with the stairs leading from the foresaid rooms in the occupation of the foresaid Charles Bradshaw up unto the foresaid two rooms in the occupation of the said Edward Merry;

§13 And also all that little room now used to lay wood and coals in, being about the middle of the said stairs westwards, which said little room last mentioned is over the foresaid buttery now in the occupation of the said Charles Bradshaw, and is now in the occupation of the said Charles Bradshaw;

§14 And also all that room or garret lying and being over the said two rooms or lofts last before mentioned in the occupation of the said Edward Merry, together with the door, entry, void ground, way and passage, and stairs leading or used to, with or from the said rooms in the occupation of the said Edward Merry up unto the said room or garret over the said two rooms in the occupation of the said Edward Merry;

§15 And also all those two lower rooms now in the occupation of the said Peter Johnson, lying directly under part of the said seven great upper rooms;

§16 And also all those two other lower rooms or chambers, now being also in the tenure or occupation of the said Peter Johnson, being under the foresaid rooms or chambers in the occupation of the said Charles Bradshaw;

§17 And also the door, entry, way, void ground and passage leading and used to and from the said great yard next the said Pipe Office, into and from the said four lower rooms or chambers;

§18 And also all that little yard adjoining to the said lower rooms, as the same is now enclosed with a brick wall, and now being in the occupation of the said Peter Johnson; which said four lower rooms or chambers and little yard do lie between the said great yard next the said Pipe Office on the north part; and an entry leading into the messuage which Margaret Poole, widow, holdeth for term of her life, now in the occupation of the said John Favor, on the west part; and a wall dividing the said yard now in the occupation of the said Peter Johnson, and the yard now in the occupation of the said John Favor, on the south part;

§19 And also the stairs and staircase leading from the said little yard now in the occupation of the said Peter Johnson up unto the foresaid chambers or rooms now in the occupation of the said Charles Bradshaw;

§20 And also all that little yard or piece of void ground, with the brick wall thereunto belonging, lying and being next the Queen's highway leading unto the River of Thames, wherein an old privy now standeth, as the same is now enclosed with the same brick wall and with a pale, next adjoining to the house of the said Sir William More now in the occupation of the right honorable the Lord Cobham on the east part, and the street leading to the Thames there on the west part, and the said yard next the said Pipe Office on the south part, and the house of the said Lord Cobham on the north part;

§21 All which premises before in these presents mentioned to be hereby bargained and sold, are situate, lying and being within the said precinct of the said late Black Friars Preachers; together also with all liberties, privileges, lights, watercourses, easements, commodities and appurtenances to the foresaid rooms, lodgings and other the premises . . . belonging or in any wise appertaining.

§22 And also the said Sir William More . . . by these presents doth . . . confirm unto the said James Burbage . . . free and quiet ingress, egress and regress to and from the street or way leading from Ludgate unto the Thames, over, upon and through the said great yard next the said Pipe Office, by the ways now thereunto used into and from the said seven great upper rooms and all other the premises, . . . together also with free liberty for the said James Burbage . . . to lay and discharge his . . . wood, coal and all other carriages, necessaries and provisions in the same great yard . . . for convenient time until the same may be taken and carried away from thence, . . . leaving convenient ways and passages . . . through the said great yard . . . to and from the said Pipe Office and to and from the garden and other houses and rooms of the said Sir William More, . . . so that the said wood, coal, carriages, and provisions so laid and discharged . . . be removed and avoided out of and from the said yard within three days next after it shall be brought thither, without fraud or further delay. . . .

§23 All which said seven great upper rooms, and all other the premises . . . above by these presents mentioned to be bargained and sold, (amongst others) Sir Thomas Cawarden, knight, deceased, late had to him, his heirs and assigns forever, of the gift and grant of the late king of famous memory, Edward the Sixth, late King of England, as in and by his letters patents under the Great Seal of England, bearing date at Westminster the twelfth day of March in the fourth year of his reign [1550], more at large appeareth; and all which said premises . . . the said Sir Thomas Cawarden, in and by his last will and testament . . . (amongst other things) did will and declare his intent to be that his executors, with the consent of his overseers, should have full power and authority to bargain, sell and alien, . . . and also . . . did ordain and make Dame Elizabeth, then his wife, and the said Sir William More . . . executors of his said last will and testament, and Thomas Blagrave and Thomas Hawe overseers of the same; . . . and all which premises . . . the said Dame Elizabeth Cawarden and William More, . . . by and with the assent, consent, agreement, and advice of the said . . . overseers, . . . did bargain and sell unto John Birch, gentleman, John Austen and Richard Chapman . . . [on] the twentieth day of December [1559], . . . and all which said premises . . . the said John Birch, John Austen and Richard Chapman did . . . [on] the two-and-twentieth day of December [1559], . . . bargain and sell to the said Dame Elizabeth Cawarden and Sir William More; . . . which said Dame Elizabeth is long sithence deceased, by reason whereof all and singular the same premises . . . are accrued and come unto the said Sir William More and his heirs by right of survivorship; . . .

§24 And the said Sir William More doth covenant and grant . . . to and with the said James Burbage . . . that he, the said Sir William More, is and standeth at the time of the ensealing and delivery of these presents, lawfully and absolutely seized of the said rooms, lodgings, yards, [etc.], . . . in his demesne as of fee simple, and that the said rooms, lodgings, cellars, [etc.] . . . are, and at all times . . . forever hereafter shall stand, continue and remain, to the said James Burbage, his heirs and assigns, forever clearly acquitted, exonerated and discharged; . . .

§25 And furthermore the said Sir William More doth by these presents authorize, nominate and appoint George Austen, gentleman, and Henry Smith, merchant-tailor, to be his lawful deputies and attorneys, jointly and severally for and in his name to enter into all the said rooms, lodgings, cellars, [etc.], . . . and peaceable possession and seizin thereof . . . to take, and after such possession and seizin thereof so had and taken, to deliver possession and seizin thereof, and of every part thereof, unto the said James Burbage. . . .

§26 IN WITNESS whereof, the parties first above named to these Indentures sounderly [*sic*] have set their seals, the day and year first above written. 1595.

[SIGNED] *James Burbage*

[Seal (a griffin) attached]

Document 20

((Sir George More's Sale of the Great House, etc.

JUNE 19, 1609

Loseley MS. No. 349, printed in type facsimile in *Blackfriars Records*, pp. 92–102.

§1 THIS INDENTURE, made the nineteenth day of June in the [seventh] year of the reign of our sovereign Lord James, . . . between Sir George More of Loseley in the County of Surrey, knight, and Sir Robert More, knight, son and heir apparent of the said Sir George More, on the one party, and George Smith, citizen and haberdasher of London, William Banister, citizen and draper of London, Richard Brooke, citizen and weaver of London, and John Freeman, citizen and haberdasher of London, on the other party, WITNESSETH: that the said Sir George More and Sir Robert More, for and in consideration of the sum of £1,300 of lawful money of England, . . . do fully, clearly and absolutely grant, bargain, sell, alien and confirm unto the said George Smith, William Banister, Richard Brooke and John Freeman: . . .

§2 All that capital messuage or tenement, with the appurtenances, called the Great House, with all chambers, rooms, kitchens, entries, stairs, easements and commodities thereunto belonging, sometime in the tenure or occupation of Sir William More, knight, deceased, father of the said Sir George, . . . situate and being within the precinct of the late friary, monastery, priory or house of the late Friars Preachers, commonly called the Black Friars, in London, . . . extending itself in length from certain rooms late of the said Sir William More, sometimes used for the Pipe Office or for the service of the said Pipe Office, unto the house now or lately used as for the parish church; . . .

§3 And also all that great garden, and all that and those grounds, courts and curtilages now or late called or known by the name of the Great Garden, to the said capital messuage or tenement belonging, . . . and also all those rooms and lodgings . . . situate within the said great garden; . . .

§4 Together with all that great vault or low room adjoining to the rooms and lodgings last above mentioned, . . . and also all that great vault or low room adjoining to the said great garden, lying and being at the south-west end of the said great garden, now used and employed for a glass-house; . . .

476

§5 And also all those two rooms sometimes used and occupied for the Pipe Office or for service of the said Pipe Office, with a loft or garret over one of the said two rooms; and also all those two low rooms and cellar lying under the said late Pipe Office, and all that yard and void room adjoining to the said two low rooms and cellar;

§6 And all that house of office, situate and being at the north end of one room lately built under the church of the Blackfriars, under the messuage of the said Sir George More, in which Stephen Egerton, preacher, now dwelleth, together with the gate standing under the said messuage in which the said Stephen Egerton now dwelleth. . . .

§7 And the said Sir George More and Sir Robert More . . . do covenant and grant . . . that as well the said capital messuage or tenement and all and singular other the premises in or by these presents mentioned . . . to be granted or bargained and sold, . . . are and be and so from henceforth forever shall remain . . . free and clear, and freely and clearly acquitted and discharged . . . of and from all former and other bargains, sales, gifts, grants, leases, [etc.], . . . except two several leases hereafter specified; that is to say, one lease of the said capital messuage or tenement called the Great House, and certain other parcels of the premises, made by the said Sir William More to Ralph Bowes, esquire, for the term of twenty-and-one years and for the yearly rent of £66 13s. 4d., by Indenture dated the last day of March, Anno Domini 1596; . . . and one other lease of the said two rooms lately used for the Pipe Office, and certain other parcels of the premises, made by Sir George More to Sir Jerome Bowes, knight, for the term of sixteen years and for the yearly rent of £14 6s. 8d. and certain glasses therein reserved and mentioned, by Indenture dated the three-and-twentieth day of April [1600–01], . . . which said several yearly rents and glasses . . . shall and may from henceforth grow payable, and due to be paid and delivered, to the said George Smith, William Banister, Richard Brooke and John Freeman. . . .

§8 In witness whereof, the said parties to these present Indentures interchangeably have set their hands and seals: given the day and year first above written.

George Smith   *Wᵐ Banester*   *RB*   *Io : freeman*

Document 21

([Hunnis's Appeal for More Funds

NOVEMBER, 1583

State Papers Domestic, Elizabeth, CLXIII, No. 88; printed in its original spelling by Wallace, *Evolution*, p. 156 n. 3; by Chambers, *Elizabethan Stage*, Vol. II, pp. 37–38; and by Hillebrand, *Child Actors*, pp. 102–104.

May it please your Honors, William Hunnis, Master of the Children of her Highness's Chapel, most humbl[y] beseecheth to consider of these few lines:

§1 First, her Majesty alloweth for the diet of 12 Children of her said Chapel daily 6*d.* apiece by the day, and £40 by the year for their apparel and all other furniture.

§2 Again, there is no fee allowed, neither for the Master of the said Children nor for his usher, and yet nevertheless is he constrained, over and besides the usher, still to keep both a man servant to attend upon them, and likewise a woman servant to wash and keep them clean.

§3 Also there is no allowance for the lodging of the said Children such time as they attend upon the Court, but the Master, to his great charge, is driven to hire chambers both for himself, his usher, children, and servants.

§4 Also there is no allowance for riding journeys when occasion serveth the Master to travel or send into sundry parts within this realm, to take up and bring such children as be thought meet to be trained for the service of her Majesty.

§5 Also there is no allowance nor other consideration for those children whose voices be changed, who only do depend upon the charge of the said Master until such time as he may prefer the same with clothing and other furniture, unto his no small charge.

§6 And although it may be objected that her Majesty's allowance is no whit less than her Majesty's father, of famous memory, therefor allowed, yet considering the prices of things present to the time past, and what annuities the Master then had out of sundry abbeys within this realm, besides sundry gifts from the King, and divers particular fees besides, for the better maintenance of the said Children and office, and besides also there hath been withdrawn from the said Children, since her Majesty's coming to the crown, 12*d.* by the day which was allowed for their

478

breakfasts, as may appear by the Treasurer of the Chamber his account, for the time being, with other allowances incident to the office, as appeareth by the ancient accounts in the said office, which I here omit.

§7 The burden hereof hath from time to time so hindered the Masters of the Children—viz., Mr. Bower, Mr. Edwardes, myself and Mr. Farrant—that notwithstanding some good helps otherwise, some of them died in so poor case, and so deeply indebted, that they have not left scarcely wherewith to bury them.

§8 In tender consideration whereof, might it please your Honors that the said allowance of 6*d.* a day apiece for the Children's diet might be reserved in her Majesty's coffers during the time of their attendance, and in lieu thereof they to be allowed meat and drink within this honorable household, for that I am not able upon so small allowance any longer to bear so heavy a burden; or otherwise to be considered as shall seem best unto your honorable wisdoms.

[*Endorsed in dorso*] 1583 November. The humble petition of the Master of the Children of her Highness's Chapel. [*and in a different hand*] To have farther allowances for the finding of the Children, for causes within mentioned.

Document 22

❨Petition of Precinct Inhabitants
to the Privy Council

NOVEMBER, 1596[1]

State Papers Domestic, Elizabeth, CCLX, No. 116; printed in its original spelling by Chambers, *Elizabethan Stage*, Vol. IV, pp. 319–20; and by Halliwell-Phillips, *Outlines*, Vol. I, p. 304. Chambers says that this document has been suspected of being a forgery, but that it is probably genuine.

§1 To the right honorable the Lords and others of her Majesty's most honorable Privy Council,—Humbly showing and beseeching your honors, the inhabitants of the precinct of the Blackfriars, London:

§2 That whereas one Burbage hath lately bought certain rooms in the same precinct, near adjoining unto the dwelling houses of the right honorable the Lord Chamberlain[2] and the Lord of Hunsdon, which rooms the said Burbage is now altering and meaneth very shortly to convert and turn the same into a common playhouse, which will grow to be a very great annoyance and trouble, not only to all the noblemen and gentlemen thereabout inhabiting, but also a general inconvenience to all the inhabitants of the same precinct, both by reason of the great resort and gathering together of all manner of vagrant and lewd persons that, under color of resorting to the plays, will come thither and work all manner of mischief, and also to the great pestering and filling up of the same precinct, if it should please God to send any visitation of sickness as heretofore hath been, for that the same precinct is already grown very populous; and besides that the same playhouse is so near the church that the noise of the drums and trumpets will greatly disturb and hinder both the ministers and parishioners in time of divine service and sermons;

§3 In tender consideration whereof, as also for that there hath not at any time heretofore been used any common playhouse within the same precinct, but that now, all players being banished by the Lord Mayor from playing within the City by reason of the great inconveniences and ill rule that followeth them, they now think to plant themselves in liberties, that therefore it would please your Honors to take order that the same rooms may be converted to some other use, and that no playhouse may be used or kept there; and your suppliants, as most bounden, shall and will daily pray for your Lordships in all honor and happiness long to live.

> *Elizabeth Russell, dowager; G. Hunsdon; Henry Bowes; Thomas Browne; John Crooke; William Meredith; Stephen Egerton; Richard Lee; . . . Smith; William Paddy; William de Lavine; Francis Hinson; John Edwards; Andrew Lyons; Thomas Nayle; Owen Lochard; John Robbinson; Thomas Homes; Richard Feild; William Watts; Henry Boice; Edward Ley; John Clarke; William Bispham; Robert Baheire; Ezechiell Major; Harman Buckholt; John Le Mere; John Dollin; Ascanio de Renialmire; John Wharton.*

1. The date of the present petition is fixed by the petition of 1619 (29:1).

2. The Lord Chamberlain at the time of the petition was William Brooke, seventh Lord Cobham. He held that office from August 8, 1596, until his death on March 5, 1597, when George Carey, second Lord Hunsdon, succeeded him. In spite of his tenure of that office, he seems never to have been the patron of the Lord Chamberlain's Men; George Carey took over their patronage at the death of his father on July 22, 1596, and they were called Hunsdon's Men until he himself became Lord Chamberlain a few months later. He was thus the patron of James Burbage and of the company when the petition was filed. His support of it, as the second signatory, is therefore surprising.

Document 23

❡ Nathaniel Giles's Commission to Impress Children

JULY, 1597

The document that follows is a memorandum issued by Queen Elizabeth I under her Privy Seal, giving instructions for the issuance of a patent under the Great Seal. It is enrolled in *Privy Signet Index* in the Public Record Office, in a bundle of parchments labeled "Privy Seals 1597 July," with a further enrollment in *State Papers Domestic*, Elizabeth, Docquets, 1597–1598. It is printed in its original spelling in Wallace's *Children of the Chapel*, p. 61 n. 1. The patent itself is dated July, 1597, and is preserved in *Patent Rolls*, 39 Elizabeth, part 9, membrane 7, dorso.

§1 Elizabeth, by the grace of God Queen of England, France and Ireland, Defender of the Faith, &c., to our right trusty and well-beloved councilor, Sir Thomas Egerton, knight, keeper of our Great Seal of England for the time being, greeting. We will and command you that under our said Great Seal ye cause our letters patents to be made forth, in form following: Elizabeth, by the grace of God, &c., to all mayors, sheriffs, bailiffs, constables, and all other our officers, greeting;

§2 For that it is meet that our Chapel Royal should be furnished with well-singing children from time to time, we have and by these presents do authorize our well-beloved servant, Nathaniel Giles, Master of our Children of our said Chapel, or his deputy being by his bill subscribed and sealed so authorized, and having this our present commission with him, to take such and so many children as he or his sufficient deputy shall think meet, in all cathedral, collegiate, parish churches, chapels, or any other place or places, as well within liberty as without, within this our realm of England, whatsoever they be;

§3 And also at all times necessary horses, boats, barges, carts, cars and wagons for the conveyance of the said children from any place, with all manner of necessaries appertaining to the said children, by land or water, at such reasonable prices as by the discretion of him or his said deputy shall be thought sufficient; and also to take up sufficient lodging for him and the said children, when they for our service shall remove to any place or places; provided also that if our said servant or his deputy or deputies, bearers hereof in his name, cannot forthwith remove the child or children when he, by virtue of this our commission, hath taken him or them,

482

that then the said child or children shall remain there until such time as our said servant, Nathaniel Giles, shall send for him or them.

§4 Wherefore we will and command you, and every of you to whom this our commission shall come, to be helping, aiding, and assisting to the uttermost of your powers, as you will answer at your uttermost perils. In witness whereof, &c.

§5 Given under our Privy Seal at our Manor of Greenwich, the third day of July in the nine-and-thirtieth year of our reign.

Document 24

⟨Henry Clifton's Complaint

DECEMBER 15, 1601

Star Chamber Proceedings, Elizabeth, Bundle C 46, No. 39; printed in its original spelling in Fleay, *Chronicle History of the London Stage*, pp. 127–32.

§1 To the Queen's most excellent Majesty: In all humbleness complaining, showeth and informeth your most excellent Majesty your Highness's true, loyal and faithful subject, Henry Clifton, of Toftrees in your Highness's County of Norfolk, esquire:

§2 That whereas your excellent Majesty, for the better furnishing of your Chapel Royal with well-singing children, by your Majesty's letters patents under the Great Seal of England, bearing date at Westminster the 15th day of July in the nine-and-thirtieth year of your Highness's reign [1597], authorized your Highness's servant, Nathaniel Giles, Master of the Children of your Highness's said Chapel, by himself or his deputy to take such children as he or his said deputy should think meet, in cathedral, collegiate, parish churches or chapels, for your Majesty's said better service,

§3 But so it is, most excellent Sovereign, that the said Nathaniel Giles, confederating himself with one James Robinson, Henry Evans, and others yet unto your Majesty's said subject unknown how [many], by color of your Majesty's said letters patents and the trust by your Highness thereby to him, the said Nathaniel Giles, committed, endeavoring, conspiring and complotting how to oppress divers of your Majesty's humble and faithful subjects and thereby to make unto themselves an unlawful gain and benefit, they, the said confederates, devised, conspired and concluded, for their own corrupt gain and lucre, to erect, set up, furnish and maintain a playhouse or place in the Blackfriars within your Majesty's City of London; and to the end they might the better furnish their said plays and interludes with children whom they thought most fittest to act and furnish the said plays, they, the said confederates, . . . hath, since your Majesty's last free and general pardon, most wrongfully, unduly and unjustly taken divers and several children from divers and sundry schools of learning and other places, and apprentices to men of trade from their masters, no way fitting for your Majesty's service in or for your Chapel

484

Royal; but the children have so taken and employed in acting and furnishing of the said plays and interludes . . . against the wills of the said children, their parents, tutors, masters and governors, and to the no small grief and oppressions [of] your Majesty's true and faithful subjects;

§4 Amongst which numbers, . . . they have unduly taken and so employed one John Chappell, a grammar-school scholar of one Mr. Spykes's school, near Cripplegate, London; John Motteram, a grammar scholar in the free school at Westminster; Nathan Field, a scholar of a grammar school in London, kept by one Mr. Monkaster; Alvery Trussell, an apprentice to one Thomas Gyles; one Philip Pykman, and Thomas Grymes, apprentices to Richard and George Chambers; Salmon Pavey, apprentice to one Peerce; being children no way able or fit for singing, nor by any the said confederates endeavored to be taught to sing, but by them, the said confederates, abusively employed, as aforesaid, only in plays and interludes.

§5 With which their said oppression they not being satisfied, . . . [they] have practiced and put in execution the same their corrupt and undue purposes against your said subject; for whereas your said subject, having Thomas Clifton, his only son and heir, being about the age of thirteen years, and having for the better education of him, his said son, placed him in a grammar school in Christ Church, London, where for a good space he had continued and been taught and instructed in the grounds of learning and the Latin tongue; and your said subject being resident and dwelling in a house which he had taken in or near Great St. Bartholomew's, London, where his son also lay and had his diet, and had daily recourse from thence to the said grammar school: the same being well known to the confederates aforesaid, and they also well knowing that your subject's said son had no manner of sight in song nor skill in music, they, the said confederates, about one year last past, and since your Majesty's last free and general pardon, did . . . unlawfully practice and conspire . . . violently and unlawfully to surprise the said Thomas Clifton as he should pass between your said subject's house and the said grammar school. . . .

§6 And accordingly, about the 13th day of December, which was in the 43rd year of your Majesty's most gracious and happy reign [1600], the said confederates . . . did . . . waylay the said Thomas Clifton as he should pass from your said subject's house to the said school, . . . and him with like force and violence did . . . hawl, pull, drag and carry away to the said playhouse in the Blackfriars aforesaid, . . . where the said Nathaniel Giles, Henry Evans, and the said other confederates . . . him, the said Thomas Clifton, as a prisoner, committed to the said playhouse amongst a company of lewd and dissolute mercenary players, purposing in that place (and for no service of your Majesty) to use and exercise him . . . in acting of parts in base plays and interludes, to the mercenary gain and private commodity of them, the said . . . confederates.

§7 Of which abuse and oppression . . . your said subject having notice, he

. . . forthwith repaired unto the said playhouse in the Blackfriars aforesaid, where he . . . then and there divers times made request to have his said son released, which they, the said Nathaniel Giles, Henry Evans and James Robinson, utterly and scornfully refused to do; whereupon your said subject then and there affirmed unto them that if he should complain unto some of your Majesty's most honorable Privy Council, they, the said confederates, would hardly answer it; whereupon [they] . . . in very scornful manner willed your said subject to complain to whom he would, and they would answer it; and in a most slight and scornful regard of your Majesty's service and the duty they owe thereunto, they then and there said further that if the Queen (meaning your Highness) would not bear them forth in that action, she (meaning likewise your Highness) should get another to execute her commission for them, and then and there used divers other contemptuous speeches, manifesting a very slight regard in them towards your Majesty's service.

§8 And your said subject, then and there also using many persuasions unto them . . . to have his said son released, alleging therein that it was not fit that a gentleman of his sort should have his son and heir (and that his only son) to be so basely used, they . . . most arrogantly then and there answered that they had authority sufficient so to take any nobleman's son in this land, and did then and there use these speeches, that were it not for the benefit they made by the said playhouse, who would should serve the Chapel with children, for them; and . . . to despite and grieve your said subject with an assurance that his said son should be employed in that vile and base manner of a mercenary player in that place, and in no other sort or manner, did then and there deliver unto his said son, in most scornful, disdainful, and despiteful manner, a scroll of paper containing part of one of their said plays or interludes, and him, the said Thomas Clifton, commanded to learn the same by heart; and in further grievance and despite of your said subject, [they] delivered and committed your subject's said son unto the custody of the said Henry Evans, with these threatening words, . . . that if he did not obey the said Evans, he should be surely whipped. In which base restraint and misusage the said Thomas Clifton . . . continued by the space of about a day and a night, until such time as, by the warrant of the right honorable Sir John Fortescue, knight, one of your Majesty's most honorable Privy Council, he was set at liberty and freed from the same.

§9 All which violent courses, despiteful usage . . . and the base restraint and employment of your subject's said son, and other the misdemeanors and offenses aforesaid, have been to the great grievance, wrong and vexation of your said subject and his said son, and have been so committed, perpetrated and done, both in abuse of the nobility of this your Highness's realm, and in abuse of your Majesty's said commission, and also to the great oppression and wrong of divers your Majesty's loving and faithful subjects, and were so committed, perpetrated and done since your Majesty's last free and general pardon, and contrary to divers your Majesty's laws in this your Highness's realm established. In tender consideration whereof, &c.

Document 25

⟨License for the King's Players

MAY 19, 1603

Patent Rolls, 1 James I, part 2; printed in type facsimile in *Malone Society Collections*, Vol. I, pp. 264–65.

Special Commission for Lawrence Fletcher and William Shakespeare and others

§1 James, by the grace of God, &c., to all mayors, sheriffs, justices of peace, bailiffs, constables, and to all officers and loving subjects, greeting.

§2 Know ye that we, of our special grace, certain knowledge and mere motion, have licensed and authorized, and by these presents do license and authorize, these our servants, Lawrence Fletcher, William Shakespeare, Richard Burbage, Augustine Phillips, John Heminges, Henry Condell, William Sly, Robert Armin, Richard Cowley, and the rest of their associates, freely to use and exercise the art and faculty of playing comedies, tragedies, histories, interludes, morals, pastorals, stage plays, and such others like as they have already studied or hereafter shall use or study, as well for the recreation of our loving subjects as for our solace and pleasure when we shall think good to see them during our pleasure;

§3 And the said comedies, tragedies, histories, interludes, morals, pastorals, stage plays and such like to show and exercise publicly to their best commodity, when the infection of the plague shall decrease, as well within their now usual house called the Globe within our County of Surrey, as also within any town halls or moot halls or other convenient places within the liberties and freedom of any other city, university, town or borough whatsoever within our said realms and dominions;

§4 Willing and commanding you, and every of you, as you tender our pleasure, not only to permit and suffer them herein, without any your lets, hindrances or molestations during our said pleasure, but also to be aiding and assisting to them if any wrong be to them offered, and to allow them such former courtesies as hath been given to men of their place and quality; and also what further favor you shall show to these our servants for our sake, we shall take kindly at your hands.

§5 In witness whereof, &c., witness ourself at Westminster the nineteenth day of May [1603].

per breve de privato sigillo, &c.

487

Document 26

⟨License for the Children of the Queen's Revels

FEBRUARY 4, 1604

Patent Rolls, 1 James I, part 8; printed in type facsimile in *Malone Society Collections*, Vol. I, pp. 267–68, and in its original spelling in *Elizabethan Stage*, Vol. II, p. 49.

Concerning a special license for Edward Kirkham and others for the Queen's Revels[1]

§1 James, by the grace of God, &c., to all mayors, sheriffs, justices of peace, bailiffs, constables, and to all other our officers, ministers and loving subjects to whom these presents shall come, greeting.

§2 Whereas the Queen, our dearest wife, hath for her pleasure and recreation, when she shall think it fit to have any plays or shows, appointed her servants, Edward Kirkham, Alexander Hawkins, Thomas Kendall and Robert Payne, to provide and bring up a convenient number of children who shall be called Children of her Revels, know ye that we have appointed and authorized, and by these presents do authorize and appoint, the said Edward Kirkham, Alexander Hawkins, Thomas Kendall and Robert Payne, from time to time to provide, keep and bring up a convenient number of children, and them to practice and exercise in the quality of playing, by the name of Children of the Revels to the Queen, within the Blackfriars in our City of London or in any other convenient place where they shall think fit for that purpose.

§3 Wherefore we will and command [you] and every of you to whom it shall appertain, to permit her said servants to keep a convenient number of children by the name of Children of her Revels, and them to exercise in the quality of playing according to her pleasure.

§4 Provided always that no such plays or shows shall be presented before the said Queen our wife by the said Children, or by them anywhere publicly acted, but by the approbation and allowance of Samuel Daniel, whom her pleasure is to appoint for that purpose. And these our letters patents shall be your sufficient warrant in this behalf.

§5 In witness whereof, &c., witness ourself at Westminster, the fourth day of February [1604].

per breve de privato sigillo, &c.

1. This heading is in Latin in the original document.

Document 27

([Petition of Precinct Officers to the Lord Mayor

CIRCA 1619

Remembrancia, v. 28; printed in type facsimile in *Malone Society Collections*, Vol. I, pp. 91–93.

§1 To the right honorable Sir Sebastian Harvey, knight, Lord Mayor of the City of London, and to the right worshipful the Aldermen his brethren, the humble petition of the constables and other officers and inhabitants within the precinct of the Blackfriars, London, showeth:

§2 That whereas in November, 1596, divers both honorable persons and others then inhabiting the said precinct, made known to the lords and others of the Privy Council what inconveniences were likely to fall upon them by a common playhouse which was then preparing to be erected there, whereupon their Honors then forbade the use of the said house for plays, as by the petition and endorsement in answer thereof may appear;

A petition of divers officers and other inhabitants in the precinct of the Blackfriars, touching the dangers and inconveniencies arising by the coaches, &c., coming to the playhouse there.

§3 Moreover, whereas, by orders of the lords and others of the Privy Council, for many weighty reasons therein expressed, bearing date the 22 June 1600, it was limited there should be only two playhouses tolerated, whereof the one to be the Bankside, and the other at a place in or near Golding Lane, exempting thereby the Blackfriars; and whereas also there was then a letter of the same date directed to the Lord Mayor and justices, strictly requiring of them to see these order[s] put in execution, and so to be continued:

§4 Nevertheless may it please your Lordship and your brethren to be advertised that, contrary to the said orders, the owner of the said playhouse doth, under the name of a private house (respecting indeed private commodity only) convert the said house to a public playhouse, unto which there is daily such resort of people, and such multitudes of coaches (whereof many are hackney coaches, bringing people of all sorts) that sometimes all our streets cannot contain them, but that they clog up Ludgate also, in such sort that both they endanger the one the other, break

489

down stalls, throw down men's goods from their shops, and the inhabitants there cannot come to their houses nor bring in their necessary provisions of beer, wood, coal, or hay, nor the tradesmen or shopkeepers utter their wares, nor the passenger go to the common water stairs, without danger of their lives and limbs, whereby also many times quarrels and effusion of blood hath followed; and what further danger may be occasioned by the broils, plots or practices of such an unruly multitude of people, if they should get head, your wisdoms can conceive.

§5 These inconveniences falling out almost every day in the winter time (not forbearing the time of Lent) from one or two of the clock till six at night, which being the time also most usual for christenings and burials and afternoons service, we cannot have passage to the church for performance of those necessary duties, the ordinary passage for a great part of the precinct aforesaid being close by the playhouse door.

§6 Wherefore our humble suit to your Lordship and your brethren is, that according to the trust which the lords and the rest of the Privy Council repose in your wisdoms for the due execution of the foresaid orders, course may be taken in the premises, and that the owner of the said playhouse may satisfy your Lordship and your brethren for his presumption in breaking the same, and also put in good assurance for the time to come that we shall not be thus endangered by such resort to this house, but that the King's Majesty's subjects may have safe and quiet passage in the common streets, and the tradesmen for uttering their wares; wherein we do the more earnestly importune for preserving the peace, which is now often broken by reason of the inconveniences aforesaid; for preserving whereof, if we shall either by turnpikes, posts, chains or otherwise, keep these coaches without our gates, great inconvenience might thereby ensue to Ludgate and the streets thereabouts. Wherefore we crave aid and direction from your Lordship and your brethren in all the premises, and will ever pray for the good and prosperous government of this honorable City.

W^m : Gouge, Minister

Humfrey Weaver *Clement Evans*	Churchwardens	We find this house a great annoyance to the Church.
Edward Ashe *Tho: Campe*	Sidemen	
Tho: Dixe *Edw: Ashe*	Constables	We find this house a great occasion for the breach of the peace.
William Waple *Richard Ellyot*	Collectors	We find this house a great hindrance to our poor.
Roger Nicholson *Richard Adams*	Scavengers	We find this house a great annoyance for the cleansing of the streets.

Document 28

❮ Petition of Precinct Inhabitants to the Lord Mayor

CIRCA 1619

Remembrancia, v. 29; printed in type facsimile in *Malone Society Collections*, Vol. I, pp. 93–94.

§1 To the right honorable the Lord Mayor of the City of London, and the right worshipful the Aldermen of the same City, his brethren.

Right honorable: We have been made acquainted with a petition which the constables and other officers within the precinct of Blackfriars intend to your Lordship and your worthy brethren, hoping thereby to procure redress of such disorders and inconveniences as arise there by reason of the playhouse in that unfit place, which being situated in the bosom of the City, we conceive will be the more tenderly considered of by your grave wisdoms, according to the trust which the State reposeth in you.

The copy of a letter of divers honorable persons and others (to the Lord Mayor, &c.) inhabiting the precinct of Blackfriars, touching the abuse and danger arising by the coaches coming to the playhouse there.

§2 We desire your Lordship and your brethren to help us to some remedy therein, that we may go to our houses in safety and enjoy the benefit of the streets without apparent danger, which now, we assure your Lordship, neither we that are inhabitants, nor any other of his Majesty's subjects having occasion that way, either by land or water, can do; for such is the unruliness of some of the resorters to that house, and of coaches, horses, and people of all sorts gathered together by that occasion in those narrow and crooked streets, that many hurts have heretofore been thereby done, and [we] fear it will at some time or other hereafter procure much more, if it be not by your wisdoms prevented.

§3 Thus much we thought it our parts to add to the petition of the said officers, whose just care (deserving commendations) we are bold also to recommend to your honorable Lordship and your brethren, upon whom they will attend for further direction in this business; and thus we rest your Lordship's loving friends.

Ja: Fullerton; S. Posth. Hoby; Mary Peyton; Agnes Clere; Agnes Finch; Wm: Rowe; Tho: Emerson; Richard Browne; Elizabeth Hill; Eliz: Onslewe; Tho: Alured; Edward Osborne; Edm: Sadler; Grace Darcy; Edw: Carr; Thomas Peyton; Katherin Bowyer; Ro: Rigdon; Ed: Curle; John Argent; Tho: Rogers; Ric⁰. Putto; L: Egerton; Paul Delane.

Document 29

⟨Order by the Corporation of the City of London for the Suppression of the Blackfriars Playhouse

JANUARY 21, 1619

State Papers Domestic, James I, Vol. 205, No. 32 (iv); printed in its original spelling by Halliwell-Phillipps, in *Outlines*, Vol. I, p. 311, and by Hillebrand in *Child Actors*, p. 155.

§1 Item, this day was exhibited to this Court a petition by the constables and other officers and inhabitants within the precinct of Blackfriars, London, therein declaring that in November, 1596, divers honorable persons and others then inhabiting in the said precinct, made known to the lords and others of the Privy Council what inconveniences were likely to fall upon them by a common playhouse then preparing to be erected there, and that thereupon their Honors forbad the use of the said house for plays, and in June, 1600, made certain orders by which, for many weighty reasons therein expressed, it is limited there should be only two playhouses tolerated, whereof the one to be on the Bankside, and the other in or near Golding Lane, exempting thereby the Blackfriars; and that a letter was then directed from their Lordships to the Lord Mayor and justices, straitly requiring of them to see those orders put in execution and so to be continued.

§2 And now, for as the said inhabitants of the Blackfriars have in the said petition complained to this Court that, contrary to the said lords' orders, the owner of the said playhouse within the Blackfriars, under the name of a private house, hath converted the same to a public playhouse, unto which there is daily so great resort of people, and so great multitude of coaches, whereof many are hackney coaches bringing people of all sorts, that sometimes all their streets cannot contain them, that they endanger one the other, break down stalls, throw down men's goods from their shops, hinder the passage of the inhabitants there to and from their houses, let the bringing in of their necessary provisions, that the tradesmen and shopkeepers cannot utter their wares, nor the passengers go to the common water stairs without danger of their lives and limbs, whereby many times quarrels and effusion of blood hath followed, and the minister and people disturbed at the administration of the sacrament of baptism and public prayers in the afternoons.

§3 Whereupon, and after reading the said order and letter of the lords showed forth in this Court by the foresaid inhabitants, and consideration thereof taken, this Court doth think fit, and so order, that the said playhouse be suppressed, and that the players shall from henceforth forbear and desist from playing in that house, in respect of the manifold abuses and disorders complained of as aforesaid.

Document 30

⟨License for the King's Players

MARCH 27, 1619

Exchequer, Treasury of the Receipt, Privy Seals, 17 James I, Bundle ix, No. 2; printed in type facsimile in *Malone Society Collections*, Vol. I, pp. 281–82.

§1 Right trusty and right well-beloved Cousin and . . . . greet you well, and will and command you that under our Privy Seal you cause our letters to be directed to our Chancellor of England, willing and commanding him that under our Great Seal of England he cause our letters to be made forth patent, in form following: James, by the grace of God King of England, Scotland, France, and Ireland, Defender of the Faith, &c., to all justices, mayors, sheriffs, constables, headboroughs, and other our officers and loving subjects, greeting.

§2 Know ye that we, of our special grace, certain knowledge and mere motion, have licensed and authorized, and by these presents do license and authorize, these our well-beloved servants, John Heminges, Richard Burbage, Henry Condell, John Lowin, Nicholas Tooley, John Underwood, Nathan Field, Robert Benfield, Robert Gough, William Ecclestone, Richard Robinson and John Shank, and the rest of their associates, freely to use and exercise the art and faculty of playing comedies, tragedies, histories, interludes, morals, pastorals, stage plays, and such other like as they have already studied or hereafter shall use or study, as well for the recreation of our loving subjects as for our solace and pleasure when we shall think good to see them during our pleasure.

§3 And the said comedies, tragedies, histories, interludes, morals, pastorals, stage plays and such like to show and exercise publicly or otherwise, to their best commodity, when the infection of the plague shall not weekly exceed the number of forty by the certificate of the Lord Mayor of London for the time being, as well within their two their now usual houses called the Globe within our County of Surrey, and their private house situate in the precincts of the Blackfriars within our City of London, as also within any town halls or moot halls or other convenient places within the liberties and freedom of any other city, university, town, or borough whatsoever, within our said realms and dominions;

§4 Willing and commanding you and every of you, and all other our loving

495

subjects, as you tender our pleasure, not only to permit and suffer them herein without any your lets, hindrances, or molestations during our said pleasure, but also to be aiding and assisting to them if any wrong be to them offered, and to allow them such former courtesies as hath been given to men of their place and quality; and also what further favor you shall show to these our servants and the rest of their associates for our sake, we shall [take] kindly at your hands.

§5 In witness whereof, &c. And these our letters shall be your sufficient warrant and discharge in this behalf. Given under our signet at our palace of Westminster, the seven-and-twentieth day of March in the seventeenth year of our reign of England, France and Ireland, and of Scotland the two-and-fiftieth.

Windebank [acting Clerk of the Signet]

[*Addressed*] To our right trusty and right well-beloved cousin and counsellor, Edward, Earl of Worcester, Keeper of our Privy Seal.

Document 31

([Official Action regarding Coaches at Blackfriars

OCTOBER 9 TO DECEMBER 29, 1633

Privy Council Register, Charles I, ix 267, 343, 355, 417; printed in type facsimile in *Malone Society Collections*, Vol. I, pp. 386–89.

SITTING OF OCTOBER 9, 1633

Touching the Playhouse in Blackfriars

§1 Upon consideration this day had at the Board, of the great inconvenience and annoyance occasioned by the resort and confluence of coaches to the playhouse in Blackfriars, whereby the streets, being narrow thereabouts, are at those times become impassable, to the great prejudice of his Majesty's subjects passing that way upon their several occasions, and in particular to divers noblemen and counsellors of state whose houses are that way, whereby they are many times hindered from their necessary attendance upon his Majesty's person and service;

§2 Their Lordships, calling to mind that formerly, upon complaint hereof made, the Board was of opinion that the said playhouse was fit to be removed from thence, and that an indifferent recompense and allowance should be given them for their interests in the said house and buildings thereunto belonging, did therefore think fit and order that Sir Henry Spiller and Sir William Becher, knights, the Aldermen of the Ward, Lawrence Whitaker, esquire, and [*blank*] Child, citizen of London, or any three of them, be hereby required to call such of the parties interested before them as they shall think fit, and upon hearing their demands, and view of the place, to make an indifferent estimate and value of the said house and buildings, and of their interests therein, and to agree upon and set down such recompense to be given for the same as shall be reasonable, and thereupon to make report to the Board of their doings and proceedings therein, by the twenty-sixth of this present.

SITTING OF NOVEMBER 20, 1633

§3 Whereas the Board hath taken consideration of the great inconveniences that grow by reason of the resort to the playhouse of the Blackfriars in coaches,

497

About going to
the Blackfriars
Playhouse in
Coaches

whereby the streets near thereunto are at the play time so stopped that his Majesty's subjects, going about their necessary affairs, can hardly find passage and are oftentimes endangered:

§4 Their Lordships, remembering that there is an easy passage by water unto that playhouse without troubling the streets, and that it is much more fit and reasonable that those which go thither should go thither by water, or else on foot, rather than the necessary businesses of all others, and the public commerce, should be disturbed by their pleasure, do therefore order:

§5 That if any person, man or woman, of what condition soever, repair to the aforesaid playhouse in coach, so soon as they are gone out of their coaches, the coachmen shall depart thence, and not return till the end of the play, nor shall stay or return to fetch those whom they carried, any nearer with their coaches than the farther part of St. Paul's Churchyard on the one side, and Fleet Conduit on the other side; and in the time between their departure and return shall either return home, or else abide in some other streets less frequented with passengers, and so range their coaches in those places that the way be not stopped; which order if any coachman disobey, the next constable or officer is hereby charged to commit him presently to Ludgate or Newgate; and the Lord Mayor of the City of London is required to see this carefully performed by the constables and officers to whom it appertaineth, and to punish every such constable or officer as shall be found negligent therein;

§6 And to the end that none may pretend ignorance hereof, it is lastly ordered that copies of this Order shall be set up at Paul's Chain by direction of the Lord Mayor, also at the west end of St. Paul's Church, at Ludgate, and the Blackfriars Gate, and Fleet Conduit.[1]

SITTING OF NOVEMBER 29, 1633

§7 A letter to the Lord Mayor of London:

We send your Lordship herewith an Order of this Board, for redressing of the inconveniences that grow by reason of the great resort in coaches to the playhouse in the Blackfriars, which Order we do hereby pray and earnestly require your Lordship to see fully and diligently executed in every point thereof, and so much the rather in regard it is of no less unseemliness to the City than of trouble and annoyance to his Majesty's subjects.

And so, expecting your Lordship's performance of these our directions, we bid you, &c.   Signed:

Lord Archbishop of Canterbury, Lord Keeper, Lord Archbishop of York, Lord Treasurer, Lord Privy Seal, Earl Marshal, Lord Viscount Wimbledon, Mr. Treasurer, Mr. Secretary Coke, Mr. Secretary Windebank.

SITTING OF DECEMBER 29, 1633

§8 Ordered the 29th, the King &c. being present.

Touching the
Playhouse in
Blackfriars

Upon information this day given to the Board, of the dis-commodity that divers persons of great quality, especially ladies and gentlewomen, did receive in going to the play-house of Blackfriars, by reason that no coaches may stand within the Blackfriars Gate or return thither during the play, and of the prejudice the players, his Majesty's servants, do receive thereby, but especially that the streets are so much the more encumbered with the said coaches,

§9 The Board, taking into consideration the former Order of the 20th of November last concerning this business, did think fit to explain the said Order in such manner: that as many coaches as may stand within the Blackfriars Gate may enter and stay there, or return thither at the end of the play, but that the said former Order of the 20th of November be duly observed in all other parts; whereof as well the Lord Mayor as all other his Majesty's officers who are prayed and re-quired to see the said Order observed, are to take notice.

1. An Order of the Privy Council, virtually identical with paragraphs 3 to 6 above, is preserved in *Remembrancia*, vii 101, and printed in type facsimile in *Malone Society Collections*, Vol. I, pp. 98-99.

Document 32

¶ Plays Protected for the King's Men

AUGUST 7, 1641

Lord Chamberlain's book 5/135; printed in type facsimile in *Malone Society Collections*, Vol. I, pp. 367–69, and Vol. II, pp. 398–99; and printed in part, in its original spelling, in Bentley, *Jacobean and Caroline Stage*, Vol. I, pp. 65–66.

After my hearty commendations. The players which are his Majesty's Servants have addressed themselves unto me, as formerly to my predecessors in office, complaining that some printers are about to print and publish some of their plays, which hitherto they have been usually restrained from by the authority of the Lord Chamberlain. Their request seems both just and reasonable, as only tending to preserve them masters of their proper goods, which in justice ought not to be made common for another man's profit to their disadvantage. Upon this ground, therefore, I am induced to require your care (as formerly my predecessors have done) that no plays belonging to them be put in print without their knowledge and consent. The particulars to which they now lay claim are contained in a List enclosed; and if any of those plays shall be offered to the press under another name than is in the List expressed, I shall desire your care that they may not be defrauded by that means, but that they may be made acquainted with it before they be recorded in your Hall, and so have opportunity to show their right unto them. And thus, not doubting of your ready care herein, I bid you heartily farewell, and rest

Aug. 7, 1641

Your very loving friend,
Essex

To my very loving friends, the
Masters and Wardens of the Company
of Printers and Stationers

A List of the Plays follows

The Wild-Goose Chase	*The Martial Maid*
The Little French Lawyer	*Beauty in a Trance*

The Loyal Subject

The Spanish Curate

The Custom of the Country

The Double Marriage

A Wife for a Month

The Island Princess

The Mad Lover

The Pilgrim

The Mayor of Quinborough, &c.

The Woman's Plot

The Woman's Prize, &c.

The Switzer

More Dissemblers Beside Women

The Widow

The Knight of Malta

The Novella

The Lovesick Maid

The Captain

The Humorous Lieutenant

Bonduca

The Inconstant Lady

Chances

The Maid of the Mill

The Bridegroom and the Madman

The Queen of Corinth

The Coxcomb

The Noble Gentleman

Beggars

The Honest Man's Fortune

The Forced Lady

Alexius

The Unfortunate Lovers

The Fair Favorite

The Emperor Valentinian

The Goblins

The Distresses

The Doubtful Heir

The Imposture

The Country Captain

The Discontented Colonel

The Brothers

Minerva's Sacrifice

The Judge

The City Madam

The Corporal

Alfonso, Emperor of Germany

The Nobleman

The Bashful Lover

Love and Honor

The 1st and 2nd part[s] of
        The Passionate Lover

The Guardian

The Duke of Lerma, or
        The Spanish Duke

The Prophetess

The Lovers' Pilgrimage

The Lover's Progress

News from Plymouth

Document 33

⟨ Plays Allotted to Sir William Davenant

DECEMBER 12, 1660

Public Record Office, Lord Chamberlain's Department, L.C. 5/137, p. 343; printed in its original spelling by Allardyce Nicoll, *A History of Restoration Drama*, pp. 314–15.

§1 "Whereas Sir William Davenant, knight, hath humbly presented to us a proposition of reforming some of the most ancient plays that were played at Blackfriars, and of making them fit for the company of actors appointed under his direction and command, viz. the plays called *The Tempest, Measures for Measures, Much Ado about Nothing, Romeo and Juliet, Twelfth Night, The Life of King Henry the Eighth, The Sophy, King Lear, The Tragedy of Macbeth, The Tragedy of Hamlet Prince of Denmark*, and *The Duchess of Malfi*, therefore we have granted unto the said Sir William Davenant liberty to represent the plays above named, by the actors under his command, notwithstanding any warrant to the contrary formerly granted. . . ."

§2 The warrant closes by granting Davenant two months' right in *The Mad Lover, The Maid in the Mill, The Spanish Curate, The Loyal Subject, Rule a Wife and Have a Wife*, and *Pericles Prince of Tyre*.

Document 34

❨Plays Allotted to Thomas Killigrew

CIRCA JANUARY 12, 1668/69

Public Record Office, Lord Chamberlain's Department, L.C. 5/12, p. 212; printed in its original spelling by Allardyce Nicoll, *A History of Restoration Drama*, pp. 315–16.

PLAYS ACTED AT THE THEATRE ROYAL

A catalogue of part of his Majesty's Servants' plays as they were formerly acted at the Blackfriars, and now allowed of to his Majesty's Servants at the new theatre.

Every Man Is His Humour	*The Pilgrim*
Every Man Out of His Humour	*The Queen of Corinth*
Cynthia's Revels	*The Spanish Curate*
Sejanus	*The Sea Voyage*
The Fox	*Valentinian*
The Silent Woman	*The Woman's Prize*
The Alchemist	*The Captain*
Catiline	*The Chances*
Bartholomew Fair	*The Coxcomb*
Staple of News	*The Double Marriage*
The Devil's an Ass	*The French Lawyer*
Magnetic Lady	*The False One*
Tale of a Tub	*The Fair Maid of the Inn*
New Inn	*The Humorous Lieutenant*
Beggar's Bush	*The Island Princess*
Bonduca	*The Knights of Malta*
Custom of the Country	*The Loyal Subject*
Love's Pilgrimage	*The Laws of Candy*
The Noble Gentlemen	*Love's Progress*
The Nice Valor	*The Winter's Tale*
The Prophetess	*King John*
The Martial Maid	*Richard the Second*

Love's Cure

Julius Caesar

The Moor of Venice

Antony and Cleopatra

Cymbeline

The Doubtful Heir

The Impostor

The Brothers

The Sisters

The Cardinal

The Duke of Lerma

The Duke of Milan

A Wife for a Month

The Wild-Goose Chase

The Elder Brother

The Faithful Shepherdess

A King and No King

The Maid's Tragedy

Philaster

Rollo, Duke of Normandy

The Scornful Lady

Thierry and Theodoret

Rule a Wife and Have a Wife

The Gentlemen of Verona

The Merry Wives of Windsor

The Comedy of Errors

Love's Labour's Lost

Midsummer Night's Dream

The Merchant of Venice

As You Like It

The Taming of the Shrew

All's Well that Ends Well

Henry the Fourth

The second part

The Royal Slave

Richard the Third

Coriolanus

Andronicus

Alphonso

The Unnatural Combat

The Guardian

Aglaura

Arviragus and Philicia 1st pt.

Arviragus and Philicia 2nd pt.

The Spartan Ladies

The Bashful Lover

Bussy D'Ambois

Brennoralt

Country Captain

The Variety

The Emperor of the East

The Deserving Favorite

The Goblins

The Fatal Dowry

The Lost Lady

The Devil of Edmonton

More Dissemblers than Women

The Mayor of Quinborough

The Northern Lass

The Novella

Osmond the Great Turk

The Roman Actor

The Widow

The Widow's Tears

Document 35

❬Newman and Hunnis vs. Farrant

COURT OF REQUESTS, 1584

Public Record Office, *Court of Requests Proceedings*, Uncalendared, Elizabeth, 1584; printed in Wallace, *Evolution*, pp. 160–68.

BILL OF COMPLAINT OF NEWMAN AND HUNNIS
JANUARY 20, 1584

§1 "To the Queen's most excellent Majesty, our dread Sovereign Lady. — In most humble wise complaining, showeth unto your most excellent Majesty your Highness's faithful and obedient subjects, John Newman and William Hunnis, of the City of London, gentlemen:

"That whereas one Anne Farrant, late of Greenwich, widow, by Indenture bearing date the twentieth day of December . . . [1581], did demise and let certain rooms, parcel of the dissolved house of Blackfriars, . . . unto your said subjects for divers years yet enduring, yielding and paying for the same such yearly rent, and at such days and times, as in the said Indenture is expressed, with other covenants by your said subjects to be performed, . . . and for the performance of the said covenants your said subjects became bound by obligation, jointly and severally, in the sum of £100: . . .

§2 So it is . . . that although your said subjects and their assigns have from time to time paid the said yearly rents . . . and, as they verily think, have observed the covenants, . . . yet notwithstanding, the said Anne Farrant, of a covetous and greedy mind, . . . hath of late . . . commenced her several suits at the common law upon the said bond of £100 against your said subjects in your Majesty's Court of Common Pleas, surmising and making speech that the said rent hath not been duly paid, . . . which your said subjects do think to have been paid at the said days, or at the least very shortly after; . . .

§3 May it therefore please your most excellent Majesty . . . to grant your Highness's most gracious Writ of Privy Seal to be directed to the said Anne Farrant, commanding her . . . personally to appear before your Majesty in your Highness's Court of Requests, then and there to answer to the premises, and farther to grant your most gracious Writ of Injunction, . . . enjoining her thereby not to proceed any farther to sue and vex your subjects. . . .

ANNE FARRANT'S ANSWER
JANUARY 27, 1584

§4 "The defendant . . . for Answer in and to the said Bill of Complaint . . . saith: that long time before that the said defendant did demise and grant, by her Indenture, the said rooms, parcel of the said dissolved house of the Blackfriars . . . to the said complainant[s], . . . one Sir William More of Loseley, in the County of Surrey, knight, was thereof seized in his demesne as of fee; and so being seized, by his Indenture of Lease bearing date the twentieth day of December . . . [1576], did amongst other things demise, grant, and to farm let unto one Richard Farrant, . . . then husband to this defendant, the said rooms . . . for the term of one-and-twenty years, . . . yielding and paying therefor yearly to the said Sir William More . . . £14 of lawful money of England, . . . in and by which Indenture the said Richard Farrant did covenant . . . to repair, sustain and amend the said rooms, . . . and that neither he nor any of his assigns should assign, demise or let the premises or any part thereof . . . but to their own use. . . .

§5 "And the said Richard . . . about three years now last past died intestate, after whose decease the administration of all the goods and chattels of the said Richard were committed to this defendant; . . . by virtue of which letters of administration, the said defendant did enter and was possessed of the things in and by the said Indenture demised, and by virtue thereof was chargeable with the same rent, condition, covenants, articles; and being a sole woman, unable of herself to use the said rooms to such purposes as her said husband late used them, . . . nor being able to sustain, repair and amend the said rooms according to the . . . articles in the Indenture, . . . at the earnest request and desire of the said complainants, she, this defendant, was content to let the rooms . . . to the said complainants, yielding and paying therefor to her yearly the sum of twenty nobles more than the said £14 due to the said Sir William More; which lease the scrivener, which by their appointment made the Indenture of the same lease, did make yielding only the yearly rent of £20 6s. 8d., . . . whereby this defendant is driven by oversight to lack one noble yearly of the rent she meant to have, for which the complainants promised her a satisfaction which she never yet could get of them.

§6 By which Indenture, also, the said complainants did covenant, grant and agree with the said defendant to repair, sustain and amend . . . the said rooms and the buildings, tilings, leads, and other the premises; . . . and further the said complainants became bound by obligation in £100 to this defendant, with condition well and truly to observe . . . all the covenants . . . which in the said Indenture of Lease . . . are mentioned; in and by which Indenture also, the said now defendant hath covenanted not only to save these complainants harmless of the said rent reserved to the said Sir William More, but also to pay or tender the same. . . .

§7 Since which demise and grant made to the said complainants, [they] . . . have granted all their estate and term in and to the premises unto one Henry Evans, citizen and scrivener of London; and they have, of and by virtue thereof, had and reaped far greater profit than the said yearly rent amounteth unto; and . . . they or some of them have sought . . . to avoid and defraud this defendant of and from the rent, . . . and . . . have not at any time since . . . paid their quarter rent due at any of the quarter days, . . . and many times have withholden the said rent for and by the space of half a year and more; and this defendant, being left very bare and poor, and with great charge of children and debts of her said late husband, . . . having great lack of money and not having money in hand to satisfy the rent due to the said Sir William More, she hath been driven . . . by humble and pitiful suit to the right honorable Lord Cobham, to obtain such favor and help of his good Lordship that one of his men would and might offer and tender to pay the rent then due; . . . and at another time this defendant hath been urged to crave and obtain of Mr. Henry Sackford, esquire, of her Majesty's Privy Chamber, to lend to this defendant so much money as would and did pay the said quarter's rent; . . . and other times this defendant hath been . . . driven for the payment of the said rent . . . to sell divers of her goods and chattels at far lesser price than they were worth, as at one time a dozen of gold buttons, and at another time a set of viols; and at some time when this defendant, for extreme need, hath borrowed of them some money, and laid some of her plate and jewels to them or some of them in pawns, they have, at the payment of the said rent to her, defalked from the rent the money to her lent, and yet detained the said pawns; and this last year . . . three quarters rents . . . were not paid until near about All Saints' Day last past.

§8 "And further, the said complainants being earnestly required by this defendant to do needful reparations upon the house, being greatly decayed by their not repairing thereof, they did drive the time so long until Sir William More was determined to come to London; whereby the said defendant . . . was constrained to amend and repair the leads of the said house, being before blown up with wind, the charges whereof did come unto 15s. 6d., and the said complainants never would pay the same; whereupon the workman did retain one of the Knight Marshal's men for arrest [of] this defendant for the same, for the avoiding whereof this defendant paid the same 15s. 6d. And further, this defendant hath divers other manifest matters . . . which do persuade her that the said complainants intend to cause this defendant to forfeit or lose her said lease. . . .

§9 Besides that the said Sir William More hath since made some entry, and a new lease of the premises, to one who by color thereof hath sued the said Evans, who hath, without the privity of this defendant, so faintly and falsely pleaded and defended the cause that judgment is like to be given against the said Evans, to the great prejudice of this defendant; and they or some of them have at some times falsely protested that they . . . had satisfied the rent due to Sir William More, when in truth the rent . . . hath not been paid; the which cause, besides divers other unfriendly and hard dealings by them . . . used to this defendant, this defendant thinketh to be such causes as this Court will vouchsafe so to consider of, that she shall not be stayed or hindered to prosecute her just and lawful actions and suits at the common law against the said complainants." The defendant reiterates that the complainants have failed to pay the yearly rents or to observe the covenants mentioned in the Indenture, and denies that a greedy or covetous mind inspired the suits which she commenced against them at the common law.

REPLICATION OF HUNNIS AND NEWMAN
MAY 27, 1584

§10 The complainants affirm the truth of everything set forth in their Bill of Complaint. They deny that they, or the said Henry Evans, have contrived to defraud the defendant of her rent or any part thereof, but say on the contrary that they have paid "the whole sum of £20 13s. 4d., according to the true intent and meaning of the said parties touching their said bargain." They say "that they have done from time to time, and were ready to have done, sufficient reparations in and upon the said premises as need required, but in one time when the said defendant willfully obtruded herself into some botching and unfit dealing in the same reparations, and did let [i.e., hinder] the sufficient and due performing thereof by the said complainants, and to their great loss and hindrance." They enter a general denial of everything stated by the defendant in her Answer, and deny specifically that "by their negligence [she was] driven to sell divers of her goods and chattels at a far lesser price than they were worth."

The Court's decision is wanting.

Document 36

⟨ The Condition of the £200 Bond

APRIL 20, 1602

The Condition of the £200 Bond is recited in (1) Hawkins' Answer in the suit of Rastall and Kirkham *vs.* Hawkins (cf. 40:2), printed in its original spelling in Wallace, *Children of the Chapel*, p. 92, n. 2, and in Hillebrand, *Child Actors*, pp. 180–81; and (2) in Evans's Answer in the case of Kirkham *vs.* Paunton *et al.* (cf. 43:30), printed in its original spelling in Fleay, *Chronicle History*, pp. 240–41.

  The original document is not extant, but its text has been preserved in the two depositions listed above. The differences between the two versions are too slight to require notice. Both versions recite the terms of Burbage's lease to Evans (cf. p. 176 above) as preamble to the Condition proper, its position being indicated by the ellipsis in the first line of the Condition as printed below.[1]

§1 "The Condition of this Obligation is such, that . . . if now the within-named William Rastall, Edward Kirkham[2] and Thomas Kendall, and every of them, their and every of their executors and administrators and assigns,[3] shall or may from henceforth, during the continuance of the said lease, have the joint use, occupation and profit, together with the within-bounden Henry Evans and Alexander Hawkins, . . . of and in the said great hall or room and other the premises, without the let or trouble of the said Henry and Alexander . . . or of any other person or persons by their or any of their means or procurement, they, the said William, Edward and Thomas . . . paying unto the said Henry and Alexander . . . from henceforth yearly during the continuance of the said lease the moiety or one-half of the said yearly rent, at the four usual feasts in the year or within one-and-twenty days next after every of the same feasts by even portions, and also bearing and paying of the moiety of such charges as from time to time shall be laid out or disbursed, for, in, or about the reparations of the premises by and according to the purport, true meaning and limitation of the said lease, and also permitting and suffering the said Henry and Alexander . . . to have joint use, occupation and profit together with them, the said William, Edward and Thomas . . . of and in the said great hall and premises, without their or any of their lets, troubles and interruptions, that then this present obligation to be void and of none effect, or else it to stand in full force and virtue."

1. The document is also recited, with minor variations, in Evans *vs.* Kirkham (cf. 42:2).

2. The Evans version incorrectly gives Edward Kirkham's first name as Richard throughout this document.

3. Subsequent ellipses indicate omissions of repetitions or variants of "their executors," etc.

Document 37

⟨The Condition of the £50 Bond

APRIL 20, 1602

The original document has been lost, but its text has been preserved in Henry Evans's Bill of Complaint in the case of Evans *vs.* Kendall (cf. 38:1), as printed by Wallace, *The Children of the Chapel*, p. 102, n. 3. It is also printed by Hillebrand, *The Child Actors*, pp. 187–88, with slight variations.

§1 "The Condition of this Obligation is such: that if the within-bounden William Rastall, Edward Kirkham and Thomas Kendall, or any of them, their or any of their executors, administrators or assigns, every week, weekly on Saturday during the space of fifteen years next ensuing the date within written, when and so often as any interludes, plays or shows shall be played, used, showed or published in the great hall and other the rooms situate in the Blackfriars, London, or any part thereof mentioned to be demised by one Richard Burbage, gentleman, to the within-named Henry Evans in and by one Indenture of Lease bearing date the second day of September in the two-and-fortieth year of the reign of our sovereign lady Elizabeth, the Queen's Majesty that now is [1600], or elsewhere, by the Children, or any called by the name of the Children of the Queen's Majesty's Chapel, or by any other children which by the consent of the said William, Edward, Thomas, Henry, and one Alexander Hawkins, gentleman, their executors or administrators of any three of them, whereof the said Henry or Alexander, their executors or administrators to be one, shall be dieted, kept or retained for the exercise of the said interludes or plays, do and shall well and truly pay, or cause to be paid, unto the said Henry Evans, his executors, or assigns, at or in the said great hall, the sum of eight shillings of lawful money of England, the first payment thereof to begin and to be made on Saturday, being the four-and-twentieth day next coming of this instant month of April within written, that then this present obligation to be void and of none effect, or else it to stand in full force and virtue."

511

Document 38

⟨Evans vs. Kendall

KING'S BENCH, EASTER TERM, 1608

Coram Rege Rolls, Easter, 6 James I, membrane 303. The document is in Latin, except for the Condition of the £50 Bond, which is in English. The text is printed in Latin in Hillebrand's *Child Actors*, pp. 332–34, and in his translation on pp. 187–89. The original document is not divided into Bill of Complaint, Answer, etc., but those divisions are obvious, and are here indicated.

EVANS'S BILL OF COMPLAINT

§1 Evans recites the Condition of the £50 Bond (Document 37), thus implying that he bases his complaint upon a violation of its terms. He gives no particulars; but in recounting the circumstances four years later, in his Answer in the Kirkham *vs.* Paunton dispute (43:36), he says that the "obligation was forfeited, . . . the arrearages being great" in the stipulated payment of 8 shillings weekly for each week that the Children should play.

KENDALL'S ANSWER

§2 Kendall says that Evans ought not to maintain his suit against him, because, beginning with "Saturday, the twenty-fourth day of the said month of April [1602], and thus every week on Saturday until the day of the suing of the said Bill, as often as any plays" were presented in the great hall in the Blackfriars by the Children of the Queen's Majesty's Chapel, he himself did well and truly pay the said Henry Evans the sum of 8 shillings of lawful money of England.

EVANS'S REPLICATION

§3 Evans protests that Kendall did not pay him "any sums of pence . . . on the Saturday being the sixteenth day of June in the second year of the reign of the lord James, now King of England" [1604], on which day "a certain play (in

512

English an interlude) was played in the said great hall . . . situate in the Black-friars . . . by boys who . . . were kept for the exercise of the said plays."

KENDALL'S REJOINDER

§4 Kendall says that no interlude was played in the said great hall on the said Saturday.

The verdict is not upon record; but Evans's Answer in the Kirkham *vs.* Paunton lawsuit says that Kirkham and Kendall gave Hawkins a new bond in the adjusted amount of £54 (43:36). On this new obligation Evans sued again, a year later.[1] Eventually the controversy was settled by Kirkham's payment of an amount that he gives as £52 10*s.* (43:3) but that Evans gives as £48 10*s.* (43:36). Incidentally, it seems strange that Evans should have brought the present action against Kendall only, without naming Kendall's more active partner, Kirkham, as codefendant.

1. King's Bench, *Coram Rege Rolls,*
Easter, 7 James I, membrane 265b. See
Hillebrand, *Child Actors,* p. 189, n. 40.

Document 39

⟨Kirkham and Kendall vs. Daniel

COURT OF CHANCERY, 1609

Chancery Bills and Answers, Ser. I, James I, K.4/33; printed in full in *The Child Actors*, pp. 334–38. This suit was brought by Edward Kirkham and Anne Kendall, widow and executrix of Thomas Kendall, for the purpose of staying a suit brought against Kirkham in the King's Bench by one John Gerrard, using Samuel Daniel's name.

BILL OF COMPLAINT OF KIRKHAM AND KENDALL
MAY 9, 1609

§1 The plaintiffs recite the essential provisions of the royal patent of February 4, 1604 (Document 26), by which Kirkham, Kendall, Hawkins and Payne were named as masters of the Children of the Queen's Revels, and by which Daniel was named as censor and licenser of the Children's plays. They say that "in regard of the pains to be taken by the said Samuel Daniel about the approbation and allowance of such plays," Kirkham and Kendall obligated themselves, about April 28 of that same year, to pay Daniel every year "one annuity or yearly sum of £10 . . . if the said Children should play or make any shows, either publicly or privately, the full time six months in every year; and if the said Children should not play or make any shows the full time of six months in every year by reason of any prohibition or pestilence in the City of London, that then the said Kirkham and Kendall should pay unto the said Daniel after the rate of 16s. 8d. a month, for such longer or shorter time as the said Children should present or do any plays or shows, either publicly or privately as aforesaid, being not the full time of six months in one year"; and for the due performance of this obligation, they gave Daniel their bond in the amount of £100.

§2 The plaintiffs say that Daniel, "having occasion to use money, would still importune and request" them to pay him his money before it became due, and sometimes to pay it to his creditors, the which things they gladly did, until October 25, 1604, at which time a new agreement was entered into at Daniel's request. It provided that Daniel should deliver up his bond to be canceled, and that thereafter he should receive 5 shillings per week for each week that the Chil-

514

dren should play; "unto which the said Daniel did agree, and for a long time after received the said 5 shillings weekly according to the said agreement; and confessing that the said bond was fully satisfied and discharged, did promise to deliver the same to the said Kirkham and Kendall to be canceled; yet notwithstanding, . . . the said Daniel hath now lately commenced suit upon the said obligation against the said Kirkham in his Majesty's Court of King's Bench, meaning to take the whole forfeiture of the said obligation against the said Kirkham; . . . and albeit your said orators have divers and sundry times earnestly required of the said Daniel to deliver the said obligation to your said orators according to his promise, and to surcease his suit upon the same, yet that to do he hath denied and refused, and still doth deny and refuse. . . ." In consideration whereof, the plaintiffs request the Lord Chancellor to issue a writ of injunction, commanding Daniel and his attorneys to proceed no further in their suit, and to summon Daniel to appear before the Court of Chancery to receive such order and direction as shall seem to his Lordship to stand with right, equity and good conscience.

DANIEL'S ANSWER
MAY 12, 1609

§3 Daniel says that it was "by the earnest suit, means and endeavor of this defendant, which he performed with his great labor, costs and expenses," that his Majesty was induced to issue the patent of February 4, 1604, and that it was "in consideration of his great pains and travel therein formerly taken" that Kirkham and Kendall became bound to him under the £100 bond. He says that he was to have received from them a new bond covering the payment of 5 shillings weekly under the revised agreement, upon receipt of which he was to deliver up the £100 bond for cancellation, but that he never received the new obligation. He thinks that he received all such sums as were due him until April 28, 1605, at which time he assigned the bond, and all future benefits under it, to one John Gerrard; but "forasmuch as the said complainants have not satisfied and paid the said annuity since the said assignment in such manner as they ought to have done according to the condition of the said bond, he, the said Gerrard, hath used this defendant's name and put the same bond in suit."

The result of this suit is not known.

Document 40

(Rastall and Kirkham vs. Hawkins

KING'S BENCH, EASTER TERM, 1609

Coram Rege Rolls, Easter, 7 James I, membrane 456. Except for the Condition of the £200 Bond, the document is in Latin. With a few ellipses of technical phrases, it is printed in translation by Hillebrand in *The Child Actors*, pp. 180–85.

RASTALL AND KIRKHAM'S BILL OF COMPLAINT

§1 In the last Michaelmas Term, William Rastall and Edward Kirkham have presented a Bill of Complaint against Alexander Hawkins in the Court of King's Bench, suing that he repay them £200 of lawful English money which he owes them and unjustly withholds. They claim that under the Condition of the £200 Bond he is held and firmly bound to them and to one Thomas Kendall, now dead, but that he has "wholly refused to pay [the said £200] to the said William, Edward and Thomas during the life of the said Thomas, and still refuses to pay the said William and Edward, to the damage of the said William and Edward of £40; and hence they bring suit, &c." They do not specify the manner in which the condition of the bond has been violated.

HAWKINS'S ANSWER

§2 Hawkins causes the Condition of the £200 Bond to be read into the record. (It is from the present context that the Condition is printed on page 509 above as Document 36.) The Condition proper is prefaced by a recital of the terms of Burbage's lease to Evans (cf. p. 176 above).

§3 ". . . By the means of which Indenture the said Richard Burbage, for and in consideration of a yearly rent expressed in the same Indenture, demised to the said Henry Evans the said great hall and other premises mentioned among other things in the said Indorsement, by the name of all that great hall or place (in English Room)[1] with places (in English rooms) above it as they were then built, adorned (in English furnished), and erected with a Theatre (in English a Stage), porticoes (in English Galleries) and seats[2] to the amount

516

specified in the schedule thereto joined,[3] situate and being toward the northern end of certain places (in English Rooms) then in the tenure and occupation of one John Robbinson[4] or his assigns, within the precinct of Blackfriars, London, and being part and parcel of those houses and edifices there which were then lately bought and purchased of Sir William More by the late James Burbage, father of the said Richard, and the said Richard Burbage, containing by estimation in length from the south side to the north sixty-six feet of assize, more or less, and in breadth from the west part to the east forty-six feet of assize, more or less.[5] . . .

§4 "And the same Alexander further declares that the said Henry Evans, for himself, his heirs, executors, administrators, and assigns, among other things agreed and conceded to and with the said Richard Burbage, his heirs and assigns, by means of the same Indenture, . . . that the said Henry Evans, his heirs, executors, administrators or assigns, at his or their own costs and expenditures, would from time to time well and sufficiently repair, support, maintain and mend the said great hall or place . . . and the said places . . . above the same, among other things by the same Indenture demised, by and through all and every necessary reparations (in English needful and necessary reparations) and emendations (in English amendments)[6] whatsoever, when and so often as need should arise or demand, or within six months after warning in this behalf to or for him or them given or left in writing at the said great hall, during the said term of twenty-one years, as by the same Indenture among other things more fully appears.

§5 "By virtue of which demise, the same Henry Evans, immediately after the said feast of St. Michael the Archangel next coming after the date of the said Indenture, entered into the said hall and tenements with their appurtenances demised in the said form, and was then in possession, and he was thus in possession until the drawing up of the said obligatory writing" (i.e., the Condition of the £200 Bond).

§6 Hawkins says that Rastall, Kirkham and Kendall had the joint use, occupation and profit, along with Evans and himself, of the great hall and other premises, from the time of the sealing of the obligatory writing until December 20, 1604; but he says that between those dates, and specifically on July 1, 1604, "the said tenements . . . were then dilapidated in various parts and unrepaired, namely in the flooring lying on the eastern side of the same hall, and in the flooring at the eastern end of the Theatre (in English the Stage) in the said hall, and in the wall there above the steps (in English the stairs), and in the window glass, and in the wooden windows as well above as below on each side of the premises specified above in the Indorsement, and in the wall at each end of the said hall, and in the leaden gutters (in English gutters of lead), and in the roof of the premises specified above in the said Indorsement."[7]

§7 Hawkins says that Henry Evans, on December 18, 1604, laid out and expended the sum of £10 for and about necessary reparations of the dilapidated parts, and that on the next day he required Edward Kirkham to pay the half of the said £10, namely £5, according to the form and effect of the said Indorsement; but Rastall, Kirkham and Kendall did not at that time pay, nor did any of them pay, the same £5; by reason of which, on December 20, 1604, Hawkins did prevent and hinder the said William, Edward and Thomas from having further joint use, occupation and profit . . . of and in the said great hall or place . . . and other the said premises, as by reason of the said condition is within his rights; . . . whence he seeks judgment as to whether the said William and Edward ought not to bring or maintain their said action against him, &c."

RASTALL AND KIRKHAM'S REPLICATION

§8 The plaintiffs protest that the said tenements were not in decay as Hawkins alleges, that Evans did not spend £10 for reparations, and that no notice was given to Kirkham of any money laid out in reparations of the said tenements. But they declare that at the time of the demise to Evans by Burbage "there was a certain chamber called the Schoolhouse above part of the said great hall, and certain other chambers above the chamber called the Schoolhouse"; and that on the last day of February, 1604, "the said Henry Evans shut up (in English locked up) the said chamber above the chamber called the Schoolhouse, and then and there expelled the said William Rastall, Edward Kirkham and Thomas Kendall . . . until the said time in which it is alleged that the said tenements were in decay in the said form; and this they are ready to prove, whence they seek judgment, and that their said debt with their said damages on the ground of the detention of the debt, be awarded them, &c."

HAWKINS'S REJOINDER

§9 "And the said Alexander declares that the said Henry Evans did not lock up the said chamber above the said chamber called the Schoolhouse, nor shut out the said William Rastall, Edward Kirkham and Thomas Kendall, or any of them, in the manner and form as the said William and Edward in their Replication above alleged; and as to this he puts himself upon his oath."

The records of the Court of King's Bench do not show the outcome of this case; but this would appear to be the action later mentioned by Evans as having been nonsuited (cf. 42:24 and 43:33). If so, Evans's attorney made an error of date in the defendant's Answer, Kirkham vs. Paunton, in referring to the suit as having been brought in the ninth year of James I (1611) instead of in 1609 (43:33).

1. ". . . tocius illius magne aule vel loci anglice Roome cum locis anglice roomes super eadem sicut tunc fuerunt erecti ornati Anglice furnished & edificati . . ."

2. ". . . cum Theatro Anglice a Stadge porticibus Anglice Galleries & sedibus."

3. Unfortunately, the schedule has been lost.

4. A John Robbinson was one of the signers of the Petition of 1596 (22:3), and a John Robinson is mentioned in Shakespeare's will as being the tenant of his Blackfriars gatehouse (cf. p. 252 above). Since each document relates to its man as a resident of the Blackfriars precinct, all may refer to the same person.

5. ". . . existens pars et parcella illorum domorum et aedificacionum ibidem quae fuerunt tunc nuper perquisitae et emptae de Willelmo Moore Milite per Jacobum Burbidge defunctum patrem praedicti Ricardi et per dictum Ricardum Burbidge continens per estimacionem in longitudine ab australe ad borealem partem eiusdem sexaginta et sex pedes assisae sit plus siue minus et in latitudine ab occidentale ad orientalem partem eiusdem quadraginta et sex pedes assissae sit plus siue minus."

This part of the Latin text, and this part only, is quoted from Wallace's *Children of the Chapel*, p. 39, n. 1. Apparently the present document was first discovered by Wallace, sometime prior to 1908. From it he quotes the text of this footnote, but nothing more. He intended to publish the document *in extenso* in a forthcoming book which, however, was never published. Hillebrand rediscovered the document later.

6. ". . . in & per omnes & omnimodas necessarias reparacciones anglice needeful and necessarie reparaciones & emendaciones Anglice amendmentes . . ."

7. ". . . fuerunt in diversis partibus inde in decasu & minime reparata videlicet in paviamento iacente super orientali parte eiusdem Aule & in paviamento in orientali fine cuiusdam Theatri Anglice the Stadge in aula predicta & in pariete ibidem super gradus anglice the Stayres & in vitrio & in fenestris ligneis tam supra quam infra in utrisque partibus premissorum . . . & in pariete in utrisque partibus & finibus predicta Aule & in gutturis plumbi anglice guttures of lead & in tegulacione predictorum premissorum . . ."

Document 41

❴Keysar vs. Burbage et al.

COURT OF REQUESTS, 1610

Court of Requests Proceedings, James I, Uncalendared; printed in its original spelling by C. W. Wallace in "Shakespeare and His London Associates," *University Studies of the University of Nebraska*, Vol. X, No. 4 (October 1910), pp. 76–100.

KEYSAR'S BILL OF COMPLAINT
FEBRUARY 8, 1610

§1 "Humbly complaining, showeth unto your most excellent Majesty your Highness's loyal and obedient suppliant, Robert Keysar, citizen and goldsmith of London:

"That whereas one Richard Burbage, gentleman, was and still is seized of an estate of inheritance in fee or fee-tail, of and in . . . one great hall or room, with certain rooms over the same, set and being in the Blackfriars, London, erected, furnished and built with stage, galleries and seats; and being so seized did, for the term of twenty-and-one years, demise the same to one Henry Evans at the yearly rent of £40, quarterly to be paid during the said term, which in effluxion of time is not yet expired by many years, by force and virtue of which lease he, the said Henry Evans, did thereinto enter and was thereof lawfully possessed;

§2 "And being thereof so possessed, he, the said Henry Evans, did for good and valuable consideration afterwards grant all or some part of the said term . . . to one John Marston, gentleman, who by force and virtue thereof did enter in and upon such part and so much thereof as was meant and intended to be to him granted, and was accordingly thereof possessed; and being so possessed, and having also one full sixth part of and in certain goods, apparel for players, properties, play-books and other things then and still used by the Children of the Queen's Majesty's Revels in and about their plays, . . . the full value of which said goods and premises was at a very low and reasonable appraisement worth £600 at the least, he, the said John Marston, and your now suppliant, did fall into speech and communication touching the buying of his, the said John Marston['s] right, title and interest of, in and to the full sixth part of the lease aforesaid, and . . . of, in and to the said sixth part of the said goods, apparel for players, properties, play-books and other things . . . and of the sixth part of all the profit and commodity to be made thereof and thereby during the continuance of the said lease; and in the end it was fully concluded and agreed . . . that for and in consideration of £100 . . . he, the said Marston, should convey his right and interest therein and thereunto to your said suppliant.

§3 "But your suppliant, understanding that there were divers partners in the said lease, goods and profit to be made as aforesaid, and fearing that by some practice and confederacy between the said Richard Burbage, Henry Evans and then [*sic*], your suppliant might be defeated and cozened of all or the greatest part thereof, and withal having heard some rumors and flying speeches to that purpose which did increase his fear, your said suppliant did make his repair to the said Richard Burbage and unto one Cuthbert Burbage, John Heminges, Henry Condell and others, being all partners and the only partners that might prejudice and wrong your suppliant in the premises, and told them that he had concluded and agreed with the said Marston for a full sixth part in the premises, . . . and both prayed them and told them that he hoped they would take no such deceitful and injurious courses to hurt or hinder him as had been reported and bruited abroad that they or some of them would;

§4 "Whereupon they all . . . promised to your said suppliant . . . that, notwithstanding that the said Henry Evans had been treating and persuading them to some such act, . . . yet that they would never yield to any such matter until all partners and parties interested in the said lease, goods and profits . . . were fully satisfied and paid whatsoever was to them due in law and conscience; . . . and upon this faithful promise so generally made by them all, your suppliant did pay his said £100 to the said John Marston, and the rather because if your suppliant would have joined to have sold his said sixth part with others that had equal interest therein, they did then offer to have given him £400 for the same.

§5 "Notwithstanding all which, . . . by the giving of some small piece of money to the said Henry Evans to the end that he would surrender up the original lease to the said Richard Burbage, . . . he, the said Evans, did surrender the same, by means whereof they, the said Richard Burbage, Cuthbert Burbage, John Heminges, Henry Condell and others, have entered in and upon the said playhouse . . . and made profit thereof to themselves to the full value at the least of £1,500, a full sixth part whereof in all equity and conscience doth of right belong unto your suppliant. . . .

§6 "In tender consideration whereof, and because . . . your said poor suppliant, in hope to have enjoyed his said bargain, hath kept boys these two years, to his exceeding charge, of purpose to have continued plays in the said house upon the ceasing of the general sickness, and hath disbursed by that means and by making provision in the said house for the purpose aforesaid £500, . . . [your suppliant prays] that therefore your Majesty will be graciously pleased . . . to call into this honorable Court the said Richard Burbage, Henry Evans, Cuthbert Burbage, John Heminges and Henry Condell, commanding them . . . to be and appear in this honorable Court of Whitehall . . . there to answer to the premises. . . ."

ANSWER OF THE DEFENDANTS
FEBRUARY 12, 1610

§7 The defendants say that true it is that Richard Burbage is seized of an estate of inheritance of and in all that great hall or room, with certain other rooms over the same, set and being in the Blackfriars in London, erected, furnished and built with stage, galleries and seats, and that he demised the same unto Henry Evans for the term of one-and-twenty years, which said term is not yet expired; but they deny that they were acquainted with any dealings and bargains made or supposed to be made by or between the said Henry Evans and John Marston, and they "utterly deny, and every one of them for and by himself utterly denieth, that the said complainant did at any time repair or come unto these defendants or any of them, and acquaint or tell them that he . . . had concluded and agreed with the said Marston for a full sixth part in the premises, and that he was presently to pay to the said Marston £100 for the same, . . . or that they, or any of them, made him, the said complainant, any such promise or replied as in and by the said Bill of Complaint is also most untruly surmised; and these defendants also utterly deny, and every one of them for and by himself utterly denieth, that they or any of them did at any time make any such offer unto the said complainant, to give him £400 or any other sum or sums of money . . . or that they or any of them did at any time advise or encourage the said complainant, either by their or any of their promise, offers or otherwise, to proceed and to pay the said Marston the said £100. . . .

§8 "But these defendants say . . . that true it is that the said Henry Evans, having entered into one bond or obligation of £400 unto the said defendant Richard Burbage, for true payment of the said rent of £40 per annum, and into divers covenants for reparations to be done in and upon the premises . . . as by the said Bond and Indenture of Lease . . . doth and may appear, and that by reason the said premises lay then and had long lain void and without use for plays, whereby the same became not only burdensome and unprofitable unto the said Evans, but also ran far into decay for want of reparations done in and upon the premises, they, the said defendants, or some of them, entered into communication with the said Henry Evans, as well for satisfaction of the said bond and covenants, then forfeited unto the said Richard Burbage, as for the repairing of the premises and so maintaining the same for and during the time to come unexpired . . . in due and necessary reparations; which he, the said Henry Evans, finding himself . . . unable to perform, and being unwilling any longer to charge himself with so great and unnecessary a burden, he, the said Evans, began to treat with the said Richard Burbage about a surrender of the said Evans's said lease, which finally, for and in regard of some competent consideration given him in recompense of his, the said Evans's, charge formerly bestowed in buildings in and about the premises, was accomplished, and the said Evans's whole estate of, in and to the premises was surrendered by the said Evans unto the said Burbage, who accepted the same surrender accordingly (without knowing of or intending to prejudice the estate of the said Marston or the complainant or either of them), as he hopeth it lawful was for him to do, especially the premises being in such decay for want of reparations as then they were.

§9 "And the said defendants confess that true it is that since the said surrender, . . . which was about the tenth of August last past,[1] they . . . have entered into, occupied and enjoyed the said great hall or playhouse, and taken the benefit and profit thereof, and have rejected the said complainant from intermeddling with them in any sort; . . . but they . . . do utterly deny that they . . . have at any time intermeddled with, had, enjoyed or received any the goods or apparel mentioned in the said Bill of Complaint. . . ."

§10 The defendants do not acknowledge that the said goods and premises were at any time worth £600 at the least, or that they have made £1,500 profit at any time since the surrender, or that Keysar paid £100 to Marston for a full sixth part of the premises, or that he has kept boys for two years past to his exceeding charge, or that he has spent £500 on the maintenance of the boys and the care of the premises.

KEYSAR'S REPLICATION
MAY 22, 1610

§11 The complainant reiterates his charge that the defendants encouraged him to proceed with his purchase of Marston's interest in the playhouse, "which they secretly meant and intended that he . . . should never enjoy." He asserts that with an inveterate and increasing malice towards him, they received Evans into their house and kept him secret from the complainant, dividing the goods and profits among themselves to his, the complainant's, exceeding loss and hindrance;

§12 "And having thereby fraudulently disappointed this complainant both of house, goods, and all his just and rightful profit to have been made thereby, then also did they, in further testimony of their malice, privately contract with the owners of all the private playhouses within the City of London for one whole year, and for the same did satisfy and pay a dead rent to the owners thereof, to their own great loss and hindrance, . . . and by that means did exceedingly hinder this complainant, who all that time had a company of the most expert and skillful actors within the realm of England, to the number of eighteen or twenty persons, all or most of them trained up in that service in the reign of the late Queen Elizabeth for ten years together, and afterwards preferred into her Majesty's service to be the Children of her Revels by a patent from his most excellent Majesty, but kept and maintained at the costs and charges of this complainant; until now, by the malicious practices of the defendants as aforesaid, they are enforced to be dispersed and turned away, to the abundant hurt of the said young men, the disappointing of her Majesty's said service, and to the loss and hindrance of this complainant at least of £1,000."

§13 Keysar disputes the defendants' assertion that they knew nothing of Evans's sale of an interest to Marston, or of Marston's ownership of a share in the house and the theatrical equipment. He repeats that he told them of his proposed deal with Marston and that they offered to pay him £400. He now claims that Evans's surrender of the lease to Burbage was made "only of malice and purpose to defraud, deceive and disappoint this complainant of his said bargain therein," and challenges their declaration that they have not intermeddled with, had, enjoyed or received any the goods or apparel in the Bill mentioned, or converted the same or any part thereof to their own use.

REJOINDER OF THE DEFENDANTS
JUNE 19, 1610

§14 The defendants say that the matters for which the complainant principally seeketh to be relieved in this honorable Court consist chiefly in two parts, of which the first is his desire to obtain an interest in and to one sixth part of the playhouse or great room and galleries used for playing, claiming it as his right through an alleged purchase of Marston's interest, which in turn is alleged to have passed to Marston from Henry Evans.

§15 "Unto which said first part, these defendants, and every of them for and by himself saith, that the said Henry Evans never granted, assigned, or set over any such estate or term at all, of, in or unto the said house, room, or galleries, unto the said John Marston, . . . neither could he so have done if he would; but the same was and would have been presently void, for that, as these defendants by their learned counsel are informed, he, the said Henry Evans, was restrained in and by his said lease . . . from granting, assigning or putting away the premises, or any part thereof, for any term whatsoever, or unto any person whatsoever; neither did the said Marston, as these defendants are credibly informed and do verily believe to be true, sell, grant or assign any part at all in the said house, room or galleries unto the said complainant, neither is there any mention at all made thereof in any deed or writing made or passed from the said Marston unto the said complainant, as these defendants are credibly informed and do verily believe to be true. . . .

§16 "And as touching the second main part of the said complainant's Bill of Complaint, by which he also claimeth to have from these defendants one full sixth part of the apparel, goods, play-books, properties for plays, and other like things, . . . these defendants say . . . that they nor any of them now have, or at any time had, any part or portion of the said goods, . . . neither did they or any of them ever meddle or have to do with them, or claim to have any interest, use or property of, in or to them or any of them; but these defendants confess that they have heard that they are in the keeping of the said Henry Evans, who hath caused the same to be appraised by honest and indifferent men, and hath made and taken a true inventory of them, as these defendants have likewise heard, according whereunto he always was, and yet is, ready to deliver such part and portion thereof unto the said complainant as his part shall or may amount unto. . . .

§17 "And these defendants further say . . . that they much marvel that the said complainant should desire so apparently to set forth his folly on record, as to charge these defendants . . . with malice towards him in contracting privately with the owners of all the private playhouses within the City of London for one whole year, and for the same to pay a dead rent to the owners thereof, to these defendants' own great loss and hindrance, but to the intent only thereby to advance their malice and to overthrow the said complainant only, . . . whenas the said complainant might in truth thereby, if the said suggestion were true, be perfectly persuaded and assured that these defendants should be not only malicious, as he . . . most injuriously suggesteth, but also malicious fools, if to do the complainant a little hurt . . . they . . . should do themselves a far greater and more certain loss; and whenas also the contract made with the owners of the said private playhouses, if any such were, hath always been, and yet is, as well to and for the use, benefit and profit of the said complainant himself and his partners . . . as to the benefits of these defendants or any of them; . . .

§18 "For these defendants say . . . that there being . . . but only three private playhouses in the City of London—the one of which being in the Blackfriars and in the hands of these defendants or of their assigns; one other being in the Whitefriars, in the hands or occupation of the said complainant himself, his partners or assigns; and the third, near St. Paul's Church, then being in the hands of one Mr. Pearce, but then unused for a playhouse—one Mr. Rosseter, a partner of the said complainant's, dealt for and compounded with the said Mr. Pearce, to the only benefit of him, the said Rosseter, the now complainant, the rest of their partners and company (and without the privity, knowledge or consent of these defendants or any of them), and that thereby they . . . might advance their gains and profit to be had and made in their said house in the Whitefriars, that there might be a cessation of playing and plays to be acted in the said house near St. Paul's Church aforesaid, for which the said Rosseter compounded with the said Pearce to give him . . . £20 per annum;

§19 "But these defendants afterwards coming to play at their said house in the Blackfriars, and the said Rosseter perceiving that the benefit of the said cessation of plays at Paul's did, or was likely to, turn as well to the benefit of these defendants and their company as to the benefit of the said complainant, the said Rosseter, and the rest of their company, . . . he, the said Rosseter, came unto these defendants . . . and entreated them that . . . they . . . be content to bear and pay one half of the charge of the said rent of £20 per annum; whereunto these defendants . . . willingly did yield, and accordingly have paid their part of the said rent. . . ."

§20 The defendants deny that they did at any time receive or keep Evans secret from the complainant, and they suggest that Keysar omitted to name Evans as a codefendant "for fear lest that he, knowing the truth of all the said complainant's untruths, should discover more than the complainant would willingly have known." They deny that the complainant had "any such company of the most expert and skillful actors within the realm of England, to the number of eighteen or twenty persons, . . . or that they were dispersed by the malicious practices of these defendants," believing rather that the actors "were dispersed, and driven each of them to provide for himself, by reason that . . . the complainant was no longer able to maintain them together" on account of the plague or other causes; and they deny finally that the complainant "hath lost by the dispersing of the said company at the least £1,000, as in and by the said Replication is most untruly and vaingloriously surmised. . . ."

An affidavit by Cuthbert Burbage is in existence (Court of Requests, Affidavits, 6–9 James I, Miscellaneous Books, 127), in which he says that the defendants have material witnesses to examine, to wit, John Marston, Henry Evans and his wife, Nathaniel Field, John Underwood, William Ostler, William Baxstead (= Barksted?), Philip Rosseter, and Margaret Hawkins, widow. The testimony of the witnesses is not upon the record, and it therefore seems likely that the case was settled out of court without their being called. The outcome is unknown.

1. If the defendants mean August 1609 when they speak of "August last past," they are mistaken; the surrender actually took place in August 1608. See page 208, footnote 33, above.

Document 42

⟨Evans vs. Kirkham

COURT OF CHANCERY, 1612

Chancery Proceedings, James I, Bills and Answers, Bundle E 4, No. 9; printed in its original spelling in Fleay, *Chronicle History*, pp. 210–22.

HENRY EVANS'S BILL OF COMPLAINT
MAY 5, 1612

§1 "To the right honorable Thomas Lord Ellesmere, Lord Chancellor of England: In all humbleness complaining, showeth unto your good Lordship your daily orator, Henry Evans of London, gentleman:

"That whereas one Richard Burbage, of the parish of St. Leonard's, Shoreditch, in the County of Middlesex, gentleman, by his Indenture of Lease bearing date the second day of September in the two-and-fortieth year of the reign of our late sovereign Lady Queen Elizabeth of famous memory [1600], hath leased and to farm letten unto your said orator all that great hall or room, with the rooms over the same, situate and being within the precinct of the Blackfriars in London, then or late in the tenure or occupation of your said orator, for the term and space of one-and-twenty years commencing at the feast of St. Michael the Archangel next ensuing the date of the same Indenture of Lease, for the yearly rent of £40, quarterly to be paid at such days and in such manner and form as in and by the said Indenture . . . it doth and may more plainly appear, by virtue whereof your said orator was truly and lawfully possessed of the demised premises for the term aforesaid;

§2 "And he, your said orator, being so possessed, one Edward Kirkham of London, gentleman, William Rastall and Thomas Kendall, late of London, deceased, earnestly labored with and entreated your said orator that he . . . would suffer them to have and enjoy some part of the demised premises; whereupon it was agreed and concluded upon between . . . [them] that they, the said Kirkham, Rastall and Kendall, should have the joint benefit and profit of all the said demised premises, excepting only one or two rooms wherein your subject then inhabited; and thereupon the said Rastall, Kirkham, and Kendall caused one obliga-

527

tion, of the penal sum of £200 or thereabouts, to be written and engrossed, ready to be sealed by your said orator and one Alexander Hawkins, late of London, gentleman, deceased, to this or the like effect following, videlicet:[1] . . . which said obligation, upon the faithful promises of the said Kirkham, Rastall and Kendall, that they would never seek or take any advantage upon the said bond in respect of any small breach of the condition of the said obligation, or in respect of your orator's dwelling or inhabiting there, he, your said orator, sealed the said bond of £200. . . .

§3 "And within one month of thereabouts next after the ensealing of the same obligation, your said orator did depart into the country, and relinquished and left all the aforesaid demised premises to them, the said Rastall, Kirkham and Kendall, only to their use and dispose as best liked them at their free wills and pleasures, for a long space and time, to their great benefit and profit, and to the damage of your poor orator at the least to the value of £300; and yet notwithstanding, the said Edward Kirkham, carrying a great spleen and malice against your said orator, in Trinity Term last arrested your said orator by writ out of the King's Bench, upon several actions of £1,000 damages, of purpose that your said orator might not find sufficient sureties to bail him; which great and undeserved malice of his, the said Kirkham's, was (although to his great trouble) avoided; for he, your said orator, did put in good bail to answer the said actions;

§4 "Whereupon the said Edward Kirkham declared against your said orator upon the above-recited bond or obligation, and your said orator, without any delay on his part, answered and came orderly to issue with the said Kirkham, ready for trial; for which, in Michaelmas and Hilary Terms last, the said Kirkham three or four times gave warning to your said orator to go to trial, and several days were appointed for the trying thereof, and your orator, with his counsel, attorney, and witnesses, at his no small charge, every several time attended; but the said Kirkham, having as it seemeth no purpose to proceed therein, doth by multiplicity of suits and vexations seek to impoverish and undo your said orator.

§5 "And to manifest the same, the said Kirkham hath commenced three several actions against your said orator and the said Alexander Hawkins upon the said bond, and now the said Kirkham seeketh to take advantage against your said orator upon the said bond of £200, upon no or very small occasions, being very little or nothing damnified; and for breach of the condition of the said obligation, the said Kirkham hath set forth that there was a certain room called the Schoolhouse, and a certain chamber over the same, demised and letten by the said Richard Burbage to your said orator in and by the said Indenture of Lease, parcel of the premises, locked up by your said orator the twentieth day of January . . . [1604]; and the said Edward Kirkham, William Rastall and Thomas Kendall, from the said twentieth day of January until the first day of May then next ensuing, [were excluded], by which . . . [they], by and during that time, had not the use, occupation and profit of the same schoolhouse and chamber with your said orator and Alexander

528

Hawkins, according to the form, effect and intent of the condition of the said obligation.

§6 "Which said schoolhouse and chamber over the same were severed from the said great hall, and made fit by your said orator, at his own proper costs and charges, to dine and sup in, and there stood divers implements of household stuff, and therefore it was not fit and convenient that the doors of the same rooms should always be unlocked and left open; and yet nevertheless the said doors were always opened at the request or desire of the said Kirkham, Rastall and Kendall, and either of them, and they might have had the joint use and occupation thereof at their will and pleasure, and they received no loss or damage . . . by the shutting or locking of any door; for that if any such door were shut or locked, as is pretended, then the same was always opened, and offered to be opened, upon every request of the said Kirkham, Rastall and Kendall, and so no damage at all unto them or any of them; yet for that the same bond is forfeited, as he, the said Kirkham, pretendeth. They, the said Rastall and Kendall, being dead, he, the said Kirkham, for matter of vexation, hath put the said bond in suit at the common law against your said orator, and threateneth to take all advantages thereupon. . . .

§7 "In tender consideration whereof, may it therefore please your good Lordship . . . to grant . . . his Majesty's most gracious writ of subpoena, to be directed unto the said Edward Kirkham," etc.

KIRKHAM'S ANSWER
JULY 19, 1612

§8 The defendant acknowledges Richard Burbage's lease of "all that great hall or room, with the rooms over the same," to Evans. He says that he, Rastall and Kendall "did treat and had communication with the said complainant to such end and purpose as in the Bill is set forth," and that thereupon Evans and Hawkins became bound to them under the £200 bond.

§9 "And this defendant denieth that he, or any of the said other defendants to his knowledge, did upon the sealing of the said bond, or at any time before or since, make any promise that they would never seek or take any advantage upon the said bond, in respect of any small breach of the condition thereof, or in respect of the plainant's dwelling or inhabiting in part of the said premises, or that the said complainant did seal and deliver the said bond upon any such promise. . . .

§10 "And whereas the said complainant . . . pretendeth that he, . . . in or about one month next after the ensealing of the said obligation, did depart into the country and relinquished and left all the foresaid demised premises to this defendant and the said other defendants . . . only to their use and dispose, to their great benefit and profit and to the damage of the plainant at least of £300, to this the defendant saith that the same is not in any part thereof true; . . . for this defendant saith, although the said complainant departed for a time into the country, yet he left

529

the said Alexander Hawkins to deal for him and to take such benefit of the said house as should belong unto him in his absence, which the said Alexander Hawkins did accordingly, so as the said complainant lost nothing to the knowledge of the said defendant.

§11 "But of the other side, by reason of the said agreement made by the said defendant and the said Rastall and Kendall with the said complainant, they were enforced to disburse and lay out for divers employments[2] the sum of £300 at the least; after which the complainant unjustly turned the said defendants out of the said house, and would not suffer them to have benefit or use thereof; for which cause . . . the said complainant . . . was arrested at the suit of him, this defendant, by writ out of the King's Bench, upon several actions of £1,000 damage, and was thereupon enforced to find and put in bail, as there was just cause he should do.

§12 "And this defendant saith that the reason whereupon he arrested the said complainant grew not out of spleen or malice . . . but upon good and sufficient cause; for the said complainant, notwithstanding his former bargain and faithful promises . . . did turn the said defendant out of the said house and premises four years together come Michaelmas next, and would not suffer this defendant or the said other defendants to take any benefit thereby.

§13 "And this defendant likewise saith that true it is that upon the plainant's putting in of bail as aforesaid, he, this defendant, did declare upon the foresaid obligation or bond, obligatory whereunto the said complainant answered and came to issue with this defendant, ready for trial. And this defendant likewise saith that . . . he . . . did at several times give warning to the complainant to go to trial, and that several days were appointed for trial thereof; but . . . it was the said complainant's own doing that the said trial was so long delayed and so often put off, for . . . he . . . made means to cross the going on thereof, and procured an order to amend his plea and so to change the issue, for which he, the said complainant, paid costs to this defendant.

§14 "And further this defendant saith that, forasmuch as this defendant hath lost threescore pounds per annum for four years at the feast of St. Michael the Archangel next coming, and is like, if the plainant may prevail in his injurious courses, to lose the profit of the said house and premises for the term yet to come, being full ten years; and for that the said complainant hath made breach of the obligation so by him and the said Hawkins entered into to him, the said defendant, as aforesaid, true it is that the said defendant hath thereupon commenced several suits against the said complainant, as he hopeth under the favor of this honorable Court it is lawful for him to do.

§15 "And this defendant saith that true it is that the said schoolhouse and chamber over the same were severed from the said great hall, and made fit by the said complainant at his own proper costs and charges to dine and sup in, as in the said Bill of Complaint is alleged; whereupon the said complainant did wrongfully withhold and detain the same from the said defendants, being of right belonging unto them as part of the demised premises; wherefore they were enforced to commence suit at the common law for remedy thereof." The defendant denies that "the said doors belonging to the said house were always opened at the request" of the defendants, or that the defendants "received no loss or damage by the shutting of the said doors."

§16 The defendant disclaims any desire to hurt the plainant's estate "by vexing him with multiplicity of suits," and says that "if in any reasonable manner he be recompensed for the money by the complainant already detained for the time past, and permitted to have the joint use and occupation of the said house and premises for the time and term to come, being full ten years," he will take no benefit or advantage of the forfeiture of the bond. He closes by praying the Court to dismiss him with his reasonable costs and charges.

EVANS'S REPLICATION
(NOT DATED)

§17 The complainant reaffirms the truth of every statement made in his Bill of Complaint, "with this: that this complainant will aver that it was meant and intended that small occasions should not, of the complainant's behalf, make breach of the said obligation, and that the doors were always (as this complainant thinketh) ready to be unlocked and left open at the public request of the defendant and the rest of his said associates, upon notice given that they or any of them meant to make any joint use, occupation and profit thereof, according to the meaning of the condition of the said obligation." And the complainant further saith that the obligation was voided by the failure of the defendant and his associates to perform "sundry payments, performances and limitations" therein specified.

§18 "Yet nevertheless the said defendant, having proceeded to issue thereupon against the complainant, delayed to procure a trial, thereby to put the complainant to trouble and charge, as in the Bill is alleged; but after the preferring of the said Bill, the said suit commenced by the defendant upon the said obligation . . . came to trial before the Lord Chief Justice of England about the end of Easter Term last past, and upon hearing of the proofs produced of the now plainant's behalf, the said defendant did then become nonsuit upon the issue so joined, as by the record thereof remaining in his Majesty's Court, commonly called the King's Bench, may appear."

§19 The complainant says that "now there is no cause why the said defendant should detain the said obligation . . . unless it were infinitely to molest this complainant; . . . or if there be any cause, upon any small trifling occasion (which this complainant denieth), as upon locking a door of a room where no joint profits to any great value could be made, . . . it standeth with the justice of this Court that the same . . . should be heard and moderated by the equity of this honorable Court.

§20 "And the complainant further for Replication saith that he was, by the defendant and his said associates, upon false information made to the late Lord Hunsdon, late Lord Chamberlain, against this complainant, commanded by his Lordship to avoid and leave the same, for fear of whose displeasure the complainant was forced to leave the country, and lost, in want of not looking to his profit there and charge otherwise, near £300, which they did of purpose to prejudice this complainant; the said Hawkins negligently, under whose title soever he pretended to take any profits, using the same.

§21 "And whereas, contrariwise, it is alleged in the defendant's said Answer that by the said agreement the said defendant, Rastall, and Kendall were enforced to disburse and lay out for divers implements[3] the sum of £300 at the least, . . . thereunto the said complainant for Replication further saith that it is not material to this complainant what the said defendant disbursed or laid out for divers implements as is alleged, neither material to be replied unto, considering that it is not showed how they were enforced so to do, or by whom, or for whom, or to whose benefit the same loss and damage grew. And this complainant . . . saith that . . . neither the said defendant or the said Rastall or Kendall did ever (to this defendant's [read complainant's] knowledge) buy any implements other than necessary apparel, after the rates and portions for to be used in and about such plays as were to be made there.

§22 "But it is true that after the King's most excellent Majesty, upon some misdemeanors committed in or about the plays there, and specially upon the defendant's act and doings thereabout, had prohibited that no plays should be more used there, that upon such prohibition the defendant and his associates seemed to go back; for no plays being used, and little or no profit made of the house, but the complainant still chargeable to pay £40 per annum for the rent thereof (whereas, without plays used there, the same rooms were not worth almost any rent), and the agreement being conditional or upon limitation that the not paying of the rent, or not performing the limitations aforesaid, could but make void the said agreement between the complainant and the defendant: therefore, the defendant willing to quit the place, as it seemed to this complainant, the said defendant, at or about the 26th of July, 1608, caused the apparels, properties and goods belonging to the copartners, sharers and masters of the Queen's Majesty's Children of her Revels (for so it was often called) to be indifferently praised [= appraised], and upon such praisement the same was divided, and so praised and divided that the praisers were at his own mere appointment; and the said complainant had the one half thereof upon such praisement and division for his part and proportion, and the defendant and the said Rastall and Kendall had the other part for their parts and proportions, which they took and accepted and seemed fully satisfied, for anything this complainant perceived.

§23 "After which partition so made (some of the boys being before committed to prison by his Majesty's command for the considerations as aforesaid), for those and other considerations before specified, the defendant said he would deal no more with it, 'for,' quoth he, 'it is a base thing,' or used words to such or very like effect; whereupon, the defendant having not performed every of the limitations tied to the complainant's said agreement of his, the defendant's, part to be performed, and so this complainant knowing the said agreement, by the breach and not performance of the same of the defendant's part, to be void; and the defendant having delivered up their commission, which he had under the Great Seal, authorizing them to play, and discharged divers of the partners and poets, as this defendant [*read* complainant] hopeth to prove, this defendant [*read* complainant][4] dealt with his Majesty's players, and contracted with them for the same, as was lawful for him to do, who entered and enjoyed and yet do enjoy the same.

§24 "And shortly after, the defendant put the said obligation in suit against the complainant as aforesaid, thinking that way unjustly to get the forfeiture thereof of this complainant; in which suit, upon trial and full hearing after issue joined as aforesaid, he was nonsuit as aforesaid."

§25 The defendant denies that he thrust the defendant and his associates out of the house unjustly, "or unjustly suffered them not to have benefit thereof, . . . but upon good and lawful means warranted by law and equity."

1. Here Evans recites the Condition of the £200 Bond substantially as it is given in Document 36, but with appropriate changes of tense, etc.

2. This word is spelled "ymploiments" in Fleay's transcription of the document in its original spelling (*Chronicle History*, p. 217). In the corresponding passage at 42:21, the word is spelled "Implements" (*ibid.*, p. 221).

3. See footnote 2 above.

4. The corresponding passage in the case of Kirkham *vs.* Paunton (43:39) makes it clear that Evans, not Kirkham, dealt with Richard Burbage about the surrender of the lease. Cf. 41:5, 43:15, 43:22, 43:27, and 44:20.

Document 43

⟨ Kirkham vs. Paunton et al.

COURT OF CHANCERY, 1612

Chancery Proceedings, James I, Bills and Answers, K 5, No. 25; printed in its original spelling in Fleay, *Chronicle History*, pp. 223–51.

KIRKHAM'S BILL OF COMPLAINT
JULY 1, 1612

§1 Edward Kirkham, of the Strand, London, addresses his complaint to the right honorable Thomas Lord Ellesmere, Lord High Chancellor of England. He recounts Richard Burbage's ownership of the Blackfriars property and his rental of it to Henry Evans, and then continues:

"By virtue thereof the said Evans into the said premises entered, and was thereof so possessed accordingly; and he being thereof so possessed, in or about [1601] it was concluded, agreed, and consented upon, by and between your said orator and one William Rastall . . . and Thomas Kendall . . . on the one party, and the said Evans on the other part, that in consideration that your said orator, the said Rastall and Kendall would disburse about the premises the sum of £400 of lawful English money, that in consideration thereof the said Evans would sufficiently assign the moiety or one-half of the said lease of the premises and the profits thereof, for and during all the term then to come and unexpired, unto your said orator, Rastall and Kendall, and the survivor of them, and to the executors and assigns of the survivor of them.

§2 "According to which agreement, your said orator, the said Rastall and Kendall, did disburse the said sum of £400 about the premises; and the said Evans did, with the assent and good liking of your said orator, the said Rastall and Kendall, assign the moiety or one-half of the premises, with the appurtenances and the profits thereof, unto one Alexander Hawkins, son-in-law to the said Evans, upon trust and confidence that he, the said Hawkins, his executors or assigns, should at all time and times, at the request of your said orator and the said Rastall and Kendall, or either of them, should reassure the said lease and the profits thereof to your said orator, Rastall and Kendall, or the survivor of them. . . .

534

§3 "By virtue of such demise . . . to the said Hawkins, . . . and upon an agreement indented, made between the said Alexander Hawkins and Evans on the one part, and your said orator, the said Rastall and Kendall on the other part, manifesting the foresaid trust, your said orator, Rastall and Kendall received the profits thereof to their own uses; and for further consideration of the said agreement, the said Evans . . . was weekly to receive of your said orator, the said Rastall and Kendall, . . . the sum of 8 shillings weekly during the said term, the which sum was paid to the said Evans accordingly by your said orator, the said Rastall or Kendall, or one of them; and likewise for the consideration of £52 10s. paid to the said Evans by the said Hawkins.

§4 "And the said Hawkins being possessed of the said lease made unto him upon trust as aforesaid, . . . Mrs. Evans, wife of the said Henry Evans, finding the said lease in the custody of the said Hawkins, her son-in-law, did very unconscionably, and without the privity of the said Hawkins, deliver the said lease to the said Burbage, Henry Evans, and John Heminges of Cripplegate, London, or to one of them; and by that means [she and they] combined and confederated amongst themselves how to defeat your said orator . . . of the said premises and of the said lease; and under color and pretense thereof, [they] have, for the space of these four years last past, received the profits of the said premises, being worth eightscore pounds by the year, besides the rents reserved thereupon, and did and yet doth deny the delivery of the possession of the premises and the said lease of the moiety to your said orator, . . . being now survivor, which is contrary to equity and conscience. . . .

§5 "The said Alexander Hawkins about two years last past died intestate; and Anne Hawkins, now wife to the said Edward Paunton, took letters of administration of the goods and chattels of the said Alexander her husband, and afterwards the said Anne Hawkins did intermarry and take to husband the said Edward Paunton, gentleman, who in the right of the said Anne his wife hath the interest of the moiety of the said premises, to the use aforesaid. And the said Rastall and Kendall died about four years last past, after whose decease the profits of which premises during the said term, to the value aforesaid, ought to come to your said orator as survivor."

§6 The complainant contends that, since Alexander Hawkins "died before the lease was reassured according to the said trust, by his death the interest thereof remaineth in the hands of the said Paunton and Anne his wife, as in the right of the said Anne, which ought to be reassured according to the trust aforesaid to your said orator as survivor; and that your said orator hath no remedy to recover the said lease, which remaineth in the custody of the said Evans, Burbage and Heminges, or one of them, ten years of which lease remaining in being and unexpired; nor knoweth not wherein the same is contained, whether in bag, box, or chest, locked or unlocked. . . .

§7 "May it therefore please your good Lordship . . . to grant to your said orator his Majesty's most gracious writ of subpoena, to be directed to the said Henry Evans, Edward Paunton and Anne his wife, Richard Burbage and John Heminges," etc.

PLEA OF RICHARD BURBAGE AND JOHN HEMINGES
JULY 8, 1612

§8 These defendants say that "the great hall in the Bill mentioned is, and at the time of the making of the lease . . . was, and ever since hath been, a common playhouse for the acting and playing of interludes and stage plays; and that the several agreements, leases and assignments in the Bill mentioned, if any such were, were made for and concerning the said playhouse, and the ordering, disposing, sharing and dividing of the said playhouse and the benefit and profit thereof, and of the plays and interludes therein to be had, coming and arising; and that the money in the Bill mentioned to be disbursed by the said complainant and Rastall and Kendall, if the same were disbursed, was by them disbursed for or about the setting forward of interludes and plays to be acted in the said playhouse.

§9 "And further say that if the said hall were converted from a playhouse to any other ordinary use, it would be of very little value, and nothing near worth the rent reserved by the said lease; and further say that the profits in the Bill mentioned, which the said complainant doth complain to have been received by these defendants, and seeketh to be relieved for the same in this honorable Court, were the profits coming by, or by means of, the said stage plays.

§10 "And these defendants further say that they never contracted or bargained, nor have had any dealing or intermeddling, with the said complainant or the said Rastall and Kendall, touching anything in the Bill mentioned.

§11 "And therefore these defendants do demand judgment . . . whether these defendants shall be compelled to make any other answer to the said Bill, and pray to be dismissed with their reasonable costs and charges," etc.

PLEA OF HENRY EVANS
JULY 10, 1612

§12 This Plea is identical with the Plea of Burbage and Heminges, except for its use of the singular "defendant" instead of the plural "defendants," and except for its omission of the paragraph numbered 10 above.

EDWARD PAUNTON'S ANSWER
JULY 22, 1612

§13 "This defendant . . . saith that true it is he lately married one Margaret Hawkins, widow of Alexander Hawkins, mentioned, as this defendant supposeth, in the said Bill of Complaint, which Margaret took letters of administration of the goods and chattels of the said Alexander; and thinketh, as in the right of the said Margaret his wife, that the interest of the said lease and of the residue of the years to come in the said great hall . . . is wholly and absolute in this defendant, and denieth the moiety only thereof was assigned to the said Hawkins by the said Henry Evans . . . upon trust, . . . to this defendant's knowledge, or that the said Hawkins, at the request of the plaintiff, Rastall and Kendall, . . . should or ought to reassure the said lease to the plaintiff, Rastall and Kendall, or the survivor of them. . . ."

§14 The defendant refers to Burbage's lease of the said great hall to Evans, and says that he verily believes that Hawkins and Evans became bound to Burbage in a bond of £400 for payment of the rent of £40 yearly during the said lease. He says further that on or about October 21, 1601, "the said Henry Evans, by good and sufficient conveyance in the law, and for good and valuable considerations therein expressed, did bona fide bargain, sell, give, grant or convey the said Indenture of Lease, and all his estate and interest therein, . . . unto the said Alexander Hawkins, his executors, administrators or assigns, absolutely; . . . of which said lease . . . the said Alexander Hawkins, as this defendant thinketh, was lawfully possessed, and so died possessed . . . of a just and true interest of, in and to the said great hall and other the premises. . . . And this defendant further saith that after the decease of the said Alexander, the interest and right of the said Alexander of, in and unto the premises, were invested as abovesaid in the said Margaret. . . .

§15 "And this defendant further saith that, . . . as he hath heard, the said Henry Evans, having gotten possession of the said Indenture of Lease, . . . did upon some private agreements between him and the said Richard Burbage, . . . after he had conveyed the same to the said Alexander, surrender the said Indenture of Lease without the privity or consent either of the said Alexander in his lifetime, in whom the estate then was, or of this defendant or his wife, since the death of the said Alexander, in whom, or one of them, . . . the estate and right of, in and unto the premises only is or ought to remain.

§16 "And this defendant further saith that the said complainant showed this defendant a copy of certain Articles of Agreement, bearing date on or about the 20th day of April, Anno Domini 1602, made between the said Alexander Hawkins and Henry Evans of the one part, and the said plaintiff and others whose names he now remembereth not, on the other part, whereby . . . the said Evans confesseth the interest and possession of the said lease to be in the said Alexander Hawkins absolutely and bona fide. . . .

§17 "But this defendant saith that he hath heard that about such trash as appertained to plays, interludes and players, the said plaintiff disbursed much money, but to what sum or upon what consideration this defendant knoweth not; neither doth this defendant think that this honorable Court will enjoin this defendant (if the said plainant were damnified in such business) to give the plaintiff any satisfaction; for he is a mere stranger to the same, neither ever had or hath any inter-meddling or profit by the same, or is like to have, otherwise than by the said lease in right of his said wife, . . . to whom in law and equity the same belongeth. . . ."

§18 The defendant says that Burbage did not, to his knowledge, demise the said hall "only to the said Henry Evans"; nor was there, to his knowledge, any agreement for the assigning of a moiety of the lease to Kirkham and his associates; nor did Evans, to his knowledge, assign only the moiety of the lease to Hawkins upon trust that he would reassign it upon request.

ANSWERS OF JOHN HEMINGES AND RICHARD BURBAGE
NOVEMBER 2, 1612

§19 Having been ordered by the Master of the Rolls to make answer to Kirkham's Bill of Complaint, these defendants jointly and severally say, and first Richard Burbage for himself saith:

That it is true that he was and is lawfully seized in his demesne as of fee, of and in a playhouse in the Blackfriars, London, and that he did, "in or about the four-and-fortieth year of the reign of the late Queen Elizabeth" [an error; should be the two-and-fortieth year, 1600], demise and to farm let it unto Henry Evans, "who intended then presently to erect or set up a company of boys . . . in the same; . . . and this defendant further answereth and saith that true it is that this defendant, considering with himself that, except the said Evans could erect and keep a company of playing boys or others, to play plays and interludes in the said playhouse in such sort as beforetime had been there used, that he was likely to be beh[ind with] the said rent of £40, for that the said house was not otherwise worth so much rent as thereupon was reserved, therefore he, this defendant Richard Burbage, did thereupon, before the said lease [was] finished and made up, require of the said Henry Evans some collateral security for the true and due payment from time to time of the said rent of £40; whereupon he, the said Henry Evans, together with one Alexander Hawkins, his son-in-law, became bound unto this defendant in a bond of £400, with condition for the payment of the said rent of £40 and for performance of other the covenants and agreements in the said lease contained.

§20 "And this defendant . . . verily thinketh that . . . after the making of the said lease unto the said Evans, he, the said Evans, did treat and deal with the complainant Kirkham and with one William Rastall and Thomas Kendall . . . about the setting and making up a company of boys and others to play plays and interludes in the said playhouse, which . . . they . . . accordingly did; and, as this defendant thinketh, the said complainant and the said other persons, in playing apparel and other implements and properties touching and concerning the furnishing and setting forth of players and plays, did disburse and dispend divers sums of money, and were, as this defendant hath heard, thereupon to be partners or sharers of such moneys, profits and commodities as should arise or be made by reason of the said plays.

§21 "Howbeit, this defendant saith that afterwards—that is to say, about the first year of his Majesty's reign [1603–1604]—there having been between that time and the time of the making of the said lease great visitation of sickness in the cities of London and Westminster and the suburbs thereabouts, and by reason thereof no such profit and commodity raised and made of and by the said playhouse as was hoped for and expected, the said Evans, as it seemed, grew weary and out of liking with the interest and term of years which he had in the said playhouse, and thereupon some speech and treaty was had with this defendant about the surrendering and giving up of the said lease, and the rather upon the importunity and earnest entreaty of the said Alexander Hawkins unto the said Henry Evans, his father-in-law, to the intent that he might be freed and discharged of the said bond of £400, wherein he was and stood bound for the payment of the said rent of £40;

§22 "Which matters continuing still for a good space of time in speech and communication, at last—that is to say, about August in the sixth year of his Majesty's reign [1608]—it was fully and absolutely concluded and agreed between the said Henry Evans and this defendant, upon labor and much importunity of the said Evans and other his special friends, that this defendant should take back again into his hands the interest and term of years before granted, and that he, this defendant, should have the same to his own use, and that in consideration thereof . . . Henry Evans should be discharged of the said rent of £40, and the said Alexander Hawkins of his bond of £400 conditioned for the payment of the said rent. . . .

§23 "Whereupon the same was done accordingly; that is to say, the said lease for one-and-twenty years was surrendered and given up, and the indenture or deed thereof given back again unto this defendant to be cancelled or otherwise done with, all at the pleasure of this defendant; and the said bond or obligation of £400 . . . was either cancelled by this defendant in the presence of the said Evans and Hawkins, or else delivered to the one of them to be defaced and cancelled at their pleasures. And so the interest of the said Henry Evans in the said playhouse, by virtue of the said lease, was fully and wholly determined; and this defendant further saith that since the time of the said last agreement, made and executed as aforesaid, he . . . did never either demand or receive the said rent of £40, nor any part or parcel thereof, of the said Henry Evans or any other person or persons for him or on his behalf.

§24 "And the said John Heminges . . . answereth and saith that he verily believeth that the Answer of the said other defendant, Richard Burbage, is in all and every matter and thing material therein contained, very just and true. . . ."

§25 Both the defendants doubt the existence of an agreement under which Evans undertook to assign the moiety or one-half of the foresaid lease of the premises to Kirkham, Rastall, and Kendall in return for their spending £400 about the premises, and they further doubt that, "according to the said pretended agreement, the said complainant, Rastall and Kendall did disburse the said sum of £400 about the said premises in manner and form as in the said Bill of Complaint is alleged; but these defendants jointly and severally say that they think that if the said complainant and the said other persons disbursed any sum or sums of money touching or concerning the said playhouse, the same was by them disbursed and laid out in playing apparel and other implements and properties touching and concerning the furnishing and setting forth of players and plays, for which they were to have their ratable and proportionable parts and shares of the profits thereby arising, and not for or in consideration of the assignment of the moiety of the said lease of the foresaid playhouse; . . . and these defendants jointly and severally deny that the said Evans did (to these defendants' knowledge) assign the moiety or one-half of the said premises, with the appurtenances, to Alexander Hawkins, . . . upon trust and confidence that he . . . should at all times upon request reassure the said lease and the profits thereof to the said complainant, Rastall and Kendall, or the survivor of them; . . . and these defendants do further traverse and . . . [deny] . . . that by virtue of the said pretended demise to Hawkins, or upon any agreement manifesting the foresaid pretended trust, the said complainant, Rastall, and Kendall received the profits thereof to their own uses, or that for further consideration of the said agreement, the said Evans or his assigns was weekly to receive of the said complainant, Rastall, and Kendall, or the survivor of them, during the said term, the sum of 8 shillings, or that the same was paid accordingly. . . .

§26 "But these defendants think it to be true that upon some such agreement as before, in the Answer of the said Richard Burbage . . . is set down and declared, the said complainant, Rastall, Kendall and the said Evans were to be partners or sharers of such moneys, profits and commodities as should arise by reason of plays or interludes made or played within the said playhouse; and so the said complainant and the forenamed persons might peradventure perceive and take some of the said profits and commodities which were gotten by the said plays or interludes within the said playhouse, but not by virtue of any assignment of the moiety of the said lease, pretended to be made as aforesaid. And these defendants further traverse and . . . [deny] . . . that Mrs. Evans, wife of the said Henry Evans, did find the said pretended lease in the custody of the said Hawkins, or did deliver the said lease to these defendants or either of them, or any other, to their knowledge, . . . or that they thereupon did combine and confederate together with the other defendant, Henry Evans . . . to defeat the said complainant, Rastall and Kendall, of the said premises and of the said lease; or that under color and pretense thereof, and of having the said pretended lease, these defendants and the said Evans have for the space of these four years last past received the profits of the said premises; or that the same are worth eightscore pounds per annum, besides the rents reserved thereupon, as in the said Bill of Complaint is alleged.

§27 "But this defendant, Richard Burbage, for himself further answereth and saith that he . . . hath, ever since the said Evans surrendered and gave up his lease, . . . perceived and taken rent for the foresaid playhouse, and some part of such profits as did arise and accrue by such plays and interludes as were there played; . . . and the said John Heminges for himself further answereth and saith that he . . . hath for the space of four years past, or thereabouts, had and received, and as yet doth receive, a certain share or portion of such profits as did or doth arise by the said playhouse and by such plays and interludes as were and are played in the said playhouse, by virtue of a demise of some part of the said playhouse, granted unto him by the said other defendant, Richard Burbage, since the surrender of the foresaid lease. . . .

§28 "And these defendants further traverse and . . . [deny] . . . that Edward Paunton, . . . in the right of Anne his wife, late wife of the foresaid Alexander Hawkins, hath the interest of the moiety of the said premises to the use aforesaid, or that the profits of the said premises, after the death of the said Rastall and Kendall, ought to come to the said complainant as survivor; . . . and [they deny] that it is material unto these defendants (the premises before alleged considered) whether the said Alexander Hawkins died before the said lease was reassured according to the pretended trust aforesaid. . . ."

ANSWER OF HENRY EVANS
NOVEMBER 5, 1612

§29 The defendant recites the terms of Richard Burbage's lease to him of "all that great hall or room, with the rooms over the same, situate within the precinct of the Blackfriars in London, then or late in the tenure or occupation of this defendant, for the term and space of one-and-twenty years, . . . by virtue whereof this defendant was truly and lawfully possessed of the demised premises for the term aforesaid.

§30 "And this defendant saith that afterward the complainant and one William Rastall and Kendall . . . entered into communication with this defendant, touching a joint benefit and profit to be made of plays and interludes to be used in or upon the premises; . . . upon which communication they . . . caused an obligation of the sum of £200 or thereabouts to be writ and engrossed and ready to be sealed by the defendant and one Alexander Hawkins, with condition subscribed, underwritten or endorsed, to this or like effect following:[1] . . . which obligation this defendant, together with the said Alexander Hawkins, sealed and delivered as their deed unto the complainant and the said Rastall and Kendall.

§31 "And the defendant further saith there were Articles of Agreement effected between this defendant and the said Alexander Hawkins on the one part, and the said complainant, Rastall and Kendall on the other part, touching such gain, profit and commodity as should be made of the said premises; as by the said Articles of Agreement being long and tedious, and therefore this defendant thought not meet to insert them at large in this Answer, which this defendant nevertheless is ready to show to this honorable Court, and whereunto this defendant referreth himself, may more fully and at large appear.

§32 "Upon which Obligation and Articles of Agreement the complainant is at liberty to seek his remedy by the course of the common laws of this realm, and not to seek relief in this honorable Court for the same, considering that this defendant hath a bill pending in this honorable Court against the complainant, showing causes why in equity and conscience the said Obligation ought to be redelivered to be cancelled, whereunto the complainant hath made his Answer, and this defendant this Term hath replied thereunto.

§33 "And this defendant . . . for further answer thereunto saith that the complainant, for righting of himself (as he supposeth) against this defendant, did in Michaelmas Term in the ninth year of the King's Majesty's reign [1611][2] commence suit upon the said obligation of £200 against this defendant, supposing the said obligation had been absolutely forfeited, meaning to take the extremest advantage thereof, whereunto this defendant pleaded the forenamed condition of the said obligation; and upon pleading between the said parties the same proceeded to issue, and trial was had thereupon in Easter Term last past before the Lord Chief Justice of England in the Guildhall, London; and upon hearing of the proofs produced of this now defendant's behalf, the said complainant did then become nonsuit upon the said issue so joined, as by the record thereof, remaining in his Majesty's Court commonly called the King's Bench, may appear."

§34 The defendant denies the existence of any agreement to the effect that if Kirkham, Rastall and Kendall "would disburse about the premises the sum of £400 of lawful English money, that in consideration thereof this defendant would sufficiently assign the moiety or one-half of the said lease of the premises, and the profits thereof, for and during all the term then to come and unexpired, unto the said complainant, Rastall and Kendall, and the survivor of them, as by the said Bill of Complaint is most falsely and untruly alleged; and this defendant doth deny that he, with the consent and liking of the complainant and the said Rastall and Kendall, did assign the moiety or half in deal of the premises to the said Alexander Hawkins upon intent or purpose that he should at all times, at request of the said complainant and the said Rastall and Kendall, or either of them, reassure the said lease and the profits thereof to [them], as in the said Bill of Complaint is also most falsely and untruly alleged."

§35 The defendant confesses that there were Articles of Agreement indented, between himself and Hawkins on the one party, and Kirkham, Rastall and Kendall on the other party; but he denies that the Articles touched upon any assignment to be made by Hawkins to Kirkham and his associates. "And this defendant further saith that the agreements and condition of the said obligation . . . being not performed on the complainant's part, and so making as well the Agreement as the said Obligation void, this defendant . . . was free and at liberty, after such breach or not performance, [not][3] to perform any agreement at all made in or by the said Articles of Agreement or specified in the Condition of the said Obligation, as he verily thinketh in his conscience, and as he is informed by his learned counsel, and as he now taketh it more fully by the said verdict already given against the said complainant.

§36 "And touching the 8 shillings weekly to be paid, and the sum also of £52 10s. mentioned in the said Bill, alleged, as this defendant taketh it, to be a consideration why the said lease should be assigned by the said Hawkins, thereunto this defendant saith that there was a bond of £50, made by the said complainant and his said partner[s], conditioned for payment of the said sum of 8 shillings weekly unto this defendant, because after the said agreements [were] made, the complainant and his said partners would at their directions have the dieting and ordering of the boys used about the plays there, which before the said complainant[4] had, and for the which he had weekly before that disbursed and allowed great sums of money, which Obligation was forfeited; and the Obligation being put in suit and ready for trial, and the arrearages being great, the said complainant and the said Kendall did by agreement take up the Obligation so made to this defendant, and they did enter into a new bond unto the said Alexander Hawkins, and he gave them thereupon a further day for the payment of £54, as this defendant thinketh, and thereupon and upon that ground the said Alexander Hawkins, by this defendant's agreement, did satisfy unto this defendant the sum of £48 10s., and not £52 10s. as in the Bill is alleged."

§37 The defendant denies that his wife found the lease in the custody of Hawkins and unconscionably delivered it to Richard Burbage or himself or John Heminges; but he confesses that, long time before any communication was had between himself and Hawkins on the one party, and Kirkham and his colleagues on the other, he, Evans, "did upon mere trust and confidence, and of intent and purpose to save harmless the said Alexander Hawkins of and from one bond of £400 which the said Alexander Hawkins entered into unto the said Richard Burbage as surety for this defendant for the said rent of £40 by the year, . . . grant and convey unto him, the said Alexander Hawkins, who married this defendant's daughter, all his goods, chattels and leases, implements, household stuff, wares, commodities, and all his goods; notwithstanding which grant, this defendant kept the said original lease made by the said Richard Burbage, and hath ever since enjoyed and continued the possession . . . of . . . the same house and rooms so leased . . . until about April last was four years; and thereupon the said Articles of Agreement, which bear date the 20th day of April, 1602, . . . were by this defendant's special appointment caused to be made, . . . because this defendant was desirous to deal honestly and squarely with the complainant. . . .

§38 "And this defendant saith that . . . the complainant and this defendant, by his Majesty's special commandment being prohibited to use any plays there, and some of the boys being committed to prison by order from his Highness, and so no profit made of the said house, but a continual rent of £40 to be paid for the same, that the same made the complainant willing voluntarily to forgo the same house, as this defendant conceived; for the defendant saith that the yearly payment of the moiety of the said rent was yearly to be paid by the complainant, and he was also tied by the Articles of Agreement to perform many other matters of charge; and . . . thereupon the complainant, as it seemed to this defendant, was willing to free himself from the same; and in pursuing his said purpose, first caused the apparels, properties and goods belonging to the copartners and masters of the Queen's Majesty's Children of the Revels (for so it was often called) to be indifferently [ap]praised, and upon such praisement the same to be divided; and this defendant had the one-half thereof, upon such praisement and division, for his part and proportion, and the complainant and his sharers (as he termed them) had the other part for their parts and proportions, . . . the complainant being then present, who seemed fully satisfied, for anything this defendant perceived.

§39 "Upon all which matters, the said complainant, withdrawing himself from dealing in the premises, returned this answer, that he would deal no more with it, for it was a base thing, or used words to such or very like effect; and the said copartnership quite dissolved, as by the said Articles will appear, the commission which he had under the Great Seal, authorizing them to play, being in his possession, was delivered up by the complainant or by his appointment, and divers of the partners and poets being by him, the said complainant, discharged and set at liberty, as the defendant hopeth plainly to prove to this most honorable Court; after which time this defendant's wife, and by the privity of the said Alexander Hawkins, dealt with the said Richard Burbage, . . . and upon agreement between them, by this defendant's consent, delivered up the said original Indenture of Lease; and upon such delivery . . . he, the said Richard Burbage, delivered up the said Obligation of £400 to be cancelled, which this defendant's wife . . . delivered unto the said Hawkins. . . ."

§40 The defendant denies that there was any confederacy between any of the defendants to defeat the complainant of any due or just right, or that the defendants have for four years last past received the profits of the premises, "or that the same so demanded by the complainant are of the yearly value of £160 over and above the rent of £40." He further denies that any interest in the premises remained in Hawkins at the time of his death or passed to his widow as executrix.

REPLICATION OF EDWARD KIRKHAM

§41 The repliant says that the several Answers of the defendants are very uncertain in all the material points therein, and that all the allegations contained in his own Bill of Complaint are most certain, true and just. "Never-

theless, for further Replication, this repliant saith that whereas the said Evans
. . . in his Answer saith that the said sum of £400 was not bestowed in such
sort as in the said Bill is mentioned, nor for the consideration therein expressed,
this repliant saith that, for the consideration in the said Bill mentioned, the
moiety of the said lease was assured to Alexander Hawkins, deceased, to the
use of this complainant and of Rastall and Kendall, his partners, and the other
moiety to the use of the said Hawkins; and this repliant hath obtained the interest of the executors of the said Rastall and Kendall, and so the whole moiety
of the said lease, and the profits thereof, . . . remaineth in this repliant.

§42 "And further this repliant saith that he and his partners have disbursed
the sum of £200, over and above the said sum of £400, for and towards the
apparel of the players and other necessaries for their provision; and without the
disbursement of the said several sums, the said Evans, Heminges, and Burbage
were not able to make any benefit or profit of the said great hall in such sort
as hath been and was made thereof; for this repliant saith, and the same will
aver and prove to this honorable Court, that during such time as the said defendants, Heminges and Burbage and their company, continued plays and interludes in the said great hall in the Friars, that they got, and as yet doth, more
in one winter in the said great hall, by a thousand pounds, than they were used
to get in the Bankside.

§43 "And this repliant doth much marvel that the said Evans doth by his
Answer challenge any interest in the said great hall, or of any other assurance
concerning the said house or plays, when that the said Evans, in or about the
three-and-fortieth year of the reign of the late Queen Elizabeth [1600], was
censured by the right honorable Court of Star Chamber for his unorderly carriage and behavior in taking up gentlemen's children against their wills, and to
employ them for players, and for other misdemeanors in the said decree contained; and further that all assurances made to the said Evans concerning the
said house or plays or interludes should be utterly void, and to be delivered up
to be canceled, as by the said Decree more at large it doth and may appear.

§44 "And this repliant further saith that whereas the said Paunton doth by his
said Answer challenge the whole interest in the said lease, by a demise from Evans
. . . to . . . Hawkins, whose relict the said Paunton married, and so in the
right of his said wife claimeth the whole interest in the said term, for answer
thereunto this repliant saith that . . . the said whole interest was assigned to
the said Alexander Hawkins, the moiety of which lease was . . . to be by him,
his executors and assigns, reassured over to this complainant and his said partners. . . .

§45 "And this repliant further saith that the said Burbage . . . did divers and
several times confess to this repliant and others that Mrs. Evans . . . did deliver
the said lease to him, . . . the said Burbage, and that after the obtaining of the
said lease, then the said Evans, Heminges and Burbage practiced amongst them-

selves how to dispossess this said repliant and his said partners of their interest in the moiety of the said great hall and of the profits thereof; and ever since, for the space of this four years and above, they have kept the possession thereof from this repliant without giving him any satisfaction, when that this repliant and his said partners have had and received the sum of £100 per annum for their part and moiety in the premises, without any manner of charges whatsoever; and after that this repliant and his said partners had received the foresaid profits, the said Children, which the said Evans in his Answer affirmeth to be the Queen's Children, were masters themselves, and this complainant and his said partners received of them, and of one Keysar, who was interest [sic] with them, above the sum of £150 per annum, only for the use of the said great hall, without all manner of charges. . . ."

THE COURT'S DECREE
NOVEMBER 14, 1612

§46 "Forasmuch as this Court was this day informed by Mr. Christopher Brooke, being of the defendants' counsel, that the plaintiff hath exhibited a bill into the Court to be relieved touching the moiety of a playhouse in the Blackfriars, which was heretofore, upon agreement between the defendant Evans and the plaintiff and one Rastall and Kendall, agreed to be conveyed unto them by the said Evans, but yet nevertheless the said conveyance was never perfected and sealed; and that since the said agreement the defendant Evans hath surrendered the lease of the whole playhouse unto the defendant Burbage, of whom he had formerly purchased the same; and that the said plaintiff, nor the said Evans, under whom he claimeth, had ever paid any rent unto the said Burbage since the said surrender; wherefore, and for that the matter between the said plaintiff and defendants is principally concerning charges and expenses disbursed in erecting a company of players and for playing apparel and other things touching plays, and the profits and commodities arising and growing by the same, as by the Articles to that purpose doth appear: it is therefore ordered by this Court that the matter of the plaintiff's Bill be clearly and absolutely dismissed out of this Court."

1. Here follows a transcript of the Condition of the £200 Bond, including the terms of Burbage's lease to Evans. The section dealing with the lease is printed on p. 176 above. The rest of the Condition is printed as Document 36.

2. As stated on p. 518 above, this suit would appear to be the case of Rastall and Kirkham *vs.* Hawkins (Document 40). If so, the scribe has made the understandable error of giving its date as the ninth year of the King's reign, instead of the ninth year of the century.

3. This word is lacking in the original, but the logic of the paragraph seems to demand it.

4. See pp. 186–87 above.

Document 44

⟨The Blackfriars Passage in
Piers the Plowman's Creed

CIRCA 1394

The text printed in the upper half of each page is that edited by the Rev. Walter W. Skeat and published by the Early English Text Society in 1867, but with the letters *th* substituted for the character þ, and with the letters *gh* substituted for the character ӡ. The text printed in the lower half of the page is a translation of the corresponding lines. It leans heavily upon Sir Alfred W. Clapham's translation as printed in "The Friars as Builders," but embodies several revisions made by the present author with the help of valuable suggestions from Professor J. B. Bessinger.

Thanne thought y to frayne the first · of this foure ordirs,	*153*
And presede to the prechoures · to proven here wille.	
[Ich] highede to her house · to herken of more;	*155*
And whan y cam to that court · y gaped aboute.	
Swich a bild bold, y-buld · opon erthe heighte	
Say i nought in certaine · siththe a longe tyme.	
Y ghemede upon that house · & gherne theron loked	
Whough the pileres weren y-peynt · and pulched ful clene,	*160*
And queynteli i-corven · with curiouse knottes,	

Then thought I to question the first of these four orders,	*153*
And pressed to the Preachers to make proof of their will.	
I hied to their house to hear more about them,	*155*
And when I came to that court I gazed all about.	
Such a boldly built building raised upon the earth	
Saw I never, in certainty, since a long time.	
I gazed on that house and eagerly looked	
How the pillars were painted and polished full bright,	*160*
And quaintly were carven with curious knots,	

547

With wyndowes well y-wrought · wide up o-lofte.
And thanne y entrid in · and even-forth went,
And all was walled that wone · though it wid were,
With posternes in pryvytie · to pasen when hem liste;   *165*
Orcheghardes and erberes · evesed well clene,
And a curious cros · craftly entayled,
With tabernacles y-tight · to toten all abouten.
The pris of a plough-lond · of penyes so rounde
To aparaile that pyler · were pure lytel.   *170*
Thanne y munte me forth · the mynstre to knowen,
And a-waytede a woon · wonderlie well y-beld,
With arches on everiche half · & belliche y-corven,
With crochetes on corners · with knottes of golde,
Wyde wyndowes y-wrought · y-written full thikke,   *175*
Schynen with schapen scheldes · to schewen aboute,
With merkes of marchauntes · y-medled bytwene,
Mo than twenty and two · twyes y-noumbred.
Ther is none heraud that hath · half swich a rolle,
Right as a rageman · hath rekned hem newe.   *180*
Tombes opon tabernacles · tyld opon lofte,

With windows well wrought, lofty and wide.
Then entered I in and forward I went,
And all walled was that dwelling place, though it were wide,
With posterns in private to pass when they list,   *165*
Orchards and arbors neatly arranged,
And a curious cross, craftily built,
With tabernacles encircled, facing all sides.
The price of a plowland in pennies so round
To embellish that pillar were little indeed.   *170*
Then hurried I forth to study the minster,
And found it an edifice wondrously built,
With arches on every side, cleverly carven,
With crockets on corners, with knots of gold,
Wide windows wrought with numberless writings,   *175*
With shapely shields shining to show all about,
With emblems of merchants mixed in between them,
More than twenty-and-two, twice numbered o'er.
There is no herald that hath half such a roll,
Such as a ragman hath reckoned anew.   *180*
Tombs upon tabernacles raised up aloft,

Housed in hirnes · harde set abouten,
Of armede alabaustre · clad for the nones,
[Made upon marbel · in many maner wyse,
Knyghtes in her conisantes · clad for the nones,] 185
All it semed seyntes · y-sacred opon erthe;
And lovely ladies y-wrought · leyen by her sydes
In many gay garmentes · that weren gold-beten.
Though the tax of ten gher · were trewly y-gadered,
Nolde it nought maken that house · half, as y trowe. 190
Thanne kam I to that cloister · & gaped abouten
Whough it was pilered and peynt · & portred well clene,
All y-hyled with leed · lowe to the stones,
And y-paved with peynt til · iche poynte after other;
With kundites of clene tyn · closed all aboute, 195
With lavoures of latun · lovelyche y-greithed.
I trowe the gaynage of the ground · in a gret schire
Nolde aparaile that place · oo poynt til other ende.
Thanne was the chaptire-hous wrought · as a greet chirche,
Corven and covered · and queyntliche entayled; 200
With semlich selure · y-set on lofte;

Placed in corners, set closely about,
In armor of alabaster presently clad,
Made out of marble in different ways
Were knights in their cognizances clad for the nonce, 185
All, it seemed, saints enshrined upon earth;
And lovely carved ladies to lie by their sides,
In many gay garments that were beaten gold.
Though the tax for ten years were honestly gathered,
'Twould not make half that house, as I truly believe. 190
Then came I to that cloister and gazed all about,
How it was pillared and painted and cunningly carved,
With roofing of lead low to the stones,
With painted tiles paved, one after another;
With conduits of clean tin, closed all about, 195
With lavers of latten lovingly wrought.
The yield of the ground in a great shire, I trow,
Would not even begin to furnish that place.
Then was the chapter house wrought like a great church,
Carven and covered and quaintly contrived, 200
With a beauteous ceiling set up aloft,

As a Parlement-hous · y-peynted aboute.
Thanne ferd y into fraytour · and fond there an other,
An halle for an heygh kinge · an housholde to holden,
With brode bordes aboute · y-benched wel clene,   *205*
With windowes of glas · wrought as a Chirche.
Thanne walkede y ferrer · & went all abouten,
And seigh halles full hyghe · & houses full noble,
Chambers with chymneyes · & Chapells gaie;
And kychens for an hyghe kinge · in castells to holden,   *210*
And her dortour y-dighte · with dores ful stronge;
Fermery and fraitur · with fele mo houses,
And all strong ston wall · sterne opon heighte,
With gaie garites & grete · & iche hole y-glased;
[And othere] houses y-nowe · to herberwe the queene.   *215*

Like a Parliament House all painted about.
Then I fared to the frater, and found there again
A hall for an high king his household to harbor,
With broad tables about, and benches to boot,   *205*
With windows of glass wrought like a church.
Then walked I further, and went all about,
And saw halls full high and houses full noble,
Chambers with chimneys, and chapels gay,
And kitchens for an high king in castles to have,   *210*
And the dorter provided with doors full strong.
Firmary and frater, with many more houses,
All walled with strong stone standing on high,
With gay garrets and great, and each opening glazed,
And other houses enough to shelter the queen.   *215*

Document 45

¶ Excerpt from the Diary of the
Duke of Stettin-Pomerania

SEPTEMBER 18, 1602

Frederic Gershow, former tutor to the young Duke Philip Julius, kept a careful diary of the Duke's travels in Germany, England, and Italy in 1602. The German text of the following excerpt was first printed in the *Transactions of the Royal Historical Society*, New Series, Vol. VI (1892), pp. 26 and 28, and was reprinted by Wallace in *Children of the Chapel*, pp. 106–107, and by Chambers in *Elizabethan Stage*, Vol. II, pp. 46–47. Translations are printed in *Transactions*, pp. 27 and 29, and in *Children of the Chapel*, p. 106 n.

§1 From there [i.e., from the Art Museum] we went to the Children's comedy, which in its argument treated of a chaste widow, and was the story of a royal widow of England.

§2 The origin of this Children's theatre is this: the Queen keeps a number of young boys who have to apply themselves zealously to the art of singing, and to learn to play on various musical instruments, and at the same time to pursue their studies. These boys have special preceptors in all the different arts, and in particular very good instructors in music.

§3 And in order that they may acquire courtly manners, it is required of them that they act a play once a week, for which purpose the Queen has built them a special theatre, and has provided them with an abundance of costly garments. Whoever wishes to see one of their performances must give as much as eight shillings of our [Stralsund] coinage;[1] and yet there are always a good many people present, and even many respectable women, because instructive plots, and many excellent lessons, as others told us, are presented there.

§4 They act all their plays by [artificial] light, which produces a great effect. For a whole hour before the play begins, one listens to a delightful instrumental concert played on organs, lutes, pandorins, mandolins, violins, and flutes, as on the present occasion, when a boy *cum voce tremula* sang so charmingly to [the accompaniment of] a bass-viol that we have not heard the like of it in the whole of our journey, unless perhaps the nuns at Milan may have excelled him.

1. One Stralsund, or Pomeranian shilling, was worth about 1½ pence of English money.

Document 46

ℂ The Sharers' Papers

1635

Lord Chamberlain's book 5/133, a book of Miscellaneous Assignments, Petitions and Warrants; printed in type facsimile in *Malone Society Collections*, Vol. II, pp. 362–73. These papers were discovered by J. O. Halliwell-Phillipps, and printed by him (but in a less accurate transcript) in his *Outlines of the Life of Shakespeare*, Vol. I, pp. 312–19.

PETITION OF BENFIELD, SWANSTON AND POLLARD

§1 "To the right honorable Philip, Earl of Pembroke and Montgomery, Lord Chamberlain of his Majesty's Household, Robert Benfield, Eliard [or Heliard] Swanston and Thomas Pollard humbly represent these their grievances, imploring his Lordship's noble favor towards them for their relief. .

§2 "That the petitioners have a long time, with much patience, expected to be admitted sharers in the playhouses of the Globe and the Blackfriars, whereby they might reap some better fruit of their labors than hitherto they have done, and be encouraged to proceed therein with cheerfulness; that those few interested in the houses have, without any defalcation or abatement at all, a full moiety of the whole gains arising thereby, excepting the outer doors, and such of the said housekeepers as be actors do likewise equally share with all the rest of the actors, both in the other moiety and in the said outer doors also; that out of the actors' moiety there is notwithstanding defrayed all wages to hired men, apparel, poets, lights, and other charges of the houses whatsoever, so that, between the gains of the actors and of those few interested as housekeepers, there is an unreasonable inequality;

§3 "That the house of the Globe was formerly divided into sixteen parts, whereof Mr. Cuthbert Burbage and his sisters[1] had eight, Mrs. Condell four, and Mr. Heminges four; that Mr. Taylor and Mr. Lowin were long since admitted to purchase four parts betwixt them from the rest, viz., one part from Mr. Heminges, two parts from Mrs. Condell, and half a part apiece from Mr. Burbage and his sisters [*sic*]; that the three parts remaining to Mr. Heminges were afterwards by Mr. Shank surreptitiously purchased from him, contrary to the

553

petitioners' expectation, who hoped that when any parts had been to be sold, they
should have been admitted to have bought and divided the same amongst themselves for their better livelihood;

§4 "That the petitioners desire not to purchase or diminish any part of Mr.
Taylor's or Mr. Lowin's shares, whose deservings they must acknowledge to be
well worthy of their gains; but in regard the petitioners' labors . . . are equal
to some of the rest . . . and yet the petitioners' profit and means of livelihood
so much inferior and unequal to theirs, . . . they therefore desire that they may
be admitted to purchase for their moneys, at such rates as have been formerly
given, single parts apiece, only from those that have the greatest shares and may
best spare them; viz., that Mr. Burbage and his sister, having three parts and
a half apiece, may sell them two parts, and reserve two and a half apiece to
themselves; and that Mr. Shank, having three, may sell them one and reserve
two;

§5 "Wherein they hope your Lordship will conceive their desires to be just
and modest, the rather for that the petitioners, not doubting of being admitted
sharers in the said house the Globe, suffered lately the said housekeepers, in the
name of his Majesty's Servants, to sue and obtain a decree in the Court of Requests against Sir Matthew Brend, for confirmation unto them of a lease parole
for about nine or ten years yet to come, which they could otherwise have prevented until themselves had been made parties.

§6 "That for the house in the Blackfriars, it being divided into eight parts
amongst the aforenamed housekeepers, and Mr. Shank having two parts thereof,
Mr. Lowin, Mr. Taylor and each of the rest having but one part apiece, which
two parts were by the said Mr. Shank purchased of Mr. Heminges together with
those three of the Globe as before, the petitioners desire and hope that your
Lordship will conceive it likewise reasonable that the said Mr. Shank may assign
over one of the said parts amongst them three, they giving him such satisfaction
for the same as that he be no loser thereby;

§7 "Lastly, that your Lordship would . . . be nobly pleased . . . to call
all the said housekeepers before you, and to use your Lordship's power with
them to conform themselves thereunto, the rather considering that some of the
said housekeepers who have the greatest shares are neither actors nor his
Majesty's Servants as aforesaid, and yet reap most or the chiefest benefit of the
sweat of their brows, and live upon the bread of their labors, without taking any
pains themselves. . . ."

Shares in the Globe			of a lease of 9 years from our Lady Day last, 1635 . . .	Blackfriars		
	Burbage	3½			Shank	2
	Robinson	3½			Burbage	1
	Condell	2			Robinson	1
	Shank	3			Taylor	1
	Taylor	2			Lowin	1
	Lowin	2			Condell	1
					Underwood	1

Document 46

FURTHER PETITION OF BENFIELD, SWANSTON AND POLLARD

§8 "Robert Benfield, Eliard Swanston, and Thomas Pollard do further humbly represent unto your Lordship:

"That the housekeepers, being but six in number, viz., Mr. Cuthbert Burbage, Mrs. Condell, Mr. Shank, Mr. Taylor, Mr. Lowin and Mr. Robinson (in the right of his wife), have amongst them the full moiety of all the galleries and boxes in both houses, and of the tiring-house door at the Globe; that the actors have the other moiety, with the outer doors; but in regard the actors are half as many more, viz., nine in number, their shares fall shorter and are a great deal less than the housekeepers' and yet notwithstanding, out of those lesser shares the said actors defray all charges of the house whatsoever, viz., wages to hired men and boys, music, lights, &c., amounting to £900 or £1,000 per annum or thereabouts, being £3 a day one day with another, besides the extraordinary charge which the said actors are wholly at for apparel and poets, &c.; whereas the said housekeepers, out of all their gains, have not, till our Lady Day last, paid above £65 per annum rent for both houses, towards which they raise between £20 and £30 per annum from the tap-houses and a tenement and a garden belonging to the premises, &c., and are at no other charges whatsoever excepting the ordinary reparations of the houses;

§9 "So that upon a medium made of the gains of the housekeepers and those of the actors, one day with another throughout the year, the petitioners will make it apparent that when some of the housekeepers share 12s. a day at the Globe, the actors share not above 3s.; and then what those gain that are both actors and housekeepers, and have their shares in both, your Lordship will easily judge, and thereby find the modesty of the petitioners' suit, who desire only to buy for their money one part apiece from such three of the said housekeepers as are fittest to spare them, both in respect of desert and otherwise; viz., Mr. Shank one part of his three; Mr. Robinson and his wife, one part of their three and a half; and Mr. Cuthbert Burbage the like. And for the house of the Blackfriars, that Mr. Shank, who now enjoys two parts there, may sell them likewise one, to be divided amongst them three.

§10 "Humbly beseeching your Lordship . . . to put an end to and settle the said business, that your petitioners . . . may proceed to do their duty with cheerfulness and alacrity; or otherwise . . . that your Lordship would be pleased to consider whether it be not reasonable and equitable that the actors in general may enjoy the benefit of both houses to themselves, paying the said housekeepers such a valuable rent for the same as your Lordship shall think just and indifferent. . . ."

§11 "The Answer of John Shank . . . humbly showeth: That about almost two years since, your suppliant, upon offer to him made by William Heminges, did buy of him one part he had in the Blackfriars, for about six years then to come, at the yearly rent of £6 5s., and another part he then had in the Globe for about two years to come, and paid him for the same two parts, in ready moneys, £156, which said parts were offered to your suppliant, and were as free then for any other to buy as for your suppliant; that about eleven months since, the said William Heminges offering to sell unto your suppliant the remaining parts he then had, viz., one in the Blackfriars, wherein he had then about five years to come, and two in the Globe, wherein he had then but one year to come, your suppliant likewise bought the same, and paid for them in ready moneys more £350, all which moneys so disbursed by your suppliant amount to £506, the greatest part whereof your suppliant was constrained to take up at interest; and your suppliant hath besides disbursed to the said William Heminges divers other small sums of money since he was in prison.

§12 "That your suppliant did neither fraudulently nor surreptitiously defeat any of the petitioners in their hope of buying the said parts, neither would the said William Heminges have sold the same to any of the petitioners, for that they would not have given him any such price for the same; . . . that your suppliant being an old man in this quality . . . and having in this long time made no provision for himself in his age, . . . did at dear rates purchase these parts, and hath for a very small time as yet received the profits thereof and hath but a short time in them; and . . . therefore he hopeth he shall not be hindered in the enjoying the profit thereof. . . .

§13 "That whereas the petitioners in their Complaint say that they have not means to subsist, it shall . . . be made apparent that every one of the three petitioners . . . hath gotten and received, this year last past, the sum of £180, which . . . is more, by above the one half, than any of them ever got or were capable of elsewhere; besides what Mr. Swanston, . . . who hath further had and received this last year above £34 for the profit of a third part of one part in the Blackfriars which he bought for £20, and yet hath enjoyed the same two or three years already, and hath still as long time in the same as your suppliant hath in his, who, for so much as Mr. Swanston bought for £20, your suppliant paid £60. . . .

§14 "That your suppliant, and other the lessees in the Globe and in the Blackfriars, are chargeable with the payment of £100 yearly rent, besides reparations, which is daily very chargeable unto them, all which they must pay and bear whether they make any profit or not; and so . . . no wise man will adventure his estate in such a course, considering . . . the many casualties and daily troubles therewith. . . .

§15 "And whereas John Heminges, the father of William Heminges, of whom your suppliant made purchase of the said parts, enjoyed the same thirty years without any molestation, being, the most of the said years, both player and housekeeper, and after he gave over playing, divers years; and his son, William Heminges, four years after, though he never had anything to do with the said stage, enjoyed the same without any trouble; notwithstanding, the complainants would violently take from your petitioner the said parts, who hath still, of his own purse, supplied the company for the service of his Majesty with boys, as Thomas Pollard, John Thompson, deceased (for whom he paid £40), your suppliant having paid his part of £200 for other boys since his coming to the company — John Honyman, Thomas Holcombe and divers others — and at this time maintains three more for the said service. Neither lieth it in the power of your suppliant to satisfy the unreasonable demands of the complainants, he being forced to make over the said parts for security of moneys taken up as aforesaid . . . for the purchase of the said parts. . . .

§16 "All which being considered, your suppliant hopeth that your Lordship will not enforce your suppliant against his will to depart with what is his own, and what he hath dearly paid for, unto them that can claim no lawful interest thereunto. And your suppliant . . . doth conceive that if the petitioners, by those their violent courses, may obtain their desires, your Lordship will never be at quiet for their daily complaints, and it will be such a precedent to all young men that shall follow hereafter, that they shall aways refuse to do his Majesty service unless they may have whatsoever they will, though it be other men's estates. . . ."

ANSWER OF CUTHBERT AND WILLIAM BURBAGE AND WINIFRED ROBINSON

§17 "To the right honorable Philip, Earl of Pembroke and Montgomery, Lord Chamberlain of his Majesty's Household: . . .

"We, your humble suppliants, Cuthbert Burbage and Winifred his brother's [Richard's] wife and William his [Cuthbert's] son, do tender to your honorable consideration for what respects and good reasons we ought not, in all charity, to be disabled of our livelihoods by men so soon shot up, since it hath been the custom that they should come to it by far more antiquity and desert than those can justly attribute to themselves.

§18 "And first, humbly showing to your Honor the infinite charges, the manifold lawsuits, the lease's expiration, by the restraints in sickness times and other accidents that did cut from them the best part of the gains that your Honor is informed they have received:

§19 "The father of us, Cuthbert and Richard Burbage, was the first builder of playhouses, and was himself in his younger years a player. The Theater he built with many hundred pounds taken up at interest. The players that lived in those first times had only the profits arising from the doors, but now the players receive all the comings in at the doors to themselves, and half the galleries, from the housekeepers. He built this house upon leased ground, by which means the landlord and he had a great suit in law, and by his death the like troubles fell on us, his sons. We then bethought us of altering from thence, and at like expense built the Globe, with more sums of money taken up at interest, which lay heavy on us many years; and to ourselves we joined those deserving men, Shakespeare, Heminges, Condell, Phillips, and others, partners in the profits of that they call the House; but making the leases for twenty-one years hath been the destruction of ourselves and others; for they dying at the expiration of three or four years of their lease, the subsequent years became dissolved to strangers, as by marrying with their widows, and the like by their children. Thus, right honorable, as concerning the Globe, where we ourselves are but lessees.

§20 "Now for the Blackfriars, that is our inheritance. Our father purchased it at extreme rates, and made it into a playhouse with great charge and trouble; which after was leased out to one Evans, that first set up the boys commonly called the Queen's Majesty's Children of the Chapel. In process of time the boys growing up to be men, which were Underwood, Field, Ostler, and were taken to strengthen the King's service; and the more to strengthen the service, the boys daily wearing out, it was considered that house would be as fit for ourselves, and so purchased the lease remaining from Evans with our money, and placed men players, which were Heminges, Condell, Shakespeare, &c.

§21 "And Richard Burbage, who for thirty-five years' pains, cost and labor, made means to leave his wife and children some estate, and out of whose estate so many of other players and families have been maintained, these new men, that were never bred from children in the King's service, would take away with oaths and menaces that we shall be forced, and that they will not thank us for it; so that it seems they would not pay us for what they would have or we can spare, which, more to satisfy your Honor than their threatening pride, we are for ourselves willing to part with a part between us, they paying according as ever hath been the custom and the number of years the lease is made for.

§22 "Then, to show your Honor against these sayings that we eat the fruit of their labors, we refer it to your Honor's judgment to consider their profits, which we may safely maintain; for it appeareth by their own accounts for one whole year last past, beginning from Whitsun Monday, 1634, to Whitsun Monday, 1635, each of these complainants gained severally, as he was a player and no housekeeper, £180. Besides, Mr. Swanston hath received from the Blackfriars this year, as he is there a housekeeper, above £30, all which being accounted together may very well keep him from starving.

§23 "Wherefore your Honor's most humble suppliants entreat they may not further be trampled upon than their estates can bear, seeing how dearly it hath been purchased by the infinite cost and pains of the family of the Burbages, and the great desert of Richard Burbage for his quality of playing, that his wife should not starve in her old age; submitting ourselves to part with one part to them for valuable consideration; and let them seek further satisfaction elsewhere, that is, of the heirs or assigns of Mr. Heminges and Mr. Condell, who had theirs of the Blackfriars of us for nothing. It is only we that suffer continually.

§24 "Therefore, humbly relying upon your honorable charity in discussing their clamor against us, we shall, as we are in duty bound, still pray for the daily increase of your Honor's health and happiness."

ORDER OF THE LORD CHAMBERLAIN[2]
JULY 12, 1635

§25 "Court at Theobalds, 12 July, 1635.

"Having considered this petition and the several answers and replies of the parties, the merits of the petitioners and the disproportion of their shares, and the interest of his Majesty's service, I have thought fit and do accordingly order that the petitioners, Robert Benfield, Eliard Swanston and Thomas Pollard, be each of them admitted to the purchase of the shares desired, of the several persons mentioned in the petition, for the four years remaining of the lease of the house in Blackfriars, and for five years in that of the Globe, at the usual and accustomed rates, and according to the proportion of the time and benefit they are to enjoy. And hereof I desire the housekeepers and all others whom it may concern to take notice, and to conform themselves therein accordingly; the which if they or any of them refuse or delay to perform, if they are actors and his Majesty's Servants, I do suspend them from the stage and all the benefit thereof; and if they are only interested in the houses, I desire my Lord Privy Seal to take order that they may be left out of the lease which is to be made upon the decree in the Court of Requests.

[Signed]   *P. and M.*"

1. "Sisters" (plural) is erroneous. Cuthbert Burbage had one sister-in-law, now Mrs. Robinson; he had no natural sisters. 2. The Lord Chamberlain's book places this order immediately after the first petition of Benfield, Swanston, and Pollard, and in doing so it is followed by Halliwell-Phillipps and *Malone Society Collections*, Vol. II. Manifestly, however, the order ought to come after all the depositions. Note that its first line mentions prior consideration of "the several answers and replies of the parties," that the three petitioners would be unlikely to file a further plea if a decision had already been reached in their favor, and that neither Shank nor Burbage refers to the issuance of an order. Cf. Bentley, *Jacobean and Caroline Stage*, Vol. I, p. 43 n. 2, and Fleay, *Chronicle History*, pp. 324–25.

BIBLIOGRAPHY

Hinnebusch, William A., O. P., *The Early English Friars Preachers*, Rome, 1951.

Jarrett, Bede, O. P., *The English Dominicans*, New York, 1921; a later version, revised and abridged by Walter Gunbley, O. P., London, 1937.

Martin, William, and Sidney Toy, "The Black Friars in London: A Chapter in National History," *Transactions of the London and Middlesex Archaeological Society*, New Series, Vol. V, Part 4 (1928), pp. 353–79.

Palmer, C. F. R., O. P., "The Friar-Preachers, or Black Friars, of Holborn, London," *The Reliquary*, Vol. XVII (1876–1877), pp. 33–39, 75–80.

———— "The Black Friars of London," *Merry England*, Vol. XIII (1889), pp. 33–43, 116–32, 191–205, 266–88, 354–66.

Tunmore, Harry P., "The Dominican Order and Parliament," *Catholic Historical Review*, Vol. XXVI (1941), pp. 479–89.

TOPOGRAPHY AND ARCHITECTURE

Abstracts of *Inquisitiones Post Mortem* Relating to the City of London, in three parts; printed for and published in *The Transactions of the London and Middlesex Archaeological Society*.

Adams, Joseph Quincy, "The Conventual Buildings of Blackfriars, London, and the Playhouses Constructed Therein," *Studies in Philology*, Vol. XIV, No. 2 (April 1917), pp. 64–87.

Baddeley, Sir John James, *The Guildhall of the City of London*, London, 1951.

Barrett, C. R. B., *The History of the Society of Apothecaries of London*, London, 1905.

Besant, Sir Walter, *Mediaeval London*, London, 1906.

Blackfriars Records, ed. Albert Feuillerat, Malone Society Collections, Vol. II, Part I, Oxford, 1913.

Bond, Francis, *An Introduction to English Church Architecture*, 2 vols., Oxford, 1913.

Clapham, Alfred W., "The Architectural Remains of the Mendicant Orders in Wales," *Archaeological Journal*, Vol. LXXXIV (1927), pp. 88–104.

———— "The Friars as Builders," a chapter in the book entitled *Some Famous Buildings and Their Story*, by Clapham and Walter H. Godfrey, Westminster, n. d.

———— "On the Topography of the Dominican Priory of London," *Archaeologia*, Vol. LXIII (1912), pp. 56–80.

Cook, G. H., *English Monasteries in the Middle Ages*, London, 1961.

Cook, Olive, and Edwin Smith, *English Abbeys and Priories*, London, 1960.

Bibliography

Crossley, Fred H., *The English Abbey*, London, 1935.

Gilyard-Beer, R., *Abbeys*, London, 1958.

Graham, Rose, "An Essay on English Monasteries," a chapter in the book entitled *Social Life in Early England*, ed. Geoffrey Barraclough, New York, 1960.

Harben, Henry A., *A Dictionary of London*, London, 1918.

Honeybourne, Marjorie B., "The Fleet and Its Neighbourhood in Early and Medieval Times," *London Topographical Record*, Vol. XIX (1947), pp. 13–87.

Jackson, Allen W., *The Half-Timber House*, New York, 1912.

James, M. R., *Abbeys*, with a chapter on "Monastic Life and Buildings" by A. Hamilton Thompson, London, 1926.

Lloyd, Nathaniel, *A History of the English House*, London, 1931, 1949.

Norman, Philip, "Mediaeval Remains Found at Blackfriars, May, 1900," *The Annual Record of the London Topographical Society* (1900), pp. 1–9.

———— "Recent Discoveries of Medieval Remains in London," *Archaeologia*, Vol. LXVII (1915–1916), pp. 13–14.

Pulsifer, William H., *Notes for a History of Lead*, New York, 1888.

Reddaway, T. F., *The Rebuilding of London After the Great Fire*, London, 1940.

The Site of the Office of the Times, London, 1956.

Wheatley, Henry B., *London Past and Present*, 2 vols., London, 1891.

POLITICAL AND ECCLESIASTICAL HISTORY

Belloc, Hilaire, *How the Reformation Happened*, London, 1928.

Brewer, J. S., *The Reign of Henry VIII*, ed. James Gairdner, 2 vols., London, 1884.

Carter, C. Sydney, *The English Church and the Reformation*, London, 1925.

Cavendish, George, *The Life of Cardinal Wolsey*, 2 vols., Chiswick, 1825.

Durant, Will, *The Reformation* (Part VI of *The Story of Civilization*), New York, 1957.

Ferguson, Charles W., *Naked to Mine Enemies*, Boston and Toronto, 1958.

Gasquet, Cardinal Francis A., *Henry VIII and the English Monasteries*, London, 1899.

Hall, Edward, *Chronicle*, eds. 1548 and 1809, London.

Holinshed, Raphael, *Chronicles of England, Scotland, and Ireland*, 6 vols., London, 1807–1808.

Hughes, Philip, *The Reformation in England* (Part I, "The King's Proceedings"), New York, 1951–1954.

Knowles, Dom David, *The Religious Orders in England* (Vol. III, "The Tudor Age"), Cambridge, 1959.

Letters and Papers of Henry VIII, 21 vols., London, 1862–1910.

Neale, J. E., *The Elizabethan House of Commons*, New Haven, 1950.

Proceedings and Ordinances of the Privy Council.

Stow, John, *Annales, or A Generall Chronicle of England*, London, 1631.

———— *Survey of London*, eds. 1618 and 1633, London.

Strype, John, *The Life of the Learned Sir John Cheke, Kt.*, London, 1705; Oxford, 1821.

———— ed., Stow's *Survey of London*, London, 1755.

Adams, John Cranford, *The Globe Playhouse*, Cambridge, Mass., 1942.

———— "The Original Staging of *King Lear*," *Joseph Quincy Adams: Memorial Studies*, Washington, 1948.

———— "The Staging of *The Tempest*, III iii," *Review of English Studies*, Vol. XIV, No. 56 (October 1938), pp. 1–16.

Adams, Joseph Quincy, "The Conventual Buildings of Blackfriars, London, and the Playhouses Constructed Therein," *Studies in Philology*, Vol. XIV (1917), pp. 64–87.

———— ed. *The Dramatic Records of Sir Henry Herbert*, New Haven, 1917.

———— *Shakespearean Playhouses*, Boston, 1917.

Albright, Victor E., *The Shaksperian Stage*, New York, 1912.

Armstrong, William A., "The Audience of the Elizabethan Private Theatres," *Review of English Studies*, Vol. X (1959), pp. 234–249.

———— *The Elizabethan Private Theatres: Facts and Problems*, London, 1957–1958.

Aubrey, John, *Brief Lives*, ed. Andrew Clark, 2 vols., Oxford, 1898.

Baldwin, Thomas W., *The Organization and Personnel of the Shakespearean Company*, Princeton, 1927.

Baskervill, C. R., "The Custom of Sitting on the Elizabethan Stage," *Modern Philology*, Vol. VIII (1911), pp. 581–89.

Bentley, Gerald E., *The Jacobean and Caroline Stage*, 5 vols., Oxford, 1941, 1956.

———— "Shakespeare and the Blackfriars Theatre," *Shakespeare Survey 1*, Cambridge, 1948, pp. 38–50.

Burney, Charles, *A General History of Music*, 2 vols., London, 1935.

Campbell, Lily B., *Scenes and Machines on the English Stage during the Renaissance*, Cambridge, 1923.

Chambers, E. K., *The Elizabethan Stage*, 4 vols., Oxford, 1923.

———— *William Shakespeare: A Study of Facts and Problems*, 2 vols., Oxford, 1930.

Collier, John P., *The History of English Dramatic Poetry to the Time of Shakespeare: and Annals of the Stage to the Restoration*, 3 vols., London, 1831.

Cowling, G. H., *Music on the Shakespearian Stage*, Cambridge, 1913.

Downes, J., *Roscius Anglicanus, or an Historical Review of the Stage from 1660 to 1706*, 1708; ed. J. Knight (facsimile reprint), 1886; ed. M. Summers, 1927.

Eccles, Mark, "Martin Peerson and the Blackfriars," *Shakespeare Survey 11*, Cambridge, 1958, pp. 100–106.

Fitzgeffrey, H., "Notes from Black-Fryers," in *Certain Elegies Done by Sundry Excellent Wits with Satires and Epigrams*, 1620, reprinted 1843.

Fitzgerald, Percy H., *A New History of the English Stage*, London, 1882.

Fleay, Frederick G., *A Biographical Chronicle of the English Drama, 1559–1642*, 2 vols., London, 1891.

———— *A Chronicle History of the London Stage, 1559–1642*, 2 vols., London, 1890.

Flecknoe, R., *A Short Discourse of the English Stage*, 1664; reprinted in Hazlitt, *The English Drama and Stage*, London, 1869.

Granville-Barker, Harley, *Prefaces to Shakespeare*; London, 1927–1937; Princeton, 1947.

Graves, T. S., "The Origin of the Custom of Sitting on the Stage," *Journal of English and Germanic Philology*, Vol. XIII (1914), pp. 104–09.

Haines, C. M., "The 'Law of Re-Entry' in Shakespeare," *Review of English Studies*, Vol. I (1925), pp. 499–51.

Halliday, F. E., *A Shakespeare Companion*, New York, 1952.

Halliwell-Phillipps, J. O., *Outlines of the Life of Shakespeare*, 2 vols., London, 1886.

Harbage, Alfred, *Annals of English Drama, 975–1700*, Philadelphia, 1940.

———— *Shakespeare and the Rival Traditions*, New York, 1952.

Hart, Alfred, "The Length of Elizabethan and Jacobean Plays," *Review of English Studies*, Vol. VIII, No. 30 (April 1932), pp. 139–54; and "The Time Allotted for Representation of Elizabethan and Jacobean Plays," *Review of English Studies*, Vol. VIII, No. 32 (October 1932) pp. 395–413.

Hillebrand, Harold N., *The Child Actors: A Chapter in Elizabethan Stage History*, Urbana, Ill., 1926.

Hotson, J. Leslie, *The Commonwealth and Restoration Stage*, Cambridge, Mass., 1928.

Isaacs, J., *Production and Stage-Management at the Blackfriars Theatre*, Oxford, 1933.

Lawrence, W. J., *The Elizabethan Playhouse and Other Studies*, First Series, Stratford-upon-Avon, 1912; Second Series, Philadelphia and Stratford-upon-Avon, 1913.

———— *The Physical Conditions of the Elizabethan Public Playhouse*, Cambridge, Mass., 1927.

———— *Pre-Restoration Stage Studies*, Cambridge, Mass., 1927.

———— *Those Nut-Cracking Elizabethans*, London, 1935.

McAfee, Helen, *Pepys on the Restoration Stage*, New Haven, 1916.

Malone Society Collections, Vol. I, Parts i–v, Oxford, 1907–1911.

Mander, Raymond, and Joe Mitchenson, *A Picture History of the British Theatre*, New York, 1957.

Murray, John Tucker, *English Dramatic Companies, 1558–1642*, 2 vols., London, 1910.

Nagler, A. M., *Shakespeare's Stage*, New Haven, 1958.

Naylor, Edward W., *Shakespeare and Music*, London and New York, 1896, rev. 1931.

Nicoll, Allardyce, *A History of Restoration Drama, 1660–1700*, Cambridge, 1923.

Prouty, Charles T., "An Early Elizabethan Playhouse," *Shakespeare Survey 6*, pp. 64–74.

Rhodes, R. Crompton, *The Stagery of Shakespeare*, Birmingham, 1922.

Sarlos, Robert K., "Development and Operation of the First Blackfriars Theatre," a section of *Studies in the Elizabethan Theatre*, ed. Charles T. Prouty, Hamden, Conn., 1961.

Smith, Irwin, *Shakespeare's Globe Playhouse*, New York, 1956.

Strafforde, the Earl of, *Letters and Dispatches*, 2 vols., London, 1739.

Thorndike, Ashley H., *The Influence of Beaumont and Fletcher on Shakespeare*, Worcester, Mass., 1901.

———— *Shakespeare's Theater*, New York, 1916, 1949.

Wallace, Charles W., *Advance Sheets from Shakespeare, the Globe, and Blackfriars*, Stratford-upon-Avon, 1909.

———— *The Children of the Chapel at Blackfriars, 1597–1603*, Lincoln, Neb., 1908.

———— *The Evolution of the English Drama up to Shakespeare*, Berlin, 1912.

———— "The First London Theatre," *University Studies of the University of Nebraska*, Vol. XIII, Nos. 1, 2 and 3 (January-April-July, 1913).

———— "The Newly-Discovered Shakespeare Documents," *University Studies of the University of Nebraska*, Vol. V, No. 4 (October 1905), pp. 347–56.

———— "Shakespeare and His London Associates," *University Studies of the University of Nebraska*, Vol. X, No. 4 (October 1910).

Wood, Anthony à, *The History and Antiquities of the University of Oxford*, trans. John Gutch, 3 vols., Oxford, 1792–1796.

Wright, J., *Historia Histrionica: An Historical Account of the English Stage . . . In a Dialogue of Plays and Players*, 1699; facsimile reprint, 1872.

INDEX